Traveller's Lit

to

The Caribbean

James Ferguson

*with chapters on Cuba and Puerto Rico
by Jason Wilson*

Traveller's Literary Companions

Read your
way around
the world

In Print

Titles in the Traveller's Literary Companion series:
South and Central America
Africa
Eastern and Central Europe
The Indian Sub-continent
Japan
South-east Asia
The Caribbean
France

British Library Cataloguing in Publication Data: A catalogue record for this book is available from the British Library.

Paperback ISBN 1 873047 51 7

Paperback cover design by Russell Townsend:
 Front cover picture shows detail from Haitian painting, courtesy of John-Paul Davidson
 Back cover picture shows detail from Haitian painting, courtesy of Louis Shelden, © Kornell Photography.
Maps drawn by Russell Townsend
Additional artwork by Zana Juppenlatz
Typeset by MC Typeset Ltd
Printed by Bell and Bain

First published in 1997 by
In Print Publishing Ltd, Coleridge House, 4–5 Coleridge Gardens, London NW6 3QH, UK. Tel: (0171) 372 2600. Fax: (0171) 372 2662.

SERIES FOREWORD

This series of *Traveller's Literary Companions* is the series I have been looking for all my travelling life. Discovering new writers and new countries is one of the greatest pleasures we know, and these books will greatly increase the enjoyment of all who consult them. Each volume is packed with scholarly and entertaining historical, geographical, political and above all literary information. A country lives through its literature, and we have here an illustrated survey not only of a country's own writers, but also of the views of foreigners, explorers, tourists and exiles. The only problem I foresee is that each volume will bring about a compulsive desire to book a ticket on the next flight out.

The writers take us back in the past to each country's cultural origins, and bring us right up to the present with extracts from novels, poems and travel writings published in the 1980s and 1990s. The biographical information about the writers is invaluable, and will give any traveller an easy and immediate access to the past and present state of each nation. Conversation with hosts, colleagues or strangers on trains will be greatly assisted. An enormous amount of work has gone into the compiling and annotating of each volume, and the balance of fact and comment seems to me to be expertly judged.

Margaret Drabble

About the authors

James Ferguson was born in London and was educated at Dulwich College and Pembroke College, Oxford. He was a Junior Research Fellow and Tutor in French at St Edmund Hall, Oxford, where he completed his D.Phil. Since 1987 he has been a researcher at the Latin America Bureau, London, specializing in the Caribbean. James Ferguson is the author of *Haiti: Nightmare Republic* (Cassell, 1996), *Dominican Republic: Beyond the Lighthouse* (LAB, 1992), *Venezuela in Focus* (LAB, 1994), *Eastern Caribbean in Focus* (LAB, 1997) and books on Grenada and Caribbean development issues. He travels regularly to the region and has written for the *Guardian*, the *Independent* and *Caribbean Week* newspapers as well as working for the BBC World Service. He lives in Oxford with his wife and two children.

Jason Wilson is a Reader in Latin American poetry at University College, London. He has published *Octavio Paz. A Study of his Poetics* (Cambridge University Press, 1979), *Octavio Paz* (Twayne, 1986), *An A–Z of Latin American Literature in English Translation* (Institute of Latin American Studies, 1989), *Traveller's Literary Companion to South and Central America* (In Print Publishing, 1993), Alexandre von Humboldt's *Personal Narrative of a Journey to the Equinoctial Regions of the New Continent* (Penguin, 1995), and numerous essays, reviews and translations. He is married, with three daughters, and has travelled widely in Latin America.

Contents

GLOSSARY

The following is a list of terms, more often than not culinary, which may be unfamiliar to readers. Elsewhere in this guide there are words whose spelling differs from that of 'standard' English, but their meaning is usually clear from their context. Unless otherwise stated, the following terms are in use in one or more of the English-speaking islands. In other cases Fr = French, Sp = Spanish, Cr = Creole.

accra: saltfish fritter
ackee: a tree, whose fruit is cooked, especially in Jamaica, as a vegetable
anchar: pickled mango
banlieue (Fr): suburb
barracoon: sheds or barracks, used for holding slaves in transit
barrio (Sp): neighbourhood, urban district
béké (Cr): a (rich) white, born in the Caribbean
blan(c) (Cr): white, more commonly foreigner
blerd naught: expression of surprise, exclamation
calabash: dried gourd of calabash tree, used as vessel
callaloo: type of spinach-like vegetable, used in soup
caudillo (Sp): strongman, chief
cerveza (Sp): beer
chapita (Sp): medals (literally 'little plates')
cocoye (Cr): fool, idiot
conkey: type of maize bread
corvée (Fr): forced labour
coucou: cornmeal and okra mix, popular in Barbados
cutlass: machete
dasheen: a root vegetable or tuber
deaders: okra
dhoti: Indian loin-cloth
dou-dou (Cr): sweetheart, darling
dutty: dirty
ganja: marijuana
gourde: Haitian currency
Gros Michel: type of banana
fete: party
finca (Sp): farm or ranch
guapa (Sp): pretty

higgler: market trader, usually a woman
janga: crayfish
jumby: ghost or spirit
Lacatan: type of banana
to lime: to hang around, waste time
loup-garou (Fr): werewolf
manumission: legal emancipation of a slave (normally by his/her owner)
mas: costumed procession (masquerade) in Trinidad Carnival
mauby: non-alcoholic drink, made from bark of mauby tree
pan: steelband drum, or steelband music
parang: form of house-to-house singing, traditional at Christmas in Trinidad
polorie: small savoury roll
Portlan: Portland, a parish in Jamaica
ron (Sp): rum
roti: chapati like pancake, popular in Trinidad
rundung: rundown, a type of fish-based stew
sancocho (Sp): meat stew
souse: pickled and stewed pig's head, similar to brawn
tapia: mud and thatch hut
tiefing: stealing
tienda (Sp): shop
washy cong: cheap sandals or sneakers
yeug: with a strange expression
zaboca: avocado

Using the Companion

Each chapter is divided into four sections: (1) a general introduction to the country and its literature, with supporting historical and cultural background; (2) a Booklist which gives details of works mentioned in the introduction or extracted; (3) Extracts from prose and poetry focusing on particular places or the country in general; (4) biographical and literary notes on the authors extracted.

The **extracts** are arranged by place, alphabetically, and each has a number to make it easy to locate from elsewhere in the chapter. A quick list of published sources can be found in the **Booklist**, where the extract numbers are highlighted in bold type. Fuller references are included under 'Acknowledgments and Citations' at the end of the book.

Title dates given in the introductions and the biographical notes normally indicate the first editions of the original works.

The **symbol** ◊ after an author's name indicates that there is a biographical entry. Where this entry is in another chapter, this is indicated after the symbol, which is then printed in parentheses: eg Walcott (◊ St Lucia).

Bold type is used throughout to highlight references to particular places, such as cities and towns, museums, writers' houses, and so on.

There is a general **index** of authors and other significant personal names at the end of the book.

INTRODUCTION

This is a dark smiling people
humble, gentle folk
descendants of slaves
and of that uncivil riff-raff
of various breeds
whom in the name of Spain
Columbus kindly ceded to the Indies.

Here are whites and blacks and Chinese and mulattoes
They are cheap colours of course
since through trade and indenture
the dyes have run and there is no stable tone.
He who thinks otherwise should step forward and speak.
Nicolás Guillén, *West Indies, Ltd*

The Caribbean is as mixed and fluid a region as Guillén's lines suggest. Even its name has different meanings. It is, of course, a sea, a sea as famed for its turquoise shades and inviting coolness as it is feared for its hurricanes and sharks. It is also the name given to an arc of hundreds of islands which stretch from Florida down to the coast of Venezuela and which enclose the sea from the Atlantic Ocean.

The Caribbean is sometimes a geo-political entity, too, including the bordering mainland states of South and Central America. During the Cold War years the 'Caribbean Basin' was seen by some as a hotbed of

Communist unrest, by others as the oppressed 'backyard' of a bullying USA. The recently formed Association of Caribbean States, for instance, counts Mexico and El Salvador among its members, although the latter does not have a Caribbean coastline.

Some parts of the Caribbean do not even refer to themselves as such, preferring to be known as the Antilles or, to a lesser extent, the West Indies. There are even different ways of pronouncing the name; you can choose between the Americanized *Ca*ribbean or the Anglicized Carib*bean*. Although we all know what the Caribbean is, it is also an elusive concept, open to differing definitions.

The Caribbean is also a set of associations and images, some historic and others more recent. Once the haunt of pirates and buccaneers, it became synonymous in the popular imagination with the 'sugar islands' and the toil of African slaves. For centuries the Caribbean was the arena for superpower conflict between European nations, each intent on expanding its empire. In modern iconography, its beaches and blue water have been consigned to a million tourist brochures, where legions of hotels offer their version of 'paradise'. The Caribbean has been reborn as a tropical playground for the wealthy and not-so-wealthy, another product offered by the global vacation industry.

But beyond the beach, there is another Caribbean, or rather a multiplicity of places with that name. There are English-speaking islands, French-speaking islands, Spanish-speaking islands. There are islands where people speak Creole, patois or Papiamento. There are islands where per capita income is less than US$400 each year and others where it is more than US$25 000. There are islands with skyscrapers, shopping malls and motorways; there are islands where the mule is still the preferred mode of transport. In some islands there are elements of all of this.

It is a place of extraordinary diversity and cultural mixing. Added to the varied legacies of indigenous civilizations, several European nations, the influence of North America and the proximity of Latin America, is the transplanted presence of Africa, India and the myriad other places of origin of its people. This 'melting pot' of disparate ideas and beliefs has produced a series of distinctive Creole societies, each with its own particular identity, each different in many ways from its geographical neighbours. Thus, Haiti and the Dominican Republic, even while sharing an island, are linguistically and culturally distant. Cuba and Jamaica are neighbours, but are separated by history and language. Barbados and Trinidad had the common experience of British colonial rule; but there the similarity ends, as staid and stable Barbados stands in striking contrast to the ethnic chaos and artistic exuberance of Trinidad.

But alongside the so-called 'balkanization' of the Caribbean are its common characteristics and concerns. Recurring and unifying themes run through its history: conquest, slavery, the plantation economy, emancipation, migration and, most recently, the almost universal advent of tourism. These common strands have touched almost all of the Caribbean, providing its different peoples with shared experience and awareness which can transcend linguistic boundaries. In areas as diverse as architecture and food, religion and family life, the Caribbean islands have a common identity which is equally reflected in their literature.

The region, of course, began its modern history as a series of non-literary societies. The first settlers from Europe were more interested in survival than books. The indigenous culture they found was mostly derided and destroyed. Slaves were not encouraged to read or write, and their masters and overseers were not, on the whole, inclined towards literature. The first writing about the Caribbean tended to come from the outside, produced by visiting priests, merchants or administrators, and hence reflected their imported assumptions and values. They reported on slavery and other aspects of colonial society and influenced opinion back in Europe. The first visitors, in turn, were followed, by Victorian travellers such as J.A. Froude or Charles Kingsley, high-minded analysts of Empire and its failings. Then came visiting writers from the USA, curious about 'exotic' phenomena such as voodoo or other folk customs.

From this stream of peripatetic authors, a genre of Caribbean travel writing eventually developed in the 1930s and 1940s, which almost invariably involved a writer's trip 'down the islands', with a chapter on each. The genre is described by Trinidadian V.S. Naipaul in his *A Way in the World*:

> 'These cruise books resembled one another. They couldn't have made much money for anybody, and I suppose they were a product of the Depression, written by hard-pressed men for public-library readers who dreamed of doing a cruise themselves one day in warm waters somewhere. Though this particular travel form required the writer to be always present, and knowledgeable, and busy, the books they wrote were curiously impersonal. That might have been because the writers had to get in everything earlier writers had got in; and also, I feel, because the writers of these travel books were really acting, acting being writers, acting being travellers, acting being travellers in the colonies.'

To some extent, the genre survives today, but in its lifetime it has also produced work by writers such as Patrick Leigh Fermor which is perceptive, enlightening, and very personal.

As for the slaves and their descendants, their fiction and philosophy were essentially oral in form, brought over from Africa and passed down through folk story-telling in African languages and patois. Indentured labourers from India added their folk literature to this mostly unwritten expression. Of interest to passing anthropologists and occasionally anthologized in folk tale form, the oral tradition was not widely appreciated outside the region. So it remained, for the most part, until the twentieth century, when literature *from* the Caribbean rather than literature *about* the Caribbean took shape and grew into an international force. There were exceptions: independent nineteenth-century Haiti was a society with many poets and printers, even if most Haitians could not (and still cannot) read; Cuba and the Dominican Republic produced significant literature. But in many islands, education and resources, publishers and readers, were in short supply. The cultural models were assumed to be elsewhere, abroad, beyond the Caribbean itself.

Caribbean literature is hence, for the most part, a relatively recent phenomenon. In the 1960s the great Barbadian novelist, George Lamming, could rightly state that it was no more than twenty years old. The 1940s did indeed see the emergence of a truly Caribbean literature, although there were isolated exceptions before then. The intellectual influence of *négritude* in the French-speaking islands and the energizing example of the Harlem Renaissance in the USA created the conditions for black writers in the Caribbean to gain access to wider audiences. At the same time, a number of journals and publishers sprang up in the Caribbean, offering a literary infrastructure which had not previously existed. From the 1950s onwards, the region began to produce writers of world stature – like Derek Walcott, Alejo Carpentier, George Lamming.

The 1950s and 1960s also witnessed one of the great waves of migration which have shaped the Caribbean's development. As hundreds of thousands of people from across the region moved to Britain, the USA and Canada, Caribbean literature became increasingly transnational, with writers based in London, New York and Ontario as often as in their 'home' islands. From this massive process of displacement have sprung some of the Caribbean's most persistent and enduring literary themes: exile, return, rootlessness.

Today, the Caribbean diaspora still claims many of the region's writers. But exile has not impoverished creativity – rather, it has contributed to the dynamism and adaptability of a literature, which, like the Caribbean's people themselves, has absorbed and transformed an infinite number of influences.

This guide aims to give an idea of some of the richness and diversity of Caribbean writing. I have included writers from outside the region – travellers, journalists, sometimes specialists – when I thought their contributions cast light on the country in question or on a particular set of attitudes towards it. But, wherever possible, I have tried to put more emphasis on authors from the islands themselves. In some cases, where a developed literary tradition exists, this has been difficult only in terms of selecting from a wide range. In others, the problem has consisted in finding extracts in English from within a non English-speaking culture. There are also some Caribbean islands whose tiny size and population prevent the existence of significant literary activity.

In the course of researching and compiling this collection, I have found several books invaluable. Eric Williams's *From Columbus to Castro: The History of the Caribbean 1492–1969* is a vital piece of scholarship, rich both in detail and analysis. Another accessible work is *A Short History of the West*

Indies by J.H. Parry, P.M. Sherlock and Anthony Maingot. The books published by Macmillan in the Warwick University Caribbean Studies series are almost invariably stimulating, while the country bibliographies published by Clio Press in the World Bibliographical Series are always useful. Among the many guidebooks available on the Caribbean, my favourite is the *Caribbean Islands Handbook*, a comprehensive and reliable guide to every corner of every island. Also highly recommended is the *Cadogan Guide to the Caribbean* by James Henderson.

The Penguin Book of Caribbean Verse in English, edited by Paula Burnett, is a lively and well-arranged selection of poetry; other collections which I found useful include *If I Could Write This in Fire* by Pamela Smorkaloff, and Nick Caistor and Anne Walmsley's *Facing the Sea*. *Anderson's Travel Companion* by Sarah Anderson provides a very helpful listing of writing on every country in the world. Two publishers have established a particular reputation for producing the best literature from the region. Both Heinemann and Longman offer a mix of classics and new fiction in their Caribbean writers' series.

I am grateful to all of the following, in Britain, the USA and the Caribbean, who helped in different ways, by steering me in the direction of sources, providing information, lending me books or suggesting new approaches: Charles Arthur, Celia Britton, Richard Burton, Nick Caistor, Kenneth Campbell, Merle Collins, Raphaël Confiant, Sean Hand, David Howard, Chris Jennings, Will Johnson, Adrian Lam, Don Mitchell, Ian Randle, Chris Searle, Lasana M. Sekou, Lucien Taylor, Ian Thomson, Audley Wright. In particular, I am indebted to the late and much missed David Nicholls and to Polly Pattullo, both of whom provided invaluable advice and access to their collections of Caribbean writing.

I should also like to thank my editors and publishers, Alastair Dingwall and John Edmondson, for their encouragement, patience and practical help. I am also grateful to my co-writer, Jason Wilson, for his contributions and for welcome advice given on other chapters. And, of course, my gratitude and much more go to Catriona, Emilie and Patrick, who shared in the making of this book in many different ways.

James Ferguson
Oxford

In memory of my mother, Sheila Mary Ferguson
14 September 1919 – 5 August 1993

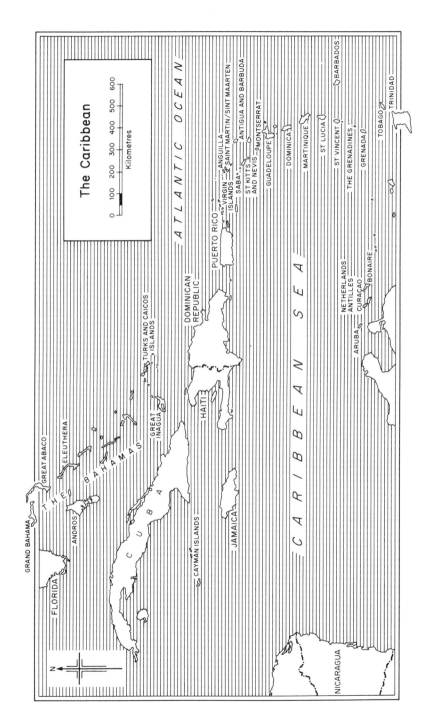

The Caribbean

THE BAHAMAS

For many tourists, the Bahamas are the very epitome of the Caribbean. With their stretches of white powder beaches framed by palm trees, their limpid water and luxurious vacation resorts, the islands seem to offer everything that the Caribbean is famous for. Add to this the attractions of water sports and the region's most opulent casinos, and it is not difficult to see why many Americans take the short flight from Florida to bask in all-year-round sunshine.

Yet some purists insist that the Bahamas are not, properly speaking, part of the Caribbean at all. Made up of some 700 islands and more than 2000 cays (pronounced 'keys'), this archipelago stretches approximately 600 miles in a south-easterly direction from near the Florida coast to within fifty miles of Haiti. Set in the Atlantic Ocean, the low-lying coral islands bear little physical resemblance to any other Caribbean territory. Their history, too, has been distinct from that of much of the rest of the region and has largely been determined by proximity to the USA. Historically separated from the English-speaking Caribbean by the French- and Spanish-dominated islands of Cuba, Hispaniola and Puerto Rico, Bahamians have tended to look north for work and cultural inspiration.

But the Bahamas also have features and influences in common with the rest of the Caribbean, not least their experience of British colonization and slavery. About 85% of Bahamians are black, the descendants of slaves, and their past and present owe much to the same forces which have created the modern-day Caribbean. People from other Caribbean nations, particularly Haiti, have gone to the Bahamas in search of better prospects, and they have increased the islands' connections with the wider region.

THE USELESS ISLANDS

Seen from the air, the Bahamas provide a spectacular panorama of blues and greens, the shallow seas around the hundreds of cays producing the

1

FACT BOX

AREA: 13 939 sq km
POPULATION: 272 000
CAPITAL: Nassau
LANGUAGES: English
FORMER COLONIAL POWER: Britain
INDEPENDENCE: 1973
PER CAPITA GDP: US$12 020

---

turquoise and ultramarine tints which decorate tourist brochures. The shallowness of the sea and the complex mass of coral outcrops and reefs traditionally made the archipelago extremely dangerous for shipping, and until the introduction of lighthouses and developed navigation technology, the Bahamas were literally a ship-wrecker's paradise.

The thin soil and lack of fresh water on the islands have always made them unsuitable for intensive agriculture, and consequently the Bahamas are among the few territories in the region which have escaped the widespread introduction of sugar-cane. Together with the navigational risks, their infertility earned them the unflattering description of the 'useless islands' from early Spanish visitors.

The 60-square-mile island called **San Salvador** looks as unpromising to any would-be settler as most of the others in the chain, with its swamps, lagoons and rocky beaches. It was here, however, that Christopher Columbus is thought to have made his first landing in the Americas on 12 October 1492. According to writer Hunter Davies ◊, there is still some dispute as to where the precise landfall took place, but, as *In Search of Columbus* (Extract 5) concludes, it seems probable that it was somewhere on this particular island.

The people Columbus chanced upon were not, as he had hoped, inhabitants of the fabled eastern realm of Japan, but the Lucayans, a branch of the indigenous Arawaks and a community of farmers and fishermen who had replaced the original inhabitants, the Siboneys. These people called themselves *Lukku-cairi* and their island *Guanahani*, but Columbus baptized it San Salvador and claimed it in the name of the King and Queen of Castile. In the first recorded encounter between the Old World and the New, the Lucayans were reportedly open and hospitable. In *Columbus: His Enterprise*, Hans Koning recalls the explorer's log entry for 12 October 1492:

> 'To win their friendship and realizing that here was a people to be converted to our Holy Faith by love and friendship and not by force, I gave some of them red caps, glass beads, and many other little things. These pleased them very much and they became very

friendly. They later swam out to the ship's boats in which we were seated, and brought us parrots and balls of cotton and spears and many other things, which they exchanged for the glass beads and hawks' bells. They willingly traded everything they owned.'

Yet, significantly, he later wrote to King Ferdinand:

'But, should your Majesties command it, all the inhabitants could be taken away to Castile, or made slaves on the island. With fifty men we could subjugate them all and make them do whatever we want.'

Finding no gold, Columbus soon left San Salvador and moved on towards Cuba. The next Spaniards to arrive were from the colony of Hispaniola, and they were in search of slave labour. The inhabitants of **San Salvador** and other islands were rounded up and enslaved. By 1520 the Bahamas were deserted.

So they remained until the middle of the following century, when an expedition of English Puritans from Bermuda settled the island of **Eleuthera**. Further English colonization gradually took place, but these communities soon had unwelcome neighbours in the form of pirates and buccaneers who thrived on the Bahamas' inaccessibility and closeness to shipping lanes. From well protected harbours the pirates preyed on laden Spanish galleons in the nearby Florida Strait *en route* from South and Central American colonies to Europe. When in 1691 the French managed to drive the buccaneers out of La Tortue (Tortuga) in their colony of Saint-Domingue, large numbers set up bases in the Bahamas. By 1715 it was estimated that there were some 1000 pirates operating in the islands, including the notorious Blackbeard.

Such was the scale of the pirate problem that in 1717 the authorities in London decided to end the piecemeal colonization of the Bahamas and to make them a Crown Colony. A Governor (himself a retired privateer) was dispatched to establish law and order, and by 1723 the buccaneers had been driven out and the Bahamas were able to claim as their motto *Expulsis Piratis, Restituta Commercia* ('With the Pirates Expelled, Trade has been Restored').

The American Revolution of 1775 had important consequences for the islands. Revolutionaries twice attacked the British colony and helped themselves to supplies and arms; the Spanish, emboldened by Britain's disarray, also invaded in 1781, only to be ejected in 1783. But, more importantly, several thousand Loyalists found refuge in the Bahamas as the USA won its independence. They represented the most reactionary strata of colonial American society and brought with them a large population of slaves, destined to work on what turned out to be unsuccessful cotton plantations in the **Exuma** islands.

Slavery provided the Bahamas with a lucrative business when the slave trade was abolished in the British Empire in 1807. Slaves were still sought after in the southern states of the USA, and illegal carriers used the

Bahamas as a base from which to supply the American market. Some ships were intercepted by the British navy, and around 3000 Africans were settled in the Bahamas, mostly on the island of **New Providence**.

SMUGGLERS' PARADISE

The Bahamas, then as now, had little to offer in terms of natural resources. Their great advantage lay simply in their closeness to the USA and their large number of secluded cays and safe harbours. Smuggling first became an important activity during the American Civil War (1861–65) when Confederate ships were able to break the Union government's blockade by using the Bahamas, and particularly **Nassau**, as a trading base. Exports of cotton and tobacco and imports of goods and war materials poured through the Bahamian capital, enriching the white merchants who became known as the 'Bay Street Boys'. When the war ended, however, so did the boom, and many Bahamians had to resort to their traditional work in sponge-production and ship-wrecking.

The Volstead Act of 1919, passed by the US Congress to prohibit alcohol, provided the 'Bay Street Boys' with another unexpected windfall. For fourteen years, **Nassau** became the centre of the bootlegging industry, supplying US drinkers with illicit supplies of rum and whisky. In his *Bahamas: Isles of June* (Extract 2), a contemporary observer, Major H. MacLachlan Bell ◊, describes how bootleg booze created a short-lived economic boom. Most famous among the rum-running captains was one Bill McCoy, who reputedly supplied 175 000 cases of spirits to the USA. The quality of his whisky, it is said, led to the expression 'the real McCoy'.

The illegal alcohol trade inevitably attracted some dubious characters from the US. In his popular 1930s travel book, *If Crab No Walk*, Owen Rutter portrays how New York's criminal fraternity descended on **Nassau**:

> 'Bay Street, the waterfront chief thoroughfare of the town, no longer was a sun-drenched idle avenue where traffic in sponges and sisal progressed torpidly. It was filled with slit-eyed, hunch-shouldered strangers, with the bluster of Manhattan in their voices and a wary truculence of manner. The faces that passed your shoulder in ten minutes on Bay Street would have given a New York cop nightmares for a week. Their owners, for the first few weeks, made existence a continual horror for the black constabulary of Nassau.'

Another American, attracted by the availability of whisky, was Ernest Hemingway (◊ Cuba), who lived on the island of **Bimini**, only 50 miles from Florida, for several years during the 1930s. The local pastimes of drinking and deep-sea fishing are memorably described in Hemingway's last and posthumously published novel, *Islands in the Stream* (Extract 3), where the autobiographical hero, Thomas Hudson, finds spiritual solace in the grandiose nature of the Gulf Stream.

Prohibition ended in 1933, but the Bahamas have remained a centre for smuggling of a different sort – cocaine. In the 1980s the islands were reputed to be used by the notorious Colombian Medellín cartel as their preferred transshipment point for supplies of cocaine from South America destined for the USA. In so-called 'cigar boats', streamlined for maximum speed, the coast of Florida could be reached 'before a milk shake melts'. A 1984 Royal Commission report stated that the Bahamas were awash with drug money and drugs, leading to an alarming increase in violent crime and money-laundering. The then leader of the main opposition party, Kendel Isaacs, melodramatically pronounced, 'The Bahamian people are selling themselves; they have become slaves of the drug traffickers.'

Among those implicated was Prime Minister Sir Lynden Pindling, who had led the Bahamas to independence from Britain in 1973. The country's first black leader, Pindling had been in power continuously since 1967, favouring the black majority and antagonizing the vested interests of the 'Bay Street Boys'. He had survived numerous scandals before, involving shady property deals and casino licences, and on this occasion, too, no hard evidence was found. But several ministers were forced to resign, and Pindling lost a general election in 1992.

TOURISM AND CULTURE

Today, tourism accounts for about 70% of Bahamian GDP, and the country is among the two or three most popular vacation destinations in the Caribbean. In 1994, 3.5 million tourists, mostly from the USA, visited the Bahamas, staying mainly in purpose-built resorts such as **Paradise Island** or **Lucaya**. Tourists have been coming to the Bahamas since the mid-nineteenth century, but the industry really exploded in the 1950s when an American entrepreneur, Wallace Groves, was leased 50 000 acres of scrubland on **Grand Bahama**, transforming it into a complex of harbour facilities, hotels and casinos called **Freeport**. The Bahamas' reputation as an exotic tourist destination was further enhanced in the 1960s by books such as *Thunderball* (Extract 1) by Ian Fleming ◊, in which double agent James Bond single-handedly defeats a super-criminal conspiracy.

Today, some of the more remote inhabited islands, known as the 'Out Islands' or 'Family Islands' retain a rustic charm, with their pine forests, empty beaches and clapboard houses. But the tourist centres have been irreversibly transformed by cruise ship terminals and duty-free shopping malls. In his poem 'Poisoned in Nassau' (Extract 4) John Updike (◊ The British Dependencies) presents a dyspeptic version of this mass-market 'paradise'. For some Bahamians, the metamorphosis has taken a terrible cultural toll. In his autobiography, *This Life*, Bahamian-born actor Sidney Poitier recalls his small-island childhood and contrasts it with his return in later life to the country:

> It disturbed me deeply that there was no cultural life expressing the history of the people – absolutely none. I did see wood carvings, but

they were imported from Haiti to sell to tourists in the Bahamas . . . It was tourism, so enormously successful over so many years, that had contaminated – diluted – debased – the shape of all things cultural in those islands, until there was no longer any real semblance of a Bahamian cultural identity.

But if tourism has removed the cultural traditions of once little-known island communities, it has also provided the resources for other expressions of identity to survive. Probably the most important of these is Junkanoo, a Christmas-time festival dating back to the rituals of newly arrived African slaves. Junkanoo entails a hedonistic blend of drink and music, and its centrepiece is the 'rush' of costumed participants down **Bay Street** in the capital. Junkanoo almost died out as a tradition, but was resurrected by tourism officials in the 1950s who saw it as an 'exotic' attraction for visitors. Now, black Bahamians can claim Junkanoo as their version of Trinidad's world-famous Carnival and as a celebration of their own turbulent heritage.

LITERARY LANDMARKS

Bimini. Set in the Gulf Stream and one of the nearest of the islands to the USA, it was intermittently home to Ernest Hemingway between 1931 and 1937. Once it was thought to be the site of the lost city of Atlantis, but Hemingway went there to escape Prohibition and to do some big-game fishing. The American writer John Dos Passos accompanied him on one expedition and recalled: 'There was a wharf and some native shacks under the coconut palms and a store that had some kind of a bar-room attached, where we drank rum in the evenings, and a magnificent broad beach on the Gulf Stream side.' Some Hemingway memorabilia can be viewed at the **Compleat Angler Hotel and Museum.** His **Blue Marlin Cottage** is now part of the Bimini Blue Water Resort.

BOOKLIST

College of the Bahamas, *Bahamian Anthology*, Macmillan, London, 1986.

Davies, Hunter, *In Search of Columbus*, Sinclair-Stevenson, London, 1991. **Extract 5**

Fleming, Ian, *Thunderball*, Jonathan Cape, London, 1961. **Extract 1**

Hemingway, Ernest, *Islands in the Stream*, Collins, London, 1989. **Extract 3**

Koning, Hans, *Columbus: His Enterprise*, Latin America Bureau, London, 1991.

MacLachlan Bell, Major H., *Bahamas: Isles of June*, Williams &

Norgate, London, 1934. **Extract 2**

Poitier, Sidney, *This Life*, Hodder and Stoughton, London, 1980.

Rutter, Owen, *If Crab No Walk*,

Hutchinson, London, 1933.

Updike, John, 'Poisoned in Nassau', in *Collected Poems, 1953–1993*, Hamish Hamilton, London, 1993. **Extract 4**

Extracts

(1) BAHAMAS: BEACHES

Ian Fleming, *Thunderball*

In pursuit of the sinister SPECTRE, James Bond still has time to visit the beach and find the elusive girl.

Bond rolled his swimming trunks into a towel, put on a dark blue sea-island shirt over his slacks and slung Leiter's geiger counter over his shoulder. He glanced at himself in the mirror. He looked like any other tourist with a camera. He felt in his trousers pocket to make sure he had the identification bracelet and went out of the room and down in the lift.

The Land Rover had Dunlopillo cushions, but the ripple-edged tarmac and the pitted bends of Nassau's coastal road were tough on the springs and the quivering afternoon sun was a killer. By the time Bond found the sandy track leading off into the casuarinas and had parked the car on the edge of the beach, all he wanted to do was get into the sea and stay in it. The beach hut was a Robinson Crusoe affair of plaited bamboo and screwpine with a palm thatch whose wide eaves threw black shadows. Inside were two changing rooms labelled 'HIS' and 'HERS'. Hers contained a small pile of soft clothes and the white doeskin sandals. Bond changed and walked out again into the sun. The small beach was a dazzling half-moon of white sand enclosed on both sides by rocky points. There was no sign of the girl. The beach shelved quickly through green to blue under the water. Bond took a few steps through the shallows and dived through the blood-warm upper water down into the cool depths. He kept down there as long as possible, feeling the wonderful cold caress on his skin and through his hair. Then he surfaced and crawled lazily out to sea, expecting to see the girl skin-diving round one of the headlands. But there was no sign of her, and after ten minutes Bond turned back to the shore, chose a patch of firm sand, and lay down on his stomach, his face cradled in his arms.

Minutes later, something made Bond open his eyes. Coming towards him across the middle of the quiet bay was a thin trail of bubbles. When it passed over the dark blue into the green, Bond could see the yellow single cylinder of the aqualung tank and the glint of a mask with a fan of dark hair streaming out behind. The girl beached herself in the shallows. She raised herself on one elbow and lifted the mask. She said severely, 'Don't lie there dreaming. Come and rescue me.'

(2) BAHAMAS: BOOTLEGGING

Major H. MacLachlan Bell, *Bahamas: Isles of June*

The prohibition of alcohol in the USA in 1919 sparked off a boom in the Bahamas, fuelled by illicit shipments of rum.

Nassau became one of the strangest by-products of Prohibition. Its contrasts grew more and more vivid as the years rolled along. Before the rum-running era there were no restaurants, no electric lighting, no sewers, no macadamized roadways. 'If you wanted to eat,' said an old-timer to me, 'you bought a can of salmon in one place and some hard tack in another and you sat on the pier and ate them.' There were the Lucerne and a few 'dumps' where men could 'doss', but outside of the Royal Victoria and the Lucerne, not a hotel to speak of. Besides, the 'Vic' opened only in winter.

At the beginning of the 'booze' era Bahamians were half eager, half afraid – were, in one word, bewildered. For a year or more Nassau folk were plainly nonplussed about the rum business. Then they woke up. Deep called unto deep. The sea became the home of men who for forty-five years had been in petty shopkeeping; the windows changed from panes of ordinary glass to plate, automobiles became as plentiful as telephone numbers; mansions grew in the skies. Nassau was 'bouncing high' once more.

Sir George Gamblin, that gentle knight who in the heyday of the traffic was an agent for the Royal Bank of Canada, told me of having eleven million dollars in the vaults one Saturday and of a telegram that came that day from Cuba to the effect that a band of 'hijackers' had left there intent on raiding the bank. Quickly a barricade was erected around the building; a platoon of police armed with rifles, bayonets and ball ammunition stood guard over the bank for a week. The bandits were scared off . . .

There were other strange results: neglected churches were renovated with liquor money, charities were refinanced, life in general took on a splendour and a spaciousness that even brought about a real estate boom remindful of Miami's great splurge. Rents on Nassau's all-important Bay Street went up like rockets, coloured workers drew pay of $6 a day, warehouses were bulging with foodstuffs, taxis replaced horse cabs, public works were undertaken, the colony's treasury soared to dizzy heights, hotels were financed with millions.

(3) BIMINI

Ernest Hemingway, *Islands in the Stream*

The tiny island of Bimini, famous for its big-game fishing, is the adopted home of Hemingway's artist-hero, Thomas Hudson.

The house was built on the highest part of the narrow tongue of land between the harbor and the open sea. It had lasted through three hurricanes and it was built solid as a ship. It was shaded by tall coconut palms that were bent by the trade wind and on the ocean side you could walk out of the door and down the bluff across the white sand and into the Gulf Stream. The water of the Stream was usually a dark blue when you looked out at it when there was no wind. But when you walked out into it there was just the green light of the water over that floury white sand and you could see the shadow of any big fish a long time before he could ever come in close to the beach.

It was a safe and fine place to bathe in the day but it was no place to swim at night. At night the sharks came in close to the beach, hunting in the edge of the Stream and from the upper porch of the house on quiet nights you could hear the splashing of the fish they hunted and if you went down to the beach you could see the phosphorescent wakes they made in the water. At night the sharks had no fear and everything else feared them. But in the day they stayed out away from the clear white sand and if they did come in you could see their shadows a long way away.

A man named Thomas Hudson, who was a good painter, lived there in that house and worked there and on the island the greater part of the year. After one has lived in those latitudes long enough the changes of the seasons become as important there as anywhere else and Thomas Hudson, who loved the island, did not want to miss any spring, nor summer, nor any fall or winter . . .

Thomas Hudson had studied tropical storms for many years and he could tell from the sky when there was a tropical disturbance long before his barometer showed its presence. He knew how to plot storms and the precautions that should be taken against them. He knew too what it was to live through a hurricane with the other people of the island and the bond that the hurricane made between all people who had been through it.

(4) NASSAU: TOURISM

John Updike, *Poisoned in Nassau*

Updike's poem is a nightmarish vision of all the horrors which Caribbean tourism can offer.

By the fourth (or is it the fifth?)
day, one feels poisoned – by
last night's rum, this morning's sun,
the tireless pressure of leisure.

The sea's pale green seems evil.
The shells seem pellets, the meals
forced doses, Bahamian cooking
as bitterly obsequious as
the resentful wraiths that serve it.

Vertigo is reading at the beach
words a thousand miles away,
is tasting Coppertone again,
is closing one's eyes once more against
the mismatch of poverty and beauty.

The beautiful sea is pale, it is
sick, its fish sting like regrets.
Perhaps it was the conch salad, or is
there something too rich in Creation.

(5) SAN SALVADOR

Hunter Davies, *In Search of Columbus*

Where exactly did Columbus first land in the New World? There are, it seems, several rival claims.

The first thing I noticed when we landed at San Salvador's little airport was a large wooden notice saying: 'Welcome to the friendly island of San Salvador, site of Columbus Landings.' It was the plural which intrigued me. The airport was bigger than I expected, the legacy of a military establishment which was set up in the 1950s as part of the US space programme. For a while, it brought work and prosperity to the island and the population doubled to 1200. No tourists were allowed during this period, as the work was classed as secret. Now they have gone. All that is left is an unnecessarily large air-strip, one road round the island grandiosely called the Queen's Highway, and a few empty army buildings. There is only one hotel, the Riding Rock Inn. The island is just twelve miles long by five miles wide. Most of the interior is as swampy and undeveloped as it was when Columbus arrived . . .

Just outside the town, at the end of a long beach called Fernandez Bay, we came to our first Columbus monument, a small pyramid-shaped white stone. The inscription read: 'Christopher Columbus made the first recorded landing in the New World on this beach, October 12, 1492. Yawl Heloise [a boat on a round-the-world cruise], Feb 25, 1951.' People who put up monuments are very confident: not just the right island, but the right spot on the right beach.

Two miles further south, on Long Beach, there is a much more impressive Columbus memorial: a large white cross, very simple, but dramatic against the bright blue of the sea . . .

The third Columbus arrival monument, and the oldest, is on the other side of the island, at Corab Cay on the east coast. 'On this spot,' so the tablet reads, 'Christopher Columbus first set foot on the soil of THE NEW WORLD. Erected by the Chicago Herald, June, 1891.'

No one seriously believes now that he could possibly have landed on that side of the island, on such a rocky, dangerous part of the first coast. The more likely landfall positions would be near one of the two monuments, on the other coast, where the long sandy beach is safe, with no rocks. There is, however, about a mile out, the inevitable Caribbean coral reef, though there are gaps. Columbus did very well, wherever he landed, to avoid any mishap.

Biographical and literary notes

DAVIES, Hunter (1936–). The author of more than thirty books on subjects ranging from Beatrix Potter to the Beatles, Hunter Davies is a popular journalist, writer and broadcaster. His *In Search of Columbus* (Extract 5), published in 1991 to coincide with the quincentenary of the explorer's arrival in the Americas, retraces Columbus's expeditions and looks at those countries in the Caribbean and Latin America where he left the most significant personal legacy.

FLEMING, Ian (1908–1964). Ian Fleming is best known for creating the archetypally suave secret agent, James Bond, who appears in twelve novels

and seven short stories. Originally a stockbroker by profession, Fleming worked as a foreign correspondent in Moscow before serving as a senior naval intelligence officer during the Second World War. His James Bond books were mostly published in the 1950s and 1960s, during which he spent most of his time at his home on the north coast of Jamaica. *Thunderball* (Extract 1) is typical of Fleming's enormously popular genre, in which a sophisticated, slightly *roué*, English secret agent invariably outwits any combination of criminals or communists.

HEMINGWAY, Ernest (see under

Cuba). In *Islands in the Stream* (Extract 3), Hemingway tells the three-part story of Thomas Hudson, a hard-drinking artist, whose life is a complex mix of personal tragedy, heroism and deep-sea fishing. Published posthumously, the novel contains most of Hemingway's familar concerns and themes, as well as what are thought to be some of the best accounts of fishing ever written. The descriptions of **Bimini** are based on Hemingway's own periods of residence there in the 1930s when he went to write, fish and drink.

MACLACHLAN BELL, Major H. MacLachlan Bell's 1930s travelogue, *Bahamas: Isles of June* (Extract 2) provides some interesting and well painted vignettes of Bahamian life and society towards the end of the Prohibition era.

UPDIKE, John (see under The British Dependencies).

CUBA

Jason Wilson

'Cuba is a peculiar exile, I think, an island-colony. We can reach it by a thirty-minute charter flight from Miami, yet never reach it at all.'
Cristina García,
Dreaming in Cuban

The Republic of Cuba lies 90 miles off Florida, is the largest island in the Caribbean ('long, beautiful, unhappy island' – Hemingway), and runs 746 miles long from west to east. The island is tropical, with a uniform temperature and abundant rain, three-quarters of the land consisting of rolling hills and plains. Cuban writer Guillermo Cabrera Infante ◊ claimed that to understand Cuba you had first to understand its geography. To the south rise the 150 mile long **Sierra Maestra**, at their highest with **Pico Turquino** (1973 metres), and densely forested. The island is lashed by hurricanes (a word derived from the Carib language) from September to October. The flora is dramatic, with the Royal Palm as the most evident, and the national tree.

On 27 October 1492, from his ship the Santa María, Christopher Columbus thought that the island of Colba was part of Japan or China. He noticed that the Arawak-speaking Tainos and the Ciboney, their vassals, smoked *tobacos*. Havana later became synonymous with the best cigars in the world (see Guillermo Cabrera Infante's witty, idiosyncratic history of cigars *Holy Smoke*, 1985). In 1992 Cuba exported over 100 million cigars.

Cuba was finally conquered in 1511 by Diego Velázquez, with the first settlement founded at Baracoa in 1515. The aborigines, enslaved under the *encomienda* system, were decimated by 1570. Already by 1517 African slaves were shipped over to work, though the bulk of the slaves arrived between 1790 and 1850 when sugar-cane became the monocrop. Slavery was not abolished until 1886. The African inheritance is enormous, with black descendants occupying some 12% of the Cuban population, and bequeathing the crucial influence of dance and music, the *son*, and *santería*, the African slave religion mixing Yoruban gods with Christianity, like

---

FACT BOX

AREA: 114 524 sq km
POPULATION: 10 900 000
CAPITAL: Havana (La Habana)
LANGUAGES: Spanish
FORMER COLONIAL POWER: Spain
INDEPENDENCE: 1902
PER CAPITA GDP: US$1170

Changó as Santa Barbara. On the African legacy see Pedro Sarduy and Jean Stubbs, *AfroCuba: An Anthology of Cuban Writing on Race, Politics and Culture*, 1993. Sarduy and Stubbs reckon that one third of today's Cuban population is non-white, and that since the revolution of 1959 Cuba has become less white. Alejo Carpentier's ◊ first novel, begun in prison in Havana in 1927, *Ecué-Yamba-O*, 1933, documented, with photos, the African part of Cuban culture, as did mulatto poet Nicolás Guillén's ◊ rhythmic poems.

COLONIALISM

During the colonial period under Spain, when Cuba was a Captaincy-General, the island was a stepping stone to the New World, from where Cortés set sail for Mexico in 1519, where Spain kept and supplied its fleet, a centre for all mail. Like all the Spanish possessions it was not allowed to trade with the other colonies, leading to much smuggling. The Caribbean islands were infested with European and American pirates and freebooters. Henry Morgan, for example, attacked Puerto Príncipe (today **Camagüey**) in 1688. In 1762 Britain captured and looted **Havana**, and after 11 months occupation swapped Havana for Florida.

Cuba was not affected by the Independence movements on the continent, and by 1825 Cuba, with a population of 533 033, and Puerto Rico were the last colonies held by Spain. There were outbreaks of revolt, especially following the Grito de Yara on 10 October 1868, finally quelled in 1878 by Spain. Cuba's great poet, chronicler and national hero José Martí (1853–1895) was killed in a skirmish with the Spanish in 1895 in a US-backed guerrilla offensive to liberate the island (he is buried in the **Santa Efigenia cemetery**, near **Santiago de Cuba**). Exiled by Spain for many years in the USA, Martí epitomized Cuba's relationship with the Giant from the North. His Havana home is a **museum**, his statue adorns the **Parque Central** (and countless other public spaces), a monument to him stands in the **Plaza de la Revolución**, and one of his poems, '*Yo soy un hombre sincero / de donde crece la palma*' gave the lyrics to the famous song 'Guantanamera'. The best glimpse of nineteenth-century Cuba is Cirilo Villaverde's anti-slavery love story *Cecilia Valdés o la Loma del Angel*, 1839 and 1882, realistically set in Havana's **La Loma del Angel** district from 1812 to 1831.

Soon after Martí's death the US warship *Maine* was mysteriously blown up in Havana harbour, precipitating the Spanish American war which lasted for 3 months and saw the Spanish finally routed, and Cuba freed, though remaining under US military rule. Writer Stephen Crane (1871–1900) was a war correspondent, and wrote a collection of short stories based on his direct experience in Cuba, *Wounds in the Rain: War Stories*, 1900. The infamous Platt Amendment (abrogated in 1934) ensured US naval presence (the base at Guantánamo), and constant interventions to 'protect' Cuba. The USA invested heavily in sugar, and later in property and vice.

DICTATORS

Three *caudillos* dominate twentieth-century Cuban history. The first was Gerardo Machado, who came to power in 1924 after five US interventions (one lasting from 1906–09, for example) until ousted in 1933. This period saw the rise of Havana student guerrillas, and street fighting, evoked in Ernest Hemingway's ◊ drama of gun-running *To Have and Have Not*, 1937, and, though not set under Machado, in Carpentier's fine short novel *El acoso*, 1957 (*The Chase*, 1990). The second *caudillo* was Sergeant Fulgencio Batista, the power behind the scenes from 1933 to 1959, and actually elected president 1933–44 and again in 1952–59. He began as a populist, and ended up a dictator. During the 1950s Havana was one of the night-time capitals of the world (the Las Vegas of the Caribbean), a fun-city depicted in Guillermo Cabrera Infante's ◊ wonderful novel *Tres tristes tigres*, 1965 (*Three Trapped Tigers*, 1971), and the background to Graham Greene's ◊ farce *Our Man in Havana*, 1958 (see Extracts 7 and 10).

The third *caudillo* is the controversial demagogue, and brilliant orator, Fidel Castro (1926–   ). A lawyer from a landed background, he came to the fore when he led 160 students in the attack on the Moncada barracks in **Santiago** in 1953. During his trial he made the famous speech beginning, '*La historia me absolverá . . .*' (History will absolve me). On the second of December 1956, from exile in Mexico, Castro set off, with Argentine Che Guevara and 80 further men, on the boat *Granma*, to liberate Cuba from Batista. Only 12 survived in the wild **Sierra Maestra**. But on the first of January 1959 Batista fled, and Castro and his *barbudos* ('bearded men') entered Havana in triumph (recorded in Norman Lewis's ◊ novel *Cuban Passage*, 1982 – Extract 13). Castro's revolution astonished the West, and proved a thorn in US interests in Latin America, spawning and supporting countless guerrilla uprisings, heralding the New Man and socialism. Castro never held elections, and closed the free press. He soon expropriated US business, so that Eisenhower passed a devastating trade embargo in 1960, forcing Castro to rely on the Russians for economic help. A US-backed invasion in 1961 called the Bay of Pigs (*Playa Girón* in Spanish) was a fiasco that reinforced Cuban determination. In October 1962 a US spy plane spotted atomic missile sights, and for four days the world stood on the brink of atomic conflict until the Russian premier Khrushchev stood down, and removed the missiles.

CHE GUEVARA

A fourth figure stands out during this period, and this is Argentine-born Ernesto 'Che' Guevara (1928–1967), the only non-Cuban to travel on the *Granma* in 1956. Guevara was an asthmatic adventurer who travelled round South America on a motorbike in 1951, graduated as a doctor in 1953, fought in Guatemala and, after Castro's remarkable victory in Cuba in 1959, became the icon of student radicals and revolutionaries worldwide through his Romantic version of the New Man purified by revolutionary violence, his love of living dangerously, and his Robin Hood appeal. He was a literate and ingenious man, with a sense of humour and a hatred of bureaucracy, who resigned from his role as president of the National Bank of Cuba and disappeared from public view to continue his anti-colonialist guerrilla activies in Zaire and then Bolivia, until he was caught and assassinated in Vallegrande, Bolivia in 1967. Although his writings are not literary, his manual *Guerrilla Warfare*, 1967, his autobiography *Reminiscences of the Cuban Revolutionary War*, 1968, his *Bolivian Diary*, 1968, and the recently published *The Motorcycle Diaries: A Journey Around South America*, 1995, all repay reading to understand the man behind the incredible myth, and the turbulent period.

CASTRO

The middle class fled to Miami when Castro aligned himself officially with Marxism in 1961. Edmundo Desnoes's ◊ novel *Memories of Underdevelopment*, 1965, caught the mood of fear in its diary of an intellectual coping with the new Cuba (Extract 9). Cuban opposition to Castro remains centred in Miami. Despite Castro's hard line with his opponents, his imprisonments, and his rhetoric of '*Patria o muerte*', the revolution brought illiteracy down to 12%, and introduced racial equality, equal rights for women, an admirable health service and effective land redistribution. But there was also rationing, paper shortage, centralized publishing, and a continuing dependence on sugar-cane.

Castro's cultural politics were more questionable. Carlos Franqui called 1960 the miracle year of the revolution, when luminaries like Jean-Paul Sartre and Simone de Beauvoir and Pablo Neruda visited the island. Western intellectuals flirted with Castro's new Cuba until the Padilla case hit the headlines. The poet Heberto Padilla was forced to confess to anti-Cuban attitudes in his poems, a confession which shocked the world, and led Octavio Paz, Sartre and Mario Vargas Llosa, among many others, to break with Cuba's hard line. During these years Cuba financed an exciting, wide-ranging literary magazine *Casa de las Américas*, and inaugurated prestigious annual literary prizes for all Latin Americans from the Casa de las Américas centre run by poet Roberto Fernández Retamar.

Good examples of the atmosphere of debate and excitement can be gauged from the late Jamaican writer Andrew Salkey's *Havana Journal*, 1971, and from British poet Tony Harrison's 1969 visit (*London Magazine*, April 1970), as well as Nicaraguan poet Ernesto Cardenal's *In Cuba*, 1974.

However, Castro stifled free expression, and ironically the best writing often came from opposition to his puritanical policies. Guillermo Cabrera Infante stands as the most eloquent creative force, a chronicler in wild and witty ways of Cuban life. In 1980, when Castro opened the prisons and dispatched undesirable prisoners, among the 120 000 sent from the port of **Mariel**, a fine Surrealistic homosexual writer Reinaldo Arenas ◊ was on board. In fact Castro did not tolerate homosexuals, and marginalized Cuba's great baroque, and obscure, essayist and poet José Lezama Lima ◊. In 1965, Beat poet Allen Ginsberg, staying in the **Havana Riviera**, pestered Castro's regime about the use of drugs like marijuana and about the fate of gay poets until he was finally deported. Even Carpentier, Cuba's grand man of letters, wrote his best work in exile before the revolution, while his attempt to write the novel of the Cuban revolution, *La consagración de la primavera*, 1978, was a relative artistic failure.

LITERARY HAVANA

San Cristóbal de la Habana, the largest city in the West Indies, was founded in 1519, and named after a Taíno *cacique* Habaguanix. The two forts on each side of the natural harbour, the long *malecón* sea-wall promenade ('the greatest sea promenade in the world', Norman Lewis), the old 16th-century and 17th-century city, now falling to pieces, the splendid hotels like the **Riviera** and the **Inglaterra**, where Federico García Lorca had his farewell party in 1930, the lovely plazas (caught in Jana Bokova's BBC documentary *Havana*) have made this a literary city, described by Carpentier as a 'city of columns', with famous bars like the vanished Sloppy Joe and Hemingway's Floridita (where he would sit under his own bust), on the corner of **Obispo** and **Monsterrat**. Hemingway's home, the **Finca Vigía**, where he wrote standing up and built a dog cemetery, is now the **Museo Hemingway** (see Extract 9). The national theatre is the **Teatro García Lorca**. The Marquesa de la Reunión's house on **calle Empedrado** (the first paved street in Havana) is today the **Centro Alejo Carpentier**. The **Casa de las Américas** is in **Vedado**, just off the **Malecón**. Good bookshops are **La Nueva Poesía** on **Obispo**, with further ones on **calle L**. Havana has been called the capital of noise, in Cabrera Infante's pun, packed with 'hablaneros' not 'habaneros'. However, Spanish poet Federico García Lorca found this tropical island a 'paradise'. In a lecture he described arriving at Havana by boat: 'But what is this? Is it Spain again?

Universal Andalusia? It is the yellow of Cádiz, but a shade brighter; the rosiness of Seville, but more like carmine; the green of Granada, but slightly phosphorescent like a fish. Havana rises up amid cane fields and the noise of maracas, cornets, bells and marimbas.'

FURTHER READING

Of books not mentioned so far, the best history of Cuba is Hugh Thomas's *Cuba, or the Pursuit of Freedom*, 1971, with Edwin Williamson's *The Penguin History of Latin America*, 1992, linking Cuba with the rest of Latin America. The most readable chronicle of Cuban cultural life is Guillermo Cabrera Infante's *Mea Cuba*, 1995. Of the myriad books on Castro see Herbert Matthews, *Castro: A Political Biography*, 1970 – Matthews was the US journalist largely responsible for the romantic way Castro was seen by the West. An insider's view is offered by Carlos Franqui, one-time editor of the paper *Revolución*, in *Family Portrait with Fidel*, 1983. On Martí, see Peter Turton's *José Martí: Architect of Cuba's Freedom*, 1986. Oscar Lewis brought his skills to *Four Women: Living the Revolution – An Oral History of Contemporary Cuba*, 1977. Two travel books that cover the revolutionary period, from among many, are Nicholas Wollaston's *Red Rumba: A Journey through the Caribbean and Central America*, 1962, and novelist Carlo Gébler's *Driving through Cuba: An East–West Journey*, 1988. Pico Iyer's novel *Cuba and the Night*, 1995, follows the fortunes of a photographer on the look-out for typical revolutionary shots, and is rich in acutely observed details of Cuban topography and social *moeurs*. An early anthology of new Cuban writing was edited by J.M. Cohen, *Writers in the New Cuba*, 1967. Poet Nathaniel Tarn edited *Con Cuba: An Anthology of Cuban Poetry of the last 60 Years*, 1969. Andrew Salkey, author of *Havana Journal*, also edited *Writing in Cuba Since the Revolution: an Anthology of Poems, Short Stories and Essays*, 1977. Margaret Randall edited *Breaking the Silence: Twentieth Century Poetry by Cuban Women*, 1982. A concise survey of Cuba today is by Emily Hatchwell and Simon Calder, *Cuba in Focus: A Guide to the People, Politics and Culture*, 1995.

Individual Cuban writers translated into English but not extracted include Humberto Arenal (1927–), *El sol a plomo*, 1958 (*The Sun Beats Down: A Novella of the Cuban Revolution*, 1959), poet Octavio Armand (1946–), *With Dusk*, 1984, and poet Belkis Cuza Malé (1942–), *Belkis Cuza Malé: Woman in the Front Line*, 1988.

Notes to map (facing page): [a]*Allen Ginsberg stayed here in 1965 until Castro had him deported;* [b]*the* **Hotel Inglaterra** *is next to the Teatro Garcia Lorca;* [c]*site of* **Sloppy Joe's** *(corner of Zulueta and Ánimas);* [d]*statue of José Martí;* [e]*location of* **La Floridita** *café, frequented by Hemingway;* [f]*José Martí* **monument;** [g]*see Extract 1;* [h]*see Extract 9.*

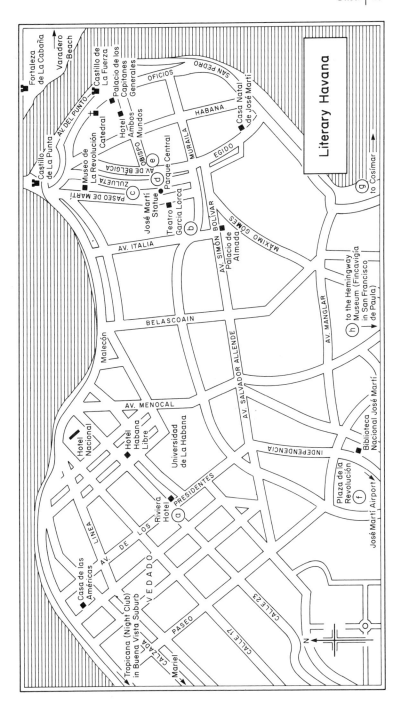

Literary Havana

Fortaleza de La Cabaña
Varadero Beach
Castillo de La Punta
AV. DEL PUNTO
Castillo de La Fuerza
Palacio de los Capitanes Generales
OFICIOS
SAN PEDRO
Castillo de La Punta
Museo de La Revolución
Catedral
Hotel Ambos Mundos
OBISPO
HABANA
Casa Natal de José Martí
Castillo de La Punta
PASEO DE MARTÍ
ZULUETA
AV. DE BÉLGICA
Parque Central
MURAILA
EGIDO
José Martí Statue
Teatro García Lorca
Palacio de Almada
AV. SIMÓN BOLIVAR
MÁXIMO GÓMEZ
to Cosimar
AV. ITALIA
BELASCOAIN
AV. MANGLAR
to the Hemingway Museum (Fincavigía in San Francisco de Paula)
Malecón
AV. MENOCAL
AV. SALVADOR ALLENDE
INDEPENDENCIA
Biblioteca Nacional José Martí
Hotel Nacional
Hotel Habana Libre
Universidad de La Habana
Plaza de la Revolución
José Martí Airport
Casa de las Américas
LINEA
AV. DE LOS PRESIDENTES
Riviera Hotel
CALLE 23
N
Tropicana (Night Club) in Buena Vista Suburb
CALZADA
Mariel
VEDADO
PASEO
CALLE 17

BOOKLIST

The following selection includes the extracted titles in this chapter as well as other titles for further reading. In general, paperback editions are given when possible. For most of the extracted works, the original publisher in English can be found in 'Acknowledgments and Citations' at the end of the volume, as can the exact location of the extracts and the editions from which they are taken.

AfroCuba: An Anthology of Cuban Writing on Race, Politics and Culture, Pedro Sarduy and Jean Stubbs, eds, Latin America Bureau, London, 1993.

Arenal, Humberto, *The Sun Beats Down: A Novella of the Cuban Revolution*, J.S. Bernstein, trans, Hill and Wang, New York, 1959.

Arenas, Reinaldo, *Farewell to the Sea: A Novel of Cuba*, Andrew Hurley, trans, Viking, London and New York, 1982. **Extract 2**.

Armand, Octavio, *With Dusk*, Carol Maier, trans, Logbridge-Rhodes, Durango, CO, 1984.

Cabrera Infante, Guillermo, *Three Trapped Tigers*, Faber and Faber, London, 1989. **Extract 7**.

Cardenal, Ernesto, *In Cuba*, Donald Walsh, trans, New Directions, New York, 1984.

Carpentier, Alejo, *Explosion in a Cathedral*, Victor Gollancz, London, 1963. **Extract 8**.

Con Cuba: An Anthology of Cuban Poetry of the Last 60 Years, Nathaniel Tarn, ed, Cape, London, 1969/Grossman, New York, 1969.

Crane, Stephen, *Wounds in the Rain: War Stories*, Ayer, Salem, NH, 1990.

Cuza Malé, Belkis, *Woman in the Front Line*, Pamela Carmell, trans, Unicorn Press, Greens-

boro, NC, 1988.

Desnoes, Edmundo, *Memories of Underdevelopment*, Penguin, London, 1971. **Extract 9**.

Fernández Retamar, Roberto, 'From the Vedado . . .', Tim Reynolds, trans, in *Triquarterly*, Fall/Winter, 1968–1969. **Extract 19**.

Franqui, Carlos, *Family Portrait with Fidel*, Vintage, New York, 1983.

García, Cristina, *Dreaming in Cuban*, Flamingo, London, 1992/Knopf, New York, 1982. **Extract 18**.

Greene, Graham, *Our Man in Havana: An Entertainment*, William Heinemann, London, 1958. **Extract 10**.

Gébler, Carlo, *Driving Through Cuba: An East-West Journey*, Hamish Hamilton, London, 1988.

Guevara, Che, *Che Guevara and the Cuban Revolution: Writings and Speeches*, A. Reynaldo and J. Muniz, trans, Pathfinder, New York, 1987.

Guillén, Nicolás, 'Heat', Robert Marquez and David Arthur McMurray, trans, in *Man-Making Words: Selected Poems of Nicolás Guillén*, Editorial de Arte y Literatura, La Habana, 1973. (Poem first published in *West Indies, Ltd*, 1934). **Extract 3**.

Hatchwell, Emily, and Simon Calder, *Cuba in Focus: A Guide to the People, Politics and Culture*, Latin America Bureau, London, 1995.

Hemingway, Ernest, *The Old Man and the Sea*, Arrow Books, London, 1993. **Extract 1**.

Hergesheimer, Joseph, *San Cristóbal de la Habana*, William Heinemann, London, 1921. **Extract 11**.

Hijuelos, Oscar, *The Mambo Kings Play Songs of Love*, Penguin, London, 1991/HarperCollins, New York, 1992. **Extract 6**.

Humboldt, Alexandre von, *Personal Narrative of a Journey to the Equinoctial Regions of the New Continent*, abridged and translated with an introduction by Jason Wilson, Penguin, London, 1995. **Extract 12**.

Iyer, Pico, *Cuba and the Night*, Quartet, London, 1995.

Lewis, Norman, *Cuban Passage*, Pantheon, New York, 1982. **Extract 13**.

Lewis, Oscar, *Four Women: Living the Revolution – An Oral History of Contemporary Cuba*, University of Illinois Press, Champaigne, IL, 1977.

Lezama Lima, José, *Paradiso*, Secker and Warburg, London, 1974/ Farrar, Straus and Giroux, New York, 1974. **Extract 14**.

Martí, José, *Major Poems: A Bilingual Edition*, Holmes and Meier, New York, 1982.

Martí, José, 'Two Fatherlands', Jason Wilson, trans. **Extract 4**.

Matthews, Herbert, *Castro: A Political Biography*, Penguin, London, 1970.

Morejón, Nancy, 'Woman in a Tobacco Factory', in Margaret Randall, ed and trans, *Breaking the Silence: 20th Century Poetry by Cuban Women*, Pulp Press, Vancouver, 1982. **Extract 15**.

Padilla, Heberto, 'I Have Always Lived in Cuba', Mark Strand, trans, in *New York Review of Books*, 23 October 1969. **Extract 5**.

Piñera, Virgilio, *Cold Tales*, Mark Schafer, trans, revised by Thomas Christensen, Eridanos Press, New York, 1988. **Extract 16**.

Salkey, Andrew, *Havana Journal*, Penguin, London, 1971.

Sarduy, Severo, *From Cuba with a Song*, Suzanne Jill Levine, trans, Sun & Moon Press, Los Angeles, CA, 1994. **Extract 17**.

Thomas, Hugh, *Cuba or the Pursuit of Freedom*, Eyre and Spottiswoode, London, 1971.

Williamson, Edwin, *The Penguin History of Latin America*, Penguin, London, 1992.

Wollaston, Nicholas, *Red Rumba: a Journey Through the Caribbean and Central America*, Hodder and Stoughton, London, 1962.

Writers in the New Cuba, J.M. Cohen, ed, Penguin, London, 1967.

Writing in Cuba Since the Revolution: An Anthology of Poems, Short Stories and Essays, Andrew Salkey, ed, Bogle-l'Ouverture, London, 1977.

Extracts

(1) COJÍMAR

Ernest Hemingway, *The Old Man and the Sea*

The old fisherman Santiago walks home in Cojímar with his young fan Manolin before setting out alone to hook his outsize marlin and lose it to sharks. This novel won Hemingway the Nobel prize.

They walked up the road together to the old man's shack and went in through its open door. The old man leaned the mast with its wrapped sail against the wall and the boy put the box and the other gear beside it. The mast was nearly as long as the one room of the shack. The shack was made of tough budshields of the royal palm which are called *guano* and in it there was a bed, a table, one chair, and a place on the dirt floor to cook with charcoal. On the brown walls of the flattened, overlapping leaves of the sturdy-fibered *guano* there was a picture in color of the Sacred Heart of Jesus and another of the Virgin of Cobre. These were relics of his wife. Once there had been a tinted photograph of his wife on the wall but he had taken it down because it made him too lonely to see it and it was on the shelf in the corner under his clean shirt.

'What do you have to eat?' the boy asked.

'A pot of yellow rice with fish. Do you want some?'

'No. I will eat at home. Do you want me to make a fire?'

'No. I will make it later on. Or I may eat the rice cold.'

'May I take the cast net?'

'Of course.'

There was no cast net and the boy remembered when they had sold it. But they went though this fiction every day. There was no pot of yellow rice and fish and the boy knew this too.

(2) CUBA: SIGNS

Reinaldo Arenas, *Farewell to the Sea*

A woman describes the Cuba she wants to escape from while on holiday with her husband, who narrates the second half of the novel.

On one side of the highway you can see the ocean; on the other a house of unplastered cinder blocks, unshaded by trees, with four windows and a tower, or something that looks like a tower – I can't imagine what it's for. I see the house from afar as we pass. It looks pathetic there in the middle of the flat field, having to take the force of the wind and the sun. The car goes on but the house stays a few seconds in my memory . . . On one side of the highway you can see the ocean; on the other a billboard with immense letters: YOU ARE ENTERING THE MONUMENTAL COFFEE BELT OF HAVANA. On one side of the highway the ocean; on the other a gigantic fence: EIGHTY THOUSAND HAVANA WOMEN TO THE CANE-CUTTING! On one side of the highway the ocean; on the other a sign: WE HAVE REACHED 100 000 COFFEE SEEDLINGS PLANTED! A sign with an athletic arm, its hand gripping a rifle. TO THE ATTACK – WITH FIDEL BEFORE US! A military post with two armed guards at the entrance. A great banner: YOUNG PEOPLE TO CAMAGÜEY FOR THREE YEARS! Two rumpled women under a bus shelter. A gas station. A gigantic placard: AT YOUR COMMAND, COMMANDER-IN-CHIEF! A sign: THE SCHOOL IN THE FIELDS IS THE BEST EDUCATION! A mural: WAR TO THE DEATH WITH LONGHAIRS AND WORMS! A faded red canvas banner arching across the highway with a smiling man planting a coffee tree drawn on it: TO DRINK IT, YOU'VE GOT TO PLANT IT! Another huge billboard with smiling men and women lifting their blades: ALL WE'VE GOT FOR TEN MILLION TONS OF SUGAR! . . .

(3) Cuba: Heat

Nicolás Guillén, *Heat*

Guillén's poem song celebrates black African roots, dance, passion, and the tropical heat of the island.

Heat splits the night.
Night falls toasted
on the river.

What cry,
what fresh cry in the waters,
the cry of burning night!

Red heat for Blacks.
Drum!
Heat for darkened torsos.
Drums!
Heat with tongues of fire
on naked spines . . .
Drum!

Water from the stars
soaks awakened
coco-palms.

Drum!
Bright starlight.
Drum!
The pole star glitters . . .
Drum!

Fire on board! Fire on board!
Drum!
Is it true? It's a lie!
Drum!
Mute coasts, mute skies . . .
Drum!

The islands sailing,
sailing, sailing,
sailing wrapped in flames.

(4) CUBA: LOSS

José Martí, *Two Fatherlands*

*Revolutionary Martí's most famous poem predicts his death in battle
to liberate his country.*

I have two fatherlands: Cuba and the night.
Or are the two one? Hardly has the sun
withdrawn its majesty, with long veils
and a carnation in her hand, than Cuba,
like a silent, sad widow, appears.
I know what the bleeding carnation means
that trembles in her hand! My chest
is empty, destroyed and empty,
where once beat my heart. Now
is the right time to begin to die. Night
is the right time to say goodbye. Light
interferes, as do human words. The world
speaks more clearly than man.
   Like a flag
that calls to battle, the red flame
of the candle blazes. I open
the windows, now tight in me. Mute, pulling
petals from the carnation, like a cloud
that obscures the sky, Cuba, a widow, passes by . . .

(5) CUBA: EXILE

Heberto Padilla, *I have always lived in Cuba*

*Some years after the scandal that became known as the Padilla
affair, with poet Padilla's apparent confession that he had been
peddling anti-revolutionary poems, he left the island to live in exile in
the USA.*

I live in Cuba. I have always
lived in Cuba. These years of wandering
in the world of which so much has been said,
are my lies, my forgeries.

Because I have always lived in Cuba.

And it is true
there were days during the Revolution
when the island could have blown up among the waves;
but in the airports,
in the places I was
I felt
that they were calling me
by name
and that I answered
I was already on this shore
sweating,
  walking,
    in shirt sleeves,
drunk on wind and foliage,
with the sun and the sea climbing the terraces
and singing their hallelujahs.

(6) CUBANS IN NEW YORK

Oscar Hijuelos,
The Mambo Kings Play Songs of Love

*The Mambo Kings (two musician brothers) left Havana in 1949 to
make it in New York.*

His nights were a disaster. He'd often come home to La Salle Street from a
job by himself, strip down and climb into bed beside Dolores, remaining
awake beside her and inviting her attentions. They would wrap their arms
around each other, caressing affectionately until they fell asleep. But he
would always awaken in the early hours, thinking that there was something
missing from his life – what, he did not know. At three-thirty in the

morning, he would get up and sit in the dark living room, softly strumming guitar chords, and stirring Dolores from her dreams, so that she would make her way down the hall.

'Nestor, why don't you come back to bed?'

He'd just keep strumming. He'd sit by the window, looking out. The street glowed like dusk with the light of a wrought-iron lamp.

'It's just a song.'

Sometimes he didn't sleep for three or four days. He didn't know what was going on. Cubans then (and Cubans now) didn't know about psychological problems. Cubans who felt bad went to their friends, ate and drank and went out dancing. Most of the time they wouldn't think of their problems. A psychological problem was part of someone's character. Cesar was *un macho grande*; Nestor, *un infeliz*. People who hurt bad enough and wanted cures expected these cures to come immediately. Cesar was quite friendly with some *santeras*, really nice ladies who had come from Oriente Province and settled on 110th Street and Manhattan Avenue. And whenever Cesar felt bad about anything, if he felt depressed about the fact that he still had to work in a meat-packing plant to maintain his flamboyant life-style, or when he felt guilty about his daughter down in Cuba, he would go see his friends for a little magical rehauling. These *santeras* liked to listen to the radio all day, loved to have children and company around them. If he felt bad, he would just go in there and drop a few dollars into a basket, lie on his stomach on a straw mat on the floor, ring a magic bell (which symbolised his goddess, Caridad or charity) and pay homage to the goddess Mayarí, for whom these women were intermediaries. And psssst! his problems would lift away. Or they would lay hands on him. Or he would just go over to 113th and Lenox, to a *botánica*, and get himself a 'cleaning' – the saint pouring magic herbs over him – guaranteed to do the trick. Going to confession at the Catholic church did the same job: a heartfelt opening of the heart and an admission of sins; then the cleansing of the soul. (and no death-bed confession either, no admission to heaven because of last rites. These Cubans died as they lived, and a man who would not confess his sins at age twenty-five was not going to do so at seventy.)

(7) HAVANA

Guillermo Cabrera Infante, *Three Trapped Tigers*

The chatty photographer meets La Estrella, the incredibly fat mulata singer, in Havana's Las Vegas night-club.

La Estrella asked me to take her home. She told me to wait a minute while she went to look for something and what she did was to pick up a package and when we went outside to get into my car, which is one of those tiny English sports cars, she was hardly able to get herself in comfortably, putting all her three hundred pounds weight in a seat which was hardly able to take more than one of her thighs, and then she told me, leaving the package in between us. It's a pair of shoes they gave me, and I gave her a sharp look and saw that she was as poor as hell, and so we drove off. She lived with some married actors, or rather with an actor called Alex Bayer, Alex Bayer isn't his real name, but Alberto Perez or Juan García or something similar, but he took the name of Alex Bayer because Alex is a name that these people always use and the Bayer he took from the drug company who make pain-killers, and the thing is they don't call him that, Bayer I mean, these people, the people who hang out in the dive at the Radiocentro, for example, his friends don't call him Alex Bayer the way he pronounced it A-leks Báy-er when he was finishing a program, signing it off with the cast calling themselves out, but they called him as they still do call him, they called him Alex Aspirin, Alex Bufferin, Alex Anacin and any other pain-killer that happens to be fashionable and as everybody knew he was a faggot, very often they called him Alex Evanol. Not that he hides it, being queer, just the opposite, for he lived quite openly with a doctor, in his house as though they'd been officially married and they went everywhere together, and it was in his house that La Estrella lived, she was his cook and sleep-in maid, and she cooked their little meals and made their little bed and got their little baths ready, little etceteras. Pathetic. So if she sang it was because she liked it, she sang for the pleasure of it, because she loved doing it, in Las Vegas and in the Bar Celeste or in the Café Nico or any of the other bars or clubs around La Rampa. And so it was that I was driving her in my car, feeling very much the showoff for the same reasons but the reverse that other people would have been embarrassed or awkward or simply uncomfortable to have that enormous Negress sitting besides them in the car, showing her off, showing myself off in the morning with everybody crowding around, people going to work, working, looking for work, walking, catching the bus, filling the roads, flooding the whole district: avenues, streets, back streets, alleyways, a constant buzzing of people between the buildings like hungry hummingbirds. I drove her right up to their house, where she worked, she La Estrella, who lived there as cook, as maid, as servant to their very special marriage. We arrived.

It was a quiet little street in El Vedado, where the rich people were still asleep, still dreaming and snoring, and I was taking my foot off the clutch, putting the car into neutral, watching the nervous needles as they returned to the point of dead rest, seeing the weary reflection of my face in the glass of the dials as if the morning had made it old, beaten by the night, when I felt her hand on my thigh: she put her 5 *chorizos* 5, five sausages, on my thigh, she put her hand on my thigh and I was amused that it covered the whole of my thigh and I thought, Beauty and the Beast, and thinking of beauty and the beast I smiled and it was then that she said to me, Come on up, I'm on my own . . .

(8) HAVANA

Alejo Carpentier, *Explosion in a Cathedral*

Alejo Carpentier's epic novel opens with a view of Havana in 1790 after the funeral of Carlos's and Sofia's father that would liberate them into turbulent Caribbean history.

It was a town constantly exposed to the invading air, thirsty for land and sea breezes, with its shutters, lattices, doors and flaps all open to the first cool breath. Then the tinkling of lustres, chandeliers, beaded lampshades and curtains and the whirling of weathercocks would announce its arrival. Fans of palm fronds, Chinese silk, or painted paper, would be motionless. But when this transient relief was over, people would return to their task of setting in motion the still air, once more trapped between the high walls of the rooms. Here light congealed into heat, from the moment the swift dawn first admitted into even the most inaccessible bedrooms, penetrating curtains and mosquito-nets; especially now, in the rainy season, after the fierce midday downpour, a regular cascade of water accompanied by thunder and lightning, which soon emptied the clouds and left the streets flooded and steaming in the returning sultriness.

In vain the palaces proudly displayed their splendid columns and coats of arms carved in stone; during the rainy months they rose out of the mud which clung like an incurable disease to their masonry. When a carriage went past, doors and railings were covered with fountains of splashes from the puddles which filled every hollow, undermined the pavements and spilled over to replenish each other with filthy water. Although they were adorned with precious marble and fine panelling, with rose windows and mosaics, and with slim voluted grilles so unlike iron bars that they looked more like iron vegetation twining round the windows, these manorial houses could not escape the primaeval slime which spattered up over them from the ground as soon as the roofs had begun to drip. Carlos reflected that many of those who had attended the wake must have had to cross at the street-corners on planks laid over the mud, or by jumping on to stepping-stones to avoid leaving their shoes behind them.

Strangers praised the town's colour and gaiety after spending three days visiting its dance halls, saloons, taverns and gambling dens, where the innumerable orchestras incited sailors to spend their money, and set the women's hips swaying. But those who had to put up with the place the whole year round knew about the mud and the dust, and how the saltpetre turned the door-knockers green, ate away the iron-work, made silver sweat, brought mildew out of old engravings, and permanently blurred and misted the glass on drawings and etchings, already curling up with damp.

(9) HEMINGWAY'S HOUSE
OUTSIDE HAVANA
Edmundo Desnoes,
Memories of Underdevelopment

The jaded narrator, abandoned by his family in Revolutionary Cuba, takes his underage mistress round Hemingway's famous house outside Havana the Finca Vigía. Miss Mary is Martha Gellhorn, and Papa was Hemingway's nickname.

The table was set for nobody. On the glass surface the dishes and forks and empty glasses, napkins with a huge H, and a floral arrangement of tiny insignificant pink and white flowers in the center. 'The table was always set exactly as you see it now, those were Miss Mary's favorite flowers,' the guide said; no one could stop him now. 'Every day the same.' 'But nobody is going to eat here now,' I said, but he kept on talking. He sounded like a wound-up toy. 'He had two fried eggs for breakfast, well-done, because he didn't like the running white of the egg. Papa liked them well done with a slice of toast, without butter. He used to sit facing that wall, right here. He always sat facing the Miró painting of a Catalonian farm, a painting Hemingway bought when he was young in Paris for three hundred dollars . . .' I asked about the painting, there was nothing on the wall. 'That painting and several others, Miss Mary took them away, after Hemingway died, she came over and took them away; but she also promised Fidel she would send first-rate reproductions as soon as possible so that the house would be kept exactly the same as when Hemingway lived there. She promised to send reproductions where you would hardly notice any difference, identical, even the same size, to be put back there.'

'But it's not the same,' I murmured. 'Reproductions are worthless and these paintings were worth millions of dollars. It's not the same.' I don't know if he heard me, but he didn't answer. 'The bullfight posters are the original ones, aren't they?' I shouted at him and he answered, still sitting on a cloud, 'Yes, those are. They haven't been touched.' Yes, those were the original reproductions. That's all we deserve, copies, we're nothing but a bad copy of the powerful and civilized countries, a caricature, a cheap reproduction.

He went through the house again and I had the feeling that everything was varnished. I saw everything just as if I was looking at a set of jewels behind glass in a museum, with the certainty that no woman would ever show them off. How corny can I get! I have mixed feelings. I feel love and hate towards Hemingway; I admire him and at the same time he humiliates me. The same as my people, it's the same feeling I have when I think of Fidel, of the revolution. Permanently split; I can't even agree with a part of myself.

'This tower Miss Mary had built,' the guide said outside while we were climbing up the spiral stairway, our hands on the rusty iron, first brushing against twisted branches of yellow and purple bougainvillea and up on top our eyes were opposite the high arched branches of a royal palm, up there were some boots, covered by a yellowish film; the heads of wild animals, a buffalo and a tiger, on the floor against the wall.

'He worked here only on the first day, when Miss Mary gave him the key, it was a present, a birthday present. After that he never came up here to work, didn't like it. He always worked in his room . . .'

While he went into the details of Papa's boring house habits, I stood staring at a bald mangy spot on the tiger's head and I thought that Cuba never really meant a fucking thing to Hemingway. Boots to hunt in Africa, American furniture, Spanish photographs, books and magazines in English, bullfight posters. Nowhere in the whole house was there anything Cuban, not even an Afro–Cuban witchcraft conversation piece or a painting. Nothing. Cuba, for Hemingway, was just a place where he could take refuge, live quietly with his wife, receive his friends, write in English, fish in the Gulf stream. Cubans, *we*, meant very little to him.

(10) HAVANA

Graham Greene *Our Man in Havana*

Wormwold, the phoney spy, goes to a Havana bar during Batista's later dictatorship in the 1950s.

So he looked in at Sloppy Joe's instead of at the Wonder Bar. No Havana resident ever went to Sloppy Joe's, because it was the rendez-vous of tourists; but tourists were sadly reduced nowadays in number, for the President's régime was creaking dangerously towards its end. There had always been unpleasant doings out of sight in the inner rooms of the Jefatura, which had not disturbed the tourists in the Nacional and the Seville-Biltmore, but one tourist had recently been killed by a stray bullet while he was taking a photograph of a picturesque beggar under a balcony near the palace, and the death had sounded the knell of the all-in tour 'including a trip to Varadero beach and the night-life of Havana'. The victim's Leica had been smashed as well, and that had impressed his companions more than anything with the destructive power of a bullet. Wormwold had heard them talking afterwards in the bar of the Nacional. 'Ripped right through the camera,' one of them said. 'Five hundred dollars gone just like that.'

'Was he killed at once?'

'Sure. And the lens – you could pick up bits for fifty yards around. Look. I'm taking a piece home to show Mr Humpelnicker.'

(11) HAVANA

Joseph Hergesheimer, *San Cristóbal de la Habana*

*In his travel book on Havana, the languorous novelist evokes one of
the city's great luxurious hotels in 1920, the same hotel in which
Lorca celebrated his farewell to Cuba in 1930.*

To illustrate further the perversity of my impulses, I was so entirely
captivated by the Hotel Inglaterra that, for the rest of the day, I was
indifferent to whatever might be waiting outside. The deep entrance with
its reflected planes of subdued light and servants in cool linen; the patio
with water, its white arches on iridescent tiles; the dining-room laid in
marble, panelled with the arms of Pontius Pilate, the bronze lustre of the
tiling, and the long windows on the Parque exactly as I had anticipated, all
created a happy effect of Spain in the tropics. The corridor on which my
room opened was still more entrancing, its arches filled with green
lattice-work, and an octagonal space set with chairs and long-bladed
plants.

Yet the room itself, perhaps one of the most remarkable rooms in the
world, easily surpassed what, until then, I had seen. There were slatted
door screens, cream-coloured with a sapphire-blue glass knob, topped in an
elaborate Gothic scrolling; and the door beyond, inconceivably tall,
opened on an interior that seemed to reach upward without any limit. It
had, of course, a ceiling, heavily beamed in dark wood; and when, later, I
speculated carefully on its height, I reached the conclusion that it was
twenty-five feet above the grey-flowered tiling of the floor. The walls were
bare, white; about their base was laid a line of green glazed tiles; and this,
except for the glass above the french window, was the only positive note.

The window, too, towered with the dignity of an impressive entrance;
there were two sets of shutters, the inner elaborately slatted, and over it
was a semicircular fanlight of intensely brilliant colours – carmine and
orange and plum-purple, cobalt and yellow. It was extraordinarily vivid,
like heaped gorgeous fruit: throughout the day it dominated the closed,
elusive interior; and not only from its place on high, for the sun, moving
across that exposure, cast its exact replica on the floor, over the frigidity of
the austere iron bed, down one wall and up another.

Havana was identified as an authentic part of my inheritance; I was – in
a purely inner manner – to understand it, to have for it the affectionate
recognition, the sense of familiarity, of which I have already spoken. The
city was wholly expressed by the fanlight sparkling with the shifting
radiance of the blazing day. It was possible, without leaving the room, to
grasp the essential spirit of the place so largely unseen.

(12) HAVANA

Alexandre von Humboldt, *Personal Narrative*

*Humboldt, the Prussian scientist, and his botanist companion Aimé
Bonpland, visited Cuba for the first time in 1801.*

The way Havana looks as you enter the port makes it one of the most
pleasant and picturesque places on the American equinoctial coasts.
Celebrated by travellers from all over the world, this site is not like the
luxurious vegetation along the Guayaquil banks, nor the wild majesty of
Rio de Janeiro's rocky coasts, but the charms which in our climates
embellish cultivated nature are here joined to the power and organic vigour
of tropical nature. In this sweet blend of impressions, the European forgets
the dangers that threaten him in crowded West Indian cities; he tries to
seize all the diverse elements in this vast countryside and contemplate the
forts that crown the rocks to the east of the port, the inland basin
surrounded by villages and farms, the palm trees reaching amazing heights,
a town half hidden by a forest of ships' masts and sails. You enter Havana
harbour between Morro fort (Castillo de los Santos Reyes) and the San
Salvador de la Punta fort: the opening is barely some 170 to 200 toises
wide, and remains like this for one fifth of a mile. Leaving this neck, and
the beautiful castel San Carlos de la Cabaña and the Casa Blanca to the
north, you reach the basin shaped like a clover. This basin links up with
three creeks, one of which, the Atares, is supplied with fresh water. The
city of Havana, surrounded by walls, forms a promontory limited to the
south by the arsenal; to the north by the Punta fort. Passing some sunken
ships, and the Luz shoals, water becomes some 5 to 6 fathoms deep. The
castels defend the town from the west. The rest of the land is filled with
suburbs (*arrabales* or *barrios extra muros*) which year by year shrink the
Campo de Marte. Havana's great buildings, the cathedral, the Casa de
Gobierno, the admiral's house, the arsenal, the Correo or Post Office, and
the tobacco factory, are less remarkable for their beauty than for their
solidity; most of the streets are very narrow, and are not yet paved. As
stones come from Veracruz, and transporting them is very expensive,
someone had recently come up with the strange idea of using tree trunks
instead of paving stones. This project was quickly abandoned, though
recently arrived travellers could see fine *caoba* (mahogany) tree trunks sunk
into the mud. During my stay few cities in Spanish America could be more
unpleasant, due to a lack of a strong local government. You walked around
with mud up to your knees, while the amount of four-wheeled carriages or
volantes so typical of Havana, carts loaded with sugar cane, and porters who
elbowed passers-by, made being a pedestrian annoying and humiliating.
The stench of *tasajo*, or poorly dried meat, stunk out the houses and
tortuous streets.

There are two fine walks, one (the Alameda) between Paula hospital and
the theatre, redecorated by an Italian artist in 1803 in fine taste; the other

between the Punta castle and the Puerta de la Muralla. This last one, also called the Paseo Extra Muros, is a deliciously fresh walk; after sun set many carriages come here. Near the Campo de Marte there is a botanic garden, and something that disgusts me, the huts in front of which the slaves are put to be sold.

(13) HAVANA

Norman Lewis, *Cuban Passage*

Two British diplomats sit in a café and discuss Cubans, their customs, voodoo, and the doomed rebellion (in fact, Castro's revolution).

Visiting the harbour café in the first cool of the evening had become a social habit of the city. People sat there to calm and steady their vision with a pacific vista of ships, and to catch a little of the emotions of travel, the gaiety of arriving and the melancholy of departure. Women believed that tar and brine in the breeze befitted their complexion, while the men who brought them here clung to the legend that the shellfish for which the café was famous improved their virility. So they chewed prawns, threw scraps to test the unerring swoop of the terns circling overhead, listened to the sweet, rootless music of the house-musicians' flutes, and sniffed at the odour of fine cigars mingled with those of the ocean, and thus the hours slipped by.

There was no better place in Havana, Hollingdale believed, to introduce a newcomer to the rich and complex flavours of local life. For this reason he had brought here the new junior man at the embassy, Sanger, who was being shown the ropes. They were discussing the national character.

'You'll find them easy to like,' Hollingdale said, 'amiable, shallow and profoundly superstitious. This must be the only capital city in the world where Woolworth's have a counter stacked with charms and voodoo paraphernalia. One of the ministers in the present government is said to belong to an African cult practising human sacrifice. Presidents start off as starry-eyed idealists and finish as monsters. They still have a law on the statute book giving a woman the right to be present when her husband is tortured.'

Sanger made a face. 'And most people speak English, you say?'

'In the city, anyway. This is virtually an American colony. Ah, yes, one thing I ought to tell you. Should you have intercourse with a local woman you must remember to thank her profusely after the act. She will do the same.'

'Useful to know,' Sanger said. Hollingdale did not join his brief laughter. A side-glance at his superior assured Sanger that he was quite serious. The information, conveyed in the driest and most matter-of-fact tone, had been made to sound like a statistic. It was something about Hollingdale that

Sanger much admired; part of the professional approach – an attitude that went with the crispness of the ill-fitting tropical suit bought off the peg at Lillywhite's. Sanger, observing him, was conscious and ashamed of the sweat-stain spreading from the armpits of the jacket.

'What about this rebellion?' Sanger asked.

'Eighty-two zealots bent on changing the face and destiny of this incorrigible land started it off in Oriente eighteen months ago. They were ready and willing to throw away their lives and most of them did.'

'But the thing still keeps going?'

'It's dead,' Hollingdale said, 'but it won't lie down.'

(14) HAVANA

José Lezama Lima, *Paradiso*

Young, asthmatic Jose Cemi is initiated into swimming by his macho father in this exuberant, tropical novel.

José Eugenio expanded his thirty-year-old chest. He seemed to be smoking the sea breeze. He widened his nostrils, drank in an epic quantity of oxygen, and then let it out through his mouth with slow puffs. The peace and innocent color of the waters awakened a shouting pride in him, one that was natural and savage. Standing in front of him he saw his five-year-old son, skinny, his ribs showing, panting as the breeze grew stronger, and then trembling as he tried to hide it, slyly watching his father as he pretended to breathe normally. José Eugenio Cemí, the Colonel, was rowing as if the wide-open box of his chest was guiding the knife of the prow. The third person in the boat was Captain Rigal's son Néstor, who was a year older than José Cemí, blond and freckled, with Holland-green eyes, who was laughing as he played in the gusty breeze. The Colonel turned to the freckled blond boy and said: 'Do you notice anything strange about Joseíto's breathing? Notice how he doesn't breathe the same way you do. It's as if something inside him is limping through the breeze. When he gets that way, I worry, because it seems as if someone is strangling him.'

José Cemí pretended not to hear. He dipped one of his hands into the cold water. As if ashamed, he dried it on his steaming trunks, which gave off a light vapor. The Colonel stopped rowing and told the blond boy to go to the bow, Then he began to splash water with his hands, wetting José Cemí too, who laughed, hiding the trouble he was having in breathing.

'I don't think you can learn how to swim by yourself,' he said. 'So I'm going to teach you today. Now, you jump into the water and hold onto this finger.' He held up his forefinger, created for the exercise of authority, strong, like a midget who was an important personage in the Tower of London. The forefinger curled like an anchor and then straightened up like a reed that jumps its moorings but then comes back to root itself in the sand once more.

José Cemí obeyed his father at once. He made the sign of the cross, a custom his mother had taught him, before jumping into the water. And, while the boat moved slowly along, propelled by the rowing of Néstor Rigal, José Cemí clutched his father's forefinger, with his whole hand, feeling the resistance of the water as it tightened like a stone against his panting chest.

'You're not afraid any more, now you can learn by yourself,' he said. The Colonel withdrew his forefinger just as a small whirlpool formed.

(15) HAVANA

Nancy Morejón, *Woman in a Tobacco Factory*

Morejón's elegy to a typical, but anonymous woman of Castro's revolution harks back to Martí, founder of Cuban independence and identity.

A woman in a tobacco factory wrote
a poem to death. Between the smoke
and the twisted leaves on the racks
she said she saw the world in Cuba.
It was 1999 . . . In her poem
she touched flowers
weaving a magic carpet
that flew over Revolution Square.
In her poem, this woman
touched tomorrow's days.
In her poem there were no shadows but powerful lamps.
In her poem, friends, Miami wasn't there nor split families,
neither was misery
nor ruin
nor violations of the labor law.
There wasn't any interest in the stock exchange,
no usury.
In her poem there was militant wisdom, languid intelligence.
Discipline and assemblies were there in her poem,
blood boiling out of the past,
livers and hearts.
Her poem was a treatise in people's economy.
In it were all the desires and all the anxiety
of any revolutionary, her contemporaries.
A woman in a tobacco factory
wrote a poem to the agony of capitalism. Yes sir.
But neither her comrades nor her neighbors
guessed the essence of her life. And they never knew
about the poem.

She had hidden it, surely and delicately,
along with some *caña santa* and *cáñamo* leaves
between the pages of a leather bound volume
of José Martí.

(16) HAVANA

Virgilio Piñera, *Cold Tales*

Piñera's dialogues capture Havana's social life.

Well, here I am . . . Since there's no one to introduce me, I'll do it myself.
My name is Rafael Sánchez Trevejo (Rafa to my wife, Rosita, my family,
and friends). And now that I remember . . . sometime around 1930, Rosita
fell in love with the *Miami*. And she would complain: 'That Rafa . . . he
never has time to take me to eat at the *Miami*.' She would say that because
we went once and she met Monona (the wife of Menchaca, the senator of
Oriente). *Girl! It's been a century since we've seen each other! I can't believe
it's you! Oh, how good you look! The years don't take their toll in you, my dear.
Monona, always the flatterer! Come on girl! I'm not the Rosita I used to be!
Look, Rafa, this is Monona. You remember her, don't you?*
Rosita warned me to bring her to the *Miami* for another one of those
chance encounters with Monona and, above all, for the ice cream. She
would say to me: 'Rafa, there's nothing like the *Miami*'s caramel chiffon
. . .'
Rosita (who now lives in New York with our daughter Caruca and Pepín,
my son-in-law) writes me fiery letters. They left about a year ago. I didn't
want to speak about this before the other stuff (the other stuff being my
past), but I have the virtue – or the defect – of saying whatever pops into
my head. So Rosita, seeing that I wasn't going to give her the husband's
consent (hoping that the government would give it to her), put to me as
the final argument in defense of her motives as an 'imminently exiled
woman', that perhaps she would run into Monona 'over there . . .'
It was for love that Rosita caught me: I caught her out of self-interest.
She became convinced a while back that I never loved her the way she
wanted: with the love of Romeo and Juliet; without – it goes without saying
– Shakespeare ever entering the picture. To her Romeo and Juliet were
nothing but a brand of cigarettes.

(17) HAVANA

Severo Sarduy, *From Cuba with a Song*

*In this experimental novel Sarduy recreates the erotic melting pot
that is Havana.*

Do you smell something? Yes, that's the smell: Cantonese rice with soya
sauce. There's something else too: dog urine (it's early); plus tea. Yes, as
you must have guessed, we're in Chinatown.

THE READER: But, what about that record of Marlene's?

1: Well, dear, not everything in life is coherent. A little disorder with
the order, I always say. You're not going to ask me to arrange a
full-feathered Chinese 'ensemble' for you right here on Zanja Street, next
to the Pacifico (yes, where Hemingway eats), in a city where there's a
distillery, pool hall, whore, and sailor on every corner. I'll do what I can.
And so:

'Chinese atmosphere, girls, come on!' – the Director steps out of a
saffron cloud smelling of burnt grass (yes, the same grass you're thinking).
He steps out of his pagoda of smoke, pensive, hair greased with sweat, eyes
of a jade bulldog – two red balls – hands crossed along a dotted line. He
shivers, turns green; the opalescent cloud crumbles in the scenery. He is
lime green, a rooster feather, he bristles; a poisonous wind has swept
through his nine orifices.

He's inspired. He calmly approaches, looking toward the stage, but in *his*
reality he's making his way through battles, he's escaping bats that are
Toledan blades, he's riding on a tortoise. For us he's taking off an earing;
but he's pulling leeches off his ears. Is he fanning himself with his hands?
On grass level he's commanding the Waters. Is he scratching his neck? He's
trying to get a gorilla off his back, or a troll who's biting his shoulder. The
Director, stoned, plays on both waves; he's an amphibian of consciousness,
the *mascalzone*.

He's wearing canvas pants, an orange sash at his waist, open sandals,
and, above all, a little aroma I'd prefer not to evoke but which is stronger
than the stench of badly digested glazed pork.

He stands on the empty proscenium, but feels looked at. He catches by
surprise, between cracks in the stage, sliding, parallel drops of mercury,
neon green eyes . . .

(Outside, the neighborhood's waking up: in the brothel's show window,
condoms with beaks, spurs, and comb, with bells; thimbles. The movie
house consumptive changes the billboard: today a moonlit bridge beneath
pine trees, a face in black and yellow stripes like an Indian fish.)

(18) SANTA TERESA DEL MAR

Cristina García, *Dreaming in Cuban*

Pilar and her daughter Celia, living in New York, return to Cuba to attend to Pilar's pro-Castro grandmother in this moving novel about three generations of the Del Pino family straddled between Cuba and the USA.

My mother inspects the bedroom she used to share with Tía Felicia, vacant now except for a frilly party dress hanging in the closet. She crosses the hallway to Abuela's room. A lace table-cloth is spread on the bed. A photograph of El Líder is on the night table. Mom turns from it in disgust.

I find Abuela sitting motionless on her wicker swing, wearing a worn bathing suit, her hair stuck haphazardly to her skull, her feet strangely lacerated. I kneel before her and press my cheek to hers, still salty from the sea. We hold each other close.

'Dios mío, what happened to you?' Mom screams when she finds us. She scurries about preparing a hot bath with water boiled on the stove.

Abuela is missing a breast. There's a scar like a purple zipper on her chest. Mom holds a finger to her lips and flashes me a look that warns, 'Pretend not to notice.'

We wash Abuela's hair and rinse it with conditioner, then we pat her dry with towels as if this could somehow heal her. Abuela says nothing. She submits to my mother like a solemn novitiate. Mom untangles Abuela's hair with a wide-toothed comb. 'You could have died of pneumonia!' she insists, and plugs in a Conair dryer that blows out the lights in the living room.

I notice Abuela Celia's drop pearl earrings, the intricate settings, the fine gold strands looping through her lobes. There's a cache of blue shadows in the pearls, a coolness in the smooth surfaces. When I was a baby, I bounced those pearls with my fingertips and heard the rhythm of my grandmother's thoughts.

'I went for a swim last night,' Abuela Celia whispers to me alone. She looks through the arched window above the piano as if searching the waves to find the precise spot. Then she squeezes my hand. 'I'm glad you remember, Pilar. I always knew you did.'

Mom places Abuela's bedding with fresh sheets and a lamb's wool blanket we brought from home. I help Abuela into a new flannel nightgown while Mom prepares bouillon and instant tapioca pudding. Abuela tastes a spoonful of each, swallows a vitamin C tablet, and falls into a deep sleep.

I pull the covers over Abuela's shoulders, searching her face for a hint of my own. Her hair turned gray since I last saw her. Her black mole has faded. Her hands are stamped with faint liver spots.

I know what my grandmother dreams. Of massacres in distant countries, pregnant women dismembered in the squares. Abuela walks among them mute and invisible. The thatched roofs steam in the morning air.

(19) VEDADO, HAVANA

Roberto Fernández Retamar, *From the Vedado, a Cuban writes to a decidedly European friend*

Poet Fernández Retamar mocks the European prejudiced view of Castro's Cuba as a tropical, tourist's paradise.

I know you want me to tell you of the tomtom in my blood,
Of the great lustrous jungle where the parrot swoops, screaming,
Of lightning fallen before my eyes
And obatala white as snow in fire
(Along with the memories I must have of jet trinkets in my shirt,
    the treasures of a twelve-year-old).

I know, friend, I know you need the savage sap
I can bring you, with a chunk of sun in one hand
And, in the other, the maraca only the milky dawn can finally silence.

But how can I write you with a busted airconditioner,
In this hotel room, this terrible summer day,
La Habana shining at my feet
Like a necklace, full of loud dusty automobiles,
With dozens of restaurants and bars and not a palm in sight?

Biographical and literary notes

ARENAS, Reinaldo (1943–1990). Born in **Holguín**, Oriente, Cuba, to a poor family, Arenas joined the Revolution, worked at the Biblioteca Nacional, and befriended poets like Lezama Lima ◊. He managed to send abroad the manuscript of his first surreal novel called *El mundo alucinado* (*Hallucinations*, 1971, with a second translation in 1987), based on the historical character friar Servando Teresa de Mier during the Independence wars in Latin America, finally published in Mexico in 1969. Arenas did not see a copy of this novel, or its many translations, until 1980. He was arrested and his manuscripts confiscated, spending 19 months in the famous **Castillo del Morro** prison as a dissident and homosexual. He tried to escape Castro's Cuba several times, and finally left with the exodus at Mariel. Suffering from AIDS, he committed suicide in New York in 1990.

His posthumously published autobiography *Antes que anochezca* (*Before Night Falls*, 1994) recreates these details. All his work is densely lyrical, epitomized by *Otra vez el mar*, 1982 (*Farewell to the Sea*, 1986 – Extract 2) where a couple spend six days at sea, narrated in parts by each one in a surreal, poetic way; and also by *Celestino antes del alba*, 1980 (*Singing from the Well*, 1987) a strange story of a poet child and a grandfather chopping down trees.

Guillermo Cabrera Infante

CABRERA INFANTE, Guillermo (1929–). Born in **Gibara**, Cuba, to parents who were founder members of the Cuban Communist Party, Cabrera Infante grew up poor in Havana. He began work as a proof corrector but soon went into literary journalism, in 1959 becoming editor of the lively *Lunes de la Revolución*. When defending his brother's short film *P.M.* about Havana night-life, Cabrera Infante got into trouble with the Castro regime and had the literary weekly closed. In 1962 he was sent to Brussels as cultural attaché. In 1965 Cabrera Infante resigned, and began his long exile from Cuba in London in 1966, becoming naturalized British. He disowned his first realist stories *Así en la paz como en la guerra*, 1960, and found his literary fame with his tongue-twisting *Tres tristes tigres*, 1967 (*Three Trapped Tigers*, 1971), a vast and chatty tableau of **Havana** night life during Batista's reign, seen through various eyes, including Coda, a photographer, the fat black singer La Estrella (Extract 7), Cue and Bustrófedon, with innumerable jokes and puns, and parodies of key Cuban writers like Carpentier ◊ and Lezama Lima ◊. One of the funniest novels written in Spanish, it won the Premio Biblioteca Breve in Barcelona in 1964, and helped launch the boom in Latin American fiction. In 1968 Cabrera Infante was finally expelled from the Cuban Union of Writers. His books are unavailable in Cuba except as samizdat. Since then Cabrera Infante's quirky and witty novels have recorded Havana filtered through his own remembered, and invented, experiences. Cabrera Infante has written film scripts (eg *Vanishing Point*), as cinema is a passion in his life, and was film critic for *Carteles* from 1954 to 1960. He collected his film criticism in *Un oficio del siglo XX*, 1963, (*A Twentieth-Century Job*, 1991). In 1979 Cabrera Infante published *La Habana para un infante difunto* (*Infante's Inferno*, 1985), an erotic biography of the capital city. He wrote *Holy Smoke*, 1985, a wonderful essay on tobacco, directly in English. His essay *Vista del amanecer en el trópico*, 1974, is essential reading on Cuba (*View of Dawn in the Tropics*, 1978). He has also collected all his writings on Cuba, with essays on the chess master Capablanca, and many gossipy tributes to friends and foes in literary Cuba in *Mea Cuba*, 1992 (*Mea Cuba*, 1994). His latest book in Spanish is *Delito por bailar el chachachá*, 1995, three overlapping stories set in Cuba about love and marriage, and fun. Cabrera Infante recently said: 'I write from my ears. I begin with sounds . . . .'.

CARPENTIER, Alejo (1904–1980). Carpentier was born in Lausanne, Switzerland, of a French father and Russian mother, and never lost his French 'r'. He grew up and was educated in Cuba, with a short time at a *lycée* in Paris, then at the University of Havana where he studied music and architecture. He began as a poet in the Afro–Cuban movement, editing *Carteles*, an avant-garde magazine. He was briefly imprisoned by dictator Gerardo Machado in 1927, when he began writing his first novel *Ecué-Yamba-O*, published in Madrid in 1933, which means 'Praise be to God' in Lucumí, a documentary novel about a poor black, with photos. He escaped from Cuba on a false passport lent by the Surrealist Robert Desnos, and lived in exile in Paris from 1928 to 1939, on the fringe of the Surrealist movement, writing musical scenar-

ios and a ballet. After returning to Cuba in 1939, he visited Haiti with Louis Jouvet, a trip which inspired his second novel *El reino de este mundo*, 1949, (*The Kingdom of this World*, 1957) – see under Haiti. From 1945 to 1959 Carpentier lived in Caracas as a journalist.

In 1946 his interest in music led to his study *La música en Cuba*. A trip up the Orinoco inspired *Los pasos perdidos*, 1953 (*The Lost steps*, 1956), following the narrating musicologist disgusted with New York, fleeing his stale marriage, and accompanied by his mistress Mouche seeking musical instruments up the Orinoco. This seminal novel illustrates his theory of *lo real maravilloso* ('Magic Realism'), with Latin America as a surreal country where all ages of history co-exist. The moral is pessimistic, the musician cannot remain in utopia with his new mistress Rosario, and is condemned to the modern city. In 1957 Carpentier published *El acoso* (*The Chase*, 1989), a tautly constructed novel about student gangsterism in 1940s Cuba. In 1959, on Castro's triumph, Carpentier returned to Cuba and published *El siglo de las luces*, 1962, (*Explosion in a Cathedral*, 1963 – Extract 8) dealing with the contradictory impact of the French Revolution in the Caribbean, with Esteban, Carlos and Sofia, all sentimentally involved with the historical character Victor Hugues in a vast tableau spanning 1790–1809. In Cuba Carpentier was appointed director of the state publishing house. In 1966 he was sent to Paris as ambassador, where he died in 1980. He has also written a long, failure of a novel about the Cuban revolution, *La consagración de la primavera*, 1978; another ironic and erudite one about a cultured dictator, *El recurso del método*, 1974 (*Reasons of State*, 1976); and many shorter pastiches.

DESNOES, Edmundo (1930–). Born in **Havana**, Desnoes worked in New York as editor of *Visión* until the

1959 revolution. He had lived for over 10 years in the USA, and knew English well enough to translate his own novel *Memorias del subdesarrollo*, 1965, (*Inconsolable Memories*, 1967, and changed to match the Spanish as *Memories of Underdevelopment* in 1971). In this novel, the 39-year-old narrator keeps his bitter thoughts in a diary about life in post-Revolutionary Cuba, with his family fled to Florida. We see him tour Hemingway's house (Extract 9), accused of making love to a minor, going to literary events, and even mocking Desnoes himself. The novel is set in 1961. It corresponds to a period of liberalization in Cuba, and can be read as a *mea culpa* of a doubting intellectual. Desnoes is an accomplished essayist.

FERNÁNDEZ RETAMAR, Roberto (1930–). Born in **Havana**, he taught at Yale in the USA, and returned to Cuba with Castro's revolution where he was appointed cultural attaché in Paris, and then Director of the prestigious centre and literary review *Casa de las Américas*. Fernández Retamar is a poet, and his influential essay anatomizing post-colonial and dependent Latin America from the Cuban revolutionary point of view, *Calibán: Apuntes sobre nuestra América*, 1971, appeared as *Caliban and Other Essays* in 1989.

GARCÍA, Cristina (1958–). Born in **Havana**, García left Cuba around 1960 and grew up in New York City. She graduated from Barnard College in 1979, with a masters from Johns Hopkins in 1981. She has been a correspondent for *Time* magazine, and currently lives in Los Angeles. Her novel *Dreaming in Cuban*, 1992 (Extract 18), deals with the break-up of a family, the grandmother staying on in Castro's Cuba, while her daughter Lourdes gets fat in New York. Her grand-daughter Pilar, a rebel, punk and painter, returns to Cuba for a holiday to visit the radical Abuela. A

quirky, poetic recreation of different versions of Cuba through three generations of women, and their dull men.

GREENE, Graham (1904–1991). See also under Haiti. After a short trip to **Havana**, Greene wrote *Our Man in Havana*, 1958 (Extract 10), 'a light hearted comedy' of errors, full of jokes, word confusions and absurd situations involving Wormwold, a vacuum cleaner rep with a sexy daughter Milly, courted by the Red Devil, police captain Segura, working under dictator Batista. At the end of this farce a vacuum cleaner is made out to be a secret installation in the **Oriente** mountains, with shootings and spying. Wormwold is recalled to London after confessing his frauds, but is promoted and given an OBE. However stilted and farcical the fairy-story plot, the Cuban background is exactly evoked. We are shown the **Vedado** suburb for the rich, Columbus's pumice stone statue, the lottery, and the thrilling nightlife of Batista's sexy Havana. In *Ways of Escape*, 1980, Greene remembered Havana as an extraordinary city where 'every vice was permissable'. On the reception of this novel in Castro's Cuba, Greene commented: 'In poking fun at the British Secret Service, I had minimized the terror of Batista's rule.' In later articles on Cuba, Greene rectified his attitudes to Castro.

GUILLÉN, Nicolás (1902–1989). Born in **Camagüey**, Guillén was a mulatto, who became the principal poet of the Afro–Cuba style, incorporating African rhythms in his *son* (a dance) poems. Influenced by the gypsy poems of Federico García Lorca, whom he met in Cuba in 1930, Guillén became well known with *Motivos de son*, 1930, and *Sóngoro Cosongo*, 1931, in accessible, populist and politicized verse. He was in Spain in 1937, the year he became a Communist, and published *Tengo*, 1964, (*Tengo*, 1974) celebrating Castro's Revolution. In 1961 he was proclaimed Cuba's *poeta nacional*, and became president of the Union of Cuban Writers, and roving ambassador. He has been translated in *Patria o muerte! The Great Zoo and Other Poems*, 1972, and *Man-Making Words: Selected Poems of Nicolás Guillén*, 1972 (Extract 3).

HEMINGWAY, Ernest (1899–1961). Born in Oak Park, Illinois, Hemingway began work as a journalist, then volunteered to serve in an ambulance unit during the First World War. His first novel appeared in 1926. That same year he made his name with *The Sun Also Rises*. He has often written about Spain, especially bullfighting, in short stories like those in *Men Without Women*, 1927, and in the novels *For Whom the Bell Tolls*, 1940, set during the Spanish Civil War, and *Death in the Afternoon*, 1932, a study of bullfighting. His terse, typewriter style is legendary, and was an enormous influence on

English and Spanish writers. Hemingway first went to Cuba to fish in 1932, and lived there with his third wife Martha Gellhorn (1908–) in the **Finca Vigía** in the Havana suburb of **San Franciso de Paula** for five years in the 1940s. The house is now the **Hemingway Museum** (see Extract 9). In the posthumously published novel *Islands in the Stream*, 1970, the painter Tom Hudson drives from the house along the route into Havana to end up in the **Floridita** bar where Hem himself drank. The novel that won Hemingway the Nobel Prize, *The Old Man and the Sea*, 1952 (Extract 1), is set in **Cojímar**, from where Hemingway set out to fish (again recreated in detail in *Islands in the Stream*, which has a map of Cuba to help readers). The earlier *To Have and Have Not*, 1937 (a nominal source only for the famous film), is an action novel about a Caribbean smuggler named after a famous pirate, Henry Morgan. It opens in Havana with a political assassination, and has violent scenes with Cuban revolutionaries. Hemingway: 'Its the Cubans run Cuba. They all double cross each other. They sell each other out. They got what they deserve. The hell with their revolutions.' Hemingway did not leave Cuba after Castro's revolution, which he supported. There is a famous photo of the two *barbudos* meeting. Hemingway shot himself in 1961.

HERGESHEIMER, Joseph (1880–1954). US novelist Hergesheimer travelled to Cuba in 1920, and wrote *San Cristóbal de la Habana*, 1921 (Extract 11), 'the best travel book I have ever read', according to Cabrera Infante ◊. His Havana is the antithesis of the night-loving vice-city of US dreams, a dilettante wandering through the city, with sharp reflections about the light, architecture, women etc. Hergesheimer also wrote the novel *Cytherea*, 1922, in which a rich business man runs off from wife and family to Cuba with his mistress

Ernest Hemingway

Savina. He sought a Cuba where 'the nakedness of passion everywhere surcharges the surface of life'. Savina suddenly dies in **Cobra**, near Camagüey. The realistic novel is a critique of 1920s America, with Cuba as the land of irresponsibility. In 1923 Hergesheimer published *The Bright Shawl*, set in 19th century Cuba, about an idealist young American who wants to fight for Cuban freedom, meets a Spanish dancer, and helps the freedom movement until his Cuban friend is killed, and he is deported. Among Hergesheimer's other novels is *Tampico*, 1926, a drama about corruption and adultery set in the Tampico oil fields of Mexico. He gave up writing novels in 1940.

HIJUELOS, Oscar (1951–). Born in New York of Cuban parents, Hijuelos is sufficiently Americanized to write in American English, after graduating from the City University of New York in 1975. He worked in advertising before he became a full-time writer in 1984. Today he is considered one of the most exciting exponents of Cuban–American fiction. His first novel *Our House in the Last World*, 1983, has budding novelist Hector writing up his immigrant family's touching history as they exile themselves from **Holguín** in Cuba to poverty in New York. The novel includes the tensions between tropical Cuba and the USA as the land of plenty, with Fidel Castro looming large as first welcomed and then execrated, with stress on laziness and the pull of the past in Cuba. Like many first novels this one has the density of painful, experienced life. Hijuelos's second saga novel *The Mambo Kings Play Songs of Love*, 1989 (Extract 6), won the Pulitzer Prize in 1989, and was made into a film. It deals with two musician brothers making it in New York from the 1950s on, with moving, detailed cameos of Cuban–American immigrant life. A third novel, *Mr Ives' Christmas*, 1995, tenderly outlines the life-history of an illustrator in New York, who, from his obscure Latin looks, befriends *latinos* in New York and whose son is shot by a Cuban thug.

HUMBOLDT, Alexandre von (1769–1859). Born at Tegel, Berlin, Humboldt was educated by tutors and at the Universities of Frankfurt, Göttingen and Hamburg, before travelling abroad to Britain. He worked in the Prussian Mines, and befriended Goethe at Jena. He travelled to Madrid with his friend Bonpland, and set sail for the New World in 1799, collecting and noting down everything for five years. On his return to Paris in 1805 he began publishing his findings in his encyclopaedic *Voyage aux régions équinoxiales de Nouveau Continent*, which appeared in 30 volumes between 1808 and 1834. He died in 1859, a bachelor, and one of the great men of Europe. His study of Cuba was translated into English in 1862 in the USA, but his plea for the abolition of slavery was censored, much to his ire.

LEWIS, Norman (1908–). See also under Haiti. Born in Enfield, North London, Lewis has travelled widely, and written novels and travel books and reportage on Spain and Latin America. As a journalist he first drew the world's attention to the plight of the Brazilian Indians in 1968. His vivid autobiography *Jackdaw Cake*, 1987, describes his marriage, and then his move out to Cuba under Batista. He refers to subsequent visits to Cuba in *This World, This World*, 1996. He has written two novels set in Cuba. *A Small War Made to Order*, 1966, is set in Castro's revolutionary Cuba just before and during the Bay of Pigs invasion (1961). An ex-fascist, bohemian Brit, Charles Fane, is paid to spy on Castro's defences, falls for his sexy Cuban interpreter, and is killed in the end. Lewis was in Cuba in 1961 himself, and wrote

Norman Lewis

newspaper articles about the situation, interviewing one of the pilots who tried to drop bombs on the Cubans. The novel can be read as a realistic introduction to Cuba for a foreigner. In 1982 he published *Cuban Passage* (Extract 13), set during Batista's last days as dictator (1959) and involving a boy of 15, Dick Frazer, learning to become a man after absconding when his beautiful mother is drugged and kept as a sex slave by a wealthy Cubano. The boy shoots the Cuban dead while hunting, is imprisoned, and then freed as Castro's *barbudos* enter Havana in January 1960. There are realistic descriptions of Havana, voodoo,

the landscape. Lewis's journalistic style packs in information, and deals with contemporary issues in the Graham Greene mode. Lewis recently published an article on his visit to Hemingway (*Granta*, 1995).

LEZAMA LIMA, José (1910–1976). Lezama Lima was born in **Havana**, and lived all his life in the same street, **calle Trocadero**, hardly ever travelling abroad. He can be considered one of Latin America's great baroque poets, as well as editor of important literary magazines like *Orígenes* (1944–1957). He wrote difficult essays on many themes, and was a densely literary man. His sole novel,

Paradiso, 1966 (*Paradiso*, 1974), created a scandal in Castro's Cuba when it appeared, especially the famous chapter 8 with its explicit homosexual scenes, though many authors, like the Argentine Julio Cortázar, came to Lezama Lima's defence. Lezama Lima was often persecuted for his same-sex tendency, as well as for not being politically supportive of the revolution. He was bitterly attacked by poet Heberto Padilla ◊. *Paradiso* (Extract 14) follows the development of sensitive, asthmatic José Cemí in a macho society; it is the narration of the growth of a homosexual in tropical Cuba, and in its family romance is clearly autobiographical. But the novel is hard to read, portentous and baroque.

MARTI, José (1853–1895). Born in **Havana** from a poor family, he spent his life fighting for the cause of Cuban independence from Spain. He was imprisoned as a boy in 1869, and was deported to Spain from 1871 to 1874 where he began his committed journalism. In 1879 he was again deported from Cuba to Spain, but escaped to France, and moved to New York in 1880 where he spent the rest of his exile living as a journalist, writing for great papers like *La Nación* in Argentina, even editing a children's magazine. He returned to Cuba as a guerrilla, and was killed in a skirmish at Dos Ríos, near Santiago, in 1895. In his life time he published two collections of poems. His prose style was modern and lively, and a great influence on aspiring writers around Latin America. His chronicles are collected for English-readers in *Inside the Monster: Writings on the United States and American Imperialism*, 1975, and *Our America by José Martí: Writings on Latin America and the Struggle for Cuban Independence*, 1977. Martí is the great figure-head of Cuban liberation, a model copied deliberately by Castro, and revered by generations of Cubans of all political

persuasions. He is famous for many battle cries, including the Pan-American '*nuestra América*'.

MOREJÓN, Nancy (1944–). Born in the old part of **Havana**, where she still lives, Morejón has a masters in French, and is a translator of French poetry. She has published several collections of poetry, and Kathleen Weaver has translated *Where the Island Sleeps Like a Wing*, 1985, into English. She has also published essays on Nicolás Guillén ◊. She works at the Cuban Union of Writers and Artists.

PADILLA, Heberto (1932–). Born in **Pinar del Río**, Padilla published his first book of poems in 1948, worked as a journalist in New York, and travelled the Eastern block during Castro's regime. He came to notoriety when he won a literary prize in 1971, which guaranteed publication, subsequently blocked because the book of colloquial and satirical poems which question the role of the poet rebel in a new revolutionary context were considered to be counter-revolutionary. His trial alerted many Western intellectuals to the possibility that Cuba might be Stalinizing its cultural life, for Padilla appeared in court after a time in prison admitting to his crimes, with black eyes. The poems that caused him so much trouble can be read in *Legacies: Selected Poems*, translated by Alastair Reid and Andrew Hurley, 1982, and *Sent off the Field: A Selection from the Poetry of Heberto Padilla*, 1971. Padilla's autobiography of his Cuban days, before his exile to the USA, with acute insights into the cultural politics, appeared in 1989 as *Autoretrato del otro: La mala memoria* (*Self-Portrait of the Other. Memoirs*, 1990). He has also had one novel translated into English – *En mi jardín pastan los héroes*, 1981 (*Heroes are Grazing in my Garden*, 1984).

PIÑERA, Virgilio (1912–1979). Born in **Cardenas**, Cuba, Piñeras studied literature at **Havana University**, and wrote for Lezama Lima's literary magazine *Orígenes*. In 1950 he went to live in Buenos Aires and befriended and translated the exiled Polish writer Gombrowicz, as well as being on the fringe of the *Sur* group, with Borges. In 1957 he returned to Cuba, and stayed on after Castro's Revolution. He was always on the breadline, and suffered persecution as a homosexual – he was even arrested in 1961 for 'moral crimes'. He never actively supported the regime, but refused to leave the island. His stories have a wonderfully bitter humour. *Cuentos fríos* appeared in Buenos Aires in 1955 (*Cold Tales*, 1988 – Extract 16). Piñera has also written novels, including *La carne de René* (*René's Flesh*, 1989), and many plays. He died in poverty in Havana. See Guillermo Cabrera Infante, *Mea Cuba*, 1995.

SARDUY, Severo (1937–1993). Born in **Camagüey**, Sarduy began publishing poems in José Lezama Lima's *Orígenes* while studying medicine. In 1960 he won a scholarship to study painting in Paris, where he lived until he died from AIDS in 1993. In Paris he befriended Roland Barthes and Philippe Sollers, wrote for *Tel Quel*, worked as a Director in Éditions de Seuil, and began his adventures as an experimental writer. In 1963 his first novel *Gestos* appeared, followed in 1967 with *De Donde son los cantantes?* (translated as *From Cuba with a Song*, 1994). This teasing pastiche of a novel (Extract 17) plays with the Chinese, African and Spanish racial roots in Cuba, mocking a reader's attempt to turn it into something realistic. It's a carnival of words, and a parodic search for identity culminating with Castro's 1959 entry into Havana. Sarduy's third novel *Cobra* came out in 1973 (translated in 1974). He was fascinated by science and wrote bizarre poems, collected as *Big Bang*. He also wrote radio plays and was a fine critic – his essays *Escrito sobre un cuerpo*, 1969, have been translated as *Written on a Body*, 1989. Another refreshing and baffling novel, *Maitreya*, based on a trip to Tibet, appeared in 1980, translated in 1987. His last novel *Colibrí*, 1986, is set in a homosexual brothel in Cuba. He once said: 'I am a Cuban through and through, who just happens to live in Paris.'

JAMAICA

'The sun etches out the minutes of my days/under my dark eyes. The train, our only/regulation, shakes down the hours stakes out/the limits of our lives/on this, my harsh and gentle island.'
Olive Senior

Jamaica is both famed and infamous. Immortalized in the languid lyrics of Noel Coward and the seductive imagery of travel agents' brochures, it is the original Eden of tropical carefreeness. Its three Rs of rum, reggae and Rastafari have come to symbolize a hedonistic and exotic escapism; tourists arrive in their hundreds of thousands each year, bound for some of the world's most beautiful beaches. The island has spectacular mountains, dramatic waterfalls and lush rainforest. Unlike many Caribbean neighbours, it even has sites of architectural interest: the Great Houses which dominated the sugar plantations, colonial towns and pirates' forts. Its culture is multifaceted, as are its people. 'Out of many one people' reads the national motto, and certainly there are influences from around the world.

And yet Jamaica is also poor, sometimes violent, and often desperate. Behind the stunning scenery of its mountains lie pockets of rural misery, ramshackle villages kept alive by dollars sent from relatives abroad. In the cities are tough ghettos where gun and drug culture often crushes ordinary family and community bonds. A two-party political system breeds fanatical loyalty and explosive confrontations. There is too little work, too much debt and a sense of social disintegration. In an island that looks like everybody's idea of paradise, life is rarely easy.

COLONIAL TIMES

The island was visited by Christopher Columbus during his second expedition in 1494 when he called it Santiago. It was, he wrote, 'the fairest isle that eyes have beheld; mountainous and the land seems to touch the sky . . . full of valleys and fields.' Characteristically, the encounter between Columbus and the indigenous Arawaks swiftly deteriorated into hostility, and the Spaniards set loose their trained dogs on the terrified

FACT BOX

AREA: 10 991 sq km
POPULATION: 2 497 000
CAPITAL: Kingston
LANGUAGES: English, Patois ('Jamaica talk')
FORMER COLONIAL POWER: Britain
INDEPENDENCE: 1962
PER CAPITA GDP: US$1340

islanders. Nor was his second visit to the island any more promising. In 1503, a badly leaking ship forced Columbus to land at what is now **St Ann's Bay**, where he and his crew spent an unhappy year awaiting rescue. Unfortunately, his reputation for cantankerous trouble-making meant that at least one ship from the colony of Santo Domingo declined to pick him up and he had to send an emissary by canoe to hire a rescue ship.

Colonization began in earnest in 1510 when a group of Spaniards founded a settlement near **St Ann's Bay**. Led by Juan de Esquivel, appointed Governor by Columbus's son Diego from Santo Domingo, their aim was to find the gold which Columbus believed to be plentiful in the island. It was a futile quest, and the colony yielded disappointing amounts of wealth. The Arawaks, meanwhile, quickly succumbed to a lethal combination of aggression and disease from the invaders. As smallpox, measles and bubonic plague swept through indigenous communities, the survivors were forced to work as serfs in the island's first plantations, where many died from overwork and ill-treatment. By the end of the sixteenth century, the Arawaks were almost extinct. Ironically, their name for the island, *Xaymaca* (meaning 'land of woods and waters'), was by now in common usage rather than Columbus's Santiago.

Under Spanish rule, Jamaica was a backwater, suitable for refitting ships *en route* to more prosperous imperial outposts such as Cuba or the South American mainland. Slaves from Africa were imported to work in the sugar-cane and cotton plantations from 1517 onwards, but for the most part the island was underpopulated and undeveloped, ideal terrain for communities of runaway slaves known as *quilombos*. Rival European powers also began to harass the Spanish colony. British ships attacked Jamaica in 1596 and 1636, and in 1655 an English expeditionary force of 38 ships and 8000 men landed near modern-day **Kingston**. Sent by Cromwell as part of his 'grand design' to defeat Spain by attacking its colonies, the force was under the command of Admiral William Penn (who founded the American State of Pennsylvania). Meeting little in the way of resistance, they advanced on the nearby Spanish capital, Santiago de la Vega (today **Spanish Town**) and burned the deserted city to the ground. The Spanish Governor, it is said, had seen the English flotilla bearing down on the island from a vantage point on the north coast. He left quickly for Cuba, and his viewing-point was renamed **Runaway Bay**.

Undisputed British rule did not come until 1670 and the Peace of Madrid which ceded imperial ownership to London. In the meantime, the first English settlers had been attacked by rebel slave guerrillas, sometimes led by Spanish troops, who had been set free by the departing Spaniards. Yet Spanish resistance was short-lived, and most of the slaves gradually withdrew to the most remote and inaccessible areas of the island to form their own free communities. Known as the Maroons (from the Spanish *cimarrón* or 'wild'), these communities were to remain a threat to the colonial system for many years.

Attracted by this foothold in the midst of the Spanish empire, a motley collection of pirates and mercenaries settled in Jamaica. The colonial authorities were at first alarmed at their presence but made a pragmatic deal, allowing them to use Jamaica as a base for their forays against ships from other nations. On the tip of the long spit of land which protects Kingston's spectacular natural harbour, the buccaneers established a 'pirate capital' at **Port Royal**. Contemporary accounts depict the place as a veritable den of iniquity, a 'gilded Hades' where the pirates' ill-gotten loot fuelled a boom-town of taverns and brothels. Colourful characters such as Bluebeard and Calico Jack Rackham were among the denizens of this unsavoury place, while Henry Morgan, perhaps the most notorious of English pirates, ended his days as Lieutenant Governor.

In 1692 the 'wickedest town in Christendom' met with what many thought was an appropriate act of divine retribution. A massive earthquake hit the Kingston area, sending a tidal wave crashing into the pirates' city. As entire streets, warehouses and ships were engulfed, about 3000 people died instantly. Port Royal never recovered its dubious lustre; a new city was founded on the other side of the bay, and what remained of the destroyed settlement was gradually rebuilt as a naval base and fort. Today, a twenty-minute boat ride from Kingston's waterfront, Port Royal is a melancholic place, where visitors can inspect eighteenth-century British cannons and visit a museum, built in the quarters where Horatio Nelson stayed in 1779.

THE KILLING FIELDS

The British were more efficient and ruthless colonizers than the Spanish had been, and their priority was the 'white gold' of sugar rather than precious metals. Following the successful cultivation of the crop in Barbados, sugar-cane spread relentlessly along the flat, fertile valleys and plains of Jamaica. In 1673 there were only 57 plantations on the island; by 1740 there were at least 430. Jamaica was soon to become the world's largest sugar producer. The wealth of its planters became proverbial. Contemporary travellers spoke in awe of their conspicuous consumption and extravagance.

The system could not function without cheap and plentiful labour, and in the absence of an indigenous workforce the planters imported slaves from Africa. Slaves arrived by the boatload every few days and were sold at a price related to how well they had survived the ordeal of the infamous 'middle passage' from Africa. Jamaica also acted as an entrepôt for other Caribbean slave societies, and many slaves were sold on into other islands. Among the various ethnic groups from Africa who found themselves sold into slavery were the Coromantees from the Gold Coast, who soon developed a reputation for fierce resistance and who swelled the ranks of the Maroons. Approximately 5000 slaves were purchased each year by Jamaica's planters, but perhaps one in three died within a year, hence ensuring the continuing profitability of the slave trade.

Some planters attempted to maintain and even increase their stock of slaves by encouraging slave women to bear children. In the years proceeding the abolition of the slave trade, some slave-owners saw this as their only means of keeping a viable workforce. In his powerful novella *Wages Paid* (Extract 9), James Carnegie ◊ recreates the brutal system of using certain male slaves as 'studs'.

The publication in 1989 of a book entitled *In Miserable Slavery* cast new and fascinating light on everyday life in an eighteenth-century Jamaican plantation. Comprising the annotated diaries of Thomas Thistlewood, a small landowner in western Jamaica between 1750 and 1786, the book reveals, for instance, some of the potential pitfalls facing the prospective slave purchaser. Reflecting on his visit to the **Savanna la Mar** slave market in January 1760, Thistlewood notes:

> 'In regard to buying of Negroes, I would choose men-boys and girls, none exceeding 16 or 18 years old, as full grown men or women seldom turn out well; and beside, they shave the men so close & gloss them over so much that a person cannot be certain he does not buy old Negroes . . . Have also observed that many new Negroes, who are bought fat and sleek from aboard the ship, soon fall away much in a plantation, whereas those which are in a moderate condition hold their flesh better and are commonly hardier.'

What is most disconcerting about Thistlewood's dispassionate jottings is the mixture of promiscuity, arbitary cruelty and occasional kindness which they record. The diarist carefully records each sexual conquest among his female slaves and casually mentions the many floggings he administers for trivial misdemeanours. Yet when he died, Thistlewood left a will stipulating that one of his female slaves should be manumitted and a small piece of land and house should be provided for her.

The Maroons

Slave resistance took many forms, ranging from feigned illness and sabotage to poisoning and even insurrection. In 1831 a revolt led by a slave and

Baptist preacher, Sam Sharpe, wreaked havoc throughout the plantations in western Jamaica. The uprising was put down with extraordinary brutality by the authorities and Sharpe was hanged (today he is a national hero and the main square of **Montego Bay** carries his name).

Others escaped and attempted to establish free communities in the wild mountainous districts of the island. The original Maroons, dating from the period of Spanish rule, were gradually joined by other runaway slaves. In 1690 a large number of Coromantee slaves escaped from **Clarendon** and banded together with Maroons to form armed groups. They were concentrated in two main areas, the so-called **Cockpit Country** in the west and the northern slopes of the imposing **Blue Mountains** near Kingston. Led by leaders such as Cudjoe and his brother Accompong, the Maroons harassed the British colonists, attacking farms and stealing livestock and crops. A series of offensives by the colonial militia failed to dislodge the Maroons from their mountain strongholds, and English soldiers were often outmanoevred by guerrilla tactics.

In 1739 the authorities finally made peace with Cudjoe, offering the Maroons freedom, land and certain rights. In return, the Maroons agreed to return any further runaway slaves to their masters. A second Maroon War erupted in 1795 after two Maroons had been publicly flogged in **Montego Bay**. This time, the authorities imported man-hunting mastiffs from Cuba and surrounded the Maroon community of **Trelawny Town**. Five hundred Maroons were captured and deported to Nova Scotia, from which most finally sailed for Sierra Leone and a return to their ancestral continent.

A Maroon community still exists in Cockpit Country today, and locals make a living from receiving tourists and relating the history of the main settlement, **Accompong**. In the 1930s the black American writer Zora Neale Hurston visited the Maroon headquarters and was moved by its aura of history. In *Voodoo Gods*, she wrote:

> 'Standing on that old parade ground, which is now a cricket field, I could feel the dead generations crowding me. Here was the oldest settlement of freedmen in the Western world, no doubt. Men who had thrown off the bands of slavery by their own courage and ingenuity. The courage and daring of the Maroons strike like a purple beam across the history of Jamaica.'

Some years later, Patrick Leigh Fermor (◊ Barbados) went to Accompong and met the same Maroon leader, Colonel Rowe, who dressed in 'a grey military jacket stiff with black braid, a Sam Browne belt, grey pantaloons with black stripes down the seams, and a helmet the same shape as those worn by colonial governors. He wore it with a nice combination of solemnity and dash.'

EMANCIPATION AND DECLINE

Controversy still surrounds the real motives for the abolition of slavery. Did a groundswell of humanitarian public opinion, encouraged by abolitionists such as William Wilberforce, really sway governments in London? Or were the forces of free trade, increasingly powerful due to the Industrial Revolution, determined to wipe out the planters' monopoly of sugar exports and the system which propped them up? Had the English colonies simply become unprofitable and slavery too expensive a system to maintain compared to the cheap labour to be found in Asia? And had the experience of the revolution in Saint Domingue and the creation of independent Haiti taught the colonial powers that slavery would inevitably destroy itself? It was a combination of all these factors which hastened the end of the slave trade itself in 1807 and then accelerated the move towards full emancipation. Fear of revolution, declining profitability, the emergence of free marketeers in Europe determined to buy sugar cheaper elsewhere: all these pressures bore down on the reluctant and resentful Jamaican plantocracy.

The 1834 Emancipation Act covered 254 310 black slaves in Jamaica, for which the planters received per capita compensation from London of £23. Freedom did not come overnight, however; first there was a four-year period of 'apprenticeship', during which the former slaves were obliged to continue their work on the plantations. When this ended, the vast majority had no desire to remain on the estates, not least because of the miserable wages offered to them. Many became smallholders, producing crops for their families, for the local market, and sometimes for export. Between 1840 and 1845 the number of freehold settlements of under ten acres soared from 883 to 20 724. A Jamaican peasantry came into being, often confined to the most marginal agricultural lands and vulnerable to debt and the threat of eviction.

Yet even the uncertainties of peasant life were preferable for most to continuing labour on the plantations. As a result, the planters became desperate for labour, shipping over immigrants from Europe and introducing indentured labourers from Africa, East India and China. From Germany and England came poor agricultural workers who settled in villages with names like **Berlin, Hanover,** and **Little London.** In **Seaford Town,** a community of Germans settled in the hope of escaping the cycle of poverty; their descendants today still carry names such as Wedermeyer and Eldermeyer. But even these new workers could not compensate for the exodus of the ex-slaves. Sugar production plummeted, depressed by labour shortages, inadequate technology and lack of investment. The 1846 Sugar Equalisation Act, removing Jamaican sugar's preferential access into the British market, came as another crushing blow. Jamaican producers could not hope to compete in a free market with countries such as Cuba or Brazil, where slavery was not yet abolished and costs much lower. Jamaica's share of the total world market fell from 15% in 1828 to 2.5% in 1850.

In 1859 Anthony Trollope ◊ visited Jamaica. His mission, he wrote, was 'to cleanse the Augean stables of our Post Office there:' In the process, he wrote a detailed description and analysis of what he saw as the colony's disastrous decline. The culprits, he believed, were emancipation and British imperial neglect, both of which had served to wreck the sugar industry and ruin the colony's prosperity:

> 'That Jamaica was a land of wealth, rivalling the East in its means of riches, nay, excelling it as a market for capital, a place where money might be turned; and that it now is a spot on the earth more poverty-stricken than any other – so much is known almost to all men. That this change was brought about by the manumission of the slaves, which was completed in 1838, of that also the English world is generally aware. And there probably, the usual knowledge about Jamaica ends.'

'The palmy days of that island are over,' he lamented, and in *The West Indies and the Spanish Main* (Extract 16), he paints a dismal picture of Jamaica's decadence.

The misfortunes of a once-glamorous plantocracy also form the main thematic motif for Jean Rhys's (◊ Dominica) most celebrated novel, *Wide Sargasso Sea* (Extract 4). Here, the madness of the narrator Antoinette develops against a desolate background of deserted estates and resentful former slaves. 'But the people here won't work,' says Antoinette's step-father. 'They don't want to work. Look at this place – it's enough to break your heart.'

In reality, the former slaves wanted to work, but for better wages than the impoverished planters could offer them. Tensions grew in the decades following emancipation, culminating in the dramatic **Morant Bay** Rebellion of 1865. The crucial issue behind the rebellion was land; suffering from the impact of droughts, high taxation and high prices (the American Civil War had cut off supplies of cheap grain and fish), landless peasants began to demand rights over unused Crown Land. When the authorities, headed by the notoriously reactionary Governor Edward John Eyre, refused to cooperate, rural communities became more organized and militant. A mulatto businessman and politician, George William Gordon, became a spokesman for the dispossessed, and through his branch of the Baptist Church he established a network of followers. Among them was Paul Bogle, a Deacon in the Church and a local leader of landless peasants at **Stony Gut** near Morant Bay.

When in October 1865 Bogle led a band of followers into town to protest at the trial of one of his supporters, fighting broke out with the police. A warrant was issued for Bogle's arrest, his men overpowered the officers sent to arrest him, and another march descended on Morant Bay. This time a full-scale riot erupted, and violence spread throughout the district, with both black peasants and white landowners murdered. In his classic novel *New Day*, V.S. Reid reconstructs the charisma and oratory with which Bogle inspired his followers into confrontation with the authorities.

Martial law was declared and Governor Eyre authorized a series of savage reprisals: some 430 rebels were executed, 600 were flogged and 1 000 homes were burned down as punishment. Paul Bogle was hanged, as was Gordon, whom Governor Eyre accused of masterminding the rebellion.

The extent of the violence, particularly the authorities' reprisals, caused consternation in Britain, where Governor Eyre was either vilified as a butcher or celebrated as a defender of civilization against anarchy. Interestingly, a significant number of writers and intellectuals supported Eyre and his actions. A defence fund was set up when he was recalled to London, and Thomas Carlyle, John Ruskin, Lord Alfred Tennyson, Charles Kingsley and even Charles Dickens spoke up in favour of Eyre and his ruthless suppression of the Morant Bay rebellion. 'The Jamaican story,' wrote Karl Marx to Friedrich Engels, 'is characteristic of the beastliness of the "true Englishman".'

EMERGENCE OF MODERN POLITICS

In the wake of the 1865 unrest, Jamaica became a Crown Colony, ruled directly from London with a Governor *in situ*, supported by a local council. This was symptomatic of Britain's belief that the island's plantocracy no longer had the authority to govern by itself. As a result, reforms in education, health and the judicial system were enacted which the conservative planters would never have contemplated, and their influence continued to decline. At the same time, a new Jamaican middle class was emerging, some black, others mulatto, who were beginning to challenge the old élite in the professions and in politics. For almost seventy years after the Morant Bay rebellion, a fragile social peace held.

With the Great Depression of 1929, Jamaica underwent an economic and political crisis. Sugar prices fell still further, banana prices plumeted and unemployment rose dramatically. A sugar workers' strike in 1938 degenerated into rioting and shootings by the police. In the midst of the disorder, the middle-class leadership of a nascent trade union movement entered the political stage. Alexander Bustamante, a strike leader, launched his Bustamante Industrial Trade Union (BITU), the Caribbean's first trade union, while his cousin, Norman Manley, founded the People's National Party (PNP). Both reformists and advocates of representative government, Bustamante and Manley set in motion a political system which has lasted to this day. As their ideological differences widened, Bustamante established his own Jamaica Labour Party (JLP) and Manley his own Trade Union Congress (TUC).

Passing through limited self-government, granted in 1944, Jamaica became a key actor in the short-lived Federation of the West Indies. Believing that the island was too small for viable independence, Manley supported the British plan for a federation of its colonies. In 1958 the Federation came into existence, with its capital in Port of Spain and its Prime Minister Grantley Adams of Barbados. But the ideal of uniting the

English-speaking territories of the Caribbean ran aground when inter-island rivalry, notably between Jamaica and Trinidad, made cooperation almost impossible. In a referendum in 1960 Jamaicans overwhelmingly voted to leave the Federation. Full independence followed quickly on 5 August 1962.

Today party politics in Jamaica are literally a matter of life or death. Walls in the slum districts of **Kingston** are covered with graffiti, praising the PNP or JLP and abusing the opposition. In the so-called 'garrison' constituencies of the capital, gunmen shoot it out for territorial control in the name of their political party, and there is no shortage of evidence that high-ranking politicians are directly involved in arming their supporters. Yet, paradoxically, Jamaica has maintained its two-party 'Westminster style' democracy since independence, with regular elections and a free press.

In the 1970s and 1980s political passions ran even higher than usual, when Jamaica became a microcosm of Cold War ideological conflict. The PNP, by now led by Norman Manley's son Michael, had espoused a form of democratic socialism, favouring land reform, higher taxes and friendship with Cuba. The JLP, on the other hand, had long abandoned its militant trade union roots, becoming a staunch supporter of Ronald Reagan's blend of free-market economics and anti-communism. The 1972–80 PNP government engaged in left-wing rhetoric and alienated opinion in Washington; as the USA expressed disquiet about relations with Havana, the economy began to falter and tensions rose. In 1980 an estimated 800 people died in election-related violence before the JLP's Edward Seaga took power, promising 'deliverance' from state intervention and socialism. His term in office was no more successful than Manley's despite massive US aid, and a series of punishing International Monetary Fund (IMF) programmes made life difficult for the majority of Jamaicans. In 1989 a chastened and 'moderate' Michael Manley returned to power, and in 1992 he handed over the premiership to Percival J. Patterson, the first black Prime Minister in the country's history.

Jamaican politics is as much about personalities as principles, and the island has produced its fair share of 'big man' politicians. Blind loyalty to the party is expected from supporters, and in return they can look forward to rewards if their side wins. In *A Boy named Ossie* (Extract 8), Earl McKenzie ◊ provides a telling fictional example of how party politics really work in Jamaica.

From Sugar to Tourism

The days of monocrop sugar cultivation are long gone. Large tracts of Jamaica are still covered with sugar-cane, much of which is exported into the European Union or goes to make the island's celebrated rum. But nowadays the economy is much more diversified, and Jamaicans work in industries which range from mining to data-processing.

The advent of the banana as an export crop did much to reinforce the growth and stability of an independent peasantry in Jamaica. The first steady export trade began in 1870 when a Captain Lorenzo Baker took a load of bananas from **Port Morant** to New York. He returned the next year and quickly developed a regular service between **Port Antonio** and the East Coast of the USA. With the arrival of refrigeration technology, the industry boomed, and soon the big US multinational, United Fruit, had substantial interests in Jamaica. Bananas meant a steady source of income for small farmers and they brought modest prosperity to many rural communities, despite the ever-present danger of hurricanes and disease. In his famous poem, 'The Song of the Banana Man' (Extract 2), Evan Jones ◊ celebrates the fruit's contribution to Jamaica's rural culture.

The discovery of bauxite (the ore used in aluminium production) in the early years of the twentieth century further diversified Jamaica's economy and provided much-needed jobs in mining. Seen from the air, the vast red scars which cut through the otherwise green landscape are the visible marks of bauxite's impact on the environment. Manufacturing has also developed, with local and foreign entrepreneurs taking advantage of the island's comparatively low wages and proximity to the North American market. In **Montego Bay**, a mostly female workforce makes electrical components and garments for US companies, while others compute credit card bills and mailshots in a data-processing centre.

The 'informal sector' is also an economic mainstay, providing work for hundreds of thousands of Jamaicans. Every town has its street vendors and market women, selling snacks, vegetables and cold drinks. In downtown **Kingston**, the pavements are almost impassable for people selling everything from bananas to hi-fi equipment. The orthodox shopkeepers bitterly resent their informal competitors, but the so-called 'higglers' or market traders are a formidable body of fiercely independent women. Many of them now travel regularly between Jamaica, Haiti, Curaçao and Panama City, in search of bargains to sell on the streets of Jamaican towns.

But it is perhaps tourism which has most changed the face of Jamaica. Once, the island was the exclusive retreat of a few well-heeled and bohemian expatriates. Writers such as Noel Coward and Ian Fleming owned properties on the north coast, while Errol Flynn bought his own private **Navy Island** near **Port Antonio**. Coward ◊ seemed to sum up the balmy atmosphere of early Jamaican tourism in his whimsical poem 'Jamaica' (Extract 11).

Since the advent of the long-haul charter flight and the down-market package holiday, Jamaica has become used to receiving in excess of one million tourists each year. Some go to the all-inclusive beach resorts and need never leave their hotel for their entire stay; others go in search of rum, reggae and Jamaica's other specialities. Older Jamaicans complain that tourism has corrupted the island's youth and brought moral and drug-related problems to once-stable communities. Economists calculate that the industry produces close to US$1 billion a year for the island's economy.

Undoubtedly a mixed blessing, tourism has become an intrinsic part of Jamaican life, and hordes of vendors, hustlers and 'guides' pursue the unwitting tourist from dawn till dusk. In his comic masterpiece, *The Lunatic* (Extract 10), Anthony Winkler ◊ paints a rather less than flattering picture of tourists, both American and European.

But despite changes in Jamaica's economic structure, the island remains poor, dependent and indebted. In the mid-1990s, the country's external debt stood at a staggering US$4.6 billion, meaning that every man, woman and child owed foreign banks and institutions more than US$1800.

'GOING FOREIGN'

As tourists flood into Jamaica, Jamaicans themselves prefer to leave the island in search of opportunities elsewhere. This has been the case for most of the twentieth century and has provided a 'safety valve' for Jamaican society, reducing levels of unemployment and providing the remittances from overseas which sustain many families. Jamaicans sometimes refer to emigration as 'going foreign', and this process of movement within the Caribbean and beyond has created distinctive cultural communities around the world.

The first wave of migration took place in the 1860s and 1870s, when Jamaican labourers went to Panama to work first on constructing the railway line and then to take part in building the canal across the isthmus. The first attempt to do so, under the command of the French engineer, Ferdinand de Lesseps, failed miserably among epidemics of yellow fever and financial mismanagement. After nine years of heavy labour in the humid and pestilential Panamanian climate, 20 000 workers had died, a large number of them Jamaican. Those who survived were left stranded in the squalid camps of Colón and Panama City and many settled there never to return.

The second bid to build the Panama Canal succeeded, and for the ten years it took to dig the waterway thousands of Jamaicans went to earn their 'Panama Gold'. Between the beginning of the century and the Canal's opening in 1914, Colón became a half-Jamaican town and the island's influence remains strong to this day. The workers who returned to Jamaica enjoyed the reputation of being rich men (in reality the black workers in Panama were paid less than their white counterparts and segregated) and their wealth and status created a sort of cocky mystique. One of Jamaica's most celebrated observers of rural life, Claude McKay ◊, draws an affectionate picture of one such Panama veteran in his classic *Banana Bottom* (Extract 6).

In the following years Jamaicans went to Cuba, Costa Rica and Honduras in search of agricultural work. But the greatest exodus occurred in the 1930s and 1940s when tens of thousands left to live and work in the USA. In the great East Coast cities such as New York, Baltimore, Boston and Philadelphia, communities sprang up which are very much still in evidence. Around 350 000 people in the eastern USA are thought to be of Jamaican origin. Today, however, entry is much less easy than it used to be and a green card is a much sought-after item. Nevertheless, many Jamaicans still go to the USA either to work (legally or illegally) or to visit friends and family. The cultural interchange between North America and the Caribbean is a two-way process, and cities such as New York have distinctive Jamaican areas where food, fashion and music are shaped by the island's influence. Conversely, North American culture has made dramatic inroads into Jamaican life, and not always with conspicuous good taste. In *Bella Makes Life* (Extract 1), Lorna Goodison ◊ provides a mocking but accurate picture of the vulgarity which can afflict some Jamaicans when exposed to a New York lifestyle.

After the USA tightened its immigration laws in the 1950s, Britain became an alternative destination for Jamaican migrants. Between 1950 and 1960, some 200 000 Jamaicans moved to Britain to fill jobs in the country's growing post-war economy. Often confined to recognizable districts of the major cities, Britain's Jamaican communities have suffered more than their fair share of discrimination and deprivation – but many second-generation Jamaicans have prospered in what has become, often reluctantly, a multicultural society, and Jamaican influences in music, sport and a range of other cultural expressions are very noticeable.

'UPTOWN' AND THE 'YARD'

Several decades after independence Jamaica remains a society of huge social divides. There is a significant middle class, comprising professionals, teachers and civil servants. In his novel *The Late Emancipation of Jerry Stover* (Extract 3), Andrew Salkey ◊ draws a wry picture of young middle-class Jamaicans in the 1960s and their impatience with the post-colonial stuffiness around them. Yet despite this middle class, there is still a dramatic gulf between a rich few and the poor majority. The wealthy minority, many lighter-skinned than the average Jamaican, live 'uptown' in prosperous suburbs with names such as **Arcadia Gardens** and **Beverly Hills**. Their lifestyle encompasses shopping trips to Miami, satellite dishes and swimming pools. In her poem 'The Lady' (Extract 13), Olive Senior evokes the neurotic lifestyle of one member of this élite.

Yet life for most Jamaicans remains a struggle, especially in the grim and violent slums of **West Kingston**. The shanty town districts of the capital are notorious for their poverty and crime, and visitors are generally warned to avoid such districts as **Trench Town** and **Denham Town**. These are the ghettos where party political allegiances are often expressed in shoot-outs and where crack cocaine has contributed a lethal new dimension of violence. Attempts have been made to modernize some of the oldest and worst slum areas, and the 1970s development known as **Tivoli Gardens** replaced the infamous **Back o'Wall** shanty town. Yet improvements for the great majority have been very slow in coming, and new clusters of tin roofs and packing-case walls break out around the city as people are evicted from their previous squatting sites. The slums go back many decades and have intrigued many writers with their aura of desperation and danger. Perhaps the most famous account of life in the 'yard' (the generic term for the tenement or ghetto) is to be found in *The Hills Were Joyful Together* (Extract 15), the classic tale of shanty town life by Roger Mais ◊.

The 'yard' has spawned countless criminals and gunmen (the legendary 'yardies' are simply the most recent gangster fraternity), but it has also produced a good number of musicians and artists who explicitly draw on their own experience of street life. In the celebrated 1972 film *The Harder They Come*, Jimmy Cliff played the part of Rhygin, the archetypal 'rude boy' turned reggae singer, whose rise to notoriety was due both to musical talent and ruthless criminality. Cliff's reggae theme song encapsulated the machismo and posturing of a young man determined to escape the stultifying poverty of the ghetto:

'And I keep on fighting for the things I want
Though I know that when you're dead you can't
But I'd rather be a free man in my grave
Than living as a puppet or a slave

So as sure as the sun will shine
I'm gonna get my share now, what's mine
And the harder they come, the harder they fall
One and all.'

The film was later adapted into a novel, *The Harder They Come* (Extract 14) by Michael Thelwell ◊, who traced in greater detail the passage from innocence to crime, from obscurity to notoriety of the gunman Rhygin.

The most internationally famous product of Jamaica's tough urban culture is reggae musician Bob Marley, whose family moved to **Trench Town** after his father had left home. Marley's musical career became intertwined with his life in the ghetto, where he combined forces with 'Bunny' Livingston, later to become a co-founder of the Wailers. When the Wailers' 1973 album, *Catch a Fire*, was released by Island records, Marley's musical talent was exposed to an international audience. Hit followed hit until 1981, when Marley, by now a reggae superstar, died tragically young of cancer. His 'Redemption Song' (Extract 5) is a classic instance of his sense of lyricism and spiritual power.

REGGAE AND RASTAFARI

The origins of the term 'reggae' are obscure and may derive from 'rags' or 'ragamuffin', in either case a reference to the music's humble social background. Musicologists agree that the genre evolved from a variety of sources, probably starting with traditional African drumming imported by Jamaica's slaves and modified by other rhythms and melodies picked up by

Bob Marley

itinerant Jamaican workers in Central America and other Caribbean islands. The first distinctive popular dance form was *mento*, a fast and normally humorous style with some similarities to Trinidadian calypso. The influences of North American big band jazz, swing and rhythm and blues in the 1950s helped to create *ska*, a more brass-based dance form which swept through Jamaica in the 1960s. The 1964 hit 'My Boy Lollipop' by Jamaican Millie Small also introduced the new wave into Britain and the USA. From *ska* came *rock steady* with a slower rhythm and a strongly emphasized bass line. Successes such as Desmond Dekker's 'Israelites' and Jimmy Cliff's 'You Can Get It If You Really Want It' brought musicians and producers to Jamaica in search of fresh talent.

Whatever the etymological roots of reggae, it gained huge worldwide popularity in the course of the 1970s with a succession of Jamaican artists such as the Wailers, Peter Tosh, Burning Spear and Gregory Isaacs. In its heyday, it was a considerable industry in its own right, with a superstructure of recording studios, record labels and world tours. Some in **Kingston** made huge sums of money, but inevitably major artists preferred to record on international labels, normally based in Europe or North America. Perhaps the zenith of reggae's domestic influence occurred in 1978 when, against a background of escalating political violence, Bob Marley brought together the PNP's Michael Manley and the JLP's Edward Seaga onstage in a symbolic act of reconciliation during the famous 'One Love' concert in Kingston.

Reggae still exists as a recognizable form, but it has evolved into various sub-genres, each with its own afficionados. *Dub* was popular in the 1980s and consisted of hypnotic backing tracks over which singers 'toasted' their own improvized lyrics. This in turn influenced the current fashion of 'dancehall', named after the venues where DJs perform their material through enormously powerful amplifiers. Influenced by US *hip hop* and *rap*, the music of the 1990s consists of the DJ talking or singing over prerecorded backing tracks. The lyrics are often explicitly sexual (*slack* in local parlance) and sometimes glorify violence and criminality. Many who appreciated the spiritual and political dimension of 1970s 'roots' reggae feel that the work of popular artists such as Shabba Ranks and Buju Banton (whose 'Boom Bye Bye' advocates shooting homosexuals) has distorted the tradition.

Reggae's international success brought to the world's attention what might otherwise have remained an esoteric spiritual cult like many others in the Caribbean. Rastafarianism became inseparable in the popular imagination from the music of Marley, Tosh and many others, and accordingly spread in influence as reggae's popularity grew. In songs such as 'Africa Unite' and 'Zion Train' Marley introduced some of Rastafarianism's central spiritual tenets to a vast international audience. The external trappings of the movement – dreadlocks and *ganja* – became fashion accessories, even if relatively few enthusiasts understood the real philosophical foundation of the movement.

The 'founding father' of Rastafarianism was Marcus Garvey (1887–1940). Garvey was born into a poor Jamaican family, but managed to escape rural obscurity and became an auto-didact, travelling widely in the Caribbean, Central America and Europe. Struck by the poverty and oppression experienced by blacks throughout the world, Garvey formed the

United Negro Improvement Association (UNIA) in 1916, with the aim of creating a strong, proud black nation in the African homeland. During the apogee of European imperialism in the continent, Garvey's message of a return to Africa struck a popular chord with black communities in the USA, Canada, the Caribbean and Europe. At its height, the UNIA had branches in 40 countries and two million members worldwide. Garvey's themes were those of organization and black redemption; his vision was of an Africa free of racism and exploitation where the world's blacks could return to build a new utopia. A hymn he wrote for the 1934 UNIA convention reads as follows:

> To Afric's shore we're bound again,
> In freedom's glory won at large,
> In thoughts we claim a just bargain,
> To sail in liberty's fair barge.

In the event Garvey's vision collapsed in the face of hostility from the authorities in the USA and Jamaica and among allegations of fraud in the Black Star Line, his shipping business which he hoped would link black people around the world. He died in London in 1940 after unsuccessful attempts to contest political power in Jamaica. Before leaving Jamaica, however, Garvey is said to have told his followers to prepare themselves for the coming of a black king in Africa. In 1930 the 'prophecy' was fulfilled when Tafari Makonnen (or 'Ras' Tafari) was crowned Emperor of Ethiopia, the only African country not to have been colonized by Europeans. Taking the name of Emperor Haile Selassie I, the 'Redeemer' claimed to be descended from King Solomon and the Queen of Sheba and thus the son of 'Jah' or God.

The fortuitous coincidence of Garvey's teachings and events in Africa inspired the beginnings of organized Rastafarianism in Jamaica, and in the 1940s the first churches and communes were established, mostly in the slum districts of **West Kingston**. As faith in the divine power of the Ethiopian Emperor grew, Rastas began to believe that he would literally despatch ships to pick them up from the dockside and transport them back to Africa. In *The Children of Sisyphus* (Extract 12), Orlando Patterson ◊ recreates the moment when thousands of Rastas waited in vain for their deliverance from hardship in Jamaica.

Based on the principle of Haile Selassie's divinity, a return to Africa and the end of oppression in 'Babylon' (the diaspora), Rastafarianism draws on an eclectic reading of the Bible and a series of strict religious codes. The unorthodox appearance of its adherents, their open use of *ganja* and their contempt for officialdom have inevitably created tensions with the authorities, and Rastas have been harassed and victimized in Jamaica and elsewhere – but the role played by Bob Marley and others helped the movement to gain wider acceptance, even if most middle-class Jamaicans today regard it with some distaste. Since the death of Haile Selassie in 1975 (an event denied by some purists), the idea of returning to Africa has become more symbolic than literal for many, even if some Rastas did manage to settle in the vicinity of Addis Ababa. There are perhaps 100 000 genuine adherents around the world, but many more so-called 'wolves' (the term used by Rastas for those who merely copy the outward appearance of the Brethren).

Absurd as it may seem to some, Rastafarianism has instilled a sense of positive self-awareness and identity in many people from Jamaica's poorest communities. It teaches that the white, colonial view of history and culture persists and that black people can find strength and inspiration out of what has been called a 'sufferer culture'.

ENGLISH AND PATOIS

Jamaica boasts a developed literary tradition and a vibrant publishing industry which manages to produce high-quality books despite constant economic difficulties. The presence of the University of the West Indies campus at **Mona** and a number of theatres, art galleries and museums in the capital ensure a lively cultural atmosphere among the intelligentsia. In recent years several highly acclaimed Jamaican writers have had their work published domestically and further afield. Interestingly, a significant number are women, including Olive Senior, Lorna Goodison, Velma Pollard, Patricia Powell, Pamela Mordecai and Christine Craig.

Jamaican writers have been able to reach English-reading audiences in Britain and North America and this has contributed to a sort of cross-fertilization. Many have dealt with issues of migration, exile and return, and some writers and artists, such as Linton Kwesi Johnson, have become permanently resident overseas.

But English, although officially the language of Jamaica, is not in reality what most Jamaicans speak. Their use of a vernacular, sometimes described as a patois, has created another, parallel literary tradition which complements that of official 'high culture'. Jamaican patois or 'Jamaica talk' is a mixture of English, Portuguese, Spanish, French and languages from the West Coast of Africa. The dominant element is English, but the speaker of 'standard English' will find it hard to get to grips with either syntax or vocabulary. As patois has evolved out of slavery as the common means of communication of different displaced people, so it has also added influences and fresh sources of expression.

This hybrid language forms the common thread of an oral tradition which stretches from the call-and-response songs of the plantation barracks to today's dub and dancehall music. An important part of this tradition are the folk tales which are directly descended from African oral story-telling. Dismissed for many years as 'uncultured' or 'folkloric', the vernacular tradition is today valued as part of Jamaica's heritage. Perhaps the first and best-known exponent of the vernacular form is Louise Bennett, known universally as 'Miss Lou'and a genuine national figure. Her poem 'Colonization in Reverse' is a wry commentary on the tide of emigration to Britain in the 1950s:

'Wat a joyful news, Miss Mattie,
I feel like me heart gwine burs
Jamaica people colonizin
Englan in reverse.

By de hundred, by de tousan
From country and from town,
By de ship-load, by de plane-load
Jamaica is Englan boun.

Dem a-pour out a Jamaica
Everybody future plan
Is fe get a big-time job
An settle in de mother lan

What a islan! What a people!
Man an woman, old an young
Just a-pack dem bag an baggage
An tun history upside dung!'

In recent years 'performance poets' and 'dub poets' such as Mutabaruka,
Oku Onuora and Linton Kwesi Johnson have taken on explicitly political
themes in their vernacular poetry. The genre also allows for the powerful
expression of everyday emotions, unfettered by the niceties of 'standard
English'. In 'Ryddim Ravings' (Extract 7), Jean Binta Breeze ◊, a
much-acclaimed oral poet, shows how the use of patois can create a
particularly intense poetic experience.

One of Jamaica's best patois poets was Michael Smith, who brought to
life the fears and enthusiasms of ordinary Jamaicans in poems such as 'I an I
alone', where the raucous pandemonium of a local market shouts from the
page:

' "Shoppin bag! Shoppin bag! Five cent fi one!"
"Green pepper! Thyme! Skellion! Pimento!"
"Remember de Sabbath day to keep it holy!
    Six days shalt thou labour,
    but on the seventh day thou shalt rest."
"Hey, Mam! How much fi dah piece a yam deh?
    No, no, dat; dat! Yes, dat!"
"Three dollars a poun, nice genkleman!" '

Smith died at the age of 29, stoned to death by four men outside a local
headquarters of the JLP. The previous evening, although he belonged to no
political party, he had heckled a JLP government minister at a public
meeting. A witness reported that when he was stopped by the four men, he
said, 'I-man free to walk anywhere in this land.'

LITERARY LANDMARKS

Kingston. The capital has not always appealed to literary visitors. Trollope
waxed indignant over its dilapidated streets and unpainted buildings. 'But

it is singular,' he wrote, 'that any man who could put bricks and stones and timber together should put them together in such hideous forms as those which are to be seen here.' Fifty years after his visit, Kingston was once again destroyed by an earthquake, which added little to its charm. In the 1950s Patrick Leigh Fermor recorded that 'The centre resembles the nastiest of London outskirts, and the outskirts are equal to the most dreary of West Indian slums.'

Port Maria. On the north coast, some 20 km east of **Ocho Rios** is **Firefly**, the house where Noel Coward spent much of the last 20 years of his life. In his diary on 3 February 1949, he writes: 'The house is entrancing. I can't believe it's mine . . . Back home, we had one more martini and sat on the verandah on rockers, looking out over the fabulous view, and almost burst into tears of sheer pleasure.' Close by is **Goldeneye**, formerly the house of Ian Fleming, who entertained the literati of the 1950s and 1960s there. Fleming's guests included Truman Capote, Stephen Spender, Graham Greene and Evelyn Waugh. Curiously, he took the name James Bond which he gave to his legendary secret agent from the author of a book on Jamaica's birds. **Firefly** is open to visitors, but **Goldeneye** is not (it is now owned by millionaire reggae entrepreneur Chris Blackwell).

BOOKLIST

The following selection includes the extracted titles in this chapter as well as other titles for further reading. In general, paperback editions are given when possible. For most of the extracted works, the original publisher in English can be found in 'Acknowledgments and Citations' at the end of the volume, as can the exact location of the extracts and the editions from which they are taken.

Bayer, Marcel, *Jamaica in Focus*, Latin America Bureau, London, 1993.

Beckford, George and Michael Witter, *Small Garden, Bitter Weed: Struggle and Change in Jamaica*, Zed, London, 1982.

Black, Clinton V., *The History of Jamaica*, Collins, London, 1983.

Breeze, Jean Binta, 'Riddym Ravings (The Mad Woman's Poem)', in *Spring Cleaning*, Virago, London, 1992. **Extract 7.**

Carnegie, James, *Wages Paid*, Casa de las Américas, Havana, 1976. **Extract 9.**

Coward, Noel, 'Jamaica', in *Collected Verse*, Methuen, London, 1984. **Extract 11.**

Goodison, Lorna, 'Bella Makes Life', in *Baby Mother and the King of Swords*, Longman, 1990. **Extract 1.**

Hall, Douglas (ed), *In Miserable Slavery: Thomas Thistlewood in Jamaica, 1750–86*, Macmillan, London, 1989.

Hurston, Zora Neale, *Voodoo Gods: An Inquiry into Native Myths and Magic in Jamaica and Haiti*, Dent, London, 1939.

Jones, Evan, 'The Song of the Banana Man', in The Penguin Book of Caribbean Verse in English, ed Paula Burnett, Penguin, London, 1986. **Extract 2.**

Kirton, Claremont, Jamaica: Debt and Poverty, Oxfam, Oxford, 1992.

Luntta, Karl, Jamaica Handbook, Moon Publications, Chico, CA, 1993.

McKay, Claude, Banana Bottom, Pluto Press, London, 1985. **Extract 6.**

McKenzie, Earl, A Boy Named Ossie: A Jamaican Childhood, Heinemann, Oxford, 1991. **Extract 8.**

Mais, Roger, The Hills Were Joyful Together, Heinemann, Oxford, 1981. **Extract 15.**

Marley, Bob, 'Redemption Song' from Uprising, Island, London, 1980. **Extract 5.**

Patterson, Orlando, The Children of Sisyphus, Longman, Harlow, 1986. **Extract 12.**

Payne, Anthony, Politics in Jamaica, Ian Randle Publishers, Kingston, 1994.

Reid, V.S., New Day, Heinemann, London, 1973.

Rhys, Jean, Wide Sargasso Sea, Penguin, London, 1968. **Extract 4.**

Salkey, Andrew, The Late Emancipation of Jerry Stover, Hutchinson, London, 1968. **Extract 3.**

Senior, Olive, 'The Lady', in Hinterland: Caribbean Poetry from the West Indies and Britain, ed E.A. Markham, Bloodaxe, Newcastle-upon-Tyne, 1989. **Extract 13.**

Thelwell, Michael, The Harder They Come, Pluto Press, London, 1980. **Extract 14.**

Trollope, Anthony, The West Indies and the Spanish Main, Alan Sutton, Gloucester, 1985. **Extract 16.**

Winkler, Anthony C., The Lunatic, Kingston Publishers, Kingston, 1987. **Extract 10.**

Extracts

(1) JAMAICA: AMERICANA

Lorna Goodison, *Bella Makes Life*

Joseph is anxiously awaiting the return of Bella, his wife, after she has spent a year earning money in New York.

He was embarrassed when he saw her coming towards him. He wished he could have just disappeared into the crowd and kept going as far away from Norman Manley airport as was possible. Bella returning. Bella come back from New York after a whole year. Bella dressed in some clothes which make her look like a chequer cab. What in God's name was a big forty-odd-year-old woman who was fat when she leave Jamaica, and get worse fat since she go to America, what was this woman doing dressed like this? Bella was wearing stretch-to-fit black pants, over that she had on a big yellow and black checked blouse, on her feet was a pair of yellow booties, in her hand was a big yellow handbag and she had on a pair of yellow framed glasses. See ya Jesus! Bella no done yet, she had dyed her hair with red oxide and Jherry curls it till it shine like it grease and spray. Oh Bella what happen to you? Joseph never ever bother to take in her anklet and her big bracelets and her gold chain with a pendant, big as a name plate on a lawyer's office, marked 'Material Girl' . . .

It was Norman, Joseph's brother, who said that Bella looked like a chequer cab. Norman had driven Joseph and the children to the airport in his van to meet Bella, because she write to say she was coming with a lot of things. When the children saw her they jumped up and down yelling mama come, mama come . . . When Norman saw her (he was famous for his wit), he said 'Blerd Naught, a Bella dat, whatta way she favour a chequer cab.' When Bella finally cleared her many and huge bags from Customs and come outside, Joseph was very quiet, he didn't know quite how to greet the new Bella . . .

Bella was talking a little too loudly. 'Man I tell you those Customs people really give me a warm time. Oh it's so great to be home though, it was so cold! in New York!! As she said this she handed her winter coat with its mock fur collar to her daughter who staggered under the weight of it. Norman who was still chuckling to himself over his chequer cab joke said, 'Bwoy, Bella a you broader than Broadway.' Bella said, 'Tell me about it . . .'

(2) JAMAICA: BANANAS

Evan Jones, *The Song of the Banana Man*

Immortalized by Harry Belafonte's Banana Boat Song, the banana industry has long been an economic mainstay for Jamaica's small farmers. Evan Jones's use of vernacular reinforces the theme of rural simplicity and pride.

Touris, white man, wipin his face,
Met me in Golden Grove market place.
He looked at m'ol clothes brown wid stain,
An soaked right through wid de Portlan rain,
He cas his eye, turn up his nose,
He says, 'You're a beggar man, I suppose?'
He says, 'Boy, get some occupation,
Be of some value to your nation.'
        I said, 'By God and dis big right han
        You mus recognize a banana man.

'Up in de hills, where de streams are cool,
An mullet an janga swim in the pool,
I have ten acres of mountain side,
An a dainty-foot donkey dat I ride,
Four Gros Michel, an four Lacatan,
Some coconut trees, and some hills of yam,
An I pasture on dat very same lan
Five she-goats an a big black ram,
    Dat, by God and dis big right han
    Is de property of a banana man.

'I leave m'yard early-mornin time
An set m'foot to de mountain climb,
I ben m'back to de hot-sun toil,
An m'cutlass rings on de stony soil,
Ploughin an weedin, diggin an plantin
Till Massa Sun drop back o John Crow mountain,
Den home again in cool evenin time,
Perhaps whistling dis likkle rhyme,
    (*Sung*) Praise God an m'big right han
    I will live an die a banana man.

'Banana day is my special day,
I cut my stems an I'm on m'way,
Load up de donkey, leave de lan,
Head down de hill to banana stan,
When de truck comes roun I take a ride
All de way down to de harbour side –
Dat is de night, when you, touris man,
Would change your place wid a banana man.
    Yes, by God, an m'big right han
    I will live an die a banana man.

'De bay is calm, an de moon is bright
De hills look black for de sky is light,
Down at de dock is an English ship,
Restin after her ocean trip,
While on de pier is a monstruous hustle,
Tallymen, carriers, all in a bustle,
Wid stems on deir heads in a long black snake
Some singin de songs dat banana men make,
    Like (*Sung*) Praise God an m'big right han
    I will live an die a banana man.

(3) JAMAICA: CONFRONTATION

Andrew Salkey,
The Late Emancipation of Jerry Stover

Jerry Stover, a young civil servant, is one of a generation of bored,
nihilistic middle-class Jamaicans, eager to challenge authority.

Jerry Stover was early. With three minutes to spare, he was leisurely climbing the winding stairs at the back of the Resident Magistrate's Courts at Half Way Tree, when he ran into the Clerk of the Courts, R.A.D. Randax-Lee, affectionately called Randy. A Negro Chinese, fifty-three, balding and a zealous civil servant, he was Jerry's only work problem. Unnoticed, socially unimportant, and entirely predictable, Randy had been the Clerk of Courts at Half Way Tree for seventeen years. He had never been thanked, praised, liked, and for seventeen years had never been promoted. Randy knew his job but he was qualified for nothing more than the position he held. Barristers came, went, and became Resident Magistrates, but Randy remained the Clerk of the Courts and served them faithfully, and in some instances, openly resentfully. He was highly sensitive about his Chinese ancestry and deeply regretted his Negro blood; altogether he disliked the way he looked.

He bullied Jerry because he could do so to no one else in the office; everybody had long ago learned to resist Randy's attacks.

Jerry and Randy passed each other, Jerry going up the stairs, Randy coming down, both silent, both watchful, until Randy said, 'I know about your exploits last night, Stover agitator. Lucky you weren't arrested, boy. Had the VPP meeting taken place in Jones Town instead of Rollington Town, you would have been up before me this morning. On the other side of the railings, I mean, Stover.'

Jerry smiled unconcernedly, innocently, while staring at Randy's large bald spot. 'Good morning, sir,' he said respectfully. 'I hadn't heard of your promotion. Congratulations.'

Randy felt assaulted. His nerves were electrified. Coolly, he asked, 'And what does that mean, Stover boy?'

'Your promotion, sir.'

'My promotion, Stover.'

'That's right, sir.'

'Being personal, Stover?'

'Hardly, sir.' Jerry was adamantly respectful.

Randy stepped up two steps to be level with Jerry; but even then, Jerry was about seven or eight inches above him. Randy quickly made up the difference by climbing another step which made him just about level with Jerry's forehead. Quite casually, he climbed yet another step.

'What exactly are you inferring, Stover?'

'*Inferring,* sir?'

'Yes. Inferring!'

'The prisoner appears before a Magistrate, not the Clerk of the Courts: before the Judge and not his Clerk, sir.'
Randy trembled.

(4) JAMAICA: DECADENCE

Jean Rhys, *Wide Sargasso Sea*

Antoinette Cosway, destined to a life of madness, recollects the neurotic intensity of her childhood in post-abolition Jamaica.

Our garden was large and beautiful as that garden in the Bible – the tree of life grew there. But it had gone wild. The paths were overgrown and a smell of dead flowers mixed with the fresh living smell. Underneath the tree ferns, tall as forest tree ferns, the light was green. Orchids flourished out of reach or for some reason not to be touched. One was snaky looking, another like an octopus with long thin brown tentacles bare of leaves hanging from a twisted root. Twice a year the octopus orchid flowered – then not an inch of tentacle showed. It was a bell-shaped mass of white, mauve, deep purples, wonderful to see. The scent was very sweet and strong. I never went near it.

All Coulibri Estate had gone wild like the garden, gone to bush. No more slavery – why should *anybody* work? This never saddened me. I did not remember the place when it was prosperous.

My mother usually walked up and down the *glacis*, a paved roofed-in terrace which ran the length of the house and sloped upwards to a clump of bamboos. Standing by the bamboos she had a clear view to the sea, but anyone passing could stare at her. They stared, sometimes they laughed. Long after the sound was far away and faint she kept her eyes shut and her hands clenched. A frown came between her black eyebrows, deep – it might have been cut with a knife. I hated this frown and once I touched her forehead trying to smooth it. But she pushed me away, not roughly but calmly, coldly, without a word, as if she had decided once and for all that I was useless to her. She wanted to sit with Pierre or walk where she pleased without being pestered, she wanted peace and quiet. I was old enough to look after myself. 'Oh, let me alone,' she would say, 'let me alone,' and after I knew that she talked aloud to herself I was a little afraid of her . . .

When evening came she sang to me if she was in the mood. I couldn't always understand her patois songs – she also came from Martinique – but she taught me the one that meant 'The little ones grow old, the children leave us, will they come back?' and the one about the cedar tree flowers which only last for a day.

(5) JAMAICA: FREEDOM

Bob Marley, *Redemption Song*

Characteristically simple but evocative, the song traces the process of emancipation from physical and intellectual captivity through faith.

Old pirate yes they rob I
Sold I to the merchant ships
Minutes after they took I
From the bottomless pit
But my hand was made strong
By the hand of the Almighty
We forward in this generation triumphantly.

Won't you help to sing these songs of freedom
'Cause all I ever had redemption songs, redemption songs.

Emancipate yourselves from mental slavery
None but ourselves can free our mind
Have no fear for atomic energy
'Cause none a them can stop the time
How long shall they kill our prophets
While we stand aside and look
Some say it's just a part of it
We've got to fulfill the book.

Won't you help to sing these songs of freedom
'Cause all I ever had, redemption songs
All I ever had, redemption songs
These songs of freedom, songs of freedom.

(6) JAMAICA: PANAMA GOLD

Claude McKay, *Banana Bottom*

At the Banana Bottom Sunday school picnic, Bita, the heroine, is struck by the ostentatious behaviour of the village's richest man.

First among the rum-shop fellows was Tack Tally, proudly wearing his decorations from Panama: gold watch and chain of three strands, and a foreign gold coin attached to it as large as a florin, a gold stick-pin with a huge blue stone, and five gold rings flashing from his fingers. He had on a fine bottle-green tweed suit with the well-creased and deep-turned pantaloons called peg-top, the coat of long points and lapels known as American style. And wherever he went he was accompanied by an admiring gang.
    For that gang everything that Tack said and did was charged with

importance. For he had not only gone to Panama like many, but had come back with the gold.

Among the older heads of Banana Bottom and other villages there were some who had sold their cows or horses, even their land, to go to Panama during the first Canal Enterprise of the eighteen eighties to try their chance. And with the breaking of the boom they had returned home with the fever, the smallpox – everything but the real thing. But Tack Tally had made good in little time and come back with the stuff all over his person.

Bita and Yoni were in charge of the fishing-pond – a lottery game where a quantity of rubbish was mixed in with a few good things and placed in a huge box, and one paid a sixpence and took his chance fishing up something. Near by Tack Tally and his boys were buying ginger beer from a higgler woman and teasing her by mixing the ginger beer with Jamaica rum and offering her a drink.

'Gwan away wid you drunken self all a you,' said the woman, 'and doan tempt a weak body. Ise a church member.'

'Theyse a lot a chu'ch members drinking likker and doings wohse,' said Tack. 'There ain't no harm in feeling good and having a good time.'

'Parson Lambert sure hard on rum-drinkers. This ginger beer is good enough foh me. I wi' drink all you treat me to.'

'Because you selling it,' laughed Tack. 'I'll treat you all you want if you let me mix it wid dis beauty of a Jamaica Old.'

(7) JAMAICA: PATOIS
Jean Binta Breeze,
Riddym Ravings (The Mad Woman's Poem)

At first sight unintelligible to those used to 'standard' English, the patois becomes clearer if read aloud. The poem tells of the confusion and longing of a 'mad woman' marooned in Kingston, with strange music playing in her head.

wen mi fus come a town
mi use to tell everybady 'mawnin'
but as de likkle rosiness gawn outa mi face
nobady nah ansa mi
silence tun rags roun mi bady
in de mids a all de dead people dem
a bawl bout de caast of livin
an a ongle one ting tap me fram go stark raving mad
a wen mi siddung eena Parade
a tear up newspaper fi talk to
sometime dem roll up
an tun eena one a Uncle But sweet saaf
yellow heart breadfruit

wid piece of roas saalfish side a i
an if likkle rain jus fall
mi get cocanat rundung fi eat i wid
same place side a weh de country bus dem pull out
an sometime mi a try board de bus
an de canductor bwoy a halla out seh
'dutty gal, kum affa de bus'
ah troo im no hear de riddym eena mi head
same as de tape weh de bus driva a play, seh

Eh, Eh,
no feel no way
town is a place dat ah really kean stay
dem kudda – ribbit mi han
eh – ribbit mi toe
mi waan go a country go look mango
so country bus, ah beg yuh
tek mi home
to de place, where I belang

an di dutty bway jus run mi aff

(8) JAMAICA: POLITICS

Earl McKenzie, *A Boy Named Ossie*

As well as sporadic violence, election time in Jamaica brings a
predictable litany of empty promises from aspiring candidates.

One day Mr James Townsend, the JLP candidate, and the sitting member
of parliament for the constituency, came to Ossie's home to ask for his
father's vote. Ossie and his father were sitting on the verandah when Mr
Townsend and his entourage entered the yard. He was a fat and
fair-complexioned man with straight hair and was the owner of a trucking
company. Ossie had seen him at their church from time to time. His father
got up and shook hands with Mr Townsend; then he called his wife from
the kitchen and introduced her. Mr Townsend began his speech:
'Our party stands for godliness and freedom. We have also built the most
roads in the entire history of the constituency. And we have big plans. We
are going to build a tank at the East River, and we are going to put in a
pump powerful enough to pump water up here. We are going to build a
cocoa factory. We plan to bring electricity and improve the transportation
system. I am asking you for your vote. Vote JLP and vote for progress.' . . .
One morning, after breakfast, Mass Delroy brought the news. They were
giving out road work and men were being signed up. Ossie's father pulled
his hoe and shovel from under the house and set off. He came home about

half-an-hour later and returned his shovel to its place under the floor. His
wife asked him what had happened, but he refused to talk . . .

Later at the shop, Ossie heard what had happened . . . His father had
arrived at the work site and found Chesty who was signing up the men.
Chesty was a muscular young man who always wore T-shirts and dark
glasses. He had a clipboard and he was writing down the names of the men
who were being employed. When it was Ossie's father's turn Chesty said:
'Which party you belong to?'

Ossie's father explained that he voted for the candidate and not the
party.

'So you are a ping-pong ball,' said Chesty. 'You bounce from one party to
the next.'

'I exercise my judgement.'

'Well, you not getting any work here. We want people who support the
cause. Only supporters of Townsend getting work.'

'Is that his wish?'

'Townsend is boss! Townsend rules!'

(9) JAMAICA: SLAVERY

James Carnegie, *Wages Paid*

> *Johnson, a slave who is used by his master, Mr Johnson, to breed
> with slave women, is a dispassionate observer of plantation life and
> its routine cruelty.*

I

The cursing came through the high window at the rear of the barracks, the
cursing that was monotonous and repetitious, the cursing that was routine.

'Get your arses up. Haul your fucking tails.'

It would not be long now before there was an even harsher noise, the
noise of the crack of the whips, but there was a difference, a difference
between the white voices of the overseer and his book-keepers and the fact
that the whips were being wielded by the black slave-drivers. Johnson
thought that the poor missionaries who had become so abundant in the last
few years didn't know what they were facing really when they were talking
about brotherhood, because the whip cut just as deep whether wielded by
black or white.

It was a day just like any other on an estate just like any other in a year
just like any other during a crop season just like any other and the work had
to be done.

Although Johnson had something of a special position, he was not one of
those slaves fortunate enough to be trusted with their own plots of land or
their own huts. Despite his reputation as a stud, he had to share the normal
stench of a barracks that was not much different, if his memory served him
well, from the barracoon where he had been kept before coming to Jamaica
15 years before as a boy of 15.

II

They moved out of the barracks in the usual way, with some brave or stupid ones remaining behind as usual pretending to be sick. Some of them were sick for true, Johnson thought, but whether they really were or not, Johnson had no doubt that by the time Mr Johnson – the fucker – in the Great House finished with them they would be a good deal sicker. Johnson respected Mr Johnson although trouble was growing between them. His name showed that Mr Johnson had once regarded him highly, since the name was only passed down normally through sons, but Mr Johnson – and Johnson in his own mind could not really leave off the title 'Mister' – now was apparently regarding him, Johnson, as a rival, although he still belonged to him, and not as a troublemaker like those far across the water in St Domingue.

(10) JAMAICA: TOURISTS

Anthony C. Winkler, *The Lunatic*

Jamaica has long been a popular tourist destination; but for many Jamaicans, including this narrator, tourists are not automatically attractive or popular.

In the old days the first tourists who came to Jamaica were English. They had pale faces, chilly manners, and distracted eyes. They were a belchless, fartless, scented people and in their presence the Jamaicans who met them and served them and who of necessity under the strictures of the Almighty's plan were bound to occasionally belch and fart and stink, felt small and worthless like unloved children. These first English tourists perpetually said 'Pardon' even when they had done nothing to be pardoned for and caused generations of Jamaicans to wince as though that innocuous word was an order for a flogging.

In the later days after the Empire had fallen the tourists were Americans: men with enormous bellies bulging through distended cotton shirts painted with shrill pictures of yellow sunsets, green parrots and pink fish; women with blood-red lips and enamelled fingernails whose bodies dripped with jewelry like fruit from a bountiful tree. The English had sniffed silently at the land like strange dogs in a strange place and gathered on verandas in the evenings to the clinking of ice and the fluorescent glow of their own whiteness; but the Americans played on the land – romping in the streets during the daytime hours like noisy schoolchildren, fornicating during the nights on dark beaches, their white rumps pumping feverishly under the tropical skies.

In these newest of days most of the tourists were Americans, and a few were English, but many were Germans – people of a growling tongue and the dogmatic mien of a parson sermonizing about hellfire to a Sunday School. Blonde, blue-eyed, these new tourists resembled the Americans in many ways, except that their big bellies were not wrapped in gaudy cotton shirts and they did not smile or laugh as easily as the Americans.

When these Germans first stepped off the airplanes the sun licked greedily at their pale skins like a hungry dog licking meat off an old bone.

(11) JAMAICA: TOURIST ADVICE

Noel Coward, *Jamaica*

Coward's witty advice to would-be visitors to Jamaica predates the advent of mass tourism and evokes a nostalgic aura of privileged expatriate life.

Jamaica's an island surrounded by sea
(Like Corsica, Guam and Tasmania)
The tourist does not need to wear a topee
Or other macabre miscellanea.
Remember that this is a tropical place
Where violent hues are abundant
And bright coloured clothes with a bright yellow face
Look, frankly, a trifle redundant.
A simple ensemble of trousers and shirt
Becomes both the saint and the sinner
And if a head-waiter looks bitterly hurt
You *can* wear a jacket for dinner.

Jamaica's an island surrounded by sea
(It shares this distinction with Elba)
It's easy to order a goat fricassee
But madness to ask for Peche Melba.
You'll find (to the best of this writer's belief)
That if you want rice you can get it
But visitors ordering mutton or beef
Will certainly live to regret it.
There's seldom a shortage of ackees and yams
Or lobsters, if anyone's caught them
But if you've passion for imported hams
You'd bloody well better import them.

Jamaica's an island surrounded by sea
(It has this in common with Cuba)
Its national tunes, to a certain degree,
Are founded on Boop-boop-a-duba.

'Neath tropical palms under tropical skies
Where equally tropical stars are

The vocal Jamaicans betray no surprise
However off-key their guitars are.
The native Calypsos which seem to be based
On hot-air-conditioned reflexes
Conclusively prove that to people of taste
There's nothing so funny as sex is.

Jamaica's an island surrounded by sea
(Like Alderney, Guernsey and Sark are)
It's wise not to dive with exuberant glee
Where large barracuda and shark are.
The reefs are entrancing; the water is clear,
The colouring couldn't be dreamier
But one coral scratch and you may spend a year
In bed with acute septicemia.
The leading hotels are extremely well run
The service both cheerful and dextrous
But even the blisters you get from the sun
Are firmly included as extras.

Jamaica's an island surrounded by sea
(*Unlike* Ecuador or Guiana)
The tourist may not have a 'Fromage de brie'
But always can have a banana.
He also can have, if he has enough cash,
A pleasantly rum-sodden liver
And cure his rheumatic complaints in a flash
By shooting himself at Milk river.
In fact every tourist who visits these shores
Can thank his benevolent Maker
For taking time off from the rest of His chores
To fashion the Isle of Jamaica.

(12) KINGSTON: RASTAFARIANS

Orlando Patterson, *The Children of Sisyphus*

Convinced of the imminent arrival of Emperor Haile Selassie's ships, Kingston's Rastafarians are waiting by the dockside for an escape from Babylon to their holy land of Ethiopia.

And the blacks of their skin were like flute-notes in the night. Deep-deep and mellow: wailing in gleaming, fluent splendour. Across the dark-brown, silty shore. Upon the undulating, stale, delicious filth. When they did not move they were so many silhouetted majesties swallowed over with all the harvest of their expectancy.

Their movements were slow, determined, god-like. Even in the quick motion of their feet as they strode between the hovels; as they ran to the top of the mounds to stare and stare across the blue, the orange-flamed, the dark, steel-grey horizon, there was the restrained gentleness of certainty. The ship would come. They talked. They laughed. The ship of the great Emperor would show itself in the morning with the glory of the sun. No, it would come in the evening-time, bursting through the molten fire of the eastern hemisphere, a conquering vessel of joy. Oh, but what did it matter? It would come. Sure as the holy land of Zion that waited now for them, it would come.

In the meantime they talked and laughed at what was past and dreamt of what was soon to be. Those of the city made friendly humour of their country brothers. The rustic Brethren laughed at themselves, but pointed out their own advantages, not that it really mattered. They had remained with the soil – the soil so small and cruel here but so fertile with everything that's joy back home in Zion. They had suffered more, had paid more for the sins of their forefathers, but at the same time had remained less tainted by the sins of the white man and of Babylon. To which the Brethren of the city retorted passionately that they had greater claims to having suffered. Look. Look at the bloated belly of the children. Look at the yellow of their eyes. Feel the scaly perversion of their skin – the skin so pure and black and beautiful in Zion, now a denizen of contempt . . . The city was the fountain-head of Babylon and they were the dogs who were soaked in its oppression.

(13) KINGSTON: THE RICH

Olive Senior, *The Lady*

Jamaica's wealthy and neurotic few are not necessarily any happier than the poor multitudes which frighten them.

At 12 Daimler Close Kingston 6 Armour Heights/ Mistress Marshall wakes late with a headache/ the light hurts her eyes/ what with pills and the whiskey/ her mouth tastes like death

She must go to the gym/ to keep fit and trim/ for her husband who's cheating with a girl/ who's not slim

Mistress Marshall calls Eunice/ bring tea and the papers/ no one dead no one born/ that she knows of/ but she turns to page eight/ and it's just as she feared/ for the columnists say that the p.m. is failing/ the country is falling/ the party is foundering/ the people are restless/ and the prophets of doom are predicting a crash/ you see what I mean Mistress Marshall doesn't know/ why her husband so worthless/ to stay on in this place/ every night the black people/ just waiting to break in/ to rob kill and worse/ but he'd have to shoot first/ no black man will get in/ except that time there/ before she knew better/ before Mister Marshall start courting/ big family and all/ his hair was so curly/ his skin almost white/ not like hers/ but it improve now she stop stand in sun at the bus stop/ at the seaside she cover with kaftan and hat/ say her skin is so delicate/ it peels if the sun rests lightly on it/ everybody wonder how naseberry/ so easy to peel/ but they dont wonder long/ her jewels are real

Mistress Marshall want to go/ every day there she nagging/ want to go to Miami where everyone gone/ for her skin would improve so/ and in climate that cool so/ her hair would grow straight/ and the shops are so full with strawberries and crystal/ caviar and silver/ real silks and satin/ ryvita and salmon/ mushrooms and gammon/ in short everything that a human could need

and the damn servant classes/ dem all is a crosses/ where the hell is Eunice?

(14) KINGSTON: RUDE BOYS
Michael Thelwell, *The Harder They Come*

Having arrived in the capital from the countryside, Ivan, soon to become the notorious 'rude boy' and singer Rhygin, is initiated into underworld culture.

Underneath their fierce rhetoric and warlike gestures their lives were not much different from his and they understood the demands of survival. Like him, many of these slick, streetwise urbanites were not long from the country either. Bogart the cool, the unchallenged leader, the man of respect, was by day Ezekiel Smith, a mechanic's apprentice. Some were apprentice carpenters, masons, or apprentice criminals like Cagney, scuffling to live any way they could. They sold newspapers, polished cars, did 'day work' or when necessary begged or stole in the streets. Some were by day garden 'boys' at the mansions and would-be mansions in the foothills, which Ivan remembered as a place of insult and fear.

But by night when the employers huddled behind iron gates and high walls, their garden boys in the little rooms out behind the servants' quarters dressed in their night finery. They pocketed their *okapis*, answered only to their war names, and headed for the ranches in search of companionship, adventure, and reputation.

These ranches surrounded the lower city. On the hills to the east, in the gulleys of the shantytowns of the center, and in the swampy mangrove wastes of the west, young men and boys sat around flickering fires in places called Dodge City, Hell's Kitchen, Boot Hill, El Paso, Durango, and even Nikosia (there was terrorism in Cyprus at the time). They smoked ganja, dreamed valiant dreams, and cursed the rich, the 'high-ups' of society, and the police, especially the elite 'Flying Saucer Squad', their sworn enemies. Periodically, almost at predictable intervals, pulpits rang with denunciations of lawless youth and wrongdoers, and editorials would call attention to the dangers represented by gangs lurking in the cracks and crevices of the social fabric. The Flying Saucer Squad would stage their well-publicized 'lightning raids' and for a while the ranches would be deserted and the gangs scattered. Until society forgot.

On the ranch Ivan served his second apprenticeship in the streets, but not as an outsider this time. He learned about madmen and badmen, dead and living, men of great reputation and short careers. He boasted and dreamed of deeds he would do. Even as they cursed the rich, they cherished fantasies of 'big money', sudden wealth of their own.

(15) KINGSTON: THE YARD
Roger Mais, *The Hills Were Joyful Together*

The yard is the communal space shared by the inhabitants of a rundown slum tenement in Kingston. It is here that Mais's drama of damnation and redemption unfolds.

Near the cistern in the yard a gnarled ackee tree reached up scraggy, scarred, almost naked-branched to the anaemic-looking sky. A thrifty black-mango tree leaned over the southern half of the front fence, its branches lopped back every so often to keep it from overhanging the narrow sidewalk. A prickly lime tree struggled up from among the earthed-in, seamy, rotting bricks in the yard; it stood against the northern row of wooden shacks right outside the room where the three Sisters of Charity lived, and crooned and gossiped and cooked and sing-sang sad hymns of wailing the livelong day.

Immediately across the street from the yard was a row of little, dowdy, huddled-together shops shut in on one side by a two-storey building that was a bar with rooms above, and on the other by an ironmongery-drygoods-and-provision store that carried a small notions department and a soft drink counter.

The sign-painter who had one of these small shops had worked on the walls of all of them, so that from a fast-moving car they looked like a row of playing card single-storey houses that a child had put together. He painted these signs at a special cut-rate, figuring it would be good advertising.

There were five of these small shops in the row. One of them flew a dirty little triangular red flag which indicated nothing more sinister than the fact that ice was sold here. It also sold newspapers as the tin sign said, and sweepstake tickets according to the amateur lettering on a piece of cardboard tacked on the wall . . .

The other three shops in the row were occupied by a cobbler, a tin smith, and a tailor, but the tailor-shop had lately given place to a fry-fish shop, and if you stood on the top tread of the brick step to the yard facing you, you could see the scaled, gutted and brined sprats hanging on a string to sun in the bit of space behind this shop. The sun made the bones of the little fish so brittle and crisp that when they were fried you ate them bones and all. Nobody bothered about the flies that buzzed them on the line, and the dust off the street and the dirt-yard that settled on them, for that was the way sprats had been handled from the morning of time.

(16) SPANISH TOWN

Anthony Trollope,
The West Indies and the Spanish Main

The ghost-town atmosphere of the administrative centre strikes Trollope as symptomatic of colonial Jamaica's malaise.

It is like the city of the dead. There are long streets there in which no human inhabitant is ever seen. In others a silent old negro woman may be sitting at an open door, or a child playing, solitary, in the dust. The Governor's house – King's House as it is called – stands on one side of a square; opposite is the house of the Assembly; on the left, as you come out from the Governor's, are the executive offices and house of the Council, and on the right some other public buildings. The place would have some pretension about it did it not seem to be stricken with an eternal death. All the walls are of a dismal dirty yellow, and a stranger cannot but think that the colour is owing to the dreadfully prevailing disease of the country. In this square there are no sounds; men and women never frequent it; nothing enters it but sunbeams! The glare from these walls seems to forbid that men and women should come there.

The parched, dusty, deserted streets are all hot and perfectly without shade. The crafty Italians have built their narrow streets so that the sun can hardly enter them, except when he is in the mid heaven; but there has been no such craft at Spanish Town. The houses are very low, and when there is any sun in the heavens it can enter those streets; and in those heavens there is always a burning, broiling sun.

But the place is not wholly deserted. There is here the most frightfully hideous race of pigs that ever made a man ashamed to own himself a bacon-eating biped. I have never done much in pigs myself, but I believe that pigly grace consists in plumpness and comparative shortness – in shortness, above all, of the face and nose. The Spanish Town pigs are never plump. They are the very ghosts of swine, consisting entirely of bones and bristles. Their backs are long, their ribs are long, their legs are long, but, above all, their heads and noses are hideously long. These brutes prowl about in the sun, and glare at the unfrequent strangers with their starved eyes, as though doubting themselves whether, by some little exertion, they might not become beasts of prey.

Biographical and literary notes

BREEZE, Jean Binta (1956–). Born in **Hanover** parish, Jean Binta Breeze studied theatre at the Jamaica School of Drama and subsequently became a teacher of English and Drama. She has worked with the Jamaican Cultural Development Commission as a coordinator for its speech and literacy programme. The author of fiction and plays as well as an actress and choreographer, Breeze can claim to be Jamaica's first woman dub poet. Her first collection, *Riddym Ravings*, was published in 1988, to be followed by *Spring Cleaning* (Extract 7) in 1992.

CARNEGIE, James (1938–). Jamaican-born Carnegie's *Wages Paid* (Extract 9) won the Cuban Casa de las Américas prize in 1976. A gritty and uncompromising narrative of sadism and revenge among slaves and master, it alienated some critics and readers at the time with its explicit language and allegedly obscene subject matter.

COWARD, Sir Noel (1899–1973). A dramatist, composer and actor, Coward was a multi-talented, theatrical artist who has come to epitomize a

Jean Binta Breeze

certain sort of British humour. His first success was an intense drama, *The Vortex*, 1924, but his classic plays were light-hearted and elegant comedies of manners such as *Hay Fever*, 1925, and *Blithe Spirit*, 1941. Coward also worked in cinema, and was closely involved in British films, such as *In Which We Serve*, 1942 and *Brief Encounter*, 1946. His poetry and songs, of which *Jamaica* (Extract 11) is a good example, remain masterpieces of urbane wit. Coward became emotionally attached to Jamaica and spent much of his last twenty years in his house on the north coast.

GOODISON, Lorna (1947–). Born in Jamaica, Goodison trained as a painter at the Jamaica School of Art and in New York. She is best known as a poet and has published three collections, *Tamarind Season*, 1980, *I Am Becoming My Mother*, 1986, and *Heartease*, 1988. She was been writer-in-residence at the University of the West Indies and at Radcliffe College, Massachusetts. The short story, 'Bella Makes Life' (Extract 1) is taken from her collection *Baby Mother and the King of Swords*, 1990.

JONES, Evan (1927–). Born in Jamaica, and educated there, in the US and at Oxford University, Jones has lived in Britain since 1956, working mostly as a script-writer for television and films. His 'Song of the Banana Man' (Extract 2) is an established favourite among his poems and was followed later by 'The Lament of the Banana Man', where the once happy farmer has become a bored ticket collector in the London underground: 'Gal, I'm tellin you, I'm tired fo true,/ Tired of Englan, tired o you./ But I can't go back to Jamaica now . . .'.

McKAY, Claude (1890–1948). Born in Jamaica and educated in the USA, McKay is now regarded as one of the earliest exponents of an authentic indigenous Caribbean literature and the region's earliest internationally recognized writer. He emigrated to the USA in 1912, moved to England in 1919, but returned to the USA two years later. Between 1922 and 1934 McKay travelled widely in Europe and Africa before eventually settling in the USA. His first works were poetry, and his fourth volume, ·*Harlem Shadows*, 1922, established his reputation. In 1928, however, his first novel *Home to Harlem* became a huge success, making him probably the first black bestselling author in the USA. He became closely associated with the so-called 'Harlem Renaissance' during the 1920s, when black radicals and writers such as Marcus Garvey and Langston Hughes set up an important intellectual movement in that area of New York. In works such as *Gingertown*, 1932 and *Banana Bottom*, 1933 (Extract 6), McKay presents an often idyllic image of turn-of-the-century Jamaica, contrasting the alien authority of colonial government with the folk wisdom and humour of ordinary rural Jamaicans.

McKENZIE, Earl (1943–) Educated in Jamaica and Canada, McKenzie is a lecturer at the Church Teachers' College, **Mandeville**. *A Boy Named Ossie* (Extract 8) is his first published collection of short stories and provides a series of seemingly simple vignettes of rural Jamaican life.

MAIS, Roger (1905–1955). Born in **Kingston**, Mais had an unconventional career, working first in the civil service, but later as a banana tallyman, an insurance salesman, a horticulturalist and a photographer. He was also a journalist, working on the *Daily Gleaner* and *Public Opinion*, the journal of the People's National Party. Mais is remembered for three novels: *The Hills Were Joyful Together*, 1953, *Brother Man*, 1954, and *Black Lightning*, 1955, all published in the three years before his untimely death.

Brother Man presents a sympathetic picture of the nascent Rastafarian movement and the social deprivation which fuelled its millenial ideal of a return to Africa, while *Black Lightning* is a more allegorical exploration of the artist's place in a colonial society, as exemplified by a peasant blacksmith and sculptor. *The Hills Were Joyful Together* (Extract 15) is his best-known work and is an uncompromisingly naturalistic portrait of life in the 'yard', the squalid tenement slums which characterize much of **Kingston**. His aim, he wrote, was to show 'what happens to people when their lives are constricted and dwarfed . . . girdled with poverty.' In a series of vivid, sometimes lurid episodes, Mais traces the disintegration into madness, violence and crime of various inhabitants of the yard. At the same time, he stresses the redeeming potential of human solidarity among Jamaica's poorest people, contrasting this spirit of resilience with the callousness of the colonial authorities. Mais's work has aged, sociologically and stylistically, but this novel in particular is still a powerful exercise in political naturalism.

MARLEY, Bob (1945–1981). Robert Nesta 'Bob' Marley was born to a white Jamaican father and black Jamaican mother and was raised in the village of **Nine Miles** in **St Ann's** parish on the north coast. His father soon abandoned the family, and they moved to the slums of **West Kingston**, where Marley at first worked as a welder. He formed the 'Wailing Wailers' in the early 1960s with Bunny Wailer and Peter Tosh, and the band was successful, recording more than 30 ska songs before breaking up. A later version of the group, the Wailers, was signed by Island Records in the 1970s and recorded a series of hugely popular albums, starting with *Catch a Fire* and including *Natty Dread*, *Exodus* (the bestseller) and *Uprising*. Marley became a Rastafarian

and popularized the movement throughout the world. His lyrics deal with the political and religious tenets of the faith – return to Africa, the oppression of 'Babylon', the omniscience of 'Jah' – and reflect a militant black consciousness, distinct from the superficiality of many other reggae lyrics. Marley became the object of attack from Jamaica's notoriously violent political gangs and survived an assassination attempt before leaving Jamaica for a period in the mid-1970s. In 1978 he returned to preside over the famous One Love concert which brought rival political leaders Michael Manley and Edward Seaga together on stage in a gesture of reconciliation. At the height of his fame, Marley was struck down with cancer and died at the age of 36. His death caused intense national mourning in Jamaica and robbed world music of one of its most influential artists. Today, Marley's **mausoleum** in the village of **Nine Miles** can be visited, as can his **Tuff Gong recording studios** in **Hope Road, New Kingston**.

PATTERSON, Orlando (1940–). Born in **Frome, Westmoreland**, and educated in **May Pen** and **Kingston**, Patterson read Economics and Sociology at the University of the West Indies before going to London to study for a PhD. In his first year in London he completed his first novel, *The Children of Sisyphus* (Extract 12), 1964. As a sociologist, Patterson has published widely on slavery and the Rastafarian movement in Jamaica and has taught at the University of the West Indies and Harvard. He is the author of several other novels, including *An Absence of Ruins*, 1967, and *Die the Long Day*, 1972. *The Children of Sisyphus* remains Patterson's most celebrated work of fiction and draws a compelling picture of the social hardship and spirituality which lay behind the growth of the early Rastafarian cult. In the notorious slum district of **The Dungle**, a cast of prostitutes, criminals and lunatics live existences of violent desperation, while the Rastafarian community, inspired by their belief in a literal 'return' to Africa, find solace in *ganja* and religious faith. Sometimes overwritten and frequently melodramatic, the novel is nevertheless a powerful and sympathetic treatment of a spiritual sect caught between idealism and delusion.

RHYS, Jean (see under Dominica).

SALKEY, Andrew (1928–   ). Born in Colón, Panama, Salkey was educated in Jamaica and then in England before working as a teacher and broadcaster. His first novel, *A Quality of Violence* was published in 1959, to be followed by *Escape to an Autumn Pavement*, 1960 and *The Late Emancipation of Jerry Stover*, 1968. In the 1970s Salkey also wrote two travel books, a volume of poetry entitled *Jamaica*, 1973, and a number of works for children. He has taught in the USA for many years and is responsible for no fewer than nine anthologies of Caribbean literature. Later works include novels, poetry and short stories, many of which reflect Salkey's fascination with the Anancy tradition of folk tales, in which the cunning spider invariably outwits his more powerful adversaries. In *The Late Emancipation of Jerry Stover* (Extract 3), Salkey dissects the social malaise in 1960s middle-class Jamaican society by following the exploits of a group of dissenting young professionals.

SENIOR, Olive (1941–   ). Born in remote rural **Trelawny** parish, Olive Senior was educated in **Kingston**, in the UK and in Canada. She has been editor of *Jamaica Journal* and director of the Institute of Jamaica Publications. Her poetry, including 'The Lady' (Extract 13) is published in the volume *Talking of Trees*, 1985, while her first collection of short stories, *Summer Lightning*, 1986, won the 1987 Commonwealth Writers' Prize. She is also the author of *Arrival of the Snake Woman and Other Stories*, 1989.

THELWELL, Michael (1939–   ). Born into an influential and politically active middle-class family in **Kingston**, Michael Thelwell was educated at Jamaica College before going to university in the USA. There he became involved in the civil rights movement, an experience which influenced much of his later writing. He has pursued an academic career in North America and has worked for many years at the University of Massachusetts. *The Harder They Come* (Extract 14) is based on the successful Perry Henzell and Trevor Rhone film of the same name (the first feature film to be made in Jamaica). It tells the story of the rise to notoriety of the singer/gangster Rhygin in the 1940s and culminates in his bloody shootout with the police. Thelwell's novel has been widely acclaimed for its sensitive portrayal of Rhygin's transformation from innocent country boy into Kingston hard man and for its authentic use of Jamaican dialect.

TROLLOPE, Anthony (1815–1882). Prodigious novelist and Post Office functionary, Trollope was also a tireless traveller. His many voyages included those to Egypt, Spain, New York and Australia. In 1858 he was sent on a postal inspection to the West Indies and returned the following year, having written his travel book *The West Indies and the Spanish Main* (Extract 16), an account of his visit to the English-speaking Caribbean, Cuba and Central America. Trollope was dismayed by the economic decline and social fragmentation which overtook the British Caribbean colonies in the mid-nineteenth century after the collapse of the sugar industry. His book is a litany of complaints about administrative incompetence, imperial neglect and bad sanitation. In a short story, 'Miss

Sarah Jack of Spanish Town', he wrote 'It is so piteous that a land so beautiful should be one which fate has marked for misfortune.'

WINKLER, Anthony C. (1942–). Born in **Kingston**, Winkler is the author of various college textbooks on English and public speaking and two novels, *The Painted Canoe*, 1983 and *The Lunatic*, 1987. *The Lunatic* (Extract 10) has been made into a film and has met with enormous popular and critical acclaim. It tells the story of the unlikely sexual relationship between Aloysius, a village madman, and Inga Schmidt, a robust German visitor to Jamaica, who has come to photograph the island's flora and fauna. Their romance deteriorates when the insatiable Inga involves the local butcher in a *ménage à trois* which in turn leads to an attempted burglary in the house of the village's wealthy landowner. Lewd and slapstick, the novel is one of the most original and successful to emerge from Jamaica in recent years.

HAITI

> 'For all this, the mysterious charm of Haiti, deriving from the innate nobility and debonair style of the oppressed majority of the population remained intact. Despite the ravages of neglect it was still a beautiful place, with an indulgent tropical grace, now only half-concealed by ruin.'
> Norman Lewis,
> To Run Across the Sea

'At first sight', wrote Hesketh Prichard ◊ in 1900, 'Port-au-Prince looks fair enough to be worth travelling 5000 miles to see; once enter it, and your next impulse is to travel 5000 miles to get away again.' Many travellers will testify to those mixed feelings of attraction and repulsion. Haiti inevitably inspires extreme reactions. Some people are fascinated by life in the raw, the extremes of beauty and suffering. Others are repelled by overwhelming poverty and the apparent anarchy which perpetuates it. Few are left unmoved by the Caribbean's poorest and most volatile country.

Haiti's reputation is legendary and mythical. No country of comparable size evokes as many images and associations in the popular imagination. Think of Haiti and it is likely that you will think of voodoo, 'Papa Doc', the Tontons Macoutes and the president–priest, Jean-Bertrand Aristide. Few of the stereotypes attached to the country are positive, and most are utterly pejorative. For many years the country was synonymous with the Duvalier dictatorship, a byword for corruption and terror. More recently, the country's notoriety has increased still further with a seemingly endless succession of coups, murders and disasters. Add to this unsavoury mixture its associations with AIDS, drug-running and the refugee 'boat people', and it is hardly surprising that most tourists would prefer to leave Haiti off their travel itinerary.

Yet there is another Haiti, a country with a distinctive culture, a proud past and a unique place in history. Once the richest colony in the world, it was ruled by the French under the name of Saint Domingue. Hundreds of thousands of slaves toiled to produce the sugar which made millions for the island's white planters and French merchants. In the course of thirteen years, these same slaves and their children rose up to overthrow not merely their masters, but also armies from England, Spain and France. From 1791

FACT BOX

AREA: 27 700 sq km
POPULATION: 6 491 000
CAPITAL: Port-au-Prince
LANGUAGES: Creole, French
FORMER COLONIAL POWER: France
INDEPENDENCE: 1804
PER CAPITA GDP: US$370

---

to 1804 the island was devastated by almost continual fighting, but finally the independent state of Haiti was forged from the only successful slave revolution in history. Even today, this sense of historical destiny weighs heavily in a country where the present is all too often unbearable.

'PEARL OF THE ANTILLES'

From Columbus's arrival in 1492 to the 1697 Treaty of Ryswick which created the separate French colony of Saint Domingue, what is now Haiti was part of the Spanish colony of Hispaniola. Its indigenous people were rapidly exterminated in the vain search for gold, and the Spanish colonists established a rudimentary plantation system based on black slavery. But Hispaniola was not a great success nor a strategic priority within the Spanish Empire, and its neglect allowed French buccaneers to establish themselves first on the island of La Tortue (Tortuga) and then to build more permanent settlements on the western side of the island. As the French presence grew stronger, the Spanish withdrew to the eastern side of Hispaniola and concentrated on raising cattle in the rich pastures around Santo Domingo, their capital.

The partition of the island gave the French what was to be their most spectacularly successful colonial venture. For a century, Saint Domingue was an economic powerhouse, exporting vast amounts of sugar, indigo, cotton and other commodities back to France. To keep the plantations and mills running, thousands of slaves were imported each year simply to replace those who died of disease or exhaustion. In 1767 Saint Domingue exported 72 million pounds of raw sugar, 51 million pounds of white sugar, 2 million pounds of cotton and a million pounds of indigo. That year, approximately 15 000 slaves were brought to Saint Domingue from Africa.

On the eve of the French Revolution, Saint Domingue was a rigidly stratified society, with the rich planters at the top of the social pyramid. Their wealth and ostentatiousness made them envied and loathed. Next came the white functionaries and tradesmen, often resentful of the élite but believing in their superiority over the caste below them – the free mulattos, who by the 1780s made up a significant section of the urban, middle-class population. The children of mixed and often illicit liaisons, the mulattos were denied the most basic of civic rights and were ostracized by a hypocritical white society. After the free blacks, mostly artisans who had been liberated as individuals, came the huge mass of slaves – half a million in 1789.

The French planters called their colony the 'pearl of the Antilles'. But this was no sophisticated replica of Paris transplanted into the Caribbean. While there were theatres and other forms of public entertainment in a few towns, life on the whole was primitive. The historian C.L.R. James (◊ Trinidad and Tobago) describes in The Black Jacobins the squalor of a society where gambling-dens and brothels were the preferred amenities:

> 'In Port-au-Prince, the official capital of the colony, the population washed their dirty linen, made indigo and soaked manioc in the water of the only spring which supplied the town. Despite repeated prohibitions they continued to beat their slaves in the public streets. Nor were the authorities themselves more careful. If it rained at night, one could not walk in the town the next day, and streams of water filled the ditches at the side of the street in which one could hear the croaking of toads.'

The massive wealth and suffering which made Saint Domingue what it was also created the conditions for an unstoppable social explosion. The catalyst was the French Revolution of 1789 which reverberated throughout the Caribbean. The whites dreaded the revolutionary rhetoric of liberty and equality, the mulattos saw in these words the key to their social advancement, and the blacks took them literally as a call to revolution. After a brief and abortive mulatto rebellion, the real uprising began on 15 August 1791. It was to last thirteen years and cost hundreds of thousands of lives.

Born in Ruins

Haiti was a country 'born in ruins'. The slave uprising which led to independence devastated the plantations on which the former colony's wealth had rested. In The Black Jacobins (Extract 9), his monumental study of the Haitian revolution, C.L.R. James shows how the slaves set out to destroy the very foundations of the system which had kept them in captivity. The plantations were swept away, towns and villages were looted and burned; the country was laid waste.

The revolution was led by men who were former slaves yet who outmanoeuvred and outfought their masters and their colonial armies. In a last attempt to reclaim Saint Domingue, Napoleon sent a massive task force of 22 000 men, the most feared army in Europe. They were defeated by yellow fever and the guerrilla tactics of the black forces. General Leclerc, the French commander and Napoleon's brother-in-law, did succeed in one respect by capturing the revolution's most important leader,

Toussaint Louverture. Louverture, who had provided strategy and discipline in what might otherwise have been an anarchic revolt, was taken prisoner in 1802 and sent to a frozen prison cell in the Jura mountains, where he died the following year. Today, his memory is venerated in Haiti. At the time, too, his heroic role in liberating Saint Domingue's slaves inspired contemporaries such as William Wordsworth, whose sonnet 'To Toussaint L'Ouverture' eulogizes 'the first among blacks':

> 'Though fallen Thyself, never to rise again,
> Live and take comfort. Thou hast left behind
> Powers that will work for thee; air, earth, and skies;
> There's not a breathing of the common wind
> That will forget thee; thou hast great allies;
> Thy friends are exultations, agonies,
> And love, and Man's unconquerable mind.'

After Toussaint Louverture came Jean-Jacques Dessalines, whose image in present-day Haiti is even more exalted. He finished the war ruthlessly and bloodily, driving the last French out of the island and declaring independence on 1 January 1804. Legend has it that Dessalines, whose back bore the scars of many a whipping, created the red and blue Haitian flag by symbolically ripping the white section from the French *tricolore*. His military strategy was one of 'scorched earth'; *koupe tèt, boule kay* ('cut off the heads, burn down the houses') was his motto. The Haitian anthem, the *Dessalinienne*, celebrates the military prowess of the leader who finally rid the country of its colonial masters. Dessalines declared himself emperor in October 1804 and assumed dictatorial powers; two years later he was ambushed on the road to **Port-au-Prince** and murdered by a group of dissident officers.

High in the mountains behind Haiti's second city, **Cap Haïtien**, stands a vast fortified castle which has been described as the eighth wonder of the world. The huge **Citadelle Laferrière** was built by Dessalines's successor, a former cook and general under Toussaint Louverture who became King Henri Christophe. Even today the Citadelle is awe-inspiring, its massive fortifications intended to repel any further attacks from the French. Its construction took a terrible toll in lives, as Henri Christophe pushed his workforce to the limits of endurance. Foreign observers reported that the King would impress visitors with the blind loyalty of his troops by ordering them to march over the parapet of the building and into the abyss. At the same time, he had the elegant **Sans Souci palace** built in the style of Frederic II's Potsdam building and created a phalanx of dukes and counts in a parody of European feudal aristocracy. In *The Kingdom of This World* (Extract 1), Alejo Carpentier ◊ recreates the aura of megalomania and paranoia which surrounded King Henri Christophe. The paranoia, moreover, was justified. As his subjects rebelled and marched on the palace, the deranged monarch shot himself with a silver bullet.

The early leaders of Haiti, heroic and grotesque by turns, were to initiate a tradition of despotic and authoritarian rule which has plagued the country's history. The slaves had fought for their freedom from slavery, and many of their leaders were inspired by the French Revolution's call for liberty, equality and fraternity. Yet what the Haitian revolution ushered in was a succession of 'providential leaders', often military men, whose commitment to freedom and equality was less strong than their taste for power and self-enrichment.

PARIAH STATE

Haiti's revolution shocked the world. It shattered Napoleonic France's self-esteem and sent a dire warning to all the slave societies of the Americas. As a result, Haiti became a pariah state, shunned by its Caribbean and Latin American neighbours who feared that the virus of freedom might spread to their own slave populations. The USA refused to recognize Haiti's independence until 1862. France, perhaps more pragmatically, recognized Haiti's sovereignty in 1825 in return for compensation of 150 million francs to be paid to the former slave-owners and planters. Inexplicably the Haitian government agreed to compensate the French and thereby saddled the nation with a vast debt which was not finally paid off until 1922.

As the world turned its back on the first black republic, the country itself turned inwards, transforming itself from a plantation economy to a peasant society. The early leaders handed out land to their troops in an attempt to quell possible discontent, while former slaves settled on smallholdings which they used for subsistence farming. The great plantations disappeared, Haiti's exports all but vanished, and the countryside reverted to traditional African agricultural techniques. Gradually, Haiti became a country of two separate and distinct societies. The great majority of black Haitians, the descendants of slaves, lived rural lives, working small farms and trading in local markets. This peasantry spoke Creole (an amalgam of French and African languages), was illiterate and mostly practised African-inspired forms of religion such as voodoo. At the same time, a small minority of coloured or mulatto Haitians, born of mixed parentage and occupying a midway position between white and black in pre-revolutionary Saint Domingue, formed the country's urban élite. These people were the merchants and functionaries who came to control much of the country's economy. They, for the most part, could speak French, were practising Catholics and looked to France as a source of cultural values. The gulf between the mulatto minority (perhaps 5% of modern Haiti's population) and the remaining 95% of blacks is still today the country's most conspicuous social feature.

Haiti's international image as a place of danger and evil stems largely from the period in which its revolution earned it so many enemies. Travellers to the country were infrequent and tended to bring back sensationalist reports of the its decline into barbarism. In the course of the nineteenth century Haiti developed an unenviable reputation for black magic and cannibalism, both of which were probably distortions of its very real voodoo religion. Turn-of-the-century visitor Hesketh Prichard ◊ was fascinated by the mystique and apparent impenetrability of the country. 'Threaded in the circle of a hundred civilised isles' he wrote in *Where Black Rules White* (Extract 13), 'she alone has drawn a veil between herself and the rest of mankind.' Other travel writers followed, producing lurid and inevitably popular accounts of bizarre rituals and depravity. Few wrote anything flattering about Haiti; most, like Prichard, concluded that blacks were simply unable to rule themselves.

ENTER THE MARINES

Haiti's first turbulent century of independence produced only limited periods of peace and stability. Ambitious would-be presidents tended to grab power by recruiting a ragbag army and marching on the presidential palace in **Port-au-Prince**. Between 1843 and 1915, Haitians suffered no fewer than twenty-two presidents, only one of whom managed to finish his term of office. Political turmoil was accompanied by economic chaos. Governments were unable to raise enough revenue by taxing poor peasants and turned to foreign governments and banks for loans. When they failed to repay them, countries such as France and the US sent gunboats to reinforce their claims. Germany, too, began to show increasing interest in Haiti, and a significant German expatriate community settled in the country, working mostly as coffee-exporters. In his fictionalized reconstruction of his grandfather's life in Haiti, *The Wedding at Port-au-Prince*, 1987, Hans Christoph Buch depicts the strange existence of a fastidious German pharmacist amidst the tropical excesses of *fin-de-siècle* Haiti.

With the completion of the Panama Canal in 1914 and the formulation of US regional hegemony in the Monroe Doctrine, Washington began to watch events in Haiti with mounting unease. German ambitions in the Caribbean were clearly unwelcome (as was remaining French influence), and chronic instability in Haiti threatened to encourage foreign intervention and perhaps wider unrest. The final straw came in July 1915 when President Guillaume Sam, who had ordered the execution of hundreds of prominent opponents, was dragged from hiding in the French legation and torn to pieces by an enraged mob. This gave US President Woodrow Wilson the pretext to occupy the troubled island (the following year the Marines also landed in the neighbouring Dominican Republic), and on 28 July the first companies of US troops landed in the outskirts of Port-au-Prince.

What was intended to be a brief intervention lasted nineteen years. At first, the American military authorities ruled directly, then through puppet presidents drawn from the mulatto élite. The occupying forces tried to improve Haiti's crumbling infrastructure, building roads, bridges and port facilities. Not that this modernization programme was entirely altruistic, as it was followed by the arrival of US investors and businessmen. Dessalines's legislation forbidding *blancs* (foreigners) from owning land was scrapped, and the Haitian–American Sugar Company (HASCO) took over large tracts of land. Worse, Haitian peasants were rounded up and forced to do unpaid work on building roads. The hated *corvée* exacerbated tensions between the occupying force (and their mulatto allies) and the majority of rural Haitians.

Resistance to the occupation really hardened from 1918 onwards, when Charlemagne Péralte mobilized a force of several thousand peasant insurgents or *cacos* to overrun the US-trained police force. Like Augusto Sandino in Nicaragua, Péralte was convinced that only peasant insurgency would drive the US 'imperialists' from his homeland. In *A Rendezvous in Haiti*, 1987, Stephen Becker conjures up the popular resentment which swelled the ranks of Péralte's *cacos*. After months of guerrilla fighting, more than 2000 *cacos* had been killed, unable to compete with the Americans' superior firepower. Péralte himself was captured and executed, and a photograph of his corpse tied upright to a door in the town of **Grande-Rivière du Nord** was circulated by the US authorities to undermine his followers' morale. To many it looked as if the charismatic Péralte had been crucified, hence enhancing his aura of martyrdom.

The US troops withdrew in 1934, leaving Haiti as divided as ever. A series of mulatto presidents ruled, while the great majority remained stuck in rural poverty and squalor. The occupation had also sharpened nationalist sentiments and fuelled a growing feeling among younger black Haitians that the time for retribution had arrived. Among them was a country doctor, who was eight years old when the Americans sailed away. Named François Duvalier, he would become better known as 'Papa Doc'.

NIGHTMARE REPUBLIC

In the 1960s, the British television journalist Alan Whicker went to Haiti to interview the country's president-for-life. In a memorable scene, Papa Doc sat in the back of his limousine throwing coins through the window as his car passed through desperate crowds of poor Haitians. It was an image which somehow typified a grotesque dictatorship which lasted almost thirty years and which again set back the cause of democracy in a country which had little experience of it.

Ironically, Papa Doc was elected president in 1957 in what by Haiti's standards was a free election. A quiet, owlish doctor with a penchant for writing poetry, he seemed to be an easy target for manipulation by the politically ambitious military. Nothing could have been further from the truth. Within seven years he had fended off several attempted coups and invasions, murdered or exiled most of his opponents and set up the dreaded paramilitary Tontons Macoutes as his private death squads and extortionists. By 1964, Duvalier felt confident enough to declare himself president-for-life, backed by a referendum in which voting papers had no space for a 'no' vote. His regime was at once murderous and comical, a sort of grotesque 'banana republic' in which corruption and violence became commonplace. Graham Greene ◊ captured this sense of cruelty and absurdity in his famous novel *The Comedians* (Extract 15). With its intense sense of place, strongly drawn characters and brooding atmosphere of despair, *The Comedians* came to sum up Duvalier's Haiti for many readers. In 1971 Papa Doc died, first having handed power over to his son, Jean-Claude, who was instantly nicknamed 'Baby Doc'. An uncharismatic and reputedly slow-witted man, Baby Doc ruled with less authority and less repression than his father. Supported by the USA, the regime was less murderous than before and began to attract foreign investment and even some tourists. Nonetheless, Haiti remained a place where opposition was not tolerated. Finally, in February 1986, after several months of rising discontent and unrest, Baby Doc was flown into exile in a US military aircraft. Abandoned by his father's followers, the economic élite, his US allies and, ultimately, the army, Duvalier *fils* had no option but to abandon the presidential palace – but not before he had removed an estimated US$250 million to ease his retirement.

THE MESSIAH

The fall of the Duvalier dynasty heralded a violent conflict between the partisans of the old order and the burgeoning democratic movement. A series of coups, short-lived presidencies and aborted elections ensured that Haiti remained in the news and that its image deteriorated further. The low point came in November 1987 when long-awaited elections were sabotaged by a brutal massacre of voters in the capital and acts of terrorism throughout the country. Then, in 1990, the impossible happened. A genuinely popular candidate was overwhelmingly elected to the presidency in free and fair elections – the first in Haiti's history. A radical priest named Jean-Bertrand Aristide, who had survived several assassination attempts and had earned the disapproval of conservatives in the Vatican, won almost 70% of the votes. His followers called him 'the Messiah', expecting miracles from this frail and soft-spoken priest. His enemies, the rich and powerful few, regarded him with the deepest suspicion.

In *No Other Life* (Extract 6), Brian Moore ◊ draws a fictionalized picture of the priest's rise to power and his struggle with the forces of reaction. Moore's novel ends with the mysterious and ambiguous disappearance of Jean-Marie Cantave following a military coup. Aristide, too, was forced out by a coup only eight months after assuming the presidency and spent three years in exile. Finally 'the Messiah' returned in October 1994 after US troops had peacefully occupied Haiti and forced out the illegal military junta. It was, as many observed, the first time that a US government had overthrown a military dictatorship to restore to power a left-wing government. Yet Bill Clinton's administration had its own reasons to intervene in

Haiti, not least to stem the tide of 'boat people' which was threatening to swamp Florida.

A COUNTRY IN CRISIS

To cross the border from the Dominican Republic into Haiti is to cross from a land of tropical forests and streams into a parched, eroded and barren landscape. This transition from fertility to desert is most dramatically witnessed from an airplane, from which the passenger sees vast swathes of green suddenly give way to the brown and grey of bare hillsides. Haiti's ecological disaster is to some extent the fruit of its historical triumph. The French colonists had already cut down and exported some of the country's best mahogany forests. When the former slaves settled on smallholdings, they cleared trees to make way for their crops. As the soil lost fertility they moved higher into the mountains, cutting and burning, turning trees into charcoal for fuel. Haiti's legal system, based on the French Code Napoléon, contributed to the process of deforestation, as it stipulated that all male heirs should inherit an equal share of a Haitian's property. Small farms became divided and even smaller. The pressure on land, water and forests became critical. Even in the 1940s, the environmental disaster confronting Haiti was apparent to the novelist Jacques Roumain ◊. In his classic *Masters of the Dew* (Extract 2), he dramatizes the struggle of one village, Fonds Rouge, to save itself from drought. According to Roumain, the gruelling poverty experienced by Haiti's peasant communities forced them to cut down trees in order to make charcoal. Today, those same pressures have transformed large parts of what is a tropical island into an arid wasteland.

The disaster befalling Haiti's countryside has fuelled the exodus to the city, most notably to the capital, **Port-au-Prince**. Once a small and relatively elegant city of several hundred inhabitants, it now contains perhaps two million, the majority of whom live in unspeakable slums. While the rich prefer the cool breezes and large gardens of the hillside suburbs, the ordinary mass of Haitians eke out a perilous existence in the sprawling shantytowns which reach down to the sea. Among the worst are the areas known as **La Saline** and **Cité Soleil**, where hundreds of thousands of shacks lie sweltering without water, electricity or sewerage. Cité Soleil was once named Cité Simone, in honour of Papa Doc's wife. In 1986 its name was changed to commemorate the Catholic Church's radio station, Radio Soleil ('Sun Radio') which played an important part in the overthrow of Baby Doc. As the US journalist Amy Wilentz ◊ records in *The Rainy Season* (Extract 17), life in La Saline can rival the worst horrors of Bombay or Lagos.

Poverty and despair drive legions of 'boat people' from Haiti towards the promised land of Florida and beyond. Large numbers of Haitians live in Miami, New York and other American cities, many of them illegal, undocumented migrants who live semi-clandestine lives. The boat trip from Haiti is expensive and dangerous; sometimes the small fishing-boats sink, and more often they are intercepted by US Coastguard patrols. Haitians, unlike Cubans, are not welcome in the USA. In *Continental Drift* (Extract 4), Russell Banks ◊ follows the desperate attempt of Haitians to leave their suffering behind them. It is an all-too-common story.

TWO NATIONS

What strikes many travellers to Haiti is the overwhelming disparity between a rich, privileged few and the poor, disadvantaged many. The country is reputed to have several hundred millionaires and perhaps five thousand very wealthy families. This clique is to be found in the chic suburb of **Pétionville**, a select enclave several miles up in the hills behind the steamy capital. There, amid expensive French restaurants and art galleries, the élite enjoys an agreeably opulent lifestyle. When Patrick Leigh Fermor (◊ Barbados) visited Haiti as part of his Caribbean travels in the 1940s, he was drawn by the 'discreet charm' of Pétionville's pale-skinned bourgeoisie. *The Traveller's Tree* (Extract 14) contains a vivid account of the gulf between Haiti's haves and have-nots. Half a century later, the country's 'social apartheid' is still firmly in place, as Herbert Gold ◊ reveals in his description of the capital city. *Best Nightmare on Earth* (Extract 16) shows how Haiti's wealthy are so hardened towards the poverty of their compatriots that they hardly even notice them.

Haiti's peasantry and slum-dwellers inhabit a completely different world. There are areas in the countryside where there are no roads and few trappings of modern civilization. These rural communities operate for the most part outside the modern economy and have little contact with what is ironically known as 'the republic of Port-au-Prince'. The Haitian peasant is both romanticized and ridiculed in the writing of foreigners and Haitians alike. In their vivid account of the Duvalier era, *Papa Doc* (Extract 8), Bernard Diederich and Al Burt ◊ recount a comic anecdote which exemplifies the cultural gulf between rural Haitian existence and the outside world.

AFRICAN SPIRITS

Like other Caribbean nations, Haiti is strongly influenced by the legacy of its peoples' African past. Yet because of its early and bloody independence, its period of isolation and the nature of its rural society, Haiti is the most African of the region's nations. Hundreds of thousands of slaves from the west coast of Africa were brought in slavery to the plantations of Saint Domingue, where they retained much of their language, culture and religion. This was largely a survival strategy and a means of resisting the horrors of plantation life. The revolution enabled the slaves to form peasant communities where African traditions and social structures remained intact. Today, as ethnobiologist Wade Davis ◊ reveals, this cultural reality is as alive as ever in the countryside of Haiti. In *The Serpent and the*

Rainbow (Extract 3), Davis shows how a whole complex of beliefs and attitudes link present-day Haiti to the ancestral departure point of Africa. Most famous and most often caricatured among Haiti's African influences is the practice of *vodou* or voodoo. For generations of foreign journalists and writers, this system of beliefs and rituals has provided a rich seam of sensationalism. In the nineteenth century, travellers hinted darkly at the appalling manifestations of black magic and cannibalism which could be seen in the country. With the US invasion and occupation came another batch of lurid travelogues which depicted voodoo as a series of frenzied, and frequently erotic ceremonies. William Seabrook ◊ produced perhaps the most successful example of this genre. His bestselling *The Magic Island* (Extract 12) contains all of the stereotypical misinterpretations which surround Western perceptions of voodoo.

In reality, voodoo is a complex and evolving belief-system which seeks to explain and influence everyday life through the role of spirits (*loas*) with whom believers hope to enter into contact. Some *loas* are associated with the personae of dead ancestors, others are more archetypal figures. The best known are those which are believed to control the elements or to hold the secret of the link between life and death. In many cases, the voodoo pantheon has become intermixed with Christian religion, the major *loas* corresponding to saints and biblical figures. Damballah, for instance, the supreme *loa*, is associated with St Patrick, while Papa Legba, who controls the crossroads (and hence the way to all things) is often depicted as St Peter or Lazarus. The centrepiece of voodoo faith is the ceremony at which the *loas* are invoked by the priest (*houngan*), who facilitates the temporary possession of an initiate by a spirit. This produces the trance and 'speaking in tongues', in which the *loa* is said to 'ride' (*chevaucher*) the believer. It is this ceremony, accompanied by music, chanting, rum and occasional animal sacrifice, that has been so often misinterpreted as an orgy.

Haitians are a religious, spiritual, and according to some superstitious, people. Haiti is reputed to have more churches per head of the population than any other country, and every village contains its *hounfours* or voodoo temples. According to the anthropologist Francis Huxley ◊, local superstitions are not confined to the uneducated and they can take extreme forms. In *The Invisibles* (Extract 10), Huxley delves into the world of magic potions and zombies which, he claims, fascinates all Haitians.

MAGICAL REALISM

A sense of the supernatural and magical runs through much of Haiti's art and literature. Haitian painting underwent a boom in the 1930s and 1940s, when it was 'discovered' by Americans who valued its colourful and naïve depictions of everyday and mystical scenes. Painters such as Hector Hyppolite and Philomé Obin became celebrities, and their work commanded high prices in New York art galleries. Haitian music also enjoys a considerable following in North America and Europe, most recently in the form of 'voodoo beat' or *racines*, a fusion of traditional drumming and rock music played by bands such as Boukman Eksperyans.

Haiti's fertile literary tradition is one of the many surprising dimensions of this misunderstood country. 'Every third Haitian is a poet' goes a well-worn saying, and in terms of sheer productivity there are few countries which can begin to compete. Until the 1950s, for instance, Haiti had produced and published more books than any other nation in the western hemisphere, with the exception of the USA. For a largely non-literate society, Haiti has also produced a number of internationally recognized writers, many of whom have lived in Paris or New York. Yet few Haitian authors have had their work translated into English, and even a significant figure such as René Depestre has not been widely translated. A recent and welcome exception is the appearance of Jean Métellus's *The Vortex Family*, a magical realist saga of a Haitian family set in the years between the US occupation and the Duvalier dictatorship.

In the nineteenth century, the country's cultural model was still very much France, and Haiti had its own ranks of romantic and symbolist poets. The US occupation opened the country to other North American influences, but also inspired a strong sense of Haitian nationalism and renewed interest in the country's African traditions. The respected ethnologist Jean Price-Mars produced the seminal *Ainsi parla l'oncle*, 1928, which stressed the cultural authenticity of peasant life, Creole language and African story-telling traditions. He was followed by writers such as Jacques Roumain ◊ who used rural themes and peasant characters as material for their political concerns.

More recently, a younger generation of Haitian authors, with close family ties to the USA and writing in English, has emerged. In 1994 two novels by young women of mixed Haitian–US backgrounds were published to widespread critical acclaim. Edwidge Danticat's *Breath, Eyes, Memory* tells of Sophie, a Haitian woman whose childhood in Haiti and adolescence in New York reveal differing facets of a complex identity. Written in a spare, understated style, the novel explores the narrator's relationship with four generations of women, from remote Haitian village all the way to New York's Flatbush Avenue. Anne-Christine d'Adesky's *Under the Bone* is a more politically explicit examination of Haiti's recent turmoil, in which the central character becomes involved in a search for a 'disappeared' peasant woman.

Haiti's most celebrated writers – Jacques Roumain, René Depestre, Philippe Thoby-Marcelin – have attempted in their different ways to convey the sense of magic and spirituality which shapes the world of the Haitian peasant. The miraculous victory of the divine over everyday poverty and despair is a recurring theme in the country's literature and one which receives powerful treatment in *Cathedral of the August Heat* (Extract 5) by Pierre Clitandre ◊. In the slums of **Port-au-Prince**, Clitandre's bizarre characters await the apotheosis, political and symbolic, which will transform their wretched lives.

INTREPID TRAVELLERS

'When I told my friends that I was going to Haiti they raised their eyebrows. "Haiti," they said. "But that's the place where they kill their presidents and eat their babies. You'd better buy yourself a large-sized gun." ' So wrote Alec Waugh (◊ Martinique) in the 1940s, and the country's poor reputation has changed little since. Because of its mystique, Haiti has attracted more than its share of travel writers, eager to expose themselves to deprivation and danger (whether imaginary or real) in search of a good story. In the twentieth century, writers such as Eric Newby, Martha Gellhorn and Norman Lewis ◊ have visited the country, and Haiti features in many Caribbean travelogues, from Patrick Leigh Fermor to Quentin Crewe (◊ Dominican Republic).

Few travellers can have experienced as much discomfort as did Ian Thomson ◊ in his exploration of remote rural Haiti. *'Bonjour Blanc'* (Extract 11) is a vivid record of the author's eventful, sometimes hair-raising, travels around the country. Norman Lewis too encountered a range of problems in his trip to Papa Doc's Haiti in the 1960s. Yet despite crumbling roads, drought and the unwelcome attentions of the Tontons Macoutes, Lewis's account of a provincial town in *To Run Across the Sea* (Extract 7) reminds us that Haiti never loses its ability to amaze.

LITERARY LANDMARKS

Port-au-Prince. The single most famous landmark for all visiting foreigners is the idiosyncratic **Hotel Oloffson**, one of the best examples of Haiti's turn-of-the-century gingerbread architectural style. Graham Greene stayed here and used it as the basis for the Trianon in *The Comedians* (Extract 15). Once the residence of President Simon Sam (not to be confused with the unfortunate President Guillaume Sam), the building was used as a hospital by the US occupying force before becoming a hotel. Eric Newby wrote of it in *A Traveller's Life*: 'It was the embellishments that made it unique. From every possible and impossible vantage point it sprouted turrets, spires, crotchets, finials and balconies, some of which appeared to have been put on upside down, all of them riddled with so much fretwork that it was a miracle that the building remained standing.' Famous for its rum punches

---

Notes to map (facing page): [a]**Kenscoff:** *'black clouds over Kenscoff and the scene of a voodoo ceremony;* [b]**Pétionville:** *Doctor Magiot's home and El Rancho hotel;* [c]**Duvalierville:** *a 'wilderness of cement' and Papa Doc's attempt to emulate Brasilia;* [d]**Port-au-Prince:** *site of the Trianon hotel and the Columbus statue where Brown meets Martha (see Extract 15)* [e]**Petit-Goâve:** *'the family tombs looked more solid than the family huts';* [f]**Aquin:** *where Jones confesses and Concasseur, the Tonton Macoute, meets his end;* [g]**Elias Piña:** *Brown meets the defeated guerrillas and learns of Jones's death.*

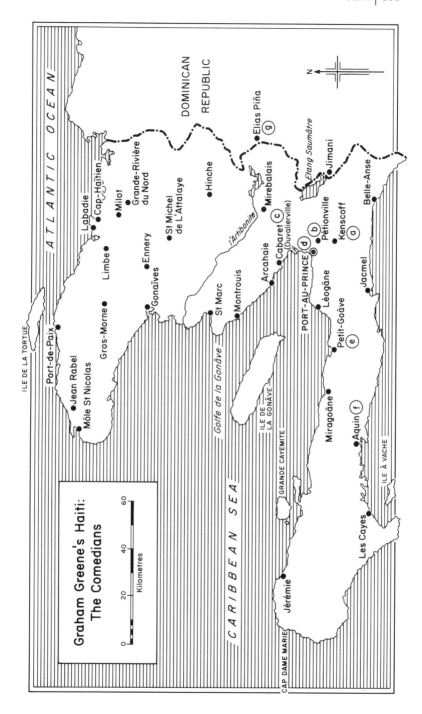

Graham Greene's Haiti:
The Comedians

0 20 40 60
Kilometres

ATLANTIC OCEAN

DOMINICAN REPUBLIC

ILE DE LA TORTUE

Port-de-Paix
Jean Rabel
Môle St Nicolas
Gros-Morne
Limbe
Labadie
Cap-Haïtien
Milot
Grande-Rivière du Nord
St Michel de L'Attalaye
Ennery
Gonaïves
St Marc
Montrouis
Arcahaie
Cabaret (Duvalierville) Ⓒ
PORT-AU-PRINCE ⓓ
Léogâne
Petit-Goâve Ⓔ
Miragoâne
Aquin Ⓕ
Les Cayes
Jérémie
Hinche
Mirebalais
Elias Piña Ⓖ
Etang Saumâtre
Jimani
Pétionville Ⓑ
Kenscoff Ⓐ
Belle-Anse
Jacmel
l'Artibonite

Golfe de la Gonâve

ILE DE LA GONÂVE

GRANDE CAYEMITE

CARIBBEAN SEA

ILE À VACHE

CAP DAME MARIE

and voodoo shows, the Oloffson is the haunt of all journalists, writers and poseurs, not least the infamous Aubelin Jolicoeur, the man who inspired the character Petit Pierre in *The Comedians* and who has lived off this dubious claim to fame ever since.

The **Presidential Palace**, situated on the **Champ de Mars**, is an unmistakeable imitation of the Washington original. With its immaculate white exterior and impossibly lush lawns, it stands in contrast to the ramshackle charm of the surrounding area. Patrick Leigh Fermor ◊ wrote of 'an immense rectangle pierced by a multiplicity of windows and crowned by a groined dome which is flanked by two attendant cupolas; and all of a white so uncompromising and refractory to the sun that it appears, in that setting of parched earth and superabaundant green, to be an edifice of snow magically transported from the polar wastes.'

Cap Haïtien. About 150 miles to the north lies the country's second city, once the elegant capital of colonial Saint Domingue. In *The Kingdom of This World* (Extract 1), Alejo Carpentier reconstructs the city's long-gone cosmopolitan charm: 'There were more tailors, hatters, feather-workers, hairdressers; there was a shop that sold violas and transverse flutes, as well as the music of *contredanses* and sonatas.' Nowadays the visitor will find only distant echos of this prosperity in the run-down city. A short drive away are the ruins of the baroque **Sans Souci palace** and the **Citadelle Laferrière**, poignant monuments to King Henri Christophe. Since 1973 attempts have been made by UNESCO to restore the grandeur of the sites, ruined by looting and earthquakes. For Aimé Césaire (◊ Martinique), author of a play about Henri Christophe, the citadel symbolizes the aspirations of the whole Haitian nation:

> Built by the whole people, men
> and women, young and old,
> and for a whole people.
> Look, its head is in the clouds,
> its feet dig into the valleys.
> It's a city, a fortress,
> a battleship of stone . . .

**Aubelin Jolicoeur at the Oloffson Hotel – Jolicoeur was the
inspiration for 'Petit Pierre' in Greene's *The Comedians*.**

BOOKLIST

*The following selection includes the ex-
tracted titles in this chapter as well as
other titles for further reading. In general, paperback editions are given when
possible. For most of the extracted
works, the original publisher in English
can be found in 'Acknowledgments and
Citations' at the end of the volume, as
can the exact location of the extracts and
the editions from which they are taken.*

d'Adesky, Anne-Christine, *Under
    the Bone*, Farrar, Straus and
    Giroux, New York, 1994.
Banks, Russell, *Continental Drift*,
    Hamish Hamilton, London,
    1985. **Extract 4**.
Becker, Stephen, *A Rendezvous in
    Haiti*, Collins Harvill, London,
    1987.
Buch, Hans Christoph, *The Wedding*

at Port-au-Prince, Faber and Faber, London, 1987.

Carpentier, Alejo, *The Kingdom of This World*, Harriet de Onis, trans, Penguin, London, 1980. **Extract 1.**

Clitandre, Pierre, *Cathedral of the August Heat*, Bridget Jones, trans, Readers International, London, 1987. **Extract 5.**

Danticat, Edwige, *Breath, Eyes, Memory*, Soho Press, New York, 1994.

Dash, J. Michael, *Literature and Ideology in Haiti, 1915–1961*, Barnes and Noble, Totowa, NJ, 1981.

Davis, Wade, *The Serpent and the Rainbow*, Collins, London, 1986. **Extract 3.**

Depestre, René , *Un arc-en-ciel pour l'occident chrétien*, Présence Africaine, Paris, 1967.

Diederich, Bernard and Al Burt, *Papa Doc: Haiti and Its Dictator*, Bodley Head, London, 1969. **Extract 8.**

Ferguson, James, *Haiti: Nightmare Republic*, Cassell, London, 1996.

Gold, Herbert, *Best Nightmare on Earth: A Life in Haiti*, Grafton Books, London, 1991. **Extract 16.**

Greene, Graham, *The Comedians*, Penguin, London, 1984. **Extract 15.**

Huxley, Francis, *The Invisibles*, Rupert Hart-Davis, London, 1966. **Extract 10.**

James, C.L.R., *The Black Jacobins: Toussaint L'Ouverture and the San Domingo Revolution*, Allison & Busby, London, 1991. **Extract 9.**

Leigh Fermor, Patrick, *The Traveller's Tree: A Journey Through the Caribbean Islands*, Penguin, London, 1984. **Extract 14.**

Lewis, Norman, *To Run Across the Sea*, Cape, London, 1989. **Extract 7.**

Métellus, Jean, *The Vortex Family*, Michael Richardson, trans, Peter Owen, London, 1995.

Moore, Brian, *No Other Life*, Bloomsbury, London, 1993. **Extract 6.**

Newby, Eric, *A Traveller's Life*, Picador, London, 1982.

Nicholls, David, *From Dessalines to Duvalier: Race, Colour and National Independence in Haiti*, Macmillan, Basingstoke, 1995.

Price-Mars, Jean, *Ainsi parla l'oncle*, Imprimerie de Compiègne, Paris, 1938.

Prichard, H. Hesketh, *Where Black Rules White: A Journey Across and About Haiti*, Thomas Nelson & Sons, London, 1910. **Extract 13.**

Roumain, Jacques, *Masters of the Dew*, Langston Hughes and Mercer Cook, trans, Heinemann, London, 1978. **Extract 2.**

Seabrook, William, *The Magic Island*, Harrap, London, 1929. **Extract 12.**

Thomson, Ian, *'Bonjour Blanc': A Journey Through Haiti*, Penguin, London, 1992. **Extract 11.**

Wilentz, Amy, *The Rainy Season: Haiti Since Duvalier*, Cape, London, 1989. **Extract 17.**

Extracts

(1) CITADELLE LAFERRIÈRE

Alejo Carpentier, *The Kingdom of This World*

The Citadelle's construction was as cruel as it was grandiose.

King Henri Christophe often went up to the Citadel, escorted by a squad of officers on horseback, to observe how the work was progressing. Heavy-set, powerful, with a barrel-shaped chest, flat-nosed, his chin half-hidden in the embroidered collar of his uniform, the monarch examined the batteries, forges, and workshops, his spurs clinking as he mounted the interminable stairways. From his Napoleonic bicorne stared the bird's-eye of a two-coloured cockade. At times, with a mere wave of his crop, he ordered the death of some sluggard surprised in flagrant idleness, or the execution of workers, hoisting a block of granite too slowly up a steep incline. His visits always ended by his having an armchair brought out to the upper terrace that overlooked the sea from beside an abyss that made even those most accustomed to the sight close their eyes. Then, with nothing that could cast a shadow or care upon him, high above all, standing on his own shadow, he measured the scope of his power. In the event of any attempt by France to retake the island, he, Henri Christophe, *God, my cause and my sword*, could hold out here, above the clouds, for as long as was necessary, with his whole court, his army, his chaplains, his African pages, his jesters. Fifteen thousand men could live with him within those Cyclopean walls and lack for nothing. Once the drawbridge of the Single Gate had been pulled up, the Citadel LaFerrière would be the country, with its independence, its monarch, its treasury and all its pomp. Because down below, the sufferings involved in its building forgotten, the Negroes of the Plaine would raise their eyes to the fortress, replete with corn, with gunpowder, iron, and gold, thinking that there, higher than the birds, there, where life below was the remote sound of bells and the crowing of roosters, a king of their own race was waiting, close to heaven, which is the same everywhere, for the thud of the bronze hoofs of Ogoun's ten thousand horses. Not for nothing had those towers arisen, on the mighty bellowing of bulls, bleeding, their testicles toward the sun, at the hands of builders well aware of the deep significance of the sacrifice even though they had told the ignorant that this represented an advance in technique of military engineering.

(2) FONDS ROUGE

Jacques Roumain, *Masters of the Dew*

After years away cutting cane in Cuba, Manuel returns to his home village, only to find that the stream which once watered the peasant farms has dried up because of deforestation and erosion.

A narrow, shallow ravine opened before him. It was dry. Tufts of weeds and all sorts of prickles had invaded its bed. The man raised his head toward a bit of sky soaked in hot steam, took out a red handkerchief, mopped his face, and seemed to reflect. He went down the path, scattering pebbles on the burning sand. Dead roots crumbled in his fingers when he examined the rough grained earth, so dry that it trickled like powder.

'*Carajo!*' he cried.

He walked slowly up the other side, his face worried, but only momentarily. Today he had too much to be happy about. Water sometimes changes its course like a dog changes masters. Who knew where the vagabond was flowing now? He strolled towards a mound crowned with macaw trees. Their crumpled fans hung inert. There wasn't a breath of air to open them and turn them into a wild play of dazzling light. This was a detour for the stranger, but he wanted to embrace the countryside from above, to see the plain spread out before him and glimpse through the trees, the thatched roofs and irregular blots of fields and gardens.

His face, drenched with sweat, hardened, for what he saw was a grilled expanse of dirty rusty color spotted by a scattering of moldy huts. He stared at the barren hill overlooking the village, ravaged by wide whitish gullies where erosion had bared its flanks to the rock. He tried to remember the tall oaks once animated with wood pigeons fond of blackberries, the mahogany trees bathed in shadowy light, the Congo beans whose dry husks rustled in the wind, the long rows of sweet potato hills. But all that, the sun had licked up, effaced with a single stroke of its fiery tongue.

He felt as though he had been betrayed. The sun weighed on his shoulders like a burden. He went down the slope into the savanna where emaciated cattle were wandering through thorny bushes searching for a rare blade of grass. Flocks of crows perched on the tall cactus flew away at his approach in a dark whirl of interminable caws.

(3) HAITI: AFRICA

Wade Davis, *The Serpent and the Rainbow*

Anthropologist Wade Davis describes the living African heritage of present-day Haiti and its relationship with voodoo.

Today evidence of the African heritage is everywhere in rural Haiti. In the fields, long lines of men wield hoes to the rhythm of small drums, and just beyond them sit steaming pots of millet and yams ready for the harvest feast. In a roadside settlement, or *lakou*, near the centre of the compound, a wizened old man holds court. Markets sprout up at every crossroads, and like magnets they pull the women out of the hills; one sees their narrow traffic on the trails, the billowy walk of girls beneath baskets of rice, the silhouette of a stubborn matron dragging a half-dozen donkeys laden with eggplant. There are sounds as well. The echo of distant songs, the din of the market, and the cadence of the language itself – Creole – each word truncated to fit the meter of West African speech. Each of these disparate images, of course, translates into a theme: the value of collective labor, communal land holdings, the authority of the patriarch, the dominant role of women in the market economy. And these themes, in turn, are clues to a complex social world.

Yet images alone cannot begin to express the cohesion of the peasant society; this, like a psychic education, must come in symbols, in invisible tones sensed and felt as much as observed. For in this country of survivors and spirits, the living and the dead, it is religion that provides the essential bond. Vodoun is not an isolated cult; it is a complex mystical worldview, a system of beliefs concerning the relationship between man, nature, and the supernatural forces of the universe. It fuses the unknown to the known, creates order out of chaos, renders the mysterious intelligible. Vodoun cannot be abstracted from the day-to-day lives of the believers. In Haiti, as in Africa, there is no separation between the sacred and the secular, between the holy and the profane, between the material and the spiritual. Every dance, every song, every action is but a particle of the whole, each gesture a prayer for the survival of the entire community.

(4) Haiti: Boat People

Russell Banks, *Continental Drift*

Driven by fear of the policeman Aubin after her nephew has stolen a ham from a wrecked truck, Vanise decides to join the 'boat people'.

The young Haitian woman, with her infant in her arms and her adolescent nephew standing behind her, watches the sea behind them slowly swallow the Haitian hills. The small, crowded boat plows northward through a choppy, slate-blue sea, towards America, Vanise believes, towards Florida, where everything will be different, where nothing except the part of her that's inside her skull will be the same, and gradually even that will change. First the village of Le Môle at the base of the green hills is devoured, then the low slopes checkered with cane fields and coconut palms go under, gone to where the dead abide, and at last the familiar dark green hills succumb. There is no known place peering back at her from the horizon, and now she faces only a point on the compass, an abstraction called south, *Adonai*, that refuses to speak to her in any voice but her own.

This is a new kind of silence for Vanise, one that frightens her, and she begins to chatter at the boy, Claude, scolding him for having stolen the ham from the wrecked truck, pointing out his stupidity in having brought it back to the cabin in Allanche, his deceit in not telling them immediately where he found the ham, before they had eaten at it, so that he could have put it back uneaten before anyone discovered that it and the rest of the meat had been stolen and Aubin came looking for him, and not finding him there would punish his mother and her and the baby, unless Aubin did find him there, in which case Aubin would have taken him off to jail. We would still be at home in Allanche, she reminds him, cooking a chicken and yams on the fire, if you were a good boy. You would have your mother, and we would all have each other, if you were not a thief.

The boy looks down at the rising and falling deck. Slowly he turns away from the south and faces north. Yes, he says, but now we are going to America.

Vanise feels the weight of a huge, swelling stone in her belly. She sighs, turns away from the southern horizon to the north and starts waiting for the sight of America rising from the sea.

(5) Haiti: The End of the World

Pierre Clitandre, *Cathedral of the August Heat*

In Clitandre's magical realist allegory of the Haitian revolution, the modern-day inhabitants of a Port-au-Prince slum eagerly await the day of reckoning.

Although they had lived through many false prophecies, people were still dazzled by this promise of all the old dreams in the world. This time the news took on such urgency that a week before the date predicted, the man-with-the-horse's-neigh caused the door of the barrack prison to be opened. And out came beings with a glassy stare, blinded by the sunlight. They disappeared into the passageways of the ghetto like sinister mummies. Seeing them pass like risen dead, a collective hysteria quickly spread. From door to door the news was repeated: Holy Virgin Mary! that Mésidor Dieusibon, dead this three years gone, had been seen again that very day drinking water from a tin cup and leaning against a shack in Seven-month-a-bawl alley. The news that Malé Dorilas, dead from gangrene these four years, had been seen again that very day by a group of washerwomen, over by where the big shed wall started, looking for something which must be the place where his carpenter's bench used to be . . .

When the great day at last arrived, from the first light of dawn, processions of women with flowers had gone to the big Cathedral Square. Then by every path and track dense groups thronged in, feeling the spirit, their heads raised towards heaven. Chanting rose up on every hand: vibrant hosannas, alleluias. But the great door of the cathedral had remained shut, and no priest dared to appear before a crowd waiting more fervently than ever for the gift of eternal life. The slums emptied of their poor, their sick, their miserly shopkeepers who hadn't thought it safe to leave their money behind and carried it with them knotted into grubby handkerchiefs. Paralytics who couldn't walk had themselves carried. And they all came down the lanes smelling of rose laurel, arms open wide to the blue, blue sky. In the ghettos the breeze blew in the depths of the passageways. They had the look of regions deserted in a great plague.

(6) HAITI: THE MESSIAH

Brian Moore, *No Other Life*

After the dictatorship of Jean-Marie Doumergue, radical Catholic priest, Jean-Paul Cantave ('Jeannot') is elected president. His former mentor visits him in the palace.

In the days of Doumergue the interior of the palace was forbidding: empty corridors, vast marbled reception rooms, the silence of a museum in early morning before it opens its doors to the public. But now it resembled a gigantic, noisy courthouse: nuns and priests, social workers, politicians, foreign consuls, street people, a few members of the elite, street merchants, peasant delegations from Mele and Cap Nord, all waited for an audience. Vendors moved through the crowds, wooden trays around their necks, selling sweet local drinks and tiny, bite-sized sandwiches. Where once the dictator's palace flunkies ruled these corridors, wearing white suits, black ties and proper shoes, now, young men in T-shirts emblazoned with Jeannot's picture laughed, beat sticks in local folk rhythms and danced up and down the corridors as they went about their self-appointed task of controlling and ordering the crowds. They knew me from the orphanage. They waved me on . . .

Two sergeants of the Garde Présidentielle, big burly men who had probably been the dictator's bodyguards, sat on cane chairs outside the shut inner door. Pelardy nodded to them and one rose to admit me. Inside, the room was large with an ornate ceremonial desk facing a double set of french windows that looked out on a hedge of pink-and-white hibiscus blossoms. Jeannot sat, not at the desk, but on a small stool in the corner of the room. A ring of empty chairs surrounded him and he was listening to an old woman, possibly a street merchant, who sat facing him. He leaned towards her, his head bent, his right hand covering his eyes as though he were hearing her confession. The old woman talked agitatedly, her voice high and angry, the Creole words jumbled so that I could not hear what she was saying. Was she denouncing someone? Jeannot leaned close and whispered to her, stopping her tirade. Rising, he put his hand on her head in a gesture of benediction. Stiffly, she got to her feet. Obedient, she took her leave of

him. As she went towards the door, she saw me, stopped, and whispered, 'C'e Mesiah, c'e Mesiah. *Deu même, t'entends?'*
Jeannot came towards me, smiling. He looked at the old woman who was now going out of the door. 'What did she tell you?'
'That you're God Himself. What's the matter, *Petit?* Isn't it enough to be President?'

(7) HAITI: THE PAST

Norman Lewis, *To Run Across the Sea*

Driving with his friend Johnson on the road to Belladère, Norman Lewis comes across an unexpected vision of the past.

For months not a drop of water had fallen from the skies of Port-au-Prince, but here the rain fell in sudden opaque showers between intervals of brilliant sunshine. We groped our way cautiously through streams and round landslides. Sometimes road and river-bed would be united for a hundred yards and large, greyish kingfishers went hurtling past on both sides of the car, and we could see little fish darting away from the front wheels. All the trees had been cut down and when the sun came out the tall, ragged poinsettias on the eroded hillsides made the day seem hotter. In rural Haiti only one couple in ten can afford to get married in church, but those who still do clothe the ceremony in dignity and panache. A bride on her way to her wedding who went splashing past on horseback in a great muslin foaming of veils and skirts was preceded by a dozen capering drummers. The name of this village was 'Peu de Chose', which in a way described it well.

The small town that followed was a piece of nineteenth-century Normandy recreated in the tropics. A clapboard version of a French church wore its spire askew like a comic hat. It was supported by a mairie, a closed-down École de Jeunes Filles, a pigmy château patched with corrugated iron, and a magnificent French pissoir enobled by its positioning at the top of a flight of wide steps. A herd of dwarf cows occupied the square, where they browsed off the fallen blossoms of the flame trees. We stopped to watch the approach of a ghostly black version of a French grandee with white Napoleon beard, cutaway coat, panama hat, spats and malacca cane. A girl had set up a stall near by, and sat smoking a cob pipe, her skirts pulled halfway up her black thighs. She sold single and half-cigarettes, olive oil by the spoonful and dried fishes' tails at one cent apiece, and cuffed away sparrows that alighted for a quick peck at the fish.
. . .
'This', said Johnson, 'is a copy of France as it once was. You won't here Creole spoken here. These people actually believe themselves to be French. Take that old man with the white beard we just saw. I know him. He has papers to prove he's a descendant of the Duc de Brantôme . . .'

(8) Haiti: Peasants and Presidents

Bernard Diederich and Al Burt,
Papa Doc: Haiti and its Dictator

During the six-year presidency of Paul Magloire, Haiti attracted a number of VIPs, not least Richard Nixon, who personally experienced the linguistic gulf between blancs (foreigners) and ordinary Haitians during his 1955 visit.

Vice President Nixon and his wife came to Haiti in the spring on the way home from a trip to the Dominican Republic. Nixon, a royally welcomed visitor, was the first guest in Magloire's new luxury marble mountain villa in Turgeau. He almost made a campaign of it. At a garden party Nixon mixed a Haitian rum (Barbancourt) cocktail for Magloire and, during a press conference, said that governments always like to show their best projects, but in Haiti he had been able to see both the 'before' and 'after' of housing projects on the outskirts of the city. Nixon praised the changes as fantastic.

He often stopped to question peasants. One such conversation was particularly memorable. He held up a young woman riding a donkey loaded with milk containers and talked with her through a government interpreter. Her first reply in Creole used a common Haitian slang expression, 'Tell this *cocoye* to let me go on my way.' The interpreter translated this as: 'She says she is happy to meet the Vice President of the United States.' Nixon then asked about her family, and the woman said she had no husband and three children, but the interpreter said: 'She is engaged.' Nixon placed a hand on the donkey's rump and asked, 'What is the donkey's name?' Her reply was: 'He is crazy. It is called a donkey.' Then she loosed a stream of complaints. The interpreter told Nixon: 'She says it hasn't got a name, and asks to be excused because it's getting late.' The official group moved on, leaving the milkmaid sucking her teeth and muttering.

(9) Haiti: Revolution

C.L.R. James, *The Black Jacobins*

The first insurrection in August 1791 heralded thirteen years of savage civil war and the end of colonial Saint-Domingue.

On the night of the 22nd a tropical storm raged, with lightning and gusts of wind and heavy showers of rain. Carrying torches to light their way, the leaders of the revolt met in an open space in the thick forests of the Morne Rouge, a mountain overlooking Le Cap. There Boukman gave the last instructions and after Voodoo incantations and the sucking of the blood of a stuck pig, he stimulated his followers by a prayer spoken in creole, which, like so much spoken on such occasions, has remained. 'The god who created the sun which gives us light, who rouses the waves and rules the storm, though hidden in the clouds, he watches us. He sees all that the white man does. The god of the white man inspires him with crime, but our god calls up on us to do good works. Our god who is good to us orders us to revenge our wrongs. He will direct our arms and aid us. Throw away the symbol of the god of the whites who has so often caused us to weep, and listen to the voice of liberty, which speaks in the hearts of us all.'

The symbol of the god of the whites was the cross which, as Catholics, they wore round their necks.

That very night they began. The slaves on the Gallifet plantation were so well treated that 'happy as the Negroes of Gallifet' was a slave proverb. Yet by a phenomenon noticed in all revolutions it was they who led the way. Each slave-gang murdered its masters and burnt the plantation to the ground. The precautions that de Blanchelande had taken saved Le Cap, but the preparation otherwise had been thorough and complete, and in a few days one-half of the famous North Plain was a flaming ruin. From Le Cap the whole horizon was a wall of fire. From this wall continually rose thick black volumes of smoke, through which came tongues of fire leaping to the very sky. For nearly three weeks the people of Le Cap could barely distinguish day from night, while a rain of burning cane straw, driven before the wind like flakes of snow, flew over the city and the shipping in the harbour, threatening both with destruction.

(10) Haiti: Superstition

Francis Huxley, *The Invisibles*

Belief in the supernatural is widespread in Haiti, even among the élite. Haitians of all social classes often turn to houngans in their houmfors (temples) to help them achieve their desires.

It's common knowledge that, before election time, politicians not only frequent houngans to do down their rivals, but try to sleep with mad-women, for luck; and if they can't find a madwoman they make do with an old granny. Everybody says so. A week before polling day the asylum at Pont Beudet becomes sporadically popular, with cars drawing up in the lanes around. I admire the stomach of any politician, willing to put himself to Bedlam even for such a desperate cause.

Many of the elite (say some of the elite) have their own houmfors, tucked away in a corner of their country estates, with a resident houngan. That way they can attend to their supernatural affairs when everyone thinks they're merely holidaying; then they can resume their own life as good anti-superstitious Catholics. There was, I soon gathered, superstition and superstition. Jean, owner of a large business who stayed at my *pension*, enjoyed talking of necromancers, zombis and poisonous herbs, and was never without an audience. Even the kitchen boy would squat on the steps outside the verandah where we sat in our squeaky rocking chairs as the darkness closed in with the scent of tobacco flowers and the occasional crack of a nut from the sablier tree, bursting as it fell. Puffing at his cigar, Jean would divulge magical recipes: how a lime fruit still hanging from its branch would produce a violent poison if pierced by a pin and left for twenty-four hours. A dreadful poison, salicylic acid. Worse was the yolk of an egg left to dry on a corrugated iron roof and then moistened by the early morning dew, and fatal a plant whose leaves, if you happened to touch them, brought you out in leprous boils. However, rub yourself with the undersurface of the leaf, and you could be cured.

'Ah, *les feuilles,*' he continued, scratching his nose. 'Did you ever hear about Heckmann? Heckmann, the great botanist, he went everywhere in Haiti, he knew everything. Heckmann was climbing the path to Christophe's castle at La Ferrière, when he stopped and let his companion go on ahead. "Why do you stop?" "I can't tell you here," he said. Up at the top he told him. "It was the tree of good and evil. I've only seen it once before, in Africa, and there it was again, by the path. But I daren't tell anyone about it. I can't tell them what it looks like. Imagine someone with a leaf of that tree in his hand, he could do anything." '

(11) HAITI: TAP-TAPS
Ian Thomson, *'Bonjour Blanc'*

Getting around Haiti by public transport can be an exciting, even alarming, experience.

The tap-tap from Jérémie to Les Cayes was four hours late in departure. A rickety piece of junk, it was named *L'Espérance* and bore the hopeful legend: '*Souviens Que Tu Es Poussière*', also to be found above the gates of the cemetery at Port-au-Prince. Haitians are generally a gracious people and one of the dubious pleasures of travel by tap-tap is the antique courtesy with which they salute one another as they clamber on board. Very soon there was standing room only, despite the sign which proclaimed in peculiar English: 'Passengers are not Permitted to Stand Forward While the Bus Is Either at a Standstill or Approaching in Motion.'

Riding tap-taps is a perilous business: accidents occur with horrific regularity owing to bald or flat tyres, and to the speed with which buses pull out in front of approaching traffic to avoid potholes. '*La Route Tue et Blesse*' is a common roadsign in Haiti, although no one pays it much attention. I felt unhappy about our driver: hunched over the open bonnet, he was pouring motor oil into the engine with a lighted cigarette glued to his lower lip, the Comme il Faut bobbing up and down as he engaged a passer-by in lively conversation.

'*Allez, chauffeur!*' An old woman grudgingly urged the driver to get a move on. Passengers continued to arrive – young girls shouldering sacks of charcoal, a man riding an ass who dismounted with a crate of Kola bottles. Then a beggar on crutches swung up to my window, rattling an old Carnation milk tin against the side of the bus: '*Blanc, blanc. Ba'moin un gourde, blanc!*'

Presently the *Espérance* lurched into life, and a tape-recorded voice graced the passengers jammed in the back with a prayer designed expressly to guard against the danger of a road accident: '*Chers clients*', it intoned. 'Let us pray to the *Bon Dieu* and to all the most merciful martyrs in heaven that we may be delivered safely unto our chosen destination. Amen.'

One more customer had yet to arrive. She waddled on board, a woman of substantial girth carrying two babies and an oil drum. In my experience the last person to mount a tap-tap is invariably very large, depriving the passengers of any remaining space. True to form, this bus would not leave until packed with more cargo than one would have thought possible. I surrendered my seat to the bulky newcomer and she eased herself on to the leopardskin upholstery with a '*Merci, chéri*', later extracting a breast for the babies.

(12) HAITI: VOODOO

William Seabrook, *The Magic Island*

Having befriended a voodoo priestess, Seabrook is invited to attend a ceremony which includes the ritual sacrifice of a bull.

From this swirling, milling ceremony of purification, figures leaped out dancing and screaming glory; here and there in the crowd a still higher, shriller, more unearthly shriek announced the pentecostal, invisible, yet flame-like descent of the *lois*, spirits of the gods and of the *mysteres*, entering the bodies of individual dancers. This final phenomenon of ultimate and overwhelming religious ecstacy, as I observed it at this and other Voodoo ceremonials seen subsequently, never became general or contagious. True, the entire crowd was now becoming frenzied and ecstatic, but they remained *themselves* in *ecstacy*. This other force, which struck a few separate individuals here and there like lightning, swept all self away, and those thus stricken became actually, in the technical, religious sense of the word, *possessed*. No need for me to insist here on the absolute subjective reality of this phenomenon. It has been common to all religions during periods of deep, mystical faith.

Not more than a dozen or at most fifteen scattering individuals that night experienced personally this ultimate and self-destroying illumination, but the coming of the *lois* was a signal to all that the gods had been appeased, and were propitiously disposed, so that they could abandon themselves without fear to joyous, savage exultation.

And now the literary-traditional white stranger who spied from hiding in the forest, had such a one lurked near by, would have seen all the wildest tales of Voodoo fiction justified: in the red light of torches which made the moon turn pale, leaping, screaming, writhing black bodies, blood-maddened, sex-maddened, god-maddened, drunken, whirled and danced their dark saturnalia, heads thrown weirdly back as if their necks were broken, white teeth and eyeballs gleaming, while couples seizing one another from time to time fled from the circle, as if pursued by furies, into the forest to share and slake their ecstacy.

(13) JACMEL
Hesketh Prichard, *Where Black Rules White*

Arriving in 1900 in the southern port city of Jacmel, Prichard suffers immediately from severe culture shock.

Through the dust and glare wizened donkeys trotted, laden with huge bundles of guinea-grass, negresses hawked about baskets of bananas and mangoes, the street was full of men and women, screaming, gesticulating, and shouting. A bareheaded negro was blowing a tin trumpet in long ringing blasts. The din was incredible. There were women carrying loads upon their heads; one was half-running with a bottle balanced on a yellow bandana tied around her brows. Most of them were dressed in white, short-kilted to the knee, and nearly all wore the turban handkerchief. As for the men, some had coats, some only trousers, and some, more ragged than the rest, affected kepis with red bands. These last, I discovered later, were policemen.

No carriages were to be seen, not even a broken-down West Indian buggy. It was my first impression of the land where Black rules White. The bawl and clatter of voices, the jostling crowd, the scream of an angry man in the hot street, the few cool stores with their sprawling side-posts, the sun, the smell, the dirt: – this was Hayti.

The British Consular Agent, to whom I had brought a letter of introduction, was most kind, and offered to put me up for the night, a proposal which I was only too glad to accept. Failing this hospitality, I should have been obliged to bivouac in the open; for Jacmel, though the principal port in southern Hayti, does not boast either hotel or rest-house where one could hope for a night's shelter.

(14) PORT-AU-PRINCE: BLACK AND WHITE
Patrick Leigh Fermor, *The Traveller's Tree*

Haiti's tiny pale-skinned élite has always enjoyed a life of ostentatious luxury, in contrast to the vast majority of black Haitians.

Smart life in Haiti – the dazzling white tropical suits, the dark heads and hands – resembles a photographic negative. Only white chauffeurs at the wheel of the grand limousines are absent to complete the illusion. *Chabane Choucoune*, the fashionable night club of Port-au-Prince, is perched on the mountain-side above the capital in the cool suburbs of Pétionville. It is a replica of an African kraal, a great cylinder of bamboo with a steep conical roof which simultaneously achieves, by a skilful twist of sophistication, the amenities, the low lights and the luxury of an expensive night club with the atmosphere of the dwelling of an equitorial monarch.

But there was nothing remotely primitive about the Christmas Eve gathering. Men in beautifully made white suits and dinner jackets danced with women dressed in the height of fashion. They were superb, far the best-looking we had seen in any of the islands: tall, broad-shouldered, narrow-waisted and long-legged, with a fine carriage of the head and great elegance of movement and gesture. What a relief to see this colour and splendour and extravagance after the shapeless dresses of the colonies! Many of our neighbours were pale in complexion, but the majority were of an imposing ebony. A woman sitting at the next table was perhaps the most beautiful in a room full of sable Venuses. She had fine dark features of extraordinary delicacy and regularity, and sat with her elbows leaning on the table, clasping and unclasping her long ringed fingers as she talked . . .

It was about an hour short of dawn before we got back to our hotel. When, at last, slightly dizzy, I went upstairs, I must have mistaken the door, for suddenly I found myself in a strange room. A small fire of logs and charcoal had been built on a sheet of tin in the centre of the floor, filling the upper half of the room with smoke. Round it squatted a peasant family, a man and three little girls of diminishing size, and an old woman who was cooking their breakfast. Their gourd-plates were being filled with ladlefuls of hot maize. Five startled black faces turned in my direction, their dark features and the whites of their eyes very distinct in the firelight. We might have been in the heart of the Congo.

(15) PORT-AU-PRINCE: GREENELAND

Graham Greene, *The Comedians*

*The narrator, Brown, has returned to the Haitian capital at the peak
of Papa Doc Duvalier's reign of terror. He meets his lover, Martha,
and they drive up to the hotel which he owns, the Trianon.*

In the public park the musical fountain stood black, waterless, unplaying.
Electric globes winked out the nocturnal message, *'Je suis le drapeau Haitïen,
Uni et Indivisible. François Duvalier.'*

We passed the blackened beams of the house the Tontons had destroyed
and mounted the hill towards Pétionville. Half-way up there was a
road-block. A man in a torn shirt and a grey pair of trousers and an old hat
which someone must have discarded in a dustbin came trailing his rifle by
its muzzle to the door. He told us to get out and be searched. 'I'll get out,' I
said, 'but this lady belongs to the diplomatic corps.'

'Darling, don't make a fuss,' she said. 'There are no such things as
privileges now.' She led the way to the roadside, putting her hands above
her head and giving the militiaman a smile I hated . . .

Suddenly, around us, above us and below us, the lights went out. Only a
glow remained around the harbour and the government buildings.

'I hope Joseph has kept a bit of oil for my return,' I said. 'I hope he's wise
as well as virgin.'

'Is he virgin?'

'Well, he's chaste. Since the Tontons Macoute kicked him around.'

We entered the steep drive lined with palm trees and bougainvillaea. I
always wondered why the original owner had called the hotel the Trianon.
No name could have been less suitable. The architecture of the hotel was
neither classical in the eighteenth-century manner nor luxurious in the
twentieth-century fashion. With its towers and balconies and wooden
fretwork decorations it had the air at night of a Charles Adams house in a
number of the *New Yorker*. You expected a witch to open the door to you or
a maniac butler, with a bat dangling from the chandelier behind him. But
in the sunlight, or when the lights went on among the palms, it seemed
fragile and period and pretty and absurd, an illustration from a book of
fairy-tales.

(16) PORT-AU-PRINCE: RICH AND POOR

Herbert Gold, *Best Nightmare on Earth*

Long-time Haiti resident Herbert Gold reflects on the curious symbiosis of the rich élite and their poor servants in the capital's wealthier districts.

Port-au-Prince erased the distinction between heaven and hell. It served nicely as both, and included endless chaotic misery along with the grace, that predatory graciousness, of the wealth found as you moved up the hillsides into purer air, the Canapé Vert and Pacot districts, and then further up towards Pétionville, the suburb of the rich. In town, the gingerbread houses of the old elite seemed to be spun out of spaghetti and lace and candy sugar, mincing and flirting and shivering in the jaws of the termites, an architectural erasure of sense. It was appropriate to a world where people flew like birds, sent messages without wire or words, sang,

> Caroline A-cao, dance till it hurts, O!
> Just dance till it hurts, O!

Streams of the poor wandered through elegant Pétionville, like ants in a fine house. Harborside in Port-au-Prince, in the Martissant district, the rich established little outposts of luxury, elaborate fortresses and fantasy mansions, complete with walls protected by broken glass and barbed wire. Protective servants lounged at the gates day and night.

Outside their gardens, often only a few steps away, there were *terrains vagues* of rotting mangoes, dead chickens, tangled underbrush and charcoal cooking fires for the lean-to shacks of those lucky enough to find work as helpers to the blessed. The rich swam through this sea almost as if the poor were invisible. It was said that many elite Haitians could make love without embarassment in a space where servants provided drinks or food or simply waited to be summoned. A friend asked, 'Would you be troubled, mon cher, to embrace your wife in the presence of a dog or a chicken?' He had a PhD in Philosophy and later went to teach at a university in Virginia.

(17) PORT-AU-PRINCE: SLUMS

Amy Wilentz, *The Rainy Season*

The slum of La Saline is Port-au-Prince's worst, a breeding ground for despair and disease. In the midst of Haiti's political turmoil, Amy Wilentz discovers the shantytown's humanity.

The day I came down from Boutilliers with the painting I had sworn never to buy, Port-au-Prince was burning and the Dominican stations were playing merengue. On the long way down Avenue John Brown, I had seen clouds of black smoke coming up from barricades all over town, mostly from the St-Martin slums and the Boulevard Jean-Jacques Dessalines, Port-au-Prince's main street, often less grandiloquently called Grande Rue. I wanted to see whether La Saline was burning, too, and I wanted to get there before the rain. I had friends in La Saline. I wondered how Mimette was, for example.

When she is not busy with her kite, Mimette likes to sit on my lap on a broken-down chair in front of her shack and ask me for presents. She knows that where I come from is called Nouyok, but she thinks it's somewhere just outside La Saline. She told me she was born in a place called Brooklyn in Cité Soleil, like her mother, but they moved to La Saline because someone got sick and her father lost his job and her mother needed to buy from a different middleman, and I couldn't really understand the whole story or even parts of it, but Mimette and her mother and a long list of brothers and sisters – each one lovingly mentioned by Mimette – ended up at the end of the whole long story very near the river of mud and sewage that runs right through the marketplace during the rainy season. The river of mud is clogged with orange peel and mango pits, with piles of rotten tobacco and decaying cattle skins, and rocks here and there to step on, steppingstones irregularly placed, and a lost yellow slipper over there, made of plastic, and another a few paces down. Mimette walks lightly through the whole thing like a thoughtless kitten, in her clean white dress, with me following awkwardly behind, splashing mud.

Biographical and literary notes

BANKS, Russell (1940–). Born in the USA, Banks is the author of ten novels and collections of short stories. He has lived and worked in Florida, Jamaica and other parts of the Caribbean. In *Continental Drift* (Extract 4), he traces the long and dangerous exodus of Haitian refugee Vanise Dorsinville to the hoped-for sanctuary of Miami. Interweaving the theme of Haiti's boat people with the story of New Englander Bob Dubois and his personal crisis, Banks uses the idea of migration as a wider metaphor for yearnings, material and emotional.

CARPENTIER, Alejo (1904–1980). See under Cuba. At first interested in the literary vogue of *negrismo*, the exploration of African popular culture, Carpentier coined the term 'magical realism' in his preface to *The Kingdom of This World* (Extract 1). The story tells of the turbulent period of Haitian independence from the first 1791 slave uprising to the creation of King Henri Christophe's short-lived kingdom. Its mix of historical detail and lyrical imagery foreshadows some of the later Latin American exponents of magical realism. Carpentier's other well known novels include *The Lost Steps*, 1953, and *Explosion in a Cathedral*, 1963.

CLITANDRE, Pierre (1954–). A writer, painter and prominent opponent of the Duvalier dictatorship,

Pierre Clitandre

Clitandre edited the opposition newspaper *Le Petit Samedi Soir* from 1978 to 1980, when he was arrested and sent into exile. He has subsequently worked as a journalist in New York and Haiti. *Cathedral of the August Heat* (Extract 5) is a fantastic account of the bizarre events leading up to 15 August, the Day of the Assumption of the Virgin and the date on which the Haitian slave revolution began in 1791. Clitandre's contemporary allegory hints at the popular uprising which was eventually to overthrow Baby Doc Duvalier in 1986. The novel is dedicated to 'my father, who disappeared in the custody of the Tontons Macoutes when going to visit a friend, July 16, 1982.'

DAVIS, Wade (1953–). A Harvard-trained anthropologist, Wade Davis's interests lie in ethnobotany, the way in which societies use plants. This led him to investigate the scientific foundations of zombification in Haiti and the relationship between voodoo and the so-called 'living dead'. Criticized in some quarters as sensationalist, *The Serpent and the Rainbow* (Extract 3) tells the dramatic tale of Davis's search for the natural ingredients used to turn people into zombies. The book was later adapted into a lurid film by Wes Craven, the director of *Nightmare on Elm Street*. Wade Davis has also written a number of scholarly books and papers on related themes.

DIEDERICH, Bernard and BURT, Al. Diederich and Burt are journalists, whose specialities have been Latin American and Caribbean current affairs. Their *Papa Doc* (Extract 8) was one of the first and fullest accounts of the Duvalier dictatorship. With an introduction by Graham Greene, the book traces the relentless rise to absolute power of the seemingly meek country doctor. Both authors were experienced journalists, Diederich having reported for the *New York Times* and *Time-Life* and Burt for the *Miami Herald*. Diederich, a veteran specialist in Caribbean politics, is also the author of a biography of the Dominican dictator, Trujillo.

GOLD, Herbert (1924–). Born in Cleveland, Ohio, and educated at Columbia University and the Sorbonne, Gold is a novelist who has tended to concentrate on Jewish American themes in books such as *My Last Two Thousand Years*, 1972. He has spent much time in Haiti, first living there in 1953 and returning frequently ever since. According to Jan Morris, *Best Nightmare on Earth* (Extract 16), 'manages to interpret the most peculiar of States in familiar human terms of empathy, compassion, and even admiration.'

GREENE, Graham (1904–1991). See also under Cuba. The author of more than 30 novels. 'entertainments', plays, travel books and essays, Greene is one of Britain's best-known and most popular twentieth-century writers. His religious, moral and political concerns stretch from meditations on original sin and redemption to the fight for social justice in Latin America. The locales for his fictional explorations of human anguish are equally diverse: his most famous novels are set in Sierra Leone (*The Heart of the Matter*), Mexico (*The Power and the Glory*), Vietnam (*The Quiet American*) and the Congo (*A Burnt-Out Case*). Greene first visited Haiti during the relatively trouble-free years of Paul Magloire's presidency (1950–56) when the country was a chic tourist destination for celebrities such as Noel Coward, Irving Berlin and Truman Capote. When he returned in 1963 it was during the darkest days of 'Papa Doc' Duvalier's 13-year tyranny, when the infamous Tontons Macoutes repressed all opposition. Greene's evocation of Duvalier's Haiti in *The Comedians* (Extract 15) is among his most powerful recreations of place and atmosphere. Against a brooding and sinister backcloth of murder, voodoo and menace, Greene's characters play out their personal dramas of infidelity, amorality and loss of faith. Greene insisted that his image of Haiti was rooted in reality. In the preface to the novel, he writes, 'Poor Haiti itself and the character of Doctor Duvalier's rule are not invented, the latter not even blackened for dramatic effect. Impossible to deepen that night.' Greene has been criticized for creating a racist picture of Haiti, with its emphasis on squalor and cruelty, but others have recognized *The Comedians* as a masterful depiction of a terrifying dictatorship. Certainly, Papa Doc himself did not approve of the novel. He personally reviewed it in the state-run *Le Matin* newspaper, concluding, 'The book is not well written. Merely the work of a journalist, the book is worthless.' Subsequently, Papa Doc paid for an elaborate and glossy brochure entitled *Graham Greene Démasqué Finally Exposed* to be distributed to the press in Europe. Rather fancifully, it described Greene as 'unbalanced, sadistic, perverted . . . a perfect ignoramus . . . the shame of proud and noble England . . . a spy . . . a drug addict . . . a torturer.' Until his death, Graham Greene re-

Graham Greene

mained interested in Haiti and a consistent supporter of democratic opposition to the Duvaliers and their military successors.

HUXLEY, Francis (1923–). Son of Julian Huxley and nephew of Aldous, Francis Huxley is an anthropologist, specializing in 'primitive' cultures and their belief systems. *The Invisibles* (Extract 10) is named after the *loas*, the voodoo deities who come to possess believers in the course of ceremonies. The book explores the role of voodoo in Haitian society and suggests that religious belief acts as a cornerstone in Haitians' everyday struggles against poverty and psychic distress.

JAMES, C.L.R. (see under Trinidad and Tobago). *The Black Jacobins* (Extract 9) has been hailed as the most important account and interpretation of the uprising and civil war which ended in the independence of Haiti. Partly a biography of Toussaint Louverture and partly a Marxist analysis of the social forces involved in the conflict, the book is a highly readable history of the world's only successful slave revolution.

LEIGH FERMOR, Patrick (see under Barbados).

LEWIS, Norman. See also under Cuba. Lewis travelled to Haiti three times during Papa Doc's regime and again in the 1970s when Baby Doc Duvalier was in power. His account of the last trip, 'Last Bus to Marmelade' (Extract 7) in *To Run Across the Sea* is an evocative snapshot of Haiti's sinister political culture and its idiosyncratic charms.

MOORE, Brian (1921–). Moore was born and educated in Belfast, a city which features prominently in several of his novels. After the Second World War he worked for the United Nations in Europe before emigrating to Canada in 1948, where he became a journalist and adopted Canadian citizenship. He now lives in California. Moore is the author of many acclaimed novels, including *The Lonely Passion of Judith Hearne*, *The Colour of Blood* and *Lies of Silence*. *No Other Life* (Extract 6) tells of the political rise and fall of a radical Catholic priest in the impoverished Caribbean island of Ganae. In an exact fictional recreation of Jean-Bertrand Aristide's dramatic accession to power in Haiti, Moore paints a highly authentic picture of the country's passion, beauty and violence.

PRICHARD, H. Hesketh (1876–1922). A former Hampshire cricketer, military man and keen hunter, Prichard travelled widely in Patagonia, Labrador, Mexico and Sardinia, producing a number of travelogues and narratives of hunting expeditions. His *Where Black Rules White* (Extract 13) typifies many of the myths and prejudices surrounding foreign perceptions of Haiti, but is also a lively and occasionally perceptive account of his expedition.

ROUMAIN, Jacques (1907–1944). A European-educated son of a wealthy mulatto family, Roumain was both a committed Marxist and champion of an indigenous Haitian literature. As a founder member of the Haitian Communist Party he spent long periods in prison and in exile. When permitted to return to Haiti in 1941, he established the Bureau d'Ethnologie as a centre for studying rural society and popular culture in Haiti. Appointed as *chargé d'affaires* to the Haitian Embassy in Mexico, Roumain was able to concentrate on prose and poetry until his tragically early death. The posthumous *Masters of the Dew*, 1944 (Extract 2) is arguably Haiti's best known novel. It tells of the return from the sugar plantations of Cuba of a radicalized peasant, Manuel, to his drought-stricken village, **Fonds Rouge**. His struggle to organize the community to find a source of water and to revive their peasant economy is a classic piece of socialist realism, extolling the virtues of collective endeavour and political consciousness. Manuel is finally murdered by another peasant in the name of some ancestral feud but only after he has discovered the water source which will save Fonds Rouge from extinction.

SEABROOK, William (1886–1945). Born in Maryland, USA, Seabrook was a widely travelled journalist who specialized in sensationalist travelogues from exotic locales such as Africa, Kurdistan, Arabia and Haiti. *The Magic Island*, 1929 (Extract 12), is typical of a vogue for voodoo stories which coincided with the US occupation of Haiti (1915–34). Seabrook's attention to titillating detail was reinforced by the pseudo–erotic drawings which accompany his text. His view of Haiti was dismissed by the eminent Haitian anthropologist, Jean Price-Mars, as 'insanity and colossal stupidity'. Nonetheless, perhaps predictably, *The Magic Island* became a bestseller.

THOMSON, Ian (1961–). Educated at Dulwich College, London and Cambridge. Thomson has worked as a journalist, writing for British newspapers including the *Independent, Financial Times, Sunday Times* and *Spectator*. He is also the author of a biography of Primo Levi. *'Bonjour Blanc'* (Extract 11) is the best modern travel account of Haiti and stands as a tribute to the author's powers of endurance. Harassed by the authorities, besieged by beggars, and initiated into a voodoo sect, Thomson travelled to parts of the country that most foreigners never see and brought back a rich store of observations and anecdotes.

WILENTZ, Amy (1958–). A Harvard-educated journalist, Amy Wilentz has worked at *The Nation, Newsday* and *Time*. In *The Rainy Season* (Extract 17) she claims that her interest in Haiti was provoked by reading Graham Greene's *the Comedians*. Arriving there in early 1986, she was able to witness at first hand

Amy Wilentz

the departure of dictator 'Baby Doc' Duvalier and the ensuing chaos which gripped the country. She has subsequently been active in pro-democracy pressure groups in the USA.

DOMINICAN REPUBLIC

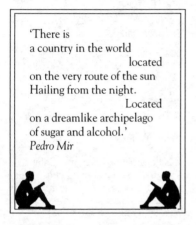

'There is
a country in the world
          located
on the very route of the sun
Hailing from the night.
          Located
on a dreamlike archipelago
of sugar and alcohol.'
Pedro Mir

In October 1992 the Dominican Republic was poised to savour a brief and rare moment of international publicity. As the 500th anniversary of Christopher Columbus's arrival in the Americas approached, the country boasted of being the site of the explorer's first settlement and the place to which he returned on every expedition. 'The land Columbus loved best' claimed the Tourism Ministry's slogan. The government confidently expected that the hyperbole surrounding the Columbus quincentenary would boost its image as a booming tourism destination and reinforce its claim to be the 'cradle of the Americas'.

To commemorate the event, the 85-year-old president, Joaquín Balaguer, had ordered the construction in **Santo Domingo** of a bizarre lighthouse, shaped like a recumbent cross, from which beams of light would be projected far up into the night sky. As expensive as it was grotesque, the lighthouse was originally commissioned in the 1930s after an international competition was held to select a monument to mark the 450th anniversary. The contest was won by Joseph Gleave, an architecture student from Manchester, but his plan was dropped for lack of money. In the run-up to the quincentenary, however, President Balaguer resurrected the plan and building started.

But from the start, the lighthouse project was marred by controversy and bad luck. A slum area near the capital's Ozama river was cleared for the site, and many people claimed that their homes had been bulldozed without compensation. The cost of the monument (put at US$250 million) was deemed obscene by critics who pointed to the country's spectacular poverty and vast foreign debt. The lighthouse, people complained, was a monument to President Balaguer's megalomania; its lights would rob the city of what little electricity it occasionally received. As protests intensified and demonstrators were killed, the Pope announced

> **FACT BOX**
>
> AREA: 48 443 sq km
> POPULATION: 7 803 000
> CAPITAL: Santo Domingo
> LANGUAGES: Spanish
> FORMER COLONIAL POWER: Spain
> INDEPENDENCE: 1844
> PER CAPITA GDP: US$1080

that he would not, after all, inaugurate the lighthouse. The King and Queen of Spain quietly withdrew from the celebrations.

Two days before the planned inauguration, President Balaguer's sister, 73-year-old 'Doña Emma', went for a last inspection of the lighthouse. Hours later, she mysteriously died. A grief-stricken President Balaguer let it be known that he would not after all attend the opening ceremony. Dominicans spoke darkly of a *fukú*, a curse, and reminded themselves that the name of Columbus is always believed to bring bad luck.

The lighthouse story somehow typifies the history of the Dominican Republic. The legacy of Columbus looms large in the country, as do the personal whims of presidential strongmen. The desire to underline the nation's European ancestry is also a dominant theme in the country's past and present, since the Dominican Republic defines itself in large part by its separateness from its overwhelmingly African neighbour, Haiti.

From Colony to Nation

The island where Columbus established his first settlement was known to its indigenous Arawak population as *Quisqueya*. It was, and is, a land of exceptional beauty, with fast-flowing rivers, high mountains and abundant forest and pasture. As Columbus reported with evident awe in the so-called *Letter of Columbus* (Extract 1), the island was 'a marvel' of tropical fertility. Columbus called the place La Española (Hispaniola) and claimed it for the Spanish Crown.

According to the publicists of the Dominican government, the island was Columbus's favourite among the whole Caribbean; in reality, it was the scene of constant squabbles between him and the other colonists and a vast disappointment in terms of the hoped-for wealth it yielded. There was some gold to begin with, and the Spanish forced the Arawaks to mine it and bring it to them, on pain of punishment or execution. But the gold soon ran out, and with it disappeared the Arawak Indians, exterminated within fifty years of Columbus' arrival by hardship, violence and disease. Attempts to import slaves from among the indigenous people of the Bahamas were largely unsuccessful.

The genocide of the indigenous population was witnessed by a Spanish priest, Bartolomé de las Casas, whose testimony remains one of the most chilling accounts of man's inhumanity to man. In *A Short Account of the Destruction of the Indies*, 1552, Las Casas recounts how the Spanish practised a sort of systematic sadism on the Arawaks:

> 'They spared no one, erecting especially wide gibbets on which they could string their victims up with their feet just off the ground and then burn them alive thirteen at a time, in honour of our Saviour and the twelve Apostles, or tie dry straw to their bodies and set fire to it. Some they chose to keep alive and simply cut their wrists, leaving their hands dangling, saying to them: "Take this letter" – meaning that their sorry condition would act as a warning to those hiding in the hills.'

Appalled by these atrocities, Las Casas called for legal protection for the Arawaks and the importation of African slaves to replace them in the mines and fields of the colony. It was too late for the original inhabitants of *Quisqueya*, whose last desperate revolt was led by the legendary *cacique* (chief) Enriquillo, but Las Casas's suggestion of using African labour was to be influential in the growth of the slave system throughout the Caribbean.

As the natural wealth of Hispaniola dried up, the colony gradually fell into decline. After gold proved a disappointment, the colonists planted sugar-cane, imported from the Canary Islands by Columbus. But with insufficient labour the plantation system could not work effectively, and the colony failed to prosper. It had the first cathedral, the first university, the first real European-style metropolis in Latin America, but the city of **Santo Domingo** had lost its prestige in comparison to the gold- and silver-rich colonies of Peru and Mexico. Within a century of its foundation, Hispaniola became a somnolent backwater of the Spanish empire.

Meanwhile, French buccaneers had begun to settle in the west of the island, and they, as well as English adventurers such as Sir Francis Drake, preyed on Santo Domingo and the other Spanish settlements. Eventually, growing French power and Spanish weakness were recognized in the 1697 Treaty of Ryswick, which ceded the western third of Hispaniola to France after a twelve-year war. This was the start of Hispaniola's partition and created the French colony of Saint Domingue, later to become independent Haiti.

While Saint Domingue became highly profitable as a slave-based sugar producer, Santo Domingo continued to languish under a series of incompetent Spanish administrations. Although its neighbour exported sugar worth more than all British Caribbean exports put together, the Spanish colony was a poor, underpopulated ranching economy, surviving on trade with its neighbour. Its relative backwardness meant that its social and cultural composition remained more stubbornly Spanish and feudal than almost anywhere else in the region. As Sumner Welles shows in *Naboth's Vineyard*, the habits and mannerisms of Spain lived on in Santo Domingo throughout the centuries.

The Haitian revolution (1791–1804) threw this sleepy colony into turmoil. As a bewildering sequence of events, involving French, British and Spanish forces, rocked the island, Santo Domingo was invaded by the French and the troops of the slave leader, Toussaint Louverture, in 1794. It was not until 1809 that the French were finally driven out of Santo Domingo, but by that time the revolutionary armies of former slaves had beaten off French and British military might to create independent Haiti. As Spain's lacklustre colonial administration continued, the Haitian regime of President Jean-Pierre Boyer decided to unify the island and Haitian troops marched unopposed into Santo Domingo.

Today, many Dominicans like to claim that the 22-year Haitian occupation was a nightmare of repression and barbarism. In fact, the Haitians abolished slavery, distributed land to poor peasants and broke up the power of the church and the old élite. Nevertheless, resentment against the occupying forces grew and a Dominican nationalist movement began to press for independence. In 1844, a secret organization known as *la Trinitaria* led a successful revolt against the Haitian authorities. Under the leadership of Juan Pablo Duarte, the new nation of the Dominican Republic came into being, the name Spanish Haiti having been considered and rejected.

DICTATORS AND DOLLARS

From the outset, the Dominican Republic was unstable and violent, fought over by competing *caudillos* (strongmen) with their armed retinues. The Haitians tried to recapture the territory on three occasions, and consequently Dominicans looked overseas for protection from what they saw as an aggressive neighbour. In 1861, after much pleading from President Pedro Santana, Spain agreed to reannex its former colony – an unprecedented event in the history of the Americas. But it was a disaster; the Spanish ruled as badly as before and alienated the majority of Dominicans who rebelled and regained independence in 1865. Even then, successive governments tried to sell or lease the republic to foreign powers, using as bait the superb natural harbour of **Samaná** on the country's north-east coast. In 1869 the Dominican Republic came close to becoming part of the USA when President Ulysses S. Grant agreed to annex the territory, only to lose a vote in the US Senate. That same year, an American journalist, Samuel Hazard ◊, visited the country and made the case for annexation. The picture he drew (Extract 9) was of a chaotic and exotic country, dilapidated and decaying but rich with potential.

In the event, the annexationists had their wishes fulfilled in 1916 when US Marines landed in **Santo Domingo**. The Dominican Republic had passed through an exceptionally turbulent period (22 governments in 17 years) and had defaulted on its foreign debt. Under the inspiration of the Monroe Doctrine, the USA moved in to clear up the country's finances, prevent further unrest and preserve the region's stability. With the Marines came large amounts of US capital, as investors rushed to buy into the country's expanding sugar industry. Sugar boomed in the wake of the First World War, which had destroyed European beet production. During the eight-year occupation, the Dominican landscape changed beyond recognition. Vast sugar plantations replaced peasant smallholdings, and the traditional *terrenos comuneros* (common lands) were broken up and sold off. In his novel *Cuando amaban las tierras comuneras* (*When They Loved the Communal Lands*), poet Pedro Mir laments the passing of the peasant's attachment to his land through the figure of *El Viejo* ('the veteran'):

> 'I know that you people can't understand this because you believe only what you see and the thing that counts most is what you don't see and roots are the most important part of a plant and they're not seen and you can cut a tree down to the ground and it will grow again because it has roots and the roots don't die as long as they're sunk into the land.'

The US occupation and the sugar boom abruptly pulled the Dominican Republic into the twentieth century. The country's infrastructure improved, roads, railways and tramways appeared, towns took on a veneer of modernization. The old landed élite, descended from the Spanish ruling class and based in the agricultural heartland around **Santiago**, prospered. But the Marines also left behind another legacy; they had trained a new 'professional' army, the Guardia Nacional, to take over when they left in 1924. Among this force was one Rafael Leonidas Trujillo, a former petty thief and plantation foreman.

Using the Guardia Nacional to force his way to power, Trujillo became one of Latin America's longest-lived and most ruthless dictators, ruling from 1930 to 1961. With his family and supporters, Trujillo effectively took control of the country and turned it into his own private fiefdom. When journalist William Krehm ◊ visited the Dominican Republic during the 1940s and asked a peasant to whom a particularly fine bull belonged, he received the simple answer '*Es del Jefe*' ('It's the Boss's'). In his *Democracies and Tyrannies of the Caribbean* (Extract 7), Krehm paints a disturbing picture of a dictatorship both sinister and comic, where everything from the capital city to the country's highest mountain was renamed after the *Jefe*.

Under Trujillo, the Dominican Republic became a parody of the region's so-called 'banana republics'. Foreign fruit companies, a bemedalled dictator, a cowed peasantry and a repressed intelligentsia: all the classic ingredients of 1940s Latin American melodrama were there. Trujillo killed and tortured at will. He even sent secret agents to kill dissidents abroad and attempted to have President Rómulo Betancourt of Venezuela, an outspoken critic, assassinated. A particularly brutal incident was the murder of the three Mirabal sisters, known popularly as the *mariposas* (butterflies), who were prominent critics of the dictatorship. In her novel, *In the Time of the Butterflies* (Extract 6) Julia Alvarez ◊ draws a compelling picture of the women's heroism and eventual martyrdom.

But there were also plenty of apologists, Dominican and foreign, who were prepared to praise the Generalisimo and the stability he brought to the country. Washington tolerated him as its 'son of a bitch' and a better option than any radical or communist. A strange personality cult grew up, and many a North American or European fellow traveller contributed to the myth of Trujillo the Benefactor. In their undistinguished 1950s travelogue, *Caribbean Cocktail*, for instance, Everild Young and K. Helwig-Larsen write in tones similar to those of admirers of Stalin's Russia:

> 'Ciudad Trujillo is now a delightful modern city, with wide avenues framed in flowers, spacious parks and large fountains, where the poor children are allowed to bathe and enjoy themselves. The inhabitants have to thank their energetic President for this, and the capital has been re-named in his honour, becoming Ciudad Trujillo, instead of Santo Domingo de Guzmán.'

As the dictatorship held on to power, opposition grew. Exiled social-democrats founded the Dominican Revolutionary Party (PRD), headed by professor and writer Juan Bosch. Discontent was also increasing among the military and the traditional oligarchy, who resented Trujillo's crude monopoly of power and wealth. On 30 May 1961, the ageing Generalisimo was gunned down by disgruntled officers in **Santo Domingo** as he went to visit one of his mistresses.

Trujillo's death created a dramatic power vacuum and a fierce struggle between the remnants of his regime and a new generation of reformists. After an interim government had been overthrown by the military, elections were held and overwhelmingly won by the PRD. Juan Bosch, the long-time exile and intellectual became president of the Dominican Republic. Yet the tensions at the heart of Dominican society were far from resolved. The conservative élite, glad to be rid of Trujillo, were also suspicious of Bosch and his promises of land reform. After only seven months, hardline officers organized a coup against the PRD government and Bosch was once again in exile.

Conflicts intensified in the aftermath of the coup and an interim *junta* was again overthrown. The armed forces divided between right-wing advocates of military rule and more progressive supporters of Bosch and the democratic constitution. In a volatile and confused process of polarization, civil war began to break out. In **Santo Domingo**, whole *barrios* were controlled by armed supporters of the PRD; they were bombarded by troops loyal to General Elias Wessín y Wessín. As full-scale insurrection seemed inevitable, US President Lyndon Johnson dispatched troops to Santo Domingo to quell the fighting. As ever, the White House feared that communism would feed on the disintegration of Dominican society (a fear later shown to be baseless) and justified its intervention as a measure to safeguard American lives. This pretext appeared hollow to many and was mocked by satirical writer Art Buchwald in the *Washington Post*, who imagined a dialogue between a US general and a hapless and mystified American tourist, Sydney, who only wants to leave the country but cannot because he is the last American left whose life must be protected:

' "Sidney, have you ever heard of the Monroe Doctrine?"

"Yeah, I guess so."

"Well, you're part of it. Your name will go down in history books with Teddy Roosevelt and Admiral Dewey. When school teachers ask their pupils who saved the Dominican Republic from going Communist, the children are going to have to answer, 'Sidney'."

Just then the phone rang. The general picked it up.

"It's the President, Sidney. He wants to speak to you."

"Yes, sir, Mr President. No, I'm just fine. I'll stay here as long as you want me to. That's nice of you to say. You're a good American too." '

On this occasion, the USA stayed only long enough to organize elections in June 1966, in which a chastened and subdued Bosch lost to Joaquín Balaguer, Trujillo's former puppet president.

OLD AND NEW

Since 1966 the Dominican Republic has had the outward appearance of a modern democracy. Elections take place every four years, the military remains in its barracks, and a lively press is able to criticize the government without ending up in one of Trujillo's torture chambers. But the old habits of dictatorship have also died hard. Every election has been plagued by allegations of fraud and intimidation, and in each contest except between 1978 and 1986, Balaguer emerged triumphant. In the 1970s Balaguer was alleged to have intimidated his opponents with a paramilitary death squad, known simply as *La Banda*; possibly a thousand activists, mostly from the PRD, were murdered. In 1996, at the age of 89, the blind patriarch finally stood down, having won yet another bitterly controversial election two years earlier. Bosch, for his part, never regained the presidency, although most Dominicans believe he won the elections of 1990. In 1994 he retired from politics at the age of 85.

If the old guard has dominated politics, the economy has been changed and rejuvenated by a dramatic process of diversification. Much of the country's dependence on sugar has gone, to be replaced by a strategy of attracting foreign tourists and foreign businesses. Almost two million tourists visited the Dominican Republic in 1995, lured by its relative cheapness, superb beaches, and, in some cases, sex tourism. At the same time, US and Asian manufacturers have come in considerable numbers to set up factories where Dominican workers can be paid a fraction of what employees at home would demand.

Not that economic transformation has brought widespread affluence.

Outside the up-market suburbs of **Santo Domingo**, the capital city has some of the region's most squalid shantytowns. A severe recession in the early 1980s led to the arrival of the International Monetary Fund and a draconian austerity programme which raised prices and cut services. The result was a traumatic uprising in April 1984 which left hundreds dead, shot down by troops. In the countryside, conditions are no better, and increasing numbers of Dominicans are tempted to flee the country altogether, attempting to reach the US via Puerto Rico in small and dangerous fishing boats. Every year thousands of Dominicans brave the 70-mile Mona Passage which separates their country from Puerto Rico. In her short story, 'The Day It All Happened' (Extract 2), Puerto Rican writer Ana Lydia Vega describes the way in which Dominicans, both legal and illegal, have imposed their identity on parts of Puerto Rico.

ENEMIES AND NEIGHBOURS

The old animosity with Haiti persists to this day. Most Dominicans will readily admit to fearing their poorer and more populous neighbour, and anti-Haitian racism is rife in all layers of society. In the 1994 election, a black candidate for the presidency was the object of a sustained propaganda campaign which sought to paint him as a Haitian sympathizer bent on unifying the two countries. President Balaguer, meanwhile, is the author of a highly acclaimed book, *La Isla al revés* (*The Island Upside Down*), which contrasts his nation's Hispanic culture with the alleged barbarity of African-dominated Haiti.

Even so, hundreds of thousands of Haitians cross the remote and porous border between the two countries each year, driven by poverty and the hope of finding work. Many work in what remains of the sugar plantations, doing hard and dangerous jobs that most Dominicans refuse to do. Living in squalid camps known as *bateyes* and often subjected to abuse and mistreatment, the Haitian *braceros* or cane-cutters have long been the lowest of the low. In September 1937, Trujillo, seeking to engineer conflict with the Haitian government, ordered the wholesale massacre of as many as 20 000 Haitians in the border area. Subsequently, the Duvalier dictatorship supplied fixed numbers of workers to the Dominican state-run sugar industry in return for a *per capita* fee.

In his powerful fictional treatment of life in the *bateyes*, Maurice Lemoine ◊ exposes the daily hardships and humiliations endured by a group of Haitian cane-cutters until they decide to escape to **Santo Domingo**. *Bitter Sugar* (Extract 10) is a startling indictment of 'modern slavery' as well as a realistic depiction of the troubled relations between the two countries.

IDENTITY CRISIS

In 1990 a book entitled *El Ocaso de la nación dominicana* (*The Decline of the Dominican Nation*) was an unexpected bestseller in the capital's bookshops.

The author, Manuel Núñez, bemoaned the loss of an authentic Dominican identity in the face of corrupting foreign influences:

> 'Everything points to the decline of the nation that we once knew
> . . . Culture, language, values – all the things that yesterday made up
> the spiritual frontier – have been submerged by changes in our
> national identity, transforming our rural culture and the spiritual face
> of our towns. We are moving further and further away from what we
> once were, while on top of the ruin of our old selves a new nation is
> born.'

Blaming the 'Haitianization of the countryside and the Americanization of the towns', Núñez gloomily predicted the end of 'Dominicanness' as a distinctive culture.

Yet Americanization has also proved to be a positive influence in Dominican culture, especially among the younger generation of Dominicans who are as much a product of North American culture as the country's older traditions. A writer such as Julia Alvarez, for example, who lives and works in the USA, draws on this complex cross-fertilization to explore questions of personal identity and belonging. In her poem, 'Homecoming: a Dominican Reverie' (Extract 5), Alvarez looks at traditional upper-class Dominican attitudes of *machismo* and snobbery both as outsider and family member. The young US–Dominican writer Junot Díaz also deals with themes of cultural displacement in his short stories, *Drown*, 1996.

Nor was earlier Dominican literature particularly distinctive in terms of its cultural or aesthetic values. In the nineteenth century, poets such as Gastón Fernando Deligne (1861–1912) wrote largely insipid imitations of the French Romantics and *fin-de-siècle* Symbolists, as in 'To Sister Mary of the Snows', a tribute to a beautiful nun:

> Such are you – a hyacinth that spends
> A day atop the grave, then dies.
> With the whiteness intact it sends
> An aroma inviolate to the starry skies . . .
>
> Ineffable serenity will trace
> On your lips a placid and enduing smile,
> At peace with you and the human race
> Without grievance, anguish or bile.

The country's best-known novel, *Enriquillo* (translated as *The Sword and the Cross*) (Extract 4) is also derivative, reminiscent of the 'noble savage' vogue which swept through Europe earlier in the nineteenth century. In the novel, Manuel de Jesús Galván ◊ resurrects the country's last Indian *cacique* and recasts him as a sentimental Romantic figure and a precursor of modern Dominican identity.

The Trujillo years were culturally barren, with all literature subject to censorship and the cult of the Generalisimo's personality. In exile, writers such as Juan Bosch ◊ and Pedro Mir were able to publish their work more freely, with Bosch specializing in gritty and atmospheric tales of peasant life. His short story 'The Woman' (Extract 3) is typical of his sense of landscape and atmosphere. Mir, whose work is unavailable in translation, has been dubbed the Dominican Republic's 'national poet' and was a founder member of the Dominican Communist Party. His work includes the epic poem *Hay un país en el mundo* (*There's a Country in the World*) which lyrically reasserts the role of the long-suffering peasantry in the nation's history. The Dominican Republic has also produced a long and distiguished line of women writers, including Salomé Ureña (1850–1897), Aida Cartagena Portalatin (1918–   ), Hilma Contreras (1913–   ) and, most recently, Julia Alvarez.

The Dominican Republic's most significant cultural contribution in recent years has been not literary, but musical. Since the 1980s, *merengue*, a traditional African dance, has become enormously popular throughout Latin America and to a lesser extent Europe and the USA. Its prime exponent, Juan Luís Guerra, is reputed to be among the world's best-paid performers and songs such as 'Ojalá que llueva café' ('Let's Hope It Rains Coffee') have become international hits.

More than five hundred years after Columbus gazed in awe at the island's lush landscape, the Dominican Republic is still a place of extraordinary beauty. Outside its ramshackle towns and straggling villages lie areas of spectacular countryside. Perhaps no area is more beautiful than the **Samaná Peninsula**, so long coveted by European powers for its natural harbour. In *Touch the Happy Isles* (Extract 8), travel-writer Quentin Crewe ◊ rightly points to the area's magnificent scenery and to a symbolic instance of human suffering which provides a poignant reminder that all is not always perfect in this 'tropical paradise'.

LITERARY LANDMARKS

Santo Domingo. The first European-built city in the Americas, the Dominican capital has fine streets of restored sixteenth-century buildings. The historian Gonzalo Fernández de Oviedo wrote in the 1550s that 'this city is so well built that there is no township in Spain generally better constructed apart from the illustrious and very noble city of Barcelona.' By the nineteenth century, many of Santo Domingo's architectural treasures were in a state of disrepair; once, noted Samuel Hazard, 'there were two or three monasteries, two nunneries, several hospitals, and a number of parochial or minor churches. All, or most of them, are now either extinct or gone to such decay as is sad to witness.' But gradual reconstruction and renovation have transformed the old colonial quarter of the capital into a fascinating historic centre. 'I loved the thickness of the walls,' wrote Quentin Crewe, 'and the way, in the evening as one passed by, they threw out the heat they had gathered in the day from the sun. I loved those long, white-washed walls, with so few windows, perhaps just one wrought iron balcony and a single doorway . . . Most of the buildings are restored, but there is nothing dead about them . . .'. The city centre may have been beautified, but the surrounding *barrios* or slum suburbs are more depressing now than a century ago. Hazard remarked that 'the outskirts of the city are composed of rather unattractive frame or semi-clay huts, roofed with palm or straw', but contemporary visitor Quentin Crewe saw a 'hopeless huddle of corrugated iron and boards all brown and grey-brown like a rusted cubist painting.'

BOOKLIST

The following selection includes the extracted titles in this chapter as well as other titles for further reading. In general, paperback editions are given when possible. For most of the extracted works, the original publisher in English can be found in 'Acknowledgments and Citations' at the end of the volume, as can the exact location of the extracts and the editions from which they are taken.

Alvarez, Julia, *Homecoming*, Plume, New York, 1996. **Extract 5.**

Alvarez, Julia, *In the Time of the Butterflies*, Algonquin Books, Chapel Hill, NC, 1994. **Extract 6.**

Balaguer, Joaquín, *La Isla al revés: Haiti y el destino dominicano*, Libreria Dominicana, Santo Domingo, 1984.

Bosch, Juan, *The Woman*, Nick Caistor, trans, in Anne Walmsley and Nick Caistor, eds, *Facing the Sea: A New Anthology from the Caribbean Region*, Heinemann, Oxford, 1986. **Extract 3.**

Columbus, Christopher, 'Letter', in Peter Hulme and Neil L. Whitehead, eds, *Wild Majesty: Encounters with Caribs from Columbus to the Present Day*, Oxford University Press, Oxford, 1992. **Extract 1.**

Crewe, Quentin, *Touch the Happy Isles: A Journey Through the*

Caribbean, Michael Joseph, London, 1987. **Extract 8.**

Díaz, Junot, *Drown*, Faber and Faber, London, 1996.

Ferguson, James, *Dominican Republic: Beyond the Lighthouse*, Latin America Bureau, London, 1992.

Galván, Manuel de Jesús, *The Sword and the Cross*, Robert Graves trans, Victor Gollancz, London, 1956. **Extract 4.**

Hazard, Samuel, *Santo Domingo, Past and Present; With a Glance at Hayti*, Editora de Santo Domingo, Santo Domingo, 1974. **Extract 9.**

Krehm, William, *Democracies and Tyrannies of the Caribbean*, Lawrence Hill & Company, Westport CT, 1984. **Extract 7.**

Las Casas, Bartolomé de, *A Short Account of the Destruction of the Indies*, Nigel Griffin, trans, Penguin, London, 1992.

Lemoine, Maurice, *Bitter Sugar*, Andrea Johnston, trans, Zed Books, London, 1985. **Extract 10.**

Mir, Pedro, *Cuando amaban las tierras comuneras*, Siglo XXI Editores, Mexico, 1978.

Núñez, Manuel, *El Ocaso de la nación dominicana*, Alfa & Omega, Santo Domingo, 1990.

Townsend, Francis E., *Quisqueya: A Panoramic Anthology of Dominican*

Verse, Editora del Caribe, Ciudad Trujillo, 1954.

Vega, Ana Lydia, 'The Day It All Happened', in Smorkaloff, Pamela Maria, ed, *If I Could Write This in Fire: An Anthology*

of Writing from the Caribbean, New Press, New York, 1994. **Extract 2.**

Welles, Sumner, *Naboth's Vineyard: The Dominican Republic 1844–1924*, Payson & Clarke, 1928.

Extracts

(1) DOMINICAN REPUBLIC: THE ENCOUNTER

Christopher Columbus, *The Letter of Columbus*

In November 1492 Columbus sighted the island which he called La Española (Spanish Isle). His letter recalls the shock of a European encountering the exuberance of tropical nature.

This island and all the others are very fertile to an excessive degree, and this island is extremely so; in it there are many harbours on the coast of the sea, beyond comparison with others that I know in Christendom, and many rivers, good and large, which is marvellous; its lands are high; there are in it many sierras and very high mountains, beyond comparison with the island of Tenerife, all very beautiful, of a thousand shapes, and all accessible and filled with trees of a thousand kinds and tall, seeming to touch the sky; and I am told that they never lose their foliage, which I can believe, for I saw them as green and lovely as they are in Spain in May, and some of them were flowering, some bearing fruit, and some at another stage, according to their quality. The nightingale was singing and other little birds of a thousand kinds, in the month of November, there where I went. There are six or eight kinds of palm, which are a wonder to behold on account of their beautiful variety, but so are the other trees and fruits and plants. In it are marvellous pine groves, and there are very wide champaigns, and there is honey, and birds of many kinds and fruits of great variety. In the interior, there are mines of metals, and the population is without number.

La Spañola is a marvel. The sierras and the mountains and the plains and the champaigns and the lands [are] so lovely and so rich for planting and sowing, for breeding cattle of every kind, for building towns and villages. The harbours of the sea here would not be believed without being seen, and so with the rivers, many and great, and with good water, most of which bear gold. In the trees and fruits and plants, there are many great differences from those of Juana: on this island, there are many spices and great mines of gold and of other metals.

(2) DOMINICAN REPUBLIC: ESCAPE

Ana Lydia Vega, *The Day It All Happened*

Filemón has successfully escaped the poverty of the Dominican Republic to start a new life in Puerto Rico. But his past is about to catch up with him.

Yes, sir. I was there that day at exactly three o'clock in the afternoon when the air outside was like a snowcone compared to the boiling inferno inside that laundry. Steam hung from the eaves, clinging like cellophane. There were more pants in there than in the army. Or, at least, it seemed that way: things were going pretty well for Filemón Sagredo, Jr, in Puerto Rico. Dirty laundry was in abundance this side of the Mona Passage, and on Arzuaga Street in Río Piedras, full of Dominican kiosks and rooming houses, the hot *sancocho* and frozen papaya shakes flowed like back in El Cibao. From time to time a wave of nostalgia for a tear-up-the-floor merengue and the sound of a down-home accent hit real hard, but you could always make a quick trip back to the Republic to see the folks and put in an appearance at the public square and even bring back a few straw mats to sell, make a little extra on the side, and get ahead, yeah.

And so in the Quisqueya Laundry luck had winked at him, from the very day he arrived, numb with fear, on the shores of Eden, just above Bramadero Bay.

That son of a bitch Grullón had let him out far from shore so as not to risk his own hide. And Filemón, along with the other five illegals, had had to swim the rest of the way in, scaring off the sharks with promises to the Virgin of Altagracia.

On the beach, another class of shark attacked him. He had to hand out wet dollars like so many blessings so he wouldn't end up in jail with all the others.

Bribes apart, the little trip had cost him well over five hundred dollars. It's a good thing that in Puerto Rico you're only poor if you want to be. There's no lack of jobs here, no. And you don't have to leave your back and your life in the damn canefields either. Anyone can get by, more or less, selling cones in a Chinese ice-cream shop, working as a short-order cook for some motherless Cuban, fixing flats in a compatriot's garage. Somehow or other, you can weather the storm. Until you get hitched to some Puerto Rican broad and clear things up with Immigration.

(3) Dominican Republic: Heat

Juan Bosch, *The Woman*

The extreme heat and aridity of parts of the Dominican Republic are powerfully evoked in Juan Bosch's short story.

The road is dead. Nothing, nobody can bring it back to life. Stretching out endlessly, not even its grey surface shows any sign of animation. The sun killed it; the metallic, burning red sun, a red so hot it turned white. Then the white metal became transparent , and there it lies, on the road. It must have died many centuries ago. Men dug it up again with picks and shovels. They sang and dug; but there were some who neither sang nor swung their picks. It all took so long. It was easy to tell they had come from far off; they sweated, they stank. At afternoon the white metal turned red, and then a tiny fire sprang up deep in the eyes of the men unearthing the road.

At its sides are thorny bushes. Sight grows weary at so much vastness around it. But the plains are bare. Reed beds in the distance. The occasional bird of prey crowning a cactus. And more cactuses, further off, stuck in the white metal.

There are shacks too, nearly all of them low adobe huts. A few are painted white, invisible in the sunshine. Only their bulky roofs, so dry they seem anxious to catch fire any day, stand out. The reeds have provided the roofing, off which water never runs.

The dead road, utterly dead, lies open to the skies. The woman was at first a black dot, then like a stone left on the outstretched corpse of the road. Lying with no breeze to stir her rags. The sun did not scorch her, only the screams of the child caused her pain. The puny boy seemed cast in bronze, his eyes dazzled with the light, as he clung to his mother and plucked at her with tiny hands. The road would soon be burning the knees of this naked, howling child.

The house was close by, but invisible.

As he drew closer, what looked like a stone left in the middle of the dead road grew and grew. Quico thought: 'It must be a calf that's been knocked down.'

He looked around him: only the plain, the grassland in the distance. A hill far off, covered in reeds, as though it were a heap of sand piled there by the winds. A river bed; the dry muzzle of the land which had water a thousand tears earlier. The golden plain split by the weight of the heavy, colourless metal. And cactuses, cactuses crowned with birds of prey.

Closer still, Quico saw it was a person. He could make out the child bawling.

(4) DOMINICAN REPUBLIC: INDIANS

Manuel de Jesús Galvan, *The Sword and the Cross*

Although in conflict with the forces of the Spanish Crown, the Indian leader, Enriquillo, is determined to show the colonists that he adheres to a chivalrous code of honour.

Again the raucous conches blew, this time giving the order to rally and break off the pursuit. Much blood had flowed and Enriquillo magnanimously decided to spare the survivors. But Tamayo was already far ahead and either did not hear, or did not want to hear, the merciful signal. After waiting for him a quarter of an hour or more, Enriquillo and many of his warriors decided to descend the steep slope down which Tamayo had run after the main body of the fugitives, like a wild beast let loose. Near the foot of the mountain, a few steps fom the path, he at last came upon Tamayo and his men, all busied with a strange task. There was a cave screened by trees, and in front of it a great pile of brushwood and fallen branches had been heaped, almost blocking the mouth. Tamayo's men were grouped in a semi-circle about it and he had just applied a resinous torch to the dry leaves at the edge. Already the flame was spreading voraciously in all directions, and a thick cloud of smoke arose. It eddied here and there, but the wind blew most of it into the cave. Tamayo stood contemplating his work with grim satisfaction.

'What is this?' cried Enriquillo, hurrying up.

'Watch, Cacique,' replied Tamayo. 'We are fumigating the men inside.'

These brutal words were hardly out of his mouth, when Enriquillo leapt on him, pushed him to one side and began to stamp out the blaze and toss the burning pieces of wood far away. His soldiers hurried to help him.

'Barbarian!' he cried indignantly. 'Is this how you interpret my instructions?'

And he shouted into the cave: 'Come out of there, Spaniards! You need have no fear. Enriquillo pledges his word that your lives will be spared!'

The unfortunate men, who were already convinced that their refuge would prove their sepulchre, came out one by one, choking and half-blinded.

Enriquillo counted seventy-two of them.

'Return in peace to La Maguana,' he bade them, 'or wherever you please. Inform the tyrants that I and my Indians know how to defend our liberty; but that we are neither executioners nor villains. You, Martín Alfaro,' he said, turning to a benign-looking Indian at his side, 'escort these men to the plain and let them go in safety. You will answer for their lives with your own.'

Preserved from certain death, the Spaniards clasped their hands in gratitude, and blessed Enriquillo's name. One of them went up to him, kissed his right hand with deep emotion, and said:

'Hear me, my lord Enriquillo. In my tribulation I vowed to God that if you saved me, I would devote the rest of my life to His service. I will keep my vow, and pray daily for your well-being.'

(5) DOMINICAN REPUBLIC: RETURN
Julia Alvarez,
from *Homecoming: a Dominican Reverie*

When my cousin Carmen married, the guards
at her father's *finca* took the guests' bracelets
and wedding rings and put them in an armored truck
for safekeeping while wealthy, dark-skinned men,
and their plump, white women and spoiled children
bathed in a river whose bottom had been cleaned
for the occasion. She was Tío's only daughter,
and he wanted to show her husband's family,
a bewildered group of sunburnt Minnesotans,
that she was valued. He sat me at their table
to show off my English, and when he danced with me,
fondling my shoulder blades beneath my bridesmaid's gown
as if they were breasts, he found me skinny
but pretty at seventeen, and clever.
Come back from that cold place, Vermont, he said,
all this is yours! Over his shoulder
a dozen workmen hauled in blocks of ice
to keep the champagne lukewarm and stole
glances at the wedding cake, a dollhouse duplicate
of the family *rancho*, the shutters marzipan,
the cobbles almonds. A maiden aunt housekept,
touching up whipped cream roses with a syringe
of eggwhites, rescuing the groom when the heat
melted his chocolate shoes into the frosting.
On too much rum Tío led me across the dance floor,
dusted with talcum for easy gliding, a smell
of babies underfoot. He twirled me often,
excited by my pleas of dizziness, teasing me
that my merengue had lost its Caribbean.

(6) DOMINICAN REPUBLIC: TRUJILLO
Julia Alvarez, *In the Time of the Butterflies*

*Forced to dance with the dictator at a social event, Minerva
Mirabal, one of the celebrated 'butterflies', inadvertently mentions
her friend and anti-Trujillo activist, Virgilio Morales.*

His face hardens, suspicion clouds the gaze. 'You know Virgilio Morales?'
What a complete idiot I am! How can I now protect him and myself?

'His family is from El Cibao, too,' I say, choosing my words carefully. 'I know the son teaches at the university.'

El Jefe's gaze is withdrawing further and further into some back room of his mind where he tortures meaning out of the words he hears. He can tell I'm stalling. 'So, you do know him?'

'Not personally, no,' I say in a little voice. Instantly, I feel ashamed of myself. I see now how easily it happens. You give in on little things, and soon you're serving in his government, marching in his parades, sleeping in his bed.

El Jefe relaxes. 'He is not a good person for you to know. He and the others have turned the campus into a propaganda camp. In fact, I'm thinking of closing down the university.'

'Ay, Jefe, no,' I plead with him. 'Ours is the first university in the New World. It would be such a blow to the country!'

He seems surprised by my vehemence. After a long look, he smiles again. 'Maybe I will keep it open if that will draw you to our side.' And then literally, he draws me to him, so close I can feel the hardness at his groin pushing against my dress.

I push just a little against him so he'll loosen his hold, but he pulls me tighter towards him. I feel my blood burning, my anger mounting. I push away, a little more decidedly, again he pulls me aggressively to his body. I push hard, and he finally must let me go.

'What is it?' His voice is indignant.

'Your medals,' I complain, pointing to the sash across his chest. 'They are hurting me.' Too late, I recall his attachment to those *chapitas*.

He glares at me, and then slips the sash over his head and holds it out. An attendant quickly and reverently collects it. El Jefe smiles cynically. 'Anything else bother you about my dress I could take off?' He yanks me by the wrist, thrusting his pelvis at me in a vulgar way, and I can see my hand in an endless slow motion rise – a mind all its own – and come down on the astonished, made-up face.

(7) DOMINICAN REPUBLIC: TRUJILLO

William Krehm,
Democracies and Tyrannies of the Caribbean

> *'Generalisimo' Trujillo ran the Dominican Republic like his own family business. Visiting the country in 1945, journalist William Krehm describes the extent of the dictator's megalomania.*

The Generalisimo collected monuments as others do stamps. Whenever he went abroad and saw an impressive monument, he had a replica built to himself. He visited France and saw the eternal flame to the Unknown Soldier: on his return he installed an eternal flame to himself under a reconstructed colonial wall. He visited Washington and the obelisk to

George Washington caught his eye; immediately he erected one to himself on the George Washington driveway in Ciudad Trujillo by the sea. Dominicans shuddered at the thought that it might occur to him to go sightseeing in Egypt. The people called the obelisk to Trujillo 'the male monument'; a few blocks away there was another monument to him of more complex form, which they called 'the female monument'. Their litters had overrun the country like Australian rabbits. White plaster busts of the Generalisimo, mass-produced from moulds, were everywhere – an estimated 1800 in the capital alone. You entered a government office and it was the first thing that you ran into; you turned a corner into the adjoining office and there was another one. Towns were constantly petitioning the Congress to have another bust of the Generalisimo set up in a naked corner of another square. And, according to the official paper, *La Nación*, Congress 'debated' the point before granting the request . . .

During my trip through the country in 1945 I took some random notes on some of the inscriptions. On a home for the aged: 'Trujillo is the only one who gives us shelter.' On the most insignificant village pumps: 'Trujillo alone gives us water to drink.' On a hospital: 'Only Trujillo cures you.' On a very ordinary town market in Santiago: 'This structure will bear witness through the centuries of the grandeur of the Era of Trujillo.' On the fortress near the new harbor in the capital, where a small area was reclaimed from the river: 'Trujillo, Hacedor de esta Tierra' (Creator of this land) – the ambiguity of the phrase was, of course, perfectly deliberate. The Dominicans prepare a delicious dessert from pineapples and eggs which they call 'Love with Jealousy'. Trujillo had a bad case of that with respect to himself.

(8) SAMANÁ

Quentin Crewe, *Touch the Happy Isles*

The Samaná peninsula, to the north-east of the country, is perhaps the most beautiful and undeveloped area of the Dominican Republic.

It seemed hardly possible that the Dominican Republic could produce any more surprises or greater pleasures. Yet the peninsula of Samaná provided both. The peninsula lies at the extreme north-east of the island. After the town of Sánchez there was a subtle change in the landscape. It was hilly rather than rugged and the road passed through exquisite palm groves, the grass beneath them dappled by filtered sunlight. The villages were poor, but gave me again that feeling that here the people were living a life that was natural to them, uninfluenced by the colonial past.

The whole peninsula was the perfect embodiment of people's ideas of the Caribbean. There were long untouched beaches, magical secret coves. Inland the hills were green and rolling, with tall trees in the deep hollows, places where the lordly ones might have dwelt. We had seen nothing which so combined gentle and wild natures since Tobago. The people were amiable and cheerful, even when we waited discreetly behind a long funeral procession, the body, wrapped only in a sheet, being carried on a litter, they waved us by, smiling. But once I saw a woman desolate with fatigue as she carried home her provisions up a long hill. Behind her trailed one daughter, tired and resigned and, some way back, another, about four years old, also carrying some cassava. Her face was twisted beyond crying, by a kind of active despair I had never seen in a child before. It was a reminder not to be deceived by the illusion of tropical paradise.

It was the town of Samaná which produced the unexpected. Tourism has made it more prosperous, though the government ran out of steam in their plans for it. The hotel was extremely simple, with a restaurant which had appalling 'Vood', as the English menu spelt it. I pondered for a long time as to who Mr Blur might be, who had inspired a dish called 'Filete Gordon Blur', before I realised what it meant. A small boy came to the door of the restaurant, begging. The waiter gave him a plate of chips, which he ate sitting on the doorstep.

(9) Santo Domingo:
Meeting the President

Samuel Hazard, *Santo Domingo, Past and Present*

Arriving in Santo Domingo, Hazard is struck by the ramshackle informality of the Dominican capital.

First impressions of such a place as St Domingo city cannot fail to be novel and strange. From the time of landing at the quay, entirely deserted of shipping, to the moment when, having secured quarters in the spacious saloons of a Government palace, the traveller has a chance to collect his thoughts, every moment brings a new, interesting, or funny sight.

Gaily-coloured walls, with dirty negroes sunning themselves against them; narrow streets, with solid-built houses, whose immense doors and spacious windows contrast forcibly with their limited height of only one or two stories; broad-brimmed-hatted horsemen on small, compact, quick-moving horses, contrast with the dusky urchin who, naked of everything but a shirt, bestrides an immense straw-saddle on the back of a very diminutive donkey, – all serve, with hundreds of other noticeable things, to strike the stranger, and impress upon him the fact that he has exchanged his Saxon associations of order, cleanliness and precision, for the peculiarities of Spanish tropical life.

Knots of men and women, mostly coloured, and busy in talk, are scattered about the quay or in the small open places called 'plazas'; odd-looking stores, with still more odd-looking assortments of goods, are entirely open to the gaze of the passer-by; while in the market-place are noticed the same peculiarities observed at Puerto Plata, only on a more extended scale. Go where one will, however, every one is cheerful, polite and communicative, while the dusky 'fair ones' presiding over piles of strange, unknown tropical productions, are merry, while obliging even in giving information.

Such are the sights that to-day first greet the traveller in the city that at one time was famous for its magnificence.

The day after my arrival I called at the palace to pay my respects to the authorities and present my letters of introduction. I was received by Mr Delmonte in the most cordial manner, and presented to President Báez, the Secretary of State, Mr Gautier, being present. They were all extremely affable and kind, and had rather a practical joke, though of a pleasant nature, at my expense; for on my happening to let drop a Spanish word, the President laughed and said – 'I must talk to them all in Spanish, as it was too *hard work* for him to talk English, and Mr Gautier did not understand it, and therefore we should get on finely as one family.' We had some pleasant words together, and I left feeling that my first had been anything but a formal call.

(10) Santo Domingo: Modern Times

Maurice Lemoine, *Bitter Sugar*

A group of Haitian cane-cutters have escaped from forced labour in a plantation, only to be confronted with the pandemonium of central Santo Domingo.

They had never seen anything like it, didn't even think it could exist. Santo Domingo hummed in their heads and everywhere all around them. An enormous city, no end in sight, houses superimposed upon houses, large avenues, automobiles that honked at every corner, and stores, especially stores. An insane array of shop windows full of shoes, records, fabric, records, shoes, household appliances, shoes, and records. Plus the *tiendas* with even more shoes. And others with records. Hawkers and peddlers. Dealers in used objects. Shoe-shiners, barefoot, bottle in hand. Mulatto women with wide derrieres and curlers on their heads. Some *guapas*, curvaceous, arching backs, *ay hombre!* And the omnipresent music, blaring forth from the toothless traps of all the booths and stalls. Bars and cafes, the crowd, going downtown or coming back, coming down or going back, turning, yelling, hustling and bustling, coming and going. 'I want to love you one more time,' shrieked a tearful singer, opening her heart and her thighs over a crackling loud speaker (raising the scorching air three more degrees). *Cerveza Presidente, Ron Bermudez*; beer and rum; rum and beer. Never saw anything like it, a veritable capital spread out under the sun . . .

They stopped, exhausted. Now what? Jean-René was gazing at the horde of vehicles surging past, unleashed by the last green light, in a blast of horns. Unable to focus his thoughts, he daydreamed for a brief moment.

He was brought back to reality by the tribulations of an old man whom the motorists, seemingly in league, could not, despite their efforts, manage to run over. The old-timer had unwisely started advancing into the street, probably in the insane hope of crossing. He was holding in his outstretched hand a more and more trembling cane, which seemed to have the same effect on the excited drivers as a cape before a furious bull. Jean-René sensed an imminent death. That of the toreador, not of the bull. A small group of Dominicans were breaking up laughing.

'I'll bet a peso on the autos!'

Biographical and literary notes

ALVAREZ, Julia (1951–). Born in the Dominican Republic, Alvarez was ten years old when her family was forced to leave the country shortly before the assassination of Trujillo in 1961. After studying English and creative writing in the US, she taught at a number of schools there and in Nicaragua. She is now a professor of English and lives in Vermont. Her first novel, *How the García Girls Lost Their Accents*, 1991, was critically acclaimed, and she has also published poetry, of which 'Homecoming: a Dominican Reverie' (Extract 5) is a good example. *In the Time of the Butterflies* (Extract 6) is a powerful recreation of the lives of the three Mirabal sisters – Minerva, Patria and María Teresa – who were murdered by Trujillo's secret police in November 1960.

BOSCH, Juan (1909–). Juan Bosch was a politician in almost permanent opposition and often in exile. A consummate conspiracy theorist, he argued that only fraud and US intervention kept him from power in the Dominican Republic. He is remembered as a writer and academic – an archetypally *déraciné* Latin American intellectual – and

also as a political reformer who was hardly given the chance to put his programme into practice. Bosch was president of the Dominican Republic for a mere seven months, before being ousted by a *coup* in September 1963. The struggle for his restoration, which led to civil war and the 1965 US invasion, gave him the symbolic stature of a radical at odds with the army, the Church and the American embassy. In reality, Bosch was a cautious social democrat who sought to modernize and democratize Dominican society after the 30-year Trujillo dictatorship ended in 1961.

The son of poor immigrant parents, Bosch had little formal education and left school before gaining any qualifications. He chose exile in preference to accommodation with the Trujillo regime, and from 1937 to 1962 made his reputation as a writer and teacher in Costa Rica, Venezuela, Cuba and the USA. During that period he became involved with a network of social democrats, many also in exile, such as future Venezuelan president Bétancourt. He also founded the Revolutionary Dominican Party (PRD) which was to win the first free elections after Trujillo's assassination.

Once in office, Bosch's liberal constitution and promise of land reform won the hatred of the Dominican oligarchy. Condemned as a communist, he also came under attack from the left of his own party. His brief administration, while honest, was considered inept and incapable of real reforms. The Kennedy administration, meanwhile, was wary of Bosch's nationalism and attempts to woo aid in Europe.

After the *coup* Bosch sacrificed popular support by remaining in Puerto Rico while the Constitutionalists fought for his cause. In US-controlled elections in 1966 he lost heavily to his perennial right-wing adversary Joaquín Balaguer. He never won office again, while Balaguer won another four elections.

Bosch's political ideas were at best unpredictable. He was at times a self-confessed Marxist but often an anti-communist. In the 1970s his social democracy gave way to a concept of 'dictatorship with popular support'and he broke with the PRD to form his personalist Partido de la Liberación Dominicana. In the 1990 election campaign he had become a born-again neo-liberal and champion of privatization. To many, however, he was first and foremost a *caudillo* – a charismatic, if mercurial, populist who taunted the so-called *tutumpotes* (his mocking term for the oligarchy) while retaining an enduring following among the poorest sectors of Dominican society. Bosch retired from active politics in 1994.

Apart from political tracts such as *Pentagonism: A Substitute for Imperialism*, 1961, a biography of Duarte and a well received history of the Caribbean, Bosch wrote a number of short stories, of which 'The Woman' (Extract 3) is one of the few to have been translated into English.

COLUMBUS, Christopher (1451–1506). Born in Genoa, Columbus was a sailor, adventurer and navigator who is conventionally credited with being the first European to arrive in the Americas. His plan to sail westwards from Europe to reach Asia was rejected by the Portuguese monarchy, and he was eventually supported by Ferdinand and Isabella of Spain. On 12 October 1492, his expedition landed on what he called San Salvador in the Bahamas. In the course of four journeys, Columbus reached Hispaniola (today Haiti and the Dominican Republic), Jamaica, Puerto Rico, Cuba and most of the Lesser Antilles as well as Venezuela and parts of Central America. He remained convinced, however, that all these territories were situated in the Asian continent. In a stormy series of relationships with his royal protectors, relatives and fellow explorers, Columbus managed to alienate most of his allies and died in comparative obscurity. In 1992, the Columbus quincentenary sparked off a lively controversy over the status and legacy of the 'Great Admiral'. Indigenous American organizations claimed that the heroic myth of 'discovery' concealed the beginning of a process of genocide and exploitation, for which Columbus could be held personally responsible. His supporters argued that he was merely a 'man of his times', who saw no contradiction between converting heathens to Christianity, enslaving them and forcibly appropriating their land. Accusations of inappropriate 'political correctness' were met with allegations of neo-colonial insensitivity. The *Letter* (Extract 1) was addressed to Ferdinand and Isabella but was intended for wider consumption and had been published in nine editions throughout Europe by 1494. Its purpose was to enumerate the physical and commercial attractions of the newly claimed territories and to encourage further investment in another proposed expedition.

CREWE, Quentin (1926–). Travel

writer, food critic and restaurateur, Quentin Crewe is the author of such acclaimed travelogues as *In Search of the Sahara* and *The Last Maharaja*. Despite being confined to a wheelchair, he specializes in journeys to difficult and inaccessible places. *Touch the Happy Isles* (Extract 8) takes him on a trip the length of the Caribbean archipelago from Trinidad to Jamaica.

GALVAN, Manuel de Jesús (1834–1910). Galván was born in Santo Domingo ten years before the establishment of the independent Dominican Republic. His childhood coincided with the period of Haitian occupation which began shortly after the withdrawal of Spain in 1821 and ended in 1844 with the rebellion of the *Trinitaria*. After youthful involvement in literary circles, he was appointed Secretary to President Pedro Santana in 1859. He supported Santana's controversial decision to re-annex the country to Spain in 1861 as a barrier against further Haitian ambitions. After the brief and unpopular period of Spanish recolonization, Galván left for exile in Puerto Rico. He returned later to the Dominican Republic, where he served as a diplomat, legislator and professor of law. He wrote widely on legal, constitutional and educational matters. His vast historical novel, *Enriquillo*, 1882, translated as *The Sword and the Cross* (Extract 4), presents an idealized picture of the Dominican Republic's long extinct indigenous population. In a fusion of historical reconstruction, drawing on the writings of Bartolomé de las Casas, and Romantic narrative, Galván evokes the aura of grandeur surrounding Enriquillo, the last Taino *cacique*. Enriquillo, who had been educated by Franciscan friars, led the last great Taino uprising against the Spanish in the 1520s. In dispute with the colonial authorities over land ownership, Enriquillo organized an insurgency which lasted for thirteen years before being settled by a formal peace treaty. In Galván's version of the story, Enriquillo's chivalrous behaviour and purity of motive make him a classic 'noble savage' in the tradition of such French Romantics as Chateaubriand. The novel also has an implicitly political and racial purpose. In his vision of reconciliation between the Taino population and the more humane elements of the Spanish colonial authorities, Galván allegorizes the case for Spanish re-annexation of the independent Dominican Republic. He also implicitly identifies the modern Dominican nation with the long-lost indigenous population of Quisqueya, thereby fuelling the myth that Dominicans are not the product of African ancestry but are somehow 'Indians'.

HAZARD, Samuel. First published in 1873, *Santo Domingo, Past and Present* (Extract 9) provides a thorough picture of the Dominican Republic during one of its more turbulent political periods. Hazard's book is also in part a plea for the annexation of the country by the USA and a warning against growing European involvement in the Dominican economy. While scathing about neighbouring Haiti ('I have been, like most persons who visit Hayti, utterly disappointed in its people and government'), Hazard praises Dominican people in glowing terms: 'I am glad to bear testimony to the fact, from personal observation, that the masses of the people of St Domingo will compare favourably with those of Great Britain, Belgium, or France.'

KREHM, William (1912–). Born in Canada, Krehm travelled extensively in Central America and the Caribbean during the 1940s, the heyday of 'banana republics', dictators and US gunboat diplomacy. His articles, some of which were published in *Time*, earned him the disapproval of the US State Department and he found himself unable to place further articles in the mainstream US media. He alleged that this censorship was largely due to pressure from US multinational companies which disliked his criticism of their operations in countries such as Honduras and Guatemala. The collection of essays, *Democracies and Tyrannies of the Caribbean* (Extract 7), was published in Mexico in 1948, but an English-language version had to wait until 1984.

LEMOINE, Maurice (1950–). A Paris-based journalist and author,

Lemoine is the author of several books on Latin American and Caribbean political and human rights issues. *Bitter Sugar* (Extract 10) is a powerful indictment of Dominican and Haitian government complicity in the near-enslavement of poor Haitian workers in Dominican sugar plantations. Translated into French and Spanish, the book did much to publicize the appalling human rights violations inflicted on Haitians inside the Dominican Republic.

VEGA, Ana Lydia (see under Puerto Rico).

PUERTO RICO

Jason Wilson

'. . . the sun carries out an ungodly vendetta here, it stains the skin, prostitutes the blood, roils the sense: here is Puerto Rico, the successive colony of two empires and an island in the Archipelago of the Antilles.'
Luis Rafael Sánchez,
Macho Camacho's Beat

Puerto Rico, meaning 'rich port' in Spanish, was originally called Boriquén ('island of the brave lord' – the Puerto Rican national anthem is called *La borinqueña*), when the Arawak-speaking Taíno Indians lived there before the conquest (leaving petroglyphs). This tropical island lies some 1600 km off the US mainland and at its widest, east to west, is 183 km, and 66 km across, slightly smaller than Corsica. The island has a range of rugged mountains, the **Cordillera Central**, reaching its highest peak, **Cerro de Punta** at 1338 m, with a generally hilly interior. The fertile plains, some 27% of the island, are given over to sugar cane (the first sugar-cane factory was built as early as 1516), though US investment in industry increased considerably from the 1940s through what was known as 'Operation Bootstrap' (*Jalda arriba* in Spanish). In a massive investment programme, over 2600 businesses took advantage of tax benefits, but they did little for the island as they gave low wages and left with their profits, bequeathing to Puerto Rico the problem of dealing with the consequent contamination. The maritime tropical climate has a mean average of 24°C, and the island lies within the hurricane belt. Interestingly, it is closer to Caracas than to Miami.

On 19 November 1493 Columbus returned some Arawak-speaking Indians to the island during his second voyage, and named the place San Juan Bautista. In 1508 Juan Ponce de León founded Puerto Rico, originally a harbour, a name later applied to the whole island. At the time of colonization there were some 30 000 Taíno natives living under local *caciques*, and these had dwindled to 2302 by the 1787 census. Today only a few native words, like *bohío* (hut), *hamaca*, *maracas*, and *batey* (porch, but

FACT BOX

AREA: 8900 sq km
POPULATION: 3 500 000
CAPITAL: San Juan
LANGUAGES: Spanish, English
FORMER COLONIAL POWER: Spain
INDEPENDENCE: 1898
PER CAPITA GDP: US$6900

originally courts for sacred ball games), with a few place names, have survived, as well as the god *Juracán* (hurricane) of the destructive wind. The population includes some 20% non-white from the negro slaves freed in 1873. An early cultural symbol of Puerto Rico was the *jíbaro*, the small independent farmer from the interior. A 19th century novel entitled *El gíbaro*, 1849, by Manuel Alonso Pacheco (1822–1889), sets out in 29 scenes to evoke Puerto Rican identity while it was still a Spanish colony. The essayist José Luis González ◊, in his *País de cuatro pisos*, 1980 (*Puerto Rico: The Four-Storeyed Country and Other Essays*, 1993) claimed that these peasants soon became share-croppers, tied to their employers by the *libreta*, or pass-book, system. The current population of the island is of Afro–Spanish origins, totalling some 3 500 000. The relationships between the different classes and races are complicated, and González argues in his metaphor of the four-storeyed house that the black slaves and *mestizos* are the true, original Puerto Ricans, and not the white immigrants from the nineteenth century. He contends that Puerto Rico's identity lies in its acceptance of its multiracial base in terms of a Caribbean link. González: 'the essentially Caribbean nature of our collective tradition and thereby acknowledge, once and for all, that the natural destiny of Puerto Rico is identical to that of all the other Caribbean peoples.'

By 1530 gold had run out, though the island continued to be attacked by pirates and Carib Indians. The Spaniards built El Morro fort in the 1540s, and later in the seventeenth century, **San Juan**, the capital founded in 1508, was fortified – Sir Francis Drake was unable to sack it in 1595. During most of the colonial period, smuggling remained the main activity. After the British failed to enter San Juan in 1797 Spain opened up trade. When the majority of the Spanish colonies broke away from Spain (except Cuba), Puerto Rico became a refuge for Spanish loyalists. In 1815 Spain passed the *Real Cédula de Gracias*, opening immigration for 'whites' with capital to exploit the collapse of the Haitian sugar business (due to the black revolution). Those who came over were mainly Corsicans and Majorcans. This influx accounts for what González called the second storey. There were some abortive independent attempts, like the Grito de Lares (23 September 1868), in which several hundred men founded a republic in the mountain village of **Lares**, with a short-lived and quickly crushed republic. In 1898, following the brief Spanish American war over Cuba, US troops landed and claimed the island from Spain. The leading nineteenth century intellectual reformist was Eugenio María de Hostos (1839–1903), an abolitionist and champion of Puerto Rico joining a West Indian federation.

In 1917 Puerto Rico joined the USA (the Jones Act), and its people became US citizens, but they could vote only if resident on the mainland. This act of joining and the resulting move to the mainland, where more than one-third of Puerto Ricans now live, have become the decisive factors in Puerto Rican culture over the rest of the century. González: 'There is no aspect of the life of the Puerto Rican people . . . that is not marked by the vicissitudes of this mass exodus . . . characterized by a constant coming and going from the home country to the seat of exile and vice-versa.' Playwright René Marqués described this situtation dramatically in an essay *El puertorriqueño dócil y otros ensayos*, 1977: 'This is a really schizophrenic society. Puerto Ricans have two languages, two citizenships, two basic philosophies of life, two flags, two anthems, two loyalties. It is very hard for human beings to deal with this ambivalence.' In 1946 Puerto Ricans voted in their first Puerto Rican governor. From 1948, through the Department of Labor, mass migration to the mainland, especially to New York, began. In 1952 Puerto Ricans voted to make the island an Estado Libre Asociado, or Commonwealth, with self-governing powers given to the island, a vote confirmed again in 1993. But there were groups (annexionists) who wanted even closer ties (like becoming the 51st state), and others who sought complete independence (*independistas*). Two black-shirted *independistas* shot the chief of police in **San Juan** in 1936 which led to Albizu Campos's imprisonment. In 1937 these *independistas* led by Campos held a protest in **Ponce**, where 21 protesters were killed ('la masacre de Ponce'). Three of the imprisoned leaders were poets: Francisco Matos Paoli (1915–), a professor of Puerto Rican literature, and translated into English in *Songs of Madness and Other Poems*, 1985; Juan Antonio Corretjer (1908–); and Clemente Soto Vélez (1905–), who spent 7 years in jail for sedition. The leading nationalist historian is Tomás Blanco (1900–1975), whose best known work is the *Prontuario histórico de Puerto Rico*, 1935. Nationalist extremists tried to assassinate President Truman in 1950. In 1952 a nationalist march on the governor's palace in San Juan led to 27 deaths. In 1954 nationalists shot at Congressmen in the House of Representatives. In 1980 only 6% of the population wanted independence. The current state of the island is that it has the lowest per capita income in the USA and a high unemployment level, it imports two-thirds of its food, and there is a steady drift away from the countryside to urban sprawls.

Between 1940 and 1960, up to one-third of the island's population left for the States. Some two million Puerto Ricans now live on the mainland, and Puerto Rican culture has to include this bilingual fact – English was the obligatory language until 1949 and only recently (1991) has Spanish been declared the official language. There are considerable differences between mainland Puerto Ricans, also known as Nuyoricans or Neoricans, writing in English, and living marginalized and unemployed in their New York ghetto of El Barrio (Spanish Harlem, the upper West Side in the 1961 musical about Puerto Ricans, *West Side Story*), and rapidly acculturalized, and the islanders for whom Spanish is the main language, though bilingualism and music still unite them. To live *allá* (over there) or *acá* (here) is a permanent dilemma. The Americanization of Puerto Rican culture is deep, and self-evident, and has led many Puerto Rican writers to turn to the Hispanic cultural tradition as a rebellion against American English and its colonial associations. A pioneering enquiry into national identity was the essay *Insularismo*, 1934, by Antonio Pedreira (1899–1939), which explored the historical discontinuity set up by the 1898 break with the Hispanic tradition, and reacted against the dominating US presence in terms of a recuperation of this Hispanic past.

The university drew many Spanish lecturers, while a group of poets on Puerto Rico turned to the Hispanic cultural tradition with their '*poesía pura*'. They were influenced by the Nobel-winning Spanish poet Juan Ramón Jiménez, in exile from Franco, who died in **Río Piedras** in 1953, leaving his library and works to the university (housed in the **Zenobia-Juan Ramón sala** in the university library). In fact, turning to Spanish institutions has always been viable, given the 'Americanization' of the island's culture, and the cultural inferiority faced by natives. Rosario Ferré ◊ best conveys the complex Puerto Rican cultural inheritance: 'As in the rest of the Caribbean, reality in Puerto Rico is so complex that it always overflows the receptacle of fiction, and it is impossible to capture it in its entirety.'

Popular music, especially *salsa* (meaning 'sauce'), unites all Puerto Ricans, whether on the mainland or on *la isla* (as dramatized in Luis Rafael Sánchez's ◊ fiction – see Extract 7 – and in Luis González's 'The Night We Became People Again' – Extract 2). The listening to and dancing of *salsa* also binds Puerto Rico to the other Caribbean islands and the Spanish-speaking mainland. *Salsa* combines Afro–Caribbean rhythms (especially the percussion instruments) with US big-band jazz – Puerto Rican Willie Colón (Spanish for Columbus!) is the best-known exponent. At the other extreme of the music spectrum is Pablo Casals (1876–1973), the great cellist, who lived his last years on the island (his house a **museum in San Juan**).

Another fascinating aspect of Puerto Rican literary culture has been the role of the woman writer. Since the 1940s the influence of North American democratic values (and feminism) has undermined the Catholic stress on women remaining at home, bearing children. Many of the most exciting writers and intellectuals in Puerto Rico, as seen in my selection here, are women experimenting on the frontiers of what is most new in Latin American literature. A recent example of such cosmopolitan and experimental writing is Giannina Braschi's *Empire of Dreams*, 1994.

In 1806, *Poesías* by Juan Rodríguez Calderón was the first book published on the island. The **university** in Río Piedras was founded in 1925, and is a source of nationalist pride, with illustrious Spanish-speaking visiting lecturers such as Ortega y Gasset, Miguel de Unamuno and the Mexican José Vasconcelos and an excellent library called the José Lazaró library. There is a **Casa del Libro** (a museum) on **calle Cristo** in **San Juan**, and an **Institute of Puerto Rican Culture** (founded in 1955) based in the **Dominican Convent**, built in 1523, with the old convent library restored. An influential view of Puerto Rican culture was that of the anthropologist Oscar Lewis, *La Vida: a Puerto Rican Family in the Culture of Poverty*, 1966, with his study of the shanty town of **La Perla**. A moving account of growing up poor in New York is provided by Piri Thomas in *Down These Mean Streets*, 1967. On US stereotyping of Puerto Ricans, there is Pedro Juan Soto's ◊ novel *Spiks*, 1973 (Extract 3). James Baldwin's novel *If Beale Street Could Talk*, 1974, also deals with blacks and Puerto Ricans in New York. Good general introductions to the island are Robert A. Crampsey, *Puerto Rico*, 1973, and Arturo Morales Carrión, ed, *Puerto Rico: A Political and Cultural History*, 1982. A lucid introduction to Puerto Rican cultural dilemmas is the playwright René Marqués's (1919–1979) collection of essays *The Docile Puerto Rican*, 1976. Diana Vélez has edited and translated *Reclaiming Medusa: Short Stories by Contemporary Puerto Rican Women*, 1988, and Julio Marzán has edited *Inventing a Word: An Anthology of Twentieth-Century Puerto Rican Poetry*, 1980 (Extracts 6 and 8). In 1974 María Teresa Babín and Stan Steiger edited *Borinquén: An Anthology of Puerto Rican Literature*.

BOOKLIST

The following selection includes the extracted titles in this chapter as well as other titles for further reading. In general, paperback editions are given when possible. For most of the extracted works, the original publisher in English can be found in 'Acknowledgments and Citations' at the end of the volume, as can the exact location of the extracts and the editions from which they are taken.

Borinquén: An Anthology of Puerto Rican Literature, María Teresa Babín and Stan Steiger, eds, Vintage, New York, 1974.

Braschi, Giannina, *Empire of Dreams*, Tess O'Dwyer, trans, Yale University Press, New Haven, CT, and London, 1994.

Burgos, Julia de, 'Rio Grande de Loíza', Grace Schulman, trans, in Julio Marzán, ed, *Inventing a Word: An Anthology of Twentieth-Century Puerto Rican Poetry*, Columbia University Press, New York, 1980. **Extract 8.**

Crampsey, Robert A., *Puerto Rico*, David and Charles, Newton Abbot, 1973.

Díaz Alfaro, Abelardo, 'Josco', in Barbara Howes, ed, *In the Green Antilles: Writings of the Caribbean*,

Panther, London, 1971. **Extract 10**.

Díaz Valcárcel, Emilio, *Hot Soles in Harlem*, Tanya Fayen, trans, Latin American Literary Review Press, Pittsburgh, PA, 1993. **Extract 1**.

Ferré, Rosario, 'The Dust Garden', in *The Youngest Doll*, University of Nebraska Press, London and Nebraska, 1991. **Extract 5**.

González, José Luis, 'The Night We Became People Again', Kal Wagenheim, trans, in *Cuentos: An Anthology of Short Stories from Puerto Rico*, Schocken Books: New York, 1978. **Extract 2**.

González, José Luis, *Puerto Rico: The Four-Storeyed Country and Other Essays*, Markus Wiener Publications, Princeton, NJ, and London, 1993.

Lewis, Oscar, *La Vida: A Puerto Rican Family in the Culture of Poverty*, 1966.

Marqués, René, *The Docile Puerto Rican*, Barbara Bockus Aponte, trans, Temple University Press, Philadelphia, PA, 1976.

Matos Paoli, Francisco, *Songs of Madness and Other Poems*, Frances Aparicio, trans, Latin American Literary Review Press, Pittsburgh, PA, 1985.

Morales Carrión, Arturo, *Puerto Rico: A Political and Cultural History*, W.W. Norton, New York, 1984.

Palés Matos, Luis, Julio Marzán, trans, in *Inventing a Word: An Anthology of Twentieth-Century Puerto Rican Poetry*, Columbia University Press, New York, 1980. **Extract 6**.

Reclaiming Medusa: Short Stories by Contemporary Puerto Rican Women, Diana Vélez, ed and trans, Spinsters/Aunt Lute, San Francisco, CA, 1988.

Sánchez, Luis Rafael, *Macho Camacho's Beat*, Gregory Rabassa, trans, Pantheon, New York, 1981. **Extract 7**.

Soto, Pedro Juan, *Spiks*, Victoria Ortiz, trans, Monthly Review Press, London and New York, 1973. **Extract 3**.

Soto Vélez, Clemente, *La sangre que sigue cantando* / *The Blood That Keeps Singing: Selected Poems of Clemente Soto Vélez*, Martín Espada and Camilo Pérez-Bustillo, trans, Curbstone, Willimantic, CT, 1991. **Extract 4**.

Thomas, Piri, *Down These Mean Streets*, Knopf, New York, 1967.

Vega, Ana Lydia, *True and False Romances*, Andrew Hurley, trans, Serpent's Tail, London, 1994. **Extract 9**.

Extracts

(1) EL BARRIO (NEW YORK)

Emilio Díaz Valcárcel, *Hot Soles in Harlem*

*Gerardo (Gery), red-haired, blue-eyed Puerto Rican, chats with his
new girlfriend, Caty, a Neorican who works in a store for her father
Lorenzo. The dialgoue captures the differences between mainland
and island Puerto Ricans.*

Dominated by a sudden flame of overpowering native happiness, Gerardo
leans over gently and embraces her uncomfortably, effusive, their foreheads
meet hotly and support one another, the girl's square hands with bitten
nails caress the recently shaved chin of the passionate Boricuan lover, his
cheeks lashed by the cold and inclemency. Caty recovers her relaxed
position and gazes at him smiling, showing her uneven row of teeth like
kernels in a poor harvest of corn.

'You're making me hungry, Caty.'

'It's the grass.'

'Does Lorenzo know you smoke?'

'*La primera vez*, he screamed at me, when he saw the bowl with the pot in
it. But *entonces* he got used to it; *yo le dije que* it's not as bad as the Camels
he smokes, that alcohol destroys brain cells. Now he don't say anything to
me. *Yo* his right hand. I help him in the store, I cook, wash the dishes, he
can't mess with me. This isn't *la Isla* where the old man *de viejas costumbres*
can hit his daughters because they have a boyfriend. Papa's still got this
idea. He says you can't teach an old dog, *tú sabes*. He listens to old Mayarí
music, Marcano, Daniel Santo, *todas estas cosas*, and Ramito, *hombre*,
the cat's from the country. *Pero* who'll tell him no. I took off one of his
records, a folk song, he asked me *por qué*, I told him this old music doesn't
make it in New York,and he started to cry *muy emocionado*, he didn't tell
me why he was crying for maybe fifteen *minutos*, but two days *después* he
tells me that he's lost me as his daughter, that he's strange to me, *que
éramos tan diferentes* that he isn't my father and I'm not like a daughter
of his.'

'Was he listening to the record?'

'Yes.'

'And you took it off?'

'I wanted to hear rock. He hates *esa música*, he lives here twenty three
years and zero English, no nothing. He only thinks about *la Isla*. A good
guy, but we're different *generaciones*.'

'Newyorican.'

'They don't have to put names on us like that, the ones from *la Isla*. They
don't know how it is. They think they know everything. They come to
teach us. You have to be here *para saber* how to make it. Papá's just like

them, think you must be sick because not talk like him and *la Isla*. He knows *todo* and he's old. I respect him because he's Papá you know but I have my ideas, he should respect me and I'll be *bien chévere* with him. Now he says he wants to go to *la Isla*, to the countryside to have a store. Then I stay here.'

'When did you go to *la Isla*?'

Caty's eyes fill, mascara streaks her face, the two dark rivers of her hair on her breasts.

'To bury Mamá. Three years ago. We lived on Flatbush then. She said bury her on *la Isla*, she always said it before she got sick.'

(2) EL BARRIO (NEW YORK)

José Luis González,
The Night We Became People Again

This short story is told by a recently arrived Puerto Rican in New York, about to become a father, and trapped during the famous black-out in the city.

So we go up the stairs and onto the roof and I find almost the whole building there. Doña Lula, the widow from the first floor; Cheo, the guy from Aguadilla, who had closed down his coffee shop when the lights went out; the girls from the second floor, who neither worked nor collected welfare, according to the tongue-waggers; *don* Leo, the Pentecostal minister who has four children here and seven in Puerto Rico; Pipo and *doña* Lula's boys, and one of *don* Leo's had formed a combo with a guitar, a *güiro*, some maracas, and even some drums, I don't know where they got them from because I'd never seen them before. Yeah, a quartet. Say, and they were really making quite a racket! When I got there, they were playing 'Preciosa', and the singer was Pipo, you know he's an *independista*, and when he got to the part where it says, 'Preciosa, preciosa, you're called by the sons of liberty,' he raised his voice so much I think they heard him in Morovis. And I'm standing there looking at all those people, and listening to the song, when one of the girls from the second floor comes over, a little heavyset, I think her name is Mirta, and she says to me, 'Say, how good it is that you're here. Come over and have a little shot.' Ah, they had bottles and paper cups atop a chair, and I don't know if it was Bacardi or Don Q, because it was dark, but right away I tell her, 'Well, if you're offering, I accept with great pleasure.' She serves me the rum and I ask, 'Say, can you tell me what the party's all about?' and *doña* Lula, the widow comes over and says, 'No, man not there. Look *up*'. And when I raise my eyes she says, 'What do you see?' 'Well, the moon.' 'And what else?' 'Well, the stars.'

Ave María, muchacho! That's when I realized! I think *doña* Lula saw it in my face, because she didn't say a thing more. She put her two hands on my shoulders and stood there looking too, nice and still, as though I were asleep, and she didn't want to wake me. Because I don't know if you're going to believe me, but it was like a dream. The moon was this big, and yellow, yellow as though it were made of gold, and the whole sky was full of stars, as though all the fireflies in the world had gone up there to rest in that immensity. Just like in Puerto Rico, 'most any night of the year'.

(3) El Barrio (New York)

Pedro Juan Soto, *Spiks*

The plight of the poor Puerto Rican is brilliantly caught in this vignette about Puerto Ricans in El Barrio (Spanish Harlem) in New York.

From the distance, if one went by its colors, it was a snappy little cart parked on the corner of 116th street. It had blue, red, and yellow stripes, and the box on top – full of cod fritters, blood sausage, and banana fritters – had glass on all four sides. From close, however, you could see that its snappiness was no more than a front that disguised the wear and tear and the rot which were consuming it from the wheels up to the push bar. On a piece of tin nailed to the front you could read in red, shaky letters: BAYAMINIÑA.

But no one paid attention to the cart. The crowd was watching the argument between the vendor and the policeman. The black women heading towards Lenox Avenue stopped in their rapid, ass-swinging tracks to see how it would all end. The customers in the nearby bar neglected their drinks and the TV set to follow the altercation through the glass window. And curiosity even turned heads in passing cars and busses.

'I pay no more,' the vendor was saying, tense. ' I pay las year other fine . . .'

The policeman only shook his head as he finished scribbling in his notebook.

'This has nothing to do with last year, buddy.'

'I got no money. I no pay more.'

'And the fine you'll have to pay next year will be a bigger one, if you don't get rid of that thing there.'

'You're killing me,' said the vendor. 'Why you do this?'

'The Department of Health . . .'

'Okay, you gimme a job an I . . .'

'. . . is after you guys.'

'I have to eat,' said the vendor. 'Don't gimme no fine, gimme a job.'

'I have nothing to do with that,' said the policeman. He put the summons in one of the vendor's pockets and added: 'You keep that . . . And remember to go to court.'

The vendor took the summons, furious, and tried to read it. But he could understand no more than the numbers.

'All right, break it up,' the policeman said to the crowd. And to the vendor: 'And you get going before I lose my patience.'

The vendor turned to the school kids, slight and cinnamon-colored like him.

'These bastards,' he said to them in Spanish. 'Sia la madre d'ehtos policías!'

'C'mon,' said the policeman. 'Get the hell out of here.'

Suddenly the vendor bent over, picked up a rock which served as the cart's brake, and stood up again with it in his fist. His face was already crumpling with a coming sob.

'Gimme a job, saramabich!'

(4) LARES

Clemente Soto Vélez,
from *Caballo de palo / Wooden Horse*

The poem recreates his father in their home town of Lares, symbolic mountain village of Puerto Rican independence ambitions.

I came to know him
gathering
early morning of Lares lost
in the brownskinned magic of quivering moons
that run
bearing a star on their shoulders,
rejuvenated in dreams,
like a mythic goddess of fireflies.

I came to know him
listening
to Indian ceremonies of drums
mounted on memories of Taíno horses
that lure
the Sicilian blossoms in the afternoons of manure,
playing a singsong game shoeless in the fountains,
like jubilant girls and boys
smelling of the fruit from delectable nights.

I came to know him
leaving
the siesta of butterflies
to toss
a handful of sky into the skirt
carrying

a sunflower that sings
in its folds
together with the solitude of the flesh hoisting itself
onto its star . . .

(5) PONCE

Rosario Ferré, *The Dust Garden*

*In a typically colloquial style Ferré has Eusebia recount her arrival in
the industrial landscape of Ponce, Puerto Rico's second town.*

Hand in hand with Eusebia, I walk under the banana trees. A layer of dust
covers them; their soft trunks have split open with the heat, exposing their
fibery, glossy flesh. Ebony beetles crawl in and out of the poinsettia's
wounds, the milk of the sweetsop drips, dries slowly into scales. We're
alone in the garden, as usual, alone except for the gardener, sweeping the
leaves and raking the dust. Limping because of her swollen leg, Eusebia
moves deeper into the frayed shadows of the banana grove and looks for a
trunk thick enough to stand the weight of her back. She searches around
on the ground, makes sure there are no fire ants, then sits and stretches out
her legs. She then begins to cut thin, moist slices of a cactus plant nearby,
and plasters them on her bunioned feet, to ease the pain. I lay my head on
her lap and listen to her snowy starched skirt crackle over her black skin.
Her cheeks glisten like wet eggplant; her hand glides back and forth over
my forehead like a mud fish, cooling and soothing. She looks at me and
smiles, making me feel content.

Eusebia pulls a half-smoked cigar out of the folds of her skirt, lights it,
and draws on it slowly. A flock of smoky blue phantoms floats over the
dusty leaves of the banana trees, she sways, eyes closed, making a deep
sound in her throat. I look into her tamarind eyes but they are dim now;
her gold tooth is also dim, sunk into the muddy whiteness of her smile.
Small, kinky wings spread out at her temples, and are combed back at the
nape of her neck. I listen as she begins her story:

'On the day Marina and I arrived in Santa Cruz,' she said, 'we drove
through the deserted streets in the De La Valle's black Packard. It was just
after noontime, the hour of the siesta, and there was nobody around. The
pink-columned houses of the town went by our car window like a row of
bawdy dancers stretching out their silk stockings before their first performance. The houses were very different from those of Guamaní; here they
were heavily decorated with gessoed fruit garlands, cupids, baskets of
flowers, and curved amphorae sitting like freshly baked cakes, covered by a
gaudy coat of sugar. Marina said the town reminded her of a huge pastry
shop and sighed with relief as we finally turned into the dusty bed of the
Portugés River.

'The river was an acknowledged boundary: it was officially recognized as the place where the town ended and the territory of the cement plant began. The Packard came to a stop before a wrought-iron gate and played its melancholy horn of chimes. No one came to greet us. We looked out the car windows, through the constant drizzle of dust, at the huge house that stood in the middle of what looked like a field of bat's dung.'

(6) PUERTO RICO:
CULTURAL CONFUSIONS

Luis Palés Matos, *Neither This Nor That*

Poet Luis Palés Matos evokes his native island and its hybrid culture in this poem song, with references to bámbula, an African dance, and ñáñigo, meaning a secret society of black Cubans.

You are my green island,
designed in pirate and black,
the pirate lending the lines,
the shadows filled in by the black.
Together drums and the harquebus
exalt your dark-skinned glory
with red gunpowder flowers
and the savage rhythms of *bámbula*.

When the hurricane folds and unfolds
its fierce accordion of winds,
over the carpet of the sea
you – agile bayadere –
with slender palmtree legs
dance on the points of your toes.

You could have gone in mantilla,
if your ardent *ñáñigo* blood
hadn't chosen madras
over Spain's airy froth.
You could have shone, shapely,
sobriety in classic mold,
if the gold force of your sun
hadn't ripened your amphora thighs
swelling their forms
wide as water jars.

You could have passed before the world
for cultured and civilized
if your armpits – flowers of shadow –

didn't spread through the plazas
the pungent odor of onions
your entrails lightly fry.

And this is you, my green Antille,
in an ambivalence over race,
neither this nor that your pedigree
that makes you so Antillean . . .
To the rhythm of the drums you dance
your pretty neither this nor that,
one half Spanish,
the other African.

(7) PUERTO RICO: GUARACHA

Luis Rafael Sánchez, *Macho Camacho's Beat*

Luis Rafael Sánchez's populist and colloquial novel about the Caribbean dance the guaracha parodies the impact of popular music (life in fact is not so phenomenal as the song states) on a mosaic of Puerto Rican life. A público is a municipal bus.

If you turn around now, a cautious turn, a cautious look, you, you'll see her sitting and waiting, calmness or the shadow of calmness passing through her. She's got a dreamer's face, a wake me up and touch me face, her legs crossed in a cross. You'll see her sitting and waiting on a sofa: her arms open, bracelets on her arms, a small watch on one wrist, rings on her fingers, over her left heel an anklet with a trinket on it, on each leg a knee on each foot a striking big shoe. A restless body, she has a body of oh cut it out, can you see?, a body that she sits down, lays out, and plops onto a sofa upholstered with a woolen material that's useful for overcoming polar chills but most unreal for any use in these tristes tropiques: the sun carries out an ungodly vendetta here, it stains the skin, prostitutes the blood, roils the sense: here is Puerto Rico, the successive colony of two empires and an island in the Archipelago of the Antilles. Sweaty too, you'll see her waiting sweaty, sweaty and plopped onto a sweaty ploppy sofa, a sweaty ploppy sofa that changes into a bed that changes into a sofa, an elegant member of a transvestite domestic cast that can do everything. The way her can can. If you turn around now, a cautious turn, a cautious look, you'll see her waiting, sweaty, in spite of the shower of a little while ago. Did they hear her showering? Impossible: she was guarachaing. Under the shower, guaracha and woman in a mating of superb agitation: voice unleashed, body bumping bathroom walls, the shower curtain's guaracha whiplash.

Turn after turn, to shoo away the buzzing of the time she has more than enough of today, today Wednesday, today Wednesday afternoon, today Wednesday five post meridiem, she hums Macho Camacho's guaracha and she makes it louder with the striking stomp of a striking big shoe: *life is a phenomenal thing*: the crowning aphorism of the guaracha that's taken over the country. The crowning aphorism or something like that, a guaracha you people have danced to or listened to or bought or asked for on some radioed program, it doesn't matter whether it's sung or hummed.

(8) Río Grande de Loíza

Julia de Burgos, *Río Grande de Loíza*

One of Julia de Burgos's best known poems explores her identity with the Puerto Rican river, and ends . . .

Río Grande de Loíza! . . . Blue. Dark. Red.
Blue mirror, fallen blue fragment of sky;
Nude white flesh that turns you black
Every time night goes to bed with you;
Red band of blood, when under the rain
The hills vomit torrents of mud.

Man river, but man with river purity
Because when you give your blue kiss you give your blue soul.

My dear Mister River. Man river. The only man
Who has kissed my soul when he kissed my body.

Río Grand de Loíza! . . . Great river. Great tear.

The greatest of all our island tears,
But for the tears that flow out of me
Through the eyes of my soul for my enslaved people.

(9) San Juan

Ana Lydia Vega, *True and False Romances*

A neighbour is telling the story of a woman whose philandering macho husband goes too far and has his balls cut off and presented to his pregnant mistress.

Things started to get what you might call interesting about two years ago into the marriage, as I recall, when he decided to bring his women home to his own house – to save money on the motel rooms, I imagine, or so as not to be so uncomfortable back there in the back seat of that car . . . Women were in and out of that house like it was a beauty parlor – they were every shape and color, I tell you, and I ought to know, because many was the day

I'd spend the whole morning out on my porch ironing – because in the morning with that sun coming in, the heat in my kitchen would melt the curlers in your hair . . . The one that came the most was a kind of albino-looking freckle-faced black woman with her hair hennaed a neon red, and she stuck out in front like this and behind even farther, the woman was something to see, and she lived out there in a place called the Bottom. Those two were shameless – he'd drive his wife to work and then in that very car he'd pick up the other one and drive her to his house. They'd drive up all cootchy-cootchy with their arms around each other, then he'd go in first, open the back door for her (why not the front door you might well ask) and bam – off to bed. How do I know? Well, what are windows for? I never saw two people more brazen – they'd leave the window half open, and what you couldn't see you could hear. There were even times – oh *Virgen Santa*, the way some people will betray you – that that hussy would come to the house in a *público*. And she wouldn't get out two or three blocks away and walk, either, she'd get out of that *público* right there in front of the house, she'd tell the driver to just let her out right there, please sir. And there he'd be, waiting for her, with his eyes just sparkling and that horniness of his (excuse my French, but that's exactly what it was, just pure horniness) coming out all over him.

The neighbors talked, of course. How could they not, if that good-for-nothing sport was in there at batting practice all day every day? Oh, not that there were any saints along Muñoz Rivera – I doubt you'd find a man in the neighborhood that hadn't played around at least once, just to keep in practice, you know. But nobody flaunted it that way – everybody else could be discreet and respectful about it, but not him . . . The women on the street were fuming – nobody spoke to him, not so much as a good morning , and if he tried to say good morning to *them* (him being the smooth-talking thing he was), they'd give him the coldest shoulder this side of the North Pole. I bet you're asking yourself why it took so long for the girl to find out. Good question . . .

One day she got sick at work. She'd get bad every month when her special friend came for his visit, and there wasn't an aspirin or a hot pad that'd do anything for it. And this particular month her belly was being twisted and ripped so bad that she asked one of the girls that worked with her to drive her home to Patillas. At twelve o'clock on the dot (I know because of the soap opera I was watching at the time) she was opening her front door. She'd seen the car in the carport, so she knew her husband was at home. She'd no more than walked in the door when she hears the bedsprings squeaking and somebody in there moaning and breathing hard enough for even *her* to finally hear it. Pain or no pain, she tiptoes over to the bedroom door, sticks just the end of her nose inside, and comes upon that scene. Her husband had that yellow-skinned redhead on all fours and he was taking her from behind, great god, and the redhead was in heaven, wiggling her backside six ways from Sunday! The things men like these days . . . Thank goodness I was widowed when I was.

(10) Toa Alta

Abelardo Díaz Alfaro, *Josco*

In this allegorical story about two bulls (one a Puerto Rican bull and the other an American one) Díaz Alfaro accurately captures the rural realities of Puerto Rico as witnessed on his grandfather's farm at Toa Alta.

The next day I saw Jincho come through the gate from the next property, leading an enormous white bull by a rope; his horns short, his powerful forehead sepia-colored; the dilated nostrils drilled through by an iron ring. Jincho came slowly along the *guayabal* path as if he were being pushed, not at all anxious to get there.

Suddenly a powerful bellow rang out over the *mayú* plantations of Los Cocos, resounding in the San Lorenzo gullies and on the jagged peaks of Farallón. A flash of joy lit Jincho's drawn face.

It was Josco's war cry, his challenge to contest, with daggers of horn, the supremacy of the herd. His head swung up and down, and he jabbed viciously at the ground, bringing up the sod and grass on his horns; blindly he lunged at the air, as if fighting with shadows.

Jincho, on the hilltop near the house, held back the white bull. Josco, striding lightly forward, came out on the path. For a moment he halted, then whirled around, agile, and began to lance the small guava trees that bordered the path, his crowned head garlanded with branches, wild flowers and rattans. On he came slowly, cautiously, with a repeated and monotonous bellow. Stretching his neck, the sound culminated in a long trumpeting roar. He raked the earth with his hoofs until clouds of golden dust rose skyward. He advanced, then stopped, immobile, hieratic, tense. On his dark spongy lips the foam erupted in bubbles of silver. For a short time he stayed thus. His neck arched, his muzzle close to the ground he snorted violently, as if tracking some mysterious scent.

At the homestead, people began appearing on the balcony. The crowd gathered from their mud huts. Urchins with swollen bellies perforated the air with shrill cries: 'Josco is fighting with the Vellillas' American.'

Biographical and literary notes

BURGOS, Julia de (1918–1953). Born in **Carolina**, Burgos began writing poems in 1938. She worked as a school teacher, and subsequently as a radio broadcaster until she was sacked. She was always a political radical, and her main themes are the problems of being a woman, social justice and being Puerto Rican. She emigrated to New York in 1940 and stayed for 11 years, in self-exile, feeling 'split in two', away from her island. She died in the street in New York from alcoholism. She was famed for having lived a scandalous life. Her complete works appeared in 1961. Her poem 'Yo soy Julia Burgos' is a feminist classic.

DÍAZ ALFARO, Abelardo (1920–). Born in **Caguas**, Díaz Alfaro studied at the University in **Río Piedras**. He taught in rural schools, was a social worker, a researcher into laws concerning minors in the Ministry of Work, and wrote scripts for the radio station WIPR. His protest stories dealing with rural Puerto Rico and the *jíbaros* first appeared in *Terrazo*, 1948 and won a prize given by the Instituto de Literatura.

DÍAZ VALCÁRCEL, Emilio (1929–). Born in **Trujillo Alto**, Díaz Valcárcel joined the army after leaving school, and fought in Korea. He was demobbed in 1953. In 1954 he began studying at the **University of Puerto Rico** while working in the publishing section of División de Educación de la Comunidad. He is one of the leading literary mentors of Puerto Rican fiction in Spanish. His first book of short stories *El asedio* appeared in 1958. He won the prestigious Spanish literary prize Biblioteca Breve for his novel *Figuraciones en el mes de marzo*, 1972 (*Schemes in the Month of March*, 1980). Another novel *Proceso en diciembre*, 1963, deals with Puerto Rican soldiers fighting in the Korean war where Díaz Valcárcel himself fought. He won a Guggenheim fellowship and wrote *Harlem todos los días* (*Hot Soles in Harlem*, 1993 – Extract 1) which follows Gerardo's picaresque journey from the island to New York. The novel is colloquial, modernistic and fun as Gerardo/Gery finds lodgings, meets fellow Puerto Rican intellectuals, and many other Latin Americans in the Babel of New York, gets a job, falls in love, etc.

Through Gerardo we see that the island traditions have vanished 'in the thunderclap of industrialization and the television era and rock and salsa' and that New York is an 'uncontrolled city full of human wreckage and lights and innumerable dangers', but that Gerardo loves it with 'an extremely extraordinary love'.

FERRÉ, Rosario (1938–). Ferré was born in **Ponce**. Her father (Luis Ferré) eventually became Governor of Puerto Rico. She comes from a family of industrialists and landowners, went to the **School of the Sacred Heart** and on to University in the USA (Wellesley and Manhattanville), married at 20, had three children, and then divorced. She returned to university in Puerto Rico in 1972, and currently lives and teaches in Washington, DC. She published the first of five collections of short stories in 1976, and has also written criticism (*Sitio a Eros*, 1980). *Papeles de Pandora*, 1976 (*The Youngest Doll*, 1991 – Extract 5) is a selection from her stories and her critical work. Her fiction deals with the dilemmas of being Puerto Rican in terms of clashes between social classes, race, and language in oral, gossipy stories where voice is predominant. She translated her own novel *Maldito amor*, 1986 (the title refers to a popular Puerto Rico song) into *Sweet Diamond Dust*, 1989. The novel evokes the De La Valle family history against the island's history, with a final burning down of the family estate by an enraged daughter. She also ran a literary magazine *Zona de carga y descarga*.

GONZÁLEZ, José Luis (1926–). González was born in Santo Domingo with a Puerto Rican father. He moved to **San Juan** when he was four years old. He has lived in New York, and curently resides in Mexico City, where he teaches at the National University (UNAM). He has written many collections of short stories, beginning with *En la sombra*, 1943, and including the influential *El hombre en la calle*, 1948. His novel *Balada de otro tiempo*, 1980, has been translated into English as *Ballad of Another Time*, 1988. His has written literary essays, and a crucial study of Puerto Rican identity *País de cuatro pisos*, 1980, translated as *Puerto Rico: The Four-Storeyed Country and Other Essays*, 1993. González joined the Communist Party in the 1940s, and for a long time was not able to enter the USA.

PALÉS MATOS, Luis (1898–1959). Palés Matos, a white, was born in **Guyama**, and died in **San Juan**. He published his first book of poems when he was 17 years old. His most important book is *Tuntún de pasa y grifería*, 1937, where he asserts himself as one of the main exponents of Afro–Antillean poetry based on popular dance and song rhythms. His complete poems were published in 1968.

SÁNCHEZ, Luis Rafael (1936–). Born in **San Juan**, Sánchez is currently a professor at the **University of Puerto Rico**. He has published short stories (*En cuerpo de camisa*, 1966) and plays, as well as his satiric and colloquial novel anatomizing the contradictions of his island through popular music, *La guaracha del macho Camacho*, 1976 (*Macho Camacho's Beat*, 1981 – Extract 7). In 1988 he published his second novel *La importanica de llamarse Daniel Santos*, in which he continues his critique of Puerto Rican manners, especially *machismo*, through popular music. Sánchez's intentions are political, describing what he calls 'colonial contamination'.

SOTO, Pedro Juan (1928–). Born in **Cataño**, Soto moved to New York aged 18 in 1946 to study at Long Island University, graduating in 1950, and further at Columbia Teachers College for his MA in 1953.

In between he was drafted into the army during the Korean war. He lived some 10 years in New York, and this became the theme of many of his stories. His first collection of short stories was *Spiks*, 1956, translated into English in 1973 (Extract 3). He has also published plays and novels, including *Usmaíl*, 1958, set on the island of Vieques where the local farmers were evicted to allow US army manoeuvres to take place. A novel *Ardiente suelo, fría estación*, 1961, was translated into English as *Hot Land, Cold Season*, 1973, and also deals with New York Puerto Ricans. He has edited the *San Juan Review*, and written film scripts and educational booklets. Since 1954, Soto has lived in **San Juan**.

SOTO VÉLEZ, Clemente (1905–). Born in **Lares**, Soto Vélez began writing poems as part of an avant-garde group which soon joined forces with the militant Nationalist Party led by Pedro Albizu Campos. Soto Vélez became editor of their newspaper *Armas*, which called for an armed struggle for independence from the USA. After participating in a sugar-cane workers' strike in 1936 he was arrested and imprisoned from 1936 to 1942. In 1943 he finally joined the Communist Party. He lived for many years in New York, working for journals and newspapers. Most of his poetry emanated from the 1950s, with his collected poems *Obra poética* appearing in 1989. Soto Vélez is a universalist, writing daring poems with humanist and revolutionary drives. His poetics are summarized in 'sing / like the peon of the subversive verb / with the hands / of the peon / that dignify / his abused body / with sprouts of gunfire'.

VEGA, Ana Lydia (1946–). Born in **Santurce**, Vega teaches French literature at the **University of Puerto Rico** in **Río Piedras** where she lives. She has won several literary prizes,

Ana Lydia Vega

including the Cuban Casa de las Américas in 1982, and the Juan Rulfo in 1984. *True and False Romances* (Extract 9) translates stories from three collections in Spanish, and includes one novella. All the stories are racy and witty, often oral, and parodic. Ana Lydia Vega offers a sharp woman's view of a culture and people divided between the USA and the Caribbean. She has also written for the theatre.

THE VIRGIN ISLANDS

'The Union Jack flew over this enchanting green hump in the blue ocean for almost two hundred years. Before that the island was Danish; before that, French; before that, cannibal. Smoky gun battles between sailing ships and the old stone fort went with these flag changes; whizzing cannon balls, raiding parties, skirmishes, and an occasional death.'
Herman Wouk,
Don't Stop the Carnival

Nobody seems too sure as to how many Virgin Islands there really are. Estimates tend to vary between 80 and 107, although most people agree that the majority of these islands are extremely small and uninhabited. When Christopher Columbus arrived on his second expedition in 1493, he named this cluster of volcanic outcrops *Las Once Mil Vírgenes*. This allusion to St Ursula and her 11 000 martyred virgins remains obscure, but is thought to refer as much to the large number of islands as to their moral rectitude.

Nowadays the Virgins are shared between the USA, which claims some 68 islands as an unincorporated territory, and Britain, which maintains a smaller eastern group as a Crown Colony. At their nearest point, the US Virgin Islands (USVI) and the British Virgin Islands (BVI) are separated by little more than a couple of miles of sea. But in terms of history, development and everyday atmosphere there is a vast gulf between them. While the USVI have grown into a mass tourism destination, welcoming some two million visitors each year, the BVI have remained relatively low-key in their approach to tourism and cater for about one-tenth of their neighbour's arrivals.

Accordingly, the USVI, and particularly the capital **Charlotte Amalie** on the island of **St Thomas**, offer the traditional tourism features of duty-free shopping, golf courses and up-market resorts. When two or more cruise ships dock at the same time in the capital's port, the streets are packed with tourists in search of souvenirs and the traffic congestion is legendary. In **Road Town**, the main settlement of the BVI, by contrast, the mood is distinctly relaxed despite an increasing number of cruise ship

FACT BOX

AREA: USVI 352 sq km; BVI 150 sq km
POPULATION: USVI 104 000; BVI 17 500
CAPITAL: USVI Charlotte Amalie; BVI Road Town
LANGUAGES: English
POLITICAL STATUS: USVI 'Unincorporated Territory of the US';
 BVI British Crown Colony
PER CAPITA GDP: USVI US$14 700; BVI US$11 200

arrivals. Visitors here tend to be from the more exclusive yachting and chartered boat sector.

Of the USVI, **St Thomas** and **St Croix** are the main islands, the latter being the site of the vast Hess petroleum refinery, while two-thirds of **St John** is given over to the Virgin Islands National Park. The main island of the BVI is **Tortola**, with smaller populations on **Virgin Gorda**, **Anegada** and **Jost Van Dyke**. There is no shortage of strange names among the Virgins, and these include **Beef Island** (once a buccaneer's cattle-hunting ground), **The Dogs** and **Dead Chest** (where Blackbeard reputedly marooned sailors to the tune of 'Fifteen men on a dead man's chest – Yo ho ho and a bottle of rum!'). The 74-acre **Necker Island** belongs to Virgin boss Richard Branson who wanted to own a private Virgin island.

ISLANDS FOR SALE

What are now the US Virgin Islands changed hands several times during the course of their early colonial history. The indigenous Caribs put up some resistance to Columbus, and although Spain claimed sovereignty to the islands, there was no real European settlement until the seventeenth century. The Dutch, the French and the British all attempted to colonize the island of **St Croix**, and at one point the Knights of Malta held a lease there. Eventually, in 1733 the French Crown sold **St Croix** to another, less likely, European power – Denmark. The Danes had already managed to take control of **St John** and **St Thomas**, the latter acting as an important entrepôt for the regional slave trade.

The Danish colony was successful and profitable for several decades. Exporting rum, sugar and cotton back to Denmark, it made fortunes for merchants, ship-owners and planters, and the sturdy warehouses and town houses of **Charlotte Amalie** bear witness to the islands' good days. By the beginning of the nineteenth century, the population had risen to 40 000 of whom 31 000 were slaves, mostly shipped over from the Danish enclave on Africa's Gold Coast. These slaves fared no better under the Danes than under British or French masters. In 1848, impatient for the enactment of abolition which was reportedly imminent, they rose up in **St Thomas** and demanded immediate freedom. As the colony's whites fled to take refuge on ships, the authorities capitulated and granted unconditional emancipation.

The problems afflicting the Caribbean sugar industry hit the Danish Virgin Islands particularly hard. **St Thomas** fared well as a free port, and ships from all around the region loaded and unloaded there. But when technological advances meant that ships no longer needed to take on coal or replenish supplies after a long Atlantic crossing, the port also fell into disrepair.

By the beginning of the twentieth century, the Virgin Islands had become a heavy burden for the Danish government. As Victorian traveller Sir Frederick Treves (♢ St Kitts and Nevis) noted in his *The Cradle of the Deep* (Extract 4), the colony was also gradually losing its Danishness. The USA, meanwhile, was keen to expand its direct territorial control over the Caribbean region, and this intensified with the completion of the Panama Canal in 1914 and fears of German intervention. In 1917 a relieved Denmark finally sold its Caribbean colony to the USA for the sum of US$25 million. Later, to the chagrin of the Danes, the Americans admitted that they would willingly have paid US$40 million. For its money, the USA acquired the strategic port of **Charlotte Amalie** and ruled out the threat of Germany buying a foothold in the Caribbean.

The Danes retired gracefully from their colonial adventure and left behind them some distinctive architecture, place names and the un-American convention of driving on the left. Not until 1993, moreover, did they finally sell their West Indian Company, which controlled land and property on the islands, to the USVI government.

The change of ownership brought few immediate benefits to the Virgin Islanders who were subjected to US military rule during the First World War and for some time afterwards. The islands were backward and bankrupt, and a series of droughts and hurricanes ruined the already flagging sugar industry during the 1930s. During that decade Herbert Hoover memorably described the islands as an orphanage and poor-house. The Second World War briefly revived the USVI's fortunes, especially with the presence of a submarine base, but peace again brought neglect and decline. It was only with the advent of the Cuban Revolution in 1959 and the subsequent US embargo that the USVI began to become developed as an alternative destination for American tourists. The 1960s witnessed a spectacular construction boom as developers transformed hitherto unspoilt coastlines into beach resorts and marinas. Sugar-cane was abandoned, and tax incentives encouraged the arrival of heavy industry from the USA. The Hess Oil Company started up its refinery on **St Croix** and was joined by an alumina processing plant.

Nowadays, the population of the USVI enjoys one of the highest standards of living in the Caribbean, with a cost of living to match. In what car licence plates describe as the 'American Paradise', islanders are US citizens (but cannot vote in presidential elections) with a Delegate to the House of Representatives. Resentment persists, however, and many people believe themselves to have a second-class colonial status. A referendum on the USVI's constitutional future in 1993 proved inconclusive as a high abstention rate reflected almost universal political apathy. There is friction, too, between 'native' Virgin Islanders and 'continentals' who have moved in from the USA, and this is compounded by hostility towards migrants from poorer neighbouring islands who have come in search of work.

'A MISERABLE SPOT'

By contrast, the British Virgin Islands have remained under more or less continuous British control since 1666, when the Dutch were driven off. In the following years, planters from Anguilla settled on **Anegada** and **Virgin Gorda** and established small-scale sugar, cotton and indigo plantations. Civil government was not established until 1773, when a House of Assembly was introduced.

The abolition of slavery and the collapse of the sugar industry in the nineteenth century sent the British Virgin Islands into a long, irreversible decline. Planters abandoned the islands, and peasant farmers settled on smallholdings, often exporting their fruit and vegetables to the more developed Danish colony. Perhaps more so than any other British territory, the Virgin Islands were left at the periphery of the empire, offering little to London and receiving even less. From 1872 they were administered from Antigua as part of the Leeward Islands Federation, but when the other British territories opted to join the short-lived Federation of the West Indies, the BVI took their own course, becoming a separate British colony. So they have remained to this day, with a Governor appointed by London but also with a large degree of internal self-government.

THE TOURIST INVASION

In 1942 the American-born journalist Martha Gellhorn ◊ arrived in **Road Town** and felt she had 'fallen off the map'. In *Travels With Myself and Another* (Extract 2) she recalls the complete backwardness of the place and its resulting charm. Thirty years later, the charm had evaporated, she writes, under the influx of tourists who had 'discovered' these distant islands (Extract 3). Shiva Naipaul ◊ also visited the British Virgin Islands in the 1970s and was contemptuous of their apparent torpor. In his essay 'Two Colonies' (Extract 1), he sees tourism and duty-free alcohol as the islands' only and pathetic forms of industry.

But tourism in the British colony has been restrained by comparison with the brash development of the USVI. According to British journalist Simon Winchester, the inhabitants of the American islands have spoiled what was once worth preserving:

> 'Their territory is a dreadful place, flashy and gaudy, loud and vulgar, with nightclubs and casinos and a thousand profitable diversions for

the overworked young of the Eastern seaboard. The charm went with the Danes, seventy years ago, and not a few islanders wish, for all the pleasures of owning an American passport, that the cool administrators from Copenhagen would come back and bring some *dignitas* with them.'

Derek Walcott (◊ St Lucia), elsewhere a critic of insensitive tourist development, writes in his poem 'The Virgins' of **Frederiksted's** transformation from a quiet Caribbean town into a tasteless tourist attraction where 'only the crime rate is on the rise / in streets blighted with sun, stone arches / and plazas blown dry by the hysteria of rumour'.

Yet not all writers have necessarily seen the growth of tourism as a matter for concern. One of the most popular novels to have been inspired by the Caribbean is *Don't Stop the Carnival* (Extract 5) by Herman Wouk ◊, who took 1950s **St Thomas** as the model for his fictional Kinja. The novel's account of the comic escapades of a would-be hotelier and the eccentricities of expatriate life was well received everywhere apart, it is said, from the USVI, to where Herman Wouk never dared to return.

LITERARY LANDMARKS

Norman Island. This uninhabited British Virgin Island is reputedly the inspiration for Robert Louis Stevenson's classic novel *Treasure Island*. Stevenson never travelled to the Caribbean, but was influenced by Charles Kingsley (◊ Trinidad and Tobago). Stevenson's father, who built lighthouses, also knew the Caribbean well.

Frederiksted, USVI. In contrast to Walcott's lament (Extract 5) stands Lafcadio Hearn's (◊ Martinique) enthusiastic description of the town in 1887, recorded in *Two Years in the West Indies*; it had, he wrote, 'the appearance of a beautiful Spanish town, with its Romanesque piazzas, churches, many arched buildings peeping through breaks in a line of mahogany, bread-fruit, mango, tamarind and palm trees.'

BOOKLIST

Gellhorn, Martha, *Travels with Myself and Another*, Allen Lane, London, 1978. **Extracts 2 and 3**.

Holdridge, Desmond, *Escape to the Tropics*, Robert Hale, London, 1937.

Naipaul, Shiva, *Beyond the Dragon's Mouth: Stories and Pieces*, Hamish Hamilton, London, 1984. **Extract 1**

Treves, Sir Frederick, *The Cradle of the Deep: An Account of a Voyage to the West Indies*, Smith, Elder and Company, London, 1897. **Extract 4**.

Walcott, Derek, 'The Virgins', in

Selected Poetry, Heinemann, Oxford, 1993.
Winchester, Simon, *Outposts*, Hodder and Stoughton, London, 1985.
Wouk, Herman, *Don't Stop the Carnival*, Fontana, Glasgow, 1987. **Extract 5**.

Extracts

(1) BRITISH VIRGIN ISLANDS

Shiva Naipaul, *Two Colonies*

For Naipaul, the British colony represents all the stagnation and futility of a forgotten imperial backwater.

Sixty miles to the west of Puerto Rico the Union Jack flaps limply over those scattered crumbs of the Empire known as the British Virgin Islands. Area: fifty-nine square miles. Population: eleven thousand. 'Tortola', said a nineteenth-century writer, 'is well nigh the most miserable, worst inhabited spot in all the British possessions.' I wouldn't go as far as that. I can think of at least half a dozen more miserable spots.

Like Puerto Rico, the islands have an internally autonomous political life and no one seems to care much for the idea of Independence – though, one gathers, the British would be only too happy to oblige. 'Give we Independence,' remarked one of the indolent, beach-combing locals, 'and you give we a dictator. No, man. We doing fine just as we is.' After which observations he offered to sell me some marijuana. The Governor sits in his house up on the hill and has little to do. Faint rumours of corruption surround the local administration. The Chief Minister, one hears, has a fondness for acquiring property. But, if some of the locals have doubts about the propriety of his real-estate transactions, the expatriates have none. To a man, these languid, sea-loving folk lavish praise on his wisdom and devotion to duty. If, I was told by one of them, the Chief Minister had done well for himself, that was only because he was a tremendously hard worker and an extremely clever man. Which, I am sure, is true.

Away from the water not much happens. Road Town, the capital, is one narrow, winding main street. Along it promenade the tourists and locally bred Rastafarians – even in Tortola they have identity problems. The chief architectural monument of the town is a white-walled jail crowned with barbed wire. What else can one say? What else can one do but wonder at an Empire reduced to this level of absurdity? that has condemned eleven thousand people to so silly an existence?

There is nothing to look at; there are no visible signs of agricultural effort. Liquor is extraordinarily cheap and, apparently, one of the hazards of expatriate life on the islands . . . The sea shines. Yachts move dreamily. At night, boat-loads of 'boat people' descend on Stanley's Beach Bar and jive to the steelband under the watchful gaze of cinematically menacing blacks who wear dark glasses and talk little.

(2) BRITISH VIRGIN ISLANDS: BACKWARDNESS

Martha Gellhorn, *Travels with Myself and Another*

In 1942, Martha Gellhorn arrived in the then undeveloped British Virgin Islands, where primitive conditions created their own charm.

My heart rose like a bird at once. It always did, incurably, except in rain, as soon as I felt I had fallen off the map. The motorboat dumped me, soaked by spray and chirpy, at Roadtown, a cluster of unpainted shacks and a single dust street. There were ten white residents on the island and 7000 blacks, no cars, few bicycles and one taxi which was a rowboat. The British Commissioner who also served as doctor, dispensing their small stock of medicines, and magistrate and editor of the mimeographed newspaper, deplored my scheme but passed me on to the local grocer, Mr de Castro, a white-haired dignified black man.

Mr de Castro introduced me to his son Carlton, owner of a potato boat, a thirty-foot sloop called the *Pilot*. A potato boat is an overgrown rowboat, with one sail and a hold for potatoes, which sold its cargo from island to island and returned carrying whatever could be brought en route, preferably rum and tobacco and preferably smuggled back into the home island . . .

I was marooned in the Social Inn, an inexplicable hostelry – why would anyone come here? – two dirty bedrooms, with beer bottles swept into corners and drifts of cigarette butts, mementoes of survivors off an English ship who had been moved on to Puerto Rico a few days earlier. Rain blew in through the shutters and under the door. There was no electric light, hardship for a reader as the only place to perch was beneath the stained mosquito net on the boards of the four-poster bed and I thought I might set fire to the place with a kerosene lamp in that tent. The Social Inn reminded me of the Palace hotel in Kweilin but there were no bedbugs and one must always be grateful for small mercies. The rain went on and on. I sat amidst my canned goods, eating them from time to time, and read detective stories while the dim daylight lasted.

(3) BRITISH VIRGIN ISLANDS: PROGRESS

Martha Gellhorn, *Travels with Myself and Another*

Thirty-five years later, Gellhorn reflects on the changes which have brought the islands prosperity, but also, as she sees it, a sense of loss.

Money, not war, destroyed the old life of the islands. War only fed in the first big dose of money. I am thankful that I knew the sleepy, lovely little islands all through the Caribbean before the dollars poured over them. At first the wintering wealthy arrived, then the reduced-rate summer tourists. Now they're coining money everywhere the year round. It's a success story; it's Progress.

The last time I saw the beautiful cove on Virgin Gorda it was full of sun-tanned bodies and ringed by boats, from swan yachts to rubber Zodiacs, and there were bottles and plastic debris on the sea-bed and picnic litter on the sand for the rich are as disgusting as the poor in their carelessness of the natural world. The Social Inn on Tortola is incredible pre-history where now you book months ahead to reserve rooms in ten hotels, or buy a luxury condominium residence; the *Pilot* is unthinkable in the two stylish marinas. St Martin, which I loved first and most, is a thriving blighted area. A great runway on the Dutch side receives Jets. Phillipsburg and Marigot are boom towns. Handsome houses of foreigners dot the hills. There are grand hotels and crummy motels, casinos and boutiques, supermarkets and launderettes, snack bars and robber restaurants, throngs of visitors and plentiful muck on the beaches. And the island, once a green bouquet of trees, looks bald. Progress uses space and is more valuable than trees.

(4) CHARLOTTE AMALIE, US VIRGIN ISLANDS

Sir Frederick Treves, *The Cradle of the Deep*

Charlotte Amalie, the beautiful capital of the US Virgin Islands, had already lost much of its Danish flavour by the end of the nineteenth century, according to this British traveller.

Charlotte Amalia, the capital of St Thomas, is without any question the most picturesque town in the whole sweep of the Windward islands. Placed within a magnificent harbour, and at the foot of a circle of green hills, Charlotte Amalia makes there a bravery of colour. The town is built about three rounded spurs which jut out from the mountain's base. It seems, therefore, to be made up of three towns joined along the sea margin, each of the three a cone of bright habitations reared against the dull green of the hill.

The walls of the houses which are thus piled one above the other are, for the most part, a dazzling white. Some are yellow or grey or orange; certain of them are blue. The roofs are always a generous bright red. Between the houses and overshadowing the roofs are clumps of green trees. Here and there can be seen stone stairs climbing up through the town, gardens with creeper-covered walls, a tufted palm, a many-arched arcade, the balustrades of shady terraces. Viewed from the sea Charlotte Amalia would seem to be a place for those who make holiday – all gaily tinted villas and palaces, where the factory chimney, the warehouse, and the woeful suburb are unknown.

Viewed from close quarters it is a little less charming. A long, level street, clean and bright, runs from one end of the settlement to the other. The remaining streets are engaged in clambering up the sides of the three hills. The town contains many handsome buildings, a few of which are dignified by age, together with shops and stores of the colonial type which breathe generally the odour of bay rum. The names of the streets are in Danish, as are also certain official notices, but with these exceptions there is little to suggest a colony of Denmark. The language of the people is English, the newspaper is in English, while the determination of the islanders to profess that tongue is shown in the following tavern wall announcement which faces the stranger on landing:

'Cool sherbert and other such sippings.'

. . . St Thomas once had an evil reputation for unhealthiness. The cemetery in the town testifies that this was not unmerited, and that there were some grounds for Kingsley's description of the place as 'a Dutch oven for cooking fever in.' Now, thanks to enlightened sanitary measures, it can claim to be quite a wholesome settlement.

(5) US Virgin Islands: Hotels

Herman Wouk, *Don't Stop the Carnival*

American Norman Paperman's dream of buying and managing the Gull Reef Club is rapidly becoming a nightmare as the problems he faces mount up.

He came awake with a bodily jerk. The knocking went on, and still the voice cried, 'Inside! Mistah Papuh! You dah?' It was a woman's voice, and not Sheila's: thin, high. The seaward window was black dark; no moonlight, no stars. His phosphorescent watch dial showed quarter past eleven.

'Inside! Inside! – Well, I guess he ain' dah.'

Another girlish voice: 'He dah.'

Hammering of several fists, and yells of two women: 'Inside! Mistuh Papuh!'

'All right, all right, one moment.'

The girls – they were the waitresses in the bar – told him that the hotel water had just run out. Church had noticed it, while washing glasses, and had immediately sent them to him.

'Okay,' said Paperman, with some elation. For once he was on top of a Gull Reef crisis. 'Tell Church he'll have water in two minutes.'

The two girls ran back to the main house and he followed in robe and flapping straw slippers. In the lobby half a dozen guests in night clothes clamoured at him. He raised both hands. 'Folks, it's a question of shifting from one cistern to another. I regret the inconvenience, but by the time you get back to your rooms you'll have water.'

Many people were drinking and laughing in the bar, all oblivious to the water crisis, and more were on the terrace, dancing to the steel band.

'Church, get the big flashlight in the kitchen and come with me. You might as well learn how to do this.'

'Yes, sir.'

He led Church to the malodorous hole under the hotel. The pump was running with a queer dry rattle. Paperman flashed the light beam along an electric cable, coiling in the darkness to a wall socket. He pulled out the plug. A fat blue spark leaped after the prongs; the pump choked, rattled, shuddered all over, gave a screech and one loud clank, and fell silent.

Paperman did not remember, at this point, whether the red valve or the green valve led to the emergency tank. It didn't matter, he thought. All he had to do was close the open one and open the closed one.

He did this.

'Now,' he said, and he plunged the plug back into the socket.

The pump reacted like a living thing, like a bull stabbbed with a sword, like a woman grasped in the dark by a strange hand. It screamed and writhed, and seemed to rise bodily off its concrete block, and shook at every point, its gauge needles dancing. Then it settled down to running noisily again.

Biographical and literary notes

GELLHORN, Martha (1908–). Born in St Louis, Missouri, Martha Gellhorn became a journalist and worked for *Collier's Weekly* as a war correspondent, covering the Spanish Civil War, the invasion of Finland and fighting in Europe during the Second World War. Her marriage to Ernest Hemingway (◊ Cuba) lasted from 1940 to 1945 and was a stormy relationship. Her later war coverage included Java (1946), Vietnam (1966) and Central America (1983–85). Apart from collected journalism, Gellhorn has published several novels, including *Liana* (◊ Saint Martin) and *The Wine of Astonishment*, 1948. She is also the author of collections of short stories. In *Travels With Myself and Another* (Extracts 2 and 3), she describes an expedition around the Caribbean during the Second

World War, when she visited the British Virgin Islands and Vichy-ruled Saint Martin.

NAIPAUL, Shiva (1945–1985). Born in Trinidad, the younger brother of V.S. Naipaul, Shivadhar Srinivasa Naipaul was educated in the island and at Oxford University. He became a writer shortly after leaving university and his first novel, *Fireflies*, was published in 1970. Several other novels followed, including *The Chip-Chip Gatherers*, 1973 and *Love and Death in a Hot Country*, 1983, as well as a travel book, *North of South*, 1978. *Black and White*, 1980, is a highly acclaimed investigation of the infamous Jonestown massacre in Guyana. A collection of essays and stories, *Beyond the Dragon's Mouth* (Extract 1) was published in 1984, one year before Naipaul's tragically premature death.

TREVES, Sir Frederick (see under St Kitts and Nevis).

WOUK, Herman (1915–). Born in New York, Wouk is a highly popular novelist, whose work includes *The Caine Mutiny*, 1951, *The Winds of War*, 1971, and *War and Remembrance*, 1978. Concerned with Judaism and the history of the Holocaust, Wouk has also written a number of plays and some science fiction. In *Don't Stop the Carnival* (Extract 6), he produced one of the most celebrated comic depictions of expatriate life in the Caribbean, featuring Norman Paperman, a would-be refugee from the stress of New York executive life who finds existence as a hotelier in a thinly disguised **St Thomas** even more exacting.

SAINT MARTIN/
SINT MAARTEN

'About ten years ago I went back there again by chance, while searching the Caribbean to see if any of it was left as once I knew it. A runway for Jumbo jets had been built on my Eden, and the island was covered by hotels, boarding houses, boutiques, eateries, villas and hordes of tourists . . . Progress: absolute ruin.'
Martha Gellhorn

Only the most modest of borders marks the dividing line between the two European enclaves which share this one island – the smallest in the world to be partitioned. The road out of **Philipsburg**, capital of Dutch Sint Maarten, has run perhaps only five kilometres through an almost unbroken line of tourist facilities before it crosses the frontier on its way to **Marigot**, the main town of French Saint Martin. A small monumental obelisk marks the spot where part of the Kingdom of the Netherlands gives way to a sub-prefecture of the *département d'outre-mer* of Guadeloupe. There is no border post, no checking of passports; the traveller crosses unnoticed from one piece of Europe to another. Saint Martin is, technically speaking, part of France. Sint Maarten is one of the six Dutch territories in the Caribbean (see The Netherlands Antilles and Aruba).

The border sneaks imperceptibly across some ten kilometres, including **Simpson Bay Lagoon**, which is neatly divided in half. The Dutch have 37 square kilometres, while the French have the larger share of 52 square kilometres. The French side is perhaps slightly wilder, with the highest point, **Pic du Paradis**, offering beautiful views over surrounding islands. Yet there is little real wilderness and hardly any agriculture. Instead, a concrete suburbia has spread over much of the island, designed for the expatriates and tourists who fuel Saint Martin's economy.

DIVIDED ISLAND

The strange status of tiny Saint Martin goes back to 1648 when Dutch and

---

FACT BOX

AREA: Saint Martin – 52 sq km; Sint Maarten – 37 sq km
POPULATION: Saint Martin – 28 500; Sint Maarten – 70 000
CAPITAL: Saint Martin – Marigot; Sint Maarten – Philipsburg
LANGUAGES: English, French, Dutch, Spanish, Papiamento
POLITICAL STATUS: Saint Martin – Sub-prefecture of Guadeloupe
and part of French Republic; Sint Maarten – Member of federal
Netherlands Antilles and part of Kingdom of the Netherlands
PER CAPITA GDP: Saint Martin – US$6200; Sint Maarten –
US$8320

French colonizers, in an uncharacteristic gesture, agreed to share the island. The French had arrived in 1629 and founded a settlement in the northern part, and two years later a Dutch expedition moved into the southern end of the island, where a large salt pond seemed a promising commercial proposition. By this time, the indigenous Carib population had been wiped out and the two communities co-existed more or less peacefully.

The Spanish, however, had designs on Saint Martin (which Columbus had sighted and named in 1493) and in 1633 they invaded the island from Puerto Rico and deported all the Dutch and French settlers. But soon the Spanish lost interest in the insignificant place, and French and Dutch colonists returned from the islands of St Kitts and St Eustatius respectively. On this occasion, the two groups agreed to share the island and signed a treaty to that effect on 23 March 1648. A probably apocryphal legend has it that the partition was decided by a race between a Frenchman and a Dutchman who set off in different directions from the centre of the island, walking around the coast until they met. The Frenchman, it is said, walked faster and gained more territory because he drank only wine, while the Dutchman was held back by his consumption of Genever or gin.

Although the Treaty of Mount Concordia was – and still is – honoured by both sides, the island was to change hands throughout the next two centuries, with the British occupying Saint Martin between 1795 and 1815. During the eighteenth century, blacks began to outnumber whites as slaves were introduced to work on sugar and cotton plantations and in cattle-raising. Dutch Sint Maarten's economic lifeline, however, was its salt industry, where slave labour was extensively used. When France abolished slavery in 1848, some slaves from the Dutch section naturally crossed the border in search of freedom, but the great majority waited a further fifteen years until 1863, when the Dutch finally decreed their emancipation.

With the end of slavery Saint Martin's already precarious plantation system more or less vanished. Some former slaves and their families moved to the Dominican Republic and Cuba to work in the sugar plantations; others found work in building the Panama Canal. Only the salt industry prospered, and an average of 200 000 250 lb barrels were exported annually, mostly to the USA.

Gradually both sides of the island became depopulated as younger people abandoned their homes to work abroad. The opening of the Shell oil refinery on the Dutch island of Curaçao in 1917 attracted many from Sint Maarten. The isolation and economic hardship experienced during both world wars did little to alleviate the island's depression. The Second World War, in particular, worsened conditions, as Saint Martin, administratively ruled from Guadeloupe, was held to be pro-Vichy and was blockaded by allied forces. Finally, the salt industry collapsed in 1949 after years of decline.

In 1942 the American journalist Martha Gellhorn (◊ The Virgin Islands) defied the blockade and German submarines and arrived in French Saint Martin. **Marigot**, she recalls in Travels with Myself and Another (Extract 1), was a gently decaying town, but not without charm. She used the landscape and atmosphere of Saint Martin for her 1944 novel, Liana (Extract 2), in which the French colony appears barely disguised as 'St Boniface'. In Liana Gellhorn explores the complexities of race and social stratification through the story of Marc Royer, a successful white local businessman, his mulatto wife Liana, and her French lover Pierre Vauclain. The triangular intrigue eventually ends in tragedy as Pierre feels compelled to return to Europe to fight for France against Germany, while Liana believes herself to be abandoned and commits suicide, alienated from her family by her social advancement.

Last Resorts

The remote and claustrophobic island life described by Gellhorn is unimaginable today. Now both sides of the island are covered in shopping malls, condominiums and beach resorts, attracting almost half a million tourists each year. As Hugh O'Shaughnessy ◊ colourfully demonstrates in his travel book Around the Spanish Main (Extract 3), the transformation of the island into a vacation paradise has not been without its problems. Another English visitor, the writer Quentin Crewe, took a similarly disapproving view in his Touch the Happy Isles (◊ Dominican Republic):

> Philipsburg struck me at once as being deeply sleazy . . . Nothing here has elegance – modern casinos, for some reason, are various hideous shades of purple and puce. In Front Street, there is a jeweller in puce, mock stone, its windows going up in steps. This next to what was once a pretty clapboard house.

Economically at least, mass tourism has been Saint Martin's salvation. In the 1950s the population of Dutch Sint Maarten had dropped to around 1500; today, as many as 100 000 find employment in the shops and hotels of Philipsburg and the other resorts. Many of these are illegal immigrants from territories such as the Dominican Republic and the poorer islands of the Eastern Caribbean. As a result, the streets of the town are filled with the sounds of different languages – English, French, Spanish, Creole, and the Spanish-influenced Dutch patois called Papiamento.

In recent years the island has produced one poet and short story writer, Lasana M. Sekou, whose preferred medium is English. His work tends to attack the commercialization of St Martin and stresses its African cultural legacy. But Sekou is most noted for his grasp of local dialect and idiom, as the short story 'Fatty and the Big House' (Extract 4) makes clear.

BOOKLIST

Gellhorn, Martha, *Liana*, Virago, London, 1987. **Extract 2.**

Gellhorn, Martha, *Travels with Myself and Another*, Allen Lane, London, 1978. **Extract 1.**

Johnson, Will, *For the Love of St Maarten*, Carlton Press, New York, 1987.

O'Shaughnessy, Hugh, *Around the Spanish Main*, Century, London, 1991. **Extract 3.**

Sekou, Lasana M., 'Fatty and the Big House', in *Love Songs Make You Cry*, House of Nehesi, Philipsburg, St Maarten, 1989. **Extract 4.**

Extracts

(1) SAINT MARTIN

Martha Gellhorn, *Travels with Myself and Another*

Arriving in 1942 pro-Vichy Saint Martin after an arduous sea crossing from the Virgin Islands, Martha Gellhorn finds an elegant, if decaying, French enclave.

We bumped rather than sailed past the breakwater into the harbour. A white house with a red roof, a white house with black shutters, a yellow house stood in a row behind the grey stone sea wall. Between the sea wall and the houses, men were playing boule. Beyond this very French Mediterranean approach, the single dust street of Marigot was lined by three-storeyed wooden houses, joined together like French town houses, each with long windows and long shutters on the second floor balconies, each decorated with whimsical fretwork. French – Caribbean – Victorian – New Orleans architecture, I thought, and it couldn't have been prettier, the houses painted in pastel shades, pink and blue and green and yellow picked out in white, though the paint was old and scabby. They could live without paint. Marigot was decaying gracefully.

Outside the town and a few straggling houses dotted along dusty paths, St Martin was jungle, not the real thing which is hideous, but great nameless (to me) plumy trees and flamboyantes, magnolias, ceiba, bread-fruit, Royal palms, and fringed banana trees, with hibiscus and bougainvillaea, gone wild and opulent, to splash colour in the rich green.

I felt rotten and looked rotten too in my dirty clothes, my hair snarled, transparent strips of skin flapping from every part not pimpled by sun blisters. A porter led me along the main street where superior Creole ladies fanned themselves on the balconies and chatted from house to house. Chatting stopped as they stared; children stopped playing in the street. Perhaps they thought I was a new type of female survivor. The porter took me to the police station; despite Vichy, no one was going to fuss about Carlton and his crew, who were fellow islanders; there was a limit to obeying nonsense regulations. If they ordered me back to the *Pilot*, I was prepared to rant or whine, or claim that my long-removed appendix had burst; I was desperate for a bed to lie on until I got my land legs again.

(2) SAINT MARTIN

Martha Gellhorn, *Liana*

> *An illicit, but as yet unconsummated, love has grown up between the black Liana (who is married to a white man) and her white French tutor, Pierre.*

The church was not far from the school on a narrow road lined with pepper trees. Pierre and Liana did not have to cross the main street nor pass the pier. The negroes saw that Monsieur Pierre had met Liana at church and walked home with her, but they would not gossip about this with the whites. It was fortunate that none of the whites saw Liana and Pierre. It would have outraged them all: no one was supposed to carry love affairs into church except the young girls of good family who could walk to and from Mass with their fiancés or those young men whom they hoped to have as fiancés.

'I did not know you went to early Mass, Pierre.'

'I couldn't sleep. I don't usually go at all.'

'You look tired. You aren't sick, are you?'

'No.' He ought to tell Liana about last night. Someone would tell her.

'It is nice to see you on Sunday.'

'Liana,' he said. He thought he must tell her that it would be better not to see her at all. He could not say that. Pierre knew that her only pleasure was their lessons which had become daily lessons, and their Saturday picnics. And my only pleasure, too, he told himself.

'What do you do on Sundays?' Pierre asked.

'I wait.'

'What for?'

'I wait for Monday,' she said and laughed.

Pierre stopped her in the road and held her elbows so that she faced him, but he did not pull her close. He saw behind her the fawn-coloured trunk of a flamboyante with its roots growing out like stretched tendons. It was cool in the shade and silent. Some black Jew-birds made a rumpus in an acacia tree and flew off, bumping across the sky. Then it was silent again.

'Liana, are you very unhappy?'

'Not now.'

'Tell me.'

'Now we have so many things to do. And the books. And everything you teach me. Are you going away, Pierre?'

'I don't want to hurt you.'

'You are going,' Liana said. She did not move and she made no sound; she only lowered her head.

Liana felt the island suddenly as. if she could see it all: green, pointed with hills and dented with valleys, oval, growing in a blue sea with reefs as its roots. It felt too small to live on. It felt so alone that beyond it there was no more land. There was only this tiny island and she could never leave it.

(3) Sint Maarten

Hugh O'Shaughnessy, *Around the Spanish Main*

The startling transformation of Sint Maarten into a tourist and consumer paradise has taken a dreadful aesthetic toll on the island.

'Wine me, Dine me, 69 me,' say the T-shirts hung out to catch the tourist eye along Front Street in Philipsburg, the capital of Sint Maarten. 'Caution: I scream when I come.' There is clearly money to be made in helping visitors to the island to advertise their need for casual sex.

There are fast food joints along the potholed Front Street and the greater part of one shopping mall is taken up by the Coliseum 'casino' where, behind a couple of plaster Grecian columns, a hundred slot machines await the onset of the cruise passengers. In shops with names like Ram and Ashok listless Indian salesmen offer lurid jewellery and cheap electronic goods.

The street, the main shopping centre of the island, rings with the cries of New Yorkers – and some French – hunting for bargains in the sun.

Sint Maarten is one of the most repellent places in the Caribbean, a graceless monument to vulgarian greed, a charmless place which should be avoided by tourists and travellers alike. It is an island of about thirty-five square miles, studded with mountains bearing names like Pic du Paradis and Mont O'Reilly. This island as a whole is a free port; you present your travel document at the police as you arrive at the international airport on the Dutch side and you are then free to roam the whole island; there are no checks on the border between the two sides. Nor are there customs inspections when you arrive because no duty is levied on anything . . .

Tourism transformed the Dutch side producing an unplanned sprawl of unsightly buildings and a business boom which sucked in workers and traders from far and wide. In 1951 there were only 1458 people in Sint Maarten, today there is a floating population of somewhere between 50 000 and 100 000 working on the Dutch side: immigrants from the other Dutch islands of Curaçao and Aruba, dogged, hard-working Haitians doing the dirtiest jobs, Indian traders, housemaids and whores from the Dominican Republic, shop assistants and bellboys from Dominica, Lebanese businessmen, European accountants, retired people from the United States and Canada. The native population is now in a tiny minority in Sint Maarten, even discounting the tourists who arrive every year in their hundreds of thousands by jumbo jet from North America and Europe.

(4) Sint Maarten
Lasana M. Sekou, *Fatty and the Big House*

After earning some money in the oil refinery at Aruba, Fatty returns to Sint Maarten, has a large house built and marries Annie. But he is going to seed and she is cuckolding him.

Then Fatty started liming heavy at Zanzi Bar and drinking. He would come home drunk, helpless as a lump on a log and fall asleep anywhere – on the cold cement floor, on the rough fish nets, on the clean kitchen table, half way on and off the bed, and that is if he made it to the soft bed he should be sharing with Annie. Annie was like the eye of Hurricane Donna which mashed up the land that year. She was not a nagging woman. She was a woman of action. Her friends were saying how Fatty was getting fat again, like when he was a boy; and how he was liming with a bunch of drunkards, and bullying people in the bar. One day during election time, Fatty well slapped off one of the other party member's wife for calling him 'nothing but a fat slobby' after he told her that her brassiere was too tight. 'Old Cassandra', who he tried to bully once to please his drinking partners, talked to the 'Bush Lawyer' who was able to settle the whole melee and keep Fatty out of trouble. His drinking pals didn't even so much as lift a finger to help him. 'Old Cassandra' said he helped Fatty only because 'the young man was Old Willay nephew.' Old Willay was a born fighter. A bold and brave one, who used to brag until his death in 1979, in Cul-de-Sac, that he was one of the only persons who dared to 'read *Winwud Ilan Opinion* openly while ahl yo' wuz skiod to lay oize on it, had to hoide to read dey oan newspaper beca' dey 'fraid Clod dem . . .'

After Fatty got off lucky he tried to behave himself. One thing about Fatty though, once he took out his drinking money from his pay, he gave Annie all the rest 'to take care of the house'.

'But Fatty, where you taking all that money?' asked the young girl in the office where the workers picked up their pay. The first time she came out of her face and asked that strange question all the others kept silent. The third time there was a light ripple of laughter, some of the workers made sounds like cows, some like goats, some attached their pointing fingers to the side of their head like horns and made butting movements at each other. Fatty, who had really let his appearance fall, paid no attention to them.

Biographical and literary notes

GELLHORN, Martha (see under The Virgin Islands). *Travels with Myself and Another* (Extract 1) contains a detailed and evocative description of French Saint Martin during the Second World War, when the colony was almost cut off from the rest of the world. *Liana* (Extract 2) is set in this archaic world of small-island prejudice and provides a sensitive depiction of a mulatto girl's doomed love affair with a French schoolteacher. Ironically, writes Gellhorn, it was her bestselling book, reaching sales of 150 000, largely because the paperback cover featured 'a picture of a beautiful light black girl, scantily clad: luscious.'

O'SHAUGHNESSY, Hugh (1935–). A journalist specializing in Latin America and the Caribbean, O'Shaughnessy has worked for the *Financial Times* and the *Observer* and has appeared in several documentary films about the region. His previous books include *Grenada: Revolution, Invasion and Aftermath*, 1984, and *Latin Americans*, 1988. His analysis of the rise and fall of the Grenadian revolution earned him a national Press Award and a Gustavus Myers award from the University of Arkansas. *Around the Spanish Main* (Extract 3) is an account of the author's travels through Cuba, Guadeloupe, French Guiana and various islands in the Eastern Caribbean.

SEKOU, Lasana M. Sekou, alias Harold H. Lake, is the only writer of note to have emerged from Saint Martin. He is the author of eight volumes of poetry, including *Maroon Lives*, 1983, and *Quimbé*, 1991, as well as the short stories *Love Songs Make You Cry*, 1989, which includes 'Fatty and the Big House' (Extract 4). Sekou is currently editor of *St Martin Newsday* and a director of House of Nehesi Publishers in **Philipsburg**.

ST KITTS AND NEVIS

When Henry Nelson Coleridge ◊ first approached the island of **St Kitts** in 1825, he was impressed from a distance by its pleasingly symmetrical landscape of mountains and canefields. Then, as now, the central peak of **Mount Liamuiga** (formerly Mount Misery), rose above the neat patchwork of fields, its upper slopes covered in dense forest and its summit lost in clouds. But once ashore, Coleridge found the town of **Basseterre** altogether less attractive. In *Six Months in the West Indies in 1825* (Extract 1), he complains bitterly about the town's main square, bemoaning its lack of trees and other ornamentation. This he interpreted as a sign of indifference on the part of Basseterre's citizens to their surroundings. Whether or not his rebuke ever reached Basseterre it is impossible to know, but Coleridge would perhaps be pleased to know that the town's main open space, **Independence Square**, is now filled with trees and even contains a central fountain decorated with gilded muses. Surrounded by a neat white wooden fence, the Square has eight converging paths, which are reputed to make the shape of the Union Jack when seen from the air. Once used as an area for slave auctions, Independence Square is today ringed by the town's finest and best-preserved eighteenth-century buildings, some of which have been converted into restaurants and art galleries.

Despite a succession of hurricanes and earthquakes, Basseterre is among the Caribbean's most attractive and architecturally valuable towns. So far, it has avoided the brutal reconstruction inflicted on cities such as Kingston, Jamaica, or Castries, St Lucia. Yet on the days that cruise ships call in the harbour, the streets are filled with tourists, and the government plans to build a cruise ship terminal in the centre of the town's waterfront.

FACT BOX

AREA: 269.4 sq km
POPULATION: 41 800
CAPITAL: Basseterre
LANGUAGES: English
FORMER COLONIAL POWER: Britain
INDEPENDENCE: 1983
PER CAPITA GDP: US$4470

Two miles across The Narrows channel lies the island of **Nevis**, whose perpetually cloud-covered peak reminded Columbus of *las nieves* or the snowy mountains of Spain. With a population of only 9000, Nevis is the other half of the Federation of St Christopher-Nevis (the islands' official, if rarely used, name). Historically poor and remote until the arrival of tourism, Nevis eyes St Kitts with some suspicion and resentment, believing that the larger island treats it is an unequal partner. When Anguilla (see British Dependencies) repudiated rule from St Kitts in 1967 and broke away from the then three-island federation, there were some in Nevis who were inclined to follow suit. Like St Kitts, Nevis has managed to preserve many of its most important historical buildings, some of which have been converted into up-market 'plantation house' hotels.

THE 'MOTHER COLONY'

St Kitts has the distinction of being the first British settlement in the Caribbean. The British first arrived in 1624 (three years before a similar expedition to Barbados), led by Captain Thomas Warner, an adventurer who had previously tried to make his fortune on the mainland of South America. Warner had briefly visted St Kitts the previous year and had found the Carib population and their chief, Tegramond, friendly and hospitable. His small expedition was swiftly followed by a rival French group commanded by Pierre Belain d'Esnambuc. The two European parties agreed to divide the island between themselves, with the English settling the centre and the French the two ends, including **Basseterre** and **Dieppe Bay Town**. From this first, shared base British and French colonial expansion gradually took place.

An uneasy peace with the Caribs lasted only until 1626, when they were reported to be planning an attack on the Europeans. In response, the British and French combined forces to inflict a massacre on the Caribs, during which 2000 indigenous people were killed at what is now known as **Bloody Point**. With the Caribs liquidated, the joint British–French territory then experienced its own setback as a Spanish expedition of over thirty ships invaded in 1629. The settlers eventually recovered and a truce held between the British and French until the 1713 Treaty of Utrecht ceded the island entirely to Britain. The 1783 Treaty of Versailles formally confirmed British sovereignty, and from 1816 until 1871 the three islands of St Kitts, Nevis and Anguilla were administered as a single colony.

The vast fortress at **Brimstone Hill** is a dramatic relic of the years of Anglo–French rivalry. With its first fortifications dating from 1690, the 'Gibralter of the West Indies' was intended to defend British territory against French ambitions. In 1782, however, a force of 8000 French troops besieged the 1000-strong garrison for a month before taking possession of the fortress. Such was the gallantry of the British troops that the French allowed them to march out of their citadel with full colours before surrendering. Today, the fortress has been restored, and its thick volcanic walls and array of cannons testify to the military importance of the colony.

Despite a history of conflict and natural disasters, St Kitts developed a reputation for being more cultured and sophisticated than most of the Caribbean's other colonies. A seventeenth-century proverb stated that the region's nobility were to be found in St Kitts, the bourgeoisie in Guadeloupe, the military in Martinique and the peasantry in Grenada. Many of the Caribbean's most eminent planter families had interests in St Kitts, and according to Patrick Leigh Fermor (◊ Barbados) staircases in Nevis 'still exist, with the iron banisters so shaped that three ladies in panniered dresses could descend them abreast.' Horatio Nelson married a Nevis heiress, Fanny Nisbet, in 1787, after having been sent to chase newly independent American traders away from the British colonies. The fashionable elegance of eighteenth-century Nevis is captured in *The Cradle of the Deep* (Extract 2), a Victorian travelogue by the physician-traveller, Sir Frederick Treves ◊.

From the outset, St Kitts was a sugar island (Nevis specialized more in cotton), and large numbers of slaves were imported to work on the plantations, whose fertile soil and gently sloping terrain were important factors in its development as a successful sugar exporter. As elsewhere, the cycle of boom and bust dominated the sugar industry, but profits were sufficient to keep the plantation system viable and to pay for fresh supplies of slaves. At the time of abolition, there were almost 20 000 slaves on the island, making it more densely populated than most of its neighbours. This large population on a small island made it difficult for the freed slaves to establish themselves as independent peasant farmers, particularly as a few large landowners kept a tight grip on the best land. As a result, many Kittitians and Nevisians continued to work on the plantations as wage labourers or emigrated to find better work elsewhere.

POVERTY AND ESCAPE

As the sugar industry declined in the twentieth century, so did social conditions, and St Kitts was considered one of the poorest outposts of the Empire. A sugar-workers' strike in 1935 was one of the first of the series of disturbances and riots which shook the English-speaking Caribbean and several demonstrators were shot and killed by police before a British warship arrived to reimpose order. One of a generation of labour organizers and politicians, Robert Bradshaw, emerged from the conflict as a popular leader and trade unionist. The St Kitts–Nevis Trades and Labour Union became the main vehicle of protest for agricultural workers and the unemployed, and Bradshaw embarked on a long political career. In later years, like his contemporaries Eric Gairy and Milton Cato, 'Papa' Bradshaw came under criticism for abusing power and forgetting his own humble origins. In his memoir of 1950s St Kitts life, *Our Love Prevailed*, James W. Sutton recalls how the former firebrand became attracted by the attentions of the island's small remaining white élite:

> 'Much of this seemed to have gone to Bradshaw's head, however, and he became one of the most bombastic and autocratic persons I had seen, to his people. He had now acquired some wealth, and to add to his prestige, he built a large, imposing mansion, called 'The White House', at The Fort, an area of town well-known as a white area. To crown it all, he left all the black women he knew, and married a wife that, although born in St Kitts, was of pure Syrian (or Lebanese) descent, and whose parents were known to be among the few millionaires of St Kitts. For a man who over the years had little but derogatory remarks to make about the rich, white people of the island, this marriage was a surprise to many.'

Despite Bradshaw's gradual political ascendency, conditions for rural workers remained stubbornly poor. Strikes took place frequently and workers emigrated in large numbers to other Caribbean territories where better wages for cane-cutting could be earned. In his autobiographical novel, *Sonny Jim of Sandy Point* (Extract 5), S.B. Jones-Hendrickson ◊ recalls how locals went to work in the Dominican Republic in the 1940s and came back with a dubious reputation.

Another exodus of emigrants took place in the 1950s and 1960s, when thousands left St Kitts for Britain. In his first novel, *The Final Passage* (Extract 3), St Kitts-born Caryl Phillips ◊ tells of the pressures and tensions surrounding a young couple's decision to abandon the island for an uncertain future in London.

A State of Independence

After the unsuccessful federal experiment of 1958–62, St Kitts–Nevis reverted to being a Crown Colony before gaining full internal self-government. In 1967 Anguilla broke away, preferring to remain a British colony, while St Kitts and Nevis moved slowly towards independence. Overcoming Nevisians' misgivings about joint independence with St Kitts, the British finally managed to rid themselves of one of their few remaining dependencies in 1983. In *A State of Independence* (Extract 4), Caryl Phillips recreates the mixed atmosphere surrounding the independence celebrations, as experienced by an islander who has spent many years in London. As Bertram Francis watches the ceremony, a downpour dampens the dignity of the occasion:

> 'As the church clock struck midnight, and the cheering and celebratory noises grew even louder, Bertram heard raindrops beginning to slap against the leaves of the trees above him. Then as the wheels of history turned, and Mount Misery became Mount Freedom, and Pall Mall Square became Independence Square (although the island had decided to keep its old colonial name), someone punched a hole in the sky and everybody ran for cover as the rain broke through.'

Today, independent St Kitts and Nevis is one of the smallest sovereign states in the world. Still producing sugar for export into the European Community, the islands, and particularly their remote rural villages, appear to have changed little in the last half century.

But modernity has not entirely passed these small communities by. In 1994, the son of the then deputy Prime Minister was shot dead. Weeks later the policeman leading the investigation was himself shot and killed, seemingly by a professional assassin. Drugs were to blame, claimed local politicians and the media, and policemen from Scotland Yard arrived to delve into what was apparently a Colombian cocaine connection. Caught up in a web of allegations and denials, the conservative People's Action Movement of Dr Kennedy Simmonds was overwhelmingly voted out of office in 1995, to be replaced by the St Kitts–Nevis Labour Party, successors to Robert Bradshaw. It was, even by the standards of Kittitian party politics, a dirty election campaign and one which tested the limits of the islands' young democracy.

Yet the system survived, and slowly St Kitts–Nevis is turning its back on a history of sugar and poverty. Tourism offers one alternative, and many now see the daily arrival of cruise-ship visitors as possible economic salvation. In Nevis, one huge luxury complex employs 600 people out of a workforce of only 5000. Few lament the waning of sugar's hold on St Kitts, but not all are convinced that tourism will single-handedly shore up its new and fragile independence.

Caryl Phillips

BOOKLIST

Coleridge, Henry Nelson, *Six Months in the West Indies in 1825*, John Murray, London, 1826. **Extract 1.**

Jones-Hendrickson, S.B., *Sonny Jim of Sandy Point*, Eastern Caribbean Institute, Frederiksted, USVI, 1991. **Extract 5.**

Phillips, Caryl, *A State of Independence*, Faber and Faber, London, 1986. **Extract 4.**

Phillips, Caryl, *The Final Passage*, Faber and Faber, London, 1985. **Extract 3.**

Shacochis, Bob, 'Dead Reckoning', in *Easy in the Islands*, Picador, London, 1985.

Sutton, James W., *Our Love Prevailed*, Sutton Publishing, Ontario, 1990.

Treves, Sir Frederick, *The Cradle of the Deep: An Account of a Voyage to the West Indies*, Smith, Elder & Co, London, 1897. **Extract 2.**

Extracts

(1) BASSETERRE

Henry Nelson Coleridge,
Six Months in the West Indies in 1825

The natural splendour of St Kitts's scenery contrasts pointedly with this author's impatient remarks on the capital's amenities.

We set sail from Nevis at three pm of the 28th, and ran down to our anchoring place before Basseterre at eleven knots under a heavy squall. We did not land until next morning, and I spent the hour before sunset in looking from the ship upon the beautiful island before us. The vale of Basseterre in softness, richness and perfection of cultivation surpasses any thing I have ever seen in my life. Green velvet is an inadequate image of the exquisite verdancy of the cane fields which lie along this lovely valley and cover the smooth aclivities of Monkey Hill. This hill is the southern termination of a range of great mountains which increase in height towards the north, and thicken together in enormous masses in the centre of the island. The apex of this rude pyramid is the awful crag of Mount Misery, which shoots slantingly forwards over the mouth of a volcanic chasm like a huge peninsula in the air. It is bare and black and generally visible, whilst the under parts of the mountain are enveloped in clouds. The height is more than 3700 feet, and is the most tremendous precipice I ever beheld. But the ruggedness of this central cluster only renders the contrast of the cultivated lands below more striking, and the entire prospect is so charming, that I could not help agreeing with the captain's clerk who said he wondered that Colon, who was so delighted with this island as to give it his own name, should not have made a full stop upon its shores. I do not uphold the pun, but upon the whole it was well enough for a hot climate and a captain's clerk.

Basseterre is a large town, with many good houses in it, and one spacious square, which, with some labor and taste expended upon it, might be made a very fine thing. Trees should be planted regularly on every side, an esplanade railed off, and a handsome stone fountain built in the centre. It would be worthy of Colonel Maxwell to look to this, and to exert his influence in effecting an improvement not less important for its utility than its beauty. It is quite extraordinary that the West Indians do not pay more attention to their comforts. The women, and the men too for the most part, never stir out while the sun shines, and thus become much more enervated than the heat of the climate would necessarily make them. Why is there not a sun-proof avenue in every town, where people might breathe fresh air and walk in the shade? Such a place of common resort would infinitely enliven the dullness of their society, invigorate their spirits and adorn their towns.

(2) NEVIS: FASHION

Sir Frederick Treves, *The Cradle of the Deep*

In the eighteenth century, Nevis was the chic watering hole for the English-speaking Caribbean's gentry.

St Kitts as it advanced in prosperity continued to keep ever before it – heedless of hot suns and hurricanes – the resolve to be, at all costs, fashionable. In entertainments, in displays of silver plate and liveries, in dress, in gewgaws, in pure dandyism, the island outdid the old country. On Nevis certain hot springs were discovered, close to Charles Town. Now a hot spring was the one thing needed to make the islands a fitting resort for people of quality, for at the commencement of the eighteenth century the life of a man of taste and breeding could not be supported without a spa.

At Nevis, therefore, a spa was established; and here, to this Tunbridge Wells of the Caribbees, came all the fashionable of the West Indies – the rich merchants with their wives and daughters, the planters, the majors and captains who were invalided or on leave, and the officers of any ship of war that could make an excuse to anchor within sight of Booby Island.

The great people arrived in schooners, with heaps of luggage and a tribe of black servants. From early to late they whirled round in one unending circle of gaiety. There were morning rides to the hills, picnic parties on Mount Pleasant, fishing expeditions to Newcastle Bay, dinners where heated men with loosened cravats proposed the toast of succeeding beauties, and dances were kept up until sunrise, and indeed until the ponies were brought round to the door again.

This led to many things – to strolls along the sands by moonlight, to many a saunter to the woods to look for fireflies that were never found, to many a whispered invitation to come out on the hill to see the Southern Cross that was forgotten before the hill was reached. Most memorable of all was the full-dress parade after the church service on Sunday; for then 'the Clarindas, Belindas, and Elviras of the period swept along, patched and painted, hooped and farthingaled *à outrance* with fly caps, top-knots and commodes, tight-laced bodices, laced aprons, and flounced petticoats, accompanied or followed by the "pretty fellows", who wore square-tailed silk and velvet coats of all colours, periwigged and top-hatted, silk-stockinged, and shoed with red-heeled shoes, their sword-knots trailing almost on the ground, and their canes dangling from the fifth button.' [Newspaper account of the year 1707]

Alas! all this has passed away. The spa is silent and in ruins. The roof of the great building has fallen in, while the balconies and verandahs, which witnessed so much simpering and such play of fans, have vanished to build cart-sheds. Still to be seen are the ball-room, the dining-hall, the overgrown Italian garden with its stucco statuary, and the court where the dowagers and chaperons gossiped and talked scandal.

(3) St Kitts: Migration

Caryl Phillips, *The Final Passage*

Michael and his wife Leila are about to leave the island and its lack of opportunities for a fresh start in England.

Michael began the slow walk down to the market, edging his way along the narrow and carelessly defined streets. Up above the gulls circled, and to them Baytown must have looked like a hot corrugated iron sea. Michael pressed on, trying not to look at the defeated faces that lined these streets, men in grease-stained felt hats and women in deceptively gay bandannas, their eyes glazed, arms folded, standing, leaning, resting up against the zinc fencing of their front yards, their children playing, racing scraps of wood in the liquid sewage, but the walk only seemed to get longer.

Though still a way off, Michael could smell the fresh fish and the tangy fruit of the market, and he could feel the growing piles of discarded rubbish under his feet. Then a ringing voice sang out above the buzzing silence of the day, and the man ran towards him, eyes bright, arms flapping wildly, shirt hanging adrift and brazen, detached from his trousers.

'Michael man, Michael! Where you going?'

The man was short and stocky. He looked wildly about himself like an animal caught in a steel trap. He skidded to a halt and began to splutter, letting his lower lip hang loose so Michael could see the bright redness of his gums against the pink of his tongue.

'Well, man, what you doing?'

Michael shook his limp hand. 'I just going pick up some yams and things for Leila.'

'Well, I surprise to see you for I hear the pair of you done gone off to England like the rest of the damn island. Boy, I sure you gone, you know. I sure, sure.'

'Next Thursday,' said Michael, eager to escape the man's enthusiasm.

'Boy, you gone on next Thursday boat then?'

'Yes, man.'

'Well, then what I hear is half-true. You really going England, you really going.'

He said nothing more and for a few moments he just looked Michael up and down in boyish admiration. Then his eyes flashed and he licked his eager lips. 'And you still has the bike and everything?'

'Yes, man.'

'Same Michael, same Michael.' He paused, then snapped to life again. 'Hey! I just think of something. You remember Footsie Walters' brother, Alphonse?'

'I hear talk of him.'

'Well, you know he just come back from England? I sure he going to be able to tell you lots of things about the place that you don't going to hear from nobody else for everybody be too much hearsay and hesay.'

(4) St Kitts: Return

Caryl Phillips, *A State of Independence*

After twenty years in England, Bertram Francis is returning to his native island for the forthcoming independence celebrations and perhaps for good.

The houses in this first village were wooden shacks painted all colours, as though a rainbow had been bent down and licked some life into the place. They were framed by green vegetation which to Bertram's eyes seemed almost plastic in its perfection. He watched as a mother furiously beat a piece of rope across the back of a child's legs, the child silent, his face twisted in concentration. And then the taxi moved on past the snarling dogs. Bertram rolled down the window and listened to the music from both radio and throat, spiritually rich music for it came from the heart where people cried when they were happy and laughed when they were sad. They passed the stove-weary mothers putting braids in their small daughters' hair with metal comb and oil for tool and lubrication, their husbands squatting on wooden boxes before a tray of dominoes. Bertram looked at the cane cutters who were now free for the day, but still walked like condemned men with neither hope nor desire, their arms swinging loosely by their sides, as if they had just witnessed the world turn a full circle knowing that fate no longer held any mystery for them. And he looked at the young girls waggling their hips crazily and throwing out their chests where breasts did not yet exist. Bertram found himself overwhelmed and disturbed by the bare brown legs, tired black limbs, rusty minds, the bright kinetic reds of the village signalling birth, the pale weary greens the approach of death. For a moment he could not admit to himself that he was home.

'People seem just as poor as they always been,' said Bertram.

The man looked back at him but said nothing, as though unsure whether his passenger spoke from embarassment or disappointment. Bertram caught the driver's look, but quickly turned away.

(5) Sandy Point

S.B. Jones-Hendrickson, *Sonny Jim of Sandy Point*

In the 1950s the west coast town of Sandy Point contained a rich variety of communities and prejudices, according to this autobiographical recollection.

The people of the Back Way, Sandy Point, were called Mingo lovers. Many people who lived down the Back Way had fathers who had gone to Santo Domingo, in the forties, to cut sugar cane. The people of Back Way also had a way of fighting and cutting up, like the people of Santo Domingo. After a time we simply called Back Way, Mingo. Mount Idle people were always idle. The people in Half Way Tree had all of their trees cut half way because they were afraid of jumbies coming from up Brimstone Hill. The people from Old Road lived on old roads. Just look at those roads going up Station Street and those roads that cut across the two rivers in Old Road.

And the people in Newton Ground and St Pauls? They were something else. They were bad. Bad people. They lived in Sodom and 'Gommarra'. If you mentioned the Hassels of Newton ground and the Lynches of St Pauls, you talking about stabbing and tiefing. Newton Ground was Sodom. St Pauls was Gommarra. Nobody could convince us, as small boys, that Newton Ground was not Sodom. Not even Mr Bradshaw, the union leader from St Pauls, could cause us not to call St Pauls, Gommarra. Nobody in our group knew how to spell Gommarra. We were not sure if it was Gommarra or Gommorra. One time Trappie asked 'Bedstead Foot Maker' how to spell Gommarra. He was not sure. But he made up something. He said, 'it was a gum and a gum, a marra and a marra, that was the way to spell Gommarra.'

Biographical and literary notes

COLERIDGE, Henry Nelson (1798–1843). A barrister by profession, Coleridge travelled to the English-speaking Caribbean and left his impressions in *Six Months in the West Indies in 1825* (Extract 1). It is a useful and well written account of social conditions during the decade which preceded the abolition of slavery.

JONES-HENDRICKSON, S.B. Born in the village of **Sandy Point**, St Kitts, Jones-Hendrikson is an economist and the author of economics textbooks and novels and poetry. His *Sonny Jim of Sandy Point* (Extract 5), an autobiographical novel of rural childhood, offers a vivid evocation of everyday life in a small village community in the 1950s and 1960s.

PHILLIPS, Caryl (1958–). Born in St Kitts, Phillips was brought up in Britain, where he lived in Leeds and then went to Oxford University. He

has written screenplays, radio and theatre plays and a number of important novels, as well as one work of non-fiction, *The European Tribe*. His novels include *The Final Passage*, *Higher Ground* and *Cambridge*. *Crossing the River*, a powerful story of slavery and the African diaspora, was shortlisted for the Booker Prize in 1993. Phillips is currently writer in residence at Amherst College, Massachusetts. *A State of Independence* (Extract 4) was published in 1986, three years after St Kitts–Nevis became a fully independent state. It tells the story of Bertram Francis and his return to the island after a long absence in England. The independence celebrations and the political machinations of his contemporaries and former friends only heighten his sense of isolation and alienation in what was once his home. Phillips's previous novel, *The Final Passage* (Extract 3), explores the relationship of a young small-island couple as they migrate to England. Contrasting the stultifying restrictions of life in a 1950s Caribbean island with the bleakness of London, the novel traces the process of disillusionment which accompanies the protagonists' physical and emotional journey.

TREVES, Sir Frederick (1853–1923). An eminent doctor, Sir Frederick Treves was Sergeant Surgeon to the King, personal physician to Queen Victoria and a founding member of the British Red Cross. He was also the author of a number of travel books, dealing with such disparate subjects as Uganda, Switzerland and Dorset. His Caribbean travelogue *The Cradle of the Deep* (Extract 2) comprises perceptive observations and a keen sense of the region's history.

ANTIGUA AND BARBUDA

'I look at this place
(Antigua), I look at these
people (Antiguans), and I
cannot tell whether I was
brought up by, and so come
from, children, eternal
innocents, or artists who
have not yet found eminence
in a world too stupid to
understand, or lunatics who
have made their own lunatic
asylum, or an exquisite
combination of all three.'
Jamaica Kincaid, A Small Place

Flat, dry and mostly featureless,
Antigua looks very different from
its more mountainous neighbours.
The island has a few hills (the
highest, at about 400 metres, is
called Boggy Peak), but compared
to St Kitts or Guadeloupe, the landscape offers little of interest. Antigua is largely made up of coral and
limestone, and this, as in Barbados,
explains its gentle, rolling topography. Looking at its 108 square miles
from the air, it is hard to believe
that the island was once covered by
dense tropical rainforest. Its original vegetation swiftly disappeared as
Antigua became the sugar island *par
excellence*. Now, sugar has also
gone, the land is mostly covered in
scrub, and tourism has become the
one and only hope. Traditionally, passing visitors saw few attractions in
Antigua and tended to hurry on to another destination. At the beginning
of the twentieth century, the American travel writer and naturalist
Frederick Ober (◊ St Vincent and The Grenadines), dismissed Antigua as
follows:

'I do not desire to treat Antigua slightingly; but taking a general
survey of its attractions, – or, rather, lack of them, – there does not
seem to be enough in the aggregate to warrant a visit.'

Nor, thirty years later, did Evelyn Waugh ◊ find anything other than a
sense of faded prosperity and decline. In *Ninety-Two Days* (Extract 2), the
British novelist describes Antigua as a forgotten and crumbling backwater.

Yet today, visitors come in their thousands each day from North
America and Europe to lie on Antigua's improbably white beaches.
Baptized by its public relations experts 'The Heart of the Caribbean', the
island claims 365 pristine beaches, one for each day of the year. To those

FACT BOX

AREA: 441.6 sq km
POPULATION: 66 000
CAPITAL: St John's
LANGUAGES: English
FORMER COLONIAL POWER: Britain
INDEPENDENCE: 1981
PER CAPITA GDP: US$6390

who stay at purpose-built tourist resorts with names like 'Blue Waters' or 'Jolly Beach' are added the ranks of one-day excursionists who descend from their cruise ships into the capital, **St John's**.

Tourism has saved Antigua from terminal bankruptcy and, together with government employment, provides almost every job on the island. Waiters, water sport instructors, beach vendors and taxi-drivers all owe their often modest living to the tourism industry. But as Lucretia Stewart ◊ observes in her travel book *The Weather Prophet* (Extract 3), tourism has also created an artificial version of Antigua, concocted for the visitor's consumption.

BARBUDA

Thirty miles to the north lies the even flatter coral island of Barbuda, adminstratively bound to Antigua since 1967. With a population of only 1500, Barbuda is the weaker partner in what many islanders consider a forced marriage, and there is persistent talk of secession. Barbudans resent Antigua's monopoly of power and resources and want greater self-government. In particular, they dislike the Antiguan-run sand-mining concern which illegally removes sand from their beaches to replace that destroyed by tourist development in Antigua and the Virgin Islands.

For almost two centuries Barbuda was the private fiefdom of a single English family, the Codringtons. They and their overseers did not try to grow sugar on the island's poor soil, but instead introduced a diversified economy based on livestock, hunting, boat-building and subsistence farming. Legend has it that the Codringtons experimented with slave-breeding programmes, intending to create a specially strong and resilient slave population, but historians have rejected the story as a myth. In any event, Barbuda developed very differently from Antigua, with its large plantations, and when the Codrington's renounced their lease in 1870, the islanders retained a distinctive form of collective land ownership. Even today, Barbuda is unusually full of wildlife and roaming domestic animals – a legacy of the Codringtons' livestock projects. Frederick Ober's account of hunting in *Our West Indian Neighbours* (Extract 4) gives some idea of the island's prolific fauna.

COLONIAL HISTORY

Columbus came across what he called Santa María la Antigua during his second expedition in 1493, but European settlement started only in 1632 when English from nearby St Kitts established a foothold on the island. At first, they came under attack from Caribs, based on other islands, who nonetheless saw Antigua as their territory. The French briefly grabbed the island in 1666, but were not encouraged by its apparent unsuitability for intensive agriculture. In 1674 Sir Christopher Codrington set up Antigua's first large-scale sugar plantation and leased Barbuda in order to grow provisions for his slaves. Slaves arrived in large numbers in the course of the eighteenth century until, in 1774, there were estimated to be 37 000. Some slaves managed to escape and form outlaw communities in the hills. In 1736 a slave conspiracy which planned to take over the island was discovered and aborted at the last moment.

Antigua gradually overtook St Kitts as the leading sugar-exporting island in the Leeward Islands, and by 1763 it was the fourth largest producer in the Caribbean. A land-owning upper class grew up, of which twenty families held estates larger than 1000 acres. By the end of the eighteenth century, Antigua had been entirely cleared of forest as sugar fields stretched in every direction. To protect their colony, the British built a system of forts and other installations, meant to deter both invasions and uprisings. The most impressive is **Shirley Heights**, where the ruins of a fortress overlook **Nelson's Dockyard**, the restored harbour where British ships could shelter from storms and attack from rival navies. A young Nelson served in Antigua for three years in the 1780s, preventing foreign ships from trading with the colony. It seems that he did not always enjoy the experience and called Antigua 'a vile spot'.

By the end of the eighteenth century, however, the halcyon days of sugar were over, and Antigua began a gradual decline. Droughts caused by deforestation reduced yields as did poor soil exhausted by over-cultivation. Cheaper sugar from other Caribbean and Latin American sources, together with European beet sugar, made Antiguan exports increasingly unviable. When slavery was abolished in 1834, Antigua's planters received almost the lowest rate of compensation in the Caribbean, reflecting the low value attached by London to the island's economy. They jumped at the opportunity to replace slavery with wage labour, reckoning that their costs would be significantly cut, and did not even bother to implement the decreed four-year period of apprenticeship. Antigua's black population was free, but economically no better off whatsoever.

The second half of the nineteenth century saw Antigua and Barbuda sink further into economic and social depression. The former slaves established villages with optimistic names such as **Freetown** or **Liberta**, but they still had to work on the sugar plantations for desperately low wages. The Antiguan planters, meanwhile, were too poor to afford indentured labour; many left the island and their properties in the hands of managers.

The First World War merely increased hardship, as prices of basic goods rose dramatically and exports were interrupted. In 1918 Antigua witnessed its first real outbreak of social conflict when the Governor ordered the militia to attack a crowd demonstrating in **St John's** against low wages. Several protestors were killed, and the planters were forced to reverse their pay cuts. Poverty persisted throughout the 1920s and 1930s, however, and the colony continued its steady decay.

BIRDLAND

When the Moyne Commission, sent from London in 1938 to report on social conditions in the Caribbean, arrived in Antigua, it noted that the island was among the most neglected and impoverished in the Empire. One of its recommendations was reform to trade union legislation, and in 1940 the Antigua Trades and Labour Union (AT&LU) was founded. In 1943, after a series of successful strikes, the union leadership was taken over by one Vere Cornwall Bird, a former Salvation Army officer who was to dominate Antigua for the next half century.

Writing in *Modern Caribbean Politics*, 1993, Tony Thorndike observes, 'Antigua has over two decades acquired the regrettable image of being the most corrupt society in the Commonwealth Caribbean, hosting a notorious amorality from top to bottom.' This assessment, by no means an isolated one, cannot be separated from the career of V.C. Bird and his political dynasty. Under the control of the Bird family, Antigua has become synonymous among journalists and other observers with drug-smuggling, gun-running and almost every conceivable form of individual and institutional corruption.

From his trade union power base, Bird formed the Antigua Labour Party (ALP) and was elected on to the Legislative Council. Backed by the great majority of poor and hitherto disenfranchised Antiguans, he presented himself as the champion of the underdog and the man who dared to confront the planters and British authorities. Like other regional demagogues, Bird managed to retain the affections of a largely rural, often illiterate, population and was popularly known as 'Papa Bird'. In 1956 he became the colony's first Chief Minister and in 1967 its first Premier when Britain introduced internal self-government. Continually in power (with the exception of the period 1971–76), he ran the island like a private company, doing deals with all manner of unsavoury entrepreneurs. In 1981 the twin state of Antigua and Barbuda finally achieved independence from Britain (with serious reservations from Barbuda) and Bird became its first Prime Minister.

In 1993 US journalist Robert Coram published a book, entitled *Caribbean Time Bomb*, which exposed in relentless detail the extent of Antigua's moral decay. Concentrating on Bird and his two eldest sons, Lester and Vere Jr, the book alleged that the family had consistently engaged in illegal and underhand activities. One of the more serious accusations was that the Antiguan government had connived in allowing a shipment of Israeli arms to break the UN embargo and reach the apartheid regime in South Africa. But even this appeared trivial compared to the revelation that Vere Bird Jr had acted as an agent for the notorious Medellín cocaine cartel, facilitating the transshipment of weapons from Israel to the drug barons. Surrounded by a rogues' gallery of swindlers and criminals, the Bird entourage seemed to revel in what British jurist Louis Blom-Cooper called 'unbridled corruption'. 'Papa Bird', once a Salvation Army stalwart, had reportedly met his mistress, Cutie Francis, when she was the thirteen-year-old winner of a beauty contest. Known as 'Evita', Cutie was for many years, wrote Coram, the power behind the throne until in 1992 she moved on to pastures new in the USA.

The USA, claimed Coram, had deliberately turned a blind eye to the Birds' activities, preferring them and their brand of conservative politics to any more radical alternative. With its military base on Antigua (operative since 1942), Washington had detailed knowledge of all developments on the island, yet chose to support the Bird government with over US$200 million of aid.

The well publicized antics of the Bird dynasty do not seem to have affected their hold on power. In 1994, Vere Cornwall Bird finally retired at the age of 84, handing over leadership of the ALP to his son, Lester. In elections that year, which were condemned by monitoring groups as manipulated by the ruling party, the ALP won for the ninth time out of ten since 1951. It was business as usual.

A Small Place

One of the Bird family's fiercest critics is Jamaica Kincaid ◊, Antigua's best-known contemporary writer. In *A Small Place* (Extract 1) she paints a remarkably unattractive picture of her native island's history and present. Appealing to the tourist to look behind Antigua's 'Heart of the Caribbean' image, Kincaid angrily denounces Britain's colonial legacy, US complicity in propping up the Birds, and the corrupt political culture of Antiguans themselves. Understandably, she is not popular in government circles and *A Small Place* is unavailable in any Antiguan bookshop.

Kincaid's concerns extend beyond the bizarre behaviour of the Bird family and encompass many themes rooted in her own West Indian childhood. In her novels and short stories, she explores the double burden of race and gender confronted by black women in cultures which remain largely racist and *macho*.

Literary Landmarks

Redonda. The state of Antigua and Barbuda also includes a one square-mile rocky outcrop called Redonda, 50 kilometres south-west of Antigua. Uninhabited and only briefly used for guano-mining in the nineteenth century, Redonda became a literary joke when an Irish adventurer, Matthew Dowdy Shiel, claimed to be its King and handed it on to his son, the popular novelist Matthew Phipps Shiel. He in turned bequeathed the imaginary kingdom to the poet, John Gawsworth, who created a 'literary aristocracy', distributing peerages to Victor Gollancz, J.B. Priestley, Lawrence Durrell and Dorothy L. Sayers. The title has subsequently been passed on to other would-be Kings, few of whom have ever visted the isolated rock. The hoax has been tolerated by the Antiguan authorities, who tried to make money by selling Redonda's own postage stamps.

BOOKLIST

Berleant-Schiller, Riva, Susan Lowes, and Milton Benjamin, *Antigua and Barbuda*, Clio Press, Oxford, 1995.

Coram, Robert, *Caribbean Time Bomb: the United States' Complicity in the Corruption of Antigua*, William Morrow and Company, New York, 1993.

Gaspar, David, *Bondmen and Rebels: A Study of Master–Slave Relationships in Antigua*, Johns Hopkins University Press, Baltimore, MD, 1985.

Kincaid, Jamaica, *A Small Place*, Virago, London, 1988. **Extract 1.**

Kincaid, Jamaica, *At the Bottom of the River*, Picador, London, 1984.

Ober, Frederick A., *Our West Indian Neighbours*, James Pott & Co, New York, 1907. **Extract 4.**

Stewart, Lucretia, *The Weather Prophet: A Caribbean Journey*, Chatto & Windus, London, 1995. **Extract 3.**

Waugh, Evelyn, *Ninety-Two Days: A Journey in Guiana and Brazil*, Penguin, London, 1985. **Extract 2.**

Extracts

(1) ANTIGUA: COLONIALISM

Jamaica Kincaid, *A Small Place*

For Jamaica Kincaid, the street names and buildings of St John's are inseparable from a history of iniquity and exploitation.

In the Antigua that I knew, we lived on a street named after an English maritime criminal, Horatio Nelson, and all the other streets around us were named after some other English maritime criminals. There was Rodney Street, there was Hood Street, there was Hawkins Street, and there was Drake Street. There were flamboyant trees and mahogany trees lining East Street. Government House, the place where the Governor, the person standing in for the Queen, lived, was on East Street. Government House was surrounded by a high white wall – and to show how cowed we must have been, no one ever wrote bad things on it; it remained clean and white and high. (I once stood in hot sun for hours so that I could see a putty-faced Princess from England disappear behind these walls. I was seven years old at the time, and I thought, She has a putty face.) There was the library on lower High Street, above the Department of the Treasury, and it was in that part of High Street that all colonial government business took place. In that part of High Street, you could cash a cheque at the Treasury, read a book in the library, post a letter at the post office, appear before a magistrate in court. (Since we were ruled by the English, we also had their laws. There was a law against using abusive language. Can you imagine such a law among people for whom making a spectacle of yourself through speech is everything? When West Indians went to England, the police there had to get a glossary of bad West Indian words so they could understand whether they were hearing abusive language or not.) It was in that same part of High Street that you could get a passport in another government office. In the middle of High Street was the Barclays Bank. The Barclay brothers, who started Barclays Bank, were slave-traders. That is how they made their money. When the English outlawed the slave trade, the Barclay brothers went into banking. It made them even richer.

(2) ANTIGUA: DECLINE

Evelyn Waugh, *Ninety-Two Days*

Evelyn Waugh's fleeting visit to Antigua, en route to Guyana, gives him a sense of lost grandeur.

And to be honest I did gaze rather wistfully as each of the islands in turn disappeared behind us. The first was Antigua and, coming on it as we did after twelve days of unbroken horizons, it remains the most vivid and most glamorous. Not that there was anything particularly remarkable about it – steep little hills covered in bush, a fringe of palm along the beach, brilliant blue water revealing, fathoms down, the silver sand of its bed; an old fort covering the bay; a shabby little town of wooden, balconied houses, its only prominent building a large plain cathedral rebuilt after an earthquake, with shining towers and a good pitch-pine interior; inquisitive black urchins in the street; women in absurd sun hats, the brims drooping and flapping over their black faces, waddling along on flat feet; ragged Negroes lounging aimlessly at corners; baskets of highly coloured fish for sale – purple and scarlet like markings of a mandril; ramshackle motor cars; and in the churchyard the memorials of a lost culture – the rococo marble tombs of forgotten sugar planters, carved in England and imported by sailing ship in the golden days of West Indian prosperity.

(3) Antigua: Tourism

Lucretia Stewart, *The Weather Prophet*

Few Caribbean islands are as dependent on tourism as Antigua, as British writer Lucretia Stewart observes.

The first thing I noticed about Antigua was the number of tourists (the island which had a population of approximately sixty-five thousand accommodated over two hundred thousand tourists a year). They poured off the cruise-ships on Thursdays and flooded the streets of the capital, St John's.

One morning, a few days after arriving in Antigua, I got up and walked out on to St Mary's Street. Something was different. I couldn't work out what it was at first. Then I realised that I couldn't see the sea. At the bottom of St Mary's Street were the duty-free tourist complexes of Redcliffe and Heritage Quays (old warehouses and slave-holding areas now transformed into restaurants and duty-free boutiques for tourists where everything was charged in US$); their location meant that the first thing the tourists encountered when they disembarked was an opportunity to spend money. You could buy postcards with a photograph of Redcliffe Quay and the consumer motto 'Shop till you drop in Antigua'. Beyond lay the sea and the deep-water harbour. That morning the harbour was completely filled by two massive cruise ships which obliterated the horizon. This, I discovered, happened every Thursday . . .

Antigua, the self-styled 'Heart of the Caribbean', seemed to exist on two levels. There was the real Antigua, the Antigua of Liberta, Bethesda, Crosbies, Cedar Grove, remote little villages scattered throughout the countryside, and of St John's, which, despite its shopping precincts and souvenir stalls, retained a certain earthy charm. And then there was the fake Antigua, the tourist Antigua, the Antigua of Sunset Cove ('where love is the setting'); Runaway Bay; Halcyon Cove; Blue Waters; Sandals (a couples-only all-inclusive resort); Harmony Hall, and so on. How people could say these names with a straight face I couldn't imagine. Places like English Harbour, Nelson's Dockyard and Shirley Heights had once been real, but were now reduced to the level of theme parks. If you rented a car, the map that was provided with it was almost exclusively of the fake Antigua, as if all anybody would ever want to do would be to drive from resort to resort.

(4) BARBUDA

Frederick A. Ober, *Our West Indian Neighbors*

*Arid and underpopulated, Barbuda was for several centuries a
remote place, famed for its profusion of wildlife.*

The first object that attracted my attention as the little sloop in which I
had taken passage from Antigua arrived within sight of Barbuda was a
quaint old martello tower, which once pertained to a castle, erected by the
buccaneers. There were no other structures of note in sight, and only after
a weary walk of about three miles was I cheered by arriving at the 'great
house', built in the flourishing times of the Codringtons. A great wall had
accompanied me along the road, broad-topped, high and deeply based,
showing that compulsory labor was at one time abundant.

The white gentlemen residing there had leased the island from the
Crown and were 'working it for all it was worth.' One of them was a
clergyman of the Church of England, and the other a planter bred to the
raising of sugar-cane and the oversight of laborers; so both together made a
very successful combination. As the 'parson' was pledged to attend to the
spiritual needs of the black people and the overseer to their physical wants,
the blacks were not neglected. They worked hard in the fields six days in
the week, under the eye of the superintendent, and on the seventh
attended services at the chapel.

As the island had been without news from outside for many moons, I was
made more than welcome, and immediately my wants were made known I
was furnished with a horse, a sable servant and dog, who accompanied me
on my excursions afield. Our first visit was to a vast inclosure where the
guinea-fowl were said to be abundant, and we arrived at their scratching
ground about mid-afternoon. The dog put up a fine male bird and I let go
both barrels at him without touching a feather. It was the same with the
second and the third bird that got up and sailed away into the dim distance,
like a railroad train making up for lost time . . .

At last, as the sun was sinking behind the sea-grapes on the shore, we
approached an old field where, my guide said, there was sure to be a flock
'dusting', and if warily approached could be taken easily. This time, as the
chattering fowl hurled themselves into the air, I caught two of them, right
and left, by firing ahead of them about half a rod, it seemed to me.
Anyway, they tumbled end over end, and I was rewarded for my hours of
toil beneath the ardent rays of a tropical sun.

Biographical and literary notes

KINCAID, Jamaica (1949–). Born in **St John's**, Antigua, as Elaine Potter Richardson, Kincaid moved to the USA in 1966 to work as a children's nanny. After a period of extensive travel she established herself as a journalist and writer. She has been a staff writer on the *New Yorker* and has contributed stories to *Rolling Stone* and the *Paris Review*. At the Bottom of *the Sea*, 1983, is a collection of short stories and her first book. *A Small Place* (Extract 1), published in 1988, is a savage indictment of the corruption which Kincaid identifies as endemic to her native Antigua as well as an attack on the legacy of British colonialism. Addressed to an imaginary tourist, it lays bare the mediocrity and cynicism which the author perceives in all aspects of Antiguan life. In the words of Salman Rushdie, 'it is a jeremiad of great clarity and a force that one might have called torrential were the language not so finely controlled.' Her novels, which deal largely with the experience of black women in the Caribbean, include *Annie John*, 1985, *Lucy*, 1990, and *The Autobiography of My Mother*, 1996.

OBER, Frederick A. (see under St Vincent and The Grenadines).

STEWART, Lucretia (1952–). Stewart was born in Singapore, but has lived mostly in Britain. A journalist, she is also the author of *Tiger Balm: Travels in Laos, Vietnam and Cambodia*. Her book, *The Weather Prophet* (Extract 3) traces her journey through several islands in the Eastern Caribbean. A perceptive observer of the region's social and cultural life, Stewart provides a highly personal account of her varied experiences.

WAUGH, Evelyn (1903–1966). One of Britain's best-known 20th-century novelists, Waugh is the author of such classics as *Decline and Fall*, 1928, *Scoop*, 1938, and *Brideshead Revisited*, 1945. In the winter of 1932 he went, 'with a heart of lead', on a voyage to British Guiana (now Guyana) and Brazil. It was not, on the whole, an experience which Waugh relished, but it provided him with material for one of his most successful novels, *A Handful of Dust*, 1934. *Ninety-Two Days* (Extract 2) is an account of what he found to be 'an arduous and at times arid experience'. He reportedly struck a deal with his brother, Alec Waugh (◊ Martinique) not to write at any length on the Caribbean islands he visited *en route*, since Alec specialized as a Caribbean travel writer.

GUADELOUPE

> 'To tell the truth, it is a completely unimportant scrap of earth, and the experts have once and for all dismissed it as insignificant. And yet it has had its bad times, its past great upsurges, fine copious bloodlettings quite worthy of educated people's attention. But all that was forgotten long ago.'
> *Simone Schwarz-Bart,*
> *Between Two Worlds*

To anybody arriving from another Caribbean island, Guadeloupe cannot fail to produce an immediate culture shock. It is, quite literally, a different world. Leaving the modern, clean airport, one finds oneself on a four-lane highway, usually crowded bumper to bumper with Renaults, Peugeots and Citroëns. This perpetually bad-tempered traffic jam gradually disperses as it crawls around the suburbs of the main city, **Pointe-à-Pitre**, passing the same hypermarkets and furniture warehouses which litter the *banlieue* of every French town. Low-cost blocks of flats alternate with comfortable clusters of villas. Billboards proclaim special offers on yoghourt or bargain mountain bikes. The names and images are all strangely familiar; it feels like some tropical version of Lille or Lyon, a little more chaotic and exotic perhaps, but nevertheless undeniably French.

Frenchness is everywhere. A profusion of pharmacies to satisfy the most anxious hypochondriac. The ubiquitous boulangerie, where baguettes are sold twice daily. Good coffee, French newspapers, horse-racing from Paris, the smell of Gitanes: all the details and rituals associated with France are here in Guadeloupe.

The illusion is enshrined in Guadeloupe's constitutional status as a full *département* of France. Like its fellow overseas *département* Martinique, Guadeloupe is no colony or dependency – it is an integral part of France. As such, Guadeloupeans are Frenchmen and Frenchwomen, enjoying identical rights to those who live in the *métropole*. They send deputies and senators to the French parliament. Since the introduction of greater regional autonomy by the Mitterand government in the 1980s they have, like other *régions*, elected regional councils. Furthermore, as French citizens they are also citizens of the European Union, subject to the same

FACT BOX

AREA: 1780 sq km
POPULATION: 390 000
CAPITAL: Basse-Terre
LANGUAGES: French, Creole
FORMER COLONIAL POWER: France
POLITICAL STATUS: *Département d'outre-mer* (French Overseas
 Department)
PER CAPITA GDP: US$6100

social legislation as Belgians or Danes. Guadeloupeans and Martinicans carry French passports and can as easily move to and from Paris as a Frenchman from Marseille.

The entire edifice of Guadeloupe's apparently First-World society is supported by subsidies from France. GDP in real terms of what is produced is relatively low. Yet Paris pumps in billions of francs each year in social security payments, development schemes and salaries for a vast civil service. As a result, the French *départements d'outre-mer* (DOMs) enjoy a standard of living out of all proportion to the rest of the Caribbean. Public-sector workers, from teachers to technicians, even receive a special 40% supplement to offset the cost of living and working in the islands, further raising salaries and prices.

In return, mainland French manufacturers have a captive market of about 800 000 people who consume large quantities of their goods. Tourists from the *métropole* spend their vacations and money inside France. Income and indirect taxes return to the French government. And perhaps most importantly, France and the French language maintain a toehold in the Americas.

Without their French status, Guadeloupe and Martinique would arguably be small and poor banana-exporting islands like their neighbours. It has been estimated that without French financial backing, the DOMs would have a per capita income of as little as US$800 a year. As it is, they enjoy educational and health provision on a par with the best in continental Europe. Yet not all Guadeloupeans are happy with an arrangement which some see as neo-colonial. In Guadeloupe, historically the poor relation of Martinique and with a stronger tradition of radical politics, there is an independence movement which places sovereignty before French subsidies. Intellectuals resent what they see as the *culture officielle*, imposed on the island by Paris. As British travel writer Zenga Longmore ◊ discovered in her *Tap-Taps to Trinidad* (Extract 1), unease with their French identity can push some Guadeloupeans into admiration for all things African.

Not all Guadeloupean culture, however, is uncritically French in inspiration. Like Martinique, the island has many painters and musicians whose influences are more recognizably African–Caribbean than European. Guadeloupe is the birthplace of *zouk* music, a hybrid popular mix of Haitian and local rhythms, electronically blended by synthesizers and drum machines. The Guadeloupean band, Kassav', is the best known exponent of *zouk*, which is listened to throughout the Caribbean and has reached Europe and North America.

SETTLEMENT AND SLAVERY

Guadeloupe is made up of two islands, separated by the narrow strait of the **Rivière Saléee**, a fact not realized by Columbus in 1493 when he named the territory after the Virgin of Guadalupe in the Spanish province of Extremadura. Confusingly, the island named Grande-Terre is largely flat and smaller than the other, Basse-Terre, which is mountainous and scenically more dramatic. Under Guadeloupe's departmental administration come also a number of smaller islands, some of which (La Désirade, Marie-Galante and Les Saintes) are visible from Guadeloupe, while others (Saint-Barthélémy and Saint Martin) are located further north in the Leeward chain (see Saint Martin/Sint Maarten).

Columbus and his Spanish successors never settled Guadeloupe, and it was the French, moving southwards from their initial Caribbean base of St Kitts, who formed the first colony in 1635. They had to contend with the indigenous Caribs who, as elsewhere, did not accept invasion without a fight. The Caribs called their island *Karukera* or 'land of beautiful waters' and to begin with defended it resolutely. However, after some five years the French had suppressed the Caribs and began to turn the flat terrain of Grande-Terre into a prosperous sugar-exporting colony. Among the first people to work on the plantations were *engagés* or indentured labourers from France, who signed up for three-year work contracts in return for the prospect of a piece of land at the end of their term. Life for these early sugar-workers was always hard and usually short, worse even than that of the black slaves. The great seventeenth-century priest–historian Du Tertre wrote in the 1660s of their dreadful conditions in his *Histoire générale des Antilles*:

> 'They are worked to excess; they are badly fed, and are often obliged to work in company with slaves, which is a greater affliction than the hard labour; there were masters so cruel that they were forbidden to purchase any more; and I knew one at Guadeloupe who had buried more than fifty upon his plantation, whom he had killed by hard work, and neglect when they were sick. This cruelty proceeded from their having them for three years only, which made them spare the Negroes rather than these poor creatures!'

Alongside the white *engagés* laboured black slaves, who in the course of the eighteenth century came to outnumber whites by more than six to one.

Much as the landowners tried to attract more white workers, they gradually came to depend on slave labour for the production of sugar. Du Tertre's humane instincts also reached out to the slaves, who, he thought, were constantly tortured by the futility of their work: 'they are well aware that all their sweat is for the profit of their masters, and that if they amassed for the latter mountains of gold, they would never get any part of it, and that, even if they lived for centuries, and worked more than they actually did, they would not derive a cent profit from all their toil.' The slaves' resentment sometimes exploded into revolt. In 1656 blacks in Grande-Terre rose up and fought for two weeks before being suppressed. Another serious uprising was recorded in 1737.

Others, meanwhile, were reaping a handsome profit. The industry was enormously stimulated by the arrival of hundreds of Dutch migrants, some Jews who were expelled from Brazil in 1654. They brought with them capital and technical know-how which helped Guadeloupe to more than double its exports in the last twenty years of the seventeenth century.

ROYALISTS AND REVOLUTIONARIES

Inevitably, Guadeloupe's thriving plantation economy soon attracted the attention of the British, who made attempts to invade in 1666 and 1703. An expedition in 1759 was more successful and the island came under British control for four years. It was a highly civilized occupation; the French planters kept control of their properties and were allowed to export sugar at advantageous prices into the British market. They also bought 40 000 slaves from British merchants at better than normal rates. At the 1763 Treaty of Paris Guadeloupe was returned to France while Britain decided to retain possession of Canada which it had also captured from the French. Apparently it was not easy to choose between the two territories and the decision to return prosperous sugar-producing Guadeloupe and keep cold, seemingly unproductive, Canada caused serious controversy. In France Louis XV's Foreign Minister Choiseul was delighted at the settlement and Voltaire mocked the British for preferring to keep 'a few acres of snow'.

The settlement, of course, did not hold for long and in 1782 Admiral Rodney led the British fleet to one of its most important victories off the coast of Les Saintes when he defeated de Grasse's French forces in a vast naval battle. Rodney's triumph marked a watershed in Anglo–French rivalry and the end of Britain's perennial struggle with a royalist adversary. The French Revolution of 1789 and its aftermath introduced a new phase in inter-imperial conflict and a clash not only of territorial ambitions but of ideologies.

The conservative planters of Guadeloupe and Martinique saw in the Revolution, with its rhetoric of liberty and equality, nothing but disaster and ruin. As in the fellow French colony Saint-Domingue, the two islands' white élites rejected revolutionary rule from Paris, preferring to retain their privileges under British protection. The British moved into Martinique and remained there for the duration of the Anglo–French war until 1815. In Guadeloupe, however, events turned out very differently, largely due to the influence of a French revolutionary named Victor Hugues.

In February 1794 the ruling Convention in Paris decreed the abolition of slavery in all French colonies. To enforce the decree the revolutionary government dispatched two Jacobin commissioners, Hugues and Pierre Chrétien, to Guadeloupe with the task of stamping out the planters' opposition. When they arrived in May, having escaped the British fleet, with only 1500 troops, they discovered that Guadeloupe was already occupied by British forces, who had accepted the planters' invitation to maintain the status quo. Hugues, a mulatto who had previously worked, according to differing accounts, as a barber, brothel-keeper and public prosecutor, managed to land his force and to issue an address which invited citizens of all colours to join revolutionary battalions. Former slaves and free mulattoes joined the force which defeated the British and their French monarchist supporters in **Pointe-à-Pitre** on 7 June 1794.

Once master of Guadeloupe, Hugues took ample revenge against those who had defied the Convention. Formerly a close associate of Robespierre, he had no doubts as to what revolutionary justice entailed. In the **Place de la Victoire**, named after the rout of the British, the guillotine was erected and some 850 royalist sympathizers were executed. A large section of Guadeloupe's white planter class was liquidated or fled, creating a shift in the social structure which even today makes the island less dominated by a *béké* or rich white minority than Martinique.

From Guadeloupe Hugues and his revolutionary troops harried the British in nearby islands, encouraging slave rebellions and preaching their brand of Jacobinism. In 1795 Hugues was reputed to be behind insurrectionary uprisings in islands as far apart as Jamaica and St Vincent and presided over a brief reign of terror in St Lucia. Eventually, as the Revolution became transformed into Napoleonic rule, Hugues was displaced from his stronghold in the Caribbean, and Napoleon's commander, General Richepanse, took control of Guadeloupe in 1802 and restored slavery.

SECOND EMANCIPATION

The slaves of Guadeloupe would have to wait another 46 years before again being granted their freedom. In that time they revolted several times against the reintroduction of forced servitude and endured the gradual decline of the sugar-exporting economy. The sugar crisis, as in the British colonies, was primarily the result of competition from other producers, especially in Europe itself, who could provide France with beet sugar more cheaply than cane sugar from across the Atlantic. Cities such as Lille and Valenciennes in northern France became huge sugar-producing centres, working with an industrial efficiency which did not exist in the Caribbean.

As a result, Guadeloupe's exports dropped steadily in the first half of the nineteenth century.

While domestic sugar producers and the free-trade lobby in France agitated successfully against Caribbean sugar imports, a humanitarian movement against slavery grew steadily in influence. In 1834 the Société pour l'Abolition de L'Esclavage was founded, which included among its members the poet Alphonse de Lamartine and the political scientist Alexis de Tocqueville. But the leading voice among the abolitionists was Victor Schoelcher, often described as the 'Wilberforce of France', who had travelled widely in the Caribbean during the 1830s and 1840s and who became an impassioned propagandist against slavery. A series of gradual reforms were introduced during the early 1840s, but it took the revolution of 1848 to usher in full emancipation. By now highly respected, Schoelcher became Under Secretary of State for the Navy, with responsibility for the colonies. He presided over a commission which recommended immediate abolition of slavery. In its report the commission stressed that the freed slaves were to become French citizens, protected by the Republic's revolutionary ideals:

> '[The Republic] . . . is making reparation to those unfortunate people for the crimes which it committed against their ancestors and the land of their birth by giving them France as their fatherland and all the rights of French citizens as their heritage, thereby bearing witness that it excludes no one from its immortal motto: "*liberty, equality, fraternity.*" '

On 27 April 1848 the provisional government of the Second Republic decreed the abolition of slavery in all French colonies. A sum of 126 million francs was paid as compensation to the owners of some quarter of a million slaves. The slaves themselves became French citizens, but only until 1851 when Louis-Napoleon's right-wing *coup d'état* rescinded the measure and sent Schoelcher and other liberals into exile. Voting rights were not restored until 1870, when Schoelcher was elected senator representing Guadeloupe.

The planters had feared that abolition would result in the final demise of the sugar industry. In fact, although some former slaves abandoned the plantations, production and exports actually increased for a period. To ensure a continued supply of labour, the planters also imported almost 40 000 East Indians to work as indentured labourers. Known disparagingly as *coulies*, the East Indians of Guadeloupe heavily outnumbered those introduced into Martinique, making the former's ethnic and social structure much more varied. The wealthy planter class (or those who had survived Hugues's Jacobin wrath) continued to live a life of conspicuous extravagance, as evoked by Jean-Louis Baghio'o in his magical-realist account of Guadeloupean history *The Blue Flame-Tree*. Gradually, though, the *békés* faced increasing competition from a rising mulatto middle class of traders and professionals.

VICHY AND DEPARTMENTALIZATION

The second half of the nineteenth century in Guadeloupe was, write the historians Parry, Sherlock and Maingot, a story of 'somnolent stagnation punctuated by occasional riots or natural disasters'. Sugar exports remained flat; in 1860 Guadeloupe sent 28 000 tons to France; in 1913, 26 000 tons. Even the outbreak of the First World War did not bring the benefits of higher prices to the island, as it did to other producers, since there was a shortage of French shipping. Thousands of Guadeloupeans and Martinicans volunteered to go and fight for France. Today, almost every village in the islands has its mass-produced memorial to those who never returned, *morts pour la patrie.*

In 1940 American writer Amy Oakley ◊ visited Guadeloupe to find a run-down, neglected corner of the French empire. In *Behold the West Indies* (Extract 5) she conveys a clear impression of the island's decline. Oakley's visit coincided with what was probably Guadeloupe's worst moment, when the island was blockaded and almost starved by the American fleet during the Second World War. After the defeat of France in 1940, the colonial authorities, as reactionary as in the past, had supported Marshall Pétain's Vichy regime. Pétain appointed Admiral Georges Robert as his military commander and sent a fleet to the region. Under Robert and the Governor, Constant Sorin, Guadeloupe endured three years of repression and hardship, as the Allied blockade prevented all imports of food and other basics. Some anti-Vichy Guadeloupeans escaped to neighbouring Dominica, eventually to join de Gaulle's Free French. Their resistance, known as the *dissidence,* laid the basis for the post-war political forces which created the modern-day DOMs. By 1943 the pro-Vichy regime had lost any remaining support, and de Gaulle's Free French representative encountered no opposition on arriving in the island.

In the political ferment which followed peace in 1945, Guadeloupeans and Martinicans overwhelmingly voted for socialists and communists in legislative elections. These deputies pressed for the islands to become full *départements* of France rather than colonies, believing that so-called departmentalization would bring rapid economic recovery. Representatives from the islands had pressed their claim to full departmental status three times before, and the idea was popular among those who saw incorporation into the Republic as a way to check the power of the local white élite. The legislation which created the DOMs in 1946 was much more the work of left-wing local politicians and their largely mulatto power bases than any old-style colonialist, determined to hang onto the islands. Their demands struck a chord with French radicals as well as Gaullists, alarmed at the prospect of growing US influence in the Caribbean.

Since 1946 a series of constitutional modifications have been introduced, usually with the aim of increasing local accountability or placating pro-independence sentiment. In the 1970s and 1980s separatist groups grew in influence and strength, claiming responsibility for a number of terrorist attacks. But there are few who genuinely advocate complete independence from France, with the economic implications that such a break would bring. As Maryse Condé ◊ reveals in her novel *Tree of Life* (Extract 4), independence remains a volatile issue, ever likely to inflame passions. Resentment against France is widespread, even if it does not lead automatically to independence politics. Guadeloupeans dislike the way in which white French technocrats tend to fly in to occupy the top jobs, while unemployment remains stubbornly high. As much as a third of the population has emigrated, living in the less salubrious suburbs of Paris or other large cities in the *métropole*. Despite the benefits of a consumerist lifestyle, many people remain suspicious of French motives and, paradoxically, fearful that the French might one day decide to cut the DOMs adrift.

WRITERS' ISLAND

Less chic and cosmopolitan than Martinique, Guadeloupe has nonetheless produced a large number of acclaimed writers, several of whom have reached a wide audience through translation into English. Perhaps the best-known, if least read, is Saint-John Perse ◊, a demanding and often obscure poet who was born in Guadeloupe in 1887 and who won the Nobel Prize for Literature in 1960. A white *béké*, Saint-John Perse left the island at the age of twelve, never to return. Legend has it that he was once aboard an airplane which landed in Guadeloupe *en route* to some other destination, but that he declined the offer to set foot on his homeland. Nonetheless, a poem such as *To Celebrate a Childhood* (Extract 2) projects an intense nostalgia for the tropical landscape of an idealized Caribbean.

More recently, writers such as Jean-Louis Baghio'o and Daniel Maximin have been translated into English. Both combine an explicitly historical approach and poetic structure to explore the vexed question of Guadeloupean identity. In *Lone Sun*, Maximin stresses the multi-ethnic, multilingual dimension of this identity in 'the story of an archipelago, mindful of our four races, our seven languages and our dozens of strains of blood'.

Interestingly, the most successful of Guadeloupe's recent writers have all been women. Apart from Maryse Condé, the island can also lay claim to Lucie Julia, Myriam Warner-Vieyra and Simone Schwarz-Bart ◊. Their work deals with a wide variety of themes, both social and personal, but certain shared concerns tend to emerge with some consistency. Both Warner-Vieyra, who has lived in Senegal since the 1960s, and Condé have centred their fiction on Africa and, in particular, racial and sexual themes within that continent. In Warner-Vieyra's *Juletane*, 1982, the experience of a West Indian woman in Africa is paralleled by her discovery of a diary written by a Caribbean girl. Condé's historical saga, *Ségou*, 1984–85, is a much more ambitious recreation of political and emotional intrigue in the Bambara kingdom.

In her *The Bridge of Beyond* (Extract 3), Simone Schwarz-Bart infuses the lives of poor Guadeloupean women with a lyrical intensity. Her celebration of seemingly ordinary experiences is intended to challenge the assumptions of 'official', Eurocentric, male-dominated history and to give those usually regarded as passive victims the significance reserved for 'great men'. The resilience and even heroism of Schwarz-Bart's female characters are responses to the harshness of their existence, but novels such as *Between Two Worlds* also explore everyday pleasures and happiness, often rooted in the beautiful landscape of Guadeloupe:

> 'And yet it was a land of verdant hills and clear waters, beneath a sun every day more radiant. When there was no wind, clouds would form and slightly veil its splendor; but usually it shone as bright as could be, the breezes and trade winds keeping heaven clear and solacing man.'

LITERARY LANDMARKS

Pointe-à-Pitre. Not all visitors grow to love the bustling main city of Guadeloupe, destroyed by an earthquake in 1843. Patrick Leigh Fermor (◊ Barbados) admits: 'We grew to loathe Pointe-à-Pitre. It was hard to choose between the day – the dust and mud and the vacuity of the streets – and the night, those interminable hours of damp torpor under a mosquito net.' Alec Waugh (◊ Martinique) wrote of 'an ineffacable impression of dejected squalor.' The veteran British traveller Quentin Crewe (◊ Dominican Republic) was no more enthusiastic about Guadeloupe as a whole: 'I was not obliged to stay on this odious island, where no one smiled and no glimmer of good taste enlivened anything.' The birthplace of Saint-John Perse in **Rue Nozières** has been developed into a small museum, commemorating the life of the poet. The **Librairie Générale** in **Rue Schoelcher** is a well-stocked bookshop which testifies to Guadeloupe's considerable intellectual life.

Basse-Terre. The administrative capital of Guadeloupe, with fine buildings dating from the seventeenth century, has survived better than its rival. It is, writes Jean-Louis Baghio'o, 'a town built like an amphitheatre round a symmetrical bay, ennobled by rounded buttresses and covered with vegetation.' Above Basse-Terre looms the volcano, **La Soufrière**, which threatened to erupt in 1976, forcing the capital's evacuation.

BOOKLIST

The following selection includes the extracted titles in this chapter as well as other titles for further reading. In general, paperback editions are given when possible. For most of the extracted works, the original publisher in English can be found in 'Acknowledgments and Citations' at the end of the volume, as can the exact location of the extracts and the editions from which they are taken.

Baghio'o, Jean-Louis, *The Blue Flame-Tree*, Stephen Romer trans, Carcanet, Manchester, 1984.

Burton, Richard D.E., and Fred Reno, *French and West Indian: Martinique, Guadeloupe and French Guiana Today*, Macmillan, Basingstoke, 1995.

Condé, Maryse, *A Season in Rihata*, Richard Philcox, trans, Heinemann, Oxford, 1988.

Condé, Maryse, *Tree of Life*, Victoria Reiter, trans, The Women's Press, London, 1994. **Extract 4.**

Du Tertre, Père J.B., *Histoire générale des Antilles habitées par les Français*, 2 vols, Paris, 1661–67.

Longmore, Zenga, *Tap-Taps to Trinidad*, Arrow, London, 1990. **Extract 1.**

Maximin, Daniel, *Lone Sun*, University Press of Virginia, 1989.

Oakley, Amy, *Behold the West Indies*, D. Appleton-Century Co, New York, 1941. **Extract 5.**

Parry, J.H., Philip Sherlock, and Anthony Maingot, *A Short History of the West Indies*, Macmillan, Basingstoke, 1987.

Saint-John Perse, *Eloges and Other Poems*, Louise Varèse, trans, Pantheon, New York, 1956. **Extract 2.**

Schwarz-Bart, Simone, *Between Two Worlds*, Barbara Bray, trans, Heinemann, Oxford, 1992.

Schwarz-Bart, Simone, *The Bridge of Beyond*, Barbara Bray, trans, Heinemann, Oxford, 1982. **Extract 3.**

Warner-Vieyra, Mìrìam, *Juletana*, Betty Wilson, trans, Heinemann, Oxford, 1987.

Extracts

(1) GUADELOUPE: AFRICA

Zenga Longmore, *Tap-Taps to Trinidad*

British-born Zenga Longmore has unwisely told her new-found Guadeloupean friend Estelle that she is an African.

Whilst Estelle and her little party sat on wicker chairs in a snug little bistro overlooking the harbour, a hapless table groaned with all manner of Frenchification. Although very few of the company could speak English well enough for me to understand, I realised I was in the midst of Guadeloupe's intelligentsia. Odd phrases from the genteel chit-chat floated to my ears: *'l'idéologie nègre'* and *'l'impérialisme de la France'*, to quote but a couple.

And then the bombshell dropped over the lobster à la couch chón chón. Estelle suddenly announced to her guests:

'I forgot to tell you, my friend here is from *l'Afrique.'*

After a breathless silence all heads turned towards me in expectation. The Indian couple in the grey tunics gaped in open-mouthed astonishment. The Guadeloupan lecturers clattered their cutlery noisily to their plates – an unforgivable sin in the eyes of the French food etiquette. The Rastafarian writer removed his gold-rimmed spectacles, then replaced them slowly, tilting his head back to get a better look. What could I do? I smirked.

'Where exactly are you from?' asked the writer, spellbound with admiration.

'Oh, a little village near Worthing.'

'Worthing?' asked one of the lecturers, 'which part of Africa is Worthing?'

'Em – ' At that point I happened to catch the eye of my hostess, Estelle, and in that one meaningful glance I knew it would be too, too cruel to give the game away.

'Nigeria,' I mumbled softly.

From that moment on I could do no wrong. Béarnaise sauce was eased over to my plate by obliging hands, cream was poured unsparingly into my tea, and my lead crystal glass was never empty of fine red claret. By now, a lot of attention had shifted towards Estelle, who hinted darkly that she had met me in Africa, and could speak numerous West African languages.

I could feel the sweat pouring from my brow in reams. Seldom have I felt so uncomfortable, apart from, that is, the time when, at the tender age of fourteen, I told a man in a train I was a lion tamer. For two and a half hours I was quizzed by the fascinated man on the finer points of taming lions, because he himself worked with the benighted beasts in a zoo.

(2) GUADELOUPE: CHILDHOOD

Saint-John Perse, from *To Celebrate a Childhood*

The poet's densely metaphorical style reveals an unmistakeably
Caribbean sense of light and landscape.

– Other than childhood, what was there in those days that there no longer
is?
 Plains! Slopes! There
 was greater order! And everything was glimmering realms and frontiers
of lights. And shade and light in those days were more nearly the same
thing . . . I speak of an esteem . . .

Along the borders the fruits
 might fall
 without rotting on our lips.
 And men with graver mouths stirred deeper shadows, women more
dreams with slower arms.

 My limbs grow and wax heavy, nourished with age! I shall not know
again any place of mills and sugar-cane, for children's dream, that in living,
singing waters was thus distributed . . . To the right
 the coffee was brought in, to the left the manioc
 (O canvas being folded, O praise-giving things!)
 And over here were the horses duly marked, smooth-coated mules, and
over there the oxen;
 here the whips and there the cry of the bird Annaô – and still there the
wound of the sugar-canes at the mill.
 And a cloud
 yellow and violet, color of the coco plum, if it stopped suddenly to crown
the gold volcano,
 called-by-their-names, out of their cabins,
 the servant women!

Other than childhood, what was there in those days that there no longer is?

(3) GUADELOUPE: HAPPINESS

Simone Schwarz-Bart, *The Bridge of Beyond*

Télumée, the novel's principal character, discovers an idyllic period
of contentment with Amboise in a tropical Garden of Eden.

 In that fine season of my life, the root of my luck came up, and the days
were like nights, the nights like days. All we planted flourished, came forth
well out of that scarcely cleared patch of hillside, full of rocks and stumps

that sprouted afresh every year, sending up bright green shoots above the sun-baked mass. After each harvest Monsieur Boissanville's representative would seize half our produce, and we lived on the rest, which provided us with oil, kerosene, and a new dress or pants when necessary. I can see nothing in those years but contentment, good words and kindness. When Amboise spoke of lemons I spoke of lemons in reply, and if I said use the knife he would use the axe as well. We enjoyed pricking out the seedlings, raising the furrows, setting the seeds in the womb of the earth. Our plot sloped gently down to the bottom of the valley, to a little stream grandly known as the torrent. At the bottom of the slope the earth was black and rich, just right for bringing forth long yams, crisp and juicy. The nearby torrent gave us its water and the shade of its trees. Amboise dug and broke up the clods of earth, and I crumbled them into a fine rain between my fingers. Every year this out-of-the-way place appealed to and attracted us more. As our sweat seeped into the soil, it became more and more ours, one with the odor of our bodies, of our smoke and of our food, of the eternal smoke, sharp and stinging, from the bonfires of green acomats. A square of paccala yams sprang up along the bank, and all around, hundreds of bindweeds intertwined their soft yet thorny creepers, like a writhing soul producing its own fetters. The yams were surrounded by a double row of gumbos, and on another patch, just nearby, malangas, sweet corn, a few standard bananas and plantains grew in a dense tangle. The garden improved every year, and we spent most of our time there. A little arbour of coconut fronds sheltered us when it was hot, and the words we spoke seemed to perch on the leaves of the trees nearby, making them stir cautiously in the wind. There under the shelter we used to speak of all things past and present, of all our eyes had seen, of all the people we'd known, loved and hated . . .

(4) GUADELOUPE: INDEPENDENCE

Maryse Condé, *Tree of Life*

A wedding feast disintegrates into a political row when talk of Guadeloupe's relationship with France inflames the guests.

It was at the moment when the sandfish was served, grilled over charcoal embers and lying on a bed of yam puree, that it all went wrong. Up until that point people had been talking about this and that. The women exchanging recipes for conch pie. One of the men recounting how a swarm of wasps had almost torn away his face while he worked his field. Who mentioned the name of the Darnel factory? No doubt Ephrem's father, who was working there after his own father and grandfather and rightly feared the loss of his livelihood. It was then that Dieudonné, until that moment silent and as ill at ease as ever in his stepmother's presence, launched into a diatribe against the plant owners and the French. For the owners were closing the plants one by one, and the French colonial power wanted to transform the country into a field of hands for its industries.

The speech was not to everyone's taste. In particular Ephrem, who in his turn launched into a diatribe against all the so-called Patriots who did nothing but talk in slogans and, if they were allowed to do so, would unerringly land the country in the hospital. Some flew to his aid by invoking the example of Haiti, that unfortunate independent neighbor whose refugees by the hundreds were to be seen toiling in our gardens.

Independence, that dangerous word was loosed, and the table was set ablaze!

The cacophony reached its height when the women shouted louder than the men to blame politics, more dangerous than a double-edged knife separating families.

Just the same, with the stuffed suckling pig a lull set in, so greatly did the animal filled with chili peppers, chives, and bay-rum leaves make mouths water.

(5) POINTE-À-PITRE

Amy Oakley, *Behold the West Indies*

In 1940 Guadeloupe's biggest town was anything but glamorous, as this visitor soon discovers.

Since the dredging of the harbour at Pointe-à-Pitre, the capital, Basse-Terre, with an open roadstead, has lost the greater part of Guadeloupe's commercial trade. Pointe-à-Pitre has been destroyed by fire, earthquakes, hurricanes, little of any worth having survived the hurricane of 1928 – one of the three worst of the thirty-two recorded since 1653.

A local guide-book (with translation for the English-speaking) describes Guadeloupe's chief cities as follows: 'Basse-Terre, the capital, silent under its grey antiquity . . . filled with sightseeings.' 'The glamorous and cosmopolitan city of Pointe-à-Pitre all crawling and swarming with 35 000 peoples.'

Glamorous! Cosmopolitan! Pointe-à-Pitre was not, as we saw it, but crawling and swarming, indeed, as a Chinese town. ('Hongkong,' my Illustrator comments.) Especially is this true of its Main Street, Rue Frébault with its metal-shuttered shops and tiers of iron-roofed balconied apartments. In full sunlight its open-air market, where humanity jostles within narrow bounds, is essentially Oriental. European notes were posters announcing Cigarettes Job, Pneus Miche, Galeries Parisiennes, and Bon Marché; while streets bore such metropolitan French names as Rue Raspail, Lamartine, Alsace-Lorraine, Gambetta, Victor Hugo.

With our host, Monsieur Party, we had come from Dolé, on a day's excursion in the invaluable battered Renault, to visit the Exposition de la Mer et de la Forêt, held in a building adjoining the Custom House upon the dock of Pointe-à-Pitre. It was an opportunity to see the town en fête. Guadeloupéennes – wide-eyed *doudous* (sweethearts) rivaling the daughters of Martinique – attired in madras and elegance of amplified Empire costumes, crowded around the cages where wild doves, ibis, and long-legged *crabiers* were on view, lizards, green or brown iguanas, raccoons. Within doors were displayed butterflies blue as those of Brazil, moths the size of bats. Here was to be seen modernistic furniture fashioned of native woods. In the section of the Sea were nets and boat models, dried fishes and conchs ingeniously utilized as lighting fixtures, tortoise-shell objets d'art.

Biographical and literary notes

CONDE, Maryse (1937–   ). Born in Guadeloupe, Condé is a highly prolific and popular writer, who has produced novels, drama, literary criticism and translations. She has lived in West Africa, the USA and France, where she taught at the Sorbonne in Paris. Her two-part epic *Ségou*, 1984–85, was followed by other fiction such as *Moi, Tituba sorcière*, 1986, and

MARYSE CONDÉ
TREE OF LIFE
TRANSLATED BY VICTORIA REITER

'Rich and dazzling.' *Cosmopolitan*

Traversée de la mangrove, 1989. In *Tree of Life* (Extract 4), originally *La Vie scélérate*, 1987, the narrator, Coco, retraces the history of her family and, in particular, her forebear, Albert, who made his fortune in the building of the Panama Canal.

LONGMORE, Zenga. Born in Britain of Caribbean parentage, Longmore recorded her idiosyncratic travel experiences in *Tap-Taps to Trinidad* (Extract 1), a humorous account of being black and British in a region where race and identity are inevitably sensitive issues.

OAKLEY, Amy. American writer Amy Oakley visited the Caribbean in the 1940s and produced a travel book *Behold the West Indies* (Extract 5), which contains interesting pictures of conditions in the region during the Second World War.

SAINT-JOHN PERSE (1887–1975). Born Alexis Léger in Guadeloupe to white parents, Saint-John Perse was educated in Paris and became a career diplomat, serving in Peking and travelling widely in the Far East. He returned to Paris after the 1914–18 war and rose to become Secretary-

General at the Ministry of Foreign Affairs. He refused to collaborate with the Vichy regime, was stripped of his French nationality and took refuge in the USA, where he lived until 1958. He never returned to his native Guadeloupe. His poetry, epic in tone and metaphysical in concerns, ranges from the the more explicitly autobiographical *Eloges*, 1911, from which 'To Celebrate a Childhood' (Extract 2) is taken, to the complex and allegorical *Anabase*, 1924. In 1960 he was awarded the Nobel Prize for Literature.

SCHWARZ-BART, Simone (1938–). Born in Charente-Maritime, France, Simone Schwarz-Bart went with her mother to Guadeloupe at the age of three. She was educated in Guadeloupe and attended university in Paris and Dakar, Senegal. Having married the Jewish writer André Schwarz-Bart, she co-wrote her first novel *Un plat de porc aux bananes verts*, 1967, with her husband. Her other novels include *Ti Jean L'horizon*, 1979, and *Between Two Worlds*, 1992. She has lived in Switzerland, Senegal and Guadeloupe. *Pluie et vent sur Télumée Miracle* (*The Bridge of Beyond*) tells of the lives of several generations of Guadeloupean women and the legacy of slavery and French colonialism in the island (Extract 3). Despite misfortunes and cruelties, Schwarz-Bart's female protagonists achieve what she has called 'victory in the heart of darkness', dramatizing Guadeloupe's 'long history, full of wonders, bloodshed and frustrations, and of desires no less vast than those that filled the skies of Nineveh, Babylon or Jerusalem.' Schwarz-Bart has been widely acclaimed for her fusion of Creole folk-tale narrative, local history and classical sense of epic.

DOMINICA

'I remember a far tall island
floating in cobalt paint
The thought of it is a
        childhood dream
torn by a midnight plaint.'
Phyllis Shand Allfrey,
The Child's Return

Dominica (pronounced 'Domineeca', official title 'Commonwealth of Dominica') is not the Dominican Republic. The confusion is easy to understand, but Domineecans are tired of receiving their mail several months late after it has been redirected from the Dominican Republic. As the island's foremost historian Lennox Honychurch remarks, most Dominicans are sadly familiar with only one Spanish phrase, *Mal encaminado a Santo Domingo* ('misdirected to the Dominican Republic').

Dominica is approximately 65 times smaller than the Dominican Republic, its population one-hundredth that of its homonym. Unlike the Spanish-speaking Dominican Republic, Dominica's official language is English, although a French Creole (*patwa*) is widely used. The island is a member of the Commonwealth, a former British colony and plays cricket rather than baseball. Some eight hundred kilometres separate Dominica from the Dominican Republic, but names notwithstanding, they are culturally much further apart.

Dominica has baptized itself the 'nature island' and it is not difficult to see why. Generations of travellers and writers have been fascinated by its looming mountains, lush rainforest and fast-flowing rivers. The island rises dramatically out of the sea, the tip of Morne Diablotin, the highest of many peaks, often lost in mist. Precipitous slopes covered in thick vegetation defy easy settlement and cultivation. Inland, mysterious lakes in craters, sulphuric springs and sheer ravines are both spectacular and threatening; names such as **Boiling Lake**, **Valley of Desolation** or **Massacre** do not reassure; the island's varied ecosystems amaze scientists of all sorts. Dominica is still largely covered by rainforest, wet, green and often impenetrable, which harbours an extraordinary profusion of flora and fauna.

Few literary visitors have remained unmoved by this awesome sight. Anthony Trollope (◊ Jamaica) passed by *en route* to Jamaica and Cuba in 1856 and gazed at the island from his ship:

FACT BOX

AREA: 750 sq km
POPULATION: 72 000
CAPITAL: Roseau
LANGUAGES: English, Creole
FORMER COLONIAL POWER: Britain
INDEPENDENCE: 1978
PER CAPITA GDP: US$2680

'To my mind, Dominica as seen from the sea, is by far the most picturesque of all these islands. Indeed it would be difficult to beat it in either colour or grouping. It fills one with an ardent desire to be off and rambling among those green mountains.'

Twenty years later, the veteran naturalist William Palgrave could hardly contain his enthusiasm:

'In the wild grandeur of its towering mountains, some of which rise five thousand feet above the level of the sea; in the majesty of its almost impenetrable forests; in the gorgeousness of its vegetation, the abruptness of its precipices, the calm of its lakes, the violence of its torrents, the sublimity of its waterfalls, it stands without rival, not in the West Indies only, but I should think throughout the whole island catalogue of the Atlantic and Pacific combined.'

Even the historian and arch-imperialist James Anthony Froude ◊ conceded in the 1880s that the island was the most beautiful of all; in his *The English in the West Indies* (Extract 5) he praises Dominica's spectacular natural beauty while berating the incompetence of its colonial administrators.

After Columbus sighted the island on his second expedition in 1493 he is reputed to have described it to Queen Isabella by crumpling a piece of paper to reproduce its jagged peaks and deep valleys. He did not stay, perhaps discouraged by this forbidding landscape. Nor did European colonization really take hold until the beginning of the nineteenth century, again because of Dominica's topography which was unsuitable for plantation agriculture. In this sense, the sheer inaccessibility of much of the island has largely determined its history and may yet still play a large part in its future as the vogue for 'ecotourism' gathers pace. A well-worn local joke has it that were Columbus to return to the Caribbean today, he would probably only recognize an unchanged Dominica.

THE CARIBS

Today the descendants of the people who watched Columbus's ships appear on the horizon still live in Dominica. Along with a small community in St

Vincent, Dominica's Caribs are the only remaining survivors of a people who inhabited the entire chain of the Lesser Antilles before the arrival of Europeans. They called the island *Wai'tukubuli* (meaning 'tall is her body') and wrested control of it and other islands from the peaceful Arawaks. Their determined resistance and fiercesome reputation as warriors and cannibals kept European colonists at bay for a further two centuries after Columbus.

The Carib community currently numbers about 2500 people, but of these only seventy or so define 'themselves as 'pure'. The others have intermarried over the generations with the island's majority black population. The Caribs have their own 3700 acre 'territory' on the north-east coast of the island, given to them in 1903 by the British colonial authorities. There are several villages, the main one named **Salybia**, and a few other settlements, surrounded by the ubiquitous clumps of banana and coconut trees. Here, in the poorest and most remote district of Dominica, the Caribs work as they have always done as fishermen, boat builders and subsistence farmers. Tourism has brought new opportunities and some members of the community make the 40 km trip from the Carib Territory to the capital, **Roseau**, to sell handicrafts to visitors.

The Caribs were, etymologically at least, the original cannibals, their name becoming synonymous with the social custom which has fascinated generations of writers. From Columbus's first encounter with them, the Caribs were to be feared and reviled for what Western observers fancifully believed to be an insatiable hunger for human flesh. Columbus's surgeon, Diego Alvarez Chanca, reported that they ate those whom they defeated in war as a matter of course: 'They say that men's flesh is so good that there is nothing like it in the world, and it certainly seems so for the bones which we found in these houses had been gnawed of everything they could gnaw.' The French Jesuit priest Jean-Baptiste Labat took a more understanding position in his 1722 *Nouveau voyage aux isles de l'Amérique*:

> 'I also know, & it is very true that when the French & English were starting to establish themselves in the islands there were many people of both nations who were killed, cured & eaten by the *Caraïbes*; but it was rage that made them commit this excess, because they were only able to avenge themselves fully of the injustice that the Europeans had done them in chasing them from their lands, by putting them to death, when they seized them, with cruelties which were not ordinary or natural to them . . .'

Thanks to their man-eating notoriety (based on a Spanish lie, say the present-day Caribs), Dominica's indigenous people have inspired curiosity and a little apprehension among visitors. In her short story 'Temps Perdi' (Extract 1), Jean Rhys ◊ tells of a visit to **Salybia** shortly after the 1930 'Carib War' when Caribs clashed with the local police and a British gunboat was summoned after accusations of smuggling led to serious fighting.

Today nobody speaks the original Carib language and anthropologists predict that the Caribs, already considerably intermixed, will not survive much longer as a distinct ethnic group. Yet the inhabitants of the Carib Territory are proud of their ancestry and continue to elect a chief who enjoys a five-year term of office. In the wake of the Columbus quincentenary, with its affirmation of indigenous identity, the Caribs are not yet ready for extinction.

COLONIAL CONFLICT

As European colonization spread throughout the islands of the Eastern Caribbean, Dominica became the last bastion of the Caribs, some of whom fled from neighbouring territories. From there the Caribs were able to launch expeditions in other islands, successfully attacking Antigua, Barbuda and Marie Galante. Ships called at Dominica to trade and take on fresh supplies, but few efforts were made to establish a permanent colonial settlement. Gradually, however, the French presence became more persistent, and settlers from neighbouring Martinique and Guadeloupe began to arrive in bigger numbers. An agreement between France and Britain in 1660 theoretically conceded control of the island to the Caribs in return for their non-aggression and Dominica was again declared 'neutral' in 1686. But conflict between the two European powers continued to simmer and all too often the Caribs were caught in the imperial cross-fire.

After a series of three-way skirmishes, the English finally occupied Dominica by force in 1761 and took formal possession two years later under the Treaty of Paris. A significant French community remained on the island and continued to dominate the plantation system. To this day, place names and language are as much French-influenced as English, and many Dominicans have more in common with people in neighbouring Martinique and Guadeloupe than with more anglicized Antigua or Barbados.

Anglo–French rivalry was not yet over, however, and France retook Dominica between 1778 and 1783 during the American War of Independence. The Treaty of Versailles restored it to Britain, only for the French to make two further invasion attempts in 1795 and 1805. Not surprisingly, the forts which protect **Roseau** and the second town of **Portsmouth** date from this period of colonial conflict.

When not rebuffing or surrendering to the French, the British authorities were under continual siege from the runaway slaves known as Maroons. This persistent conflict dated back to the importation of African slaves which began to gather pace under British rule from 1763. Many slaves escaped the rigours of the sugar-cane and coffee plantations and settled in the inaccessible mountainous interior. There they often joined forces with Carib groups, launching devastating raids on farms and villages. The French were happy to encourage this drain on British military resources and even went so far as to arm the Maroons during their 1778–83 occupation of the island. The Maroon Wars rumbled on until 1814, when a large force of specially assembled rangers attacked runaway slave communities, killing or capturing at least 500 Maroons, including their veteran leader Jacko.

'TYPICAL DOMINICA'

Despite this debilitating background of unrest, Dominica became a modest agricultural exporter in the first half of the nineteenth century, with coffee and sugar bringing prosperity to some landowners. But then, in 1829, a coffee blight effectively wiped out the industry, reducing exports to a trickle. Sugar took over as the major export crop, with increasing numbers of former slaves turning to subsistence farming after emancipation in 1833. They joined an already substantial number of ex-slaves who had been freed before abolition. When the Baptist minister Joseph John Gurney visited the island in 1840, he was gratified to witness what he perceived as a peaceful transition from slavery to small-scale farming and wage labour. His *A Winter in the West Indies* paints an idyllic picture of natural splendour and social harmony.

Yet sugar, like coffee before it, was doomed to failure, and when the Caribbean colonies lost their monopoly in the British market in 1846 the rot began to set in. Because of its rugged terrain, Dominica was in any case hardly an ideal plantation island, and as sugar prices fell, widespread poverty and hardship began to emerge. As European beet sugar production eclipsed tropical sugar-cane, Dominica's economy stagnated.

In 1887, at the peak of the sugar slump and during a period of intense social unrest and dramatic out-migration, Froude visited Dominica and saw it as the epitome of British imperial neglect. Looking at **Roseau's** dilapidated housing and the rural slums of the interior, the advocate of empire despaired:

> 'The British flag was flying over the fort, but for once I had no pride in looking at it. For the last half-century we have left Dominica in desolation, as a child leaves a toy that it is tired of.'

Other crops came to replace sugar, notably limes, but they invariably proved disappointing. There was a brief six-year period of reform and infrastructural development under the enlightened colonial administrator Henry Hesketh Bell, but decline set in again after 1905. In the latter part of the nineteenth century, Rose & Co came to Dominica and set up a lime production and extraction industry. Fluctuating prices and a series of disastrous hurricanes damaged the industry before an outbreak of disease in the 1920s destroyed most of the island's lime trees. Attempts to plant cocoa and other crops proved little more successful.

Such was Dominica's poverty that in 1929 only 96 people out of the population of 43 000 were considered wealthy enough to be eligible to pay income tax. The Second World War, with its shortages and disruptions, merely worsened the situation. As the influential Moyne Commission report, published in 1945 pointed out: 'Of all the British West Indian Islands Dominica presents the most striking contrast between the great poverty of a large proportion of the population and the beauty and fertility of the land.' This view was endorsed by James Pope-Hennessy ◊ in his impressions of Dominica in the early 1950s. Like Froude, this English writer loathed what he saw as the stifling mediocrity of the colonial authorities and the resulting impoverishment of most Dominicans. *The Baths of Absalom* (Extract 6) remains a powerful indictment of colonial neglect.

Dominica developed a reputation for failure and bad luck; to some, it seemed that the island was jinxed. 'Typical Dominica' became a cynical catchphrase among the growing expatriate community of artists, nature-lovers and drop-outs as the island suffered yet another setback. To those convinced of some malevolent influence, Dominica's strange and haunting beauty seemed disquieting. The travel writer Alec Waugh (◊ Martinique) wrote in the 1940s of a 'Dominica legend':

> ' "Everyone goes crazy down there," they say. "All that rain and those mountains shutting them in and everything going wrong. Did you hear about that fellow who tried to dig a hole through the centre of the earth because his wife was buried in Australia? He dug it with a cutlass, carrying the earth up in a calabash. You can still see the hole. That's typical." '

New Beginning

By the time Dominica approached independence, it had been fought over by Britain, France and the Caribs, had been briefly a member of a federal 'Southern Caribee Islands', had enjoyed limited self-rule, had been tacked on to the Leeward Islands and had reverted to Crown Colony status. During this time and particularly during the period of self-rule an increasingly powerful middle class of coloured merchants and professionals (the so-called 'mulatto ascendancy') had arrived on the political stage, challenging the influence of the old white élite. In 1939 the island was transferred from the Leeward to the Windward Islands Federation and in 1967 won full internal autonomy after participating in the ill-fated West Indies Federation.

The main force behind the drive towards political independence was the Dominica Labour Party (DLP), led at the time by the idiosyncratic Patrick John. During the run-up to independence in 1978 Prime Minister John allegedly approved a secret deal with a company which planned to construct a trans-shipment terminal for 'laundering' petroleum to the then embargoed South African government. Other fanciful and shady schemes involved the sale of Dominican passports to international businessmen and strange dealings with mercenary forces interested in invading other Caribbean territories. The introduction of repressive legislation aimed at preventing 'subversion' did little to enhance his standing. By 1979 the whiff of scandal had become overpowering and John was removed by a general strike, quickly finding himself in prison on charges of corruption. Elections in 1980 brought the doughty conservative, Eugenia Charles, to power. Known as the Caribbean's 'iron lady', Miss Charles took a robustly right-wing line on most issues, including providing conspicuous support for the US invasion of Grenada in October 1983.

Dominica's short history of stable, multi-party democracy (Eugenia Charles lost peaceful elections in 1995 and retired) has coincided with a period of relative prosperity, thanks to the latest of the island's export crops – the banana. Dominica has been exporting bananas, mostly into the British market via the Geest company, since the 1950s, but it was really only in the 1980s that a 'banana boom' occurred, fuelled by a combination of rising prices and protected entry into the British market. The flow of cash into the island paid for many a Japanese truck or television set and created a new generation of small farmers, politically influential and highly dependent on the banana industry.

Since then the boom has faded, although not yet into real bust, and prices have dropped alarmingly. The prospect that Dominica may lose its privileged access into the European market and hence face an unwinnable price war with large Latin American producers fills many Dominicans with dread, since bananas have accounted for more than half of export earnings during the 1990s. After so many failed crops in the past, the omens are not good. Only 'ecotourism' promises an alternative economic future, but all too often tourism destroys the beauty which sustains it.

BEAUTY AND HORROR

Strangely, of the two internationally known writers from Dominica, both were women and both were white, daughters of the tiny European planter and professional class. Jean Rhys ◊ was born 25 years before Phyllis Shand Allfrey ◊ and the two women never met (although they corresponded extensively), but there is a certain thematic similarity between them, not least in their treatment of Dominica itself. Although Rhys is much more widely read than Shand Allfrey, her association with the island was much less lasting as she left at the age of sixteen, only to return on one brief visit. Despite this separation, Dominica continued to haunt Rhys and the island appears, whether named or not, throughout her work as a metaphor for a more general feeling of loss and rootlessness. In her autobiography *Smile Please* (Extract 2) she recalls how its landscape and people came to shape her literary imagination and, in particular, her sense of tragedy.

Through Rhys, and to a lesser extent Shand Allfrey, comes the idea of Dominica as a place of beauty but also of fear, melancholy and death. In *Wide Sargasso Sea* (see Jamaica), her best-known work, Rhys traces the emotional disintegration of Antoinette Cosway (later to become the Mrs Rochester of *Jane Eyre*) and the parallel breakdown of her husband. As he leaves the island (described merely as 'one of the Windward Islands') after the honeymoon period which has revealed Antoinette's madness, Rochester sees its mysterious beauty as somehow a mirror image of his anguish:

> 'I hated the mountains and the hills, the rivers and the rain. I hated the sunsets of whatever colour, I hated its beauty and its magic and the secret I would never know. I hated its indifference and the cruelty which was part of its loveliness. Above all I hated her. For she belonged to the magic and the loveliness.'

In Shand Allfrey's *The Orchid House* (Extract 4) the sinister leitmotiv of beauty and horror prefigures that of *Wide Sargasso Sea*. The tuberculosis of cousin Andrew, the opium addiction of 'the Master' are reflected in the island's over-lush, decadent landscape:

> 'Beauty and disease, beauty and sickness, beauty and horror: that was the island. A quartering breeze hurried eastward, over cotton tufts of clouds; the air was soft and hot; colour drenched everything, liquid turquoise melted into sapphire and then into emerald.'

The destructive force of Dominica's nature is more than a purely literary device. The island has been struck many times with unusual ferocity by hurricanes in the course of the twentieth century, each wreaking havoc on farms, fields and houses. In 1979 Hurricane David smashed into Dominica, killing 37 people and leaving 60 000 homeless. What was left standing was flattened by Hurricane Allen the following year. As artist and Dominica resident Stephen Hawys ◊ reports in his autobiographical *Mount Joy* (Extract 3), the hurricane season inspires real and justifiable anxiety among disaster-prone Dominicans.

LITERARY LANDMARKS

Roseau. On Cork Street, in the centre of the ramshackle capital, stands the clapboard and tin-roofed house where Jean Rhys was born in 1890. Now a guesthouse, the building has survived countless hurricanes.

Geneva Estate. Rhys's mother was born on this estate, 'a two-hour journey from Roseau.' It provided the inspiration for the setting of her best-known novel. 'Geneva was an old place, old for Dominica. I tried to write about Geneva and the Geneva garden in *Wide Sargasso Sea*.'

BOOKLIST

The following selection includes the extracted titles in this chapter as well as other titles for further reading. In general, paperback editions are given when possible. For most of the extracted works, the original publisher in English can be found in 'Acknowledgments and Citations' at the end of the volume, as can the exact location of the extracts and the editions from which they are taken.

Cracknell, Basil, *Dominica*, David & Charles, Newton Abbot, 1973.

Froude, J.A., *The English in the West Indies*, Longmans, Green & Co, London, 1888. **Extract 5**.

Gurney, Joseph John, *A Winter in the West Indies, Described in Familiar Letters to Henry Clay, of Kentucky*, John Murray, London, 1840.

Hawys, Stephen, *Mount Joy*, Duck-worth, London, 1968. **Extract 3**.

Honychurch, Lennox, *Dominica: Isle of Adventure*, Macmillan, Basingstoke, 1991.

Hulme, Peter and Neil L. Whitehead, *Wild Majesty: Encounters with Caribs from Columbus to the Present Day*, Clarendon Press, Oxford, 1992.

Pope-Hennessy, James, *The Baths of Absalom*, Allan Wingate, London, 1954. **Extract 6**.

Rhys, Jean, 'Temps Perdi', in *Tales of the Wide Caribbean*, Heinemann, London, 1980. **Extract 1**.

Rhys, Jean, *Smile Please: An Unfinished Autobiography*, André Deutsch, London, 1979. **Extract 2**.

Shand Allfrey, Phyllis, *The Orchid House*, Virago, London, 1990. **Extract 4**.

Extracts

(1) Dominica: Caribs

Jean Rhys, *Temps Perdi*

The narrator has gone to visit the Carib Territory out of curiosity to see a people supposedly on the verge of extinction but still capable of rioting against the government.

Round another bend in the road we saw below us the big clearing where the police-station stood with five or six other houses, one of them a Catholic church.

In the station the rifles were stacked in a row, bayonets and all. The room was large, almost cool. Everything looked new and clean, and there was a circular seat round the palm tree outside.

'We had trouble here,' our policeman told us. 'They burnt the last station and they burnt twenty feet off this one while it was being built.'

'Why?'

'Well, it seems they thought they were going to have a hospital. They had asked the Government for a hospital. A petition, you know. And when they found out that the Government was giving them a police-station and not a hospital, there was trouble . . .'

'There is a beautiful Carib girl,' the policeman said, 'in the house over there – the one with the red roof. Everybody goes to see her and photographs her. She and her mother will be vexed if you don't go. Give her a little present, of course. She is very beautiful but she can't walk. It's a pity, that . . .'

When you went in it was like all their houses. A small room, clean, the walls covered with pictures cut from newspapers and coloured cards of Virgins, saints and angels, Star of the Sea, Refuge of the Distressed, Hope of the Afflicted. Star of the Sea again, Jesus, Mary and Joseph . . .

The girl appeared in the doorway of the dark little bedroom, posed for a moment dramatically, then dragged herself across the floor into the sun outside to be photographed, managing her useless legs with a desperate, courageous grace; she had white, lovely teeth. There she sat in the sun, brown eyes fixed on us, the long brown eyes of the Creole, not the small, black, slanting eyes of the pure Carib. And her hair, which hung to her waist and went through every shade from dark brown to copper and back again, was not a Carib's hair, either. She sat there smiling, and an assortment of brightly-coloured Virgins and saints looked down at her from the walls, smiling too. She had aquiline features, proud features. Her skin in the sun was a lovely colour.

(2) DOMINICA: CHILDHOOD

Jean Rhys, *Smile Please*

In her autobiography, Jean Rhys tells how her nanny instilled in her the sense of menace which colours much of her writing on the Caribbean.

Now it is time to talk about Meta, my nurse and the terror of my life. She had been there ever since I could remember: a short, stocky woman, very black and always, I thought, in a bad temper. I never saw Meta smile. She always seemed to be brooding over some terrible, unforgettable wrong. When I wasn't old enough to walk by myself I can remember the feel of her hard hand as she hauled me along to the Botanical Gardens where she was supposed to take me every afternoon. She walked so fast that I had to run to keep up with her, and most of the time, her face turned away, she muttered, curses, I suppose.

She dragged me past Miss Jane's sweet shop. I'd often been there with my older sister before she left. Miss Jane was an old coloured lady whose small house was on the way to the Botanical Gardens and her sweets were not only delicious but very cheap. There you could get a small jar of freshly made guava jelly for a penny. The base of most of the other sweets was syrup – mixed with shredded coconut, a tablette, with ginger, a ginger cake. The most expensive were made of clarified sugar and cashew nuts. Those, I think, were threepence. The strangest was a sweet which was called lassi mango, if that is how it is spelt. When it was broken it would stretch indefinitely. The game was for one child to take one end, the other child the other, and go in different directions. At last it would be an almost invisible thread, and the joke was to watch someone walk into it and slap themselves, trying to account for the stickiness. Past all these delights Meta would drag me, taking not the faintest notice of my efforts to escape and jerking me if I looked back.

It was Meta who talked so much about zombies, soucriants, and loups-garoux. She was the only person I've heard talk about loups-garoux (werewolves) in the West Indies. Soucriants were always women she said, who came at night and sucked your blood. During the day they looked like ordinary women but you could tell them by their red eyes. Zombies were black shapeless things. They could get through a locked door and you heard them walking up to your bed. You didn't see them, you felt their hairy hands round your throat.

(3) DOMINICA: HURRICANES

Stephen Hawys, *Mount Joy*

> *On several occasions, Dominica has been flattened by the hurricanes which afflict the Caribbean. The anxiety of the hurricane season, writes Stephen Hawys, is tempered by the knowledge that nature invariably recovers.*

We are always a little jumpy in September, even if we have not been consciously worrying about hurricanes. Subconsciously hurricane has been with us for two months and every little rumour of it registers a little more in September than at any other time. Rumour has it that there is a hurricane somewhere near Barbados which in a few hours is reported as bad weather in the Martinique channel. We run to nail up faulty shutters and windows, tighten bolts upon swing-arms and see that the place can be battened down to withstand the ever-possible siege. Then either the hurricane gun is heard and the great rain and wind rises out of a still calm, or nothing happens. When it comes mankind and animals wait until the genie has passed, they await his return again to beat down what he has already shaken loose – it is on a hurricane's return journey that houses fall down. Or nothing happens and we go out presently to pull out nails and take down boards, rather sheepishly telling one another that the barometer looked dangerous. In a few days we shall hear what happened.

I have seen through sunlit air a curtain of deep indigo – almost black – creep up from the south and pass across to the west of the island leaving blue sky in its wake. That was a hurricane passing two hundred miles away. I have not been through a hurricane myself – yet. I have seen paths cut through huge forest trees and houses deroofed in our valley and have been shown where the sheets of galvanised iron were found, a quarter of a mile from their place of origin . . .

What is even more amazing than the hurricane is the speed with which the earth recovers. It survives the defoliation, the shaking of the roots of its trees – it survives the fear which holds every plant in its grip no less than our own throats. They are stirred up to put out leaves at once, to flower and fruit more abundantly unless they are mortally injured, while some of us sit disconsolate upon the wrecked veranda feeling that there is no use in doing anything while such evil things are abroad and may come at any time.

(4) Dominica: Return
Phyllis Shand Allfrey, *The Orchid House*

Returning from America, Stella is intoxicated by the sensual exoticism of Dominica and drawn towards the mysterious and consumptive Andrew.

In Stella's sick dreams of home the island had been a vision so exquisite that she was now almost afraid to open her eyes wide, lest she might be undeceived and cast down, or lest confirmation would stab through her like a shock. Treading the black damp earth of the bridle-path, brushed by ferns and wild begonias, experiencing the fleet glimpse of a ramier flying from the forest floor through branches into the Prussian blue sky, it was impossible not to look and look and drink it in like one who had long been thirsty. *It is more beautiful than a dream, for in dreams you cannot smell this divine spiciness, you can't stand in a mist of aromatic warmth and stare through jungle twigs to a spread of distant town, so distant that people seem to have no significance; you cannot drown your eyes in a cobalt sea, a sea with the blinding gold of the sun for a boundary!*

Stella put her arms round the trunk of a laurier cypre and rubbed her cheek softly against the bark. *I've come back*, she said to the tree. A little yellow lizard jumped out of a hole at the trunk-base, sliding across her path, and above her there was the sweet frightened fuss of humming-birds' wings. *I've come back*, said Stella, squeezing the laurier cypre as if she would strangle it for joy.

Her sandals made a noise in the rutted narrow way, which was simply a river bed in the rainy season. She descended into the valley, crossed a stream by stepping stones, bending to cool her hands in the sparkling water, and began her ascent towards Petit Cul-de-Sac. The way was not very familiar to her for she had only ridden there on a donkey once or twice during her grandfather's lifetime, yet she felt so strong (had she not learned to be a farm-hand and braved the rigours of zero weather?), that the sharpness of the incline meant nothing to her, and she was surprised to find beads of sweat on her forehead when she arrived at the clearing.

Cornélie's house was very small, a wooden shingled shack with a verandah and outhouses covered with palm-leaf roofs – it was so small that it looked like an old dolls' house, dwarfed by the immense trees which leant towards it lovingly. On the verandah stood a child's wicker cot on wheels, covered with mosquito-netting. In the middle of the clearing, stretched out in a canvas deck-chair of purple and green stripes lay Andrew.

(5) ROSEAU

James Anthony Froude,
The English in the West Indies

Victorian traveller and eminent historian, Froude is entranced, like most visitors, by the grandeur of Roseau's physical setting.

The situation of Roseau is exceedingly beautiful. The sea is, if possible, a deeper azure even than at St Lucia; the air more transparent; the forests of a lovelier green than I ever saw in any other country. Even the rain, which falls in such abundance, falls often out of a clear sky as if not to interrupt the sunshine, and a rainbow almost perpetually hangs its arch over the island. Roseau itself stands on a shallow promontory. A long terrace of tolerable-looking houses faces the landing place. At right angles to the terrace, straight streets strike backwards at intervals, palms and bananas breaking the lines of roof. At a little distance, you see the towers of the old French Catholic cathedral, a smaller but not ungraceful-looking Anglican church, and to the right a fort, or the ruins of one, now used as a police barrack, over which flies the English flag as the symbol of our titular domination. Beyond the fort is a public garden with pretty trees in it along the brow of a precipitous cliff, at the foot of which, when we landed, lay at anchor a couple of smart Yankee schooners and half a dozen coasting cutters, while rounding inwards behind was a long shallow bay dotted over with the sails of fishing boats. White negro villages gleamed among the palms along the shore, and wooded mountains rose immediately above them. It seemed an attractive, innocent, sunny sort of place, very pleasant to spend a few days in, if the inner side of things corresponded to the appearance. To a looker-on at that calm scene it was not easy to realise the desperate battles which had been fought for the possession of it, the gallant lives which had been laid down under the walls of that crumbling castle. These cliffs had echoed the roar of Rodney's guns on the day which saved the British Empire, and the island I was gazing at was England's Salamis.

(6) Roseau

James Pope-Hennessy, *The Baths of Absalom*

The ramshackle frontier-town ambiance of Roseau is not to everybody's taste, as Pope-Hennessy's disgusted account makes clear.

Never before in my life had I been so naggingly conscious of two harmless everyday substances – wood and tin. What is not made of wood in Roseau seems made of tin, what is not made of tin seems to be wood, and most frequently, as in the majority of the dwelling-houses, these two materials are joined in an unhealthy, almost sinister union. For the third element, paint, which might have rendered the other two less offensive, is totally and notoriously lacking throughout the town. The wooden houses and shacks and cabins and sheds and shops have, some of them, a rudimentary basic foundation of stone: but most are of worn unpainted wood and many are covered by a grey skin of shingles, stained and curling from the rain, and giving the outsides of the houses a diseased, half-leprous look. The tiny verandahs and miniature gables – for most Roseau buildings are on a doll's house scale – are moreover decorated with elaborate fretwork patterns which make them impossible to keep clean. Fences protecting backyards are made of bits of packing-case, and everywhere, all the day long, people were chipping and tinkering away at pieces of wood with an aimless, slow, fanatic zeal. Youths squatted happily in the gutters ripping crates apart to nail them together as crates again, or to construct little wheeled push-carts. On some days every child in Roseau seemed to be gripping a piece of wood in its hand. As for the tin element, this was if anything more noticeable. It began with the rusted roofs of old corrugated iron sheeting, patched with other bits of tin and darned with wire, roofs with an absence of chimneys which made one think of them as covering summer-houses or potting-sheds, and on which the tropical rain battered a noisy tattoo. And one was kept constantly aware of other bits of tin – old oil-drums, old biscuit tins, cigarette tins, sardine tins, tins that had contained meat from Australia or pilchards from Liverpool, all were requisitioned, hoarded and put to some unexpected and usually unattractive use . . . Fundamentally there is a dreadful pathos about this collection of rubbish-heap material, just as there is about the ragged clothes spread out to dry by washerwomen on the shores of the Roseau River, which daily and publicly proclaim the inexcusable poverty in which the working people of Dominica are maintained.

Biographical and literary notes

FROUDE, James Anthony (1818–1894). A distinguished historian and Regius Professor at Oxford University, Froude visited the British Caribbean colonies in 1887 and produced a book which created enormous controversy. As well as being an elegant travelogue, *The English in the West Indies* (Extract 5) was also a polemic in favour of British colonial rule and against black self-government. Espousing the conventional social Darwinism of the period, Froude argued that the Caribbean's black colonial subjects were inferior to their white masters and that Britain should reinvigorate its relationship with this part of the empire. Lamenting imperial decline, Froude wrote, 'The bow of Ulysses is unstrung . . . They [the colonial subjects] cannot string the bow. Only the true lord and master can string it.' His clear sympathy for the white plantocracy and his disdain for black culture caused a considerable backlash in the Caribbean. The black Trinidadian intellectual, John Jacob Thomas, wrote a devastating riposte entitled *Froudacity: West Indian Fables Explained*, 1889, which accused Froude of colonialist impertinence and racism. Arguing against imperialist rule from London and championing the Caribbean's distinctive cultural identity, Thomas asked: 'Does Mr Froude in the fatuity of his skinpride, believe that educated men, worthy of the name, would be otherwise than resentful, if not disgusted, at being shunted out of bread in their own native land, which their parents' labour and taxes have made desirable, in order to afford room to blockheads, vulgarians, or worse, imported from beyond the sea?'

HAWYS, Stephen (1878–1968). An English painter, Hawys moved to Dominica in 1929 after spells in Paris, the Pacific and East Africa and bought a tumbledown, former plantation estate, **Mount Joy**. His autobiographical account of his life in remote rural Dominica, *Mount Joy* (Extract 3), evokes the island's spectacular natural beauty and its ramshackle colonial administration. His reminiscences and expatriate philosophizing can occasionally grate, but his descriptions of Dominican flora and fauna are detailed and perceptive.

POPE-HENNESSY, James (1916–1974). After completing a degree at Oxford and working for a London publisher, Pope-Hennessy became private secretary to the Governor of Trinidad and Tobago. He spent the Second World War in British Intelligence, and in 1947 became literary editor of *The Spectator*, a post he resigned in order to travel and write. Apart from the slim essay, *The Baths of Absalom* (Extract 6), Pope-Hennessy wrote a number of histories and essays, including an account of the Atlantic slave trade, *Sins of Their Fathers*, 1967. *West Indian Summer*, 1943, is a reconstruction of the lives and impressions of several British travellers in the Caribbean, including Raleigh, Trollope and Froude. Like Froude, Pope-Hennessy was a stern critic of Britain's imperial neglect in the Caribbean. His writing continually emphasizes the incompetence and insularity of the colonial administrators and the degrading poverty experienced by the majority of black islanders. *The Baths of Absalom* forcefully contrasts the decay and demoralization of British-owned Dominica with the relative prosperity and dynamism of French-governed Martinique. In the French territories, he writes, Froude 'would have found much to support his conviction that with intelligent thought and care a European government can make these islands at once prosperous and truly civilised.' His impressions of Dominica and St Lucia are unremittingly negative. 'Pathetically loyal to this country, pathetically proud of being British, these little islands constitute a stain on England's record which should long ago have been erased.' Pope-Hennessy's critique, while undoubtedly idiosyncratic in its obsessive dislike of tropical vegetation, architecture and climate, nonetheless gives an interesting flavour of the economic and political *malaise* which preceded independence in the English-speaking Caribbean.

RHYS, Jean (1890–1979). Born Ella Gwendoline Rees Williams to a white Creole family in Dominica, Jean Rhys came to England in 1907. Her early years in London and Paris were unhappy and provided the material for her early fiction. In 1924 she began using the pen-name Jean Rhys. Her first collection of short stories, *Left Bank*, was published in 1927, followed by four novels including the much-acclaimed *Good Morning, Midnight*, 1939. Yet her writing career was mostly unsuccessful until the publication of *Wide Sargasso Sea* in 1966, which followed almost thirty years of obscurity. This imaginative reconstruction of the life of Antoinette Cosway, the first and mad wife of Mr Rochester in Charlotte Bronte's *Jane Eyre*, was rapturously received and established her reputation. The novel traces the hereditary insanity and traumatic childhood which lie behind Antoinette's madness and eventual suicide. Its sense of brooding menace and sinister inevitability draws closely on Rhys's own experiences in colonial Dominica, as revealed in her unfinished autobiography *Smile Please* (Extract 2). Otherwise, references to Dominica are normally oblique and fleeting in Rhys's work, an exception being the short story, 'Temps Perdi' (Extract 1), which evokes a long-past encounter with the island's Caribs.

SHAND ALLFREY, Phyllis (1908–1986). Like Jean Rhys, a white Creole born in Dominica (where her father was Crown Attorney), Shand Allfrey left the island to study in Europe and later lived in Britain and the USA. In Britain she became involved in the Labour Party and Fabian Society, and when she returned to Dominica in 1954 she co-founded the Dominica Labour Party and was elected as an MP for Dominica in the short-lived West Indian Federation. Between 1958 and 1962, Shand Allfrey was Minister of Labour and Social Affairs in the federal government, based in Trinidad. When the Federation collapsed in 1962, she returned to Dominica to edit the weekly *Dominica Herald*, and later the family-owned *Dominica Star*. In her later life, tragedy struck twice with the death of her daughter in Africa and the devastation wrought on Dominica and the Shand Allfreys' house by Hurricane David in 1979. Her best-known work, *The Orchid House* (Extract 4), was first published in 1953, reprinted in 1982 and serialized on television in 1991. It tells of L'Aromatique, a 'house empty of men' and the sensuous and beguiling influence of Dominica on three white sisters, all of whom love the same man. The story, rich in tropical evocation, is largely seen through the eyes of Lally, the girls' black nurse, who watches as they leave the home and island, only to be drawn back. With their father shell-shocked from the First World War and addicted to the opium supplied by the sinister Mr Lilipoulala, Stella, Natalie and Joan represent three very different personalities, but each is attracted to Andrew, their cousin, himself dying of tuberculosis. Natural beauty, sickness and evil are intermixed in this extraordinarily rich and atmospheric novel which suggestively depicts the decline of a colonial culture.

MARTINIQUE

Arriving in Martinique in the 1950s from run-down Dominica, James Pope-Hennessy (◊ Dominica) marvelled at the sheer Frenchness of the capital **Fort-de-France**, with its Parisian fashions and *pissoirs*. In 'The Baths of Absalom', he concludes, 'you could easily believe yourself in France'. In the 1960s, V.S. Naipaul (◊ Trinidad) made the same disconcerting discovery. 'Martinique is France,' he wrote in *The Middle Passage* (Extract 5). For both writers, the crossing from the English-speaking Caribbean into the French Antilles entailed a disorienting shift in European influence and style.

Today Martinique is even more a version of France than then. For fifty years the island has been a full *département* of the French Republic, and its tropical-Gallic flavour is perhaps even more pronounced than that of Guadeloupe. Its landscape may be typically Caribbean, with volcanic mountains, rainforest and steamy banana plantations, but amidst the exotic stand the familiar symbols of French consumerism: the Crédit Agricole, Euromarché, Délifrance. Television brings the latest news from Paris; seven 747s a day link the island with the *métropole*; the shops are crammed with over-priced French goods.

Martinique is the consumer society *par excellence*. Martinicans reputedly own more cars per head of population than anywhere else in the world. The island boasts the highest recorded *per capita* consumption of French yoghourt and, more significantly, champagne. In Martinique's Shell petrol stations, a dazzling array of champagne waits alongside engine oil to tempt the passing motorist. In the hypermarkets which ring **Fort-de-France**, French apples and tomatoes are delivered daily. 'Local' produce such as limes, bananas and yams is mostly imported from poorer neighbours like Dominica or the Dominican Republic.

There are areas of poverty, tumbledown hillside shantytowns which occupy otherwise useless land around the capital. There are mean suburbs,

---

FACT BOX

AREA: 1128 sq km
POPULATION: 372 000
CAPITAL: Fort-de-France
LANGUAGES: French, Creole
FORMER COLONIAL POWER: France
POLITICAL STATUS: *Département d'outre-mer* (French Overseas Department)
PER CAPITA GDP: US$6700

---

with ugly tin-and-concrete shacks and squalid tenements. But up in the hills beyond Fort-de-France are the spacious homes and well-ordered gardens of Martinique's large middle class. And in the exclusive *quartier* of **Didier** are the often palatial gingerbread residences of the *békés*, the traditional white élite which dates back to the seventeenth century.

One of the most celebrated of Martinique's *béké* caste was Marie-Josèphe Rose Tascher de la Pagerie, later rechristened Joséphine by her husband, Napoleon Bonaparte. From 1796 when she married Bonaparte to 1809 when they divorced, Joséphine wielded enormous influence and created for herself an aura of legend. Today, La Pagerie, the ruined plantation house at **Trois-Ilets** where the Empress Joséphine was brought up, is open to the public, who can inspect letters, portraits and other memorabilia in a small museum.

Joséphine, it is widely believed, was responsible for persuading Napoleon to reintroduce slavery in the French Caribbean in 1802, eight years after the revolutionary Convention had abolished it. Her mother still owned plantations both in Martinique and Haiti, and she saw nothing reprehensible in the system which had created the prosperity of her *béké* forebears. For this reason at least, Joséphine's memory is not widely venerated in modern-day Martinique. Her statue which stands in **La Savane**, the capital's central park, has had its head knocked off and is splattered with red paint. 'Respect to Martinique', somebody has scrawled in Creole. It is far removed from the languorous associations evoked by Lafcadio Hearn ◊ in his influential travel memoir *Two Years in the West Indies* (Extract 6).

Hearn's picture of Martinique as a sun-soaked sensual Eden forms part of a longer tradition of exoticism attached to the island. French Romantic poets imagined the Antilles as a place of unfettered pleasure among dream-like landscapes, and Paul Gauguin enthused about Martinique's natural beauty before going on to his other earthly paradise in Tahiti. The myth of the *belle Créole*, or beautiful Creole woman, became a potent image of desire among French writers. The Creole term of affection *dou-dou*, meaning *chéri* or darling, was imagined by writers and travellers to be a signal of sexual availability, and Martinican women, exemplified by

Hearn's picture of Joséphine, achieved legendary status as objects of desire. Later, exotic literature of this sort was derided by critics as *doudouiste*, but Martinique's reputation as a sophisticated and hedonistic place has lived on. In an essay such as 'Music for Chameleons' (Extract 3) by Truman Capote ◊ Martinique is pictured as both chic and somehow sinister. A more frivolous, Anglo–Saxon, interpretation of the island's charms is provided by Noel Coward in his poem 'Martinique' (Extract 9).

Whites and Blacks

Martinique's history in many ways parallels that of Guadeloupe, but there have been important divergences which have created distinct societies and cultures. Martinique's white upper class is still today stronger and more cohesive than Guadeloupe's; it has a much smaller East Indian population than its fellow *département d'outre-mer*; it is wealthier, more developed and is traditionally looked upon with suspicion and envy by Guadeloupeans.

There is some disagreement as to whether Columbus chanced upon the island in 1493 or 1502. Before his arrival, it was called *Madinina* or 'island of flowers' by its Carib population, but Columbus opted for Martinica in honour of St Martin. It was, wrote the explorer, 'the most beautiful thing I have ever seen. My eyes never tire of contemplating such greenery.'

It was not until 1635 that a French expedition, led by Pierre Belain d'Esnambuc, settled on the north-west coast and founded what was to become the infamous city of **St Pierre**. At first the Caribs put up resistance, but superior European weaponry and epidemics of unfamiliar diseases wiped out the indigenous population. Slaves were imported, and Martinique, like Guadeloupe, swiftly developed into a highly profitable sugar economy. The British occupied Martinique in 1762, only to return it to the French the following year under the Treaty of Paris.

Martinique's history took a dramatically different course from that of Guadeloupe during the period of political ferment which followed the French Revolution. In 1789 the island's Governor received a message signed 'All the Negroes'; it read:

'We know that the King has made us free and, if there is any resistance to giving us our liberty, we shall set fire to the whole colony and drown it in blood; only the Governor and the religious houses will be spared.'

Such threats made the already paranoid land-owning class even more fearful. Hostile to the revolutionary proclamations emanating from France, the *békés* invited the British to occupy Martinique and ensure the continuation of the status quo. Between 1794 and 1802 (the eight years in which Guadeloupe's slaves enjoyed their first, short-lived emancipation before Napoleon revoked it), Martinique and its slave system were protected from revolution by Britain. While Victor Hugues enthusiastically guillotined Guadeloupe's royalists, Martinique's aristocracy remained untouched.

But the *békés* could not escape the gradual decline of the sugar industry which preceded full emancipation in 1848, nor the act of abolition itself. Despite stubborn opposition from the Martinican planters, Victor Schoelcher's abolition decree liberated the island's slaves and turned them overnight into French voters and citizens.

POMPEII OF THE CARIBBEAN

The latter half of the nineteenth century was, for the most part, as uneventful in Martinique as in Guadeloupe. The end of slavery did not bring anarchy, as the *békés* had feared, nor did it bring great improvements to the lives of the former slaves. Sugar cultivation continued as the colony's mainstay, but old-fashioned techniques and lack of investment meant that Martinique fell behind bigger sugar islands such as Cuba. Rum became an increasingly important export and was much appreciated in France.

But, despite its slow decline, Martinique still boasted its capital city, **St Pierre**, 'the Paris of the Antilles', a lively, cosmopolitan place. It was, writes Alec Waugh ◊:

'A lovely city, with its theatre, its lamplit avenues, its *Jardin des Plantes*, its schooners drawn circlewise along the harbour. Life was comely there; the life that had been built up by the old French *émigrés*. It was a city of carnival. There was a culture there, a love of art among those people who had made their home there, who had not come to Martinique to make money that they could spend in Paris.'

Unlike the ugly utilitarian towns of the English colonies, St Pierre was elegant and charming. Its theatre was modelled on that of Bordeaux and had a lively programme of drama and music. Its school, the Lycée St Pierre, was founded in 1882 to educate the children of the white élite. It was renowned throughout the Caribbean as a loose-living city where all the pleasures could be easily obtained.

It was also a doomed city. For several days in early May 1902 the huge volcano, **Mont Pelée**, which hangs over St Pierre, began to give warning signs: cinders floated over the city and blew as far away as Dominica, rivers were reported to be boiling, crops were scorched and blackened in the fields. The authorities reassured the population that nothing worse would happen, that Mont Pelée would soon quieten down. There was no evacuation, and instead people prepared to celebrate Ascension Day on 8 May.

On that morning at 8 am the volcano erupted with an explosion which was heard in Guadeloupe and St Pierre was engulfed in a cloud of toxic ash, mud and flames. Within less than a minute, some 30 000 people, the city's entire population, died. Ships moored in the harbour were incinerated; one managed to limp back to St Lucia, its deck covered with charred bodies. In her short story 'Heat' (Extract 10), Jean Rhys (◊ Dominica) evokes a childhood memory of the catastrophe. Only one man is recorded as having survived the eruption. A certain Antoine Ciparis, convicted of murder and awaiting execution, was saved, although badly burnt, by his underground cell. Pardoned by the Governor, Ciparis spent the rest of his life in America as a Barnum & Bailey circus act, telling his story and displaying his burns.

Today, St Pierre is a melancholic site – a small modern town has risen from the ashes of the old. New buildings stand side by side with the slowly disintegrating shells of what were once wealthy warehouses and mansions. An exhibition shows clocks with their hands welded at 8 am, petrified plates of food, a church bell melted like wax. Alec Waugh's 1920s description of the ruins in *The Sugar Islands* (Extract 11) holds true to the present day.

From Colony to Département

The disaster at St Pierre abruptly destroyed a large section of Martinique's social and cultural élite, further accentuating the island's backwardness. For the next few decades, it quietly vegetated on the periphery of the French empire.

As in Guadeloupe, Martinique's planter class initially embraced the Vichy regime after the French defeat in the Second World War, and Pétain kept 300 tons of gold from the Banque de France in safe-keeping there. Cut off from the outside world by the Allied naval blockade, Martinique faced considerable deprivation and its people became highly resourceful as they learned to live without the most basic imports.

It was also a period of intense intellectual activity, as writers and political activists debated the post-war future of France's Caribbean colonies. Central to this debate was Aimé Césaire ◊, a Paris-educated radical and poet, who emerged at the end of the war as the most powerful advocate of 'departmentalization'. Standing as the French Communist Party's candidate for mayor of Fort-de-France and *député* to the French Assembly, Césaire won both elections on a tide of anti-*béké* sentiment. Although perhaps not communist sympathizers, many Martinicans supported Césaire's vision of their island as an integral part of the Republic, where power lay more in the institutions of Paris than with the local white élite. In his allegorical novel *The Ripening* (Extract 2), Edouard Glissant recalls the excitement of election day, when Martinicans voted for a black radical candidate.

Once elected, Césaire, together with left-wing *députés* from Guadeloupe and French Guiana, pressed for full incorporation into the Republic, arguing that it was the logical extension of Schoelcher's abolition decree of 1848. With the Communists in a strong position in the National Assembly and the Gaullists suspicious of US ambitions to annex Martinique and Guadeloupe, the law was unanimously approved. In theory, the territories were transformed overnight from colonies to full and equal parts of France.

In practice, the legislation took several years to implement as those expecting instant rewards from Paris became increasingly impatient. In the half century following departmentalization, Césaire remained a consistent advocate of the system. He broke with the French Communist Party in 1956 to found his own Parti Progressiste Martiniquais (PPM), which argued not for independence, but for greater autonomy within the relationship with France. This concept was intended to defend Césaire against charges that he accepted wholesale assimilation while preserving the all-important economic lifeline with Paris. Pro-independence parties have accused the PPM of abandoning Martinique's identity for second-class dependency, but few voters have been tempted to opt for a clean break with the *mère patrie*.

The dilemma of Martinican identity remains unresolved to this day. On the one hand, France provides massive subsidies without which an unproductive economy would rapidly unravel. On the other, official 'Frenchness' is viewed by many as an unwelcome imposition on people whose cultural history is often more African than European. Assimilation, say its critics, robs Martinicans of what makes them different from French people and, by implication, of their true identity.

Négritude and Since

Ironically Aimé Césaire, the great defender of departmentalization, was also the writer most associated with the militantly anti-assimilationist movement known as *négritude*. The movement had its roots in 1930s Paris, where black students and artists from French-speaking Africa and the Caribbean devoted themselves to political and aesthetic anti-colonialism. Already in 1921 a Martinican-born writer, René Maran, had won the prestigious Prix Goncourt with his novel, *Batouala*, based on his experiences in West Africa. The appearance of the iconoclastic manifesto *Légitime défense*, 1932, and the one and only issue of the journal *L'Etudiant noir*, 1935, are viewed by literary historians as seminal moments in the formulation of a revolutionary black aesthetic which sought to reject the cultural dominance of the European tradition and celebrate a long-repressed 'black consciousness'. Césaire's celebrated poem, 'Cahier d'un retour au pays natal', translated as 'Return to My Native Land' (Extract 8) is arguably *négritude*'s most powerful poetic expression. Lambasting French colonial arrogance, the poet evokes his childhood poverty and the suffering of blacks during slavery while asserting a sort of transcendental African-ness:

> 'Give me the sorcerer's savage faith
> give my hands the power to mould
> give my soul the temper of the sword
> I will stand firm. Make of my head a prow
> and of myself make neither a father

nor a brother nor a son
but the father, the brother, the son
do not make me a husband, but the lover of this
unique people'

A follower of Césaire's revolutionary *négritude*, if not his assimilationist politics, was Frantz Fanon ◊, who left his native Martinique to fight for the cause of the Algerian Revolution. His explosive study of the psychology of racism in Martinique, *Black Skin White Masks* (Extract 7), exposes the neuroses and complexes of a society where skin colour permeates all human relations. For Fanon, the uncritical embracing of French values, and particularly language, by Martinicans was not the solution to their psychological conflicts, but more probably the cause.

More traditional in its form of social protest, but also aware of the debilitating effect of cultural alienation, was *Black Shack Alley* (Extract 1) by Joseph Zobel ◊. Published in 1950 shortly after Martinique's transformation into a *département d'outre-mer*, Zobel's novel contrasted the hardships of a Creole-speaking black peasantry with the French-speaking white or mulatto élite of **Fort-de-France**. Its protagonist, José, learns that to succeed in life he must turn his back on his humble origins and become a Frenchman.

Over the years, *négritude* has come to be seen by some Martinican writers as the 'official' ideology of the island and too closely associated with the figure of Césaire. The contradiction between a French-subsidized, Western consumer society and the cultural ideal of black Africa was too glaring for Edouard Glissant, for example, who developed the concept of *antillanité* to describe the specifically Caribbean nature of Martinican culture. Neither Eurocentric nor Afrocentric, Glissant's aesthetic stressed the peculiar fusion of Europe and Africa in Creole societies.

Critics of Césaire have also pointed out that the champion of African identity writes exclusively in the most classical of French. Césaire himself has admitted that he could write in no other language, opening himself to the charge of linguistic Eurocentrism. Subsequent Martinican writers have developed Glissant's idea of *antillanité* into what has been called *créolité*, a literary theory which stresses not just Martinique's Creole culture, but its Creole language. Like Fanon, they see the imposition and adoption of the French language as undermining Martinique's true identity, which can be expressed most authentically through Creole. Some authors, such as Raphaël Confiant, have written entire novels in Creole (hence cutting themselves off from the French market) as well as in French. Others, such as Patrick Chamoiseau ◊, have introduced Creole vocabulary, idiom and syntax into their writing in French, making it comprehensible but nonetheless unmistakably Martinican in flavour. In *Creole Folktales* (Extract 4), Chamoiseau recreates the essentially oral structure of traditional Martinican story-telling, complete with stock characters and folk wisdom.

The French literary establishment officially blessed *créolité* in 1992 when

Chamoiseau's novel, *Texaco*, was awarded the Prix Goncourt. The complexity of its linguistic form meant, however, that a translation into English was dogged with problems and disagreements. Nonetheless, the elevation of Chamoiseau and Confiant into the French literay canon has meant that Martinican and Guadeloupean writers can reach a much wider audience than within the region itself.

LITERARY LANDMARKS

Fort-de-France. The capital's main open space, **La Savane**, contains the now mutilated statue of the Empress Joséphine, once idolized by Lafcadio Hearn. 'So many pens have described the details of that statue,' wrote Alec Waugh in 1947, 'it is not easy to be unmoved by it.' Among the pens was that of Hart Crane, the emotionally tortured American poet who committed suicide at the age of 33. His poem '*To the Empress Josephine's Statue*' celebrates Joséphine's aura of mythic femininity:

'You, who contain augmented tears, explosions,
Have kissed, caressed the model of the hurricane,
Gathered and made musical in feathery fronds
The slit eclipse of moon in palm-lit bonds,
Deny me not in this sweet Caribbean dawn –
You, who have looked back to Leda, who have seen the Swan.'

Predictably, Frantz Fanon provides a rather less elegaic picture of the area: 'This Savannah seems to have its own poetry. Imagine a square about 600 feet long and 125 feet wide, its sides bounded by worm-eaten tamarind trees, one end marked by the huge war memorial (the nation's gratitude to its children), the other by the Central Hotel; a miserable tract of uneven cobbles . . .'

St Pierre. The terrible events of 1902 have moved and inspired many writers, from Jean Rhys to Patrick Leigh Fermor (◊ Barbados). The latter's only novel, *The Violins of Saint-Jacques*, reworks the St Pierre catastrophe into fictional form, as related by Berthe, the sole survivor of a volcanic eruption which destroys the island of Saint-Jacques: 'The streets had fallen silent. The citizens had been halted in their flight and then laid low in swathes, as though one invisible sweep of a sickle had reaped them all, by the descending gas which had invaded the capital the moment the mountain-side opened.'

BOOKLIST

The following selection includes the extracted titles in this chapter as well as other titles for further reading. In general, paperback editions are given when possible. For most of the extracted works, the original publisher in English can be found in 'Acknowledgments and Citations' at the end of the volume, as can the exact location of the extracts and the editions from which they are taken.

Burton, Richard D.E. and Fred Reno, *French and West Indian: Martinique, Guadeloupe and French Guiana Today*, Macmillan, Basingstoke, 1995.

Capote, Truman, 'Music for Chameleons', in *A Capote Reader*, Abacus, London, 1987. **Extract 3**.

Césaire, Aimé, *Return to My Native Land*, John Berger and Anna Bostock trans, Penguin, Harmondsworth, 1969. **Extract 8**.

Chamoiseau, Patrick, *Creole Folktales*, Linda Coverdale, trans, The New Press, New York, 1994. **Extract 4**.

Chamoiseau, Patrick, *Texaco*, Gallimard, Paris, 1992.

Coward, Noel, 'Martinique', in *Collected Verse*, Methuen, London, 1984. **Extract 9**.

Fanon, Frantz, *Black Skin, White Masks*, Charles Lam Markmann, trans, MacGibbon and Kee, London, 1968. **Extract 7**.

Glissant, Edouard, *The Ripening*, Michael Dash trans, Heinemann, London, 1985. **Extract 2**.

Hearn, Lafcadio, *Two Years in the West Indies*, Harper & Brothers, New York, 1923. **Extract 6**.

Leigh Fermor, Patrick, *The Violins of Saint-Jacques*, Oxford University Press, Oxford, 1985.

Naipaul, V.S., *The Middle Passage: The Caribbean Revisited*, Penguin, London 1969. **Extract 5**.

Pope-Hennessy, James, *The Baths of Absalom*, Alan Wingate, London, 1954.

Rhys, Jean, *Heat*, in *Tales of the Wide Caribbean*, Heinemann, London, 1980. **Extract 10**.

Waugh, Alec, *The Sugar Islands*, Cassell, London, 1958. **Extract 11**.

Zobel, Joseph, *Black Shack Alley*, Keith Q. Warner, trans, Heinemann, London, 1980. **Extract 1**.

Extracts

(1) MARTINIQUE: CLASS

Joseph Zobel, *Black Shack Alley*

Having succeeded in reaching the Lycée at Fort-de-France, José is now painfully aware of his humble family background and the sacrifices made by his grandmother, M'man Tine.

Perhaps it was because of her heart, more penetrable at that time, that M'man Tine's condition became apparent to me with painful, abnormal acuteness. Abnormal and shameful, since that scene at the *lycée*. A teacher had asked each student his identity and the name and profession of his parents. Without any hesitation, I had naively given those of my mother, washer-woman, with my address in town; and just as naively it was the name of M'man Tine that had come from my mouth as next of kin. But, at her 'profession', I had faltered. First of all, I didn't know, in French, the name of the job she held. No, it certainly did not exist in French.

'Profession!' the teacher shouted, impatient.

'Doctor, school-teacher, cabinet-maker, office worker, tailor, seamstress, pharmacist,' the other students had said.

For me, impossible to find the name of the work my grandmother did. Were I to say: 'she works in sugar cane fields,' the whole class would burst out laughing. There was nothing like such things to have those students in stitches.

'Farmer,' I finally stammered out.

That word, on its own, had slipped from my mouth and I was grateful that it had come to my rescue.

Fortunately, the opportunity to give my parents' profession never again presented itself.

But this time, stronger and deeper than when I used to accompany her to the fields, a feeling of compassion came over me every time, on evenings, during that stormy month of September, M'man Tine came home, her rags and her skin weather-beaten, soaked like a sponge, and every time that, wanting to send me to the store, she looked in vain for the missing cent in every corner of the room . . .

Thus, at an age when I felt myself naturally given to a carefree existence, all my impulses were at the same time thwarted by the constant suffering, by a sort of oppression that weighed more and more despicably on my grandmother.

The more I looked at M'man Tine, the more I felt within me that she was subjected to an unjust punishment which, at times, made her appear more frightening than pitiful.

Why? Why not live in a house, why not wear dresses without holes, why not eat bread and meat, without always having to mumble those long, sad words that stuck in my throat and strangled me?

And who forced her to be like that?

(2) MARTINIQUE: ELECTION DAY

Edouard Glissant, *The Ripening*

*After the isolation and hardship of the Second World War, a mood
of radical change is sweeping the island as elections approach.*

The first Sunday of the month of September 1945, the life of the entire region was concentrated in the town. Election day had come at last. Emerging from the black hole of the war, which had brought to a terrible conclusion years of indifference and privation, the people were eager to affirm their rebirth. These elections had a lot at stake: it was not only a matter of electing a Representative, the important question was whether the long night was over and a new dawn at hand . . .

From all directions, crowds of men and women converged. From Bellem, a distant hillside in the depths of the forest where the inhabitants, stocky men, had a mysterious, secretive appearance like the shadows of their forests. From Pays-Mêlés, an area stretched out along the old colonial main road; inhabitants of this area accustomed to seeing the world go by were noisy and extrovert, they called to everyone. From the great mountains to the west dominated by the white mansion: a hardy community, used to climbing that steep slope, wished to free themselves of that prison over their heads. From Morne au Diable, where Lomé came from, where the land was rocky in parts and crumbly in others, a mixture of moodiness and bursts of joy. From Californie, where body and soul were washed by sand and sea; hard muscles and stubborn determination.

And in the town there was a great surge of these various communities. White suits, white shirts, red ties. Flowers in buttonholes. Beyond all doubt, victory was assured. As early as ten o'clock, everyone knew how things would go. At the polling stations these ties and flowers began to gather: neither stuffed ballot boxes nor fraudulent voting lists could prevail against such a tide of support. Calm, orderly voting made it a law-abiding affair and prevented the powers that be from resorting to the army. The watchword was: stay calm, stay calm, do not react, do not get into trouble, just vote. The majority of the electorate thronged the streets and they visibly suppressed their impulse to burst into enthusiastic shouts of triumph. It would have been an amazing sight for an uninformed observer to see such a surprisingly self-contained crowd, reserved and well-behaved, but which was clearly quivering with excitement.

(3) MARTINIQUE: EXOTICISM

Truman Capote, *Music for Chameleons*

Capote's travel piece presents Martinique as an intriguing blend of Parisian sophistication and dark superstition.

She is tall and slender, perhaps seventy, silver-haired, soigné, neither black nor white, a pale golden rum color. She is a Martinique aristocrat who lives in Fort de France but also has an apartment in Paris. We are sitting on the terrace of her house, an airy, elegant house that looks as if it were made of wooden lace: it reminds me of certain old New Orleans houses. We are drinking iced mint tea slightly flavored with absinthe.

Three green chameleons race one another across the terrace; one pauses at Madame's feet, flicking its forked tongue, and she comments: 'Chameleons. Such exceptional creatures. The way they change color. Red. Yellow. Lime. Pink. Lavender. And did you know they are very fond of music?' She regards me with her fine black eyes. 'You don't believe me?'

During the course of the afternoon she had told me many curious things. How at night her garden was filled with mammoth night-flying moths. That her chauffeur, a dignified figure who had driven me to her house in a dark green Mercedes, was a wife-poisoner who had escaped from Devil's Island. And she had described a village high in the northern mountains that is entirely inhabited by albinos: 'Little pink-eyed people white as chalk. Occasionally one sees a few on the streets of Fort de France.'

'Yes, of course I believe you.'

She tilts her silver head. 'No, you don't. But I shall prove it.'

So saying, she drifts into her cool Caribbean salon, a shadowy room with gradually turning ceiling fans, and poses herself at a well-tuned piano. I am still sitting on the terrace, but I can observe her, this chic, elderly woman, the product of varied bloods. She begins to perform a Mozart sonata.

Eventually the chameleons accumulated: a dozen, a dozen more, most of them green, some scarlet, lavender. They skittered across the terrace and scampered into the salon, a sensitive, absorbed audience for the music played. And then not played, for suddenly my hostess stood and stamped her foot, and the chameleons scattered like sparks from an exploding star.

Now she regards me. '*Et maintenant? C'est vrai?*'

'Indeed. But it seems so strange.'

She smiles. '*Alors.* The whole island floats in strangeness. This very house is haunted. Many ghosts dwell here. And not in darkness . . .'

(4) MARTINIQUE: FOLKTALES

Patrick Chamoiseau, *Creole Folktales*

Ti-Jean, the traditional epitome of cunning, has decided to avenge himself on his godfather (in reality, his father) by playing on his credulity.

He got his godfather to take him on as a kind of handy boy, handy for better or worse. Once installed in the Béké's shadow, Ti-Jean bided his time. Which came on the occasion of a party that the Béké could not postpone, even though his cook was confined to bed with a difficult pregnancy. '*Manjé mwen sé mwen menm,*' announced Ti-Jean. 'Cooking is my speciality.' His godfather left him in charge of everything: hunting the manicous, seasoning them just right; slaughtering chickens, sheep, ducks, and game; preparing the meats and pâtés; cleaning the offal; picking the herbs and spices, chopping and grating them; and popping all this into fifteen stewpots over a nice spread of glowing charcoal. Hubble-bubble, the pots were boiling hard. The guests waited, enjoying the punches and the savory fritters. Their nostrils flared, tantalized by delightful aromas. Soon their bellies began to bite them, and they asked if the food was going to spend the day in the kitchen. Their host went off laughing to see how things were coming along.

A strange sight greeted him: the fire was out, and the pots were sitting on the floor, bubbling away beneath the crack of Ti-Jean's whip. He had removed them from the coals only a moment before, and now he persuaded his godfather that they were boiling by the heat of his whip. 'Cook, cook, cook away,' he sang to the pots, snapping his whip. Not a man known for his sparkling intellect, the godfather said to himself, 'But this is a magic whip!' He demanded that Ti-Jean sell it to him. The boy protested, '*Parin ô, fwèt tala ké poté'w dévenn!*' 'Oh, Godfather, this whip will bring you nothing but trouble!' Instead of paying him heed, the white man paid Ti-Jean the first – and certainly not the last – money he ever received in his life, stashed the whip away, and went off to celebrate with his fellow Békés. Over desert he exclaimed, 'Gentlemen, this was good, but next Sunday, on the Feast of Saint Peter, it will be better. Don't make any other plans, because the best eating anywhere will be right here!' He was thinking, of course, of his marvelous whip.

(5) MARTINIQUE: FRANCE

V.S. Naipaul, *The Middle Passage*

Martinique's 'Frenchness' impresses every visitor. Here, Naipaul gently mocks the cultural contortions of an island which believes itself to be part of France.

Martinique is France. Arriving from Trinidad, you feel you have crossed not the Caribbean but the English Channel. The policeman are French; the street nameplates in blue-and-white enamel are French; the cafes are French; the menus are French and are written in a French hand. The landscape, in the south, is not stridently tropical. Rolling pasture land, worn smooth and unfruitful by cultivation, with dark blobs of scattered trees, and little claws and tongues of land sticking out into the clear sea, suggest a gentler Cornwall. Unlike the other islands, which have one main town to which everything gravitates, Martinique is full of little French villages, each with its church, *mairie* and war memorial (*Aux Enfants de – Morts pour la France*), each with its history and its illustrious, for whose descendants pews are reserved in the church. The radio station announces itself as 'Radio-diffusion Française'. The political posters – *Voter Oui à de Gaulle* (the referendum had taken place not long before) and *Meeting de Protestation: Les Colonialistes Ont Assassiné Lumumba* – are of metropolitan France and unlike anything else in the Caribbean. The tobacco kiosks stock Gauloises; and the advertisements are for Cinzano and St Raphael and *Paris-Soir*. Only, most of the people are black.

They are black, but they are Frenchmen. For Martinique is France, a legally constituted department of France, so assimilated and integrated that France, or what is widely supposed to be that country, is officially seldom mentioned by name. 'M. *Césaire est en métropole*,' the *chef-de-cabinet* said to me, as though M. Césaire had simply motored down to the country for a long week-end and hadn't flown 3000 miles to Paris. The myth of non-separation is carried to the extent that *routes nationales*, which presumably lead to Paris, wind through Martiniquan countryside . . .

In a restaurant during a tourist invasion I saw a white woman turn to a sun-glassed black Martiniquan and say, '*Nous sommes les seuls français ici.*' 'You are English?' a white Martiniquan asked me. No, I said; I came from Trinidad. 'Ah!' he said, smiling. '*Vous faites des nuances!*'

(6) MARTINIQUE: JOSÉPHINE

Lafcadio Hearn, *Two Years in the West Indies*

*For Hearn, Joséphine's statue epitomizes the exotic and sultry charm
of the French Antilles.*

You reach Fort-de-France, the capital of Martinique, by steamer from St
Pierre, in about an hour and a half . . . There is an overland route – *La
Trace*; but it is a twenty-five mile ride, and a weary one in such a climate,
notwithstanding the indescribable beauty of the landscapes which the lofty
road commands.

. . . Rebuilt in wood after the almost total destruction by an earthquake
of its once picturesque streets of stone, Fort-de-France (formerly Fort-
Royal) has little of outward interest by comparison with St Pierre. It lies in
a low, moist plain, and has few remarkable buildings: you can walk all over
the little town in about half an hour. But the Savane, – the great green
public square, with its grand tamarinds and *sabliers*, – would be worth the
visit alone, even were it not made romantic by the marble memory of
Josephine.

I went to look at the white dream of her there, a creation of
master-sculptors . . . It seemed to me absolutely lovely.

Sea winds have bitten it; tropical rains have streaked it: some microsco-
pic growth has darkened the exquisite hollow of the throat. And yet such is
the human charm of the figure that you almost fancy you are gazing at a
human presence . . . Perhaps the profile is less artistically real, – statuesque
to the point of betraying the chisel; but when you look straight up into the
sweet creole face, you can believe she lives: all the wonderful West Indian
charm of the woman is there.

She is standing just in the centre of the Savane, robed in the fashion of
the First Empire, with gracious arms and shoulders bare: one hand leans
upon a medallion bearing the eagle profile of Napoleon . . . Seven tall
palms stand in a circle around her, lifting their comely heads into the blue
glory of the tropic day. Within their enchanted circle you feel that you
tread holy ground, – the sacred soil of artist and poet; – here the
recollections of memoir-writers vanish away; the gossip of history is hushed
for you; you no longer care to know how rumor has it that she spoke or
smiled or wept; only the bewitchment of her lives under the thin, soft,
swaying shadows of those feminine palms . . . Over violet space of summer
sea, through the vast splendor of azure light, she is looking back to the
place of her birth, back to beautiful drowsy Trois-Islets, – and always with
the same half-dreaming, half-plaintive smile, – unutterably touching . . .

(7) MARTINIQUE: LANGUAGE

Frantz Fanon, *Black Skin, White Masks*

The inferiority complexes suffered by many Martinicans, writes Fanon, is reinforced by their received belief in the superiority of 'classical' French.

The Negro who knows the mother country is a demigod. In this connection I offer a fact that must have struck my compatriots. Many of them, after stays of varying length in metropolitan France, go home to be deified. The most eloquent form of ambivalence is adopted toward them by the native, the one-who-never-crawled-out-of-his-hole, the *bitaco*. The black man who has lived in France for a length of time returns radically changed. To express it in genetic terms, his phenotype undergoes a definitive, an absolute mutation. Even before he had gone away, one could tell from the almost aerial manner of his carriage that new forces had been set in motion. When he met a friend or an acquaintance, his greeting was no longer the wide sweep of the arm: With great reserve our 'new man' bowed slightly. The habitually raucous voice hinted at a gentle inner stirring as of rustling breezes. For the Negro knows that over there in France there is a stereotype of him that will fasten on to him at the pier in Le Havre or Marseille: 'Ah come from Mahtinique, it's the fuhst time Ah've eveh come to Fance.' He knows that what the poets call the *divine gurgling* (listen to Creole) is only a halfway house between pidgin-nigger and French. The middle class in the Antilles never speak Creole except to their servants. In school the children of Martinique are taught to scorn the dialect. One avoids *Creolisms*. Some families completely forbid the use of Creole, and mothers ridicule their children for speaking it.

> My mother wanting a son to keep in mind
> if you do not know your history lesson
> you will not go to mass on Sunday in
> your Sunday clothes
> that child will be a disgrace to the family
> that child will be our curse
> shut up I told you you must speak French
> the French of France
> the Frenchman's French
> French French

Yes, I must take great pains with my speech, because I shall be more or less judged by it. With great contempt they will say of me, 'He doesn't even know how to speak French.'

In any group of young men in the Antilles, the one who expresses himself well, who has mastered the language, is inordinately feared; keep an eye on that one, he is almost white. In France one says, 'he talks like a book.' In Martinique, 'He talks like a white man.'

(8) Martinique: Négritude

Aimé Césaire, *Return to My Native Land*

Amidst the violent and bizarre metaphors of Césaire's epic poem, a vision emerges of the poverty and squalor which filled the poet's childhood.

At the end of the small hours: life flat on its face, miscarried dreams and nowhere to put them, the river of life listless in its hopeless bed, not rising nor falling, unsure of its flow, lamentably empty, the heavy impartial shadow of boredom creeping over the equality of all things, the air stagnant, unbroken by the brightness of a single bird.

At the end of the small hours: another house in a very narrow street smelling very bad, a tiny house which within its entrails of rotten wood shelters rats by the dozen and the gale of my six brothers and sisters, a cruel little house whose implacability panics us at the end of every month, and my strange father nibbled by a single misery whose name I've never known, my father whom an unpredictable witchcraft soothes into sad tenderness or exalts into fierce flames of anger; and my mother whose feet, daily and nightly, pedal, pedal for our never-tiring hunger, I am woken by those never-tiring feet pedalling by night and the Singer whose teeth rasp into the soft flesh of the night, the Singer which my mother pedals, pedals for our hunger night and day.

At the end of the small hours, my father, my mother, and over them the house which is a shack splitting open with blisters like a peach-tree tormented by blight, and the roof worn thin, mended with bits of paraffin cans, this roof pisses swamps of rust on to the grey sordid stinking mess of straw, and when the wind blows, these ill-matched properties make a strange noise, like the splutter of frying, then a burning log plunged into water with the smoke from the twigs twisting away . . . And the bed of planks on its legs of kerosene drums, a bed with elephantiasis, my grandmother's bed with its goatskin and its dried banana leaves and its rags, a bed with nostalgia as a mattress and above it a bowl full of oil, a candle-end with a dancing flame and on the bowl, in golden letters, the word MERCI.

A disgrace, Paille Street, a disgusting appendage like the private parts of this town, whose sea of grey-tiled roofs extends to left and to right all along the colonial road; whereas here there are only roofs of straw, stained brown by sea-spray, worn thin by the wind.

(9) MARTINIQUE: SMELLS

Noel Coward, *Martinique*

Coward's comic verse aims to puncture Gallic pride in the Caribbean département with a familiar repertoire of English prejudices.

No Frenchman can forbear to speak
About the charms of Martinique
It seems it is a land of spice,
And sugar, and all things nice
A veritable Paradise
Un endroit fantastique.

The Compagnie Transatlantique
Sends lots of ships to Martinique
Because, they say, it's nicer far
Than many other places are
More glamorous than Zanzibar
Cleaner than Mozambique.

They also say it has more 'chic'
Than Tunis in the Nord d'Afrique
Possessing 'Plagues' with finer 'sable'
A climate 'Toujours admirable'
In fact, they say, it's 'Formidable'
This God-damned Martinique.

In praising this celestial Freak
They, one and all omit to speak
About its flat cathedral bells
Its indescribable hotels
The noisesome and disgusting smells
That make the island reek.

(10) MONT PELÉE

Jean Rhys, *Heat*

The eruption of Mont Pelée, Jean Rhys recalls, was widely interpreted as divine retribution against the loose-living Martinican city of Saint Pierre.

In the afternoon two little friends were coming to see us and to my surprise they both arrived carrying large glass bottles. Both the bottles had carefully written labels pasted on: 'Ash collected from the streets of Roseau on May

8th, 1902.' The little boy asked me if I'd like to have his jar, but I refused. I didn't want to touch the ash. I don't remember the rest of the day. I must have gone to bed, for that night my mother woke me and without saying anything, led me to the window. There was a huge black cloud over Martinique. I couldn't ever describe that cloud, so huge and black it was, but I have never forgotten it. There was no moon, no stars, but the edges of the cloud were flame-coloured and in the middle what looked to me like lightning flickered, never stopping. My mother said: 'You will never see anything like this in your life again.' That was all. I must have gone to sleep at the window and been carried to bed.

Next morning we heard what had happened. Was it a blue or a grey day? I only know ash wasn't falling any longer. The Roseau fishermen went out very early, as they did in those days. They met the fishermen from Port de France, who knew. That was how we heard before the cablegrams, the papers and all the rest came flooding in. That was how we heard of Mont Pelée's eruption and the deaths of 40 000 people, and that there was nothing left of St Pierre.

As soon as ships were sailing again between Dominica and Martinique my father went to see the desolation that was left. He brought back a pair of candlesticks, tall heavy brass candlesticks which must have been in a church. The heat had twisted them into an extraordinary shape. He hung them on the wall of the dining-room and I stared at them all through meals, trying to make sense of the shape.

It was after this that the gossip started. That went on for years so I can remember it well. St Pierre, they said, was a very wicked city. It had not only a theatre, but an opera house which was probably wickeder still. Companies from Paris performed there. But worse than this was the behaviour of the women who were the prettiest in the West Indies . . .

(11) SAINT PIERRE

Alec Waugh, *The Sugar Islands*

The ruins of St Pierre still stand, like those of Pompeii, as a testament to the horror of 8 May 1902.

Once we went to St Pierre.

From Fond Lahaye it is a three hours' sail in a canoe, along a coast indented with green valleys that run back climbingly through fields of sugar cane. At the foot of most of these valleys, between the stems of the coconut palms, you see the outline of wooden cabins. So concealed are these cabins behind that façade of greenery that were it not for the fishing nets hung out along the beach on poles to dry you would scarcely suspect that there was a village there. Nor, as you approach St Pierre, would you suspect that in that semicircle of hills under the cloud-hung shadow of

Mont Pelée are hidden the ruins of a city for which history can find no parallel.

At first sight it is nothing but a third-rate, decrepit shipping port, not unlike Manzanillo or La Libertad. It has its pier, its warehouses, its market; its single cobbled street contains the usual dockside features. A café or two, a restaurant, a small wooden shanty labelled 'Cercle', a somewhat larger shanty labelled 'Select Tango'. A hairdresser, a universal store. At first sight it is one of many thousand places. It is not till you step out of that main street into the tangled jungle at the back of it that you realize that St Pierre is, as it has always been, unique.

Even then you do not at first realize it. At first you see nothing but greenery, wild shrubbery, the great ragged leaves of the banana plant, with here and there the brown showing of a thatched roof. It is not till you have wandered a little through those twisted paths that you see that it is in the angles of old walls that those thatched cottages are built, that it is over broken masonry, over old stairways and porticoes, that those trailing creepers are festooned; that empty windows are shadowed by those ragged leaves. At odd corners you will come upon signs of that old life: a marble slab that was once the doorstep of a colonial bungalow; a fountain that splashed coolly through siestaed summers; a shrine with the bronze body broken at its foot. Everywhere you will come upon signs of that old life; '*le Pays des Revenants*' they called it. With what grim irony has chance played upon the word.

Biographical and literary notes

CAPOTE, Truman (1924–1984). Born in New Orleans of Spanish descent, Capote became internationally famous with *Breakfast at Tiffany's*, 1958, which was successfully adapted into a film, and *In Cold Blood*, 1966, a 'non-fiction novel' about a murder in Kansas. His collection of short pieces, *Music for Chameleons* (Extract 3) reveals his range of cultural and literary interests.

COWARD, Noel (see under Jamaica). The poem 'Martinique' (Extract 9) is doubtless based on some unfortunate tourist experiences by a writer who preferred what he saw as the eccentric 'Englishness' of Jamaica to the 'Frenchness' of Martinique.

CESAIRE, Aimé (1913–) Césaire was born into a poor peasant family in **Basse Pointe**, northern Martinique. His family moved to **Fort-de-France**, where Césaire attended the Lycée Schoelcher and in 1931 he won a scholarship to study in Paris. There he met and worked with a group of black students and intellectuals from both Francophone Africa and the Caribbean, contributing his writing to various radical journals. Césaire is normally credited with coining the term *négritude*, which became an influential literary and philosophical set of ideas in the 1930s. Essentially, it combined rising anti-colonialism with a radical reappraisal of black culture and consciousness. Rejecting the dominance of Western rationalism, with its view of Europe as the centre of civilization, *négritude* argued that Africa and the African diaspora had their own authentic cultural values, which white racism had always denigrated. Placing lyricism at the centre of this new aesthetic, Césaire and his colleagues found Surrealism, at that time a major literary vogue in Paris, a suitable form for their vision of a new black consciousness.

In 1939, Césaire returned to Martinique, where he taught at the Lycée Schoelcher. Attracted to Marxism during his stay in Paris, he was now a member of the French Communist Party. In 1942 the eminent French Surrealist André Breton arrived in Martinique, where he befriended Césaire. Breton was largely responsible for establishing his reputation in Paris, and Césaire went back in 1944 to considerable acclaim. In 1946, he was elected as a *député* to the French National Assembly and as Mayor of **Fort-de-France**, a position he held for more than fifty years. Césaire became one of the most important exponents of 'departmentalization', the belief that incorporation into the centralized French state was the best option for the former colonies. Martinique's status as a *département d'outre mer*, an integral part of the French Republic, is largely Césaire's handiwork. In 1956, he left the French Communist Party and two years later became leader of the Martinican Progressive Party (PPM), continuing to reject independence from France in favour of increased autonomy within the departmental relationship. He has written a number of essays, plays, biographies, as well as other collections of poems. His *Toussaint Louverture*, 1960, situates the Haitian slave leader within the period's Third World anti-

colonialism and makes him a precursor of later independence struggles.

Césaire's *Cahier d'un retour au pays natal*, 1939, translated as *Return to My Native Land* (Extract 8), has been described by critic Roberto Márquez as 'perhaps the single most celebrated, sustained, and representatively compendious lyrical monument to *négritude*.' According to legend, a roneoed copy of the poem was discovered by Breton in a haberdasher's shop in **Fort-de-France**. Breton was responsible for its republication after the war, and the poem became the standard text of *négritude*. In a series of discordant, and often discomforting images, Césaire spurns the French colonial concept of assimilation ('Accommodate yourself to me/I won't accommodate myself to you') before tracing the route back from Martinique to Africa, the origin of the slaves whose descendants make up the majority of Martinicans. The poem's tone is both apocalyptic and lyrical as it demands the end of Eurocentric arrogance and the beginning of a new black solidarity: 'No race holds a monopoly of beauty, intelligence and strength/ there is room for all at the meeting-place of conquest.'

CHAMOISEAU, Patrick (1953–). Born in **Fort-de-France**, Chamoiseau is the leading Martinican writer of the post-Césaire generation. His thematically and linguistically complex novel *Texaco*, 1992, received the Prix Goncourt, marking an important breakthrough for French West Indian literature. Chamoiseau is the author of two earlier novels, *Chronique des sept misères*, 1986, and *Solibo Magnifique*, 1988, and an autobiographical account of his childhood, *Antan d'enfance*, 1990. He also co-authored with Raphaël Confiant and Jean Bernabé the influential *Eloge de la créolité*, 1989, a manifesto championing a new form of cultural and linguistic awareness in Caribbean literature. His own fiction is full of Creole words, expressions and constructions, some of which are explained to the non Creole-reader, others which must be guessed at. A well known ecologist and critic of assimilation, he writes a regular column for the pro-independence journal *Antilla*. In *Creole Folktales* (Extract 4), Chamoiseau recreates some of Martinique's traditional stories, which feature characters such as the cunning Ti-Jean, the antithesis of the rich and stupid *béké*.

FANON, Frantz (1925–1961). Frantz Omar Fanon was born in Martinique and was educated in France, studying medicine and specializing in psychiatry. His first book, *Black Skin, White Masks* (Extract 7), was published when he was only 27 years old and provided an incisive critique of the psychology of racism in his native island. In 1953 Fanon was assigned to work in a hospital in Algeria at the time when a popular independence struggle against the French colonial régime was gathering impetus. He took the side of the National Liberation Front (FLN) and soon became one of its most articulate spokesmen. His experience of anti-colonial insurrection led to his theory, expressed in *The Wretched of the Earth*, 1961, that national liberation could only take place through violent revolution. This book, together with *Studies in a Dying Colonialism*, 1959, became handbooks for a generation of Third World revolutionaries, and Fanon was hugely influential throughout Africa, if less so in Martinique itself. Fanon died of leukaemia in 1961, having delayed treatment because of the pressure of political commitments. He did not live to see the independence of Algeria which took place the following year.

GLISSANT, Edouard (1928–) Born in rural Martinique, Glissant attended the Lycée Schoelcher in **Fort-de-France**, where, with his con-temporary Frantz Fanon, he was influenced by the radical *négritude* of Aimé Césaire. Later, in Paris, he was active in anti-imperialist and Marxist circles. Returning to Martinique in 1965, Glissant founded the Institut Martiniquais d'Etudes and continued to campaign against French cultural domination of the island, while producing a series of novels, poems and theoretical works. In his best-known novel *La Lézarde* (*The Ripening*), Glissant evokes the atmosphere of 1945 Martinique (Extract 2), when Césaire's populism won him an overwhelming electoral victory as Mayor of Fort-de-France. His novel centres on the political awakening of a group of young Martinicans and their decision to prevent fraud in the election by killing the reactionary symbol of the *ancien régime*, Garin. This is by no means an exercise in socialist realism, however, and is constructed around a densely metaphorical and lyrical narrative style. The merging of landscape, popular language and a specifically Caribbean consciousness make up what Glissant calls *antillanité* ('Caribbeanness'), a phenomenon common to all territories of the region, irrespective of colonial legacies.

HEARN, Lafcadio (1850–1904). An Irish–Greek novelist and travel writer, Patricio Lafcadio Tessima Hearn was born in Greece, educated in France and England, and migrated to the USA in 1869 to work as a full-time writer. He specialized in the exotic, and in 1890 travelled to Japan where he became a Japanese citizen, took the name Koizumi Yakumo, and wrote a series of books about Japanese life. His *Two Years in the West Indies* (Extract 6) presented an alluring picture of Martinique as a sensuous and morally relaxed tropical refuge but also contains interesting observations on Creole language and culture.

NAIPAUL, V.S. (see under Trinidad). In *The Middle Passage* (Extract

5), Naipaul presents a characteristically acerbic vision of the Caribbean, where, in the case of Martinique, 'mimic men' ape the cultural norms of France.

RHYS, Jean (see under Dominica). Rhys's short story, 'Heat' (Extract 10) is quite probably autobiographical (she was twelve years old at the time of the Mont Pelée eruption) and powerfully evokes the magnitude of St Pierre's calamity.

WAUGH, Alec (1898–1981). The older brother of Evelyn, Alec Waugh was a popular novelist and travel writer who wrote widely on the Caribbean. His best known book is *Island in the Sun*, 1956, a novel set in the imaginary island of Santa Marta. The novel recreates some of the political and racial intrigue prevalent in the English-speaking colonial Caribbean on the eve of independence. *The Sugar Islands* (Extract 11) is a collection of travel pieces written between 1928 and 1953 before the Caribbean became a mainstream holiday destination.

ZOBEL, Joseph (1915–). Born in Martinique, Zobel wanted to become an interior designer but in 1937 began work as a civil servant. His first novel *Diab'la* was published in 1942, followed the same year by *Les Jours Immobiles*. When Martinique joined Free France, Zobel worked as a press attaché to the Governor, later leaving the island to study at the Sorbonne.

Joseph Zobel

Black Shack Alley (*La Rue Case-Nègres*) was published in 1950 and won the Prix des Lecteurs. It was later made into a highly acclaimed film. It tells the story of José, brought up on a poverty-stricken sugar plantation by his grandmother, M'man Tine. As José progresses through the colonial education system to a scholarship at a **Fort-de-France** lycée (Extract 1), he becomes increasingly aware of his humble background and of the social injustices on which the island is based. Like the female characters of Simone Schwarz-Bart and Maryse Condé in Guadeloupe, M'man Tine stands as a symbol of the suffering and resilience of black women in post-slavery plantation society.

St Lucia

'It is a place where the villages are blessed with names like Patience and Repose; where two bays are called Great Hole and Little Hole; and where a peninsula, pointing forever across the Atlantic to Africa, is called Cinnamon. The people are gentle like the names they give to their small pieces of hillside and riverbank.'
Earl G. Long, *Consolation*

St Lucia's **Pitons** are among the Caribbean's most famous and spectacular landmarks. Two forest-clad volcanic plugs which rise 2500 feet out of the sea, they are breathtakingly beautiful. The Pitons' uniqueness has earned them a place on St Lucia's national flag and has made them recognizable around the world. Like Peru's Macchu Pichu or Tanzania's Kilimanjaro, the Pitons have become a sort of tourist trademark and have acquired an almost religious aura. Generations of travellers and writers have looked in wonder at the twin peaks. The Victorian traveller E.A. Hastings Jay is but one of many visitors to wax lyrical over the Pitons in his *A Glimpse of the Tropics*, 1900. More recently, the *Caribbean Islands Handbook* (rarely inclined to hyperbole) advises that 'the scenery is of outstanding beauty, and in the area of the Pitons it has an element of grandeur.'

The Pitons are believed to be of considerable ecological and cultural importance. Their distinctive ecosystem harbours a profusion of plant and animal life. They are the site of potentially invaluable pre-Columbian remains – the island's Arawaks used the area as sacred ground. Experts have speculated that the Arawaks celebrated astronomical phenomena such as the solstice there; archaeologists have unearthed finds of petroglyphs and pottery. There is evidence that fires have been lit at the top of the Pitons for 1000 years, perhaps in homage to the gods.

Yet all too often in small, poor Caribbean societies financial imperatives outweigh environmental and aesthetic considerations. In 1992, after a long and bitter battle, the **Jalousie Plantation Resort and Spa** opened its doors. The luxury hotel (US$400–500 'all-inclusive' per night) is situated in the valley between the two Pitons, precisely on the site of the supposed Arawak burial ground. With sports, sauna, cable televison and a plethora of eating

---

FACT BOX

AREA: 617 sq km
POPULATION: 142 000
CAPITAL: Castries
LANGUAGES: English, Creole
FORMER COLONIAL POWER: Britain
INDEPENDENCE: 1979
PER CAPITA GDP: US$2900

---

and drinking facilities, Jalousie is custom-built for well-heeled tourists from Europe and North America.

Part-owned by an Iranian business group, which bought the land from an English aristocrat, Lord Glenconner (formerly the owner of Mustique), Jalousie inspires deep and divisive emotions. In her book *Last Resorts*, Polly Pattullo describes how its advent split an entire community. For the unemployed youths of nearby **Soufrière**, the complex offered the welcome prospect of work. For its opponents, the construction of a hotel between the Pitons was tantamount to an act of desecration. St Lucian Nobel laureate Derek Walcott ◊ fulminated against the project in the local newspaper. 'To sell any part of the Pitons,' he wrote, 'is to sell the whole idea and body of the Pitons, to sell a metaphor, to make a fast buck off a shrine.' It was, he concluded, like opening 'a casino in the Vatican or a take-away concession inside Stonehenge.'

The Jalousie controversy says a good deal about the impact of tourism on small islands like St Lucia. The industry brings jobs and foreign capital to places which otherwise have little prospect of investment or development. But it also brings more insidious influences, as Martin Amis ◊ discovered during his vacation in St Lucia. Confessing to the author's sense of detatched unreality, Amis's essay, 'St Lucia' (Extract 7), evokes much of the scarcely concealed tension surrounding tourism and tourists.

COCKPIT OF EUROPE

Uncharacteristically, Christopher Columbus appears to have missed St Lucia, and the first European expedition to reach the island is thought to have been Dutch. At the time of the earliest attempt to settle the island in 1605, it was inhabited by Caribs who had already driven out the indigenous Arawaks. The Caribs, who called the island *Iouanalao* or *Hewanorra*, were typically – and quite understandably – inhospitable to the Europeans who tried to establish themselves on their island. In 1638 a group of English settlers from Bermuda and St Kitts managed to win a toehold on St Lucia but three years later they were attacked and nearly all killed by the Caribs.

Despite these inauspicious beginnings, St Lucia was to become the most fought-over Caribbean territory in the struggle for supremacy between England and France. So prepared were governments in London and Paris to dispatch fighting forces to invade the island, that St Lucia became known as the 'Helen of the West Indies'. In a period between 1660 and 1814 St Lucia changed hands no fewer than fourteen times.

The French claimed sovereignty in 1642 and Cardinal Richelieu offered St Lucia to the French West India Company. The first French settlement took place in 1650 and ten years later the French successfully concluded a treaty with the Caribs. This merely ushered in a long period of fierce rivalry with the English, who recognized the island's economic and strategic potential. Admiral George Rodney, commander of the British fleet, wrote in 1778 that St Lucia was a far greater prize than neighbouring Martinique, since the latter 'though possessing four harbours, has none equal to the Carénage of St Lucia or so secure and capable of being defended, which alone is of the utmost consequence to a maritime Power.'

True to his convictions, Rodney battled tirelessly to keep St Lucia English. His forces had taken the island in 1762, only to lose it the following year. In 1778 war erupted again, and a particularly bloody encounter took place in February 1789, when French generals tried to lead 5000 troops through English lines. According to the contemporary British historian Bryan Edwards:

> 'The struggle was long and terrible. At last the French were driven back with heavy slaughter: seventy of them are said to have fallen within the works at the very first onset. In spite of this fierce repulse they paused only to rally and recover breath; and then hurried back with undiminished fury. The second conflict was no less violent than the first: it terminated in the same manner. Though their ranks were sorely thinned by this double discomfiture, they were induced to make a third charge; but they had no longer that ardour which originally inspired them. They were speedily broken, overwhelmed and scattered in complete and irretrievable disorder.'

Two years later, the French were back and tried, unsuccessfully, to invade St Lucia. In 1782 Admiral Rodney again led the English fleet in an epic set-piece attack on the French navy which has become known as 'the battle of the Saints' (after the French islands, Les Saintes, near where the conflict took place). The battle marked a turning-point in Anglo–French rivalry and tilted the balance firmly in London's favour. On this occasion some 14 000 French were killed or wounded after Rodney skilfully broke the enemy formation, allowing his ships to encircle and fire broadsides into helpless French vessels. In the Treaty of Versailles which followed, English supremacy in the Caribbean was recognized, but ironically St Lucia was restored to France as part of the settlement.

The fighting continued, especially during the French revolutionary period when Victor Hugues, the scourge of the English in the Caribbean, used his base in St Lucia to support insurrections in nearby islands. The guillotine was erected in **Castries** and St Lucia, apparently full of revolutionary fervour, was baptized by the French *St Lucie la Fidèle*. Again, the English invaded, in 1796, and fought a protracted campaign against a guerrilla force of white and black republicans known as the *armée dans les bois*. Eventually, this force was pacified by General John Moore (later the hero of Corunna), and an exhausted St Lucia finally discovered peace.

Over 150 years the island had become an emblem of British imperial ambition and military prowess. Thirteen British regiments bore the name of St Lucia on their colours; as Jan Morris remarks in *Pax Britannica*, 'the Northumberland Fusiliers wore a white plume in their hats because here, in 1778, their men had triumphantly plucked the white favours from the headgear of the defeated French.'

Defeated the French may have been, but they left a linguistic and cultural legacy as strong as almost anywhere in the Caribbean except their overseas *départements*. Creole is still the everyday language of most St Lucians, and family and place names are overwhelmingly Gallic in inspiration. **Castries** itself is named after an eighteenth-century French Minister of the Colonies. A drive along the west coast will take you past places called **Marigot, Anse la Raye** and **Choiseul**, while surnames like Chastenet, St Omer or Hippolyte are not unusual. St Lucia is largely Roman Catholic rather than Anglican, its architecture more like that of Haiti and Martinique than that of Barbados, and its musical tastes tend as much towards Martinican *zouk* as towards Jamaican reggae. The French maintain an Alliance Française establishment in **Castries**.

BLACK GOLD AND GREEN GOLD

With the advent of continuous British rule, St Lucia became another outpost of empire and another exporter of sugar. The abolition of slavery in 1834 and the decline in sugar prices affected the island as badly as its neighbours, but in 1885 St Lucia was chosen as one of the English Caribbean's two main coaling stations. Placed conveniently on the trade routes between north and South America and endowed with the region's best deep water harbour, the island found a new role in selling Welsh coal – 'black gold' – to passing steam ships. It was a lucrative business; in 1897, 947 ships entered **Castries** harbour, 620 of them steam-powered. That year, **Castries** was the fourteenth most important port in the world in terms of tonnage handled. In the 1920s, the veteran Caribbean traveller, Algernon Aspinall ◊, found the harbour to be thriving in his *A Wayfarer in the West Indies* (Extract 1).

Gradually, however, oil came to replace coal, and Castries lost its imperial role. A strike of coalers in 1935 was met by a show of strength when the Governor summoned a British warship. Marines patrolled the streets and the warship played its searchlights over the town at night. A commission of enquiry into wages was promised, but it offered no increase. Two years later, workers on the sugar plantations also went on strike for higher wages. This time, slight increases were forthcoming, a small success which encouraged the formation of St Lucia's first trade union in 1939. From the union movement grew the St Lucia Labour Party which won the first full elections in 1951 and which has competed since independence in 1979 with the conservative United Workers' Party of former lawyer John Compton.

The decline of both sugar and coal prompted the rise of St Lucia's banana industry from the 1950s onwards. Advocated by the colonial authorities as appropriate for smallholder production, the banana business completely dominated St Lucia's economy. The British company Geest sent its banana boat regularly to the island, buying all fruit of acceptable quality for the protected British market. By the 1980s bananas accounted for 70% or more of the island's exports. 'Green gold' was a mixed blessing, however. As small farmers benefitted from the regular payments from Geest, they also chose to overlook the risk to their livelihoods from hurricanes and dependency on a single crop. As the future of St Lucia's banana exports hangs in the balance in the 1990s, so too does the welfare of the majority of the rural population.

Only tourism competes with bananas in St Lucia. The island now plays host to hundreds of thousands of tourists each year, many of whom stay in luxury 'all-inclusive' enclaves such as Jalousie, where everything is prepaid and where there is no need to leave the hotel grounds.

THE COST OF CHANGE

The destructive impact of 'development' has become a recurring theme in St Lucia's literature. Over the years, a combination of natural disasters (the last of four major fires occurred only in 1948) and bad planning has transformed large parts of **Castries** into ugly, concrete blocks. A few streets of three-storey Victorian gingerbread buildings, with fretwork balconies, remain but much has been replaced with functional architecture, which Patrick Leigh Fermor (◊ Barbados) described as 'a brisk and shoddy piece of work.' In Kendel Hippolyte's ◊ poem 'Castries' (Extract 2), the changed urban landscape becomes a metaphor for the adulteration and corruption of other cultural values such as language and community.

This anxiety over the deleterious effects of rampant modernization finds expression, too, in writing about the countryside. In his novel *Consolation* (Extract 5), St Lucian-born Earl Long ◊ plots the encroaching influence of a North American-style, tourism-based culture on a rural backwater. Long's vision of the village Consolation is one of community and humanity under threat from a baleful concept of progress. This sense of St Lucia's particular cultural vulnerability emerges strongly in Derek Walcott's 1993 Nobel Prize lecture, published as *The Antilles: Fragments of Epic Memory* (Extract 4). Here Walcott counterposes what he sees as a dominating European/North American concept of 'development' with the fragility of St Lucia's Creole culture.

Derek Walcott

PRIZES AND POETS

St Lucia probably has more Nobel Prize winners per capita than any other nation. From its 140 000 population have emerged two Nobel laureates – the economist Arthur Lewis, and the poet and playwright Derek Walcott. Lewis (1915–1991) won the 1979 Economics Prize after a distinguished academic career and was the first black man to win such an award other than the Nobel Peace Prize. Walcott received the Nobel Prize for Literature in 1993 after producing an impressive collection of poems and plays which culminated with *Omeros* in 1990.

St Lucia and Trinidad (where Walcott moved in 1958) feature throughout his extensive poetic output. Rural landscapes such as that of the **Roseau Valley** form a central thematic and metaphorical strand in his work, as exemplified by 'Sainte Lucie' (Extract 3), a poem which evokes the strangely monotonous lushness of one of St Lucia's biggest banana plantations and the moving and religious work of art which stands among it. For Walcott the Caribbean landscape – and often the island seascape –

acts as a starting-point for his particular sense of the mythic. In *Omeros*, the lives and language of ordinary fishermen and their communities are elevated into epic stature in a reworking of the classical Homeric legend of journey and discovery.

Walcott's quest for Caribbean self-definition (in the context of a history of dispossession and colonial culture) is inseparable from his central concern with language. The everyday cadence of St Lucian Creole is fused with the rigour of classical English to create a singularly Caribbean voice, where the Western literary tradition is both enriched and subverted. Robert Graves said that 'Walcott handles English with a closer understanding of its inner magic than most (if not any) of his English-born contemporaries.'

Less well known than Derek Walcott, but nevertheless important literary figures are his brother Roderick Walcott (1930–), a dramatist and theatre director who was St Lucia's first director of culture, and Garth St Omer ◊, a novelist. St Omer, whose *The Lights on the Hill* (Extract 6) has been likened to James Joyce's *Dubliners*, paints an often negative picture of small-island stasis and the paralysis of 'outsider' protagonists in such societies. Other significant writers from St Lucia are the poet John Robert Lee (see under Barbados), Kendel Hippolyte and the promising US-based Earl G. Long.

LITERARY LANDMARKS

Castries. The central square in the older part of town, previously Columbus Square, was renamed **Derek Walcott Square** in 1993. On one side is **Castries Cathedral**, which contains paintings by the acclaimed St Lucian artist, Dunstan St Omer. St Omer's work can also be seen in a large mural on the sea wall at **Anse La Raye** and in the **Roseau Valley** church.

The Pitons. Hardly a visiting writer has failed to notice what Patrick Leigh Fermor described as 'two lonely spikes jutting out of the coast of the island, each shaped like the Matterhorn.'

BOOKLIST

The following selection includes the extracted titles in this chapter as well as other titles for further reading. In general, paperback editions are given when possible. For most of the extracted works, the original publisher in English can be found in 'Acknowledgments and Citations' at the end of the volume, as can the exact location of the extracts and the editions from which they are taken.

Amis, Martin, 'St Lucia', in *Visiting Mrs Nabokov and Other Excursions*, Cape, London, 1993. **Extract 7**.

Aspinall, Algernon, *A Wayfarer in*

the West Indies, Methuen, London, 1928. **Extract 1**.

Edwards, Bryan, *The History, Civil and Commercial, of the British Colonies in the West Indies*, John Stockdale, London, 1794.

Hastings Jay, E.A., *A Glimpse of the Tropics: or, Four Months Cruising in the West Indies*, Sampson Low, Marston & Company, London, 1900.

Hippolyte, Kendel, 'Castries' in *The Labyrinth*, The Source, Castries, 1993. **Extract 2**.

Long, Earl G., *Consolation*, Longman, Harlow, 1994. **Extract 5**.

Morris, Jan, *Pax Britannica: The Cli-*

max of an Empire, Penguin, London, 1979.

Pattullo, Polly, *Last Resorts: The Cost of Tourism in the Caribbean*, Cassell/Latin America Bureau, London, 1996.

St Omer, Garth, *The Lights on the Hill*, Heinemann, London, 1986. **Extract 6**.

Walcott, Derek, *The Antilles: Fragments of Epic Memory*, Faber and Faber, London, 1993. **Extract 4**.

Walcott, Derek, Extract from 'Sainte Lucie', in *Sea Grapes*, Cape, London, 1976. **Extract 3**.

Walcott, Derek, *Omeros*, Faber and Faber, London, 1990.

Extracts

(1) CASTRIES

Algernon Aspinall, *A Wayfarer in the West Indies*

Aspinall's perception of St Lucia's capital is coloured by the fierce Anglo–French rivalry which ended only a century previously.

Castries, the capital of St Lucia, stands near the head of a landlocked bay aptly described by the colony's motto as 'Statio haud malefida carinis' – a safe haven for ships. Originally called Carénage, the town received its present name in 1784 in honour of Maréchal de Castries, the French Colonial Minister. Thereafter, it was Carénage to the English, and Castries to the French, except during the revolution in 1792, when the National Convention conferred upon it the title of 'The Faithful' as a mark of recognition of the thorough manner in which the inhabitants accepted and carried out the doctrines imparted to them by the republican agents from France. The bloodstained Tree of Liberty found congenial soil in St Lucia, and anarchy and terror prevailed throughout the island.

After entering the harbour by bottle-necked straits you see on the right the wooded heights of Morne Fortuné and on the left the hilly promontory known as the Vigie, or 'Look Out'. On a plateau near the summit of the

Morne, the Union Jack flies over Government House, the residence of the
Administrator, who must be counted fortunate to live on such a pleasant
spot. It commands one of the finest views in the West Indies. Far below lies
Castries basking lazily in the sun, the water of its fair harbour as smooth as
glass except where it is broken into ripples by craft moving in and out.
Alongside the wharf a steamer is being coaled, and you can hear the
laughter and song of the black women as they swing in an endless
procession up the gangway, each of them with a basket of coal on her head.
To the east are rumpled masses of forest-clad mountains as far as eye can
see, and across the harbour the historic Vigie with its orderly row of
barracks, some of which had only just been completed when the garrison
was peremptorily withdrawn in 1905 in pursuance of the 'blue water' policy
which then prevailed. Beyond the narrow promontory is the grand sweep of
Choc Bay, the romantic Pigeon Island off the entrance to Gros Islet Bay,
and, in the distance, the hazy form of Martinique shimmering in the
tropical heat – altogether an enchanting scene.

(2) Castries: Change
Kendel Hippolyte, *Castries*

*Hippolyte's lament for a town spoilt by modernity is also a lament
for lost youth and love.*

i.

i came upon this town
i came upon this town while she was changing
out of her cotton country Sunday-best
into synthetic pearls and leatherette;
stripping off delicate, eaved French architecture
to struggle into high-heeled blocks and functional pillboxes.

Everything was changing:

people, the way they walked, why,
how they waved at you
more and more from a passing car
going who the hell knows – where it ceased to matter
after a time. The very language changed.
Even the river festered to a swamp.
The stone lions on the bridge started to lose their teeth.
Then someone closed the wharf from where i used to watch the sunset
making miracles with water, a few clouds and a sea-gull.

It all happened so fast:

i was talking Creole love-talk to a girl just down from Morne La Paix –
we finished, bargaining how much it would cost, in American accents.
i've probably resigned myself to it all now
except sometimes – like on a day when rain
blurs everything else but memory – i remember
and, in a French ruin overtaken by the coralita
or a girl i knew from Grand Riviere –
Solinah, whose voice still makes a ripple of my name –
i glimpse her again, naked and laughing.

(3) ROSEAU VALLEY

Derek Walcott, from *Sainte Lucie*

Dunstan St Omer's altarpiece in a St Lucian country church is a celebrated fusion of biblical and Caribbean images. These lines are from Part II of 'For the Altar-piece of the Roseau Valley Church, St Lucia'.

Five centuries ago
in the time of Giotto
this altar might have had
in one corner, when God was young
ST OMER ME FECIT AETAT whatever his own age now,
GLORIA DEI and to God's Mother also.

It is signed with music.
It turns the whole island.
You have to imagine it empty on a Sunday afternoon
between adorations

Nobody can see it and there it is there,
nobody adores the two who could be Eve and Adam dancing.

A Sunday at three o'clock
when the real Adam and Eve have coupled
and lie in re-christening sweat

his sweat on her still breasts
her sweat on his panelled torso

that hefts bananas
that has killed snakes
that has climbed out of rivers,

now, as on the furred tops of the hills
a breeze moving the hairs on his chest

on a Sunday at three o'clock
when the snake pours itself
into a chalice of leaves.

The sugar factory is empty

Nobody picks bananas,
no trucks raising dust on their way to Vieuxfort,
no helicopter spraying

the mosquito's banjo, yes,
and the gnat's violin, okay,

okay, not absolute Adamic silence,
the valley of Roseau is not the Garden of Eden,
and those who inhabit it, are not in heaven,

so there are little wires of music
some marron up in the hills, by AuxLyons,
some christening.

A boy banging a tin by the river,
with the river trying to sleep.
But nothing can break that silence,

which comes from the depth of the world,
from whatever one man believes he knows of God
and the suffering of his kind,

it comes from the wall of the altar-piece
ST OMER AD GLORIAM DEI FECIT
in whatever year of his suffering.

(4) St Lucia: Change

Derek Walcott,
The Antilles: Fragments of Epic Memory

Walcott's Nobel Prize lecture warns of the soulless erosion of cultural identity through tourism and celebrates the simplicity of an 'undeveloped' rural St Lucia.

Before it is all gone, before only a few valleys are left, pockets of an older life, before development turns every artist into an anthropologist or folklorist, there are still cherishable places, little valleys that do not echo with ideas, a simplicity of rebeginnings, not yet corrupted by the dangers of change. Not nostalgic sites but occluded sanctities as common and simple as their sunlight. Places as threatened by this prose as a headland is by the bulldozer or a sea-almond grove by the surveyor's string, or, from blight, the mountain laurel.

One last epiphany: a basic stone church in a thick valley outside Soufrière, the hills almost shoving the houses around into a brown river, a sunlight that looks oily on the leaves, a backward place, unimportant, and one now being corrupted into significance by this prose. The idea is not to hallow or invest the place with anything, not even memory. African children in Sunday frocks come down the ordinary concrete steps into the church, banana leaves hang and glisten, a truck is parked in a yard, and old women totter towards the entrance. Here is where a real fresco should be painted, one without importance, but one with real faith, mapless. Historyless.

How quickly it could all disappear! And how it is beginning to drive us further into where we hope are impenetrable places, green secrets at the end of bad roads, headlands where the next view is not of a hotel but of some long beach without a figure and the hanging question of some fisherman's smoke at its far end. The Caribbean is not an idyll, not to its natives. They draw their working strength from it organically, like trees, like the sea almond or the spice laurel of the heights. Its peasantry and its fishermen are not there to be loved or even photographed; they are trees who sweat, and whose bark is filmed with salt, but every day on some island, rootless trees in suits are signing favourable tax breaks with entrepreneurs, poisoning the sea almond and the spice laurel of the mountains to their roots. A morning could come in which governments might ask what happened not merely to the forests and the bays but to a whole people.

(5) St Lucia: Development
Earl G. Long, *Consolation*

*The idyllic rural community of Consolation has been 'discovered' by
an American entrepreneur, who is building a tourist resort.*

The surveyors came soon after, knocking iron stakes into the ground, and
cutting paths through the red, fragrant *ti-baume* scrub. Then came the
bright, yellow bulldozers that shaved the slope as if the soil were as soft as
ashes. They did not even hesitate at trees and rocks. The villagers came to
watch, uncertain whether to be excited or frightened. The children
welcomed the entertainment at first, with the boys all wishing to be tractor
operators. Then they sensed their parents' unease and stopped coming.
Even Brazil Pascal stopped going to see the transformation of his old
property, although he knew it would be the last spectacle he would witness.
He stayed indoors after the first week of construction and his neighbours
seldom saw him again. He died one year later. Molasses protested that the
decision had been his father's alone, but he maintained his distance from
the older men in the village and he never ventured near Estephan St
Pierre's home.

The capital suddenly discovered Consolation, and people who had
abandoned the village many years ago, began remembering their relations
there. Carloads of strangers arrived at weekends, especially on Sundays, to
visit old friends and relatives, to ask with agonized nonchalance about the
extent and ownership of family lands, and to lavish assurance that they had
never left Consolation in spirit.

The beaches at Great Hole and Little Hole were crowded again at
weekends when the young people discovered that their water was cleaner
and bluer than at other beaches they had rushed to. And to make their own
beaches as comfortable as the old ones, they littered the sand with paper,
bottles, cans and plastic.

(6) St Lucia: Rural Life
Garth St Omer, *The Lights on the Hill*

*Stephenson, the novel's intellectual hero, recalls his childhood, when
during school holidays he spent time with his brother and father in the
island's poor rural district.*

Carl was now much bigger and stronger than he was. He had never been to
school and spoke only the patois of the island. Stephenson joined him and
his father when they went to make charcoal. In the evening they returned.
They walked over the steep tracks, hard underfoot (he was barefoot, too)
because of the lack of rain. Around them hills arose from crevices deep as
the one they seemed continually to be climbing out of. A shout sounded.

Sometimes the blow of an axe. The sounds echoed. Parts of the hill were in shadow. Slowly the cloud moved. The hill was like a cat awakening. On the other side of a gorge, from another charcoal pit, smoke rose in the air. They passed men in tattered trousers and old felt hats with dirty singlets or old jackets and their cutlasses in their hands. Sometimes they carried bags of charcoal on their heads. The boys wore nothing above their torn shorts. The bigger ones carried loads almost as heavy as those of the men. Through the holes of their old frocks the slips of the women showed. They greeted one another in patois as they passed and those who happened to be descending the slope stood aside to allow the others to climb. Then the sun set. The hills were in shadow and dead trees stood white on them everywhere. Bare patches of earth, cultivated with yam or dasheen, lay between areas of stunted bush. Only on the tops of the highest of the hills to the West did the light from the sun still show.

They threw down their loads and washed their feet with as little water as possible. The breadfruit and salted fish pushed steam upwards through the leaves and the piece of cloth that covered them. Later they ate sitting on low stools in the open space before the house, the fowls coming out of their sleeping places to peck at their feet. Then the lamps were lit. The thick unchimneyed smoke disappeared into the night. They sat out in the now pleasant warmth for a little while.

(7) St Lucia: Tourists

Martin Amis, *St Lucia*

Beyond the safe confines of the beach resort lies another island: beautiful, but also ambivalent towards its tourists.

But it transpires that St Lucia, for now, is both beautiful and innocuous, like its people. In the small towns (and small towns are the only kind of towns there are here) you sense a strange air of poverty and prettiness. Most of the 'traditional' timber houses, while inconceivably tiny, are primped, made much of, tirelessly adorned. You pull up for a soft drink and find that the Coke and 7-Up signs are there for decoration. The children lining the rural roads are trimly uniformed, healthy-looking, well-ordered – and above all numerous. Dennery and Micoud, the more neglected townships on the island's Atlantic coast, lie soaked and puddled in rainy-season boredom. There is much unemployment, and no welfare. People are poor, but nature is rich; it would be hard to starve. The street-wanderers of Micoud regard us with ambiguous levity. We stop for a can of orange juice and are unsmilingly overcharged. Although you wouldn't call them hostile, they are no more friendly than I would feel, if a stranger drove down my street in a car the size of my house.

Even at its most rank and jungly, St Lucia has a kiddy-book harmlessness. The leaves and palms seem greased with baby oil. You expect to encounter Babar the Elephant, smiling tigers, naughty monkeys. Even the real dangers ('minor only!') are Disneyish: poison apples, falling coconuts. Swooningly the vegetation topples into the bluer green of the sea. The Pitons, twin larval peaks, look elemental – a land that time forgot – but cinematic too; King Kong would feel at home with them, clambering from one to the other. At the 'unique' drive-in volcano our gaptoothed Rasta led us through the smells and steam of Sulphur Springs. Now here was blackness and menace. The dark cauldrons bubble at 300°F. Fall in there and you would be dead five times over in a couple of seconds. Everywhere the ground fizzed and simmered (busy counter-space in hell's kitchen), containing with effort the fury of its nethers . . . As we returned to town the locals waved at the car or gazed at us with languid scepticism. In your capacity as a tourist, you feel tolerated as something crucial to the health of the economy. You sometimes feel like a banana trader, a banana planter, a banana expert. Indeed, you sometimes feel like a banana.

Biographical and literary notes

AMIS, Martin (1949–). Martin Amis is one of Britain's foremost novelists. His fiction includes *Other People*, 1981, *London Fields*, 1989, and *Time's Arrow*, 1991. He has also written numerous articles for newspapers and magazines which have been published in the collections *The Moronic Inferno*, 1986, and *Visiting Mrs Nabokov and Other Excursions*, 1993. 'St Lucia' (Extract 7) is a fine example of Amis's perceptive and caustic commentary.

Martin Amis

ASPINALL, Algernon (1871–1952). Eton and Oxford educated, Sir Algernon Aspinall had a lifelong interest in the Caribbean, specializing in tropical agriculture. He served on many commissions and committees and was Vice-President of the influential London-based West India Committee. He wrote a guide to the Caribbean, edited a collection of traditional folk tales, and combined history and contemporary observation in his *A Wayfarer in the West Indies* (Extract 1).

HIPPOLYTE, Kendel (1952–). Born in St Lucia, Hippolyte was educated there and at the University of the West Indies, Jamaica, before returning to work primarily in local theatre. A teacher of English and theatre, he is the author of two previous collections of poetry: *Island in the Sun – Side Two*, 1980, and *Bearings*, 1986. A collection entitled *Birthright* was published in 1996 by the Peepal Tree Press. *The Labyrinth* (1993), from which *Castries* (Extract

2) is taken, explores a series of themes ranging from St Lucia's rapid modernisation to the collapse of the Grenadian revolution.

LONG, Earl G. (1959–). Born in St Lucia, Long studied at the London School of Hygiene and Tropical Medicine before going to work as a microbiologist in Georgia, USA. *Consolation* (Extract 5), his first published novel, tells the story of a small country village and the emotional ties which bind its people together. Its simple charm is threatened when an American developer decides to construct a tourist resort by the beach, but nature wreaks its revenge on the scheme and Consolation survives as a close-knit and idealized version of a small-island community.

ST OMER, Garth (1931–). Born in Castries, St Omer was educated in St Lucia before teaching for several years in schools in the Eastern Caribbean. In 1956 he went to Jamaica to study at the University of the West Indies and then taught in schools in France and Ghana. After several years of full-time writing, St Omer went to Columbia University, followed by a PhD at Princeton. He subsequently joined the English Department at the University of Santa Barbara, California, where he became Professor. He has received a number of awards and fellowships. His other works include *Nor Any Country*, 1969, and *J-, Black Bam and the Masqueraders*, 1972. *The Lights on the Hill* (Extract 6), originally published in 1968, is a study of the protagonist's existential *Angst* as the claustrophobia of small-island existence weighs heavy on a sensitive and emotionally unfulfilled personality. Although much of the brief novella deals with Stephenson's inner turmoil, it also offers finely drawn vignettes of St Lucia's landscapes and society.

WALCOTT, Derek (1930–). Walcott's stature as one of the most important figures in world literature was confirmed in 1993 when he was awarded the Nobel Prize for Literature. Born in **Castries** into what he has described as 'genteel, self-denying Methodist poverty', he was the son of a painter father and a mother who produced Shakespearean plays at the local Methodist school. His father died when he and his brother Roderick were still very young. By the age of eighteen, Walcott had produced his first collection of poems, *25 Poems*, 1948, as well as a play, *Henri Christophe*, 1950. After taking a degree in English, French and Latin from the University of the West Indies in Jamaica, he studied theatre in New York before working in Trinidad as a full-time writer and director of the Trinidad Theatre Workshop, which he founded in 1959. For the next two decades he was based mainly in Trinidad, where he produced a considerable corpus of poetry and theatre. The best-known poetry from this period includes *In a Green Night*, 1962, *The Castaway and Other Poems*, 1965, and *The Gulf*, 1969. At the same time, he wrote and produced many plays, the most successful of which was *Dream on Monkey Mountain*, 1971.

In 1976 Walcott left the Trinidad Theatre Workshop and embarked on a more academic career, teaching at various US universities, and since 1981 he has taught creative writing at Boston University. Since 1976 he has produced several volumes of poetry, including *Sea Grapes*, 1976, *The Fortunate Traveller*, 1982, *Midsummer*, 1984, and *Omeros*, 1990. The last of these is widely considered to be his greatest achievement and preceded the award of the Nobel Prize.

In 'Sainte Lucie' (Extract 3), taken from *Sea Grapes*, Walcott recreates the landscapes of St Lucia as well as the particular Creole constructions of his fellow islanders. His concern for the island's distinctive language and

Garth St Omer

culture forms the central theme of his Nobel Prize speech, published as *The Antilles: Fragments of Epic Memory* (Extract 4). Here, Walcott rejects the view exemplified by V.S. Naipaul that the Caribbean is a place without history or culture and at the same time emphasizes the vulnerability to mass tourism of small, as yet unspoiled, rural communities.

ST VINCENT AND THE GRENADINES

'Come nearer, focus on one dot of an island/I was born there, on the rim of a volcano/on the edge of a large full stop/where the sand is black/where the hills turn a gun-barrel blue/where the sea perpetually dashes at the shoreline/trying to reclaim it all.'

Philip Nanton, 1

Halfway up the rugged east coast of St Vincent, and about twenty kilometres north of the capital **Kingstown**, lies the melancholic settlement of **Georgetown**. Its name evokes its former colonial importance, and in the nineteenth century the town was the centre of a thriving sugar industry. In the 1960s Georgetown's sugar factory was closed and its *raison d'être* disappeared with it. Today, **Georgetown** looks like the archetypal Wild West ghost town, its houses mostly closed up and dilapidated, its gardens unkempt and overgrown. Weeds grow freely in the streets, and few people are to be seen among the once-imposing merchants' houses which line the main road northwards.

A few minutes out of **Georgetown** and the road begins to deteriorate. To the west looms the imposing silhouette of the **Soufrière** volcano, which last erupted in 1979 and which has covered the landscape in solid lava. Often cars cannot negotiate the **Rabacca Dry River** which cuts across the road and which, in the rainy season, is anything but dry. Beyond lie a handful of villages amid banana plantations. Poor, isolated and a world away from the capital, places like **Sandy Bay**, **Owia** and **Fancy** are reputed to be the last redoubts of the island's Carib community and of the legendary Black Caribs.

Only thirty kilometres to the south is Mustique, one of St Vincent's 32 sister islands and cays, known collectively as the Grenadines. Here, a night at the Cotton House Hotel can cost US$750, probably the annual income of a Sandy Bay inhabitant. Mustique is privately owned and those Vincentians who live there make up the team of cooks, gardeners and maids who look after a clientele of celebrities such as Mick Jagger and

> ## FACT BOX
>
> AREA: 389.3 sq km
> POPULATION: 110 000
> CAPITAL: Kingstown
> LANGUAGES: English
> FORMER COLONIAL POWER: Britain
> INDEPENDENCE: 1979
> PER CAPITA GDP: US$2130

Princess Margaret. Under the terms of Mustique's ownership, Vincentians are not allowed to give birth or be buried on the island.

The contrasts between mainland St Vincent and its Grenadine dependencies are clear. While St Vincent remains a largely rural, undeveloped society, places such as Mustique, Bequia (pronounced Beck-way) and Union Island have become favoured enclaves for the wealthy yachting élite. Most visitors to the Grenadines no longer even stop off in St Vincent itself, but land on the private airstrips in their secluded island paradises.

THE CARIB WARS

St Vincent was first called *Hairoun* (now only the name of a local beer), and when Columbus visited the island during his third voyage in 1498 it was inhabited by the Caribs who had already overpowered the indigenous Arawaks, killing the men but interbreeding with the women. As in Dominica, the Caribs were determined to resist European colonization and met any incursions into their territory with ferocity.

The Caribs were more hospitable to escaped African slaves from other islands, however, and in 1675 when a passing Dutch slave ship was wrecked between St Vincent and Bequia, they took the surviving slaves into their community. According to some historians, the black slaves were welcomed as equals. According to Sir William Young ◊, however, the Caribs merely intended to re-enslave their captives. In *An Account of the Black Charaibs in the Island of St Vincent's* (Extract 1), Young describes how the Africans and Caribs developed into implacable enemies. Whatever the truth, a process of intermarriage produced the so-called 'Black Caribs', distinct from the indigenous 'Yellow Caribs', both of whom were resolutely opposed to European designs on the island.

Like its neighbours, Grenada and St Lucia, control of St Vincent was hotly disputed between Britain and France in the course of the eighteenth century, and this rivalry was further complicated by the hostility of Caribs and Black Caribs. The island was settled first by the French, then by the British in 1722, and in 1763 St Vincent was officially ceded to Britain by the Treaty of Paris. The French invaded again in 1778 but restored the island to the British in 1783 under the Treaty of Versailles.

Now, however, the Black Caribs took up the offensive against the British colonists. An initial treaty of 1773 had been honoured by neither side and the 'Carib Wars' ran parallel to Anglo–French conflict. The French, complained the British, encouraged the Caribs to revolt, and in 1795 the revolutionary French agitator, Victor Hugues, was behind a renewed outbreak of fighting. As the so-called 'Brigands' War' intensified, reinforced British forces responded harshly, driving the Black Caribs northwards and cutting off their supplies until they were forced to surrender *en masse*. Eventually the survivors were rounded up, held on the tiny island of Balliceaux (where half of them died) and deported to the British-controlled island of Roatán off the coast of Honduras. A contemporary observer, Alexander Anderson, witnessed the defeat and destruction of the Black Caribs:

> 'About 6000 surrendered, and we may readily allow one third of them to have been killed and perished in the woods by wounds, hunger and fatigue. The shocking state a number of them were found in [in] the woods was awful, some expiring half putrid, many dead in their hammocks, some partly eaten by rats and their own dogs. Like all savages, they paid no attention to their sick and infirm on their march from the windward of the island.'

A century later, a Vincentian cleric by the name of Horatio Nelson Huggins composed what is probably the first Caribbean epic poem. Looking back to the downfall of the Black Caribs, *Hiroona* gives voice to their chief, Warramou, as he curses the British and predicts their eventual loss of St Vincent:

> 'Ah! wronged Hiroon, my country, then
> Shall Heaven be known as just – white men
> Flung forth from thee, O ocean gem,
> As we are now flung forth by them!
> Your very negro-slaves shall gain
> Their freedom, fling away the chain
> And claim to shake you by the hand,
> And strut your equals in the land.'

On a high promontory to the north of **Kingstown Bay**, stands the imposing outline of Fort Charlotte, which was gradually built over the course of the turbulent eighteenth century. Strangely, many of the cannons point not out to sea, but look inland towards the steep wooded hillsides which encircle the capital. The fort somehow symbolizes the precarious nature of colonial St Vincent, vulnerable both to attack from the French and to sudden deadly raids from the Black Caribs in the island's remote interior.

Not that the deportation meant the end of the Carib presence in St Vincent. In the first years of the twentieth century, Frederick Ober ◊ visited **Sandy Bay** and found both Black and 'Yellow' Caribs. In *Our West Indian Neighbours* (Extract 2) he describes the remaining community and compares them to the North American Indians, displaced and dispossessed by the white man. Today, both Carib and Black Carib villages remain in the north of St Vincent, the last remnants of the island's first inhabitants. Those who were deported to Roatán, meanwhile, spread into Guatemala and Belize where they have maintained their own distinct identity.

IMPERIAL BACKWATER

The departure of the Black Caribs brought a measure of peace, and St Vincent adopted the familiar features of a plantation economy. But the island was a latecomer to the sugar industry, and the slave population and sugar exports were noticeably smaller than in other islands. Land ownership was extraordinarily restricted and absentee landowners were the norm. Some English-descended families came to St Vincent, notably from overcrowded Barbados, to manage estates and work in the colonial bureaucracy with the result that today there are more whites in the island than in most neighbouring territories.

Abolition brought the usual labour shortages, and significant communities of Portuguese and East Indian labourers arrived to work in the fields. As sugar declined in importance, smallholders began to grow other crops such as bananas, coconuts and cotton. St Vincent also became the world's largest producer of arrowroot, traditionally used as a food thickener but now more widely used in manufacturing computer paper.

The island's relative poverty and backwardness were compounded by its mountainous landscape and a succession of natural disasters. In May 1902, just two days before the catastrophe at Martinique's Mont Pelée, the **Soufrière** volcano unexpectedly erupted, killing over 2000 islanders and covering much of the best land with lava and ash. In Barbados, more than 150 kilometres away, the sky reportedly turned pitch black.

As a remote backwater in the British empire, St Vincent remained little visited for much of the twentieth century. In *The Sugar Islands* (Extract 5), Alec Waugh (◊ Martinique) gives an evocative account of a dreary Sunday morning in deserted **Kingstown**. A Legislative Council was inaugurated in 1925, but universal suffrage did not materialize until 1951. The island was one of the British colonies shaken by labour unrest in the 1930s; when the Legislative Council proposed increased taxes, a crowd of unemployed islanders attacked the Council Chamber, roughed up the Governor and looted some shops. A British warship was summoned, and three rioters were killed by police.

In 1951 one of the Eastern Caribbean's archetypal small-island politicians, Ebenezer Joshua, was elected to the Legislative Council and formed his People's Political Party, having left another rather grandly named party, the Eighth Army of Liberation. A trade unionist and rabble-rouser, Joshua is probably the model for Jerry Mole, the anti-hero of G.C.H. Thomas's *Ruler in Hiroona* (Extract 3), although Grenada's Eric Gairy, Antigua's Vere Bird or St Kitts's Robert Bradshaw could just have well provided

Thomas's inspiration. Like Joshua, Jerry Mole develops a reputation as the people's champion through leading a series of strikes, although his own tastes tend more towards an easy life of luxury. Like Joshua, too, Mole takes the precaution of making his wife a minister in his own government before meeting with a well deserved downfall.

INDEPENDENCE AND SINCE

Since Joshua's retirement in 1980, Vincentian politics has been a two-horse race between the St Vincent Labour Party and the New Democratic Party of Sir James 'Son' Mitchell, a race more usually won by Mitchell. Not that the island's politics have lost their rumbustious flavour, with allegations of one-party rule, corruption and drug-running livening up political debate in the tiny parliament building. Was it sheer coincidence, sceptics ask, that St Vincent (once, but no longer, a whaling nation) voted with Japan to oppose a 'no-whaling' sanctuary in Antarctica? Japan, after all, provided the money for Kingstown's new fish market (known as 'little Tokyo') and was reportedly generous enough to pay St Vincent's membership of the International Whaling Commission.

Independence, finally achieved in 1979, has done little to improve St Vincent's precarious economic position, and the island is by far the poorest in the Eastern Caribbean. Despite the legendary fertility of areas such as the lush **Mesopotamia Valley**, many Vincentians hardly make ends meet, and remittances sent from workers overseas are an important contribution to the island's economy. A series of violent hurricanes in the 1970s and 1980s, as well as another volcanic eruption, badly damaged St Vincent's agricultural production.

In recent years two Vincentians have established literary reputations outside the Caribbean. Shake Keane, who now lives in New York, is the author of several volumes of poetry, of which *One a Week with Water*, 1979, won the prestigious Casa de las Américas prize in Havana. His *Volcano Suite* recalls the day in 1979 when **Soufrière** again erupted, this time without fatalities but with considerable damage and widespread evacuation:

'The thing split Good Friday in two
and that good new morning groaned
and snapped
like breaking an old habit

Within minutes
people
who had always been leaving nowhere
began arriving nowhere
entire lives stuffed in pillow-cases
and used plastic bags
naked children suddenly transformed into citizens'

More recent is the arrival of H. Nigel Thomas ♭, who currently teaches literature in Canada. His novel, *Spirits in the Dark* (Extract 4), dissects the psychological complexities of a young man growing up in a small island, burdened by the double difficulty of expressing his precocious intelligence and homosexuality in a restricting social milieu.

BOOKLIST

Hulme, Peter and Neil L. White-head, *Wild Majesty: Encounters with Caribs from Columbus to the Present Day*, Clarendon, Oxford, 1992.

Ober, Frederick A., *Our West Indian Neighbours*, James Pott & Company, New York, 1907. **Extract 2.**

Price, Neil, *Behind the Planter's Back: Lower Class Response to Marginality in Bequia Island, St Vincent*, Macmillan, Basingstoke, 1988.

Thomas, G.C.H., *Ruler in Hiroona:*
A West Indian Novel, Macmillan Caribbean, Basingstoke, 1989. **Extract 3.**

Thomas, H. Nigel, *Spirits in the Dark*, Heinemann, Oxford, 1993. **Extract 4.**

Waugh, Alec, *The Sugar Islands*, Cassell, London, 1958. **Extract 5.**

Young, Sir William, *An Account of the Black Charaibs in the Island of St. Vincent's*, Frank Cass, London, 1971. **Extract 1.**

Extracts

(1) ST VINCENT: BLACK CARIBS

Sir William Young,
An Account of the Black Charaibs
in the Island of St Vincent's

The history of the warlike Black Caribs is recorded by the head of the official British commission, sent to establish peace on the island.

The Negroes, or Black Charaibs (as they have been termed of late years), are descendants from the cargo of an African slave ship, bound from the Bite of Benin to Barbadoes, and wrecked, about the year 1675, on the coast of Bequia, a small island about two leagues to the south of St Vincent's.

The Charaibs, accustomed to fish in the narrow channel, soon discovered these Negroes, and finding them in great distress for provisions, and particularly for water, with which Bequia was ill supplied, they had little difficulty in inveigling them into their canoes, and transporting them across the narrow channel to St Vincent's, where they made slaves of them, and set them to work.

These Negroes were of a warlike Moco tribe from Africa, and soon proved restive and indicile servants to the less robust natives of the western ocean.

The Charaibs, incommoded by the refractory spirit of their slaves, and apprehending danger should their numbers increase, came to a resolution of putting to death all their male children which should be born; still, according to their national custom in war, reserving the females.

This cruel policy occasioned a sudden insurrection of the Blacks, who massacred such of the Charaibs as they could take by surprise, and then fled, accompanied or followed by their wives and children, to the woods and rocks which cover the high mountains to the north-east of St Vincent's.

In these almost inaccessible fortresses they found many other Negroes from the neighbouring islands, who, murderers or runaways, had fled from justice, revenge, or slavery.

Incorporating with these Negro outlaws, they formed a nation, now known by the name of Black Charaibs; a title themselves arrogated, when entering into contest with their ancient masters.

The savage, with the name and title, thinks he inherits the qualities, the rights, and the property, of those whom he may pretend to supersede: hence he assimilates himself by name and manners, as it were to make out his identity, and confirm the succession. Thus these Negroes not only assumed the national appellation of Charaibs, but individually their Indian names; and they adopted many of their customs: they flattened the foreheads of their infant children in the Indian manner: they buried their dead in the attitude of sitting, and according to Indian rites: and killing the men they took in war, they carried off and cohabited with the women.

(2) St Vincent: Caribs

Frederick A. Ober, *Our West Indian Neighbours*

Returning to visit St Vincent's Carib community at the beginning of the twentieth century, Ober anticipates – and receives – a warm welcome.

Christmas week was well along toward its ending when I descended the windward slopes of the Soufrière and sought the shores of Sandy Bay, where lived the last remnants of the Carib Indians. But the Christmas rejoicings were by no means over, for they last a fortnight in that favored land down near the equator; and, moreover, word had been sent and passed along that I was coming, so if necessary the festivities would have been protracted. For this was my second visit to the Caribs; and as on the first one I had remained for weeks, had hunted with them, fished with them, eaten at their tables, and, in fact, had been as good an Indian as I knew how to be, on this my second coming I was more than welcome.

I was met at the 'dry-river' (a stream the bed of which had been filled with lava from the volcano in a previous eruption) by the sub-chief, old Rabacca, who conducted me to Overland, a village of mixed Indians and blacks, whence my trip to Sandy Bay was a continuous ovation. Rabacca was descended from an Indian giant, who, after killing many white men of the island more than a hundred years ago, was finally captured and gibbeted in chains, surviving a week in dreadful torment and dying with imprecations against the English on his shriveled lips. Rabacca, however, had inherited no animosity against the white man, his worst enemy being that West Indian substitute for 'John Barleycorn', aguardiente, or native rum. When not in his cups Rabacca was the best worker on the windward sugar plantations, none other, be he white, red or black, being his equal at loading a 'moses boat' in the heavy surf that beats continuously on the island's east shore.

Rabacca conducted me to a little hut of reeds, wattled and thatched with palm leaves, where, after my hammock had been swung and my effects installed, he acted as master of ceremonies and reintroduced me to the old friends of many years agone. This done, I was invited to accompany the assembled Caribs to the banquet hall, a little distance away, where the feast was already set out that had been prepared against my arrival. The 'hall', by the way, was merely a vast roof of palm thatch set upon stout poles, open on every side, shaded by palms, with entrancing views outspread around of smiling sea and gloomy, forest-clad mountain slopes. Beneath the thatch was a long table of rough boards, covered with plantain leaves, upon which were spread not only such products of land and sea as bounteous nature has lavished on dwellers in the tropics, but many viands imported from abroad. For instance, there was 'tinned' mutton from London, genuine Southdown, flanked with heaps of breadfruit, roasted as well as boiled. And, by the way, if there is anything more palatable – at least to a hungry hunter – than boiled breadfruit with Southdown mutton and drawn butter, it is that same fruit similarly served after having been roasted in the ashes of a campfire.

(3) St Vincent: Politicians
G.C.H. Thomas, *Ruler in Hiroona*

Jerry Mole is the classic small-island, rabble-rousing politician. He recalls his first big demonstration.

I turned, trot-walked to the pavilion, ran up the steps to the gallery and grabbed the microphone.

'Comrades,' I boomed, 'you ready to march?'

'Yeahse! Yeahse!'

The park was all sound and colour – khaki, cheap cotton frocks; red, blue, green, white banners; placards; 'AWAKE HIROONA!'; 'DOWN WITH THE ADMINISTRATOR'; 'WE TIRED WITH MUD HUTS'; 'FORBES MUST GO!'; 'WE SPIT ON IMPERIALISM'; 'OUR GOAL IS MOLE' – and so on and so forth. Steel bands tentatively ping-ponged like orchestras tuning up, their metallic notes co-mingling with the lively babel.

'Comrades! Comrades! Too much noise! Please! Comrade Marksman, your group sagging out of line . . . Now . . . quiet please! . . . That's better. Now, listen carefully. We marching from here, straight up Kingsland Main Street, right through town, straight up Happy Hill. Then over the hill, down Merry Vale Hill, through Merry Vale village straight on to Merry Vale pasture. There we will join our comrades from the Central and Windward districts. We will then rest a while, have a little jump-up dance and some light refreshment provided for you on the pasture. Then the Central and Windward districts will march back with us right back here in this park. Then I and a few comrades will address you from this gallery here. Then we will have our feast. You understand?'

'Yeahse! Yeahse! *Ping-pong. Ping-pong. Boom. Bong!* said the steel bands.

'Comrade Southwall, please quiet those steelbands . . . Fine. Now one last word, comrades. I notice that some of you seem to be having trouble with your shoes. If you don't feel comfortable in shoes, take them off now, so you can march at ease.'

My words had a similar effect to that of a spitting machine-gun trained on a crowd of people. Almost the entire assembly dropped to the ground and began to fumble with their footwear. When they got up again, some had their shoes strung across their forearms; some tied the laces together and hung the shoes around their necks. Some of the men had their shoes sticking out of the side or hip pockets of their trousers. Even some of the members of the Committees of Management took advantage of this opportunity to revert to type.

(4) St Vincent: School

H. Nigel Thomas, *Spirits in the Dark*

Miss Anderson, known as 'the Bulldog', is the terror of Jerome's school, beating the children for the slightest misdemeanour.

She shook her head, looking a little like a pawing bull. 'You all think I was born big.' She gave a third problem and remained in the class. Everyone got it wrong. This time she beat them all without bothering to count the lashes. But they noticed that the blackest and smallest students got the most.

Just after she got through, they heard a loud voice saying, 'Show me where the fucker is.' It was a cane-cutter with bits of burnt sugar cane stalks sticking out of his hedgehog hair. There were tiny runnels in the black cane dust that covered his face. He barged into the classroom. 'That is the fucking bitch?' he asked the little girl accompanying him.

'Get out!' Miss Anderson ordered him, her hands on her hips.

'Yo' ever swallow your teeth?' he asked her.

Miss Anderson was quiet and her arms were now hanging.

The cane-cutter bent down and pointed to the girl's left leg, which looked satiny and was almost twice the size of the right one. 'Yo' call this teaching?' he asked Miss Anderson, thrusting a finger in her face. 'Yo' fucking call this teaching?'

Miss Anderson began to tremble and to back away from him.

'Don't move!'

Miss Anderson stood still.

'I don' ever have to beat this child. She is the obedientest child there is. You don' ever put yo' fucking hands on she again. If yo' do, so help me God, I will knock every fucking teeth outta yo' head! What yo' trying to prove? Yo' don' know is the cane crop? Yo' don' know the children have fo' carry their parent food? How the fuck yo' think we feed and clothes them?' He stopped and wrinkled his brow. 'Ain't yo' mother name Melda?'

Miss Anderson gasped. The cane-cutter laughed and shook his head. He spat on the floor in front of her.

'You is as common as dirt. You is nobody. Miss Anderson! Huh! Yo' better find out who yo' father is.' He became silent, then pulled at his daughter's sleeve and turned to leave. Then he stopped at the door. 'I sure didn' want for hurt yo' feelings, but I hope yo' 'preciate that we have fo' earn we living, that the children have fo' bring we food.' He left.

(5) ST VINCENT: SUNDAY

Alec Waugh, *The Sugar Islands*

*First impressions of Kingstown harbour on a rainy morning are not
entirely positive for the veteran Caribbean traveller, Alec Waugh.*

I first saw it on a wet mid-November morning. I was on my way to
Grenada. I was planning to return later to St Vincent. I woke to the sight
through my cabin porthole of a semicircle of jagged mountains banked with
cloud. At the base of the mountains ran the wharf – a long colonnade,
bisected by a wooden jetty. It was raining steadily. A dozen streams,
pouring their silt into the harbour, sent a long tide of mud towards the ship.
'Another wasted morning,' the purser grumbled. Despondently, he leant
against the taffrail. We had lost two days already at Barbados. West Indians
only work when it is fine. Today they had not even bothered to send out
lighters. Heaven knew how many more hours we would not have to waste
before we docked finally at Kingstown. Inaction fretted the purser.
Impatiently, he tapped the top of his white buckskin shoe against the deck,
answering at random the passengers' enquiries. St Vincent? A poky little
place. Pretty enough if you liked scenery, but nothing more. One of those
small places that had gone to seed. One of the Empire's liabilities. What
did they raise here? Oh, most everything. Sugar, coconuts, bananas, with
arrowroot and sea-island cotton as their steady standbys. Was there
anything to see on shore? Was there ever anything to see in the Caribbean
except sunlight? And this was November: a month too soon for that.

His tone of denigration matched the scene. I had never seen anything
less typical of a boat day in a tropic port. There was none of the traditional
noise or bustle; no boys diving for pennies; no boatmen plying vociferously
for hire; no bargaining vendors of fruit and cushions; only a couple of silent
salesmen standing in a corner of the deck beside a small store of local
mahogany, bead bags, Coronation stamps, and sharks'-bone walking sticks.
The two anchored schooners in the harbour, motionless beside their
moorings, were appropriate interpretations of the atmosphere of general
inanimation. It was not till I was actually on shore that I found the
explanation. During a long voyage one loses one's sense of the calendar. I
had forgotten – everyone else on board had forgotten – that it was a Sunday
morning.

Biographical and literary notes

OBER, Frederick A. (1849–1913). Born in Massachusetts, Ober was an acknowledged expert in the field of ornithology, working from the early 1870s at the Smithsonian Institute. He spent two years (1876–78) in the Lesser Antilles, discovering 22 new species of birds new to science. He was also the author of several popular travel books, notably *Camps in the Caribbees: The Adventures of a Naturalist in the Lesser Antilles*, 1880, and *Our West Indian Neighbours* (Extract 2). Ober became particularly interested in the Carib communities of St Vincent and Dominica, which he visited on several occasions.

THOMAS, G.C.H (1932–1995). Born in Trinidad, Thomas is best known for his successful novel, *Ruler in Hiroona* (Extract 3), which has also been adapted into dramatic form.

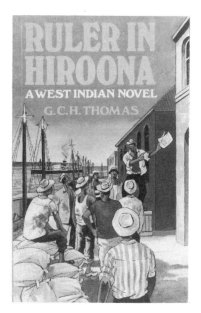

Although Thomas denied basing the novel on any real place or people, the name Hiroona and the escapades of its anti-hero Jerry Mole are full of allusions to St Vincent and its mercurial former leader, Ebenezer Joshua. Mole starts his confessions thus: 'I shall be writing about the nineteen-fifties and sixties, and the West Indian islands were incredible places during those times. They still are in some respects.' There follows a comic account of Mole's sordid political career and richly deserved downfall.

H. Nigel Thomas

THOMAS, H. Nigel (1947–). Born in St Vincent, Thomas left the island in 1968 to live and work in Canada. His poems and short stories have been published in many anthologies and he has written widely on American, African and Caribbean literature. He is currently associate professor at Université Laval in Quebec City. *Spirits in the Dark* (Extract 4) tells of the childhood, youth and early adulthood of Jerome Quashee in the fictional Caribbean island of Isabella. Jerome's repressed homosexuality and sensitivity, exacerbated by the stifling confines of a racist, post-colonial society, lead to a nervous breakdown, from which Jerome attempts to recover through retrospective analysis and spiritual commitment.

WAUGH, Alec (see under Martinique).

YOUNG, Sir William (1749–1815). Sir William Young was the son of the Governor of Dominica (also named Sir William Young) and one of the biggest landowners in St Vincent. Head of the commission sent to in-

vestigate unrest in St Vincent in the 1790s, Young analysed the tensions between indigenous Caribs and the mixed-race Black Caribs as well as the competing colonial claims of France and Britain. His report, *An Account of the Black Charaibs in the Island of St Vincent's* (Extract 1), concluded that either the British would have to abandon St Vincent or the Black Caribs would have to be deported *en masse*. He was also the author of a travel account, *A Tour Through the Several Islands of Barbadoes, St Vincent, Antigua, Tobago, and Grenada in the Years 1791 and 1792*, 1801. In 1807 Young was appointed Governor of Tobago, where he remained until his death.

GRENADA

'Grenada is moving fast
We reaching somewhere at
                    last,
Our motto we must remember
"Forward ever and backward
                    never!" '

Lord Melody

For a brief, bizarre moment in October 1983, the tiny island of Grenada stood at the very centre of the Cold War. The world's greatest super-power had decided, in the name of national and regional security, to invade a nation of fewer than 100 000 people. As Marines streamed ashore and helicopters clattered over the pretty little town of **St George's**, journalists around the world struggled to find this 350 sq km pinprick in the atlas. Television news in Moscow solemnly reported that the USA had invaded Granada, and a map of southern Spain duly appeared behind the newsreader. In Britain, people were surprised to find out that the Americans were landing in a territory where the head of state was still, in theory at least, Queen Elizabeth II.

The US invasion of Grenada (the Reagan administration and some Grenadians preferred to call it an 'intervention' or even 'rescue mission') marked the dramatic culmination and disintegration of almost five years of revolution. That revolution, begun in March 1979 when a small band of armed activists had taken control of the island in a coup, is to date the only successful seizure of power in the English-speaking Caribbean. It ushered in a period of rapid social change, of considerable economic development and, some said, of human rights abuses. It also created a political culture in which a small vanguard party sought to lead a largely rural and undeveloped society into what it believed to be 'consciousness'. In the ideological climate of the early 1980s these goals and methods found little favour in Washington. For its short life, the Grenadian revolution was on an inevitable collision course with the United States. That many Grenadians were inspired by the 'revo' is beyond doubt; that the revolution finally devoured its own children is also sadly true.

ISLAND OF CONFLICT

Grenada is picturesque in a way that neighbouring islands are not. Its rainforests are perhaps less dramatic than Dominica's and it has nothing to

---

FACT BOX

AREA: 348 sq km
POPULATION: 91 800
CAPITAL: St George's
LANGUAGES: English, Patois
FORMER COLONIAL POWER: Britain
INDEPENDENCE: 1974
PER CAPITA GDP: US$2410

---

compare to the sheer grandeur of St Lucia's Pitons. Yet its landscape is an almost perfect blend of wildness and cultivation, where the terrain changes from one valley to the next in a succession of hills, rivers and fields. Often the sea appears unexpectedly through a valley or around a hillside, a reminder that Grenada lives from both fishing and tourism. As Hugh O'Shaughnessy remarks in his travel book entitled *Around the Spanish Main*:

> 'I pick my words carefully when I say there is no more beautiful island in the Caribbean than Grenada. Some perhaps can equal it, none can surpass it. In this Eden Nature has been wildly prodigal with gifts. Man for his part has done nothing to spoil and what little he can to embellish. Life may not be easy in Grenada and for many it may be less than fulfilling but it is lived in among finest surroundings, in different spots tranquil, pleasant, languid, rugged and fertile.'

Grenada is known as the 'spice isle' and spices, particularly nutmeg, form a large part of its income. The nutmeg appears on the national flag, and many Grenadians cultivate the trees from which not only nutmeg but the even more valuable surrounding spice, mace, fall in profusion. Popular folklore states that an entire family can live from the proceeds of a single nutmeg tree simply by picking up and selling the fruit which drops from it. Alongside nutmeg, small farmers grow cocoa, bananas and the vegetables which arrive by the vanload in the **St George's** Saturday market.

Such images of tropical self-sufficiency are alluring but conceal a turbulent history and a difficult present. Grenada may look like many people's idea of Eden, but its past consists all too often of upheaval and bloodshed.

Columbus sighted the island on his third expedition in 1498 and called it Concepción. Amerigo Vespucci (who gave his name to the entire continent) passed by several years later and named it Mayo. For some reason not quite understood, the island began to appear on sixteenth-century maps as Granada, later to be modified by the French as La Grenade and anglicized as Grenada. Two small dependencies became attached to Grenada in due course, **Carriacou** (a small fishing island of some 4000 people) and **Petit Martinique** (smaller still).

Like the others of the Lesser Antilles, Grenada was fought over from pre-Columbian times onwards. The Caribs displaced the Arawaks with their usual brutality and fended off the first European attempts at settlement. Expeditions by English colonists in 1609 and French in 1638 ended in bloody confrontation and retreat. In 1650 a group of French settlers from Martinique established a foothold on the island and bartered with the Carib population. Initially friendly relations deteriorated and the Caribs were eventually exterminated. As the indigenous population was driven northwards, Carib warriors made a final stand at a place which is known today as **Sauteurs** or **Leapers' Hill**. Surrounded and unwilling to surrender, forty Caribs jumped from the cliff to their deaths in an ultimate gesture of defiance.

With the Caribs gone, the French developed a plantation economy, where tobacco and indigo, and then sugar, depended upon slave labour. Within a century the island had a hundred sugar mills and 12 000 black slaves. In 1763, however, the British took control of Grenada, lost it again to the French, and finally consolidated their presence in 1783 under the terms of the Treaty of Versailles. Under British rule, nutmeg was introduced from the Dutch East Indies and cocoa replaced sugar as the dominant crop.

France made one last bid to retake Grenada in 1795 in the throes of its revolutionary expansionism. From the territory of Guadeloupe, Victor Hugues and his agents encouraged the remaining French planters in Grenada to rise up against the British. The revolt was led by Julien Fédon, the mulatto son of a French planter and black slave mother who owned a coffee and cocoa estate. Fédon and a force of slaves attacked the town of **Grenville** and then took the British Lieutenant-Governor and fifty other notables hostage. All of the prisoners were executed before British reinforcements could arrive and crush the rebellion. Fédon simply disappeared, fuelling speculation that he had escaped to another island or had drowned in trying to do so. Later, this landowner who freed his own slaves became one of the heroes of a subsequent revolutionary movement.

The abolition of slavery in 1834 and the gradual establishment of a peasant economy did little to break the power of the landowning élite. Poverty and deprivation persisted in the countryside throughout the century following abolition, and the small merchant and professional middle class of the capital, **St George's**, looked down on 'country folk' who were largely illiterate and who spoke a French-based patois. According to Grenadian historian and politician, George Brizan, the 1930s were particularly difficult years:

> 'The 1938 Commission on Economic Conditions among Wage-earners described the peasant's housing as disgraceful, his clothing as wretched and his body as emaciated by hookworms, venereal disease and tuberculosis. His children were ravaged by yaws and gastro-enteritis.'

If the great majority of Grenada's small farmers and agricultural labourers endured conditions such as these, life for the urban middle class was certainly more attractive. In her autobiographical *A Grenadian Childhood* (Extract 4), Nellie Payne ◊ recounts the quaintly old-fashioned customs of 1920s **St George's** in an age before modern amenities arrived. This aura of old-world charm also features prominently in Patrick Leigh Fermor's (◊ Barbados) account of Grenada's capital in the 1940s. In *The Traveller's Tree* (Extract 5), **St George's** takes on the nostalgic charm of a west country market town.

HURRICANE GAIRY

Into the depressed and occasionally violent society of 1940s Grenada stepped Eric Gairy, a black Grenadian who had worked in the oil refineries of Aruba and returned with experience of organizing trade unions. Gairy founded his Mental and Manual Workers' Union in 1949 and the following year led a successful island-wide strike for better pay and conditions for agricultural workers. In 1951 he set up a political party, the Grenada United Labour Party (GULP) and was elected to the colony's Legislative Council in Grenada's first exercise in universal suffrage.

Gairy exerted an extraordinary influence over his following of poor rural Grenadians. He became known simply as 'Leader' and was revered for the way in which he dared to take on the power of the white plantocracy and colonial authorities. A dapper, vain man, normally dressed in white suits, cravats and gold jewellery, Gairy caught the popular imagination of marginalized communities who had never hoped to have such a charismatic spokesman. His methods and style infuriated the island's traditional political class; he was repeatedly suspended from the Legislative Council for disruptive behaviour and was the subject of several commissions into corruption. Yet between 1951 and 1974 he won five out of seven elections, becoming Chief Minister and then Prime Minister as Grenada assumed full independence in 1974.

Gairy's idiosyncratic rule was a potent mix of populism, mysticism and sheer thuggery. He rewarded supporters with jobs and money and threatened opponents. He established a paramilitary group known as the 'Mongoose Gang' who terrorized, beat and sometimes killed those who spoke out against him. He openly admired General Pinochet in Chile and the Duvaliers in Haiti, while repressing any political activists at home. He amassed a considerable fortune from various business interests and also from the dues exacted from his trade union membership. In *Angel* (Extract 2), Grenadian poet and novelist Merle Collins describes the unscrupulous tactics used by 'Leader'. He also, rumour had it, took a more than statesmanlike interest in Grenada's successful entrant to the 1969 Miss World contest.

As time went by, 'Uncle Gairy' became more eccentric and violent in his methods. A state broadcast in October 1972 gives a flavour of the paranoid delusions and mysticism which had replaced his campaigning populism:

> 'I call upon my mystic brothers and sisters, Fratres and Sorores of the Rosicrucian Order, and certainly, all other mystic and spiritual bodies to join in meditative and other metaphysical exercises at this time. We must remove the enemies from our paths of progress. We all owe an obligation for the maintenance of peace and quiet within our dear State.'

In 1975 Gairy embarrassed many Grenadians by delivering a rambling and incoherent speech to the General Assembly of the United Nations on his favourite topic of unidentified flying objects. In 1978 the Government Printery published 'Four Years Today', a poem to celebrate Grenada's fourth anniversary of independence:

> 'The Doctor is interested in humanity
> From the cradle to the cemetery
> A home all around for aged and needy
> Oh how we love the doctor very sincerely.'

'REVO'

Not all Grenadians loved 'Doctor' Gairy as much as his doggerel proclaimed. During 1973 and 1974 opposition to his megalomania hardened with a series of strikes and demonstrations. At the forefront of the anti-Gairy movement was a group of younger Grenadians, some educated abroad, others influenced by radical currents within the regional churches and Black Power. Out of these small groups and individuals emerged the New Jewel Movement (NJM), a small left-wing party committed to ending Gairy's semi-dictatorial rule. Gairy responded brutally; NJM activists were beaten up by the Mongoose Gang and the party was driven underground. In January 1973 Rupert Bishop an anti-Gairy businessman was shot dead as he protected children during a demonstration in **St George's**. His son, Maurice, a London-educated lawyer, was already head of the NJM. Three years later he was elected to parliament and became leader of the opposition after an election in which Gairy had flagrantly cheated.

On 13 March 1979 Gairy's reign came to an end when 46 armed NJM supporters took over the army barracks and radio station in an almost bloodless coup. Gairy was out of the country and had, it is alleged, left instructions for his thugs to deal with the NJM in his absence. In any case, the NJM met with almost no opposition and with a huge outpouring of relief and celebration. Jubilant crowds filled the streets of the capital and Mongoose Gang members were swiftly rounded up and imprisoned.

Once in control, the NJM formed the People's Revolutionary Government (PRG) and pledged to introduce sweeping social reforms after the long years of Gairy's neglect. With limited resources but with considerable popular goodwill, the PRG concentrated on improving the lives and conditions of the island's rural poor. Roads were built or repaired, making it easier for farmers to transport crops. Housing grants were made available, enabling poor families to buy building materials. Free health services were introduced in a series of rural clinics, while Grenada's crumbling schools were patched up and money spent on teacher training and new, more relevant textbooks.

Economically, the PRG sought to develop a mixed economy, where state intervention supported private enterprise. In an attempt to escape the limitations of being a mere exporter of tropical produce, the government set up an agro-industrial plant to produce tinned fruit and conserves. Most importantly, recognizing the importance of tourism as a regional industry, the PRG planned a new international airport capable of handling modern wide-bodied jets.

The emphasis was on popular participation. Policy, even the national budget, was debated at local parish meetings. Organizations were set up to represent women and young people, and rallies, marches and meetings became regular events. Voluntary labour was used for island-wide literacy schemes which brought education to people who had never been to school. For many, particularly the youth of hitherto isolated and depressed villages, it was an exhilarating experience. British teacher and writer, Chris Searle, who worked at the Ministry of Education, recalls the joy of the 'revo':

> 'There was the joy of education, of seeing your children achieving free secondary schooling and your illiterate mother learning how to read and write, the joy of seeing wasted, unemployed youths forming co-operatives and planting the idle land. There was the joy of free health care, of walking to see a doctor or dentist in your local health clinic and knowing that the few dollars you had would stay in your pocket that morning . . .'

The sense of excitement, of living through real change, was an intrinsic part of the Grenadian experience. Yet some were frightened and resentful, others suspicious of the PRG's high-profile anti-imperialist rhetoric. According to critics of the 'revo', young boys with guns became zealots and bullies. Certainly, some critics were treated harshly and found their way all too easily to the prison at **Richmond Hill**. But real human rights abuses were rare, especially given the paranoia which grew out of terrorist bombings and other apparently counter-revolutionary attacks. These attacks even strengthened popular support for the PRG and pride in a small island's sudden international importance. In her famous poem 'Callaloo' (Extract 3), Merle Collins captures the thrill of a people unexpectedly thrown into the political limelight.

With the revolution came a flourishing of language and expression. Literacy classes encouraged older Grenadians to record their memories, and popular education methods rescued patois from the second class status given to it by the colonial system. Poets proliferated (as they did in revolutionary Nicaragua) and the state publishing house issued collections of their work. Some were propaganda but there were also poems and calypsos which reflected popular sentiments and aspirations.

The World Bank, rarely a friend of revolutionary governments, praised the PRG in a 1982 report for 'laying better foundations for growth within the framework of a mixed economy.' Even so, the Reagan administration viewed the Grenadian experiment with the deepest suspicion. After Washington had greeted the 'revo' with hostility, the PRG had found an ally in the form of Cuba, which supplied the island with aid, advice and political support. Grenadians were trained as doctors in Havana, while the Cubans sent engineers and large amounts of money to help construct the new international airport at **Point Salines** near the capital. Hostility between the USA and Grenada sharpened, with the PRG accusing Washington of old-fashioned imperialism and destabilization tactics. The White House, meanwhile, insisted that Grenada was a pawn of Cuban expansionism in the Caribbean and a Marxist threat to the region's stability.

In reality, the PRG did contain hardline Marxists who advocated close links with Cuba and the Soviet Union. But it also contained pragmatists who recognized that a backward rural society could not be dragged into some revolutionary utopia overnight. More significantly, the tiny size of the NJM (it had only 65 full members) put enormous strains on its activists and exacerbated tensions and rivalries within the party. The charismatic and hugely popular Maurice Bishop found himself increasingly under attack from the more doctrinaire Marxist wing of the NJM, led by Bernard Coard. Arguments erupted over Bishop's style of leadership and the direction of the revolution. Coard and his followers suggested joint leadership, with Bishop remaining as a figurehead but Coard's faction dictating policy. As animosities deepened and tension grew, the 'revo' began to unravel.

REVOLUTION IN REVERSE

No Grenadian will ever forget the events of October 1983. As the conflict within the NJM's Central Committee broke out into open warfare, Prime Minister Bishop was arrested and put under house arrest by military personnel loyal to Bernard Coard. Hearing the news, a huge crowd marched on Bishop's house on the 19th and forcibly liberated him, taking him down into **St George's' Market Square** to address the people. As troops were reported to be approaching, Bishop, some of his ministers and crowds of supporters took refuge in **Fort Rupert**, an old colonial bastion which Bishop had had renamed in memory of his murdered father. Suddenly the military opened fire on the fort, spreading panic among the crowd, many of whom leapt over the fort's walls to death or injury. Finally, taking control of the fort, the troops led Bishop, his mistress and Education Minister Jacqueline Creft and several other NJM leaders to an inner courtyard and shot them.

As a stunned island listened in disbelief to the news, General Hudson Austin announced the formation of a Revolutionary Military Council (RMC) and a 24-hour curfew. The RMC ruled for just six days, rounding up opponents and threatening to shoot anybody who broke the curfew. Yet by now US military might was steaming towards Grenada, warships having been diverted from their existing mission in the Lebanon. On the morning of 25 October the first US troops landed on Grenada in a massive show of force. Merle Collins's poem 'Rock-Stone Dance' evokes the sense of horror and powerlessness felt by many Grenadians:

> 'I watched
> like easter-morning
> through the egg-whites
> of our scattered dreams
> the ships that came
> to scorn my tears
> to mock our dreams
> to launch the planes
> that dropped the bombs
> that ripped the walls
> that raped the land
> that burnt the earth
> that crushed the dreams
> that we all built'

The rationale for the invasion was a familiar one: regional stability was under threat and US citizens (a group of students at a second-rate private medical faculty) were in danger. To maintain the constitutional niceties, the Governor-General – who had remained *in situ* throughout the revolution – backdated a letter requesting urgent US assistance. Regional governments, with an eye to cordial relations with Washington, endorsed the invasion and sent a few troops to participate in an 'international peacekeeping force'. Britain turned its back on the invasion, despite its historical links, claiming that it had not been consulted.

The invasion took longer and was bloodier than had been expected. Some Grenadian militiamen fought back, and US troops ill-advisedly attacked a group of Cuban construction workers at the airport who defended themselves. It took five days, 6000 troops, nineteen US fatalities (most in 'friendly fire') and US$75 million of American taxpayers' money to crush what President Reagan fancifully described as 'a growing tyranny'. One US bomb hit the island's mental hospital, killing between 20 and 50 patients. The secret Soviet–Cuban installations which the PRG was thought to have built simply did not exist. The Grenada which the USA invaded was, as it still is, a tiny island of ramshackle villages, pretty beaches and nutmeg trees.

A traumatized island welcomed the 'rescue mission'. Promises of extensive US aid and investment encouraged hopes that Grenada would become

Merle Collins

a showcase of free-market prosperity. Elections were held and US-backed politicians took power. But little of the expected aid bonanza materialized. With the passing of time, Grenada became less and less of a foreign policy priority. Some investors came and then left again, attracted by cheaper labour elsewhere. The island returned to obscurity. Today, Grenada continues to export nutmeg, bananas and cocoa, while tourists arrive at the airport which was finally finished with US money.

A memorial to Maurice Bishop stands in an overgrown graveyard on a hill overlooking the red-tiled warehouses and bustling waterfront of **St George's**. Little else remains of the 'revo' and the man who led it, as his body has never been discovered. Yet for those who lived through it, the period of the PRG remains a powerful memory of what a small island could achieve and how badly the experiment could end. In *Snowflakes in the Sun* (Extract 1), Jean Buffong ◊ lets the elderly couple Uncle Dolphus and Aunt Sarh recall the pain of Grenada's brief moment of fame. That fame is long gone, but many Grenadians are still coming to terms with events which put tiny Grenada, albeit fleetingly, on the world map.

Literary Landmarks

St George's. At the mouth of the harbour stands **Fort George**, now police headquarters and formerly Fort Rupert, where Maurice Bishop and his closest supporters were executed in 1983. The building's grim past is evoked in Howard Fergus's poem 'Lament for Maurice Bishop': 'They say ghosts march past in silence/at Fort Rupert/sire's sepulchre/son's doomed altar/revolution's wasted rampart.'

BOOKLIST

Brizan, George, *Grenada: Island of Conflict*, Zed, London, 1984.

Buffong, Jean, *Snowflakes in the Sun*, The Women's Press, London, 1995. **Extract 1**.

Collins, Merle, *Angel*, The Women's Press, London, 1993. **Extract 2**.

Collins, Merle, 'Callaloo', in *Callaloo: Four Writers From Grenada*, Young World Books, London, 1984. **Extract 3**.

Ferguson, James, *Grenada: Revolution in Reverse*, Latin America Bureau, London, 1990.

Leigh Fermor, Patrick, *The Traveller's Tree: A Journey Through the Caribbean Islands*, Penguin, London, 1984. **Extract 5**.

Lewis, Gordon K., *Grenada: The Jewel Despoiled*, Johns Hopkins University Press, Baltimore, 1987.

Payne, Nellie, *A Grenadian Childhood*, in *Jump-Up-and-Kiss-Me: Two Stories From Grenada*, The Women's Press, London, 1990. **Extract 4**.

Searle, Chris, *Words Unchained: Language and Revolution in Grenada*, Zed, London, 1984.

Extracts

(1) GRENADA: HISTORY

Jean Buffong, *Snowflakes in the Sun*

Returned after years in London, Uncle Dolphus and Aunt Sarh spend much of their time reminiscing with their neighbours, Mr Alvar and Mr Joe. They remember the events of October 1983 and happier times.

The day was slowly closing its door. The early evening buses were starting to go up. The road was alive. 'Evening Miss Dolphus.' 'Howdy Mr Dolphus.' 'Mr Alvar oye you spend the whole day with you neighbour.' 'Aye aye Mr Joe I don't know when I see you.' The greetings from the people passing along the road went on and on. Buses hooted their horns, cars peep a peep peep. The passage on the sea was beginning to be operative. The fishermen were coming in one by one. Soon the island hopper with steelband blasting would be making its way to St George's from Carriacou and Petit Martinique. Life went on and on at its meandering pace.

'Lord that morning when Sarh finished talking on the phone was then she bawled. I tell you my lady bawled, she bawled I thought she was going mad.' Uncle Dolphus again broke the silence.

'Aye aye I bawl oui. How you mean? I bawling and praying, thanking God at the same time.'

'That was a time, that was a time,' Mr Alvar stressed. 'We make history. We always making we own history but that was something else. I expect the whole world was looking at us if it on television. Everybody eye on little Grenada. Some people never hear the name before.'

'When they heard the Americans involved that made them more interested. Watching, waiting, waiting, watching.' Uncle Dolphus raised his voice all of a sudden, vex with somebody or the other.

'People funny, was not the first time they hear about Grenada on the television but they don't remember,' Aunt Sarh started again.

'When?' Devon turned his head yeug to face Aunt Sarh.

'The time when we win the Miss World contest. I don't remember what year but . . .'

'Woye o woye,' Uncle Dolphus clapped his hands. 'Woye o yoye that night you'd think was my wife win beauty contest. Sarh jumped she danced, she danced. I never see her so happy.'

'How you mean, she must feel good. She must feel real good to see she people winning beauty show,' Mr Joe like he wake up. 'And the girl come from right here you know. Right here in Victoria. All Grenadian must feel good that time.'

(2) GRENADA: 'LEADER'

Merle Collins, *Angel*

Regal, Doodsie's brother and Angel's uncle, has been inspired to work on behalf of 'Leader''s trade union. Then he has a disillusioning encounter with his hero.

During the two years that Allan was away, Doodsie closed down the little shop she could not afford to keep stocked with goods. Regal was around at first, organising for the union. Then he and Leader quarrelled.

One night, during a union dance for which Regal had spent his own money organising, intending to get back his outlay from the profits, he said, Leader appeared, stayed a few minutes and then walked through the door carrying the entire bag of money. The dance had been a huge success. Regal, standing with a noisy group of friends, had been watching Leader circulating. He stared for a few shocked moments at the doorway through which the elegant upright back had disappeared. Recovering his presence of mind, he ran outside to talk to Leader. He took from his pocket the list of expenses and the receipts for his purchases. He asked for his money from the total. Leader laughed.

'Man, you are not serious.'

'How you mean? I spent my own money. You could see in here. But the dance successful. Even after I get back mine, the union will still make.'

Leader laughed again, placed one hand on Regal's shoulder.

'Man, you're a joker. Look around.'

He took a few steps back. He stood facing the dance hall outlined in the soft moonlight behind Regal. He flung his arms wide.

'Look at how many people there are out there, man. You think all of those people would turn out if it weren't for me and my union? Don't get greedy, man.'

Leader grinned. He lifted one hand in a gesture of farewell. Regal stared as though mesmerised at the encircling gold of the ring on the middle finger. He watched the car leave. Behind him the music stopped as the band came to the end of a rousing tune. From inside the hall came shouts and whistles. 'Play dat one again!' The night breeze went unexpectedly cold. Regal shivered. The shiver came a second time, unexpectedly. Regal muttered, 'Somebody walkin over my grave.'

(3) GRENADA: REVOLUTION

Merle Collins, *Callaloo*

The Grenada revolution inspired an outpouring of national pride and enthusiasm. Merle Collins uses the spicy national delicacy, callaloo, as a metaphor for this short-lived excitement.

> Mix up
> Like callaloo
> Not no watery callaloo
> But a hot
> thick
> Sweet callaloo
> Burnin' you tongue
> Wid dem
> chunk
> O'dumplin
> Goin'down
> Nice
> An'wid coconut
> Wid
> or widdout deaders
> As de case may be
> As de taste may be
> As de pocket may be
> But sweet
> An'hot

Dat is what
It feel like
To be part o'dis
Revolution reality
O'dis
wakin'up reality
O'dis
No more hidin'you passport
reality
no more
Hangin'you head
An'shufflin you foot
An'trying to hide
Behin'de person
in front o'you
Like little Janet
Behin'she mudder skirt

When de man ask

Way you from?

No more
Playin'you doh hear
Or sayin'some shit like
A . . .
A . . .
A island
Near by Trinidad
Or
A . . .
A few mile
Off Venezuela
But out
Loud an'bole
Like you make de name
Grenada!

An
Wid you head in de air
Becus de world is yours
An'you know is yours
An'you not go be
meek
meek
meek

An'wait to see
If somebody
Go let you
Inherit de earth
Becus you know arready
Is yours
So you say
Loud
An'clear
An'proud
Grenada!

An'you silent scream
Which he mus'be hear
Becus he look up
Into your claimin'eyes
Says
Dat mean
Revolution
Dat mean
Progress
Dat mean
Forward!

Dat mean
Sharin'
An'carin
An'believin'
An'livin'
An'lovin'
Dat mean
A country
In de Caribbean
In Latin America
In de Americas
In de struggle
In de world

Dat mean
Comrade
A people
Like de people
In Cuba
In Nicaragua
In Zimbabwe
In struggling South Africa

In all dem countries
Where de people know
Dat de donkey say
De world aint level
Even donkey heself
Mus'be does shake he head
To feel dem bumps
An know how ting
So hard for some toe
An so sof'
for others

All o'we
In all o'dis world
So mix up
Like callaloo
An'yet
So not like callaloo
An' dat is why
De change
An'de promise o'de change
Is sweet
An'strong
Like de soup
When Grannie
Cover it down dey
An let it
Consommé
Like dat
Hot
Sweet
Burnin'
Heavy
Heavy
Callaloo!

(4) ST GEORGE'S : THE NIGHT BRIGADE

Nellie Payne, *A Grenadian Childhood*

In the days before modern sewerage reached St George's, a hardy band of women – the Night Brigade – did an unenviable job.

How well I remember the Night Brigade! You see, we were then still literally in the dark. No electricity, no sewerage system, very little ice.

For lights we used kerosene lamps, candles and Coleman gas lamps and lanterns.

Ice was made by an engineer called Mr Eric Smith and amusing tales circulated in St George's of people buying a pennyworth of ice and sending it by schooner to their families in the eastern town of Grenville who felt cheated on receiving a soggy piece of newspaper; of others packing a few pounds in their suitcases to take as a treat to their less fortunate friends in Sauteurs, another town twenty-five miles away in the north of the island: on arrival they found their clothes mildewed and ruined!

. . . No sewerage meant pôt chambres under the beds. There were enamelled ones and china ones. The china ones were beautifully decorated by the artist in the family and I recall bending forward to examine a spray of forget-me-nots, overbalancing and making a horrible mess on the floor . . .

The closet was a room in which there was a throne-like chair with a hole in the seat. Under the hole a giant pail stood, waiiting to receive the contents of pôt chambres . . .

The women who toted the pails were the simple, fearless type with ribald humour.

They made a weird procession, all jacketed and with large, floppy headgear. With pails, buckets and kerosene tins balanced on their heads, they performed their duties with incessant chatter.

Most people tried to be off the streets when the Night Brigade passed. If one happened to encounter them, the scented handkerchief, ever in readiness, was put to one's nose and one could expect a comment from one of the carriers.

Mother, on leaving the library at closing time – nine p.m. – put her hanky to her face as she saw the procession approaching. A voice from the bottom of a pan cackled, 'No stap yo'nose, is you own mess ah hauling.'

We never knew who those women were, but I do know we changed our woman once as Cook told Mummy, 'She dead, ah get anoder one for you ma'am.' . . .

Sometimes the bottom of a bucket would cave in and the woman to whom this happened (and after her head was clear) would say, 'Blarst! Is only boiled corn and split peas dey eat dis week, oui!'

(5) St George's: Nostalgia

Patrick Leigh Fermor, *The Traveller's Tree*

Arriving in the capital after the sprawling chaos of Trinidad's Port of Spain, Leigh Fermor is charmed by St George's small-town ambiance.

The capital of Grenada and the pinnacled belfries under the rain, the steep streets and the wet stone columns and fanlights of Adam houses, the glimpses along the lanes of a grey and turbulent sea – all this resembled a beautiful eighteenth-century Devonshire town in mid-winter. The car drove into the yard of a small hotel that might have been a coaching inn.

Dashing indoors through the downpour, we expected to plunge into a world of crops, goloshes, toby-jugs, superannuated advertisements for Apollinaris Water, and copies of Pears' Cyclopaedia; which was, indeed, more or less what we found.

By the time we woke up, the rain had stopped and the little capital wore a different, but no less charming, aspect. How dissimilar everything in Grenada was from the immensity, the trams and the ugliness of Port of Spain! The change in atmosphere, tempo, mood and scenery was complete.

Like Roseau, St George's is a large village that has evolved easily and slowly into a small country town, but the houses, instead of wood and lattice and shingle, are built of stone: fine, solid dwellings, with graceful balustraded staircases running up to pilastered doorways supporting fanlights and pediments. The burnished knockers and door-knobs and letterboxes reflect the morning sunlight. So steep is the hillside on which the town clusters that the cobbled lanes and streets twist in many directions, and it was only by climbing to the top of the town that we could get an idea of its economy as a whole.

The coast is a succession of volcanic craters, of which one of the largest, the Carenage, is the harbour of St George's. The capital itself is built on the steep crater's rim, which is submerged at its outer segment to form a gap over which the ships can sail out and in; the broken circumference, emerging from the water in bluffs, ascends under its load of houses and churches, to unite with the forested slopes inland. Lagoons engrail the coast with pale blue crescents and discs, and from their landward circumferences the island soars in a steep and regular geometry of volcanic peaks. Old fortresses lie along the hilltops commanding the town, and on the escarpment of the crater's rim that ends and completes St George's – rising into a final knoll before its steep plunge under water – the old French Fort (later re-baptized Fort George) rears its defences.

Biographical and literary notes

BUFFONG, Jean (1943–). Born and educated in Grenada, Buffong moved to Britain in 1962 and has since worked as a civil servant. She is active in various writers' associations and community arts groups. Her first published work was *Jump-Up-and-Kiss-Me*, 1990, a fictional account of Grenadian village life which appeared alongside Nellie Payne's *A Grenadian*

Childhood. Snowflakes in the Sun (Extract 1) tells of the return to the island from Britain of a retired couple and their reintegration into a rural community after the rigours and alienation of years abroad.

COLLINS, Merle (1950–). Merle Collins is Grenada's best known writer, producing both fiction and poet-

Jean Buffong

ry. Born in Aruba and brought up in Grenada, she studied at the University of the West Indies and has a PhD in Government from the London School of Economics. She worked first as a teacher, then during the period of the People's Revolutionary Government, worked at the Ministry of Foreign Affairs and was a member of the National Women's Organization. She was a popular performer at rallies and meetings, reading poems such as 'Callaloo' (Extract 3) which draw upon elements of patois and everyday vernacular. After the collapse of the PRG, Merle Collins moved to London, where she performed her poetry with the group New Dawn. She has contributed to several anthologies and has edited a collection of writing by black women in Britain. Her first novel *Angel* (Extract 2), traces the lives of three generations of Grenadian women from the social unrest of the 1940s to the US invasion of October 1983. Angel, the daughter of humble parents, goes to university in Jamaica and returns, politicized, to play a role in the revolution. Through her, her

mother Doodsie and her grandmother Ma Ettie, we follow the vicissitudes of a family under strain and the political development of a woman, impatient with her parents' attitudes but ultimately committed to them and her community. Merle Collins is also the author of a collection of short stories, *Rain Darling*, 1990, and a poetry collection, *Rotten Pomerack*, 1992. She now teaches at the University of Kentucky.

LEIGH FERMOR, Patrick (see under Barbados).

PAYNE, Nellie. Payne was born and grew up in Grenada, 'blessed with a West Indian father of African descent and an English mother.' She moved to Trinidad when she married, but returned to Grenada in 1978, when she started working at the School of Continuing Studies at the University of the West Indies. Her account of growing up in a middle-class family in 1920s Grenada, *A Grenadian Childhood* (Extract 4), is full of colourful anecdotes and a sense of long-lost innocence.

Nellie Payne

BARBADOS

'The Barbadian is a problem . . . he is English in a way that the rest of us are not . . . Barbados is a sunburnt piece of England, modified by the tropics, but still and stubbornly a corner of the English countryside, and Barbadians, black and white, have clung to that Englishness.'

John Hearne (Jamaican novelist)

'Little England'. 'Bimshire'. The quaint and hackneyed nicknames given to Barbados proclaim a quintessential and nostalgic Englishness about the island. Tourist brochures often describe it as some tropical version of the home counties, where tea is invariably taken at four o'clock and cricket is played on the village green. Nameplaces add to the illusion – coastal resorts are called Worthing, Hastings, Dover or Brighton. Other names to be seen on signposts include Newbury, Bath and Newcastle.

The idea that Barbados, more than thirty years after independence, is still somehow part of England has become a recurring motif among travel writers and visitors. Some have compared the island's gentle, undulating hills to the more familiar rural landscape of Dorset. Others see in the rugged Atlantic coast a replica of Cornwall or Scotland. In **Bridgetown**, the capital, the comparison is intensified by the presence of a Trafalgar Square, where a statue of Lord Nelson stands among ranks of eager taxi drivers, erected 36 years before its London equivalent.

The 'Englishness' of Barbados is not, of course, simply the invention of whimsical visitors or the local tourist board. Uniquely among the Caribbean territories, the island underwent 340 years of unbroken British rule. Unlike its neighbours, it was never colonized or fought over by Spanish, French or Dutch competitors and so experienced a continuum of colonial influence which is unparalleled in the region.

The evidence of this influence is difficult to ignore. Religious, sporting, culinary preferences all reflect the long domination of London. Barbados is overwhelmingly Anglican, its often pretty parish churches built in 'tropical Church of England' style. Cricket, horse racing and (English) football are the national sports. Hotels offer such English staples as shepherd's pie or

311

FACT BOX

AREA: 430 sq km
POPULATION: 264 000
CAPITAL: Bridgetown
LANGUAGES: English
FORMER COLONIAL POWER: Britain
INDEPENDENCE: 1966
PER CAPITA GDP: US$6240

Yorkshire pudding to their guests, many of whom come from Britain. Barbadians, known also as Bajans, pride themselves on their 'Westminster-style' parliamentary democracy which has provided peaceful and orderly government since independence in 1966. The British Queen still appears on postage stamps as the nominal head of state.

Some travellers have found in this apparent parody of England a disconcerting, even irritating, reflection of the least attractive qualities of the 'mother country'. Patrick Leigh Fermor ◊, for instance, memorably compared Barbadian expatriate life in *The Traveller's Tree* (Extract 9) to a home counties golf club, while the Guyanese writer Edgar Mittelholzer, an acerbic observer of late British colonial society, painted a far from attractive picture of social snobbery in his *With a Carib Eye*. But these accounts, from the 1950s, to some extent predate the waning of British influence in Barbados and elsewhere in the Caribbean. Today, cultural inspiration is more likely to come from North America, and Barbadian television, like the region as a whole, is filled with CNN broadcasting and US game shows.

Not all visiting writers, moreover, have subscribed to the 'Little England' interpretation of Barbados. When Aldous Huxley ◊ passed through the island *en route* to Central America, it was the unfamiliarity of the place, with its tropical langour, pungent smells and strange night-time noises, which affected him. In *Beyond the Mexique Bay* (Extract 8), Huxley's vision is not one of comforting Englishness, but of 'unspeakable melancholy'.

Nor is the colonial legacy uncritically accepted by all Barbadians. In 1995 a columnist in the *Barbados Advocate* proposed removing Lord Nelson from his pedestal in the centre of **Bridgetown**. The statue, he wrote, was an offensive symbol of slavery (which Nelson enthusiastically defended) and should be replaced with a Barbadian hero. Elsewhere, artists and writers have successfully introduced a revaluation of Barbadian cultural influences, stressing instead the traditions of African art and music and the permanence of 'resistance culture'.

SUGAR, SERVANTS AND SLAVES

The myth of 'Little England' necessarily plays down the inevitably cruel history of slavery and exploitation which has made Barbados what it is today. If the first English colonizers encountered no indigenous people on the island, it was probably because the communities there had already been raided and displaced by Spanish slavers before the mid-sixteenth century or had fled to the greater safety of neighbouring islands where mountainous terrain offered greater protection. In any event, archaeological research has revealed the presence of successive waves of Amerindian settlers from mainland South America up until the arrival of Europeans. Portuguese adventurers visited the island in the 1530s and named it *os Barbados* ('the bearded ones') because of the Bearded Fig trees which they found on the beaches.

The flat limestone topography of Barbados separates it from the volcanic and mountainous islands of the Windward chain, and it stands to the east of the chain, almost apart from the rest of the Caribbean islands. Its position and the prevailing easterly winds seemingly made the island extremely difficult to attack during the heyday of colonial rivalry. Hence Barbados remained English and never underwent 'foreign' invasion or occupation.

By the time the earliest English colonizing expedition arrived in 1627, the island was reportedly uninhabited. This enabled the colonists to escape attack from indigenous populations and to engage in the lucrative business of growing and exporting tobacco. When tobacco prices dropped in 1631, planters turned to cotton and then to indigo. Sugar-cane only began to appear as a major crop in the mid-1630s.

The absence of indigenous people also meant that there was no readily available labour force on the island. As black slaves were at first hard to obtain and expensive, the planters opted for white indentured labourers from Britain. In the 1630s and 1640s thousands of indentured servants arrived, having agreed to seven-year contracts of labour with the landowners. Many of the restrictions and hardships associated with slavery were experienced by the poor white servants, who were in essence the property of their masters.

The importation of African slaves really accelerated as indentured servants began to become more expensive and slaves were perceived as better value. Between 1640 and 1700 it has been estimated that Barbadian planters imported some 135 000 slaves. Their role was to work on the large sugar estates which began to emerge as the viability of large-scale production became apparent. With its flat terrain, Barbados was ideally suited to plantation sugar-cane cultivation. Furthermore, conflict in Brazil between Portuguese settlers and Dutch merchants meant that Brazilian sugar, which had accounted for 80% of the European market, became scarce, allowing Barbadian planters to export sugar at attractive prices. Dutch capital and technology helped the industry to develop, and in return the local planters bought more black slaves from the Dutch. It was a profitable business; between the 1650s and 1670s Barbados was the pre-eminent British sugar colony, accounting for 65% of Caribbean exports.

Rich and Poor Whites

The sugar boom created a generation of local magnates, who dominated Barbadian politics and society. Some of these families, known as the 'plantocracy', maintained their property and interests into the nineteenth and twentieth centuries and still form part of the social élite. Land holdings became more concentrated as richer planters took over smallholdings previously owned by freed servants or poorer farmers. The 1680 census revealed that 54% of the island's land was controlled by 7% of property-owners and that this wealthy minority owned 60% of the island's slaves.

According to Barbadian historian Hilary Beckles, the plantocracy took over political power in the colony and tried to secure as much autonomy in financial and government matters from Britain as was possible. At the same time, the landed gentry adopted aristocratic airs, seeking and receiving knighthoods and baronetcies from London. In this way, they created a rigid social hierarchy and strong sense of class which, say many Barbadians, has survived to the present day.

Other white settlers were less fortunate. As sugar prices declined in the 1660s, thousands of poorer whites decided to abandon Barbados, with its shortage of land, for other colonies, in mainland America or in the Caribbean. The wealthy often returned to England to live comfortably as absentee landowners, but the poor usually moved on in search of another, more promising, opportunity.

Others, however, remained. Brought over as indentured servants, they were unable to acquire their own properties at the end of their contract and formed a sort of rural sub-class, disparaged and exploited by the plantocracy. Some poor whites formed the ranks of the local militia, set up to control the growing black slave population. To their number were added a group of approximately 100 prisoners, transported to Barbados in 1686 in the wake of the abortive Monmouth rebellion and the infamous 'Bloody Assizes' of Judge Jeffreys. The poor whites, known also pejoratively as 'redlegs', formed communities in the more marginal, less fertile areas of the island. Visitors were often shocked by the squalor of these settlements and by the apparent degradation of the poor whites. During the 1790s, for instance, Dr George Pinckard toured the region and was dismayed by the poverty he encountered:

> 'Besides the great number of hospitable mansions found on the plantations, in the different parts of the country, many humble dwellings attract the notice of the traveller . . . They are the cottages of a poorer order of white people – of obscure individuals, remote from the great class of merchants and planters, and who obtain a scanty livelihood by cultivating a small patch of earth, and breeding-up poultry or what they term stock for the markets. They are descended from European settlers, but from misfortune, or misconduct, in some of the race, are reduced to a state far removed from independence.'

More than 150 years later, Patrick Leigh Fermor saw in the poor whites a pathetic and decadent community, unable to improve its situation in the same way as blacks had achieved. In *The Traveller's Tree* he distinguishes between the white people of the French islands and those seemingly doomed to extinction in Barbados:

> 'These pale, Nordic people, standing barefoot in the dust with loads of sugar-cane on their heads and gazing listlessly as the trim limousines go bowling past, are pathetic and moving figures, and their aspect has none of the cheerfulness of the inhabitants of the Saints or of the pleasant solidity of the whites of the Guadeloupean hinterland. They look like poor devils and nothing else.'

SLAVERY AND RESISTANCE

Even more desperate was the lot of the black slaves, who by the beginning of the eighteenth century outnumbered whites by more than three to one. As elsewhere, a structure of control and repression was put in place to contain this potentially revolutionary majority. A militia patrolled the island, punishments for escape and sabotage were fierce, and the price of rebellion was public execution. Even so, insurrections took place in 1649, 1675 and 1692. In the eighteenth century, uprisings were much less common than in other slave societies, probably because Barbados, as an important military and naval base, had a more visible and developed machinery of repression than elsewhere. There is some evidence, too, that slavery itself was less harsh in Barbados than in other territories. Nonetheless, escape from the plantation was a common form of resistance, even if it was difficult to remain at large for long in the flat and well-populated Barbadian countryside.

As the move towards abolition gathered pace, inspired as much by the decreasing profitability of slavery as humanitarian concerns, Barbados was facing economic crisis. Poor sugar yields and low prices had ruined many smaller planters; a series of droughts and hurricanes had disrupted production. There were periods of high prices, especially when rival producers were experiencing their own difficulties, but the general trend was downwards. Nonetheless, in 1754 Barbadian-born Nathaniel Weekes published what is probably the first long (1000 lines) poem in the English language on a Caribbean theme. Entitled *Barbados*, the poem sings the praises of sugar-cane and urges the planters to treat their slaves humanely:

> 'To urge the Glory of your *Cane*'s success,
> Rich be your Soil, and well manur'd with Dung,
> Or, *Planters!* what will all your Labours yield?
> A faithless Profit, and a barren Crop.'

Faced with the abolition of the slave trade towards the end of the eighteenth century, Barbadian planters began to see the logic of improving slaves' conditions. In particular, they wanted to maintain their stock of labour by persuading female slaves to bear as many children as possible. Payments were made and work concessions were offered as incentives to women to have children. Through the process of 'amelioration' the planters believed that they could retain a system of slavery even after the trade itself had come to an end. As breeding replaced purchasing, Barbados became self-sufficient in slaves and was able to re-export those who arrived from Africa during the last decade of the slave trade.

But despite a gradual softening of conditions, the slaves themselves were impatient for emancipation. The example of the Haitian revolution of 1791–1802 reverberated as far as Barbados, as did reports of abolitionist meetings and pressure in England. While the planters nervously noted increased hostility among their slaves, they did not suspect that a full-fledged rebellion was possible.

Such a rebellion broke out on Easter Sunday 1814 and rapidly covered half the island. Canefields were burned as the slaves signalled their movements to one another. In her short story 'Freedom Come' (Extract 4), June Henfrey ◊ reconstructs the role of Nanny, reputedly one of the rebellion's ringleaders and an associate of the slave leader, Bussa. In the event the insurrection was rapidly put down, and an estimated 1000 slaves were killed by militia or in subsequent court martials.

A series of reforms followed the uprising, as the conservative Barbadian plantocracy tried to put off the arrival of full emancipation. When this became inevitable, they settled for compensation and a period of apprenticeship during which the 'freed' slaves continued to work for them without wages. On 1 August 1838 final emancipation took place and slavery ended in Barbados.

Trade and Emigration

Determined to cling on to economic and political power, the plantocracy made few concessions to their former slaves in the wake of emancipation. Labour laws favouring the plantation owners were quickly introduced, as was draconian legislation against 'vagrancy'. Land was all but unavailable to the newly emancipated blacks, as most of it was owned by the large planter families, and many former slaves had no choice but to return to the fields as labourers. Others emigrated, to British Guiana and other colonies where employment prospects were believed to be better.

Despite their gloomy predictions, the planters did not meet with economic catastrophe in the wake of abolition. Sugar prices held up, and it was not until the 1880s and the appearance of subsidized European beet sugar that the Barbadian industry really declined. At the same time, a rising merchant class, based in **Bridgetown**, began to ally itself with the traditional plantocracy, strengthening the old élite with its growing financial and political power. At the beginning of the twentieth century,

Barbadian planters and merchants also began to trade in significant terms with the US and Canada, lessening their dependence on the British market.

Increasing numbers of poor Barbadians, meanwhile, continued to emigrate. Between 1904 and 1914, an estimated 20 000 Barbadian labourers went to work on the Panama Canal. Many 'Panama men' returned with considerable savings, able to start small businesses or buy land. Those who remained were able to bargain for better wages, as the planters saw the local pool of labour diminish. The Panama experience had widespread consequences, forcing the planters to modernize the sugar industry through fear of inadequate labour and creating the beginnings of a significant black middle class.

Towards Independence

As in other Caribbean countries, the move towards political independence in Barbados can be traced back to the social conflicts of the 1930s. A stubborn plantocracy still dominated the island's legislature, blocking reforms wherever possible, while an increasingly impatient black and coloured middle class was pressing for representation. In 1937 an incident occurred which sparked off a series of important social changes. Clement Payne, an associate of the Trinidadian trade unionist Uriah 'Buzz' Butler, arrived in Barbados in order to set up a similar trade union organization in the island. The government, alarmed at his popularity, had him arrested on a technicality and deported. His supporters were furious and rioted in **Bridgetown** and country districts. Widespread looting took place and crowds smashed shop windows and cars. Eventually, after police shot dead 14 demonstrators and arrested more than 400, an uneasy peace returned. A subsequent royal commission identified poverty and unemployment as key factors in the social unrest and recommended reforms such as pensions and trade union rights.

Out of the Clement Payne affair emerged the political movement which still dominates the island's politics. Formed in 1938, the Progressive League (later to become the Barbados Labour Party) represented the reformist aspirations of the black and coloured middle class. Its leader, Grantley Adams, called for gradual social change but stopped short of demanding the nationalization of the sugar industry. Elected to the House of Assembly in 1934, Adams and his party and trade union worked for the constitutional changes which led to internal self-government in 1958. Adams was the first and only Prime Minister of the short-lived Federation of the West Indies between 1958 and 1962. His allegedly autocratic tendencies forced some BLP members to leave, setting up the rival Democratic Labour Party (DLP) in 1955. Under the leadership of Errol Barrow, the DLP won elections in 1961 and steered Barbados towards full independence in November 1966.

THE ANTI-COLONIAL VOICE

The years preceding full independence, when educational reforms and greater social mobility were challenging the old hierarchy, produced a number of important literary works which explored the nature of colonial society in Barbados. Two very different novels of childhood reflect the still enormous gap between the white planter class and the majority of poor black Barbadians. *Christopher* (Extract 2), by Geoffrey Drayton ◊, explores the world of a planter's young son as he comes to terms with personal relationships and the social reality beyond his comfortable daily life. In one scene, Christopher is approached by a beggar and tells him he has spent his pocket money:

> 'The head withdrew with a shrill guffaw. "Heh! That's rich," it said. "Spent it all, he says." The voice approached again, menacing. "Spent it all didja? Well, do you know where you got it all to spend? – From bastards like me, slaving from first of January to last of December for you friggers . . ." '

George Lamming ◊'s *In the Castle of My Skin* (Extract 3), published six years before *Christopher*, is also a novel of childhood, but one which tells of the growing understanding on the part of a poor village boy of the mediocrity and occasional repression of colonial society. Beyond the narrator's observations of the village characters and the forces that they represent lies the wider theme of a social order in the process of transformation. As distant **Bridgetown** is shaken by riots, G and his fellow schoolchildren learn of 'Little England''s undying loyalty to the 'mother country'.

This period is also atmospherically evoked by Austin Clarke ◊ in his memoir of Barbados during World War Two, *Growing Up Stupid Under the Union Jack* (Extract 7). For Clarke, the absurdity of the colonial education system prefigures the end of British domination in Barbados. Mocking the 'Little England' myth, the narrator admits: 'We all wanted to be either Americans, or else to live in America. So, we lived through the defeats and victories of the British Empire and her allies.'

BAJAN CULTURE

The founding of the literary magazine *Bim* by Frank Collymore ◊ in 1942 gave generations of Barbadian and other Caribbean writers an important outlet for their poetry, short stories and criticism. Given as its title the nickname applied to the planters by their slaves, *Bim* achieved regional influence and helped to launch the careers of several leading authors. Collymore himself was among other things an accomplished writer of short stories and keen social observer; his 'RSVP to Mrs Bush-Hall' (Extract 5) combines these attributes in a comic dissection of snobbery and pretentiousness.

One author whose work first appeared in *Bim* is Timothy Callender ◊,

Timothy Callender

whose collection of short stories, *It So Happen* (Extract 6) introduces
another aspect of Bajan culture. Callender's focal point is the Barbadian
village, with its gallery of eccentrics and rum shop loud-mouths. Drawing
on local vernacular and a particularly Bajan sense of comedy, Callender
exposes the foibles of his fictional village in a series of moral fables, where
sins are usually punished in humorous fashion.

Alongside the island's tradition of comic and satirical writing stands a growing collection of poetry. Probably the most important contemporary Barbadian poet is Kamau Brathwaite ◊, who has been producing highly acclaimed and demanding work since the 1960s. In *Sun Poem* (Extract 1), Brathwaite adopts a more than usually autobiographical tone with his evocation of childhood in rural Barbados. Brathwaite has spoken of his distaste for the 'official' version of Barbadian culture which tends to downplay the island's African legacy and the determining role of slavery. As a corrective, his poetry draws on his personal experience of Africa and the more authentic identity which he discovered there. Among Africans, he has written:

> 'I came to connect my history with theirs, the bridge of my mind now linking Atlantic and ancestor, homeland and heartland. When I turned to leave, I was no longer a lonely individual talent . . . And I came home to find that I had not really left. That it was still Africa; Africa in the Caribbean. The middle passage had now guessed its end.'

Brathwaite's consciousness of his African antecedents is perhaps typical of a wider reassessment of the past in Barbadian popular culture. One of the island's most popular festivals Crop-Over, a weekend celebration of parades and calypsos which leads up to Kadooment Day on the first Monday of August, is based on the slaves' traditional rejoicing at the end of the cane-cutting period. Now commercialized and aimed at the tourism industry, the resurrection of the festival in the 1970s was at least a gesture of recognition to Barbados's painful past.

THE COST OF SUCCESS

Today Barbados is one of the Caribbean's success stories, with per capita income levels which equal those of such countries as Greece or Portugal. It is a highly literate society, and nearly all Barbadians have access to piped water and a telephone. In the early 1990s the economy underwent a recession, due largely to economic depression in the US which adversely affected the tourist trade. Since 1994, however, growth has returned and the economic outlook is positive. Although social inequalities still exist and a remnant of the old white plantocracy still holds disproportionate power, Barbados has progressed immeasurably since the conflicts of the 1930s. A stable multi-party democracy, it has, in the words of respected journalist Rickey Singh, avoided the corrosion of 'personality cults and partisan politics.'

Sugar is now much less important than manufacturing and tourism, and Barbados struggles to produce the 54 000-tonne quota which it is allowed to export at preferential prices into the European Community. Many planters have abandoned sugar altogether, selling their land for new housing or tourism development. At the same time, Barbados has built an important manufacturing sector, producing foods, clothing and electrical goods for domestic and export markets.

But the biggest money-earner on the island is without doubt tourism, which brought US$550 million into Barbados in 1995. About half a million tourists come to the island each year, and about the same number arrive by cruise ship for a day trip. All around the south and west coasts an almost unbroken succession of hotels, guesthouses and restaurants cater to the tourist invasion.

But with a population density of 1600 per square mile, Barbados is one of the world's most crowded countries and the tourism industry has taken a heavy toll on the island's natural resources. Few places, except perhaps on the more remote east coast, are untouched by tourism. In 'Skeete's Bay, Barbados' (Extract 10), St Lucian poet John Robert Lee paints an elegaic picture of one of the island's last 'unspoilt' idylls.

LITERARY LANDMARKS

The rugged Atlantic coast of Barbados is more picturesque and less developed than the southern coastline with its rows of hotels. The small villages of **Cattlewash** and **Bathsheba** feature in the poetry of Kamau Brathwaite, representing the importance of the sea and fishing communities in his evocation of a Barbadian childhood. Near **Bathsheba** is the legendary **Atlantis Hotel**, currently somewhat dilapidated, where the outstanding Barbadian novelist George Lamming resides when he returns to the island. Further south and slightly inland stands **Codrington College**, one of the Caribbean's most striking historical buildings. Founded at the beginning of the eighteenth century by Christopher Codrington, Governor-General of the Leeward Islands and *de facto* owner of the island of Barbuda, the College was for many years a seminary where Barbadians and others trained for the Anglican priesthood. Patrick Leigh Fermor described it as follows: 'In a hollow beyond a spinney of tall mahogany, south of the township of Bathsheba, a beautiful Palladian building, reclining dreamily on the shores of a lake among lawns and balustrades and great shady trees, suddenly appeared, its columns and pediments conjuring up, in the afternoon sunlight, some enormous country seat in the Dukeries.'

BOOKLIST

The following selection includes the extracted titles in this chapter as well as other titles for further reading. In general, paperback editions are given when possible. For most of the extracted works, the original publisher in English can be found in 'Acknowledgments and Citations' at the end of the volume, as can the exact location of the extracts and the editions from which they are taken.

Beckles, Hilary, *A History of Barbados: From Amerindian Settlement to Nation-State*, Cambridge University Press, Cambridge, 1990.

Brathwaite, Kamau, *Sun Poem*, Oxford University Press, Oxford, 1982. **Extract 1**.

Callender, Timothy, *It So Happen*, Heinemann, Oxford, 1991. **Extract 6**.

Clarke, Austin, *Growing Up Stupid Under the Union Jack*, McClelland and Stewart, Toronto, 1980. **Extract 7**.

Collymore, Frank, 'RSVP to Mrs Bush-Hall', in *The Man Who Loved Attending Funerals and Other Stories*, Heinemann, Oxford, 1993. **Extract 5**.

Drayton, Geoffrey, *Christopher*, Heinemann, London, 1972. **Extract 2**.

Henfrey, June, 'Freedom Come', in *Coming Home and Other Stories*, Peepal Tree, Leeds, 1994. **Extract 4**.

Hoyos, F.A., *Barbados: A History from Amerindians to Independence*, Macmillan Caribbean, London, 1978.

Huxley, Aldous, *Beyond the Mexique Bay*, Flamingo, London, 1988. **Extract 8**.

Lamming, George, *In The Castle of My Skin*, Longman, Harlow, 1987. **Extract 3**.

Lee, John Robert, 'Skeete's Bay, Barbados', in Anne Walmsley and Nick Caistor (eds), *Facing the Sea: A New Anthology from the Caribbean Region*, Heinemann, Oxford, 1986. **Extract 10**.

Leigh Fermor, Patrick, *The Traveller's Tree: A Journey Through the Caribbean Islands*, Penguin, London, 1984. **Extract 9**.

Mittelholzer, Edgar, *With a Carib Eye*, Secker & Warburg, London, 1958.

Extracts

(1) BARBADOS: CHILDHOOD
Kamau Brathwaite, from *Sun Poem*

*Brathwaite's autobiographical evocation of a school outing captures
all the excitement and euphoria of the event.*

ii

to cattlewash on the sunday school excursion . . .

expectation blowing up like a balloon for weeks before until at last: d-day:
bank-holiday: with all the boys in coloured home-made shirts now blowing
out behind like yellow pink red blue balloons . . .

o all the best buses in the world were there

sunny loo . . .black belle . . .breakneck jane . . .

iii

aaaamen
to the godspeed prayers in the church and then they were off

looking at everything they passed/shouting at everything they passed/
clapping at everything they passed/bugle horns blowing as the world
unfurled . . .

the jumping houses/the hedges in bunches/telephone poles like slim/
crucifixions dip up/dipping down/shining black wires/dip up/dipping down/
thread on a spool . . .

*we're going to a wonderful place
we're going to a won der ful place
over the hills and far away
we're going to a wonder full place*

the jumping houses/the hedges in bunches/scampering lady-hens/lifting
their skirts/fields spinning past them/like painted wheels/green red brown/
green yellow and brown/the lanes between them/ turning like spokes

*we're going to a won der ful place
we're going to a wonder full place*

over the hills and far away
we're going to a wonderful place

o the trees and/the breeze and/the fields spinning past clear/holiday
weather/and mother behind in the following bus/with baskets of sweet-
drink and/conkey and/ham so they shouted when/there was shouting to
do/and sang nearly all the songs that they knew/and they clapped and were
happy like birds in a bush/till well away in the morning

18

All the boys in the sunday school bus lived on the sunset side of the island
where the land was low and the sea was calm except in september when the
    hurricane
season roof-ripping came and the fishermen hauled their boats up the beach
    as high

as their boats would go. but the rest of the year it was calm. the west
of the island was calm. the land where the little boys lived
was as calm and as green and as soft as the sea at low tide

(2) Barbados: Childhood
Geoffrey Drayton, *Christopher*

Christopher, a young white boy, confides in his black nurse, Gip,
that he has had nightmares.

'Oh, dear!' Gip raised her eyes to heaven, then looking at Cinder for
sympathy. 'What you been dreaming now?'

Christopher decided that he'd better not tell. Nightmares did not
frighten him in the morning; and he did not want to be told about the
cholera again.

'Witches and grubs and things,' he volunteered in an off-hand fashion –
they being his pet aversions. Perhaps, though, he'd better be a little more
specific. 'I was swallowed by a – a – cow,' he added.

Gip looked doubtful.

'A cow can't swallow nothing big as you . . .'

Gip asked no more. She would not encourage him in his fancies. She did
not believe he had dreamt about cows at all. And Master Chris was
altogether too fanciful. For her little distinction lay between imagining and
lying. Both condemned their perpetrators to eternity of hell-fire –
somewhere inside the earth, where Satan kept his kingdom, as the negro
pastor had taught her. They never said anything much about hell in the
parish church where she took Christopher at eleven o'clock; but the

Sunday-night sessions at her own chapel had made her very aware of its existence.

This was not the Sunday for church however. Once a month the family had breakfast with a sister of Mr Stevens who lived by the sea – a huge breakfast at eleven o'clock, consisting of black pudding, souse, and other kinds of offal from the pigs that had been killed on the preceding Saturdays. Christopher was not interested in the breakfast. But he loved the sea, and felt in kinship with its infinite moods and inhabitants. He knew this was one of those special Sundays because Gip took a brightly coloured shirt out of the drawer instead of a white one. He would wear sandals and no socks, and could be perfunctory about washing because he would wash in the sea later. He barely restrained himself from jumping up and down. It seemed such a long time since he had been to the sea.

(3) Barbados: The English

George Lamming, *In The Castle of My Skin*

The narrator, G, has gone on a crab-hunt with his friends Bob, Trumper and Boy Blue. The expedition turns into an impromptu history quiz.

'But what about America?' Trumper asked.

'America?' Bob got up from the rocks.

'You talking about the olden times,' he said. 'You talkin' about a way back in 1492. But Barbados wus discovered by the English in 16 something or the other, an' that is modern times.'

'An' who discover America?' Trumper asked.

'The English too,' Bob said quickly.

'An' where the English come from?' Boy Blue asked.

'From England,' Bob said, making the question seem ridiculously simple. And now we knew we had him cornered.

'An' where's England?' Boy Blue asked.

Bob smiled and to our utter astonishment spoke with a kind of religious conviction: 'Barbados or Little England, an island of coral formation set like a jewel in the Caribbean Sea.'

We heard the words, and we knew they weren't Bob's.

'That ain't in no Michael John hist'ry book,' Trumper said.

''Cause 'tis no joke,' Bob answered. ' 'Tis facts. Facts.'

We walked away from the sea in silence through the hot afternoon. The surface of the street was soft where the asphalt had cracked and swollen in the sun. We crossed our heads with paper and grape leaves. Everything was quiet and hot, but the wet and ooze of the sea. The tide turned gently till it ruined itself against the rocks. In the distance beyond the harbouring ships the water was level and still. On one side of the street the school garden blazed with roses in the sun. Fire spilled from the petals along the green leaves and down the thorny barks of the black branches. The grass was a strong brown, low-cropped like a moustache in stubble. On the side by the sea the shade was deep and soothing over the esplanade. It was an open square with beaches and a grass plot trimmed into a circle around the small stone fountain. The area was gravelled with a surface of asphalt. A large grape tree sprawled its branches over the benches. At the other end the black-branched evergreens bunched together to make a deeper shade. The leaves were close and thick. In the centre between the shades and in front of the fountain was the small bandstand. It had a brief flight of five steps curving into the flat arena where the police band played once a week in the afternoon and once a month at night. It was like a picture in a book.

(4) BARBADOS: REBELLION

June Henfrey, *Freedom Come*

The famous 1816 insurrection brings hopes of liberation for Nanny, a slave woman who has lost faith in the prospect of peaceful abolition.

As ever, the Easter weather was hot and breezy. It got windier as the canes were cut down, and the now open fields offered no resistance to the breezes that sprang up over the sea and travelled far inland over the flat south side of the island. Here and there a line of mahoganies braced themselves against the buffeting, pushing their branches out towards the land and forsaking all growth on the other side, so they seemed like half trees. Nanny welcomed the wind, knowing that it would feed the fires once they were lit and aid their spread.

She took up a position at an east-facing bedroom window. She had come to the room on the pretext that she was checking on the work of the maid who had cleaned and polished the furniture, this being part of her housekeeper's role. She could not be sure that the first coil of smoke which she saw from there was the agreed signal, but soon others appeared at various points along the horizon, and she knew it had started. She rushed down the stairs and out into the yard, dragging off her headtie and waving it like a banner. The commotion that ensued in the house and in the yard quickly spread to the mill, and the slaves working there rushed out to help break down the outhouses and get at the tools which were stored inside them. With these weapons, they set off to join the main body of slaves who were gathering, further west, under Bussa. As they ran across the fields, their numbers grew, with cane-cutters and some drivers joining them.

For the next few hours Nanny's excitement mounted. She dashed this way and that, shouting to the other slaves that they did not have to work any more, and making loud plans for the way they would live when this day was over. She had never felt so strong or so happy. She was even glad that in the confusion the family had fled, unhurt so far. There'd be time enough later to settle old scores and to bring the owners to book for their wrongs. As she rushed about, trying to read the signals from the fires and picking up stray bits of information about the progress of Bussa's march, she caught up young children in her arms and told them that they were the generation who would be free and never know the indignities endured by their parents and grandparents..

(5) Barbados: Snobbery

Frank Collymore, *RSVP to Mrs Bush-Hall*

Social climber and snob par excellence, Maude Bush-Hall has planned an ostentatious party at which to announce the engagement of her daughter Pyrlene to Lucas Traherne, who claims to be an English aristocrat and poet.

How happy she was, how proud of it all – the weather, the stars, the lights, the gay assembly! How delightful everyone had been! Everyone, including Sir Charles Charles, that paragon of the old Barbadian order about whose acceptance of the invitation she had entertained some misgiving. How very gracious he and his wife, Lady Emma, had been to her: 'Charmed, charmed to meet you, Mrs Bush-Hall,' he had boomed, and had somehow managed to infuse into his greeting the fact that he had only at that moment achieved a life-long desire. Breeding will always tell, she thought: good old B'adian blood. She was more than ever proud of her birthright. Little England and Big England for ever.

Audible, very slim and very elegant in his fawn tropicals, mounted the steps and joined her.

'Ain't it all too good to be true, Audie?' she murmured.

Audible grunted approval. 'You certainly giving them one hell of a good time, Maudie. But why you up here all by your one? Where Pyrlene and Lucas?'

She pointed them out where they stood in the centre of a little knot of people whom Pyrlene had previously referred to as 'the literati'. 'I going jine them now,' she said.

The two of them walked down the steps to the lawn.

Smiles greeted her everywhere. Mrs Zimmerbloom, the American sculptress, again assured her what a wonderful time she was having and admired her cute frangipani-coiffure, the Beethoven Smalls were effusively appreciative of the pleasantly modulated effect of the steel band, the Honourable Boysie Scantlebury congratulated her in his warmest and moistest tone on the excellence of her whisky, Mrs Orgie Wilde, the secretary of the HIYA, was moved to ecstatic ejaculations of 'Divine, my dear, too too divine' as she caught sight of her. Mr Hathaway Withym could not forbear introducing her for a second time to his most recently acquired friend, a young German, Herr Panzi, and even Lurleen DaCourcey felt it incumbent upon her to confess it was as good as an evening at Government House.

(6) BARBADOS: VILLAGE LIFE

Timothy Callender: *It So Happen*

King claims to have been to England and to have picked up a measure of sophistication which astounds his fellow villagers.

Everybody was impressed with the things King seem to know, and when he went in the rumshop all the men come around him, talking to him, just to show one another that they could talk intelligent with a man like King, who had travelled in the outside world. And it turn out that one or two of the others say that they had travelled too, although nobody had never hear about them before that time. One man call to mind the time that he did drift to St Lucia in a fishing boat, and another man boast about an avalanche of snow that come down the mountains and nearly kill him when he was living in Costa Rica. But all in all, King had the best travel stories, and he had the best accent too. And he explain to them that the way he was speaking was the right way to speak.

'These is things that we got to learn and understand,' another man say. 'Is only recently that I find out too that all these years we been talking to one another, we been talking wrong. King have the right idea; is always right to speak as proper as possible.'

'In this island,' King say, 'it is not at all difficult to tell where anybody come from, once you observe them and listen carefully to the way they speaks. When you listen to the way a intelligent, educated man speak, and the way other people speaks, you recognizes who is a fool from who is not no fool.'

'Where you learn to speak like that?' another man enquire.

'In England, where you think?'

It was surprising how suddenly everybody get interested in culture and education. They start to practise how to speak properly, and to discuss big things, like Current Affairs and Politics and Religion and Histry and Sociology. Was surprising, too, how many of them you coulda seen walking about with newspapers and magazines under they arm or in they back-pocket. One fellow named Gerald, who had do well in Elementary School, even take to walking up and down the street with a book in he hand with he finger stick between the pages, like he so interested in what he reading that he couldn't put down the book.

(7) BARBADOS: WORLD WAR TWO

Austin Clarke,
Growing Up Stupid Under the Union Jack

Far from the 'mother country', the war created privation, improvisation and a comical sense of self-importance.

Hitler must have been winning the War. For all of a sudden sugar which we produced, was rationed. It became almost impossible to get, and very difficult to buy, unless the shopkeeper liked you. Flour, rice, corn meal for making *coucou*, a delicious weekend delicacy; matches; butter from Australia; salt beef and English potatoes, all of a sudden, these foodstuffs disappeared from Barbados . . .

We turned to the green bushes among us. 'If you don't have a horse,' my mother said, 'ride a cow.' So, we made teas from the bushes we normally left growing wild. Miraculous Bush, made into tea, was all of a sudden, discovered to be good for the bowels. We ground sweet potatoes into flour. We processed, with the help of some homemade graters, cassava root. Both the 'poisonous' cassava and the 'sweet' cassava; and we turned these formerly despised roots into the most delicious *staple foods*. We had to turn our kerosene lamps down, if not out, at a certain time of night. Blackouts reached us from up in the Mother Country, and from the various 'theaters of war'. The Germans, the British said, were now in Caribbean waters. We got scared. *Sirens* sounded throughout the night, throughout the country. Searchlights would point into the sky at nightfall, and we would follow the line, and imagine German planes in it, and shoot them down, with our mouths. The three or four hundred men who were enlisted in the Barbados Volunteer Force were called into barracks, at the Garrison, to live and to prepare themselves for the defense of the British Empire, and to eat bully-beef and biscuits. All of a sudden we had an Army. The Police were put on alert. Sea-scouts became self-important, as they were taken deeper out into the Harbor, and told a few things by the Harbor Police. And our leader, Grantley Adams, sent a cable up to the King, His Britannical Majestical George the Sixth, King of England, Northern Ireland, and the British Possessions Beyond the Seas, and told the King, 'Go on *England, Little England is behind you.*' And from that day, we were known, with pride or with embarassment, as 'Little England'.

(8) Bridgetown
Aldous Huxley, *Beyond the Mexique Bay*

For all its apparent familiarity, Barbados can still seem tropical, alien and even unsettling to the foreign visitor.

Bridgetown is not a large place; ten minutes of slow walking brought us to the suburbs. It was evening and the hot air was perfectly still. We walked through a vertical stratification of sewage smells and flowers, through minglings of tuberose and stale fish. Gigantically tall thin palms, bending down with their own lankiness, had been drawn, so it seemed, by a very vulgar but extraordinarily accurate and laborious artist – drawn in Indian ink, on the pale orange expanses of the West. There was a yelling of frogs; and the insects were like an invisible but ubiquitous orchestra, incessantly engaged in tuning up.

It was six years since I had been in a hot country, and I had forgotten how unspeakably melancholy the tropics can be, how hopeless, somehow, and how completely resigned to hopelessness. The feet of the negroes shuffled along the pavements. Small black children played in the gutters, silently. Squatting on the kerb, their fathers were reading the local newspaper by the light of the street lamps. And between the lamps, in the thickening night, every passing form was disquietingly without a face, and handless; blackness melted into blackness; men were suits of clothes walking. Every now and then we passed a chapel – always lighted up and always full of people singing hymns. For half a minute, perhaps, the noise of 'Abide with Me' would drown the noises of the tropical night; then, as one moved further away, the frogs and the cicadas would reassert themelves, and one was aware of both noises vibrating with an equal hopelessness under the first stars.

(9) Bridgetown
Patrick Leigh Fermor, *The Traveller's Tree*

Some visitors find Barbados a little too English, almost suburban, in architecture and atmosphere.

The more one sees of the little capital, the more it resembles a London suburb. But, after leaving the thoroughfares of the centre – all of which bear homely names like Broad Street, Chapman's Road, Trafalgar Square or Lightfoot Lane – and when the region of the Women's Self-Help Association and the Ladies' Lyceum Club had fallen behind, glimpses are caught of fine wooden houses in the Regency style retreating from the road among groups of trees. A large savannah encircled by a racecourse encloses a grandstand and a polo ground where grooms walk blanketed race-horses under the palms. The little contiguous towns of Hastings and Worthing faithfully echo in miniature the seaside resorts of England; and the Marine Hotel, the Windsor, the Ocean View and the Balmoral, bask placidly in the sunshine like advertisements of Torquay. Old gentlemen in tussore suits and panama hats sniff the ozone, and pink Anglo–Saxon babies, safe under their muslin mosquito nets, slumber in prams. The cricket pitches and golf links melt into the open country.

The rest of the island is a low, rolling panorama of cane-fields, 166 square miles in area – the size of the Isle of Wight or of a small English county which, in many ways, it closely resembles. For the omnipresent sugar-cane, sweeping and ruffling across the undulations, is wonderfully reminiscent of an English pastureland under a wheat harvest, and the turning sails of occasional windmills further an illusion which only the colonnades of palm trees belie. This gentle landscape, with the silver-grey arrows of the sugar-cane puffing and bending in the breeze, possesses a smooth and restful charm . . .

The term 'Little England' which the Barbadians apply to their home is no empty boast; and if the verdict of modern opinion has gone against the sort of English life on which the Barbadians have modelled theirs, it is not the Barbadians' fault. But it is hard to stay long in the island without feeling that Barbados reflects most faithfully the social and intellectual values and prejudices of a Golf Club in Outer London, for example, or of the married quarters of a barracks in Basutoland, which are not England's most interesting or precious contributions to world civilisation. Many travellers find in the island a tropical exuberance of exactly those values to which they had most joyfully bidden farewell in England.

(10) Skeete's Bay

John Robert Lee, *Skeete's Bay, Barbados*

Can this isolated, as yet 'unspoilt', part of Barbados resist the advent of tourism and the changes it brings?

One always missed the turning, but found, in time
The broken sign that pointed crookedly, loath to
Allow another stranger here. Perhaps this Tom
Or Dick has plans for progress that will tow
The boats away and make them 'quaint'; that will tame
This wild coast with pale rheumatics who tee

Off where sea-eggs and fishermen
Now lie with unconcern. Naked children
   And their sticks flush crabs from out their holes
   And a bare-legged girl, dress in wet folds
Wades slow towards a waning sun.

And the sea tossed angrily
For it knew that freedom here was short.
It remembered other coasts
Made mod by small-eyed men in big cars.

And as before it knew she'd vanish
The bare-legged girl; the children and their crabs
Would leave; a better world would banish
Them to imitation coconut trays.

But those small eyes reflecting dollar signs
Have not yet found the crooked finger to this peace;
And down the beach the women bathe their sons
Who'll never talk, like Pap, of fishing seasons past.

Only memory will turn down this way
When some old man somewhere recalls his day
On this beach where sea-eggs once lay.

Biographical and literary notes

BRATHWAITE, Kamau (1930–   ).
Born Lawson Edward Brathwaite in
Barbados, he studied at Cambridge
University and then at the University
of Sussex, where he wrote a PhD
dissertation on the development of
creole society in Jamaica (published
by Oxford University Press in 1971).
Brathwaite taught at a university in
Ghana for seven years before returning to the Caribbean, where he now
teaches history at the University of
the West Indies, Jamaica. His poetry
has become increasingly well known
since the late 1960s and has won him
a series of awards and a reputation as
one of the Caribbean's foremost modern poets. Often complex and densely
allusive, Brathwaite's work is largely
concerned with the creation and
celebration of an African identity
within Caribbean culture. *Sun Poem*
(Extract 1) is more accessibly auto-

biographical than much of Brathwaite's work.

CALLENDER, Timothy (1946–
1989). Born in Barbados, Callender
was educated at Combermere High
School and the University of the
West Indies. After teaching in St
Kitts and completing his MA in London, he returned to Barbados to teach
at the Cave Hill campus of UWI. A
musician, poet and playwright, Callender had his first short stories published in *Bim* magazine (see Frank
Collymore). *It So Happen* (Extract 6)
was first published in 1975, and at the
time of his early death Callender was
working on a series of epic story
poems for local radio. *It So Happen* is
a sharply observed, often comic series
of vignettes, based around village life
in Barbados. With a strong sense of
register and dialect, Callender mocks

the pretensions and foibles of the people who inhabit his fictional **St Victoria**.

CLARKE, Austin (1934–). Born and educated in Barbados, Clarke moved to Canada in 1955 to attend university. His career has been mostly academic, but he has also worked in radio and television in Canada and the USA. He has also served as Barbadian cultural attaché in Washington DC. His books include *Survivors of the Crossing*, 1964, and *The Prime Minister*, 1977. His 1980 memoir of schooldays in 1950s Barbados, *Growing Up Stupid Under the Union Jack* (Extract 7), is a scathing and often comical account of an education system dominated by colonial mediocrity and snobbishness.

COLLYMORE, Frank (1893–1980). Frank Collymore was born in **St Michael**, Barbados, and attended the prestigious Combermere High School, where he later taught English and French for fifty years. In the 1940s and 1950s he was editor and publisher of the influential literary magazine *Bim*, which played an important role in the growth of Caribbean literature. As well as being a teacher, poet, lexicographer, painter, actor and broadcaster, Collymore was also an accomplished short-story writer. His stories were published in a collected volume only in 1993, 35 years after he was awarded the OBE. 'RSVP to Mrs Bush-Hall' (Extract 5) is typical of Collymore's satirical presentation of Barbadian eccentricities. The story tells of a former prostitute turned society hostess who hopes to impress local society with her daughter's engagement to a self-styled English aristocrat. Unfortunately, Lucas Traherne is merely a con-man and thief who robs Mrs Bush-Hall and jilts her daughter at the engagement party itself.

DRAYTON, Geoffrey (1924–).

Born in Barbados, Drayton was educated at Cambridge University and went on to live in Canada, working as a research economist and teacher. He has since worked as a journalist with *Petroleum Times* and the Economist Intelligence Unit, both in London. *Christopher* (Extract 2) tells of a young white Barbadian's experiences of growing-up in a still rigidly segregated society. The son of an unsuccessful and unaffectionate sugar planter, Christopher becomes dependent on his relationship with his black nanny, Gip. Drayton is the author of two other novels – *Three Meridians*, 1951, and *Zohara*, 1961 – as well as various short stories.

HENFREY, June (1939–1992). Henfrey, née Gollop, was born and brought up in the village of **St David's**, Barbados before moving to England to study. She later settled in England where she raised her family. *Coming Home and Other Stories* (Extract 4) was written in the two years before her death. The stories cover a wide range of historical and emotional themes, but concentrate on the personalities of women at odds with the double oppression of race and gender.

HUXLEY, Aldous (1894–1963). The author of such twentieth-century classics as *Point Counter Point*, 1928, *Brave New World*, 1932, and *Eyeless in Gaza*, 1936, Huxley travelled to Central America via the Caribbean in the early 1930s and recorded his impressions of the region in *Beyond the Mexique Bay* (Extract 8). While impressed by the cultural richness of Mexico and Guatemala, with their Mayan traditions of spirituality, Huxley was dismissive of the British Caribbean colonies. 'Jamaica,' he writes, 'is the Pearl of the Caribbean – or is it the Clapham Junction of the West? I can never remember. But, anyhow, pearl or junction, it made us both feel extremely ill, and we were

Aldous Huxley

thankful to be off on a small Norwegian banana boat, bound for British Honduras and Guatemala.'

LAMMING, George (1927–). Born and brought up in **Carrington's Village** in Barbados, Lamming uses elements of his childhood experience to create the imagined Creighton Village, the focal point of his first novel and masterpiece *In the Castle of My Skin*, 1953. He went on to be educated at Combermere High School, after which he left for Trinidad in 1946 to work as a teacher. Four years later he migrated to London in order to become a full-time writer. His other major works include *Natives of My Person*, *Season of Adventure* and *The Pleasures of Exile*, 1960. *In the Castle of My Skin* (Extract 3) is arguably one of the Caribbean's most influential novels: Drawing on Lamming's understanding of village life in colonial Barbados, it develops what is a recurring theme in the region's literature: the emergence of authentic values within the constraints of an externally imposed ideology. The ideology in question is that of British

colonialism, and it is against the background of traditional grammar school education and the inculcation of 'Little England' loyalties that the narrator, G, becomes aware not only of social inequality but also his own artistic temperament. The novel traces the transformation of Creighton Village from a place of semi-feudal acceptance into an arena of social and political unrest. In a series of set-piece scenes, Lamming shows how the old village, dominated by the landlord and an ethos of subservience, falls under the sway of Slime, the epitome of a new post-colonial leadership. At the same time, G prepares for his 'setting forth' from the confines of village life and into the wider world. As an account of a community's social transition and an individual childhood, *In the Castle of My Skin* has few equals in any literature.

LEE, John Robert (1948–). Born in **Castries,** St Lucia, John Robert Lee studied at the University of the West Indies in Barbados before returning to St Lucia to direct a theatre group. He has since worked as a librarian and is active in the Church, preaching and writing. His poems and short stories have appeared in several anthologies and in various volumes of poetry, including *Vocation*, 1975, *Dead Season*, 1978, *The Prodigal*, 1983, and *Possessions*, 1984. 'Skeete's Bay, Barbados' (Extract 10) typifies Lee's affinity with Caribbean landscapes.

LEIGH FERMOR, Patrick (1915–). Born of mixed English and Irish ancestry, Leigh Fermor was educated at King's School, Canterbury. At the age of eighteen, he demonstrated his lifelong penchant for adventure by walking from Rotterdam to Constantinople. After several years in the Balkans, he joined the Irish Guards in 1939 and took part in operations in Albania, Crete and Greece, and spent two years disguised as a shepherd organizing the capture and

kidnapping of the German commander. Leigh Fermor is the author of
numerous books of travel writing and
the novel *The Violins of Saint-Jacques*,
1953. His *Traveller's Tree* (Extract 9)
is now established as a classic outsider's account of the region. He went to
the Caribbean in 1947 to produce
what he described as 'a personal, random account of an autumn and winter
spent in wandering through these islands.' Leigh Fermor's interests and
style are idiosyncratic and engaging,
although some have detected the
patrician attitudes of a worldly upper-
class European. A perceptive review
of the book in *Newsweek* in 1951
identified 'a spirit common to postwar
English writers, a sort of polite disin-
terest, a willingness to learn coupled
with a suspicion of false enthusiasms,
a civilized friendliness and a conscien-
tiousness that apparently led him to
every village, landmark, museum and
library, coupled with doubt that the
whole business was worth doing.'

TRINIDAD AND TOBAGO

'Hell is a city much like Port of Spain,/What the rain rots, the sun ripens some more,/ all in due process and within the law,/as, like a sailor on a spending spree,/we blow our oil-bloated economy.'
Derek Walcott,
The Spoiler's Return

Port of Spain, writes Trinidad's most celebrated author, V.S. Naipaul ◊, 'is the noisiest city in the world . . . You have been here only an hour, but you feel as exhausted as though you had spent a day in some Italian scooter-hell.' Trinidad's capital, it is true, is not for those in search of peace and quiet. Unlike calm Tobago, with its tranquil beaches and gentle countryside, Trinidad, and particularly Port of Spain, is a brash, raucous place, where traffic, music and high-decibel conversation relentlessly assault the eardrums. This steamy city is the home of calypso and the steelband and the epicentre of Caribbean festivities, the Carnival. As musician, broadcaster and journalist Henry Shukman reports in *Travels with My Trombone*, it is a chaotic blend of old and new, a cacophonous mish-mash of styles. Port of Spain is arguably also the most dangerous place in the world in which to drive – and to be a pedestrian, according to Amryl Johnson ◊ in her *Sequins for a Ragged Hem* (Extract 5). It is the meeting point, too, for a unique fusion of cultures, brought together into a sometimes volatile social mix by the country's history.

In Trinidad there are the descendants not only of African slaves, but of Indian and Chinese labourers, European settlers from Britain, France and Spain, Portuguese and Madeirans, Syrians and Lebanese and more recent immigrants from South America and the rest of the Caribbean. This 'melting pot' has produced one of the most cosmopolitan populations in the world, where radically different cultures sometimes mix or more often co-exist more or less harmoniously. Trinidadians, according to people from the other Caribbean islands, are mostly insane. Many Trinidadians would not refute the charge, but they also see their island as more modern, developed and influential than their smaller neighbours. They are also, Naipaul notwithstanding, mostly proud of its extraordinary cultural energy and noise.

336

FACT BOX

AREA: 5130 sq km
POPULATION: 1 260 000
CAPITAL: Port of Spain
LANGUAGES: English, Hindi, Urdu, French and Spanish
FORMER COLONIAL POWER: Britain
INDEPENDENCE: 1962
PER CAPITA GDP: US$3300

The twin-island state comprises two very different territories. Trinidad, once a part of mainland South America, is the most southerly of the Caribbean islands and lies only ten kilometres from the Venezuelan coast. Its area of 4828 sq km is large enough to contain a variety of landscapes, including the northern mountain range, fertile plains and mangrove swamps. Tobago, by contrast, is only 300 sq km and is largely volcanic in origin. Thirty-five kilometres to the north of Trinidad, Tobago is dwarfed by its oil-producing sister island and has occasionally expressed secessionist ambitions.

Trinidad was sighted by Columbus on his third expedition in 1498 and was either named in honour of the day of the Holy Trinity or after a group of three hills which the explorer saw on the horizon. At the time of Columbus' sighting there were significant communities of indigenous inhabitants on the island, of whom the peaceful Arawaks comprised a majority, living in the south. In the northern hills and rainforest, however, were settlements of Caribs, who put up tenacious resistance to the encroachment of European settlers. It was not until the end of the eighteenth century that the Spanish gained a real foothold on the island. In 1783, a census recorded a population of 126 Europeans, 605 Africans and 2032 indigenous Amerindians. That year, organized settlement began, with large numbers of French-speaking Royalist migrants subsequently arriving to escape the French Revolution and the slave rebellion in Saint Domingue.

The British took control of Trinidad in 1797, and Spain formally ceded the island in the 1802 Treaty of Amiens. Britain also took over Tobago in that year after the smaller island had changed hands some 29 times in a dizzying succession of invasions and counter-invasions. The period of Spanish–French–British imperial rivalry is recreated in Naipaul's epic *The Loss of El Dorado*, where Trinidad appears as a coveted but endlessly disappointing mirage, promising access to the fabled riches of El Dorado. Claimed, settled and fought over by the Dutch, French and British, Tobago was finally added to the British Empire and was later amalgamated with Trinidad in 1888. Yet with its mix of Spanish, French and British influences, Trinidad was essentially a cosmopolitan Creole society. In 1859

Anthony Trollope (◊ Jamaica) petulantly complained that 'the fact is they all speak French.' Even today, French patois is spoken in some districts, and Catholicism remains the largest religious denomination.

Meanwhile, as the remaining indigenous population disappeared through disease and dispossession, the colonists began to import larger numbers of African slaves to work on the sugar plantations which the French had established. But compared to other Caribbean islands, large-scale sugar production had come late to Trinidad because of the difficulties encountered in pacifying the island. As a result, when the slave trade was abolished in 1807 and emancipation took place in 1834, the planters confronted a serious labour shortage. Parliament in London voted Trinidad's slave-owners £1 039 119 in compensation for losing their slaves, but this, they complained, did not offset their losses. With the former slaves unwilling to work as low-wage labourers in the sugar fields, Trinidad's plantation owners began to look elsewhere for their workforce. By 1845, 10 000 immigrants had arrived from other Caribbean islands, where there were fewer opportunities and lower pay, while considerable numbers of Madeirans migrated in the 1830s and 1840s. Even with this influx of labour, however, the sugar estates of the **Caroni Plain** were short of hands. In 1845, the first members of Trinidad's new agricultural workforce arrived from another corner of the British Empire.

FROM CALCUTTA TO CARONI

Rural Trinidad is in many ways a different world from that of the capital and other big towns. Here, among what remain of the sugar plantations and the newer rice paddies, is the heartland of Indian Trinidad. Villages in the sugar belt have Hindu temples and Muslim mosques rather than churches, their houses surrounded by red and white Hindu prayer flags. In the fields herds of buffalo graze among coconut palms. The scene is like India transplanted into the Caribbean, and indeed this landscape is largely the result of the massive migration of Indians in the post-emancipation period.

Between 1845 and 1917 approximately 140 000 'East Indian' (to distinguish them from the indigenous 'Indians') labourers crossed the 'black waters' from Calcutta or Madras to Trinidad. Thousands more went to British Guiana and smaller numbers to Jamaica and other islands. The British government had approved a scheme in 1844 whereby Indian workers would be shipped over for five-year periods of 'indentureship' or apprenticeship. The idea was that they would work on the plantations for that period and thereafter either return to India or remain in Trinidad as smallholders. Although most came from Uttar Pradesh, they were by no means a homogeneous group and were themselves divided by caste, language and religion. There were two men for each women and nearly all were between ten and thirty years old. To the European planters and former black slaves, however, they were simply 'coolies', a derogatory term which lives on today. The black community in particular resented their willingness to work for low wages, thereby depressing rates of pay. In 1869 Charles Kingsley ◊ visited Trinidad and was impressed by the 'coolies' and the system of indentureship (Extract 9).

Yet not all were so pleased with East Indian indentureship. The British Anti-Slavery Society produced scathing reports of harsh conditions and exploitation on the plantations, and some Indians talked of 'a new form of slavery'. Additionally, Chinese labourers were also brought to Trinidad in the 1850s and 1860s, further exacerbating inter-racial tensions. In the 1890s the right of free passage back to India was withdrawn and thousands of migrants were effectively stranded in Trinidad. The decline of the colony's sugar industry in the 1920s and 1930s created widespread hardship among those Indians who had remained dependent on cane-cutting. In *The Jumbie Bird* (Extract 12), Indo–Trinidadian novelist Ismith Kahn ◊ tells of the devastating consequences among rural communities and the disillusionment felt by those who know they will never return to India. In *A Way in the World* V.S. Naipaul recalls the sight of homeless Indians in **Woodford Square** in Port of Spain:

> 'They were utterly destitute. They were people who had been, as in a fairy story, lifted up from the peasantry of India and set down thousands of miles away – weeks and weeks of sailing – in Trinidad. In the colonial setting of Trinidad, where rights were limited, you could have done anything with these people; and they were tormented by the people of the town.'

The Indian diaspora and a sense of betrayal and rootlessness are powerful themes in Trinidad's literature. In Clem Maharaj's *The Dispossessed*, the sugar estate, Highlands, is closing down because of a price slump. Abandoned in its ruins are the descendants of the indentured labourers, who are now reduced to penury and despair:

> 'In 1917, the last boat brought its passengers, coolies bound for estates everywhere, Highlands getting its quota. These people, the passengers of the last boat, remained; there were no return passages. Whatever this estate had taken to build in terms of pain, suffering and displacement was of no account when the end came. The children of the last boat were adrift again.'

Yet the experience of East Indians has by no means been an entirely negative one. In the bustling streets of **Tunapuna** or **San Fernando**, the rows of shops and bazars selling Indian clothes, food and clothes testify to a vibrant commercial presence. Alongside calypso and soca, Indian melodies blare out of shop-doors and buses, while the curry-filled chapati known as *roti* is the ubiquitous national snack. Many Trinidadians of Indian origin consider themselves to be simply Trinidadians and are receptive to the complimentary cultural influences which surround them. In Sam Selvon's

A *Brighter Sun*, the East Indian hero, Tiger, is asked whether he wants to 'return' to India:

> 'What I would go back there for, Joe? I born in this country, Trinidad is my land . . . It have so many different kinds of people in Trinidad, boy! You think I should start to wear dhoti? Or I should dress as everybody else, and don't worry about Indian so much, but think of all of we as a whole, living in one country, fighting for we rights?'

Significantly, in November 1995 a politician of East Indian ancestry, Basdeo Panday, found himself Prime Minister of the country after his party had narrowly won a general election. The country's first East Indian premier, Panday, a dynamic and charismatic labour organizer, proved that his ethnic constituency had the power and determination to take over government.

THE MELTING POT

The Chinese in Trinidad have also encountered mixed fortunes. As many as 17 000 came to the British Caribbean between 1835 and 1866, when the Chinese government insisted that the islands' authorities pay a return passage for its nationals. Partly because most Chinese migrants were men, they intermarried more quickly than the East Indians and became part of a mixed Creole society. But some Chinese did not and remained apart from mainstream Trinidadian society. Traditionally they have become small traders, shopkeepers and restaurant-owners. As Noel Woodroffe ◊ shows in his short story, *Wing's Way* (Extract 8), the Chinese may be despised in small rural communities but are nevertheless preferred to the East Indians.

If the extraordinarily mixed ethnic heritage of Trinidad has at times created conflict and alienation, it has also brought about a truly Creole society where people from four continents find themselves neighbours and sometimes friends. In *Miguel Street* (Extract 4), V.S. Naipaul draws a series of vignettes of life in a working-class **Port of Spain** district, where people of African and East Indian descent live in a spirit of communal identity, where eccentrics and lunatics enliven the drabness of poverty. 'A stranger could drive through Miguel Street and just say "Slum!" because he could see no more,' writes Naipaul:

> 'But we, who lived there, saw our street as a world, where everybody was quite different from everybody else. Man-man was mad; George was stupid; Big Foot was a bully; Hat was an adventurer; Popo was a philosopher; and Morgan was our comedian.'

This cast of characters, drawn with both irony and affection, symbolizes much of the humanity of Naipaul's early perception of Trinidad. The same sense of warmth is evident in *Crick Crack Monkey* (Extract 14), where Merle Hodge contrasts the intimacy and solidarity of working-class **Port of**

Spain life with the pretentiousness and tedium of an aspiring 'professional' middle class.

Winds of Change

The discovery of oil at the beginning of the twentieth century gradually changed the face of Trinidadian society. As sugar slowly declined in viability, the petroleum industry grew in importance. The workforce in the oil sector was predominantly Afro–Trinidadian, with workers brought in from smaller islands such as Grenada to work for lower wages. The Depression of the 1930s fuelled a growing sense of militancy among the oil workers, and a series of strikes and disturbances challenged the colonial government. The southern city of **San Fernando,** the nearby oil town of **Fyzabad** and the refining area around **Pointe-a-Pierre** became hotbeds of political militancy. In *Crown Jewel* (Extract 13), Ralph de Boissière ◊ recreates the wave of industrial unrest which swept through 1930s Trinidad. The unrest brought with it demands for greater democracy and for independence. Reforms were gradually introduced, and political parties and trade unions gathered in strength. A legendary figure who emerged at this time was Grenadian-born Turbal Uriah 'Buzz' Butler, a trade union leader who led a hunger march in 1935 from the southern oilfields into Port of Spain. In 1937 Butler was among the leadership of a general strike which paralysed Trinidad's industrial and agricultural production. The colonial authorities had him arrested, riots broke out, both demonstrators and police were killed, and British Marines landed to restore law and order.

The outbreak of the Second World War slowed the pace of political reform but quickened that of social change. The arrival of US troops to protect the strategic oil industry exposed Trinidadians to North American culture and provided a different influence from that of London. The US naval base at **Chaguaramas** became a mecca for those in search of the 'Yankee dollar', and prostitution as well as other service industries thrived. With the end of the War and the prospect of the naval base's closure, Trinidad's best-known calypsonian Mighty Sparrow ◊ ironically lamented the fate of Port of Spain's good time girls:

> 'Well the girls in town feeling bad
> No more Yankees in Trinidad
> They going to close down the base for good
> Them girls have to make out how they could
> Is now they park up in the town
> In for a penny, in for a pound
> Yes, is competition for so
> Trouble in town when the price drop low.'

Yet the Americans were to return in force, this time attracted by the island's oil deposits and petroleum refining capacity. In his celebrated calypso 'The Yankees Back' (Extract 6), Mighty Sparrow provides an acerbic commentary on the motives and methods of companies such as Texaco.

The disturbances of the 1930s and the gradual withdrawal of British influence in the Caribbean fuelled the movement towards independence. Self-government and universal suffrage were introduced in the post-war period, and in 1956 the People's National Movement (PNM), led by the brilliant and eccentric Dr Eric Williams, won Trinidad's first elections. As Chief Minister, Williams led the country into the short-lived Federation of the West Indies with nine other English-speaking Caribbean islands. When the Federation collapsed in 1961 due to Jamaica's withdrawal, Williams uttered his famous judgment 'one from ten leaves zero' and Trinidad abandoned the federal path. Full independence from Britain followed swiftly on 31 August 1962.

Under the dominant personality of Eric Williams, the PNM held a monopoly of power for thirty years. The Oxford-educated Prime Minister was also a formidable historian, writing several volumes on slavery and Caribbean history in general. His *British Historians and the West Indies*, 1964, is a polemical onslaught on much of the work of eighteenth- and nineteenth-century British historians such as Thomas Carlyle and James Anthony Froude (◊ Dominica). Of the latter he wrote, 'No British writer, with the possible exception of Carlyle, has so savagely denigrated the West Indian Negro as Froude did in his analysis of Negro character.' The object of the book, he stressed, was to reinforce Trinidad and Tobago's status as an independent nation by exploding the myths of an 'old, tired, tiresome world, whose historian representatives, adorning the greatest of the metropolitan universities, have sought only to justify the indefensible and to seek support for preconceived and outmoded prejudices.'

Williams was also adept at maintaining power through appeals to Trinidadian patriotism and by mobilizing the country's African population behind his version of black nationalism. His rise to prominence and early prestige were in part due to his campaign to force the USA to return the **Chaguaramas** base (which eventually happened in 1962). Williams's party also articulated the aspirations of black Trinidadians and, consequently, was viewed with suspicion by the East Indian population. While the PNM coopted some East Indians, its strength lay in the organized, industrial and Afro–Trinidadian working class. In a series of meetings and rallies in the capital's **Woodford Square**, Williams developed a reputation as a compell-ing orator and, some would say falsely, as a defender of poor people's interests. Eric Williams held on to power until his death in 1981, during which time Trinidad, and to a lesser degree Tobago, underwent a dramatic process of boom and bust.

'CAPITALISM GONE MAD'

In 1973 the Organisation of Petroleum Exporting Countries (OPEC) quadrupled oil prices and Trinidad suddenly found itself awash with petrodollars. As revenue from Texaco and the other oil companies flowed into the government's coffers, Williams decided to invest in modernizing the economy. Steelworks and other heavy industries sprang up, as the government rushed into diversifying the island's exports. Modern tower blocks sprouted up in Port of Spain and the luxurious suburbs around the capital acquired larger and more ostentatious mansions.

In an atmosphere of corruption and conspicuous consumption, much of the windfall was spent on imports such as new cars and luxury items. As Trinidad's per capita income outstripped the rest of the Caribbean, its import bill increased eleven-fold. The poor, however, remained poor. The slums of **Laventille** and other urban districts grew ever bigger during the 1970s as migrants from the countryside and other islands flocked to join in the apparent bonanza. Middle-class Trinidadians revelled in what they called the *fete* (party). The poor, meanwhile, struggled with rising prices, land shortages and a crumbling infrastructure. At this time, Mighty Sparrow's 'Capitalism Gone Mad' seemed to sum up the country's delirium:

'You have to be a millionaire
Or some kind of petty bourgeoisie
Anytime you living here in this country
You have to be a sculduggery
Making your money illicitly
To live like somebody in this country

It's outrageous and insane
The crazy prices here in Port of Spain . . .
Where you ever hear a television cost seven thousand dollars?
Quarter million dollars for a piece of land
A pair of sneakers two hundred dollars
Eighty to ninety thousand dollars for motor cars
At last here in Trinidad we see capitalism gone mad . . .'

Nor was Earl Lovelace ◊, a Trinidadian novelist, any more cheerful about the boom. **Port of Spain**, he wrote in 1983, had become 'a hustler's paradise, a fairground with pirates at large, music booming, New York trinkets on the sidewalk, everybody on a hustle . . . our mad directing traffic or otherwise engaging with their demons and singing "Capitalism gone mad".' That same year, *Moses Migrating* (Extract 3) by Sam Selvon ◊ was published, telling of the disorientation felt by a Trinidadian returning to the island after 25 years in London and finding it blighted by modernization and money.

By 1981, the year of Williams's death, the boom was already over. In the course of the 1980s recession took hold and living standards declined relentlessly. Having borrowed with abandon during the good years, Trinidad was now heavily in debt. Worse, the island's oil reserves seemed to be smaller than had previously been thought. In 1986 Trinidadians took their revenge on the PNM by voting it out of office and elected a makeshift coalition known as the National Alliance for Reconstruction (NAR). But Trinidad's decline continued and even worsened. By 1991 the NAR was broken into warring factions and hopelessly unpopular, and the PNM returned to power with promises of economic recovery. The promises proved hollow, however, and in the close-fought elections of November 1995, Basdeo Panday's United National Congress (UNC) scraped into power with the coalition support of the NAR.

BLACK POWER

In the early years following independence, it seemed that Trinidad and Tobago might become a model constitutional democracy, with free and fair elections and political stability. In 1970, however, Trinidad, was rocked by the so-called Black Power uprising, led by a disparate group of intellectuals and black nationalists who were critical of the PNM's allegedly 'colonial' politics. Shortly after that year's Carnival, a series of student demonstrations and clashes with police escalated into a full-scale crisis and a State of Emergency. When part of Trinidad's 750-strong Defence Force mutinied against its superiors, it seemed that violent change was inevitable. Yet the uprising subsided quickly, its leaders divided between revolutionary action and wringing concessions from the government. Prime Minister Williams, meanwhile, had taken the precaution of summoning US and Venezuelan warships which waited offshore while a curfew was enforced. The episode was a traumatic reminder of the fragility of Trinidad's democracy and the potentially explosive nature of its social inequalities. In his poem 'Port of Spain', Nobel Prize-winner Derek Walcott (◊ St Lucia) suggestively evokes the atmosphere of menace and latent violence which hung over the city long after the revolt died away.

In July 1990 the spectre of violent insurrection returned to Trinidad, when the self-styled Imam Yasin Abu Bakr and a group of 100 black fundamentalist Muslims stormed parliament and captured the Prime Minister A.N.R. Robinson, eight cabinet members and other hostages. Their call to Trinidadians to rise up against the government was universally ignored. In a drama which lasted five days, Robinson was shot and wounded, while 23 people were killed in the initial assault and the army's retaking of the parliament building. As the country was paralysed by these extraordinary and violent events, people in **Port of Spain** went on the rampage, smashing shops and looting. According to V.S. Naipaul's A Way in the World:

> 'As soon as the siege began there was no effective government. It took a little while for this to be understood; and then the effect on black communities – local and immigrant, in the capital and all those contiguous settlements at the foot of the Northern Range, north of the mainly Indian countryside, which remained quiet, untouched by the frenzy to the north – the effect on these communities was extraordinary. They were like people who have

been granted a moment of pure freedom. They formed looting gangs. It was of this – of the inflamed, unrecognizable faces of the looters, the glittering eyes – as much as of the siege at the Red House that people spoke when I went back.'

In the end, Robinson and his Cabinet were released as the Muslim group surrendered. For several days, it had been, as Naipaul puts it 'the end of things, a world without logic.'

CRICKET

'Whoever and whatever we are, we are cricketers.' C.L.R. James's remark on the centrality of cricket in the English-speaking Caribbean holds particularly true for Trinidad. Brought to the islands by British colonialism, cricket has become almost an icon of West Indian achievement and pride. The emergence of local cricketing talent coincided with the growing self-confidence of the independence movement, and cricket has come to be seen as the historic revenge of the once colonized over their former masters. Certainly, in recent years West Indian teams have humiliated their English opponents with predictable regularity, and the names of cricketers such as Garfield Sobers, Vivian Richards and, most lately, Brian Lara (a Trinidadian) have become legendary.

In her portrait of the **Queen's Park Savannah**, the capital's great outdoor meeting-place, Jan Morris ◊ rightly detects the undertones of racial conflict which run through even the national obsession with cricket. In 'Howzat? and Mr Morgan' (Extract 11), Morris describes the city's playing fields as being the symbolic centre of myriad cricket games played all around the island.

The Marxist historian and theoretician C.L.R. James ◊ was perhaps the Caribbean's greatest cricket writer and exponent of the sport's wider social implications. As the British historian E.P. Thompson remarked of him, 'I'm afraid that American theorists will not understand this, but the clue to everything [in James] lies in his proper appreciation of the game of cricket.' This is really no exaggeration, as James's writing uses cricket to explore the ideas of nationhood, political activism and regional identity. In his article 'Cricket' (Extract 10), James provides some insight in a light-hearted anecdote into the importance of the game not merely at national level but in the context of everyday local rivalries.

CALYPSO

'It's a feeling which comes from deep within,
   A tale of joy or one of suffering,
It's editorial in song of the life we undergo,
   That and only that I know is true calypso.'
Mighty Duke

Calypso is Trinidad's most distinctive and internationally famous creative form. It is above all a critical, subversive medium, in which the singer pokes fun at those in positions of power and influence. This tradition of satire stretches back to the African songs of praise and derision which accompanied the black slaves to Trinidad. The African influence became merged with linguistic and stylistic elements from French, Spanish and English sources, and at the end of the eighteenth century the first 'shantwell' (in itself a French–English construction), Gros Jean, earned a reputation for entertaining the wealthy planters with his *risqué* musical commentaries. Calypso has spread throughout the Eastern Caribbean, but Trinidad remains the true home of the genre and the place where would-be calypsonians must come if they wish to be taken seriously.

The key elements of calypso are topicality, humour and satire. As such, calypsonians have often fallen foul of those in authority, as in the 1930s when the British colonial regime tried to ban several calypsos for being 'profane'. Even in the 1980s governments in Antigua and Barbados tried to censure particularly critical calypsos aimed at their incompetence or political misjudgment. The songs tend to concentrate on scurrilous aspects of behaviour such as corruption or sexual misdemeanour, but they are also a vehicle for the performer's own self-deprecating humour. Mighty Sparrow's repertoire is typical of this mix of social commentary and witty self-denigration. His rise to prominence corresponded with the growing political dominance of Eric Williams and the PNM, and Sparrow became closely associated both with the Prime Minister and his party. Yet, in calypso's best traditions, the singer was not afraid to castigate Dr Williams when he saw that he was breaking his election promises to hold down prices:

> 'They raise up the taxi fare
> No, Doctor, no
> And the blasted milk gone up so dear
> No, Doctor, no
> But you must remember
> We support you in September
> You better come good
> Because I have a big piece o'mango wood.'

Calypso is capable of creating considerable controversy and of articulating popular grievances into a potent form of protest. In his short story, 'They Better Don't Stop the Carnival' (Extract 2), Michael Anthony ◊ shows how the hugely unpopular decision of the colonial government to ban Carnival during the War acts as a catalyst for Lord Invader's equally popular calypso song of 1942.

The genre is also highly competitive, and each year calypsonians battle it out for a series of prizes and honours which coincide with Trinidad's Carnival. Anthony's Lord Invader is an accurate portrait of the typical calypsonian who usually originates from the working-class, Afro–

Trinidadian districts of **Port of Spain**. With comically grandiose sobriquets such as Atilla the Hun, Black Stalin or Lord Kitchener, they launch their particular song each year in January during the run-up to Carnival. In calypso 'tents' or halls the performers compete against one another, frequently improvising on the failings of their fellow calypsonians. At the same time, the island's media continually broadcast the best of the year's entries. As songs are gradually eliminated by a process of public opinion, the contest culminates on Dimanche Gras, the Sunday immediately before the official opening of Carnival. The artist who wins the Calypso Monarch's crown becomes to all extents and purposes the provider of that Carnival's theme tune. There are also other competitions, such as the Roadmarch contest, where the Carnival bands play tunes as they process through the capital city. The calypsonian whose melody is played most often as the bands pass the judging stages is deemed to have won. Lord Kitchener (Aldwyn Roberts), for instance, specializes in steelband music for marching bands and has won the Roadmarch title on eleven occasions.

Since the beginning of the twentieth century calypso has often been merged with another tradition, that of the steelband or more popularly 'pan'. Evolving from the tamboo-bamboo musical form, in which lengths of bamboo were used to beat out rhythms on pots, pans and dustbins, the steelband really took off after the Second World War when it was discovered that large oil drums could be turned into musical instruments by beating them into particular shapes. Any range of notes can be played across the spectrum of 'pans', and bands practise all year round for their entry into the Carnival competitions. The climax of the steelband year is the 'Panorama' contest on the **Savannah**, where the last eight bands, each containing as many as fifty musicians, fight for the title.

As Earl Lovelace ◊ makes clear in his celebrated evocation of shanty-town life, *The Dragon Can't Dance* (Extract 1), calypso is the lifeblood of Trinidad's urban poor. Acting as a transcendental means of escapism as well as social protest, it retains its centrality in Trinidadian culture several generations after its first appearance. With the emergence of rival forms of musical commentary such as rap, calypso has to some extent evolved with the times and has produced popular 'soca' music as well as so-called 'rapso' artists, yet long-standing favourites such as the Mighty Sparrow remain firmly entrenched in Trinidadians' affections.

CARNIVAL

The origins of Trinidad's particular Carnival tradition are said to lie in the period of French colonial rule when the rich planters and their families would visit one another dressed in fancy costumes for pre-Lenten masked balls. With the emancipation of the island's black slaves in 1834, the newly liberated peasants and workers took over the idea of masquerade, transforming it from an élitist gathering to a massive outdoor celebration. As Carnival grew in popularity, the colonial authorities reacted with alarm, attempting to suppress it and banning it altogether during the Second World War. Nowadays, however, Carnival is a vast tourist attraction (accommodation is almost impossible to find during the Carnival period) and is part of the national calendar. Some purists complain that it has lost its radical, subversive edge with the proliferation of commercial sponsorship. Yet the size and sheer extravagance of the occasion show no sign of decreasing.

After the release of the calypsonians' songs in early January, work begins in earnest on the costumes and props to be used by the competing Carnival groups (known as 'Mas Camps'). They process on the weekend preceding Lent in spectacular theme costumes, normally with giant King and Queen characters at the rear. Attired in ingenious combinations of sequins, stilts, feathers and lycra, the players follow their particular steelband. Everywhere in the capital, steelbands. Mas Camps and calypsonians are feverishly active.

Carnival Monday is perhaps the most important day, and it starts with 'J'Ouvert' (a corruption of the French *jour ouvert*) in the early hours of the morning. In his short story 'King Sailor One J'Ouvert Morning' (Extract 7), Lawrence Scott ◊ captures the intense excitement of the day on which hundreds of thousands descend on **Port of Spain** for an exhausting session of dancing, drinking and revelry. The traditional roots of Carnival are most clearly evident in J'Ouvert, when mischievous 'jab-jabs' (from the French *diable* or devil) smear the unsuspecting with grease or paint, while 'mokojumbies' attempt the arduous circuit on stilts. The following day, Mardi Gras, sees the main processions and judging at different points on the circuit in **Independence Square**, **Woodbrook** and the **Savannah**. This is the most spectacular part of Carnival, as the Carnival bands, often comprising thousands of costumed participants, wind their way through the congested streets in their dance formations. Amidst floats and lorries blasting out the latest soca and calypso hits, Trinidadians and visitors alike 'jump up' in one of the world's most exuberant and exhausting street parties.

LITERARY LANDMARKS

Woodford Square. At the centre of downtown **Port of Spain** is the square, which, according to Naipaul, 'the Spaniards had laid out in the 1780s as the main city square, and which the British had later embellished; where the destitute Indians from the plantations had slept until they died out; and where later the black madmen had come to camp.' Named after the British Governor, Sir Ralph Woodford (traditionally credited with or blamed for the idea of Indian indentureship), the Square is bordered on one side by the Anglican Cathedral and on another by the Red House, the seat of Trinidad's House of Representatives and Senate. Woodford Square became the focal point for Eric Williams's political movement and it was where he held his popular meetings and rallies. It was also the scene of Abu Bakhr's spectacular, albeit unsuccessful, coup attempt in 1990.

Queen's Park Savannah. Several blocks up from the nowadays scruffy Square is a large expanse of open space with playing fields and a race course. On the west side of the **Savannah** are the ornate Edwardian mansions built in the first decade of the twentieth century which house government offices, private schools and the Archbishop. Of this 'company of legendary Trinidadian mansions', writes Jan Morris ◊:

> 'One is gorgeously Gothic, one exotically Moorish, one predominantly blue: but the most stylish of them all is No 25 Maraval Road, where Mr Morgan lives. It is a big white house surrounded with balconies, like an eccentric gunboat on the China Station, and it is encrusted with every kind of ornament, towers and turrets and filigree and wrought iron and balustrades and flagstaffs and weathercocks and all possible fractions of elaboration.'

The Pitch Lake. On the south-west coast near **San Fernando**, lies a 50-hectare area of hot black tar. The lake, which constantly refills itself and is used for road maintenance, is a tourist curiosity and has been visited by many writers. Charles Kingsley likened it somewhat ornately to 'that black Bolge beneath the baking rays of the tropic sun'. Aldous Huxley (◊ Barbados) was less impressed: 'For the real pitch lake is simply about two hundred asphalt tennis courts, in very bad condition, set in the midst of some gently undulating green meadows. I felt inclined to ask for my money back.'

BOOKLIST

The following selection includes the extracted titles in this chapter as well as other titles for further reading. In general, paperback editions are given when possible. For most of the extracted works, the original publisher in English can be found in 'Acknowledgments and Citations' at the end of the volume, as can the exact location of the extracts and the editions from which they are taken.

Anthony, Michael, 'They Better Don't Stop the Carnival' in *The Chieftain's Carnival and Other Stories*, Longman, Harlow, 1993. **Extract 2.**

De Boissière, Ralph, *Crown Jewel*, Picador, London, 1981. **Extract 13.**

Cross, Malcolm, *The East Indians of Guyana and Trinidad*, Minority Rights Group, London, 1980.

Henry, Paget and Paul Buhle, eds, *C.L.R. James's Caribbean*, Duke University Press, Durham, NC, 1992.

Hodge, Merle, *Crick Crack Monkey*, Heinemann, Oxford, 1981. **Extract 14.**

James, C.L.R., 'Cricket', in *Trinidad & Tobago*, Michael Anthony and Andrew Carr, eds, André

Deutsch, London, 1975. **Extract 10.**

Johnson, Amryl, *Sequins for a Ragged Hem*, Virago, London, 1988. **Extract 5.**

Khan, Ismith, *The Jumbie Bird*, Longman, Harlow, 1985. **Extract 12.**

Kingsley, Charles, *At Last: A Christmas in the West Indies*, Macmillan, London, 1900. **Extract 9.**

Lovelace, Earl, *The Dragon Can't Dance*, Longman, Harlow, 1986. **Extract 1.**

Maharaj, Clem, *The Dispossessed*, Heinemann, Oxford, 1992.

Mighty Sparrow, 'The Yankees Back', in *The Penguin Book of Caribbean Verse in English*, Paula Burnett, ed, Penguin, London, 1986. **Extract 6.**

Morris, Jan, 'Howzat? and Mr Morgan: Port of Spain 1958', in *Among the Cities*, Penguin, London, 1986. **Extract 11.**

Naipaul, V.S., *A House for Mr Biswas*, Penguin, London, 1961.

Naipaul, V.S., *A Way in the World*, Minerva, London, 1995.

Naipaul, V.S., *Miguel Street*, Penguin, London, 1971. **Extract 4.**

Naipaul, V.S., *The Loss of El Dorado*, Penguin, London, 1987.

Scott, Lawrence, 'King Sailor One J'Ouvert Morning', in *Caribbean New Wave*, Stewart Brown, ed, Heinemann, Oxford, 1990. **Extract 7.**

Scott, Lawrence, *Witchbroom*, Allison & Busby, London, 1992.

Selvon, Sam, *A Brighter Sun*, Longman, Harlow, 1985.

Selvon, Sam, *Moses Migrating*, Longman, Harlow, 1983. **Extract 3.**

Shukman, Henry, *Travels with my Trombone*, Harper Collins, London, 1992.

Walcott, Derek, 'Port of Spain', in *The Fortunate Traveller*, Faber and Faber, London, 1982.

Eric Williams, *British Historians and the West Indies*, André Deutsch, London, 1972.

Williams, Eric, *From Columbus to Castro: The History of the Caribbean, 1492–1969*, André Deutsch, London, 1970.

Woodroffe, Noel, 'Wing's World', in *Best West Indian Stories*, Kenneth Ramchand, ed, Nelson, Walton-on-Thames, 1982. **Extract 8.**

Extracts

(1) Port of Spain: Calypso

Earl Lovelace, *The Dragon Can't Dance*

For the inhabitants of Port of Spain's hillside shanty towns, Carnival and calypso are celebrated with pride, passion and the prospect of fleeting oblivion.

Up on the hill with Carnival coming, radios go on full blast, trembling these shacks, booming out calypsos, the songs that announce in this season the new rhythms for people to walk in, rhythms that climb over the red dirt and stone, break-away rhythms that laugh through the groans of these sights, these smells, that swim through the bones of these enduring people so that they shout: Life! They cry: Hurrah! They drink a rum and say: Fuck it! They walk with a tall hot beauty between the garbage and dog shit, proclaiming life, exulting in the bare bones of their person and their skin.

Up on the hill with Carnival coming and calypso tunes swimming in the hair of these shacks, piercing their nostrils, everybody catches the spirit and these women with baskets and with their heads tied, these women winding daily down the hill on which no buses run, tramping down this asphalt lane slashed across this mountain's face, on their way, to Port of Spain city, to market, to work as a domestic, or to any other menial task they inherit because of their beauty; these women, in this season, bounce with that tall delicious softness of bosom and hip, their movements a dance, as if they were earth priestesses heralding a new spring.

The children dance too, coming home from school in the hot afternoon when the sun has cooked the castles of dog shit well, so that its fumes rise like incense proper to these streets. They dance, skipping along, singing calypsos whose words they know by heart already, swishing their skirt tails, moving their waists, laughing, their laughter scattering like shells into the hard flesh of the hill. Dance! There is dancing in the calypso. Dance! if the words mourn the death of a neighbour, the music insists that you dance; if it tells the troubles of a brother, the music says dance. Dance to the hurt! If you catching hell, dance, and the government don't care, dance! Your woman take your money and run away with another man, dance. Dance! Dance! Dance! It is in dancing that you ward off evil. Dancing is a chant that cuts off the power from the devil. Dance! Dance! Dance! Carnival brings this dancing to every crevice on this hill.

(2) PORT OF SPAIN: CALYPSO

Michael Anthony,
They Better Don't Stop the Carnival

The rumour that the 1942 Carnival is to be abandoned to help the allied war effort both appals and inspires calypsonian Lord Invader.

Invader took a bus to Carenage, and all the while music kept drumming in his head and words kept flowing into his mind. He had wanted another number for the calypso season and he got it. Yes, he got it. He sat on the bus and he was not seeing anything, although his eyes were wide open. The conductor had to touch him in order to collect the fare from him. In his mind, Invader was hammering the tune into shape as the words flowed. The bus rolled on, and with his head turned towards the sea, he was thinking of what Birdie had been saying; and cutting the phrases, trimming and fitting in his mind, he felt sure he had got the first verse. His eyes became more glassy and vague. His lips began moving slightly, and as his eyes closed, he did not feel the jerking of the bus for he was in the calypso tent. The melody joined with the words, and he was strutting across the stage and declaiming to hundreds of people:

> *The Governor stop our festival*
> *But some say they'll still play their Carnival,*
> *The Governor stop our festival*
> *But some say they'll still play their Carnival,*
> *So the Lord Invader went out of town,*
> *I was afraid they'd shoot me down,*
> *So I went down Carenage Water*
> *Playing hide and seek with my neighbour's daughter.*

> *To San Fernando . . .*

The bus came to a brusque and noisy stop, throwing Lord Invader against the seat in front of him. Some of the passengers looked back and the conductor was standing in the passageway looking at him impatiently. The conductor said, 'Ain't you say you going Carenage? You sleeping, man.' Invader looked outside and saw that indeed it was Carenage. He hastened out of the bus, his guitar under his arm, his handkerchief inside the neck of his shining silk shirt. Somebody on the bus said, 'That's Lord Invader.' As the bus moved off, everybody turned back to look.

(3) PORT OF SPAIN: CHANGE

Sam Selvon, *Moses Migrating*

After 25 years in London, Moses has returned to Port of Spain, only to find many unexpected changes in his old haunts. Coca-cola has taken the place of the traditional drink mauby.

Distance is relative. To a Trinidadian walking from de-Hilton to the shops in Frederick Street might seem endless, but to a Londoner like me, who walk countless miles either from missing the last bus or not having the fare, it was just a stroll. If wasn't for the hot sun I might of enjoyed it; I minimised the perspiration by taking my time and making one-today-one-tomorrow steps. White people really lucky, because science say white does repel heat, whereas black does attract it. That's the true reason why some black people wish they was white: to keep cooler, nothing racial.

I reach down by Park Street, and went in a parlour to have a glass of mauby to cool off. It was one of the local refreshments I was yearning for – a tall glass of mauby, with shave-ice, made frothy at the top with a lay-lay stick.

'A tall glass of mauby, please, with plenty shave-ice, swizzle it up nice and frothy,' I say to the girl attendant in a green and white uniform.

She laugh. 'Mauby! We don't sell mauby, mister.'

'How you mean you don't sell mauby?' I ask.

'We got milk-shake, Cokes, Pepsi, orange juice, sweet-drinks and ice cream, but we don't sell mauby.'

I look around the establishment. It wasn't like the kind of parlour I remember in the old days. It was all spick and span, a few people was sitting at tables, and it had some more girls behind the counter to serve customers, and a cash register machine. It even had machines dispensing the drinks she mention. And no flies was buzzing around.

'How you mean, no mauby?' I ask again. When I was in Trinidad everybody used to drink mauby.

'Nobody don't drink that any more. You got to go by the market, or look for one of them small parlours in a sidestreet.' She looked at me suspiciously, as if she explain too long and unnecessarily, then ask: 'Where you from?'

'London.'

'Oh.' She turn to another girl and say, 'This mister asking for mauby!' and both of them laugh as if is a joke, and even some of the others in the shop.

'Okay, okay, give me a Coke,' I snap.

(4) PORT OF SPAIN: STREET LIFE

V.S. Naipaul, *Miguel Street*

The narrator's uncle, Bhakcu, is a compulsive and hugely incompetent amateur car mechanic. He has gone to buy a new car, and the street's inhabitants eagerly await its arrival.

So we waited for the new car.

Midday came, but Bhakcu didn't.

Hat said, 'Two to one, that man taking down the engine right this minute.'

About four o'clock we heard a banging and a clattering, and looking down Miguel Street towards Docksite we saw the car. It was a blue Chevrolet, one of the 1939 models. It looked rich and new. We began to wave and cheer, and I saw Bhakcu waving his left hand.

We danced into the road in front of Bhakcu's house, waving and cheering.

The car came nearer and Hat said, 'Jump, boys! Run for your life. Like he get mad.'

It was a near thing. The car just raced past the house and we stopped cheering.

Hat said, 'The car out of control. It go have a accident, if something don't happen quick.'

Mrs Bhakcu laughed. 'What you think it is at all?' she said.

But we raced after the car, crying after Bhakcu.

He wasn't waving with his left hand. He was trying to warn people off.

By a miracle, it stopped just before Ariapita Avenue.

Bhakcu said, 'I did mashing down the brakes since I turn Miguel Street, but the brakes ain't working. Is a funny thing. I overhaul the brakes just this morning.'

Hat said, 'It have two things for you to do. Overhaul your head or haul you arse away before you get people in trouble.'

Bhakcu said, 'You boys go have to give me a hand to push car back home.'

As we were pushing it past the house of Morgan, the pyrotechnicist, Mrs Morgan shouted, 'Ah, Mrs Bhakcu, I see you buy a new car today, man.'

Mrs Bhakcu didn't reply.

Mrs Morgan said, 'Ah, Mrs Bhakcu, you think your husband go give me a ride in his new car?'

Mrs Bhakcu said, 'Yes, *he* go give you a ride, but first *your* husband must give *me* a ride on his donkey-cart when he buy it.'

Bhakcu said to Mrs Bhakcu, 'Why don't you shut your mouth up?'

Mrs Bhakcu said, 'But how you want me to shut my mouth up? You is my husband, and I have to stand up for you.'

Bhakcu said very sternly, 'You only stand up for me when I tell you, you hear.'

(5) PORT OF SPAIN: TRAFFIC

Amryl Johnson, *Sequins for a Ragged Hem*

Fuelled by its oil economy, Port of Spain's traffic problems are legendary, not the least the etiquette of the driver–pedestrian relationship.

'They does cross the street as if they in their bedroom.'

Another day-time trip to Port of Spain. This time in a friend's car. The indignant exclamation had been provoked by a pedestrian stepping out in front of our car and sauntering nonchalantly across the street. Under normal circumstances, I would have taken little notice. There was something almost suicidal about the way he had stepped out in front of the car. But that wasn't it. He wanted to cross the street so he crossed, knowing the cars would have to stop for him. Far more practical than running him over to teach him a lesson. The laws on homicide are taken as seriously in Trinidad as they are anywhere else.

I watched and made mental notes. There was a rapport between driver and pedestrian. It was like a game being acted out. I would see it between clerks and customers, between audiences and performers. It had everything to do with action and response or clever repartee. Parrying with words.

I saw pedestrians react to drivers in a second way. There was indignation from one middle-aged gentleman when a car's bumper touched the crease in his trousers.

'Bounce me down! Bounce me, nah! You see what I go do you.'

The note of dare in his voice was matched by the action of rolling up his sleeve. The hand closed into a fist. The driver put on a mask of remote preoccupation and waited for the man to move away from his windscreen.

(6) TRINIDAD: AMERICANS

Mighty Sparrow, *The Yankees Back*

The profit-obsessed oilmen who came to Trinidad after the Second World War were a different breed from the philandering GIs.

Well, the day of slavery back again!
Ah hope it ain't reach in Port of Spain.
Since the Yankees come back over here
They buy out the whole of Pointe-a-Pierre.
Money start to pass, people start to bawl,
Pointe-a-Pierre sell, the workmen and all.
    Fifty cents a head for Grenadians,
    A dollar a head for Trinidadians;
    Tobagonians free, whether big or small;
    But they say, they ain't want Barbadians at all.

Well, it look as if they going mad
To sell the refinery in Trinidad.
Ah hear they tackling the Pitch Lake,
But ah keeping cool for Heaven's sake.
Next time they will buy Ste Madeleine Cane –
Then it's easy to capture Port of Spain.
But when they buy Trinidad and you think they stop,
They taking Tobago for lagniappe.
    Fifty cents a head *etc*.

Ah watching me girl friend, Lillian;
They have a funny intention
Bunching with Olga and Doris
Who intend to start their foolishness.
But if they think the Yankees making joke,
This time, ain't no fun: it's strictly work!
Not because they come back in barrage,
Remember the Sparrow still in charge.
    Fifty cents a head *etc*.

Whenever this place have Yankees
Women does make we suffer like peas,
But now it's entirely different,
The Yankees don't want entertainment.
The way they pack up in Pointe-a-Pierre,
They entertaining one another down there.
To any woman who want Yankee money,
Turn Grenadian and work like a donkey!
    Fifty cents a head *etc.*

(7) TRINIDAD: CARNIVAL

Lawrence Scott, *King Sailor One J'Ouvert Morning*

*Returning to Trinidad after a long absence, Philip Monagas feels
alienated from the island's culture until the start of Carnival, when
he resolves to take part in J'Ouvert.*

Four o'clock Monday morning. That was the magic hour. It felt like going
to bed and getting up for midnight mass. It had that feeling like going to
church. And instead of the litany: Tower of Ivory, House of Gold, Ark of
the Covenant pray for us, it was his carnival mantra, 'Come down J'Ouvert
morning, find yourself in a band.' Jam Jam Jam.

He shut the door behind him easy and went out into the four o'clock
darkness resplendently white with ribbons and pom poms: King Sailor,
with only the amber street light for a moon. He was walking down into
town from up in the Cascade Hills. Dogs barking. Cock was crowing since
midnight so that was nothing special. Shuffling feet. He could hear the slap
of washy cong on the pitch. People coming down. Massing. More people by
the savannah. This was more people than midnight mass Christmas time
even with the parang mass they have now. This was more people than
Easter vigil, even if they giving new fire and water.

Already he thought that everyone was watching him. And then it was
easy because he was watching everybody. People coming out, showing
themselves. There was no distinction now. Some people might think that
he was a tourist, but they have plenty black tourists too from Brooklyn and
Queens, he thought.

People were looking good. Even those who were not playing mas and just
had on jeans and T-shirt looked special. This was it. He had been told
about it and he had read about it: Carne Vale, Canboulay, Emancipation.
J'Ouvert was all these and he was here in the long line and belonging to it.
The little steel bands were coming down from the hills behind Port-of-
Spain and there was the sound ahead; a sound which was the massing of
people and the scraping of pans on the ground, the hooking up of pans on
to their sheds and then the final tuning and the fringes on the pan sheds
fluttered in the dawn breeze and glittered. A strange quiet. He saw a bat

and a skeleton float by. And then it was sudden, in absolute union, pan pan pan, jam jam jam, as Invaders began to move down Tragarete Road.

(8) TRINIDAD: CHINESE
Noel Woodroffe, *Wing's Way*

An important, but often despised, ingredient in the Trinidadian melting-pot are the Chinese. Wing, the small village grocer, lives a life of cultural alienation.

Throughout the day Wing sat at his ancient till while his wife served at the counter, parcelling out the flour and the rice and the half-pounds of sugar; the sides of salt-fish and the bootblack, the razor blades and the hairnets, the rat-poison and the face-cream, and the thousand other things that flowed out of Wing's shop and helped to flesh out the lives of the villagers whose houses cluttered up the High Road, backed up four to a yard, squashed into almost inaccessible corners of back lots, straggling down to the fishermen's huts by the sea. These people, Wing's customers, mingled curses with their cooking smells and incestuously depended on their physical nearness to each other. They directed a stream of ill-concealed hostility towards the new, concrete houses built by the oil company for its workers at the other end of the village. These houses were serviced by a new-type supermarket owned by Indians who had magically appeared when the housing development was completed. The Indians' supermarket, with its little carts which customers wheeled down the aisles between the shelves picking out their own goods, was avoided with grim determination by the residents of Old Village, as the older section of La Negra was called. They preferred to deal with Wing only.

Wing was not fooled by the people's faithfulness to his shop. He knew that they came to him because in their eyes he was neuter. They would not buy from the Indians, and the new supermarket with its efficient check-out lanes and new cash registers robbed them of the contempt they always felt for the shopowners. Wing knew the people well enough after so many years, to be aware of the fact that it was only their contempt for the man behind the counter that kept at bay, for a little while at least, the deep anxiety of seeing their hard-earned dollars disappear for a few paltry, perishable items. So that when they called for a quarter pound of butter (as they called margarine) in loud, impatient tones, Wing cashed their few cents into the jaws of his till with a face as masked and as impassive as a Chinese statue. Wing sometimes matched contempt for contempt and spread their change with a fanning motion of his hand across the counter-top. He sneered then in his mind as he watched washer-women struggle to pick up the small flat coins off the counter with finger-ends swollen, pitted and blunted by too many years in harsh soap.

(9) Trinidad: 'Coolies'

Charles Kingsley, *At Last*

Victorian traveller Charles Kingsley reiterates the conventional contemporary beliefs about the proverbial thrift and industry of Indian indentured labourers.

After·he has served his five years' apprenticeship, the Coolie has two courses before him. Either he can re-indenture himself to an employer for not more than twelve months, which as a rule he does; or he can seek employment where he likes. At the end of a continuous residence of ten years in all, and at any period after that, he is entitled to a free passage back to Hindostan; or he may exchange his right to a free passage for a Government grant of ten acres of land. He has meanwhile, if he has been thrifty, grown rich. His wife walks about, at least on high-days, bedizened with jewels: nay, you may see her, even on work-days, hoeing in the cane-piece with heavy silver bangles hanging down over her little brown feet: and what wealth she does not carry on her arms, ankles, neck and nostril, her husband has in the savings' bank. The ship *Arima*, as an instance, took back 320 Coolies last year, of whom seven died on the voyage. These people carried with them 65 585 dollars; and one man, Heerah, handed over 6000 dollars for transmission through the Treasury, and was known to have about him 4000 more . . .

Very interesting was the first glimpse of Hindoos; and still more of Hindoos in the West Indies – the surplus of one of the oldest civilisations in the old world, come hither to replenish the new; novel was the sight of the dusky limbs swarming up and down among the rocks beneath the Matapalo shade; the group in the water as we landed, bathing and dressing themselves at the same time, after the modest and graceful Hindoo fashion; the visit to the wooden barracks, where a row of men was ranged on one side of the room, with their women and children on the other, having their name, caste, native village, and so forth, taken down before they were sent off to the estates to which they were indentured. Three things were noteworthy; first, the healthy cheerful look of all, speaking well for the care and good feeding which they had had on board ship; next, the great variety in their faces and complexions. Almost all of them were low-caste people . . .

(10) TRINIDAD: CRICKET

C.L.R James, *Cricket*

Cricket offers the Caribbean a way to settle old scores against the English. It is also a matter of life and death between rival local teams, who will resort to any tactic.

My father was a member of the cricket club which had been formed by the young men of the area, who used the new overarm instead of the old underarm bowling. But another team in the area still bowled underarm. So they professed great contempt for the new-fangled players, who played overarm, and kept to their underarm bowling. The overarm bowlers challenged them to a match. The older ones refused.

Even in those days there was a cricket competition every Saturday, organized from Port of Spain. From Tunapuna, the underarm players and my father's team both joined. Thus, they had to play against one another after all.

My father was a teacher, and the head of his school was a man called Mr Waddell, a great underarm cricketer in his day, but he sided with my father's team. Every afternoon, after school, he had the senior boys bowling to my father, while he bowled underarm, the kind of bowling my father would have to meet. Friday afternoon, Mr Waddell told my father, 'Robert, open out now and make your strokes.'

On the match day great numbers of people came around to see the competition between the older generation and the new. My father went in first wicket down, made forty-eight not out, and they beat the old gentlemen by eight wickets.

One of the older generation was Mr Blenman, the butcher. Mr Blenman did not play cricket any more but he told my father gravely, 'Robert, we're not finished with it. We'll play you another match one day.' My father was triumphant: 'Whenever you are ready.'

After a year or two Mr Blenman informed my father his team was now ready to play a challenge match. As usual many of the neighbourhood turned up for the match. In Mr Blenman's team was a stranger.

He batted and batted. Ninety-five runs. And he would have made a hundred but that he got run out at ninety-five. Worse still; when the young men went in to bat the stranger bowled almost as well, and the older generation won the match in great style. My father's team wondered who the stranger was. And only a year or two afterwards when the West Indian team was chosen to go to England they learnt that Mr Blenman's stranger was C.A. Ollivierre, one of the famous family of cricketers from St Vincent. It seems that Mr Blenman had probably paid his passage from St Vincent and then back again. Ollivierre distinguished himself greatly in England. Such was the temper of cricket in a West Indian village nearly a hundred years ago.

(11) Trinidad: Cricket

Jan Morris, *Howzat?* and *Mr Morgan*

At the heart of Port of Spain lies the Savannah, the arena for the capital's cricket contests and the scene of occasional racial tension.

Wherever you look, from the hills to the city, they are all playing cricket. To be sure, they are playing the game all over the island, in numberless unmapped clearings in the bush, overhung by lugubrious banana trees or gorgeous flamboyants: but this is the very heart of Trinidadian cricket, where the game is played today with more dash and delight than anywhere else on earth. There may be thirty or forty games, all at the same time. The thud of the balls echoes like muffled fireworks across the green, and wherever you look there are the crouching fielding figures, the big stylish black batsmen, a game suddenly collapsing in theatrical laughter, or the poised theatrical expectancy, all white eyes and quivering arms, that follows the magical cry of '*Howzat?*'

Some of these sportsmen are grand and mannered, with spotless whites and rolled wickets; but they trail away through immeasurable gradations of clubmanship to the raggety small boys on the edge of the field, with an old bit of wood for a bat, and a stone for a ball, and the wicket-keeper peering with breathless expectancy over a petrol can . . . Many a strand of culture or tradition contributes to the texture of Port of Spain, and one of the strongest is that tough old umbilical, cricket.

Not all the cricketers are black. Many of these citizens are Indian by origin, and many are a *mélange* in themselves, part European, part African, with a touch of Chinese and a Hindu grandparent on the mother's side. Racial rivalries are still potent, especially between brown and black, and sometimes you may catch a hint of them on the Savannah. An Indian father, for instance, shoos away a small black boy anxious to play kites with his son. 'Go away, sonny,' he says crossly, 'this is a private game we are playing, you see, and we do not want other people coming and playing here.' The black boy gazes stubbornly into the middle distance. he is wearing an old Army forage cap, much too big for him. 'I'se not playing with you anyway,' he says. 'I'se playing here all by myself. This ain't no private garden' . . . And you can see a spasm of annoyance cross that Hindu's smooth face, a spasm that runs through the society of Trinidad, and gives an extra vicious animation to the politics of the city.

(12) TRINIDAD: EAST INDIANS

Ismith Khan, *The Jumbie Bird*

*A group of elderly Indians gather in Woodford Square to smoke and
to discuss their favourite topic: the dreamed-of return to Hindustan.*

'Khan Sahib,' Mongroo said, 'even if we ain't go back to Hindustan, these
children should go. I does feel too bad when I watch them and see that they
is Indian. I does say, "But what right these children and them have to stop
here?" We old people was foolish, man, bu the children an' them shouldn't
have to suffer for we wrongs.'

'This boy have to go back, mus' go back to learn what kind people he
born from . . .one day . . .' Kale Khan's voice trailed off as he passed some
of the herbs to the other two men.

They massaged the herbs in the palms of their hands, the two men
pressed their thumbs upon their palms with the herbs between, and Kale
Khan pressed the herbs from one spot to another until he had a flat disc,
which he rolled into a ball, and pressed it out again, doing this over and
over. Then they put the three wads together, and Kale Khan stuffed it into
the clay pipe with three or four quick sharp nudges with his finger. A look
at the mouth of the pipe, a few more quick nudges, this time his finger
entered the mouth of the pipe, then he set it down at his side in the grass.

'You mean to say all you boys didn't have sense to know it was only dry,
dry lies those rascals tell you when they say that you would get rich and
make plenty money plantin' sugar cane in Trinidad?'

'Baba,' Kareem said respectfully, addressing Kale Khan, 'we was young
boys, we thought we would run away from home, make big fortune, and
then we go back to we village; how we could ever know that when we come
here they would give we cutlass and hoe to work in this hot sun? First day
Mongroo get so much big, big blisters on his hands, he couldn't even hold
the hoe the next mornin'.'

'You hear that boy . . . you hearin' well what that worthless scamp
Woodford tell these boys? Fool them and bring them come Trinidad side,
you ain't go learn all that in History book . . .'

(13) TRINIDAD: REBELLION

Ralph de Boissière, *Crown Jewel*

*A wave of social unrest is spreading across the plantations and
oilfields of 1930s colonial Trinidad. The reformist leader, Boisson,
is losing ground to revolutionary agitators such as Payne.*

The promises of government had been like so many promises, light as the
cotton that flies from the silk-cotton tree in March, but seedless, fruitless.
In the south the idle thickened, spread like a pestilence, infecting the land

with demands and questions no one heeded. The official world was so convinced we were a happy people, needing little, and paid no great attention when men went hat in hand, in vain, from boss to boss. They did not seem to notice when men gave up hope. Whey-whey gambling, the illegal manufacture and sale of rum, petty thefts of every kind, highway robbery – these must be stamped out. A menace to the law-abiding!

On the sugar estates the white overseers – and how well they knew the Indians, riding among them all day long, not shy of enjoying the comforts some black-eyed daughters could provide – yes, they knew, they were convinced the peasants were content with a half-day's work. Three days' work a week for eight months of the year, it was all the sugar trade would carry. Doctors often found the bodies full of hookworm. Independent doctors claimed the hookworm was due to ill-nourishment and filth; company doctors claimed the ill-nourishment was due to the hookworm. Perhaps both were right, but it was beyond question that the family cow with uncovered ribs was healthier than they. For carting canes a man earned fifty-five cents a day, the highest wage. And six cents a day for the children, the weeders. And still ingratitude. One could not please them. Grumbling and threats when, by Jove, if you'd given them a whole week's work they'd have gone off in the afternoon to sleep or fish, or tend their vegetable gardens.

The best that Boisson's dozens of hangers-on could do was to point with pride to his picture in court dress when in May he attended the coronation of George the Sixth. But Workers' Welfare was growing apace. Payne got a job as a truck driver on one of the smaller fields. He formed branches of the party in the Point Fortin area, to the south-west of Fyzabad, and in Pointe-a-Pierre, the big refinery twenty miles north. The drivers flocked to meetings. Their quarrel was chiefly with overtime. Instead of getting it from the ninth hour they got it only from the tenth, and even then not time and a half but time and a quarter. Further, they claimed that if they must sleep 'on call' in the companies' barracks instead of at home they were entitled to pay from the time of entering the barracks. They were demanding, in addition, extra pay for Sunday work.

(14) Trinidad: Social Embarrassment

Merle Hodge, *Crick Crack Monkey*

Cynthia has been awarded a scholarship and has left Tantie's poor but happy home to live with her wealthy and snobbish Aunt Beatrice. Tantie has announced unexpectedly that she is coming to visit.

I waited in pain for the sound of a car drawing up at our gate. Carol and Jessica were agog with wicked expectation; Auntie Beatrice moved about the house with her worst dragon-face on. Several times I nearly fainted at the sound of a car braking. But when they came they stood darkening the front door before I was aware of anything . . .

'Tee! Dou-dou!' Tantie swept into the drawingroom with the whole band in tow. Horrors, they had brought Doolarie, what would Auntie Beatrice say to that afterwards? And Uncle Sylvester coarse and repulsive, his over-fed stomach tipping out over the top of his pants. They sat themselves down as though they had every right to make themselves comfortable in these surroundings. In fact the tone of Auntie Beatrice's drawingroom did not seem to make the slightest impression on them . . .

I realized afterwards that I had sat on the edge of my chair for the whole time, with my head hung. The worst moment of all was when they drew forth a series of greasy paper bags, announcing that they contained polorie, anchar, roti from Neighb' Ramlaal-Wife, and accra and fry-bake and zaboca from Tantie, with a few other things I had almost forgotten existed, in short, all manner of ordinary nastiness . . .

I sat with the bags poised gingerly on my knee Tantie suggested: 'Well yu don' want to eat a polorie or something? What yu waitin for?' I declined in alarm: the very thought of sitting in Auntie Beatrice's drawingroom eating coolie-food! And accra! Saltfish! Fancy even bringing saltfish into Auntie Beatrice's house! When I refused Uncle Sylvester, to my disgust, leaned over and said familiarly: 'Awright, dou-dou, lemme help yu out them,' and reaching into a greasy bag drew out a thick spotted roti; he settled back with sounds of satisfaction and opening his jaws wide enough to accommo-date Government House (this was a dictum of Auntie Beatrice's in the context of table-manners) proceeded to champ away. A strong smell of curry assailed the drawingroom. That was another thing I would pay for afterwards, I thought miserably. And I hoped Auntie Beatrice wasn't looking on too, with Uncle Sylvester sitting on the sofa eating roti and curry with as much reverence as if he were sitting on a tapia-floor.

Biographical and literary notes

ANTHONY, Michael (1930–). Born and brought up in **Mayaro**, Anthony attended school in **San Fernando** before working at the oil refinery at **Pointe-à-Pierre**. In 1954 he emigrated to England where he had various short stories broadcast on the BBC's Caribbean Voices programme. In 1963 his first novel, *The Games Were Coming* was published and since then a number of other novels and short story collections have appeared, including *The Year in San Fernando*, *Green Days by the River* and *Cricket in the Road*. In 1970, Michael Anthony returned to live in Trinidad.

DE BOISSIERE, Ralph (1907–). Born in Trinidad, de Boissière emigrated to Australia in 1948, where he worked as a salesman, clerk and car-assembler. *Crown Jewel* (Extract 13), first published in Australia in 1953, was an international success (translated into nine languages). An explicitly Marxist critique of the colonial system, it tells of the unrest and hardship of the 1930s which spawned trade union and left-wing militancy in Trinidad's oilfields and propelled the island further towards independence. Interweaving political commentary with romantic intrigue, the novel introduces a wide variety of characters – British, black, Indian, Chinese, South American – mirroring Trinidad's complex social and ethnic structures.

HODGE, Merle (1944–). Born in Trinidad and educated there, Hodge won the Girls' Island Scholarship in 1962 and read French at University College, London. She has also lived in France and Denmark. She has taught French at the University of the West Indies and has worked in secondary schools in Trinidad and Grenada, notably during the period of the People's Revolutionary Government. *Crick Crack Monkey* (Extract 14) is an account, both poignant and humorous, of a young girl's coming to terms with social and intellectual snobbery in Trinidad. Having been brought up in the boisterous, warm but working-class household of her aunt, Tantie, after her mother's death, Cynthia wins a scholarship to a good school. Her other aunt, the vain and pretentious Beatrice, takes her into her home in an attempt to teach her the appropriate social graces. Gradually, Cynthia loses touch with what had been a happy childhood and enters the alienating world of middle-class suburban Trinidad.

JAMES, C.L.R. (1901–1989). Historian, novelist, critic, political activist and cricket enthusiast, Cyril Lionel Robert James was born in **Tunapuna**, near Port of Spain. The son of a schoolteacher, he attended Trinidad's main government secondary school, where he became a teacher himself in the 1920s. Among his pupils was the young Eric Williams, later to become independent Trinidad's first Prime Minister. In 1932 James went to London, where he was active in the growing African nationalist movement. His contacts included orthodox Communists such as George Padmore, Moscow's chief agent in charge of African and Pan-African affairs and a wide variety of Trotskyists and other revolutionaries. He published widely on political and cultural issues and was cricket correspondent for the *Manchester Guardian* and *Glasgow Herald*. His influence among radical black thinkers, nationalists and Marxists, was enormous. In 1938 James moved to the USA, where he became active in the Trotskyist Socialist Workers' Party. He was interned on Ellis Island in 1952 and was expelled the following year, returning to England. In 1958 he went to Trinidad and spent four years there in the period leading up to independence. During that time he was associated with Eric Williams, by now the leader of the People's National Movement (PNM). Attracted by the PNM's anti-imperialist stance, James became editor of the party newspaper, the *Nation*. Yet within two years he and Williams had split over ideological differences and Williams left Trinidad. From 1962 onwards, James was mostly based in London, where he died aged 88 in 1989. His stature as a leading twentieth-century Marxist thinker grew throughout his long and distinguished career. A prolific writer, James' many works include the novel *Minty Alley*, 1936, the play *Toussaint Louverture*, 1936, a collection of political and cricket writing, *Beyond the Boundary*, 1963, and *Nkrumah and the Ghana Revolution*, 1977. His 1938 classic, *The Black Jacobins* (see under Haiti) is perhaps the most important study of the Haitian revolution of 1791–1804, placing the slave revolution in the context of the emerging black nationalism of the 1930s. James is also remembered for his uniquely politicized cricket writing. In 'Cricket' (Extract 10), we see the lighter side of the sport which fascinated him throughout his life.

JOHNSON, Amryl. Trinidad-born Johnson came to Britain when she was eleven. She has worked as a poet in schools and as a lecturer in arts education. *Sequins for a Ragged Hem* (Extract 5) tells of her six-month trip around the Caribbean and what she describes as a 'quest for memory'. The book looks closely and wryly at social life in the region, particularly Trinidad, and the ever-present legacy of slavery and colonialism.

KHAN, Ismith (1925–). Ismith Khan was born and brought up near **Woodford Square** in **Port of Spain**, the haunt of eccentrics and down-and-outs. His grandfather, Kale Khan, on whom a principal character in *The Jumbie Bird* (Extract 12) is based, was a Pathan, one of the proud and independent people whose traditional homelands straddle Pakistan and Afghanistan. He came to Trinidad as a free craftsman, but, like his fictional counterpart, formed part of a wider East Indian community evolved from indentureship. Ismith Khan recreates the defiant anti-Britishness of his grandfather in the novel, as well as the collective sense of exile and loss which characterizes the Indian diaspora in the Caribbean. The 'jumbie bird' of the title is the symbolic portent of death, whose cry is superstitiously thought to bring tragedy to this exiled community. The young hero, Jamini, is caught between the nostalgia of his grandfather and the need to adapt himself to the realities of modern-day, multi-cultural Trinidad. Ismith Khan is also the author of *The Obeah Man*, 1964.

KINGSLEY, Charles (1819–1879). British clergyman, supporter of 'Christian socialism' and author of *The Water Babies*, Kingsley visited Trinidad in 1869–70, returning to publish his impressions of the then British colony. *At Last* (Extract 9) reflects many of the racial and cultural attitudes of the time, and Kingsley repeatedly stresses the 'civilizing mission' of the British in the Caribbean. His account is enthusiastically in favour of East Indian migration to Trinidad and praises the 'Coolies' as industrious, sober and community-minded. His impression of Trinidad's African population is less flattering. Despite many such views, as a keen naturalist, Kingsley provides a fascinating account of the island's flora and fauna and the workings of its colonial government.

LOVELACE, Earl (1935–). Born in **Toco**, in northern Trinidad, Lovelace was brought up in Tobago, returning to Trinidad for his secondary education. He worked on the *Trinidad Guardian* before becoming an agricultural extension officer. In 1964 he won the Trinidad and Tobago Independence literary competition with his first novel, *While Gods Are Falling*,

Earl Lovelace

1965. *The Dragon Can't Dance*, 1979, was followed by *The Wine of Astonishment*, 1982. Since returning to Trinidad from the USA in the 1970s, Lovelace has worked in community theatre projects and has lectured at the University of the West Indies. *The Dragon Can't Dance* (Extract 1) is possibly one of the most influential modern novels of the Caribbean. With its acute depiction of the suffering and squalor of shantytown life and the redemptive quality of Carnival, it goes directly to the core of Trinidadian popular culture. The novel follows a cast of characters who inhabit the same slum 'yard' near **Port of Spain** and the way in which Carnival galvanizes a community which lives on the margins of Trinidadian society. C.L.R. James was not exaggerating when he wrote: 'Nowhere have I seen more of the realities of a whole country disciplined into one imaginative whole.'

MIGHTY SPARROW (1935–). Born Slinger Francisco in Grand Roy, Grenada, 'Mighty Sparrow' has been undisputed champion of calypso in Trinidad from the mid-1950s onwards. His lyrics are a salacious blend of political satire, humour and innuendo, and have been recorded on more than forty albums of calypso songs. Sparrow was the first calypsonian to move from exclusively live performances to the recording studio and accordingly earned an international reputation as a singer and lyricist. 'The Yankees Back' (Extract 6) is a celebrated example of his mix of wit and social commentary.

MORRIS, Jan (1926–). One of Britain's best-known travel writers, Jan Morris has written about Wales, Venice, Oxford, Manhattan, Spain, Canada, Hong Kong and Sydney. Her travel pieces have been published in six collections, and she is also the author of autobiographies and the novel, *Last Letters from Hav*, 1985.

'Howzat? and Mr Morgan' (Extract 11) is a typical piece of acute observation, affectionately describing **Port of Spain** as a place of 'raw and raucous celebrations'.

NAIPAUL, V.S. (1932–). Vidiadhar Surajprasad Naipaul is one of the most prominent, and sometimes controversial, writers to have emerged from the Caribbean. He is the author of several novels and collections of short stories dealing directly with Trinidad and the Caribbean, including *The Mystic Masseur*, 1957, *The Suffrage of Elvira*, 1958, *Miguel Street*, 1959, and *A House for Mr Biswas*, 1961. Naipaul came to England in 1950, where he studied at Oxford before starting his literary career. The early fiction is characterized by an ironic and often humorous tone, drawing on personal experiences of life in the East Indian community of Trinidad. *Miguel Street* (Extract 4) is a collection of vignettes, some comic and other poignant, of a working-class, multiracial community in **Port of Spain**. With *The Mimic Men*, 1967, however, Naipaul seemingly abandoned his hitherto affectionate, if ironic, depictions of the Caribbean experience, turning to what his critics have seen as a patrician and condescending dismissal of the region's social and cultural life. In works such as *The Middle Passage*, 1962, and *The Loss of El Dorado*, 1969, Naipaul returns to the history and present-day (then largely colonial or newly independent) society of the Caribbean, painting a dispiriting picture of poverty, racism and insularity. For him, the Caribbean is a place of rootless and hence cultureless people, unable to sustain authentic forms of artistic and political expression and condemned to mimic the dominant influences of the colonial and neo-colonial powers. In *The Middle Passage*, he concludes, 'Every day I saw the same things – unemployment, ugliness, overpopulation, race – and every day I heard the same circular arguments. The young intellectuals, whose gifts had been developed to enrich a developing, stable society, talked and talked and became frenzied in their frustration. They were looking for an enemy, and there was none.'

Naipaul's disparaging depiction of the Caribbean has made him a controversial and often unpopular figure in the region. He remains adamant, however, that 'history is built around achievement and creation; and nothing was created in the West Indies.' In *A Way in the World*, 1994, he returns to some of his dominant themes, reflecting on what he senses is the Caribbean's lack of a meaningful past. This he describes in personal terms: 'Many years later I thought that the feeling of the void had to do with my temperament, the temperament of a child of a recent Asian–Indian immigrant community in a mixed population: the child looked back and found no family past, found a blank. But I feel again now that I was responding to something that was missing, something that had been rooted out.'

Naipaul has also travelled widely in India, Africa, the American Deep South and the Far East, writing on the political and ethnic conflicts he encountered. He now lives in Britain. In 1990 he received a knighthood for his services to literature.

SCOTT, Lawrence. Scott was born in Trinidad and came to England to become a Benedictine monk. Choosing instead to study English, he has since taught English, drama and creative writing in London and Trinidad. His first novel *Witchbroom*, 1992, is a rich and exotic reconstruction of the Caribbean region's history as told by a multifaceted narrator and last of a Creole dynasty, Lavren Monagas de los Macajuelos. In the short story 'King Sailor One J'Ouvert Morning'

(Extract 7), the *déraciné* white Trinidadian Philip Monagas, returning to the island after a long absence, finds himself drawn into the apotheosis of J'Ouvert morning, the explosive high point of Port of Spain's Carnival.

SELVON, Sam (1923–1994). Born in **San Fernando** of East Indian parents, Selvon worked at the **Pointe-à-Pierre** oil refinery and as a journalist on the *Trinidad Guardian* before emigrating to Britain in 1950 (coincidentally on the same ship as the Barbadian George Lamming). His experiences in London inspired his masterpiece *The Lonely Londoners*, 1956, a wry account of West Indian immigrant life in a cold and unwelcoming city. *Moses Migrating* (Extract 3) is the third novel in the Moses trilogy (after *The Lonely Londoners* and *Moses Ascending*, 1975). His other acclaimed works of fiction include *A Brighter Sun*, 1952, and *The Plains of Caroni*, 1970. In 1978, Selvon moved to Canada, where he taught literary criticism and creative writing. His death in 1994 brought many tributes to his literary career and particular mastery of humorous dialogue. Beneath the comic use of dialect and vernacular, however, lies a serious concern with the poverty of Trinidad's East Indian agricultural labourers and the racism faced by Caribbean immigrants in Britain.

WOODROFFE, Noel (1952–). Born in Tobago, Woodroffe spent his childhood in the famous **Pitch Lake** village of **La Brea**. He studied at the University of the West Indies where he completed a PhD. He has worked as a teacher, a civil servant, a salesman and a tour guide. His short story 'Wing's Way' (Extract 8), is an atmospheric account of a Chinese store-keeper's double life of everyday usury and private dreams.

THE BRITISH DEPENDENCIES

'Across the wave, along the wind,/Flutter and plough your way,/But where will you a Sceptre find/To match the English Sway?/Its conscience holds the world in awe/With blessing or with ban;/Its Freedom guards the Reign of Law,/And majesty of Man!'
Alfred Austin

Strewn across the Caribbean lie some of the last remnants of the once mighty British Empire. Nowadays they are mere pinpricks on the atlas, a few isolated colonial outposts among the independent nations of the Caribbean. Yet as recently as fifty years ago, a map would have shown many of the islands in imperial red, ranging from the sweeping archipelago of the Bahamas to the solid outline of Trinidad, almost touching the South American mainland.

It was also fifty years ago that the British resolved to rid themselves of their Caribbean colonies. After centuries of colonial conflict and control, the possessions had become a burden to Britain by the end of the Second World War, and it was with undisguised relief that London granted independence to the great majority of its territories. In the course of the 1960s and 1970s, new sovereign states regularly came into being, with the last – St Kitts and Nevis – waiting until 1983 to cut its ties with Britain. By then, British influence and aid had declined, and small-island states saw a brighter future under the influence of the USA and the multilateral donor organizations.

Yet today the Union Jack still flies over a handful of Caribbean territories. In these islands, Governors still live in elegant residences, decorated with ornamental cannons and well tended lawns. Meanwhile, in London's Foreign and Commonwealth Office civil servants discuss how to control expenditure on the last crumbs of empire. Britain's withdrawal has not been as complete as perhaps it wanted, and certain obligations persist.

Those who live in the last colonies, however, do not enjoy the rights and benefits taken for granted by the inhabitants of French Martinique and Guadeloupe or the Dutch islands. They cannot, for instance, live in Britain, even though they hold a form of British passport. Nor can they expect free medical treatment or education in the 'mother country'. Theirs is a second-class British citizenship.

368

FACT BOX

AREA:
Anguilla – 96 sq km
Cayman Islands – 260 sq km
Montserrat – 63 sq km
Turks and Caicos Islands – 266 sq km
POPULATION:
Anguilla – 8960
Cayman Islands – 30 000
Montserrat – 11 600
Turks and Caicos Islands – 12 500
CAPITAL:
Anguilla – The Valley
Cayman Islands – George Town
Montserrat – Plymouth
Turks and Caicos Islands – Cockburn Town
LANGUAGES: English
POLITICAL STATUS: Anguilla, Montserrat and the Turks and
Caicos Islands are British Dependent Territories; the Cayman
Islands are a British Crown Colony.
PER CAPITA GDP:
Anguilla – US$15 500
Cayman Islands – US$27 480
Montserrat – US$4846
Turks and Caicos Islands – US$6252

There are five dependent territories (the accepted euphemism for colonies) left: **Anguilla, The British Virgin Islands** (see The Virgin Islands), **The Cayman Islands**, **Montserrat** and **The Turks and Caicos Islands**. Each has a distinctive history and each has its own reasons for wishing to remain attached, however tenuously, to the old imperial power. For most it is the economic and political security derived from the attachment and the belief that genuine independence cannot be achieved by vulnerable micro-states which determine the relationship. But there are also other, more specific, grounds for putting off a divorce that most others saw as inevitable.

ANGUILLA

You can, say the locals, stand at one end of Anguilla and see the sea at the other end, so flat and featureless is this 34 square mile island. Hurricane Luis, which smashed into it in the Autumn of 1995, removed the few trees and telephone poles which might have obscured the view. Apart from its superb beaches, around which are clustered a handful of up-market hotels, Anguilla arguably has little to offer. The main town, **The Valley**, is a small settlement of shops, a bank, government offices and the island's only traffic light; most Anguillans live in tiny villages or isolated houses scattered across the rolling scrub-covered landscape.

Anguilla's poor soil was never suitable for plantation cultivation, and colonization was a piecemeal affair, starting in 1650 with a British settlement. There had previously been indigenous communities living on the island (there have been significant discoveries of petroglyphs and other artefacts), but they were driven away by the British. The Caribs tried to attack the British in 1656 and the French made invasion attempts in 1745 and 1796, but these were only brief interruptions to continuous British rule. Anguilla was no great prize compared to many of the surrounding islands, and as a result it was left to itself. Its poverty was its best defence against pirates and rival European powers. In 1825 when Henry Nelson Coleridge (◊ St Kitts and Nevis) visited the island, he described the Anguillans as 'a good sort of folks, although they have been living in a curious state of suspended civilization.'

The island escaped large-scale slavery, and when abolition arrived in 1834 the freed slaves joined the ranks of small peasants, growing tobacco, fishing and building boats. Land was not difficult to obtain, and Anguillans mostly became smallholders. As V.S. Naipaul (◊ Trinidad and Tobago) points out in his essay 'The Shipwrecked Six Thousand' the island's lifeblood was money sent back from men working abroad. They went to the Dominican Republic and Jamaica to cut cane, to the refineries of Aruba and Curaçao, or, for some obscure reason, to the English town of Slough.

To simplify their colonial bureaucracy the British ruled Anguilla in conjunction with St Kitts and Nevis, viewing the three islands as an entity despite being seventy miles apart. St Kitts, the largest of the three, was naturally chosen as the administrative centre. When the prospect of independence drew closer in the 1960s, London proposed that St Kitts–Nevis–Anguilla become a State in Association with the UK prior to complete independence. This seemed a neat formula for joining three tiny islands into a viable single state.

But the British had not counted on the Anguillans' strong sense of their own island identity and, more importantly, a traditional suspicion of St Kitts. Since the mid-nineteenth century the people of Anguilla had resented being ruled via St Kitts and on several occasions had petitioned London to treat them on an equal footing. Kittitians, for their part, had always mocked Anguillans, seeing them as country bumpkins living primitive lives on an undeveloped island. This mutual hostility worsened when Robert Bradshaw, the demagogic former sugar workers' leader, became Premier of St Kitts. Affronted that Anguillans had not voted for his St Kitts Labour Party, Bradshaw reputedly promised to turn Anguilla into a 'desert'. Islanders complained that the government in St Kitts vindictively withheld resources allocated by London and even used grants destined for Anguilla for projects in St Kitts.

Nonetheless, Britain pressed ahead with its plans, and in February 1967 the three-island grouping became self-governing. The arrangement was to last only a matter of weeks, and in May after a series of disturbances a group of some 250 armed Anguillans rounded up seventeen policemen from St Kitts, put them in a boat and pushed them out to sea. The following month Anguilla voted overwhelmingly in a referendum for independence from St Kitts. At one point, a group of seventeen Anguillan men even attempted an invasion of St Kitts, but fortunately arrived late, having become lost *en route*.

All attempts at compromise failed. Anguillans resolutely rejected 'St Kitts imperialism' and London's pleas for a settlement. Their unilateral secession left St Kitts powerless and presented the British with an unwelcome constitutional crisis. In February 1968 the American writer John Updike ◊ visited the island and wrote in his 'Letter From Anguilla' (Extract 1) of its strange mix of parochialism and paranoia.

That paranoia was perhaps justified, for in March 1969, six weeks after another referendum had reconfirmed Anguillans' desire for independence, a British force of 300 paratroopers, 40 Marines and 50 policemen invaded the island in what Updike describes as a 'Lilliputian exercise of gunboat diplomacy'. Not a life was lost, and not even an injury was recorded, as Anguillans welcomed the British as liberators. The invasion was widely derided as colonial comic opera; *Time* magazine described it as Britain's 'Bay of Piglets', and the *Times* regretted that 'a British Government is still capable of replaying Suez not as tragedy but as farce'.

If the British authorities thought that they could persuade Anguilla to accept control from St Kitts, they were mistaken. The islanders stoutly resisted any renewed relationship with their old adversary, and eventually Britain reluctantly agreed to resume formal control of the island. So it has remained to this day, a colony which wanted to be independent from St Kitts but not from London.

Anguilla is now largely self-governing, with a Chief Minister who works in consultation with a Governor. The Chief Minister naturally complains that London does not provide enough financial assistance. The Governor is too diplomatic to agree, but does his best to remind the Foreign and Colonial Office of its responsibilities.

THE CAYMAN ISLANDS

The Cayman Islands, statistics show, have more fax machines per head of population than anywhere else in the world. With a population of just under 30 000, the islands are also home to more than 500 banks, 20 000 registered companies and 350 insurance companies. The Yellow Pages telephone directory lists six pages of banks; the modern office blocks which have sprung up in the capital, **George Town**, are bedecked with the brass plates of mysterious finance companies.

The Cayman Islands are literally awash with money. They constitute the largest offshore banking centre in the world and enjoy the Caribbean's highest per capita income (US$27 500). Nearly all the financial activity takes place on Grand Cayman, the biggest of the three islands. Cayman Brac and Little Cayman are smaller, quieter and considered among the best diving destinations in the region.

Flat, arid and with no supply of fresh water, the Cayman Islands were not originally destined for economic greatness. Christopher Columbus chanced upon the islands in 1503 when he called them Las Tortugas after the large turtles which abound there. Later they became known as Las Caymanas, the Carib word for the salt-water crocodiles which were also to be found in large numbers. The first European visitors were normally in search of turtle meat, and ships passed by especially in order to hunt the creatures. English settlers from Jamaica arrived in the 1660s but were harried by Spanish pirates. In turn, English pirates used the islands as a base from which to attack Spanish and other foreign ships. Large-scale slavery never really took hold as the islands were too dry and barren to support plantation production.

From 1670 the islands were administered from the British colony of Jamaica, although there was a measure of internal self-government. The Governor of Jamaica was hence also the Governor of the Cayman Islands, and as a result the islands were very much at the periphery of the British Empire. The account provided by 1930s traveller Karl Baarslag ◊ in his *Islands of Adventure* (Extract 2) gives some idea of their remoteness and backwardness. Turtle fishing provided some income, but most Caymanian men left home to work aboard ships. When Jamaica opted for independence in 1962, the Cayman Islands chose to become a direct dependency of Britain.

The dramatic transformation of the islands into an international tax haven took place mainly in the 1970s, and by 1987 foreign company assets in the Caymans were valued at US$200 billion. Much of this money was legitimate, being held in bank accounts for legal tax or investment purposes. But millions also flowed into the islands from dubious sources in Miami and Latin America. Writing of the Caymans just before Queen Elizabeth's official visit in 1983, *Sunday Times* journalist Simon Winchester likened them to a 'Switzerland in the Caribbean'.

Tourism has accompanied the offshore banking boom, and the Caymans now promote themselves in British and American newspapers as an up-market vacation destination. The rush to build hotels, condominiums and marinas has created jobs for poorer locals as well as for illegal immigrants from Haiti and other islands.

MONTSERRAT

With place names like **Wapping**, **Dagenham** and **Streatham**, Montserrat seems to owe more than a little to the influence of suburban London. Yet the island's claim to fame is rather more its supposed Irishness than its Englishness. Those arriving at its airport will find a shamrock emblem stamped into their passports; the island's flag is adorned by a harp-bearing maiden; there are villages called **Cork Hill** or **St Patrick's**. Montserrat likes to be known as the 'Emerald Isle', its greenness being both a result of its lush vegetation and its Irish connections.

Columbus sighted Montserrat in 1493 and named it after the monastery in Spain where the Jesuit Ignacio de Loyola founded his order. The Caribs who lived there knew it as *Alliouagana*, meaning 'land of the prickly bush', which perhaps explains why there were relatively few of them. They had totally disappeared by the mid-seventeenth century when Sir Thomas Warner, founder of the neighbouring colony of St Kitts, ordered dissident English and Irish Catholics to move onto Montserrat. There a thriving Catholic community grew up, safe from the bigotry of other islands. Its ranks were swelled by refugees fleeing religious persecution in Virginia and by convicts expelled from Ireland by Cromwell.

But the Irish settlers were as prepared to import slaves as any other colonists, and in the course of the eighteenth century the island became a sugar-exporter, with whites outnumbered ten to one by black slaves. A rebellion in 1768 was ruthlessly suppressed, and although the French made several attempts to grab the island – with the help of the Irish settlers – it remained English from 1783 onwards.

The sugar economy gradually declined during the nineteenth century, and Montserrat became yet another depressed corner of the British Empire. People survived through subsistence farming and by emigrating to other islands, but Montserrat was among the poorest of many poor Caribbean territories. Its fortunes revived somewhat with the advent of tourism, particularly up-market retirement homes, and with the growth of an offshore banking sector in the 1980s. But massive fraud and allegations of money-laundering led to a crackdown by the FBI and Scotland Yard in 1989, and most of the 350 banks registered in Montserrat had their licences revoked. Nor did the havoc wreaked by Hurricane Hugo in 1989 help Montserrat's economic stability. An estimated 95% of buildings were damaged and losses were estimated at US$260 million.

Today Montserrat has largely recovered from the hurricane damage which uprooted almost every tree and removed every roof on the island. Tourism provides most of its income, and a significant number of expatriate Americans and Europeans have chosen to build second homes there. Its social stability is attractive to those people, as is its apparent attachment to its colonial status. In his survey of the surviving British Empire, *Outposts* (Extract 3), Simon Winchester observes that Montserrat remains probably the most English of the colonies.

In recent years, Montserrat has produced two poets of considerable talent: Howard Fergus, a historian and teacher, and E.A. Markham, a much-travelled theatre director and editor. In 'Late Return' (Extract 4), Markham deploys a complex cluster of natural images to represent the sense of rootlessness and alienation which accompanies a return to his native island.

THE TURKS AND CAICOS ISLANDS

'Where on earth are the Turks & Caicos Islands?' went the islands' tourist board slogan in the 1980s, and it was a good question. One of the more remote corners of the Empire, the forty low-lying islets and cays situated at the southern end of the Bahamas and 200 kilometres north of Haiti, had until then had a mostly uneventful history. But in 1985 the colony's Chief Minister, Norman Saunders, was arrested in Miami on charges of drug smuggling and was subsequently imprisoned. A photo of the disgraced politician, head bowed and being led away by a US anti-narcotics agent, appeared around the world. It was the islands' moment of notoriety.

The Turks and Caicos Islands claim to be the site of Columbus's first landing in the Americas, although this is hotly disputed by the Bahamas. In any case, Spanish adventurers rapidly wiped out the indigenous Lucayans (a branch of the Taino Arawaks) by sending them as slaves to Hispaniola or by infecting them with disease. The first settlers were of British origin and moved from Bermuda, producing salt with black slave labour on the dry southern islands of Grand Turk and Salt Cay for sale to the British colonies on the American mainland. The islands were also infested by pirates, who used the protected natural harbours as bases from which to attack Spanish shipping. Shipwrecking became a regular and sometimes profitable activity, as the islands present notoriously difficult navigational problems, with shallow sand banks and extensive reefs. In his novel *The Island* (Extract 5), Peter Benchley ◊ situates a story of modern-day piracy and religious fanaticism in these dangerous waters.

After control had passed hands from Spain to France and then to Britain, the Turks and Caicos were attached to the Bahamas. This proved unpopular with the islanders, who preferred links with Jamaica, and in 1874 the territory was annexed to the larger colony to the south. So it remained, eking a modest living from salt production and fishing, until 1962 when Jamaica became independent. A federal arrangement with the Bahamas followed until they, too, gained independence, and in 1973 the Turks and Caicos became a British Crown Colony.

The sale of postage stamps and a small amount of tourism were not enough to generate much prosperity, and in the 1980s the islands turned, like their fellow dependencies, to offshore finance. With few taxes and fewer regulations, they attracted some 9000 companies, each paying for the privilege of being registered there. Drug transshipment also proved to be a lucrative activity; the report which followed Saunders's arrest concluded that high-ranking officials had taken large bribes for allowing small planes to land and refuel on their way to Florida. Other investigations unearthed a wide range of corrupt and unsavoury practices including arson, and the

Guardian newspaper berated British neglect of what it called 'rotten islands in the sun'.

Spurred into action, the British government suspended constitutional rule in 1986 and abandoned hopes that the islands might choose to become independent. A semblance of normality returned with elections in 1988, but the issue of independence has never resurfaced – much to the relief of most islanders. In the meantime, tourism has expanded dramatically, with more than 50 000 visitors arriving each year on the island of Providenciales.

BOOKLIST

Baarslag, Karl, *Islands of Adventure*, The Travel Book Club, London, 1944. **Extract 2**.

Benchley, Peter, *The Island*, André Deutsch, London, 1979. **Extract 5**.

Markham, E.A., From 'Late Return', in *Human Rites*, Anvil Press, London, 1984. **Extract 4**.

Naipaul, V.S., 'Anguilla: The Shipwrecked Six Thousand', in *The Overcrowded Barracoon and Other Articles*, André Deutsch, London, 1972.

Petty, Colville L. and Nat Hodge, *Anguilla's Battle for Freedom, 1967*, Petnat, Anguilla, 1987.

Updike, John, 'Letter From Anguilla', in *Picked-Up Pieces*, André Deutsch, London, 1976. **Extract 1**.

Winchester, Simon, *Outposts*, Hodder and Stoughton, London, 1985. **Extract 3**.

Winchester, Simon, 'What the Queen Should Know About the Cayman Islands', in *The Sunday Times*, London, 2 January 1983.

Extracts

(1) ANGUILLA: POLITICS

John Updike, *Letter From Anguilla*

During the uneasy stand-off between secessionist Anguilla and 'imperialist' St Kitts, John Updike visited Anguilla to report on its eccentric politics.

A population of six thousand is the size of a small American town. Like small-town politics everywhere, Anguillan politics appears to an outsider an inscrutable tangle of personalities, old grudges, and bad habits. The island, for instance, is geographically divided into the East End and the West End, and white and mulatto East Enders dominated the drive for independence. Is this resented? Anguilla surely is one of the most color-blind places left in an increasingly racist world, but an egalitarian tolerance bred by centuries of colonial obscurity may well be strained by the opportunities and adversities of independence. And what of nepotism, where every third person is named Rey, Richardson, or Gumbs? We attended a political rally on the cricket field and heard a young man called Artlin Harrigan try to defend, under some vicious badgering, his newspaper, the *Beacon*, which had asked for new elections and an expanded council, and had implied graft and log-rolling in the present council. 'I am in a fearful bind,' he said into the microphone, 'for if I print half of what I know, I fear Bradshaw will use it to prove that Anguillans cannot govern themselves.' In turn, a council member, Mr Wallace Rey, rose up and claimed it was highly improper for the *Beacon* to be printed on the Anglican Church's duplicator. This demand for separation of church and state strikes a rather new note on an island governed for generations as an adjunct of the Anglican Church, and may not be unrelated to the whiteness of the present rector. Although the crowd of several hundred acted much like any bored and amused small-town rally, two old ladies came to blows beneath a mahogany tree, and some of the speakers, including an urbane refugee from one of Bradshaw's jails, seemed all too expertly demagogic. When the council secretary spoke suavely of the council's right to secret discussion and of its wisdom of choice as to what 'the people' should know, I myself, as children scampered around the mustered trucks in the tropic twilight, felt chilled by a whisper of Fascism. The crowd seemed puzzled and somewhat cynical, and voiced unity only at the mention of the hated name of Bradshaw, a bogey whose usefulness cannot be infinite.

(2) THE CAYMAN ISLANDS: 1930S

Karl Baarslag, *Islands of Adventure*

Today's traveller to Grand Cayman would have difficulty recognizing the poor and forgotten island which this writer discovered.

I was up with the dawn for my first sight of Grand Cayman. From the sparkling blue Caribbean, the flat, low little island was as unimpressive as the coast of Belgium or the mud flats of the Elbe and Weser. We sounded our way cautiously to an anchorage off Georgetown, for the edge of the shelf is only four hundred yards from the shore and drops off steeply to tremendous depths. The island appears densely wooded with small growth or scrub palmetto, which halt within a few hundred feet of the blue sea in a fringe of gleaming white beaches. Georgetown, a collection of small but neat cottages and a few prominent government buildings and stores all built of wood, did not appear particularly impressive from our anchorage. There was a small stone jetty with a tiny light, a boat being built up on ways, and a few natives gathering at the landing; otherwise one would have thought the town deserted. I could make out no other signs of industry or life.

Although still early in the morning, the sun was already unbearably hot, and I decided that an hour or two ashore in this dull little place would probably be more than sufficient for all the sight-seeing I would want to do. After passing the usual customs and other entry formalities we were welcomed ashore by the boarding officer, a fine-looking mulatto of dignified and courteous mien. I had hardly landed and strolled a few hundred feet along the hard, white coral road, before I sensed that I was on the threshold of making a profound and happy discovery, that I was stumbling on a tiny bit of never-never land forgotten by centuries, a rare gem of an island happily overlooked by the great, bustling, harried, outer world. Globe-trotters, writers, and escapists are constantly searching for some small, unspoiled spot, only to find that the ravages of the civilization they are trying to flee have already preceded them. And here was a spot they had not yet discovered! . . .

There were no radio or cable connections with the outer world. Some years ago the inhabitants petitioned the Governor at Jamaica for a small radio station, but their request was turned down on the grounds that the islands did not really need a station and that wireless communication would be 'merely a toy.' A few years before, I was told, the islands had been swept by a disastrous hurricane and the worried Jamaican government had had to charter and dispatch an airplane to the islands to see if they were still there.

(3) MONTSERRAT

Simon Winchester, *Outposts*

Even in post-colonial times, Plymouth, the capital of Montserrat, retains an aura of imperial belonging.

Plymouth, the tiny Georgian town with the well-proportioned houses made of Portland stone that was shipped in as ballast on the early sugar boats, is a pretty and dignified place – an Imperial capital that has been cared for, and of which the local people are proud. They are forever repairing the roofs and touching up the pointing, painting the old walls in whites and blues and yellows, keeping the place cheerful and spotless, even though they have few visitors and have very little money to spend.

It is a very English town, despite the supposed Irishness of the countryside. The suburbs are called Dagenham and Amersham and Jubilee Town, and there is a Richmond and a Streatham, and St George's Hill overlooks the place. In the town centre, where John Street and George Street meet Strand Street and Marine Drive, there is a war memorial. Nearby is the old Custom House, the market, the abattoir, the post office, the prison and the clock tower. There always is a war memorial, and here in Plymouth it is where the Boy Scouts and the Montserrat Volunteers and the Guides paraded on Empire Day each May, when the schools were all closed and the Governor could be seen in his white uniform and his feathery hat, and when the children sang 'God Save the King' and fidgeted during the speeches and then lined up for sticky buns and lemonade. Empire Day seems less appropriate now, so they celebrate the Queen's birthday instead, in June; but the war memorial is the focus of it all, as it is in every remaining outpost of the Empire. Some memorials are in shabby and forlorn corners; some, like those in Jamestown, the capital of St Helena, and here in Plymouth, the almost-perfect capital of Montserrat, seem more properly Imperial, and the children and their parents seem to have an extra spring in their step and sing just a little more heartily, believing, as they look around at all the lovely constructions of their mother country, that they do in fact possess something of which they can be proud.

(4) MONTSERRAT

E.A. Markham, from *Late Return*

The ruins of a house suggest a lost childhood and the ambiguity of return to an island by the poet who is both insider and foreigner.

'What an odd name, Markham, for a Montserratian!' – Canadian tourist in Montserrat
'There is no Markham in the Directory.' – Telephone Exchange

I

The ruin, at least, was something; the yard
with face half-rutted was the boy no girl would kiss
except in retrospect; blotches of soil erupting
like teenage lust: a tangle of green – sugarapple,
mango, sour now, outgrowing the graft of family name;
other fruit, near-fruit . . .
With no young scamp to lizard vertical for juice,
Your nuts are safe: weeds cling
in parody to trunk (like boys born after you, tall,
or long-abandoned sons made good, defying dad
to wish them better) unharnessed
by Nellie's line on which the great, white
sheets of the house would flap their wings in rage.
Fringed Afro of arrogance:
their better view of the sea taunts us, close to earth, flaunting
fruit too high to get at;
some beyond-the-milk stage bunched as if in decoration.
Well before dark, my challenge from below, half-
remembered, no-more-to-be-taken-up, peters out:
mine is a garden, not of Eden, but of youth.
Suspecting things to be as honest, as accurate as they seem,
that this bit of family, untended, past its best
season, reflects something in me, I reach
for the camera I don't possess. Someone in Europe,
in America, will find this quaint. For me, a tourist-
polaroid to arrest decline.

II

I am home again, perhaps two generations late.
I think, when the jumble of accusation, of longing,
clears: I am the juvenile not yet exiled.
This rock is a springboard
into water, into sea.
Sea is a safe mattress
for the pole-vaulter, beyond sand;
my ocean-liner, vast and reliable, absorbing
shock, proof of completed journeys near to risk,
knowing the way to 'abroad'. The jump
is voluntary as coming to a road which forks:
sudden pressure from behind makes you choose
without benefit of signpost. Now this:
Montserrat has caught up with the world,
impatient of late-comers, of its children, foreign-ravaged,

straggling home without humility. (High-flying
Concorde boxing people's ears, is enough.)
Others have been unpersoned
through the idiocies of politics. I, who seek no public
cut to advancement, am an Economic
not a political dissident.

(5) THE TURKS AND
CAICOS ISLANDS: SHIPWRECKS

Peter Benchley, *The Island*

Intrepid journalist Maynard is flying to one of the islands with an alcoholic pilot to investigate rumours of ships disappearing without trace.

Miles away, to the east, Maynard saw several large islands. Remembering the chart, he guessed that one was Navidad, one North Caicos, one Grand Caicos. There were countless smaller islands to the west, uninhabited, covered with scrub, pounded by surf. Directly beneath were the Caicos Banks, an endless plain of sand and grass, no more than six feet deep. The western edge of the Banks ended abruptly, shelving to forty feet, then shearing down to five thousand feet.

Maynard recalled something Michael Florio had said: in the days of sail – especially the days of the cumbersome, unmanoeuvrable square-rigged ships – the Caicos Banks were among the most treacherous in the hemisphere. Ships storm-driven off course would seem to be in the relative safety of deep water. Their sounding leads would find no bottom. And then someone would hear, above the howl of the wind, a strange thunderous roar. It sounded like surf, but it couldn't be surf, not in the open ocean. They would proceed ahead until, at last, a lookout – his eyes stinging from a film of salt – would see the impossible, an explosion of towering breakers dead ahead. It was too late. There would be recriminations and keening and prayers. The ship would hit the rocks and, within minutes, be gone. Most of it would be scattered across the Banks. Some pieces would float, and some survivors might cling to the floating pieces. Twenty-seven men had survived one such wreck, Florio had said. They had ridden a section of decking thirty miles over the Banks and had washed ashore on Grand Caicos. Twenty-one had died of thirst or exposure. Four had committed suicide, driven mad by bugs. Two had lived.

An airport lay ahead: Great Bone Cay. Whitey finished off his flask and banked hard right, then hard left, lining the plane up with the runway. 'Flaps down,' he said to himself and pushed a switch. 'Flaps down.' The plane slowed. 'Wheels down.' Another switch. A light blinked on. 'Wheels down.'

The plane hit the runway too hard, bounced, hit again, and settled.

Whitey taxied up to a rectangular concrete building, where two pickup trucks and perhaps a dozen people, including two who carried clipboards and wore epaulets on their starched white shirts, were waiting.

Whitey shut off the engine and said to Maynard, 'If you got any grass, dump it now. They are friggin' *lunatics* about grass, and the jail got no screens on it.'

Biographical and literary notes

BAARSLAG, Karl. Baarslag's obsession with islands around the world produced a book, *Islands of Adventure* (Extract 2), covering territories in every ocean. His account of the 1930s Cayman Islands provides an informative contrast with the finance-fuelled boom of the 1970s and 1980s.

BENCHLEY, Peter (1940–). Born in New York, Benchley attended Harvard University before working as a reporter and associate editor on the *Washington Post* and *Newsweek*. In the 1970s he became a full-time novelist and scriptwriter, producing a string of successful thrillers which include *Jaws*, 1974, *The Deep*, 1976, and *White Shark*, 1994. Like most of his fiction, *The Island* (Extract 5) is concerned with dark and sinister forces, in this case a bizarre religious community descended from shipwrecked sailors on a remote island among the Turks and Caicos.

MARKHAM, E.A. (1939–). Born in Montserrat, Markham moved to Britain in 1956, where he studied English and philosophy before

E.A. Markham

teaching in London. He has since lived and worked in France, Scandinavia, Northern Ireland, the Caribbean and Papua New Guinea, where he was employed as a media coordinator. Markham has edited various magazines, has directed theatre companies and is the author of a collection of short stories, *Something Unusual*, 1986. He has published several collections of poetry, including *Human Rites*, 1984, from which the poem 'Late Return' (Extract 4) is taken, *Living in Disguise*, 1986, and *Towards the End of a Century*, 1989. Markham's poetry reflects his wide and varied experience, but, as he admits, childhood memories of Montserrat and, in particular, his grandmother are a recurring topic in his work: 'That house, that childhood environment which seems to grow richer and more bizarre over the years – returning in poems, stories, radio talks, plays – the grandmother long dead, the house now a ruin, is an important part of my London/Ulster/Stockholm/Port Moresby reality.'

UPDIKE, John (1932–). Updike was born in Shillington, Pennsylvania, and went to Harvard University and the Ruskin School of Drawing in Oxford. He worked on *The New Yorker* before producing a highly acclaimed series of novels, short stories, poems and essays. His best-known fiction is the Rabbit sequence of novels which charts the progress of a salesman in surburban middle America. Other significant works include *Couples*, 1968, *The Witches of Eastwick*, 1984, and *Brazil*, 1994. 'Letter From Anguilla' (Extract 1) is taken from *Picked-Up Pieces*, 1976, a collection of journalism and essays which reflects Updike's wide range of interests. His account of Anguilla's Lilliputian revolution against St Kitts is sympathetic to the islanders' predicament and told without the condescension which coloured many other journalists' view of the event.

WINCHESTER, Simon (1944–). A journalist and travel writer, Winchester has worked for the *Sunday Times* and is the author of several books on South East Asia. His *Outposts* (Extract 3) records a tour around Britain's last remaining colonial possessions, including St Helena, the Falkland Islands and Hong Kong.

THE NETHERLAND ANTILLES
AND ARUBA

'Curaçao might easily be a suburb of Amsterdam . . . The streets are narrow, noisy and busy, weltering in a confusion of autos, pushcarts, wheelbarrows and bikes blundering through the crowds, just as they do in old Holland. It is truly, frankly and even proudly Dutch, with the substantial quality, energy and order characteristic of its motherland.'
Hendrik de Leeuw,
Crossroads of the Caribbean

The Dutch were probably the Caribbean's most efficient, some might say ruthless, colonialists. They were the moving force behind the slave trade in its heyday and were responsible for the transportation of millions of Africans to work in plantations from Cuba down to Trinidad. They were the merchants *par excellence*, trading in every manner of commodity and manufactured good, matching supply and demand with outstanding efficiency. The Dutch were also expert financiers, bringing their business acumen and technological knowhow to sugar production around the region. Operating among rival colonial superpowers such as Britain, France and Spain, the Dutch played one off against the other while always making a handsome profit. Yet the Netherlands has left less of a mark on the modern-day Caribbean than any of the other European nations. It never owned large colonies among the islands, nor tried to encourage full-scale settlement. Unlike in the Dutch East Indies, its possessions were modest in size and unpromising in terms of resources. Dutch was never widely spoken in the region; the country's institutions and culture have not been much imitated. When the mainland South American state of Suriname became independent in 1975, the main Dutch connection with the region seemed severed.

But the Dutch link with the Caribbean persists. Although, like London, The Hague may have wished to divest itself of its colonies, it did not manage to do so. Instead, like the French, the Dutch opted to incorporate their Caribbean territories into the 'mother country', but at the same time

---

FACT BOX

AREA: 993 sq km
  Aruba – 193
  Bonaire – 288
  Curaçao – 444
  Saba – 13
  Sint Eustatius – 21
POPULATION: 265 100
  Aruba – 72 100
CAPITAL:
  Aruba – Oranjestad
  Bonaire – Kralendijk
  Curaçao – Willemstad
  Saba – The Bottom
  Sint Eustatius – Oranjestad
LANGUAGES: Dutch, English, Papiamento
POLITICAL STATUS: autonomous members of Kingdom of the
  Netherlands; Aruba is separate from the Netherland Antilles.
PER CAPITA GDP: US$8320
  Aruba – US$14 000

---

giving them much more internal autonomy than France accords to its *départements d'outre-mer*.

There are six islands in the Caribbean which belong to the Kingdom of the Netherlands. Five – **Bonaire, Curaçao, Saba, Sint Eustatius** (known universally as Statia) and **Sint Maarten** – make up the federal grouping of the Netherland Antilles, with its own parliament in Curaçao. The other, **Aruba**, withdrew from the Netherland Antilles in 1986, seeking separate status within the Kingdom of the Netherlands. A total of approximately 265 000 people live in the six islands, making a series of mini-states rather than a viable single entity. These people hold Dutch passports and are eligible for the same rights and benefits in Holland as any citizen. At the same time, the Dutch government pays to each of them the equivalent of US$500 each year in aid.

The islands are further divided into two groups, separated by some 880 kilometres of sea. The so-called 'ABC' islands of Aruba, Bonaire and Curaçao lie about 70 kilometres off the coast of Venezuela. For the most part flat and dry limestone terrain, their history has been closely intertwined with that of oil-producing Venezuela. To the north are the three small territories of Saba, Sint Eustatius and Sint Maarten (see Saint Martin/Sint Maarten), known as the 'three S's'. These islands are largely volcanic in formation and have survived through the centuries as trading posts and sea-faring communities.

The distance between the ABC group and the three S's is more than merely geographical. Culturally, the ABC islands have more in common with South America, and language, food and music are all heavily influenced by proximity to Venezuela. The three S's, on the other hand, owe more to generations of English and Scottish settlers who came to the islands in the course of the eighteenth century. English is the *lingua franca* in Saba, Statia and Sint Maarten, and Anglo-Saxon-inspired protestantism outweighs the majority Catholicism to be found in Aruba or Bonaire.

Few writers from the Netherlands Antilles have managed to reach a readership outside the region, and those who write in Dutch or Papiamento have not been widely translated. With the exception of Tip Marugg ◊, no significant Dutch Antillean author has been published in English.

ARUBA

Aruba hardly corresponds to any conventional image of a tropical island. It has little rainfall, almost no vegetation, and is largely made up of desert, broken only by rocks, cacti and the distinctively gnarled and windswept *divi-divi* trees. Its inhospitable terrain meant that it held no potential as a sugar-producing island, and as a result Aruba was one of the few Caribbean territories not to experience African slavery. Instead, the indigenous Arawak Indians mixed with early Spanish and then Dutch settlers to create a *mestizo* (mixed-blood) population more akin to that of Venezuela than other islands. Nowadays there are no 'pure' Indians left in Aruba, but the Arawak legacy is still visible in people's features.

Aruba's economic fortune was made in 1929 when a subsidiary of the US Exxon oil company opened its refinery at **San Nicolas**. The Americans were worried that a future Venezuelan government might wish to national-ize the oil industry (as the Mexicans had done) and wanted to site their refinery in a more politically stable offshore location. The refinery brought 8000 jobs and attracted migrant workers from the whole of the Eastern Caribbean.

In 1985, however, Exxon closed the refinery, just as Aruba was pressing its claim for separate status. Faced with the prospect of massive unemploy-ment, the Aruban authorities rapidly diversified into tourism, building large numbers of hotels and promoting the island specifically as a destination for divers and watersports enthusiasts. The result was spectacu-lar; a construction boom and vastly increased tourist arrivals revived Aruba's economy. The growth of offshore finance and the partial reopening of the oil refinery further strengthened the island's position.

Aruba's decision to leave the Netherlands Antilles in 1986 was a reaction to Curaçao's perceived domination of the grouping. For years Arubans had resented its bigger and richer neighbour's monopoly of power and resources, and a referendum strongly backed what became known as *status aparte* (separate status). Aruba was meant to go on towards full independence, but subsequent election results have not favoured pro-independence parties and the island seems set to remain a part of the Dutch Kingdom.

BONAIRE

Bonaire is larger than Aruba, but has only about one-sixth of its population. Like the other 'ABC' islands it is arid and flat, its main traditional economic activity having been salt mining. The island was first chanced upon by Amerigo Vespucci's Spanish-backed expedition in 1499, and early Spanish involvement consisted largely of rounding up the Arawak Indians living there and enslaving them to work in Hispaniola. The Dutch arrived in 1636 and began to produce salt, using African slave labour. They also used the island as a livestock rearing centre and sent the animals to the main colony of Curaçao.

Bonaire is a harsh, unwelcoming place, and in its history it has been used as a prison and slave centre. The salt pans on the south coast some ten kilometres from the main village, **Kralendijk**, lie near a cluster of tiny stone houses, set in a barren landscape of scrub and rocks. These are the shelters given to the slaves who produced the salt and they have recently been restored as a monument to the slave system. Later, Germans and suspected Nazi sympathizers were interned in Bonaire during the Second World War.

Men from Bonaire went to work in the oil refineries of Aruba and Curaçao, and until the 1970s the island had little economic activity of its own. The construction of an oil transshipment terminal and the development of a tourism industry has changed that, however, and today about 50 000 tourists visit the island every year, attracted by its diving and unique bird-watching opportunities.

Bonaire was the birthplace of Cola Debrot, probably the best-known of the region's writers, who was Governor of the Netherlands Antilles in the 1960s as well as being a novelist and poet. His *Mijn zuster de negerin* (*My Sister the Negress*) was a success in Holland in the 1930s and brought attention there to the literary possibilities of Papiamento.

CURAÇAO

The biggest and most populous of the Netherlands Antilles, Curaçao is also the most obviously Dutch. The pastel-coloured buildings which stand alongside the port at **Willemstad**, complete with gables, elaborate façades and red tiled roofs, are like some canalside street of Amsterdam transplanted into the tropics. The bustle of Curaçao's capital, with its seventeenth-century colonial architecture and constant maritime activity, has attracted visiting writers for centuries. Christopher Isherwood ◊ wrote in his travel memoir *The Condor and the Cow* (Extract 1) that Willemstad inspired in him fantasies of escapism:

'All this colour and movement, all this going and coming, are a natural part of the surrounding atmosphere, the immmensity of sun-lit water and blue windy sky. Laughter and light, the sea-breeze and the human gestures, the sparkle of waves and eyes, seem to blend into each other and create the very element of happiness. The tourist on the balcony, with his passport and his money in his pocket, readily accepts Willemstad as a paradise and slips into day-dreams of a voluntary exile.'

Curaçao was the hub of the Dutch Caribbean empire. A fleet from the Netherlands took possession of it in 1634 after the Spanish had given up their search for gold. The Dutch were more interested in its strategic location between their interests in Pernambuco, Brazil, and what is now New York, and recognized its potential as a trading centre and base for attacking the Spanish. The government was in fact a company, the Dutch West India Company, which ran Curaçao and the other territories as a business. Within a half century, Curaçao had become a thriving free port and a profitable regional slave market. The arrival from the 1650s onwards of Jews escaping persecution in Spain and Portugal further enhanced the island's role as a commercial centre. The synagogue in Willemstad is the oldest in the Americas and gives some idea of the colony's prosperity in the seventeenth and eighteenth centuries. While attempts at sugar-cane cultivation failed because of the dry climate, banking, trading and slaving flourished.

Curaçao also experienced instability and violence. A slave revolt in 1795 was brutally put down. Five years later the British took control of the island, only to withdraw three years later and then reinvade in 1807. The British finally abandoned claims to Curaçao in 1816, and from 1828 to 1845 the island, along with the other Dutch territories, was ruled from the colony of Suriname, the Dutch West India Company having ceded control to the Dutch government. In 1845 the six islands were incorporated into a single unit, named Curaçao and Dependencies, a move which confirmed Curaçao's pre-eminence and the resentment of the others.

The abolition of slavery in the Americas removed much of Curaçao's prosperity and it went into decline for fifty years. The discovery of massive oilfields in Venezuela early in the twentieth century halted the downward spiral and again transformed Curaçao into an economic powerhouse, as the Dutch–British Shell Oil Company set up a refinery on the island in 1915 to avoid political instability on the mainland. Curaçao's fortunes improved still further during the Second World War, when an influx of US troops, sent to protect the oil installations, laid the basis for a tourism industry. At the same time, Dutch businesses, anticipating the German invasion of the Netherlands, transferred assets to the colony and thus began the vast offshore finance industry which still brings wealth to Curaçao. In the 1930s, Dutch–American travel writer Hendrik de Leeuw remarked in his *Crossroads of the Caribbean* on the island's bustling commercial ambiance.

Today, oil remains important to Curaçao, despite the uncertainties caused by the volatile international market. Banks, insurance companies, and other corporations are registered in their thousands on the island, escaping taxes and transferring money between Europe, North America and Latin America. Tourism brings hundreds of thousands of visitors, many of them cruise passengers, each year to browse in the duty-free shops of Willemstad. And the eponymous blue liqueur, Curaçao, made from sun-withered orange peel, spreads the island's name around the world.

Curaçao has produced more literature than any of the other Dutch islands. Tip Marugg ◊ locates his novel *Weekend Pilgrimage* (Extract 2) in a small rural community in Curaçao, while Frank Martinus Arion, a prolific poet and playwright, has developed a Dutch version of *négritude*, stressing his people's cultural affinity with Africa.

SABA

Saba (pronounced 'Say-bah') is not for the nervous flier. Its 400-metre airstrip is about as long as an aircraft carrier's flight deck and is flanked by a precipitous drop into the sea. It was built in 1963 on the only flat piece of land on this 8 square kilometres of mountain rock. Until then, the island was linked to the outside world only by boats which moored at the bottom of sheer and forbidding cliffs. Now, small planes from Sint Maarten make the stomach-churning landing several times daily, depositing passengers at what must be one of the world's smallest and friendliest airports.

It is hard to imagine why people should have wanted to colonize Saba in the first place. An extinct volcano which emerges almost vertically from the sea, it is enormously picturesque but hardly suitable for agriculture or any other livelihood. Lush and green, with a central peak almost always hidden by cloud, it has little cultivable land and no beaches. Only one inlet among the looming cliffs allows ships to reach a small pier.

The peculiar topography of the place is matched by its distinctive mix of cultural influences. About half the population of 1100 are white, descended from Dutch, English and Scottish settlers. The other half are black, their ancestors having been slaves who worked, for the most part, as domestic servants. Remarkably, there are few brown-skinned Sabans. And stranger still, nearly all islanders, whether black or white, seem to share two predominant surnames: Hassell and Johnson. They live in four picture-book villages of white clapboard houses, with green shutters and red roofs, set among neat suburban gardens and atypically clean streets. Everybody speaks English; Dutch is restricted to a few official notices and street signs.

The history of Saba has been one of human struggle against a spectacular but ungiving nature. There is evidence of early Carib communities, but they had disappeared by the time Columbus passed the island on his second voyage in 1493. The first European settlers were Dutch, who arrived in the 1640s, ignoring French claims to the island. Between then and 1816 it changed hands no fewer than twelve times (ten fewer than neighbouring St Eustatius). On one occasion, the British pirate Thomas Morgan took possession of the island and ejected all the resident Dutch. Some of his crew are thought to have stayed behind, giving rise to modern Sabans' claim that they are descended from pirates.

With few alternatives, Sabans have traditionally made their living from the sea and many worked until recently as merchant seamen. Of these a large number went to the USA to work aboard American steamships, often as captains. This maritime tradition kept the island alive, as Saban sailors returned with money and, more often than not, a wife.

On the island itself, life was rugged and simple. Until the construction of a road linking the tiny port and the main village, **The Bottom**, goods had to be carried from boats by man or donkey up a steep path, with 200 steps carved out of the volcanic rock. In the 1930s the American writer Glanville Smith ◊ recorded in his *Many a Green Isle* (Extract 4) the unusual system of transporting arriving visitors to Saba's modest capital.

The road itself was impossible to build – or so said the Dutch engineers invited to examine the project. But one Josephus Lambert Hassell was not so easily discouraged and took a correspondence course in civil engineering before starting on the roadworks with local, part-time, and sometimes voluntary, labour. The road took five years to link the port and The Bottom and another thirteen to reach the next village of **Windwardside**. Eventually cars replaced donkeys, and Saba belatedly entered the twentieth century. In his *Saban Lore* (Extract 3), Saban historian and politician Will Johnson recalls the curious social customs which predated the advent of modernity.

The car offered this remote island a short-lived economic sideline when Dutch motorists started coming here to take their driving tests. As part of the Kingdom of the Netherlands, Saba presented a legal and ideal alternative to the complexities of Rotterdam or The Hague. Buying packages of lessons and accommodation, Dutch 'licence tourists' were usually able to master the island's single road – although its steep descents and hairpin bends were presumably of little relevance to driving conditions in Holland. The practice eventually stopped, sabotaged, it is claimed, by pressure from Dutch driving instructors.

Tourism today is limited by the island's airstrip and by the absence of beaches. Some visitors come for the diving, which is among the best in the region, and others for the extraordinary scenery. Mass tourism, as experienced by Sint Maarten (which can be clearly seen about 40 kilometres away), is not likely to touch Saba in the foreseeable future – to the relief of nearly every islander.

SINT EUSTATIUS

Few places can have suffered such a disastrous economic downfall as Sint Eustatius or Statia, the poorest of the Dutch islands. Looking today at the rundown settlement of **Oranjestad,** it is hard to imagine that Statia was once known as the 'Golden Rock', one of the busiest and wealthiest colonies in the world. A few crumbling ruins are all that is left of the warehouses and merchants' offices which lined the **Lower Town.**

Statia's prosperity was mostly ill-gotten. The tiny island was well situated on major trade routes and became an entrepôt for merchant ships travelling to and from Europe and the other colonies. Goods changed hands with few questions asked, and traders escaped the tedious obligation of returning their cargoes of sugar, tobacco or cotton to the European metropoles. Slavery was another booming business, and in the best years of the eighteenth century, Statia's tiny harbour received more than 3500 ships a year. A Scottish woman named Janet Schaw ◊ visited Statia in 1775 and recorded in her *Journal of a Lady of Quality* (Extract 5) the commercial mayhem of a thriving free port.

The American War of Independence provided another welcome business opportunity. Statia became an important staging post for weapons and supplies which were taken by ship to Boston or New York and delivered to George Washington's troops in defiance of the British naval blockade. In 1776 the island became the first territory in the world to recognize American independence when the cannons at **Fort Oranje** fired an official salute to an approaching ship, the *Andrew Doria*, flying the new state's colours. The Statian authorities later claimed that this was a mistake and the Governor was recalled to the Netherlands, but the action incurred the wrath of the British. In 1781 a British fleet led by Admiral Rodney arrived and took control of the colony. For a month Rodney kept the Dutch flag flying on the island, luring unwitting ships into the harbour and impounding their cargoes. Finally, some 150 ships were captured, their goods confiscated, and Rodney sent back £5 million of booty back to England – much of which, ironically, was plundered by the French in a battle around the Scilly isles.

Rodney's revenge spelled the end of Statia's glittering reputation as the 'Golden Rock'. The French captured it from the British the following year and the island changed hands a few more times before the Dutch eventually reclaimed sovereignty in 1816. By then, the illicit trading lifeline with the USA had disappeared and the slaving industry was on the wane. Statia slipped into disrepair, its population dwindled, and ships stopped calling in at the once-congested port of Oranjestad. To this day, the island has never recovered from its sudden downfall. Its tiny population lives on Dutch aid, a little tourism and a small-scale oil storage facility. It is a sad place, broken and bankrupt, one of the more pathetic victims of a long-forgotten European rivalry.

BOOKLIST

De Leeuw, Hendrik, *Crossroads of the Caribbean Sea*, Julian Messner, New York, 1935.

Isherwood, Christopher, *The Condor and the Cows*, Methuen, London, 1949. **Extract 1.**

Johnson, Will, *Saban Lore: Tales From My Grandmother's Pipe*, privately published, Saba, 1989. **Extract 3.**

Marugg, Tip, *Weekend Pilgrimage*, Roy Edwards trans, Hutchinson, London, 1960. **Extract 2.**

Schaw, Janet, *Journal of a Lady of Quality: Being the Narrative of a Journey from Scotland to the West Indies, North Carolina, and Portugal, in the Years 1774 to 1776*, Yale University Press, New Haven, Connecticut, 1992. **Extract 5.**

Smith, Glanville, *Many a Green Isle*, The Travel Book Club, London, 1945. **Extract 4.**

Extracts

(1) CURAÇAO

Christopher Isherwood, *The Condor and the Cows*

En route to South America from the USA, Isherwood's ship calls in at Willemstad, Curaçao, allowing the writer to appreciate the port's unmistakeably Dutch atmosphere.

September 23. Curaçao: the long barren island, shaped like a ship hit broadside by a gale – it seems to be listing. On the west, the land slopes up gently to a central range of sharp-peaked hills; on the east, it falls steeply away to the shore. Almost no vegetation and hardly any houses, until you round the cape and see Willemstad. The toy-like prettiness of the town makes you gasp. It is absurdly gay; orange, crimson, scarlet, parrot green and canary yellow. I don't know if this architecture is typical of the Caribbean, but it is extremely individual: ridiculous little classical porches, window-frames decorated with bold slapdash festoons of colour, an air of mock grandeur, of Negro high spirits, and something of the décor of the Russian ballet.

On the waterfront are an old Dutch fort and a row of tall seventeenth-century houses which might have been lifted bodily from a canal-side in Amsterdam. They have the same narrow gables and bas-relief figures, the same hooks for hauling furniture and goods to the windows of the upper storeys. The harbour is within and behind the town, a large lagoon called the Schottegat. To enter it, you pass down a long channel which is like a main street. Your arrival has an atmosphere of welcome and triumph. Ships' sirens hoot their greetings. The ancient pontoon-bridge, the 'Queen Emma', swings back like a gate to let you through. Everybody waves – Dutch and Chinese schoolboys, negro women with baskets on their heads, Venezuelan girls on the vegetable-boats from La Guaira, American sailors washing their dungarees. The ship seems to have grown suddenly enormous; from the boat-deck you can look out over the roof-tops.

Around the Schottegat are the plants and storage tanks of the oil-refineries. The place reeks sourly of oil. The water of the lagoon is covered with a thin rainbow film and its shores are funereally edged by yards of shining jet-black scum. You might as well be in Wilmington, California. This is the main source of Willemstad's wealth. A grimy utilitarian backyard behind a pretty showcase of imported goods.

(2) CURAÇAO: WIND

Tip Marugg, *Weekend Pilgrimage*

The narrator recalls the thrills and fears of his childhood and the permanent presence of the wind which sweeps across the island of Curaçao.

Sometimes, though, I went up to the attic on my own; sometimes even when it was already quite dark. Now I come to think of it, that was odd, for there were hundreds of small things I was frightened of in those days, or which I didn't dare to do alone; but I was never frightened in that big dark attic. When I went there by myself, I usually lay on one of the big window seats and gazed outside. If there was a moon, the sight could be marvelous. Then I would gaze at the gleaming sea in the distance; it really looked as if there were stars in the black water, too, gathered together in a broad path of light that reached from the coast to the horizon and then climbed up along the sky, right up to the moon. Or I would look at the waving, rustling treetops, or at the mysterious will-o'-the-wisps which moved at such lightning speed from one place to another. Sometimes, too, I would close my eyes and listen to the wind. I had never paid any attention to it before, but I discovered then that the wind could make a thousand different sounds.

Even now, I still like listening to the wind, at silly moments. The wind's a part of the island. It's a wind which never gets tired, and which blows over Curaçao like a stimulating breath, fresh and thin in the cool rainy period, languid and hot in the warm September days, heavy and strong in the hurricane season. The wind which makes the tough acacia and divi-divi trees bow their heads in defeat; which takes on its wings the small boats laden with fruit and makes them cleave the waves; which sometimes sweeps the heat away like a great invisible broom and drives the coolness of the sea onto the land in its stead; the wind which catches the cotton-covered seeds that burst from the oblong pods of the kapok tree and sends them floating like little brown birds above the croton shrubs.

(3) Saba

Will Johnson, *Saban Lore*

Until the recent advent of roads and telephones, the inhabitants of remote Saba lived old-fashioned, often geographically constrained, lives.

Among the local customs which have now disappeared was that of making up poems and songs about people who had done something bad or stupid. Some of these poems and songs were so to the point that this too caused enmity between families for years.

Crime was limited to petty theft and cursing out one another. In our long history of colonization of Saba, murder and other serious crimes have been vary rare. Sometimes, if one wanted to tell a person off without too much ado, an anonymous letter was written and dropped in a spot where any member of the public could find it, read it, and pass it on. This system of drop-letters has now completely disappeared. An anonymous letter to the Editor can serve the same purpose!

Contact between villages was infrequent. One of my grandmothers, who was born and lived in the village of Hell's Gate, never visited The Bottom until she was fifty years old. Incidentally her husband's parents came from that village. Although this could have been a case of not liking her inlaws, as a boy I often heard old people saying that they never had the time, inclination or desire to visit any other village. There are still a number of people both young and old, even with all the means of transportation today, who have never been off Saba . . .

There were no comforts in the old *rum shops*. One would walk inside and up to the counter of a local grocery-rum shop et alia, order a glass of rum or gin, then return outside and sit on a stone wall. The town drunk of those days must have eventually acquired a very calloused derriere.

Poor people could earn some money by gathering firewood and selling it or by fetching tubs of water and bringing it on their heads up the mountainsides from the springs located close to the sea.

(4) SABA

Glanville Smith, *Many a Green Isle*

Volcanic Saba fascinates visitors with its strange topography and picture-postcard quaintness.

Saba, a Dutch island to the east of the Anegeda Passage, makes a show on maps, because for all its small circumference it sticks too high into the air for the cartographers to overlook. One of the Antilles' best and oldest jokes is that Saba's capital, at the top of a toilsome nine-hundred foot series of flagstone stairs, is called The Bottom. But 'the bottom' it is, in Saban terms; the other towns are all up farther flights – St John's, Windward Side, or (nearest to heaven of all) Hell's Gate.

Up these formidable stairs a few circus horses have been trained to climb. The captain of my ship had hired the lot for himself, his Dutch guests, Dutch wife, and dainty small Dutch daughter. The party viewed their mounts with some trepidation and the road ahead with more: horses' backs at home stayed usually at a level. Poor Netherlanders! their trip up was anxious enough, but when Dobbin turned round and skipped downstairs with rump up and head in China, there was nothing to do but cover the eyes with one hand and catch at the saddle with the other.

Unhampered by a horse, I got on much more nimbly. Here was The Bottom, with morning's dews yet fresh upon it – a town half provision garden in a hollow. And here was Windward Side on its ridge, another nine hundred feet nearer to the sky. In illimitable miles of bright sun-glitters the Caribbean quivered far below; up from its surf the steep cliffs leaned, then steep slopes of grass studded with bursts of sisal; next, tropical shrubs, woods growing at a frightful angle, and then pastures more moderately tilted. And here was the town and I puffing into it, while Saba's peak still loomed above, piercing a soft mist of cloud.

What a town! For sweet looks it was a veritable lollipop. Begonias and slim crocuses bloomed atop the mossy walls, fat cows posed majestically in paddocks the size of parlour carpets. As for the houses, so spotless-white, with their masonry gable ends and hooded chimneys – their shutters, iron lamps, picket gates, and flowers – obviously they had been grouped as they were to stage an operetta . . . But there seemed to be no performance scheduled for that morning. Instead, sheds were being painted, gardens were being weeded, windows were being washed. On verandas pretty girls in their prettiest frocks were busy at the drawn work for which the island is famous.

(5) SINT EUSTATIUS

Janet Schaw, *Journal of a Lady of Quality*

This diary from the 1770s gives some impression of St Eustatius's pre-eminence as a trading centre, if not as a place of beauty.

In a few hours after we left St Kitts, we landed on St Eustatia, a free port, which belongs to the Dutch; a place of vast traffick from every corner of the globe. The ships of various nations which rode before it were very fine, but the Island itself the only ugly one I have seen. Nor do I think that I would stay on it for any bribe. It is however an instance of Dutch industry little inferior to their dykes; as the one half of the town is gained off the Sea, which is fenced out by Barracadoes, and the other dug out of an immense mountain of sand and rock; which rises to a great height behind the houses, and will one day bury them under it. On the top of this hill I saw some decent-looking houses, but was not able to mount it, to look at them nearer. I understand however that the whole riches of the Island consist in its merchandize, and that they are obliged to the neighbouring Islands for subsistence; while they in turn furnish them with contraband commodities of all kinds. The town consists of one street a mile long, but very narrow and most disagreeable, as every one smokes tobacco, and the whiffs are constantly blown in your face.

But never did I meet with such variety; here was a merchant vending his goods in Dutch, another in French, a third in Spanish, etc etc. They all wear the habit of their country, and the diversity is really amusing . . .

From one end of the town of Eustatia to the other is a continued mart, where goods of the most different uses and qualities are displayed before the shop-doors. Here hang rich embroideries, painted silks, flowered Muslins, with all the Manufactures of the Indies. Just by hang Sailor's Jackets, trousers, shoes, hats etc. Next stall contains most exquisite silver plate, the most beautiful indeed I ever saw, and close by these iron-pots, kettles and shovels. Perhaps the next presents you with French and English Millinary-wares. But it were endless to enumerate the variety of merchandize in such a place, for in every store you find everything, be their qualities ever so opposite . . .

We were treated with great hospitality at this place, but they have nothing of the gentility of the neighbouring Islands. I slept or rather lay two nights under the hill, which seemed to threaten me every moment from its Neighbourhood, and the Musquatoes [mosquitos] too are very hearty and strong, so that we had enough of amusement to keep us from sleep, and were not a little pleased to get aboard the Rebecca again.

Biographical and literary notes

ISHERWOOD, Christopher (1904–1980). Born in Cheshire, Isherwood attended university at Cambridge before going to work as a teacher in Berlin, an experience which inspired his best-known works, *Sally Bowles*, 1937, and *Goodbye to Berlin*, 1939. In 1939 he emigrated to California where he worked as a scriptwriter. In 1947 he travelled down the west coast of South America, keeping a diary of his experiences which later became *The Condor and the Cows* (Extract 1). Curaçao was the first port of call after leaving the USA, and its mix of Caribbean colourfulness and oil-dominated squalor is perceptively observed.

JOHNSON, Will (1931–). Born in Saba and educated in Curaçao, Johnson worked in St Martin as a journalist before returning to Saba to found and edit the *Saba Herald*. Since 1969 he has been actively involved in politics – he was commissioner and acting administrator of Saba in the 1970s and 1980s. He has also represented Saba in the legislature of the Netherlands Antilles in Curaçao and is currently a Senator. *Saban Lore: Tales From My Grandmother's Pipe* (Extract 3) is a history of this tiny and beautiful island as well as an affectionate record of some of its eccentricities.

MARUGG, Tip (1923–). Silvio A. 'Tip' Marugg was born in Curaçao and has worked as a magazine editor as well as producing fiction and poetry. His best-known work, translated as *Weekend Pilgrimage* (Extract 2), nostalgically portrays the transformation of Curaçao from a rural and stable community into its modern, industrial form.

SCHAW, Janet (1730s?–1780s?). Little is known about Janet Schaw, who was born in Edinburgh, the daughter of a local landowner. She left, however, an extraordinary account of her voyage through the British colonies of the Caribbean and North America in the *Journal of a Lady of Quality* (Extract 5). Her description of St Eustatius, where her ship called after leaving St Kitts, is one of the fullest from the period and shortly predates the famous moment when the island became the first to salute American colours.

SMITH, Glanville. American writer Smith travelled widely in the Caribbean in the 1930s and 1940s in search of his 'perfect' island. In *Many a Green Isle* (Extract 4), he gives an atmospheric account of 1930s Saba, in a period when visitors were a rarity.

ACKNOWLEDGMENTS AND CITATIONS

The authors and publisher are very grateful to the many literary agents, publishers, translators, authors and other individuals who have given their permission for the use of extracts and photographs, supplied photographs, or helped in the location of copyright holders. Every effort has been made to identify and contact the appropriate copyright owners or their representatives. The publisher would welcome any further information.

EXTRACTS

THE BAHAMAS: (1) Ian Fleming, *Thunderball*, Jonathan Cape, London, 1986. © Glidrose Productions Ltd. By permission of Glidrose Productions. (2) Major H. MacLachlan Bell, *Bahamas: Isles of June*, Williams and Norgate, London, 1934. (3) Ernest Hemingway, *Islands in the Stream*, Scribner, New York, pp 3–4. © 1970 by Mary Hemingway. By permission of Scribner, a Division of Simon & Schuster, and HarperCollins Publishers Ltd. (4) John Updike, 'Poisoned in Nassau', in *Collected Poems 1953–1993*, Hamish Hamilton, London, 1993, pp 133–134. © 1993 by John Updike. By permission of Penguin Books Ltd and Alfred A. Knopf, Inc. (5) Hunter Davies, *In Search of Columbus*, Sinclair-Stevenson, London, 1991, pp 110–112. By permission of Reed Books. **CUBA:** (1) Ernest Hemingway, *The Old Man and the Sea*, Scribner, New York, pp 15–16. Copyright 1952 by Ernest Hemingway. Copyright renewed © 1980 by Mary Hemingway. By permission of Scribner, a Division of Simon & Schuster. (2) Reinaldo Arenas, *Farewell to the Sea*, Andrew Hurley, trans, Viking, London and New York, 1982, p 25. Copyright © by Andrew Hurley and Reinaldo Arenas, English language translation. By permission of Viking Penguin, a division of Penguin Books USA, Inc. (3) Nicolás Guillén, 'Heat', in *Man-Making Words: Selected Poems of Nicolás Guillén*, Editorial de Arte y Literatura, La Habana, 1973, pp 63–64. (4) José Martí, 'Two Fatherlands', Jason Wilson, trans. (5) Heberto Padilla, 'I have always lived in Cuba', in *New York Review of Books*, 23 October 1969, p 6. (6) Oscar Hijuelos, *The Mambo Kings Play Songs of Love*, Penguin, London, 1991, pp 114–115. Copyright © 1989 by Oscar Hijuelos. By permission of Farrar, Straus & Giroux, Inc. (7) Guillermo Cabrera Infante, *Three Trapped Tigers*, Faber and Faber, London, 1989, pp 64–65. By permission of Faber and Faber Ltd. (8) Alejo Carpentier, *Explosion in a Cathedral*, Gollancz, London, 1963, pp 11–12. (9) Edmundo Desnoes, *Memories of Underdevelopment*, Penguin, London, 1971, pp 58–60. By permission of Penguin Books Ltd. (10) Graham Greene, *Our Man in Havana*, Heinemann, London, p 26. By permission of David Higham Associates. (11) Joseph Hergesheimer, *San Cristóbal de la Habana*, Heinemann, London, 1921, pp 6–9. (12) Alexandre von Humboldt, *Personal Narrative . . .*, Penguin, London, 1995. (13) Norman Lewis, *Cuban Passage*, Pantheon, New York, 1982, pp 5–6. Copyright © 1982 by Norman Lewis. By permission of the author c/o Rogers, Coleridge & White Ltd, 20 Powis Mews, London W11 1JN. (14) José Lezama Lima, *Paradiso*, Secker and Warburg, London, 1974, pp 127–128. Translation copyright © 1974 by Farrar, Straus & Giroux, Inc. By permission of Farrar, Straus & Giroux, Inc. (15) Nancy Morejón, 'Woman in a Tobacco Factory', in *Breaking the Silence: 20th Century Poetry by Cuban Women*, Pulp Press, Vancouver, 1982, p 145. (16) Virgilio Piñera, *Cold Tales*, Eridanos Press, New York, 1988, pp 207–208. (17) Severo Sarduy, *From Cuba with a Song*, translated by Suzanne Jill Levine, Sun & Moon Press, Los Angeles, CA, 1994, pp 26–28.

© 1994 by Sun & Moon Press. By permission of Sun & Moon Press. (18) Cristina García, *Dreaming in Cuban*, Flamingo, London, 1992, pp 217–219. Copyright © 1992 by Cristina García. By permission of Alfred A. Knopf, Inc. (19) Roberto Fernández Retamar, 'From the Vedado . . .', *Triquarterly*, Fall/Winter 1968–69, p 141. **JAMAICA:** (1) Lorna Goodison, 'Bella Makes Life', in *Baby Mother and the King of Swords*, Longman, Harlow, 1990, pp 80–82. By permission of the Longman Group Ltd. (2) Evan Jones, 'The Song of the Banana Man', in *The Penguin Book of Caribbean Verse in English*, Penguin, London, 1986. (3) Andrew Salkey, *The Late Emancipation of Jerry Stover*, Hutchinson, London, 1968, pp 15–16. By permission of Random House UK Ltd. (4) Jean Rhys, *Wide Sargasso Sea*, Penguin, London, 1968, pp 16–17. Copyright © Jean Rhys, 1966. By permission of Penguin Books Ltd, and W.W. Norton & Company, Inc. (5) Bob Marley, 'Redemption Song', from *Uprising*, Island, London, 1980. (6) Claude McKay, *Banana Bottom*, Pluto Press, London, 1985, pp 65–66. (7) Jean Binta Breeze, 'Riddym Ravings (The Mad Woman's Poem)', in *Spring Cleaning*, Virago, London, 1992, pp 20–21. By permission of Little, Brown & Co. (8) Earl McKenzie, *A Boy Named Ossie: A Jamaican Childhood*, Heinemann, Oxford, 1991, pp 9–10. By permission of Heinemann Educational, a division of Reed Educational and Professional Publishing Ltd. (9) James Carnegie, *Wages Paid*, Casa de las Américas, Havana, 1976. (10) Anthony C. Winkler, *The Lunatic*, Kingston Publishers, Kingston, 198, pp 43–44. By permission of Kingston Publishers Ltd. (11) Noel Coward, 'Jamaica', in *Collected Verse*, Methuen, London, 1984, p 402. © 1984 The Estate of Noel Coward. By kind permission of Michael Imison Playwrights Ltd. (12) Orlando Patterson, *The Children of Sisyphus*, Longman, Harlow, 1986, p 173. (13) Olive Senior, 'The Lady', in *Hinterland: Caribbean Poetry from the West Indies and Britain*, E.A. Markham, ed, Bloodaxe, Newcastle-Upon-Tyne, 1989. (14) Michael Thelwell, *The Harder They Come*, Pluto Press, London, 1980, pp 200–201. By permission of Grove/Atlantic, Inc, and Pluto Press. (15) Roger Mais, *The Hills Were Joyful Together*, Heinemann, Oxford, 1981, pp 9–10. Originally published by Jonathan Cape. By permission of Random House UK Ltd. (16) Anthony Trollope, *The West Indies and the Spanish Main*, Alan Sutton, Gloucester, 1985, pp 12–13. **HAITI:** (1) Alejo Carpentier, *The Kingdom of This World*, Penguin, London, 1980, pp 74–75. (2) Jacques Roumain, *Masters of the Dew*, Heinemann, London, 1978, pp 35–36. (3) Wade Davis, *The Serpent and the Rainbow*, Collins,

London, 1986, p 72. By permission of HarperCollins Publishers. (4) Russell Banks, *Continental Drift*, Hamish Hamilton, London, 1985, pp 106–107. (5) Pierre Clitandre, *Cathedral of the August Heat*, Readers International, London, 1980, pp 114–155. By permission of Readers International. (6) Brian Moore, *No Other Life*, Bloomsbury, London, 1993. (7) Norman Lewis, *To Run Across the Sea*, Cape, London, 1989, pp 86–87. Copyright ©1989 Norman Lewis. By permission of Norman Lewis, c/o Rogers, Coleridge & White Ltd. (8) Bernard Diederich and Al Burt, *Papa Doc: Haiti and Its Dictator*, The Bodley Head, London, 1969, p 69. (9) C.L.R. James, *The Black Jacobins*, Allison & Busby, London, 1991, pp 87–88. By permission of Allison and Busby Ltd. (10) Francis Huxley, *The Invisibles*, Rupert Hart-Davis, London, 1966, pp 43–44. By permission of Francis Huxley. (11) Ian Thomson, 'Bonjour Blanc', Penguin, London, 1992, pp 148–149. Originally published by Hutchinson. By permission of Random House UK Ltd and Ian Thomson. (12) William Seabrook, *The Magic Island*, 1929. (13) H. Hesketh Prichard, *Where Black Rules White: A Journey Across and About Haiti*, Thomas Nelson & Sons, London, 1910. (14) Patrick Leigh Fermor, *The Traveller's Tree: A Journey Through the Caribbean Islands*, John Murray, London, 1984, pp 231–232. By permission of John Murray (Publishers) Ltd. (15) Graham Greene, *The Comedians*, Penguin, London, 1984. By permission of David Higham Associates Ltd. (16) Herbert Gold, *Best Nightmare on Earth: A Life in Haiti*, Grafton, London, 1991. Copyright © 1991 by Herbert Gold. By permission of HarperCollins Publishers Ltd, and Simon & Schuster. (17) Amy Wilentz, *The Rainy Season*, Cape, London, 1989, p 91. By permission of Random House UK Ltd. **DOMINICAN REPUBLIC:** (1) Christopher Columbus, 'Letter', in Peter Hulme and Neil L. White, eds, *Wild Majesty: Encounters with Caribs from Columbus to the Present Day*, Oxford University Press, Oxford, 1992, pp 10–12. (2) Ana Lydia Vega, 'The Day It All Happened', in Maria Pamela Smorkaloff, ed, *If I Could Write This in Fire: An Anthology of Writing from the Caribbean*, New Press, New York, 1994, pp 212–213. Copyright 1995. By permission of The New Press. (3) Juan Bosch, *The Woman*, Nick Caistor, trans, in Anne Walmsley, ed, *Facing the Sea: A New Anthology from the Caribbean Region*, Heinemann, Oxford, 1986. By permission of Nick Caistor. (4) Manuel de Jesús Galván, *The Sword and the Cross*, Robert Graves, trans, Victor Gollancz, London, 1956, pp 221–222. By permission of the University of Indiana Press. (5) Julia Alvarez, *Homecoming*, Plume, New York, 1996. Copyright © 1984, 1996 by Julia

Alvarez. Published by Plume, an imprint of Dutton Signet, a division of Penguin Books USA, Inc. Originally published in a slightly different version by Grove Press. By permission of Susan Bergholz Literary Services, New York. All rights reserved. (6) Julia Alvarez, *In the Time of the Butterflies*, Algonquin Books, Chapel Hill, NC, 1994, pp 99–100. Copyright © 1994 by Julia Alvarez. Published by Plume, an imprint of Dutton Signet, a division of Penguin Books USA, Inc and originally in hardcover by Algonquin Books. By permission of Susan Bergholz Literary Services, New York. All rights reserved. (7) William Krehm, *Democracies and Tyrannies of the Caribbean*, Lawrence Hill & Company, Westport, CT, 1984, pp 169–170. (8) Quentin Crewe, *Touch the Happy Isles: A Journey Through the Caribbean*, Michael Joseph, London, 1987, pp 260–261. By permission of Penguin Books Ltd. (9) Samuel Hazard, *Santo Domingo, Past and Present; With a Glance at Hayti*, Editora de Santo Domingo, Santo Domingo, 1974. (10) Maurice Lemoine, *Bitter Sugar*, Zed Books, London, 1985, pp 85–86. By permission of Zed Books. **PUERTO RICO:** (1) Emilio Díaz Valcárel, *Hot Soles in Harlem*, Latin American Literary Review Press, Pittsburgh, PA, 1993, pp 144–145. (2) José Luis González, 'The Night We became People Again', in *Cuentos: An Anthology of Short Stories from Puerto Rico*, Schocken, New York, 1978, p 139. (3) Pedro Juan Soto, *Spiks*, Victoria Ortiz, trans, Monthly Review Press, London and New York, 1973, pp 59–60. Copyright © 1973 by Monthly Review Press. By permission of Monthly Review Foundation. (4) Clemente Soto Veléz, 'Caballo de palo/The Wooden Horse', in *La sangre que sigue cantando/The Blood That Keeps Singing: Selected Poems of Clemente Soto Vélez*, Martín Espada and Camilo Pérez-Bustillo, trans, Curbstone, Willimantic, CT, 1991, p 49. By permission of Curbstone Press. (5) Rosario Ferré, 'The Dust Garden', in *The Youngest Doll*, University of Nebraska Press, London and Nebraska, 1991, pp 19–20. Copyright © 1976 by Rosario Ferré. Copyright © 1991 by the University of Nebraska Press. By permission of the University of Nebraska Press. (6) Luis Palés Matos, 'Neither This Nor That', Julio Marzán, trans, in *Inventing a Word: An Anthology of Twentieth Century Puerto Rican Poetry*, Columbia University Press, New York, 1980, p 55. (7) Luis Rafael Sánchez, *Macho Camacho's Beat*, Gregory Rabassa, trans, Pantheon, New York, 1981, pp 5–6. (8) Julia de Burgos, 'Río Grande de Loíza', in *Inventing a Word: An Anthology of Twentieth Century Puerto Rican Poetry*, Columbia University Press, New York, 1980. (9) Ana Lydia Vega, *True and False Romances*, Andrew Hurley, trans, Serpent's Tail,

London, 1994, pp 133–135. By permission of Serpent's Tail. (10) Abelardo Díaz Alfaro, 'Josco', in Barbara Howes, ed, *In the Green Antilles: Writings of the Caribbean*, Panther, London, 1971, p 278. **THE VIRGIN ISLANDS:** Shiva Naipaul, 'Two Colonies', in *Beyond the Dragon's Mouth: Stories and Pieces*, Hamish Hamilton, London, 1984, pp 397–398. (2) and (3) Martha Gellhorn, *Travels with Myself and Another*, Allen Lane, London, 1978, pp 67–68 and pp 106–107. By permission of Martha Gellhorn. (4) Sir Frederick Treves, *The Cradle of the Deep: An Account of a Voyage to the West Indies*, Elder & Co, London, 1897. (5) Herman Wouk, *Don't Stop the Carnival*, Fontana, Glasgow, 1987, pp 146–147. By permission of HarperCollins Publishers Ltd, and Peters Fraser & Dunlop Ltd on behalf of the author. **SAINT MARTIN/ SINT MAARTEN:** (1) Martha Gellhorn, *Travels with Myself and Another*, Allen Lane, London, 1978. By permission of Martha Gellhorn. (2) Martha Gellhorn, *Liana*, Virago, London, 1987, pp 55–56. By permission of Martha Gellhorn. (3) Hugh O'Shaughnessy, *Around the Spanish Main*, Century, London, 1991, pp 70–71. Copyright © 1991 Hugh O'Shaughnessy. By permission of the author c/o Rogers, Coleridge & White Ltd. (4) Lasana M. Sekou, 'Fatty and the Big House', in *Love Songs Make You Cry*, House of Nehesi, Philipsburg, St Maarten, 1989, pp 24–25. By permission of Lasana M. Sekou. **ST KITTS AND NEVIS:** (1) Henry Nelson Coleridge, *Six Months in the West Indies in 1825*, John Murray, London, 1826. (2) Sir Frederick Treves, *The Cradle of the Deep: An Account of a Voyage to the West Indies*, Smith, Elder & Co, London, 1897. (3) Caryl Phillips, *The Final Passage*, Faber and Faber, London, 1986, pp 98–99. By permission of Caryl Phillips. (4) Caryl Phillips, *A State of Independence*, Faber and Faber, London, 1986, pp 18–19. By permission of Caryl Phillips and Faber and Faber Ltd. (5) F.B. Jones-Hendrickson, *Sonny Jim of Sandy Point*, Eastern Caribbean Institute, Frederiksted, USVI, 1991, pp 16–17. **ANTIGUA AND BARBUDA:** (1) Jamaica Kincaid, *A Small Place*, Virago, London, 1988, pp 24–26. By permission of Richard Scott Simon Ltd. (2) Evelyn Waugh, *Ninety-Two Days: A Journey in Guiana and Brazil*, Penguin, London, 1985, pp 14–15. By permission of Peters Fraser & Dunlop Ltd. (3) Lucretia Stewart, *The Weather Prophet: A Caribbean Journey*, Chatto and Windus, Loondon, 1995, pp 185–186. By permission of Random House UK Ltd. (4) Frederick A. Ober, *Our West Indian Neighbours*, James Pott & Co, New York, 1907. **GUADELOUPE:** (1) Zenga Longmore, *Tap–Taps to Trinidad*, Arrow, London, 1990, pp

165–166. By permission of Hodder & Stoughton Ltd. (2) Saint-John Perse, *Eloges and Other Poems*, Louise Varèse, trans, Pantheon, New York, 1956, p 152. (3) Simone Schwarz-Bart, *Between Two Worlds*, Barbara Bray, trans, Heinemann, Oxford, 1982, pp 146–147. Originally published by Victor Gollancz. By permission of Victor Gollancz Ltd. (4) Maryse Condé, *Tree of Life*, Victoria Reiter, trans, The Women's Press, London, 1994, pp 361–362. By permission of The Women's Press Ltd. (5) Amy Oakley, *Behold the West Indies*, D. Appleton-Century Co, New York, 1941. DOMINICA: (1) Jean Rhys, 'Temps Perdi', in *Tales of the Wide Caribbean*, Heinemann, London, 1980, pp 159–160. By permission of Penguin Books Ltd. (2) Jean Rhys, *Smile Please: An Unfinished Autobiography*, André Deutsch, London, 1979, pp 29–30. By permission of Penguin Books Ltd. (3) Stephen Hawys, *Mount Joy*, Duckworth, London, 1968, pp 132–133. By permission of Gerald Duckworth & Co Ltd. (4) Phyllis Shand Allfrey, *The Orchid House*, Virago, London, 1990, pp 64–65. Copyright © Phyllis Shand Allfrey, 1953. By permission of Little, Brown & Co (UK), and Curtis Brown Ltd on behalf of The Estate of Phyllis Shand Allfrey. (5) J.A. Froude, *The English in the West Indies*, Longmans, Green & Co, London, 1888. (6) James Pope-Hennessy, *The Baths of Absalom*, Allan Wingate, London, 1954, pp 31–32. MARTINIQUE: (1) Joseph Zobel, *Black Shack Alley*, Keith Q. Warner, trans, Heinemann, London, 1980, pp 135–137. By permission of Joseph Zobel. (2) Edouard Glissant, *The Ripening*, Michael Dash, trans, Heinemann, London, 1985, pp 146–147. By permission of Éditions du Seuil and Heinemann Educational, a division of Reed Educational and Professional Publishing Ltd. (3) Truman Capote, 'Music for Chameleons', in *A Capote Reader*, Abacus, London, 1987, pp 356–357. (4) Patrick Chamoiseau, *Creole Folktales*, Linda Coverdale, trans, The New Press, New York, 1994, pp 93–95. Copyright 1995. By permission of The New Press. (5) V.S. Naipaul, *The Middle Passage: The Caribbean Revisited*, Penguin, London, 1969, pp 211–212. Copyright © V.S. Naipaul, 1962. By permission of Aitken & Stone Ltd, and Penguin Books Ltd. (6) Lafcadio Hearn, *Two Years in the West Indies*, Harper & Brothers, New York, 1923. (7) Frantz Fanon, *Black Skin, White Masks*, Charles Lam Markmann, trans, MacGibbon and Kee, London, 1968, pp 19–21. (8) Aimé Césaire, *Return to My Native Land*, John Berger and Anna Bostock, trans, Penguin, London, 1969, pp 46–47. (9) Noel Coward, 'Martinique', in *Collected Verse*, Methuen, London, 1984. © 1984 The Estate of Noel Coward. By

kind permission of Michael Imison Playwrights Ltd. (10) Jean Rhys, 'Heat', in *Tales of the Wide Caribbean*, Heinemann, London, 1980, pp 41–42. By permission of Penguin Books Ltd. (11) Alec Waugh, *The Sugar Islands*, Cassell, London, 1958, p 46. ST LUCIA: (1) Algernon Aspinall, *A Wayfarer in the West Indies*, Methuen, London, 1928. (2) Kendel Hippolyte, 'Castries', in *The Labyrinth, The Source*, Castries, 1993, p 7. By permission of Kendel Hippolyte. (3) Derek Walcott, 'Sainte Lucie', in *Sea Grapes*, Cape, London, 1976, pp 52–53. Copyright © 1976 by Derek Walcott. By permission of Farrar, Straus & Giroux, Inc. (4) Derek Walcott, *The Antilles: Fragments of Epic Memory*, pp 27–29. Faber and Faber, London, 1993. © The Nobel Foundation 1992. By permission of The Nobel Foundation. (5) Earl G. Long, *Consolation*, Longman, Harlow, 1994, pp 131–132. By permission of the Longman Group. (6) Garth St Omer, *The Lights on the Hill*, Heinemann, London, 1986, pp 96–97. Originally published by Faber and Faber. By permission of Faber and Faber Ltd. (7) Martin Amis, 'St Lucia', in *Visiting Mrs Nabokov and Other Excursions*, Cape, London, 1993, pp 71–72. By permission of Random House UK Ltd and Random House, Inc. ST VINCENT AND THE GRENADINES: (1) Sir William Young, *An Account of the Black Caraibs in the Island of St Vincent's*, Frank Cass, London, 1971. (2) Frederick A. Ober, *Our West Indian Neighbours*, James Pott & Company, New York, 1907. (3) G.C.H. Thomas, *Ruler in Hiroona*, Macmillan Caribbean, Basingstoke, 1989, pp 67–68. By permission of Macmillan Publishers Ltd. (4) H. Nigel Thomas, *Spirits in the Dark*, Heinemann, Oxford, 1993, pp 8–9. (5) Alec Waugh, *The Sugar Islands*, Cassell, London, 1958, pp 235–236. GRENADA: (1) Jean Buffong, *Snowflakes in the Sun*, The Women's Press, London, 1995, pp 175–176. By permission of The Women's Press Ltd. (2) Merle Collins, *Angel*, The Women's Press, London, 1993, pp 53–54. By permission of The Women's Press Ltd. (3) Merle Collins, 'Callaloo', in *Callaloo: Four Writers from Grenada*, Young World Books, London, 1984, pp 41–43. By permission of Young World Books. (4) Nellie Payne, *A Grenadian Childhood*, in *Jump-Up-and-Kiss-Me: Two Stories from Grenada*, The Women's Press, London, 1990, pp 83–84. By permission of The Women's Press Ltd. (5) Patrick Leigh Fermor, *The Traveller's Tree: A Journey Through the Caribbean Islands*, Penguin, London, 1984, pp 175–176. By permission of John Murray (Publishers) Ltd. BARBADOS: (1) Kamau Brathwaite, *Sun Poem*, Oxford University Press, Oxford, 1982, pp 39–41. By permission of Oxford

University Press. (2) Geoffrey Drayton, *Christopher*, Heinemann, London, 1972, pp 34–35. (3) George Lamming, *In the Castle of My Skin*, Longman, Harlow, 1987, pp148–149. (4) June Henfrey, 'Freedom Come', in *Coming Home and Other Stories*, Peepal Tree, Leeds, 1994, pp 82–84. (5) Frank Collymore, 'RSVP to Mrs Bush-Hall', in *The Man Who Loved Attending Funerals and Other Stories*, Heinemann, Oxford, 1993, p 129. By permission of Heinemann Educational, a division of Reed Educational and Professional Publishing Ltd. (6) Timothy Callender, *It So Happen*, Heinemann, Oxford, 1991, pp 34–35. By permission of Heinemann Educational, a division of Reed Educational and Professional Publishing Ltd. (7) Austin Clarke, *Growing Up Stupid Under the Union Jack*, McClelland and Stewart, Toronto, 1980. Copyright 1980 by the author. By permission of the author via The Bukowski Agency. (8) Aldous Huxley, *Beyond the Mexique Bay*, Flamingo, London, 1988, pp 5–6. Originally published by Chatto and Windus. By permission of Random House UK Ltd on behalf of Mrs Laura Huxley. (9) Patrick Leigh Fermor, *The Traveller's Tree: A Journey Through the Caribbean Islands*, Penguin, London, 1984, pp 131–133. By permission of John Murray (Publishers) Ltd. (10) John Robert Lee, Skeete's Bay, Barbados', in Anne Walmsley and Nick Caistor, eds, *Facing the Sea: A New Anthology from the Caribbean Region*, Heinemann, Oxford, 1986. By permission of John Robert Lee. **TRINIDAD AND TOBAGO:** (1) Earl Lovelace, *The Dragon Can't Dance*, Longman, Harlow, 1986, pp 148–152. By permission of André Deutsch Ltd. (2) Michael Anthony, 'They Better Don't Stop the Carnival', in *The Chieftain's Carnival and Other Stories*, Longman, Harlow, 1993, pp 81–82. By permission of the Longman Group. (3) Sam Selvon, *Moses Migrating*, Longman, Harlow, 1983, pp 80–81. By permission of Mrs Althea Selvon. (4) V.S. Naipaul, *Miguel Street*, Penguin, London, 1971. Copyright © 1971 by V.S. Naipaul. By permission of Aitken and Stone and Penguin Books Ltd. (5) Amryl Johnson, *Sequins for a Ragged Hem*, Virago, London, 1988, pp 29–30. By permission of Little, Brown & Co (UK). (6) Mighty Sparrow, 'The Yankees back', in *The Penguin Book of Caribbean Verse in English*, Paula Burnett, ed, Penguin, London, 1986. (7) Lawrence Scott, 'King Sailor One J'Ouvert Morning', in *Caribbean New Wave*, Stewart Brown, ed, Heinemann, Oxford, 1990, pp157–158. By permission of Heinemann Educational, a division of Reed Educational and Professional Publishing Ltd. (8) Noel Woodroffe, 'Wing's World', in *Best West Indian Stories*, Kenneth Ramchand, ed, Nelson, Walton-on-Thames, 1982, pp 140–141. (9) Charles Kingsley, *At Last: A Christmas in the West Indies*, Macmillan, London, 1900, pp 148–152. (10) C.L.R. James, 'Cricket', in *Trinidad & Tobago*, Michael Anthony and Andrew Carr, eds, André Deutsch, London, 1975, pp 112–113. (11) Jan Morris, 'Howzat! and Mr Morgan: Port of Spain 1958', in *Among the Cities*, Penguin, London, 1986, pp 290–291. By permission of A.P. Watt Ltd on behalf of Jan Morris. (12) Ismith Khan, *The Jumbie Bird*, Longman, Harlow, 1985, p 16. By permission of the Longman Group. (13) Ralph de Boissière, *Crown Jewel*, Picador, London, 1981, pp 308–309. By permission of Ralph de Boissière. (14) Merle Hodge, *Crick Crack Monkey*, Heinemann, Oxford, 1981, pp 106–107. Originally published by André Deutsch. By permission of André Deutsch Ltd. **THE BRITISH DEPENDENCIES:** (1) John Updike, 'Letter From Anguilla', in *Picked-Up Pieces*, André Deutsch, London, 1976, pp 71–72. Copyright © 1972 by John Updike. By permission of Penguin Books. (2) Karl Baarslag, *Islands of Adventure*, The Travel Book Club, London, 1944. (3) Simon Winchester, *Outposts*, Hodder and Stoughton, London, 1985, pp 235–236. (4) E.A. Markham, 'Late Return', in *Human Rites*, Anvil Press, London, 1984. By permission of Anvil Press Poetry Ltd. (5) Peter Benchley, *The Island*, André Deutsch, London, 1979, pp 81–82. By permission of André Deutsch Ltd. **THE NETHERLANDS ANTILLES AND ARUBA:** (1) Christopher Isherwood, *The Condor and the Cows*, Methuen, London, 1949, pp 4–5. Copyright Christopher Isherwood, 1947. By permission of Curtis Brown Ltd, London, on behalf of The Estate of Christopher Isherwood. (2) Tip Marugg, *Weekend Pilgrimage*, Roy Edwards, trans, Hutchinson, London, 1960. (3) Will Johnson, *Saban Lore: Tales from My Grandmother's Pipe*, privately published, Saba, 1989, pp 72–73. By permission of Senator Will Johnson. (4) Glanville Smith, *Many a Green Isle*, The Travel Book Club, London, 1945, pp 206–207. (5) Janet Schaw, *Journal of a Lady of Quality . . .*, Yale University Press, New Haven, CT, 1922.

PICTURES

p 40 – Guillermo Cabrera Infante, courtesy of Faber and Faber; p 61 – Bob Marley, by Adrian Boot, © Adrian Boot, used by his permission; p 83 – Jean Binta Breeze, courtesy of Virago Press; p 103 – Aubelin Jolicoeur, by Julio Etchart, © Julio Etchart/Reportage, used by his permission; p 120 – Pierre Clitandre, by Alix Ambroise, Jnr, courtesy of Readers International; p 121 – Graham Greene, by William Karel; p 123 – Amy Wilentz, courtesy of Jonathan Cape; p 166 – Ana Lydia Vega, courtesy of Serpent's Tail; p 191 – Caryl Phillips, by Horace Ore, courtesy of Faber and Faber; p 262 – Joseph Zobel, by Catriona Davidson, used by her permission; p 268 – Derek Walcott, by Nigel Parry, © Nigel Parry, courtesy of Faber and Faber; p 277 – Martin Amis, by Chris Steele-Perkins/Magnum, courtesy of Jonathan Cape; p 279 – Garth St Omer, courtesy of Heinemann Educational Publishers; p 291 – H. Nigel Thomas, courtesy of Heinemann Educational Publishers; p 301 – Merle Collins, by Jacob Rose, © Jacob Rose, courtesy of The Women's Press; p 310 – Jean Buffong, by Robert Goldong, © Robert Golding, courtesy of The Women's Press, and Nellie Payne by Jim Rudin, © Jim Rudin, courtesy of The Women's Press; p 319 – Timothy Callender, courtesy of Heinemann Educational Publishers; Earl Lovelace – by Debra Blackwood, © Debra Blackwood, courtesy of Faber and Faber; p 381 – E.A. Markham, by Tony Ward, © Tony Ward 1993, courtesy of Anvil Press Poetry Ltd.

INDEX

This is an index of authors and other significant people mentioned in the text. (A number of other authors are included in the booklists.) **(E)** = extract, **(B)** = biographical entry.